Dragon by the Tail

BY THE SAME AUTHOR

Foreign and Other Affairs

Dragon by the Tail

AMERICAN, BRITISH, JAPANESE, AND RUSSIAN ENCOUNTERS

WITH CHINA AND ONE ANOTHER

John Paton Davies Jr.

W · W · NORTON & COMPANY · INC ·

NEW YORK

Library of Congress Cataloging in Publication Data

Davies, John Paton, 1908-
    Dragon by the tail.

      1. China—Politics and government—1912-1949.
2. China—Foreign relations—U.S. 3. U.S.—
Foreign relations—China. I. Title.

DS775.D37   327   68-20817

ISBN 0-393-05455-1

3 4 5 6 7 8 9 0

For Patricia

Contents

Photographs appear between pages 224 and 225
Front Endpaper: Map of China as of 1945
Back Endpaper: Map of Asia as of 1945

Prologue

THIS IS THE STORY OF the breakup of traditional Chinese society. It is also the story of how Americans, pushing westward across the Pacific, Britons northward from the spice islands, Japanese southward from their gnarled archipelago, and Russians eastward from out of the Siberian steppe, intruded upon China, collided with one another, and triggered the implosion and what followed—the fusion of a new order in China and East Asia.

Because a cataclysm of such magnitude is complex, the focus of this narrative moves back and forth from Asia, to the United States and to Europe. But the center of the story is China and its transformation through ideas and violence, foreign and domestic.

The time span for the implosion, the collapsing inward of a civilization, was about a century and a half. Traditional China—backward-looking, ponderous and smug—began to experience the disruptive impact of the maritime West at the end of the eighteenth century. The fission accelerated on into the twentieth century, reaching a climax in the 1940s when the Pacific War, followed by civil war, fired the collapse of the old order and fused a new China.

In telling this story I interpose personal experiences and observations, for in a sense I was caught up in the latter phases of the collision of power and implosion.

My parents were American missionaries in China, a part of a righteous and consecrated crusade that strove with love to win China to Christ and, in so doing, did much to shatter a civilization that had endured for millennia. I was born in 1908, during the last years of the Chinese Empire, and spent my boyhood amidst this proselytizing endeavor and the transition from imperial to republican to warlord rule. My college education was in the United States, excepting for one year at Yenching University, near Peking. During the 1930s, as an American Foreign Service officer, I observed the Japanese occupation of Manchuria and invasion of Central China.

As the collision of external forces and the internal implosion culminated in the Pacific War, I was detailed to the American commanding general in China, Burma, and India, Joseph W. Stilwell, for whom I functioned as a political adviser. This kept me moving between Chungking, Washington, New Delhi, London, and Yenan, headquarters of the Chinese Communist movement, which even then had begun the fusion of a new order in China. In 1945 I went to the American Embassy at Moscow on assignment and from there observed the Soviet assault upon the Japanese in Manchuria and Korea, the end of World War II, and the first two years of the Chinese Civil War.

I do not carry the autobiographical asides in this narrative beyond my tour in Moscow. What followed is another story. It is sufficient to say here that I was transferred in 1947 to the Department of State as a policy planner; that I was accused by Senator Joseph McCarthy and like-minded politicians and publicists of having contributed to the American "loss" of China; then, when I declined to resign under attack, John Foster Dulles, secretary of state, fired me in 1954 as a risk to the security of the United States; and that in 1969 the State Department reexamined my case and granted me security clearance.

Acknowledgments

For reading all of this volume in manuscript and generously offering criticism and encouragement, I express my gratitude to Professor John K. Fairbank, Professor Rodney C. Loehr, Mr. Raymond P. Ludden, and Mr. John S. Service.

Likewise, for constructive comments on various segments of the manuscript I owe warm appreciation to Colonel David D. Barrett, Major General Haydon L. Boatner, Mr. Caleb Davies, Jr., Mr. Donald Davies, Brigadier General Frank Dorn, and Mr. John K. Emmerson. And for his recollections of times of stress and storm, I thank my father, at ninety-three, for his long, long memories.

Dragon by the Tail

CHAPTER *I*

The Great Rivers

CHINA IS SECLUDED from the rest of the continent of Asia by encircling mountain ranges and deserts. And deep within China is an area of inner seclusion, surrounded by barricades of mountains, separating it from the rest of the country.

This is the Red Basin of Szechuan province. It is so called because of the color of its underlying sandstone and because its seventy-five thousand four hundred square miles lie below the jagged escarpments rising around it.

Lodged in the westernmost part of the Red Basin, far back from the China coast, in the foothills of the great mountain ranges and the snow peaks that pile up yet further back into Tibet, is the town of Kiating. My parents ventured that far from Ohio and Manitoba in 1906 as Baptist missionaries. There I was born.

In that time, before modern means of transport had penetrated or soared over the upthrust encirclement of the Red Basin, Kiating and the rest of the area dwelt in isolation. This apartness, intimidating to other Chinese, troubled the inhabitants little. For there were some forty million of them. Kiating itself was perhaps a mere fifty thousand people. But the capital of Szechuan, Chengtu, was about half a million, and so was Chungking. And the density of population per cultivated square mile rose, in the Chengtu plain, to something like two thousand, as against, for example, some eight hundred in Rhode Island.

Furthermore, the Red Basin was remarkably self-sufficient. The land was fertile, the climate benign, giant pandas infrequent, monkeys plentiful, and the range of crops wide because of the varying altitudes. The farms on the plains were irrigated by a system developed more than two thousand years ago; those on slopes were terraced, and all were tended meticulously, as gardens. Kiating and the rest of the Red Basin, notwithstanding their hideaway parochialism, were a distillation, the essence of China.

Thus nestled in seclusion, Kiating lay at the junction of two rivers. One was boisterous, rushing down from the highlands to the west. So shallow it was that only bamboo rafts, laden with tea, wood, oil and other produce from the uplands, could navigate its churning, rock-strewn waters. The raftsmen made a brave and strident occasion of their safe arrival at Kiating, shouting and posturing as they poled the long, sluggish platforms in from the swift current to the landings beneath the town's walls.

The second river, the Min, was less headlong as it meandered out of the wide Chengtu plain to the north. It was also a little deeper so that flat-bottomed, shallow-draft junks could navigate it even upstream. Against the current, boatmen rowed, sailed, poled, or pulled bamboo cables—or any combination of the four—to move the craft on its way.

On land, over narrow dirt or flagstone roads, transport was by wheelbarrow or man acting as a beast of burden, for there were few pack animals in this part of China. On the flatlands, goods, pigs, or people were balanced on either side of the big wooden, and invariably squeaking, wheelbarrows as the staggering barrow-man shoved his cargo along ancient, endless ruts. Or carriers transported produce, dangling from the two ends of limber slats across their shoulders, or their fellow men in sedan chairs.

More often, and almost without exception in hilly country and on mountain trails, goods, swine and human beings were carried on the bent backs of porters. These men were, for the most part, sturdy fellows with bulging leg muscles, varicose veins, welts on their shoulders, a temperate addiction to opium, and a rated speed, loaded, of 20–30 miles per day, depending on the burden and the gradient.

Sedan chairs were another mode of passenger transport. The chair was carried by means of two parallel poles more or less twelve feet long, with crossbars joining the ends fore and aft. In the case of two bearers, the crossbars rested directly on the men's shoulders, not in the effete eighteenth century French fashion with the chair slung low from shoulder straps. With three bearers, a short pole was attached to the crossbar, one end of which lay on a shoulder of the lead man, the other on a shoulder of the second man, behind the crossbar and between the shafts. With four bearers, the same arrangement was lined up to the rear of the chair.

There were three basic models in sedan chairs: bent-pole, standard, and mountain. The bent-pole was the luxury model used only in cities by high functionaries and the very rich. It was characterized by arched carrying shafts that raised the lacquered and silk-curtained palanquin, and its privileged occupant, high above the gawkers in the street. The two, three, or four bearers were accompanied by an extra shift which alternately took over with admirable dexterity, in nowise slowing the swift, mincing pace, nor tipping in the slightest the proud conveyance.

The standard model, enclosed with plain materials, was usually carried by two men. If the passenger was stout or wished to have accompanying luggage strapped behind the chair, three or four bearers might be employed. The standard model was used not only for moving about town, but also on journeys lasting days and even weeks. About thirty miles a day was considered to be satisfactory when traveling over reasonable terrain.

The mountain chair was a stripped-down model open to the elements, with a small swing for a footrest, which could be pulled up when the path was particularly steep or boulders had to be gone over. It was a jaunty conveyance that provided the passenger with little sense of security but much exhilaration.

A dozen or so roads, little better than trails in many stretches, crawled out over the jagged rim of the Red Basin to connect Szechuan with the rest of China and the world. But the main line of communications with the outside was the Yangtze.

The houseboat *Eloise* belonged to the Baptist mission at Kiating. She was a plump little thing, about thirty feet long with a forward deck of perhaps fifteen feet, a thatched cabin, and a helmsman's deck. The oarsmen rowed standing up, facing the bow and pushing their long oars against the water. She was used by my father and his fellow-missionaries to travel the Min on evangelistic visits to nearby towns.

In September 1911, the *Eloise* was readied for a longer than ordinary voyage. For the first rumbles of the oncoming Republican Revolution had been heard. So most of the missionaries prepared to flee before the storm. Five days after my brother was born, we boarded the *Eloise* and were rowed out into the river, downstream.

From Kiating to the China coast by river was about seventeen hundred miles, further than from Montreal to New Orleans. The journey was made in four stages. As I was three years old at that time and do not remember the 1911 voyage from Kiating to the sea, I reconstruct the journey from oft-told tales by my parents and my own vivid recollections of later travels on the Yangtze and its tributaries.

Some four days after leaving Kiating, traveling only in daylight because of navigational hazards, we reached the point at which the Min flowed into the Yangtze. Here the Yangtze was already eighteen hundred miles from its source high in the Tibetan borderland. It had begun above sixteen thousand feet and had cascaded down through canyons, one of them thirteen thousand feet deep, nearly thrice the depth of the Grand Canyon of the Colorado. In these upper reaches, the Yangtze was called the Chin Sha Kiang, the River of Golden Sand. On a stretch near China's border with Burma, before turning eastward, it plunged along a course parallel to and, by the caprices of geology, only fifty miles from the Salween River, which later veered to the west to pour into the Bay of Bengal. Between these two, separated by sheer ranges, a third great river, the Mekong, rushed southward to its sluggish delta on the shores of the South China Sea.

By the time that the Yangtze was fed by the Min, it had come down to little more than eight hundred feet above sea level. But it was still not tamed. The *Eloise* passed through stretches of white water, lunging and creaking through rapids, in the week's voyage to Chungking.

At Chungking, we left the *Eloise* and went ashore to join other evacuees awaiting the formation of a convoy of larger houseboats and the arrival from downriver of a midget British gunboat to escort us on our way. When all was arranged, we set off on a less cramped vessel but on a somewhat more adventurous voyage. Below Chungking, the Yangtze forced its way through the mountain barrier blockading the Red Basin. The mountains constricted the river into narrow gorges between cliffs rising as much as 2,000 feet on either side. Thus pressed in upon themselves, the waters roared and fought their way past confining walls and great boulders in their course. Likewise, changes in volume from the headwaters caused the level of the river to rise and fall, at times 200 feet. The record, in the Windbox Gorge, in 1871 was 275 feet, nearly the height of the United States Capitol.

In these fierce passages, there were more than crags in the ever-changing channels. There were also whirlpools that would appear, change, and disappear, and into which even the largest houseboats, from time to time, would slip and then in dizzying circuit descend and vanish. When we saw thunderous rapids before us, we disembarked, walked around them on thin trails, breathlessly watched the houseboat shoot the course, the oarsmen shouting, stamping, and rowing like madmen to keep headway, and the helmsman lunging at his tiller this way and that, as best he might, to steer the vessel clear of both rocky crests and maelstroms.

Finally, we were through the mighty barrier. A fortnight or so after leaving Chungking, the convoy arrived at Ichang at the beginning of the gently sloping Yangtze Plain, four hundred miles from Chungking, a thousand miles from the coast, and less than three hundred feet above sea level. There we boarded a small Japanese steamer. We had emerged from medievalism and now rode the brand new twentieth century, the era of steam power, fueled by coal.

Thus in a relatively stately fashion, we steamed down the broadening Yangtze. To the north, the Yangtze Plain was flanked by spurs of Tibet's massive Kunlun system which, by the time they reached their ultimate extension in East China, were prosaic, bumpy hills. To the south were more hills.

The flat lands and water of the Yangtze Plain totalled some seventy-five thousand square miles. Three lakes, each of more than a thousand square miles, lay to the south of the river. The Yangtze's largest tributary, the Han, joined the great river, not in the highlands or the Red Basin, but in the plain. And in the lower reaches of the Yangtze the countryside was crisscrossed by networks of canals.

The third stage of our outward voyage took about three days to Hankow, the main transshipment port in Central China. Hankow was at the junction of the Han River and the Yangtze. Across the Han from Hankow was Hanyang, and across the Yangtze was Wuchang. Together, the three cities were called Wuhan.

The revolution that led to the overthrow of the empire had erupted at Wuchang not many days before our arrival. It was still sputtering. We heard gunfire but saw no disturbances because our steamer docked alongside the Japanese concession at Hankow and we transferred to a larger ship, flying the Union Jack, moored at the British concession. These foreign-administered enclaves were usually respected as neutral in Chinese civil conflicts.

Below Hankow, the Yangtze was now a majestic river, a mile wide, with a huge volume of fast-flowing water. It was deep enough to carry ocean-going ships, drawing twenty-five feet, all the way to Hankow, six hundred and thirty miles from the Pacific. It was pigmented ochre from the soil burden it carried—six hundred million tons a year of dirt, pebbles, and rocks wafted in suspension or rolled along its river bottom. This sediment had been washed down into the mainstream from a drainage system of seven hundred and fifty square miles.

A few rivers in the world, including the Mississippi, were longer than the Yangtze. A few carried a larger volume of water. And a few had a larger drainage basin. Only the Amazon, empress of rivers, exceeded the Yangtze in all three. But none of them nourished, transported, and bathed so many people. Not all of these bigger rivers put together could equal the Yangtze river system in the number of people served—some two hundred million.

The traffic on the river, all seventeen hundred miles from Kiating to Shanghai, acted out man's intimate relationship with this imperious waterway and its tributaries. A constant procession of craft moved up, down, and across stream —rafts, houseboats, big matronly cargo junks, ferryboats, steamers, gunboats, small craft loaded with vegetables on their way to market, and fishing boats tending weirs or nets or cormorants with strands of straw tied around their necks so that they could not swallow the fish that they caught for their master. There was the constant kaleidescope of villages along the river banks and women washing clothes, children swimming, almost any male contentedly answering the call of nature, and farmers treading paddles in sluices to bring water up over the banks to irrigate their fields.

Toward the end of the long voyage, the river widened so that we seemed to be moving through a large tawny lake. In the estuary we came to the squat Whangpoo, a scullery maid river to the splendid Yangtze. Fourteen miles up its drab, overworked course lay Shanghai, seventy years before a scrawny fishing village, by 1911 well on its way to becoming the biggest city on the continent of Asia.

From Shanghai we steamed across the Pacific to a year's furlough in America. After that it was back to Shanghai and, reversing our passage of the Yangtze, up against the current to Kiating. This was a slower voyage, particularly above Ichang, where the houseboat was pulled by trackers. We left Shanghai in February. It was April before we reached Kiating.

The second great river basin in China is that of the Yellow River, the Hwang Ho. In the history of man and ancient Chinese culture, it is more significant than the Yangtze Basin. For if there is a cradle of Chinese civilization, the Yellow River is it. But, as a river, the Hwang Ho lacks the protean grace of the noble Yangtze.

The Yangtze and Yellow River basins are divided by the eastward spurs of the Kunlun Mountains, by the lower elevations of that massive system originating in Tibet up against the Afghan border. The most sharply defined of these spurs is the Chin Ling. South of the Chin Ling, the climate is subtropical, with abundant, dependable rainfall and plenty of vegetation. To the north of the range, winters are cold, summers hot, the rainfall irregular, and the terrain nearly bare of forests. The Hwang Ho basin lies north of this central belt of mountains.

In the mid-1930s, as a vacationing language officer from the American Legation in Peking, I went into the eastern front of the Chin Ling and climbed one of its peaks. It was the 7,000-foot sacred mountain of Hua Shan—the kind of mountain that Chinese delight in, leaping perpendicularly from the plain, precipices, raw rock, jutting crags, and here and there stunted, contorted trees. In the early mornings, strands of mist trailed across the peak. Not surprisingly, a monastery perched on the ridge, at once defying and communing with nature.

Peering down through wreathing mists, down the northern face of the mountain to the deep valleys and extended yellow plain below, was to participate in a Chinese painting, to be a part of a landscape having no depth perspectives into the scene, only perpendiculars, only a flat up and down representation of nature—fey and contrived.

Turning around and looking south was a return to the reality of geography. Masses of mountains rigidly rose and fell to the farthest horizons, like a sea petrified in a gale. This was the Yangtze Valley's tall, thick barricade against the dry, bleak winds from Mongolia and Siberia.

From the Chin Ling due north to the low hills of Inner Mongolia lay the central portion of the Yellow River Basin. Like all of the basin, the total area of which is nearly three hundred thousand square miles, it was exposed to the inclement continental climate. But more than that, it included the heart of the loess country.

Loess is wind-borne silt whose particles are larger than those of clay but finer than sand. It is blown all over north China in windstorms, making the sky amber. It settles finely and loosely in layers of yellow dust. In some areas, the loess is several hundred feet thick, with roads ground down into deep ditches from the passages of carts, wheelbarrows, horses and men over the course of centuries. So gouged out are some roads that the traffic cannot be seen from adjacent fields—excepting as implied by clouds of loess sent billowing up over the rims of the cleft.

Millions of Chinese in Shensi and Kansu provinces live in caves dug into the face of loess cliffs. Loess has a vertical cleavage, it slices nicely, and so lends itself to being dug into for habitation. Yenan, the capital of the Chinese Communists before they seized power, was mainly a town of cave houses carved into the faces of cliffs.

Cave dwelling has its hazards—earthquakes. The loess provinces of Shensi and Kansu are in an earthquake belt. A particularly bad shake in 1920 collapsed caves, burying the occupants, and caused loess slides that entombed many people outside of the caves. Those who escaped were without food, tools, and livestock because all of these had been stored in caves. The death toll of those crushed and those starved was estimated to have been about a quarter of a million people.

The 120,000 square miles of loess country does not occupy all of the Yellow River Basin. The upper portion of the basin is in the western wildernesses, grasslands, and marshes. There on the eastern frontiers of Tibet, the Hwang Ho gets off to a good start at 14,600 feet. The course lying before it is 2,890 miles to the sea. It dashes down through canyons in the Kunlun range, rather like the Yangtze in its upper reaches. By the time the river reaches the capital of Kansu, Lanchow, it has gone down to less than 5,000 feet and has lost some of its élan. Up to then, it has such velocity that it is able to carry a heavy load of sediment, products of erosion gushed down into it from its upper slopes. But at Lanchow, it has already entered the loess zone.

It then begins to take on the added load of the airborne silt. As it slumps to thirty-five hundred feet and begins the great horseshoe loop around the Ordos Desert, it loses its youthful impetuosity and drags on a slow gradient, dropping sediment on its course. It is then in trouble. Sandbars form and the listless river meanders, looking for the easy way out. But the loess is remorseless.

Relentlessly, too, the tributaries of the Hwang Ho dump sediment into the river. The two big contributors are the historic Wei and the Fen, so that below them the Hwang Ho in high water carries as much as a phenomenal 40 percent of silt. Thus burdened, the Yellow River at just under four hundred feet above sea level enters the Yellow Plain, nearly four hundred and eighty miles from the Yellow Sea.

This great plain itself was the product of the Hwang Ho—land made over tens of thousands of years by its ever eastward extending delta. Upon entering the prehistory delta land, the Yellow River began its frustration at the hands of man. For if it had been permitted to follow its natural inclination, it would have snaked its way back and forth across the flat land, raising the level of the plain as it extended its delta ever further into the ocean. This would have meant, of course, that the huge fan over which it swept, now here, now there, could not support a settled population and farms. No one could know with surety where the river might next turn.

So man made a faulty but, under the circumstances, a very human decision. For some two thousand years, the Chinese have tried to control the Yellow River with dikes, defining a fixed channel. Thus thwarted, the river took due vengeance, breaking dikes and changing its course. Over the centuries, it has drowned and starved millions of Chinese. Yet they continue to cluster within its wide reach, more than eighty million of them on the Yellow Plain.

Man could not master the river with dikes, notwithstanding the enormous effort put forth, because it carried thirty-five billion cubic feet of silt into the plain every year. As it crossed the flatlands between dikes, it dropped twenty billion cubic feet along its artificial channel, discharging only fifteen billion in the ocean for delta building. The twenty billion cubic feet were deposited in low-water season, when the flow was not vigorous enough to flush the full load of sediment to the sea. Inevitably, this raised the river bed. If the next year's flood waters were moderate, they did not overflow or breach the dikes. But if they were in full spate, the dikes were in acute danger, unless they had been raised and strengthened.

Being fairly foresighted in such matters, the Chinese tended to build up the dikes. The result was that as the river bed rose, so did the levees. Thus the Hwang Ho flows above the Yellow Plain, rather as a gigantic aqueduct, with the water-level well above the bordering countryside.

When the Yellow River took its vengeance, it often was as a small break, without much damage being done and no lives lost. Sometimes it poured down on the farmlands lying beneath it. Fifteen times in recorded history, it has raged off onto a new course. The earliest reference to its course, long before the Christian era, indicated that the Yellow River emptied into the Gulf of Chili. It has since ranged as much as six hundred miles south of its first-known estuary to empty into the inoffensive Huai River and thence, with effrontery, into the Yangtze.

This last happened in 1938 when the Chinese, retreating before the Japanese invasion of Central China, breached the dikes as a defensive stratagem. The Japanese were thereby delayed in their southward advance, but not halted. Approximately six million Chinese peasants and town people were, however, cast adrift as refugees and an estimated half million died in one manner or another from the inundation.

Theoretically, a compromise might have been worked out between man and the Hwang Ho if the slopes of the Yellow River Basin had been reforested, or the course of the river straightened to speed up its flow and thereby carry off its load and scour its channel, or if silt basins had been made next to the river and designed to draw off successively the surplus water and collect its sediment. But none of these remedies was applied. This was not for want of engineering skill, as witness the Great Wall and the Grand Canal, dug from near Peking to south of the Yangtze. In any event, the Yellow River continued to be China's Sorrow.

In addition to devastating floods, this unfulfilled river took its revenge on man in quite an unusual fashion, considering its size and the volume of water it carries. Most of it was unnavigable. Parts of it, back in the mountains, bore rafts of inflated animal skins. And some short sections carried small junks. But there was nothing on the Hwang Ho like the shipping that used the Yangtze. The river was too shallow, too treacherous, or too subject to unmanageable rises and falls of water levels. So there it flowed, a misery to itself and a menace to its people.

Transport in the Yellow River area, then, has been mostly by land. Little of it has moved by manpower. For this was the region of pack animals and two-wheeled springless carts drawn by Mongolian ponies or mules. Both ponies and mules were also used as pack animals, as were burros and camels, not dromedaries with one hump but bactrians with two.

Historically, the Yellow River Basin has been the region of long roads— fifty days, more or less, by cart from Peking to Lanchow, the capital of Kansu. Thence northwestward, out of the Yellow River Basin, through the passes of the mountains that flanked ancient China, through the Jade Gate, last outpost of the

Great Wall, around the edge of Chinese Turkestan's desert, over more mountains, skirting more desert, pausing at oases; and one hundred and fifteen days after leaving Lanchow, with luck, the traveller reached Kashgar on China's Central Asian frontier.

This was the fabulous Silk Road of antiquity, the Chinese section of the route that connected the empire with civilizations to the west, with those of Central Asia and the Mediterranean world. Contact between these cultures began as early as the second century B.C. along the incredible trail stretching across the middle of Asia. Thus silk and other luxurious novelties went out of the Yellow River Valley by caravans. In exchange, the grapevine, the influence of Alexander's Greece, Buddhism from India, and Marco Polo from Venice entered China.

Then, too, over this route Chinese armies twice marched, in the first century B.C. and the eighth century A.D., as conquerors into the valleys of the Oxus and Jaxartes, not far from a locality that in the middle of the twentieth century became a Soviet space and missile test center.

CHAPTER *2*

Beyond the Passes and the Jade Gate

THE STRETCH OF DESERT, mountains and grasslands lying beyond the Jade Gate was but a segment of the vast arc of barbarian territory spreading around China proper. Beginning in Tibet, this expanse beyond the Chinese pale extended northward through Turkestan, to the east through Mongolia, and thence into Manchuria. For the most part, this was nomads' land.

It was inhabited by restless, martial peoples—rude herdsmen, horsemen, and hunters. When made desperate by drought on the grasslands or when feeling strong enough to invade, pillage, and occupy, they raided and overran the sedentary Chinese farmers and townspeople. The Chinese, after infusions of barbarian virility, would eventually retaliate by pushing out into the wilderness to subdue the tribes and secure their frontiers. Then a new barbarian invasion would sweep into China. Thus it went on, intermittently back and forth, for more than two thousand years.

The Koreans, Vietnamese, Thai, and Burmese were not in this category because they were generally not aggressive in their relationship with the Chinese. They endured vassaldom when imposed on them and did not invade, nor usurp the throne. In fertile plains and valleys fed by ample rains, they were not under compulsion to range in search of uncertain pasture or game. Nor did they possess the aggressive military skill of the steppe people.

The pattern of interinvasion between the barbarians and the Chinese benefitted both. To the civilized, highly conventionalized Chinese, the coarse horsemen out of the northern wilderness, who walked with a spread-legged roll and never bathed because water had been scarce on the steppe, were uncouth and repulsive. But they taught the Chinese how better to defend themselves and to invade the steppe. Eugenically they improved the Chinese stock, which had a tendency toward effeteness in both its virtues and its vices.

For the barbarians, too, the alternating aggression had beneficial effects. Chinese counterattacks and subjugation of the tribes peoples rubbed off rough edges on those subdued. Not a few of the barbarian chiefs invading China showed themselves to be semi-civilized by Chinese standards and adept at some of the more urbane forms of political connivance and treachery.

The human ecology of the frontier was essentially in balance. It was a balance of persisting unlikes. The nomads of the steppes could not in their grasslands become truly Chinese because the land-climate combination would not support a Chinese kind of agricultural society and because their tribal style of leadership, with the strong man chief commanding only so long as he was strong man, did not jibe with the ingrained Chinese system of hereditary rule in family and dynasty. The barbarians became like the Chinese when they stopped roaming, stayed off horses, and saturated themselves in China for a generation or two.

The self-satisfied Chinese were not tempted to become barbarians. They were of the only civilization. Those who penetrated the regions beyond the pale clung to their native culture. Where the land was fertile and watered, as in Manchuria and the oases of Central Asia, they colonized in Chinese agricultural communities. Otherwise, they were in the wilderness in military formations or as enforced settlers in exile to keep the barbarians in check. They were on the frontiers of Chinese power in a defensive capacity to maintain, with fluctuating success, a buffer zone protecting China proper.

China was not a well-defined political entity. For more than two millennia, its borders expanded and contracted. The size of the empire varied like that of an accordion. By the seventeenth century, during which the Manchus established their dynasty in Peking, barbarian strength on the steppes began to fade. A new power was rising in the far north. It was Russia and it was surging eastward toward the Pacific. As it did so over the next two centuries, the Turki and Mongolian tribesmen were ground between the upper and nether millstones of Russia and China. Thus the new barbarians pressing upon China from the north came to be slavic.

The swell and squeeze of empire in recent times was particularly noticeable in the region known to us as Manchuria and to the Chinese as the Northeast. It was an ample, diverse, rich, and thinly populated area with China proper to its south, Mongolia to its west, Russia to its north, Korea and Japan to its east. So surrounded, Manchuria has been a tensely significant piece of contested—and contesting—territory. Its principal natural resource—and enticement—was its whereabouts.

One of its many tribes, the Manchus, ruled Manchuria and China too, but lost both. The Mongols conquered both, along with most of Asia and a little of Europe, and then lost everything. The Russians detached pieces of Manchuria but were repeatedly frustrated in their efforts to absorb all of the region. Arriving late on the scene, the Japanese contested the Russians for domination of Manchuria, eventually taking it over in 1931.

But it was the Chinese, after conquering and then losing it several times over during the past two thousand years, who ended up holding Manchuria under typically tortured circumstances. In 1945, the Japanese, overlords of

Manchuria, were defeated by the Americans in the Pacific, their troops in Manchuria surrendered to a tardily invading Soviet Army, which then reluctantly withdrew, leaving the region to competing Chinese factions, who thereupon fought furiously over the prize that neither had won.

Viewed in long perspective, Manchuria has been the ground over which conflict has persistently ebbed and flowed. Taking a short historical span, the fifty-five years from 1895 to 1950, there emerges a pattern of concentrated and varied violence.

In those fifty-five years, five wars were fought on Manchurian soil. They were the Chinese-Japanese war (1894–95), the Russo-Japanese War (1904–05), the so-called Manchurian Incident of 1931 when the Japanese Army took over the Northeast by force, the Soviet invasion in the closing days of World War II, and the Civil War between the Chinese Nationalists and Chinese Communists.

In addition to wars, most of Manchuria was occupied without significant hostilities by Russian troops from 1900 to 1903. Japanese forces moved into parts of North Manchuria during the civil war in Russia. Soviet troops drove across North Manchuria in 1929. And in 1950, Manchuria was used as a base from which the Chinese Communists intervened in the Korean War, when General MacArthur advanced incautiously northward to the Korean-Manchurian border on the Yalu River.

As delineated during the first thirty years of this century, Manchuria was about four hundred thousand square miles in extent. This is approximately equal to the size of Iowa, Nebraska, the Dakotas, and the southern half of Saskatchewan. In latitude and climate, the two zones are similar. Both originally had prairie and forests and were sparsely populated. But there the similarities cease.

Manchuria was rich in minerals, by the 1930s had a heavy industry base and was a hub of international transportation. It also had a sea coast on two gulfs of the Yellow Sea. And its population by mid-twentieth century was over forty million.

Although under several dynasties Manchuria had been included as part of the Chinese Empire, it always was, on into this century, *k'ou wai*. To be *k'ou wai* was to be outside of the pass, to be beyond the passes in the mountains crested by the Great Wall. It was to be beyond the pale of civilization, at the best to be colonial.

For the conventional Chinese mind, the Great Wall was a barrier against barbarian incursion. Stretching more than fourteen hundred miles from the Jade Gate, on the frontier with Turkestan, to the sea, it protected the Chinese from unwelcome attention only when the dynasty was bristling and alert. But when the human defenses were slack, it was no serious impediment to invaders. It was really a monument in brick, stone, and mud to a usually static point of view.

Going *k'ou wai*, through the pass into Manchuria, in 1930 was not like crossing a provincial boundary within China proper. It was still suggestive of venturing forth into another and less cultivated land. The difference was not as sharp as going through the pass northwest of Peking into Inner Mongolia. For there one climbed up over mountains onto a bare plateau, parched, clear, and infinitely spacious. Going into southern Manchuria along the coastal route presented no visual contrasts to North China. It was to the eye simply more of North China, briefly interrupted where the mountains and the Great Wall came wearily down to the shore. The difference was subjective for most Chinese—remembrances of teahouse legends from the past.

Until the last years of the nineteenth century, the eastern and western borders of Manchuria were casually defined. In the east, heavily forested mountains extended to the Sea of Japan and the Gulf of Tartary. The eastern zone was inhabited by perhaps one million Tungusic tribesmen, including the Manchus, and a few hundred thousand Koreans who had senselessly migrated that far and come to regret it for generations. The Tungusi were hunters, herdsmen and part-time farmers. Various Chinese dynasties had claimed all of this territory to the east, embracing the long strip along the gulf and the sea, which is now part of the Soviet Union, from Vladivostok to beyond the mouth of the Amur.

The western borderland was forested only in part. Most of it was bare mountains and rolling grasslands frequented by about two million seminomadic Mongols who had little concept of and even less respect for boundaries decreed by Peking, unless maintained by superior force.

In the sixteenth century, before the Russians began their epic expansion across Asia to the Pacific, the northern boundaries of what we call Manchuria fuzzed off indefinitely into the tribal wilderness lying north of the Amur River. This waterway now delimits the upper border of China's Northeast. But then it was for fishing and transport and the Tungusic tribes that lived along its tributaries in eastern Manchuria were related to tribes living far to the north of the Amur. It was the Russians who eventually induced Peking to accept a boundary delimited by the Amur and two of its tributaries, the Argun and the Ussuri.

Northern Manchuria is dominated by the Amur system. The Chinese call the river the Heilung Kiang, the Black Dragon River. Some twenty-seven hundred miles long, it is the third biggest in China, exceeded only by the Yangtze and the Yellow River. With its tributaries, the Amur provides two thousand miles of navigable waterways. This is farther than from New York to Cartagena, Colombia. However, because of ice, the normal navigation season is only from May to October.

Down the center of Manchuria spreads a six-hundred mile long plain that averages some three hundred miles in width. It is formed by the wide valleys of two large rivers and their affluents. One of them is the Sungari which flows northeast to join the Amur. The other is the Liao which wanders southward into Liaotung Bay. The plain which they form is the agricultural heartland of Manchuria—soybeans, sorghum, millet, and wheat grown in such abundance that they provide surpluses for the rest of China and, in the case of soybeans, for export.

It was the fertility of the Manchurian plain, much of it in natural grasslands as recently as fifty years ago, that attracted Chinese immigration. The Manchu emperors in Peking had tried at first to keep the Chinese from migrating to Manchuria and then to limit their entry into the Manchus' homeland. After the fall of that dynasty, land-hungry Chinese settlers and seasonal workers from south of the Wall streamed into the Northeast, amounting for a short time to about one million a year. This fairly well filled up Manchuria by mid-century to something like forty million. It is the overwhelming ethnic majority of the Chinese that, more than anything else, makes Manchuria now an integral part of China.

Manchuria's spectacular economic development during the twentieth century was due to both its rich natural resources and the industrious immigrant population. But there was another reason for progress. It was foreign capital, skills, and management. The Russians and the Japanese brought war, destruction, and oppression. But they also built and ran a network of railroads far superior to that in China proper, contributing in a large measure to the rapid development of the region. And the Japanese introduced large-scale mining and heavy industry more advanced than any south of the wall.

Of the three biggest cities in Manchuria, two were created as by-products of imperialist aggression. Harbin, well over one million by 1960, started as a company town created by the Tsarist-controlled Chinese Eastern Railway. Dairen, which also grew to more than one million, was likewise started by the Russians, but developed into a thriving, efficient port city by the Japanese. Even Mukden, *Shenyang* to the Chinese, owes to Japanese exploitation much of its expansion from a lumpish Manchu capital to an industrial metropolis of about two million five hundred thousand people. This is not to suggest that the population growth in these cases represent qualitative progress. It is only to indicate that by the measure of prevalent values in virtually all countries, these were considerable accomplishments.

Harbin was unique among Chinese cities. It was not only a manifestation of Russian colonial initiative, it also was a center to which many of the White Russian émigrés, fleeing the civil war in their country, gravitated—if only temporarily until they could move to some other haven. Thus, when I first visited Harbin in 1930, about one-third of the population of three hundred thousand was Russian. The rest were Chinese.

White Russians crowding the streets, onion-domed churches, solid Tsarist buildings, street signs in Russian, restaurants with borscht, vodka, smoked salmon, and blue-tinted cut glass goblets—the old Russian way of life was here, suffused in nostalgia, in the depths of Manchuria. Even to the extent of a flash-by scene: a brightly complected slavic beauty in a black fur coat and hat, sitting like a young duchess in her glistening droshky, drawn by a rather vain black horse.

Six years later, on my next visit, the scene had changed. The Japanese had come. They had taken all of Manchuria. The Soviet Government had sold its inherited interests in the Chinese Eastern to the Japanese. Harbin was drab and subdued. Now the White Russian reveries were even more pathetic, their present realities a grinding humiliation, their prospects in this alien land of sojourn utterly desolate. The era of Russian influence in Manchuria was over—until Stalin flung in the Soviet Army in 1945.

Mukden, where I was stationed during the mid-thirties as an American vice-consul, was a big, busy, ugly city. As a commercial, banking, and rail center operated by the Japanese, it dispensed most of the produce of Manchuria. Through Mukden passed trainloads of soybeans, grain, hides, lumber, coal, metals, and manufactured goods. It was the hub of railroads radiating into Korea and so to Japan; to Harbin and thence to the Trans-Siberian and to Europe or to Vladivostok; to Peking and the rest of China; to Fushun and its huge open-pit coal mine; to the forests and Ever White Mountains on the Korean border; and to the wharves of Dairen, beyond which lay the oceans of the world.

Mukden was a city without spirit, without light. Dominated by two institutions, the Japanese Army, which ruled Manchuria, and the South Manchuria Railway, which administered the economy, Mukden was a remarkably depersonalized human agglomeration. There were two strata of society. The elect were the Japanese, from generals to peculiarly odious carpetbaggers. The oppressed were the Chinese, systematically exploited by the grimly efficient Japanese, pliantly bending before crude force, discreet, opportunistic, fawning but deceptive and surviving.

Cultural life centered in a number of dance halls that favored the tango. From time to time all fifty of the Japanese and Korean hostesses at The Star, which was my favorite, would appear in bridal gowns with paper orange blossoms entwined in their well-oiled raven locks. This was regarded as particularly elevating by those interested in the finer things of life. Some of the patrons, on leave for rest and rehabilitation from frontier posts, wore felt boots, quilted breeches, and sidearms onto the dance floor. Although considered gauche in a metropolitan cultural center, these lapses were overlooked in the interests of getting on with the dance.

The only other manifestation of refinement was the annual Ball of the Turco-Tatar Ladies. In spite of its name, this was an all-European function, rather snobbish, to which Asians were not invited. The ladies were from the small, sadly frayed Russian émigré community. They were of ambiguous age and comported themselves with the brittle pride of those who brood upon the injustice of their downfall. The throng of thirty or forty celebrants in this cultural exchange were alert to emotional tensions. Those of us who were not Turco, nor Tatar, nor slavic, participated with skittish sympathy lest the merriment, under the solvent of vodka, unpredictably melt into tears.

CHAPTER 3

South China

SOUTH CHINA—that is, China south of the Yangtze Basin—is the China that we of the maritime West knew first. To be sure, Marco Polo and a handful of other western Europeans journeyed to North China long before the Portuguese, the English, and the Dutch sailed to South China ports to open commercial relations with the empire in the sixteenth century. But it was the eighteenth and nineteenth century China trade concentrated at Canton that created our first widespread impression of China: a pretty, quaint, and antique land of willow-pattern teahouses, knobby little hills, jasmine, and sleek brocades.

It is true that South China is pretty—verdant, hilly, and laboriously tended. Whether it is quaint is a subjective judgment. But in terms of Chinese civilization, it is not ancient. Even southeastern Manchuria was settled by Chinese before most of South China. The Chinese expansion southward from the Yellow River and Yangtze Basin was a tardy and fitful process, forced by barbarian pressures from the north and famines in the sometimes drought- or flood-stricken center of Chinese civilization. Unlike the Americans and Russians who exulted in expanding their frontiers, the Chinese seemed to have colonized southward grudgingly. They were a people who believed that it was virtuous to die where you were born and who were transfixed by their defensive frontier against the northern barbarians, rather than captivated by the easy opportunities for expansion to the south.

Although the Ch'in Empire in the third century before Christ conquered a long corridor to what is now Canton and beyond, most of South China continued to be inhabited by aboriginal tribes living in rain forests. The last large part of China proper to be brought within the empire was the plateau which became the province of Yunnan, meaning South of the Clouds. The scattered tribes of these highlands were more or less conquered, not by a native Chinese dynasty, but by Khublai Khan in 1253. Khublai, the Mongol, made himself a Chinese emperor and so Yunnan became part of China, thanks to the enterprise of a northern barbarian usurper.

Yunnan was not really incorporated in the empire, however, until the seventeenth century. Even in 1933, when I was stationed there as a vice-consul, the Chinese were still racially in the minority and their writ did not run throughout the province. Chinese dared not enter some aboriginal areas without military escort for fear of being buried alive.

As the Chinese expanded into South China, the original inhabitants had three basic choices. They could retreat further southward. They could move aside into the hills and let the Chinese flow past them in the valleys. Or they could mix with and be assimilated by the Chinese.

Some did the first. But many of the aborigines moved back into the hills as cultural hold-outs. They lived apart from the Chinese, did not intermarry, and kept their own language, customs, and dress—in the case of the Miao tribeswomen, elaborately and brightly embroidered. The tribes people numbered in the millions. And in several instances they were related to tribes in Southeast Asian countries.

Finally, other aborigines adapted themselves to dealing with the settlers from the north. They adopted Chinese ways, intermarried, and their descendants became the bulk of the Chinese population of South China. The results of this intermixture are apparent. The Chinese from the south is slighter and shorter than the northerner, who is a mixture of Chinese and barbarians from outside of the Great Wall.

South China is not a distinct unit like the Red Basin of Szechuan with its encircling mountains, nor the Yangtze or Yellow River basins, each unified by its drainage system. South China's common characteristics are hilly topography, generous rainfall, and plenty of solar warmth. It is a semitropical and tropical zone.

The up and down landscape, much of it delightfully eccentric limestone formations rising sheerly from constricted little plains, leaves scant land for cultivation. In some areas, as little as ten percent of the countryside is cultivated. Wherever the slopes permit, the hillsides are terraced and irrigated. Rice is the principal crop.

It was in the hills that mark South China's border with the Yangtze Basin that Mao incubated the peasant armies of the Chinese Communists and established his first base areas. There he also began to learn the rudiments of administering people and territory. And moving westward to escape overwhelming government pressure, the Communists fought through these hills on their Long March to the northwest loess country and a new base area from which they later battled their way to power over all of China.

Its seacoast, as much as any other distinctive characteristic, sets South China apart from the rest of the country. Below the mouth of the Yangtze, the coast is indented with numerous good harbors and the population along it is seafaring to an extent unknown along the silt-formed shores of North China. For more than a thousand years, the southern shore folk have been fishermen and seafarers. Inland communications in South China were primitive and slow because of mountains. But junks wallowed up and down the coast carrying produce and passengers with comparative ease. And boat populations developed in port cities, people who spent their lives afloat, but not adrift, engaged in short hauls of produce and ferrying passengers.

Indian and Middle Eastern traders had ventured by sea to the South China coast as many as two thousand years ago. But these were tenuous contacts compared with the overland connections through Turkestan. By the eighth century, ocean commerce had begun to grow, not through Chinese seafaring but from the visits of Korean, Persian, and Arab ships. This encouraged the Chinese to the degree that, about three hundred years later, they had captured the trade with Japan, Korea, and as far south as Sumatra. Some Chinese, at least, were fairly launched on salt water beyond coast hugging and could see farther than the Great Wall.

How well they had been launched was demonstrated in 1405, when a fleet of sixty-two Chinese ships and twenty-eight thousand men sailed through the Straits of Malacca to India. These vessels, some of which were imposing four-deckers, were navigated with the aid of the compass—which the Chinese had invented perhaps as much as a thousand years earlier. Five expeditions followed, sailing as far as Aden, the Persian Gulf, and the coast of East Africa. Their purpose seems to have been to extract tribute, trade, and collect for the delectation of the Ming Emperor Chu Ti (sometimes referred to as Yung Lo, the name of his reign period) such curiosities as giraffes.

The impresario of these semi-goodwill tours was Chêng Ho, a eunuch of the Yung Lo court. Having made China the greatest maritime power of that time —for his exploits had never been equalled—Chêng Ho was forced to abandon his voyages at the end of the sixth of them in 1433. No single reason for the opposition is known.

What is known is that the literati-bureaucracy was against him because it was hostile to the notorious graft and intriguing of the court eunuchs. The traditional Confucian contempt of mercantilism—trade is vulgar—assumably played a part in the decision. There was also a popular conviction that the rest of the world had nothing worthwhile to contribute to China. The Middle Kingdom was self-sufficient, the center of civilization; things from abroad were at best mere baubles. Furthermore, the ponderous capers of Chêng Ho were mounted in an extravagant fashion and so were a heavy drain on the treasury. Finally, and most importantly, the bogey of the barbarians on the northern frontiers again preoccupied the court. So China turned inward again, away from brilliant achievements on blue water, back to the Yellow River Valley, with eyes fixed on the Great Wall and the wilderness beyond.

The eunuch's feat was one of those atypical Chinese performances that make the Chinese essentially unpredictable. Against all tradition and totally at variance with the stereotype of the Chinese as a race of land-minded farmers, they casually demonstrated that they could be the world's preeminent maritime power. And having shown what they could do on the high seas in grand style and on distant voyages of exploration, they abruptly abandoned these enterprises and reverted to type.

Being of a somewhat more adventurous disposition than the northern Chinese, those of the south were more apt to emigrate overseas. And many of them did. They went to Formosa and to the islands and mainland of southeast Asia. The emigration to the Western Hemisphere was later, in the nineteenth century. Wherever they went, they proved themselves to be industrious, frugal, and not readily assimilable. In Southeast Asia, the overseas Chinese formed large communities that remained fundamentally foreign to their adopted countries. And being shrewder businessmen than the natives, the merchants of the Chinese community tended to be disliked by the host people.

By the end of the nineteenth century, the overseas Chinese, who never lost an interest in their homeland and who all aspired to burial in their family graveyards, had come to support reform and revolutionary movements back in the Middle Kingdom. The nationalist revolution against the Manchu (Ch'ing) Dynasty received financial backing from many Chinese living abroad.

Sun Yat-sen, the so-called father of that revolution, spent his youth and young manhood mostly in overseas communities. During Chiang Kai-shek's years as a cadet in Japan, he naturally sought out Chinese living in Japan and so came in contact with revolutionaries, whose cause he joined. Subsequently, Chinese living abroad have contributed to the support of political factions in the homeland; first to the Kuomintang and later to both the Nationalists and the Communists.

In geographical summary, China is one of the giant countries of the world, larger than the United States. Being big does not necessarily make a country diversified in its geographical characteristics. Canada, for example, is slightly larger than modern China, and Brazil somewhat smaller. Yet they do not have the range of climate and topography that China has. In the case of China, its northeastern corner has a Siberian climate with frigid winters. In contrast, the island of Hainan is tropical, in the same latitude as Haiti or Port Sudan, half way down the Red Sea.

With Tibet, China has the northern slopes of Mt. Everest and the loftiest highlands in the world. China's eastern boundary is formed, in part, by the wide deltas of the Yellow River merging in ooze with the sea. In the Northwest is Koko Nor, an azure lake of more than six hundred square miles, ten thousand feet above sea level. Even further west, deep in the Chinese portion of Central Asia, is the Turfan Depression, a desert oasis nearly one thousand feet below sea level.

Notwithstanding all of its land, only a small fraction of China has been cultivated, some twelve percent. The reason is that most of the land is too dry, too leached, too steep, or too high. Because about one-half of China is more than a mile high, the margin for expansion of farming is small.

With the Soviet Union, China shares the longest common frontier in the world. In addition, China borders on eleven other countries. Some of those along its southern frontier—Laos, India, Bhutan, Sikkim, Nepal, Pakistan, and Afghanistan—have only limited contact with China across their jagged boundaries in the clouds. But with Korea, Mongolia, Vietnam, and even Burma, there have been extensive interchanges across the borders.

China was and is the most populous country in the world. At the beginning of the Manchu dynasty, in the seventeenth century, the population was probably not above one hundred million. At the close of the nineteenth century, it was probably at least four hundred million. By the nineteen seventies, something in the neighborhood of eight hundred million people live in China.

The Chinese are not racially "pure." The original inhabitants of the Yellow River Valley mixed with barbarian and southern aboriginal stock. The Chinese speak of their country as being inhabited by five distinct peoples: Chinese, Manchus, Tibetans, Mongols, and Mohammedans (of Turkic-speaking Central Asian extraction). Although China is not the melting pot that we are, nor even as multiracial as the Soviet Union, still it is not homogeneous. The Japanese, for example, are less mixed in their origins, at least since the beginning of recorded history.

The languages spoken by the inhabitants of China are quite as varied as the ethnic composition of the Chinese. The so-called "mandarin" Chinese, or the "national language" as the Chinese call it, is dominant and is spoken, in diverse dialects, by more people than any other language in the world. Further apart than dialects are the various Chinese languages, mostly in the south. Cantonese is one of them. The differences here are as great as between Italian and Spanish.

The combination of geographical and language barriers emphasized and perpetuated regionalism. Broadly speaking, the differences between southern and northern Chinese have been sharper than those between the deep South of the United States and Yankees of the North. But the particularism was much more than a simple north-south or east-west matter. It has been fractionized into many regionalisms, with neighboring localities none too tolerant of one another.

Two powerful forces were a unifying influence in China's diversity and regionalism. One was the written Chinese language. The other was the imperial government, more the civil service than the emperor.

CHAPTER *4*

Traditional Beliefs and Governance

THE REPUBLICAN REVOLUTION of 1911 was a breakdown in the progressive disintegration of traditional China. But it was only one seizure in a degenerative process. Other symptoms of organic decline had preceded that revolution. Others would follow. The most severe to come would be the Communist Revolution.

By 1911, the Manchu dynasty was played out. This was to be expected. It had lasted 267 years, a respectable life as dynasties go. But the ruling house and the court had become decadent. The time had come, in the pattern of the Chinese past, for the overthrow of the dynasty, whereupon a new dispensation would be the lot of the Chinese people.

The debilitation, however, went deeper than the dynasty. It affected Chinese civilization as a whole in which the rise and fall of dynasties were merely episodic. Chinese civilization was old, more than four thousand years old. It had long been backward-looking, conventionalized, even stagnant. It had lost the intellectual freshness and creativity that had characterized earlier Chinese thought, particularly the thousand years from Confucius to the diffusion of Buddhism, from the fifth century B.C. to the fifth century A.D.

The patterning of life on an idealized past and the high-minded practice of administering public affairs by a civil service of classical scholars had contributed to the extraordinary durability of traditional Chinese civilization. It is even conceivable, had external circumstances continued as they had been for thousands of years, with the Middle Kingdom challenged only by cultures inferior to its own, that traditional Chinese civilization might have continued on and on through our times—a fascinating vestige of antiquity.

But China was challenged by a more vital civilization, the maritime West, beginning in the nineteenth century. The combination of anachronistic society, dynastic decay, and western dynamism was too much for the old order. By the middle of the nineteenth century, it had begun to crack up. By 1912 the imperial system had collapsed. By 1927 the Red Army had germinated in the hills south of the Yangtze. By 1945 the Communists had begun a furious, systematic attempt to destroy traditional Chinese society through violence.

Such a transition, culminating in revolution, is not like changing a suit of clothes—the past hung up in a closet, the present neatly pressed and complete with a second pair of pants. A revolution is an organic reaction to the past. And although it changes the present, the future proves that a revolution cannot fully divest itself of the past. Thus traditional China, the China repudiated by the Communists, was first a progenitor of the Communist revolution, then its adversary, and finally a part of its living self.

Two features of traditional China have not always been taken fully into account by Westerners. One is that it was often turbulent. Much has been written in the West—and will again be said here—about the rationality, equanimity, and mellowness of Chinese civilization. This emphasis is altogether natural, for the orderly, constructive phases of Chinese history were probably the more significant, and certainly the more satisfying to contemplate.

But the periods of turmoil—some lasting for generations—are also important to an understanding of China, past and present. Not only barbarian conquests, but also dynastic wars, peasant uprisings, and unadorned chaos swept over parts of and occasionally all of the country. The Chinese have always been keenly aware of these times of strife, for episodes out of such epochs were vivid in their folklore, literature, and theater. With all of their conservatism and devotion to harmony, the Chinese often lapsed into frenzies and violence.

Another fundamental characteristic was that traditional China functioned on two planes. The two levels were interrelated, but they were quite different. On one plane was the culture of the common people. On the other was the culture of the privileged. The root difference between the two was that one was illiterate, the other literate. The difference was greater than class distinction, as we now use the phrase. It was a distinction between cultures.

We of the West have been so bemused by what we have been told of the refinements of the higher culture—Confucianism, the elegance of Chinese painting and poetry, the grandeur of old Peking—that we do not take fully into account the other China. This other China, the Middle Kingdom of the illiterates and semiliterates, was by far the more populous. It was no less than ninety-nine percent of the inhabitants of traditional China.

These, the untutored, were virtually all of the peasantry, craftsmen, fishermen, laborers, tradesmen, and soldiers. By far the largest element, some ninety percent, was the peasantry. For China was, wherever the land allowed habitation and cultivation, a vast mosaic of small farms. The wealth of the nation came from the farms. The towns and cities were administrative and commercial centers for an agricultural society.

Thus the peasantry dominated the culture of the uneducated by sheer numbers, if by nothing else. Craftsmen, tradesmen, and urban workers formed subcultures, adapted to lives in congestion. But they were closer to the farmer than to the culture of the literati and officialdom.

What the Chinese peasant knew, he had learned through the ear, not through the written word. He learned it from other peasants, itinerant story tellers, Taoist or Buddhist monks, traveling theatrical troupes, or passing chairbearers, wheelbarrow men, or muleteers. He learned it in the form of legends, fables, maxims, tales of the supernatural, incantations, and gossip. In this respect, the culture of the untutored was closer to prehistory China than was that of the literati, who preened themselves on behaving like the ancients.

For the peasant, his culture was a cosmos teeming with good spirits to be wheedled and evil ones to be propitiated; of misty heroes and murky villains out of China's folk ages; of placid contentment when the times were peaceful and nature bountiful; of stoic patience and endurance when the times were bad and nature perverse; of fatalistic resignation when war or famine or pestilence bore down upon him. Seldom did he rise in revolt. But when he did, he fought with fury.

The traditional Chinese tiller of the soil was a husbandman, more conservative than the American farmer, more diligent than the Indian ryot, more frugal than the French peasant, more independent and self-respecting than the Russian serf. He was more than a gardener, but not much more. For his plot of land was a few acres which he cultivated intensively. It was the tiny axis on which his scant world turned, and it had been so for generations. On the outer rim of that world was a nearby market town to which he would go with his produce, but rarely beyond, unless driven by desperation or conscripted by force.

The imperial capital was utterly remote. All that the capital represented was remote—even the magistrate in the nearest district town. The unlettered ones looked up to this resident representative of erudition and authority, and to the few literati living there, with distant awe. These were men apart, of another station in life, another culture, who spoke in a style unfamiliar, even incomprehensible, to the rustic commonalty.

While the lower culture was most of China, the higher culture ran China. The higher was, essentially, a culture of aristocracy. During the mythological era and the initial centuries of recorded history, the aristocracy was exclusively hereditary. Confucius (conventionally assigned 551–479 B.C.) developed the idea of a governing aristocracy of merit serving the throne and selected on the basis of scholarship. Thus he preceded Plato in advocating rule by philosophers.

Confucius was not a religious teacher. His outlook was agnostic, mundane, and ethical. Although the Chinese worshipped a multitude of spirits—among them a supreme deity called Shang Ti, and then T'ien (Heaven)—Confucius advised respectful skepticism toward the supernatural. "Not yet understanding life," he said, "how can you understand death?" He was scrupulous in observing age-old rites to the supernatural while declining to speculate on its nature.

Living in a chaotic era, Confucius was appalled by man's relationship to man. This was his central concern. He wanted a moral order on earth. It was attainable because an ideal society, he thought, had existed some five hundred years earlier. If such an utopia had existed, then it should be possible to recreate it if only mankind would follow the example of the ancients. Responsible for ethical tutelage and example were the lettered élite—and the sovereign. It was for them to manifest and inculcate virtues such as righteousness, straightforwardness, and benevolent love of fellow men.

But the practice of virtue should be in accordance with propriety because, as Confucius observed, to be straightforward without the restraints of propriety would be rude. Decorum was therefore an influence for moderation and urbanity, tempering the excesses of absolute virtue. The Confucianists codified propriety in elaborate rules of etiquette.

Confucius had little success in persuading the rulers of the petty kingdoms of his time to adopt his precepts. But later the Confucian outlook gradually came to be accepted, elaborated upon, contested, modified, and finally sanctified. Confucianism became the core of the higher culture of traditional China.

In the process of development, Confucianism adopted ideas from conflicting philosophies. For the Chinese had an unusual capacity for syncretism. One school of thought influencing the Confucianists was that of the so-called Legalists. Having a low opinion of mankind, the Legalists believed in strictest law and order, rewards and punishments, collective responsibility for the behavior of the individual, and the duty of the people to produce wealth and military strength for the authoritarian state. While disapproving of the Legalists, the Confucian literati assimilated some of their tenets.

Similarly, the agnostic Confucianists came to coexist with Taoism and Buddhism. Both religions, as they were popularized for and by the commonalty, were debased into lush animism, sporting eighteen Buddhist hells, and eighty-one Taoist and thirty-three Buddhist heavens. But for the less credulous élite, the appeal of Taoism and Buddhism was intellectual and aesthetic.

The Taoist notion of a mystic oneness with Nature through passivity, and the serene Buddhist belief in release from the sorrows of this world through denial of desire and ultimate union with the infinite, these quite un-Confucian trains of thought fascinated, outraged and, to a greater degree than they liked to admit, captivated Confucianists. It was not uncommon for a purposeful scholar-bureaucrat as he grew old to relax his austerity and happily take on the comfortable Taoist belief in the importance of doing nothing or the Buddhist virtue of thinking about nothing. In so doing, or more precisely, not doing, he remained a Confucianist, at least in his own estimation.

Neither level of Chinese culture was troubled by belief in Original Sin and the Fall of Man. Nor did Confucius develop any idea resembling these Christian doctrines. Consequently, the Chinese were not driven by a sense of guilt, an anxious need for its expiation, or a thirst for salvation by a personal God. Neither level was a guilt culture. Compulsions of guilt were introduced to the Chinese later by Christianity, and then by Communism.

The idea of human advancement toward utopia through mortal collision of dialectical materialism, class struggle, revolution, and dictatorship of the proletariat—such a formula would have seemed preposterous to the classical Chinese.

Only somewhat less farfetched would be the western concept of democracy—progress without violence toward a better life through ensuring the equality of all men, and the amiable submission by the minority to the will of the majority.

To the Confucianists, utopia lay behind, not ahead. The best had passed; it was not to come. So progress was regression. To advance was to return to the fancied perfection of the ancients.

In the past perfect society not all men were equal. They were distinctly unequal and so classified. In the classic five relationships of Confucius, all but the last listed were between superior and inferior: ruler and subject, father and son, husband and wife, elder brother and younger brother, friend and friend.

People were also classified according to their occupation. At the top of the scale was, of course, the emperor. Below the imperial family came the literate élite, those of the higher culture, sometimes referred to as the gentry. Most esteemed among them were the literati officials. These had attained high rank from having passed the more advanced examinations leading to government office. On a lower plane were those of lesser scholastic attainments, many of whom were of slight learning but of ample wealth in land holdings. These are sometimes designated as "lower gentry," but are here referred to simply as gentry.

After the gentry came the cultural gap. Heading the list of the untutored were peasants, followed by artisans. Both were regarded with favor because they were producers. Merchants, because they merely bought, sold, and profited, were held in disdain and sometimes even regarded as beyond the bounds of Chinese society, along with jugglers, soldiers, slaves, harlots, and actors. Those wealthy merchants who performed meritorious deeds were able to cleanse themselves of the stigma of trade and become members of the gentry upon judicious payment of contributions to sympathetic circles in the imperial court.

Class distinctions, therefore, were sharply defined. They were not, however, extravagantly discriminatory as in the Indian caste system, with its severe social and religious taboos and sanctions. At the other extreme, there was nothing in traditional China remotely resembling the concept of class struggle, unless vaguely manifested in occasional peasant uprisings in times of acute economic distress. As a preindustrial society, the Middle Kingdom had neither capitalists nor proletariat in the Leninist sense of the proletariat's being the class engaged in the production of goods in large-scale capitalist industrial enterprises.

The social ideal in traditional China was highly stylized. The political choreography required order and harmony. Each individual and each group had an assigned role in relation to others. No one was to transgress his role and all were to perform in harmony.

The ruler should be a ruler. The subject should be a subject. The father should be father and the son a son. Each should perform what his role called for. This is what the Confucianists called "rectification of names."

Thus, the emperor, and not the will of the majority, reigned. The common man was unsheltered by any bill of rights. The emperor was the ruler and he, the subject, was at the mercy of such benevolence as the sovereign chose to bestow. The emperor, therefore, was an absolute monarch—with one reservation. He was answerable to heaven. He ruled under its mandate, not unlike an imperial driver's license issued from on high and subject to withdrawal if abused by reckless behavior endangering the public.

This ingenious theory was contrived before the unification of China as an empire, in the third century B.C. Its authors were the founders of the Chou dynasty, who justified their usurpation by asserting that the preceding dynasty had lost the "Mandate of Heaven" because of its deficiency in virtue. This had made it unfit to govern. Thereupon, they proclaimed, the Mandate had passed to the Chou rulers. Chou virtue, having been yet untested, was assumably intact. To clinch the claim, the first Chou king described himself as Son of Heaven, a celestial pretension of which his successors in that and subsequent dynasties made no attempt to divest themselves.

The presumption regarding the Mandate of Heaven became a tenet in the political philosophy of traditional China. It was more than a sanctimonious justification for usurpation, reflecting unfavorably on the preceding ruling house. It also gained considerable acceptance as a right, suggested by Mencius, to popular revolt against any ruler whose behavior violated the canons of benevolence and righteousness.

For if the sovereign thus exhausted the Mandate of Heaven, he lost that which qualified him as sovereign and became "the robber and ruffian we call a mere fellow." Such "a mere fellow" deserved to be put to death by the people. "I have never heard," added Mencius, "that this was assassinating a ruler." As this stern proposition worked out in Chinese history, an emperor killed by a revolt that succeeded became "a mere fellow." But if the revolt failed, he was the Son of Heaven, most foully assassinated, and the unsuccessful rebels suffered the nasty consequences.

Irrespective of these postmortem considerations, the emperor was restricted, at least in principle, by a high moral code. A great deal was expected of him. He was the exalted intermediary between mankind and an impersonal heaven which, in this relationship, was constituted of primordial moral principles and the forces of nature. Thus the sovereign had dual responsibilities. He was to set a moral example to the people. And he was charged with making sure that nature stayed on the side of the farmer. If natural calamities occurred, it was because of some imperial deficiency in virtue.

The emperor was expected in theory not only to comport himself as a paragon of morality before his subjects. His also was the responsibility to perform rites to the forces of nature, to heaven and to earth so as to fend off droughts, floods, and other natural disasters. These ceremonies were less of a strain on the Son of Heaven than the day-to-day obligations of morally keeping up to snuff. Certainly, the petty rulers whom Confucius met gave him little reason to anticipate exemplary ethical conduct by royalty. And so it proved to be with latter-day emperors. Most of them praised the Sage and discharged their liturgical functions. Very few of them measured up to his precepts, any more than various of our most Christian kings took after the teachings of Jesus. Many emperors were best remembered for their debauchery.

Confucius was really directing himself more to his own kind—the scholars —than to the kings, princes, and hereditary aristocracy. He expected the literati to enlighten and guide the rulers, whether the scholars were granted official positions or not. Those selected as officials would directly affect the administration of government. Those who failed would still, through teaching and example, make an impact on the court and the people. Together, if they were models of wisdom, virtue, and propriety, their influence could be compelling.

In their relationship with the sovereigns, the literati had one decisive advantage. They were indispensable to the throne. For they had a monopoly on education and so were the only ones equipped to serve as administrators. Because of the exacting nature of the written Chinese language, the monopoly of literacy held by the scholars was securely theirs. The literati were not displeased that this was so.

Written Chinese began as pictographs, representing things, not the sounds of spoken names of the things. From there it developed gradually to ideographs or characters, retaining traces of their pictorial origins, but ever more abstract and esoteric. Written Chinese is like a mathematician's language of symbols and formulas which stand for things, actions, and ideas, no matter how pronounced in English, German, Russian—or Chinese. It is not like our alphabetical language which spells out, more or less phonetically, the sounds of words.

To become a scholar, a man had to memorize something like eight or nine thousand characters. But that was only the beginning, for ideographs were fluid in definition, depending on context or other characters used with them. For example, the ideograph which we ordinarily translate as "word" can also mean among other things: the special name taken by a Chinese man at the age of twenty, or to betroth a girl, or to bring forth and give suckle to, or (in connection with the ideograph for "people") to love and care for the masses.

The ideograph which we translate as "righteousness" may also mean, depending on context: morality, duty to one's neighbor, adopted (in the sense of a child or slave-girl), and false (in the sense of a hairpiece). Even the surname of Confucius, K'ung, in the original Chinese, may also mean an opening or a hole, great, very urgent, and a peacock.

In the spoken language, there are other multiple pitfalls. They need not be gone into here. The point here is that only a student who had devoted years to the study of written Chinese and become familiar with the classical literature could hope to understand and then himself compose in the language of the literati, strewn with literary allusions and scholastic exhibitionism. It is no wonder, therefore, that education was viewed with awe and that men of learning were greatly honored as quite apart and superior to the untutored.

Learning by memorization, reciting aphorisms by rote, steeped in scholasticism, and marinated in moralism, the traditional student emerged with a mind that was ripe and refined. It was seldom, after this process, an original mind nor was it receptive to new ideas. It was well-suited to the administration of a secluded, sedentary civilization, so long as the only threat to its existence came from those less civilized.

The literati considered themselves to be the transmitters and protectors of Confucianist culture. For them, this was the only civilization. All non-Chinese societies were uncivilized, barbarian. However, those barbarians who subjected themselves to the discipline of acquiring Confucianist culture were indulged and accepted as civilized, as sharers in the only civilization.

The scholar officials also regarded themselves as the administrators of a universal empire. The emperor whom they served held a mandate from Heaven, and moreover, was the Son of Heaven. These were sufficient credentials for assuming that he held sway over, not only Chinese, but all on earth. Because of this assumption, fragmentation of China, as often happened in Chinese history, was particularly distressing to the Confucianists. For such a breakup was more than a political disaster. It was also a violation of the moral order prescribed by Heaven.

Another imperial and literati concept that flowed from the notion of China as a universal empire was that there could be no other equal, sovereign state. There was China, the Middle Kingdom. Around it, beyond the beneficence of its civilization, were vassal or tributary states which paid tribute to it in recognition of its supremacy. What the Chinese emperor gave in return was bestowed as gifts.

Having taken for granted for generations upon generations the overwhelming preeminence of Chinese civilization and the Dragon Throne, the scholar bureaucrats seemed to the westerners who encountered them in the eighteenth and nineteenth centuries uncommonly self-possessed at best, and insufferably haughty, at worst. The British, who were then the most persistent claimants for "normal" relations with Peking, underwent considerable humiliation in return for their enterprise. In response to the request of Lord Macartney in 1793 for resident diplomatic relations and trading facilities, the emperor deigned to issue a series of special mandates directed to King George III.

Ch'ien Lung opened with the salutation, "You, O King, live beyond the confines of many seas, nevertheless, impelled by your humble desire to partake of the benefits of our civilization, you have dispatched a mission respectfully bearing your memorial. . . . To show your devotion, you have also sent offerings of your country's produce."

Having put George III at ease, in the position of a favor-currying vassal, the Son of Heaven complimented the British monarch, noting that his memorial revealed "a respectful humility which is highly praiseworthy." Whereupon Ch'ien Lung rejected the British proposals presented by Lord Macartney. "Our Celestial Empire," he patiently explained, "possesses all things in prolific abundance. . . . There is therefore no need to import the manufactures of outside barbarians." But ever indulgent, the emperor hastened to soften the blow: "I do not forget the lonely remoteness of your island, cut off from the world by intervening wastes of sea, nor do I disregard your excusable ignorance of the usages of Our Celestial Empire."

Further on in the mandates, the Son of Heaven reminded King George that, "My capital is the hub and center about which all quarters of the globe revolve." In this tone, he admonished the British sovereign: "It is your bounden duty reverently to appreciate my feelings and to obey these instructions henceforward for all times, so that you may enjoy the blessings of perpetual peace." Ch'ien Lung closed his communications with: "Tremblingly obey and show no negligence."

These sentiments of the emperor were shared, if not composed, by his scholar-bureaucracy. And yet, with all of their disdain for barbarian chieftains, the literati had usually displayed a remarkable suppleness in putting themselves at the service of those barbarians who conquered China. Throughout Chinese history, barbarian invasion and occupation was followed, after initial literati revulsion, by scholar-bureaucrat and gentry collaboration with the alien conquerors. In some cases, the barbarians were slow to accept the Chinese administrators. The Mongols at first brought in Saracens and other foreigners as civil officials, but then as the Mongols themselves took to Chinese ways, they came to rely on the Chinese scholar officials.

Thus the bureaucracy provided continuity through dynastic changes, even after the disruption of alien invasion and rule. The invaders found that although they might conquer the Chinese, they could not alone administer the multitudinous, evasively intractable Chinese. Consequently, sooner or later, they turned to the only ones who knew how to do so.

The barbarian rulers' conclusion that they needed Chinese collaboration was in considerable part due to their having themselves succumbed to a polished culture, tended and exemplified by the literati. It follows that with the maturing of an alien dynasty, the emperors became progressively more Chinese in their outlook. Ch'ien Lung, whose ancestors were barbarian invaders from Manchuria, had himself so partaken of the benefits of Chinese civilization that he treated the barbarian George III with an arrogant suavity which was a model of its celestial kind.

With all of their haughtiness, the literati were not a completely closed group. To a remarkable extent, the Confucianists kept entry into this highly privileged class on the basis of merit. Notwithstanding many exceptions, qualification was by examinations at several levels, depending on the degree being sought. This being generally so, the way to power and prestige lay open to talented peasant boys, provided that their families could or patrons would finance their tutoring. But the path was not easy for them. Youths of the lower culture were at a disadvantage not only because of the cost of education but also because lads growing up in the higher culture had important environmental advantages over those from simpler circumstances.

The bureaucracy in traditional China was on a more modest scale than those in modern industrialized states. The number of civilian officials during the Ch'ing dynasty, for example, hovered around twenty thousand. The American Department of Agriculture alone has five times that number of employees.

An explanation for the Chinese economy of effort in government was that the common man was pretty much left alone, save for taxes and occasional impressment for public works or military service. The imperial civil service did not itself extend down to the village level. Essentially, the local gentry administered everything below the district or county seat. This required no great effort. The population was normally well behaved. The patriarchal family system made for stability. And Confucian ethics and emphasis on the hierarchical five relationships influenced popular conduct in the direction of orderliness. Custom, compromise, and consensus governed most behavior.

To ensure public order, however, and to provide for military conscription and training, there existed a system called *pao chia* whereby families were organized in groups of ten. Each group chose its headman and through him the ten families were held collectively responsible for the misconduct of any one of their members. Likewise, through the headman, the group was required to supply its quota of manpower for public works or military service.

Collective responsibility for the misdeeds of an individual does not jibe with our ideas of justice. It was, however, economical and efficient for the government. The Japanese recognized this during their occupation of parts of China in the 1930s and 1940s and used the *pao chia* system with brutal effectiveness. The Communists also saw its utility, applying it in their own terms.

The cultural gap between the governing élite and the common people extended beyond the difference between literacy and illiteracy, etiquette and rustic manners. It stretched to the difference between ruler and subject, in which the subject was unprotected by law and consequently was dependent upon such ethical restraints as the ruler, whether emperor or district magistrate, chose to impose upon himself. In the hierarchical society of traditional China, this gap between those who ruled and those who were ruled was not bridged. There was no real communication between the two levels.

Therefore, if those who governed dispensed not benevolent paternalism but oppression, the only recourse for the unprivileged was revolt. When successful, peasant revolts led only to a partial change of rulers, not to the creation of a new system to replace the hierarchical one of Confucian paternalism. It remained for the Communists, in their rise to power, to close the gap between ruler and ruled, to organize the mass potential, to give the peasants a feeling of significant participation, even of control over their destinies, in so doing to smash the old system, and then to subject the peasants to a new and disciplined order.

The marvel is that the Confucian style of government lasted as long as it did —some two thousand years. The reasons that it did are manifold. For one thing, the self-perpetuating civil service, based on intellectual merit and selected through competitive examinations, provided an administration of competence and continuity. Then too, the original Confucian formula was humanistic, moderate, and stabilizing. Furthermore, Confucianism was at crucial times in its development relatively flexible, adapting itself to changes in popular attitudes and borrowing from other philosophies. It early drew selectively on the authoritarian ideas of the Legalists and accommodated itself to Taosim and Buddhism.

Confucianism was easily as humorless as any other political system—for they all take themselves with absurd solemnity. It indulged in bouts of intolerance towards opposing ideas. Yet, on the whole, it bore with equanimity persistent ridicule from critics, particularly the Taoist intellectuals, who did have a sense of humor and who professed to believe that political and social institutions corrupted the inborn harmony of man with nature. Chuang Tzu, when invited to become prime minister, likened that position to that of a sacrificial ox, fatted, bedecked with embroidered trappings, and treated with honor. "Defile me not," he told the king's emissary. The lot of an uncared for piglet was preferable—"I would rather disport myself in the mire . . ."

Two Confucian institutions placed traditional China ahead of the rest of the ancient and medieval world in the art of government. The examination system for entry to official position was one—introduced during the first century B.C. The second was the imperial Board of Censors, developed some seven centuries later. The board acted as an inspectorate against corruption and other misdeeds within the bureaucracy. It had direct access to the emperor. Occasionally it reproved the emperor himself—at times with fatal consequences to the critic.

The censor device had its weaknesses. It was susceptible to intimidation by the throne and bribery by fellow bureaucrats. But on the whole, it had a salutary influence on the government.

CHAPTER 5

The Family and the Individual

IN TRADITIONAL CHINA, the state was less important than Chinese civilization. After all, dynasties rose and fell, the empire was several times overrun or riven asunder by barbarian hordes. Furthermore, the state apparatus was never close to the people and it, too, on occasions had been shattered. But the Chinese people and their civilization endured.

Such broad allegiances as the Chinese held were more to race and civilization than to the nation. The Chinese spoke of themselves as the Han people, with strong connotations of race and culture. It was not until their nineteenth century contact with the nation states of the West that they described themselves in nationalistic terms as men of the Middle Kingdom. Traditional China, therefore, was ethnocentric rather than nationalistic, more culturally proud than patriotic.

The state also occupied second place to the family. The institution of the family was the cornerstone of Chinese society, and, whatever claims the emperor might make on his subjects, their deeper loyalty was to the elders of the family. Filial piety, if not the root of all virtue, was at least a prime manifestation of virtue.

Confucius set the tone on this score when one of the petty rulers of his time told the Sage that there was in his part of the country a man so upright that he bore witness against his own father when the old man appropriated a sheep. Confucius did not think much of this concept of rectitude. He observed that in his part of the country "a father would screen his son and a son his father." "In that," Confucius declared, "lies uprightness." It was not that Confucius would condone cattle-rustling or stealing sheep. It was that he put fidelity within the family as the higher law.

The traditional Chinese family was a highly formalistic institution. Each member had his place in the patriarchal system, graded by age and sex. Grandfather ruled the family and the youngest granddaughter was the lowliest of the lot. This was not a family circle; it was a family pyramid.

The son owed his father obedience and veneration. As a child, he owed his mother both, but in a lesser degree than to his father. After the death of the father, the mother owed obedience to her son. Filial piety carried beyond the death of parents. For then they joined the considerable assemblage of ancestors whose spirits were worshipped by the entire family.

The husband had complete authority over his wife. He was free to indulge himself by taking one or several concubines, if he could afford the luxury and the domestic strain. The wife had to put up with concubines with as good grace as her disposition permitted. Although a woman could be returned to her family as unsatisfactory, there was no other arrangement similar to divorce. And should a woman be widowed, the social pressure against her remarrying was tremendous. Some bereaved and constant women were lucky enough to be honored, posthumously, with stone or wooden arches spanning thoroughfares and proclaiming them to have been virtuous widows.

Ordinarily, women found full scope for their executive drive only after they acquired daughters-in-law. These hapless young women had minimal rights in the families into which they were married. And their husbands, stifled by filial piety, were obligated, if it came to a choice, to side with their parents against their wives. The solace for a daughter-in-law was to stick it out in anticipation of the day when she, too, would be a mother-in-law.

Relations between brothers, one of the five Confucian relationships, were less taxing than the other family ties. The elder brother was distinctly superior and next in line of authority after the father. But unless there was conflict over inheritances or wives, the relationship was likely to be fairly companionable.

Members of a traditional Chinese family were, consequently, members of an organization. It was an authoritarian, systematized organization, insistent on conformity and gradual promotion on the basis of seniority and specialization, men in the men's department and women in theirs. It stood, closely knit, against outside encroachments and its collective interests had priority over the individual interests of its members.

The family provided social security for all who belonged to it, insofar as the collective means permitted. It was the responsibility of the group that no member suffered want. From this grew the prevalence of nepotism in traditional Chinese society. Most Chinese took the favoring of relatives in employment as normal and proper.

Marriage was arranged between families, not left to the giddy impulses of the immature. All girls were to be married, and nearly all were, if for no other reason than that the head of the family did not wish to have the embarrassment and expense of an unmarriageable daughter on his hands. There were, therefore, scarcely any old maids in traditional China. The few who could not be married off were the obligation of their families—to be supported within the household until the end of their days. And so it was with widows. Which, everything considered, was not so much worse a fate than that of the lone, emancipated modern woman.

When a family was too poor to support all of its members, the first to be discarded was a female. Outside the walls of Kiating was a small tower-like structure. Parents who had decided to unburden themselves of an infant daughter deposited her in this installation. There she was left to die of exposure. If the baby was not so disposed of, she still ran the risk that poverty would later impel her parents to sell her as a slave girl to some well-to-do household, or as a prostitute. Such transactions in any part of China were widespread in times of famine when small girls and young women were taken out of their own districts for sale in unafflicted areas.

Young males, in contrast, were cherished. They were their parents' guarantee of support in old age and worship after death—the Confucianist substitute for immortality. Although daughters participated in ancestor worship, they did not perform the essential rites. Furthermore, once married off, they tended their husbands' parents and worshipped their husbands' ancestors.

The principal function of a woman was procreation, more precisely to produce sons. She produced them not for herself, excepting as a filial son was expected to care for an aged mother, but for her husband and his forebearers so that the male line would not be broken and the ancestral rites not neglected. Her secondary function was household service for her husband and family. Because she was regarded as intellectually incompetent, she rarely was taught to read or write and was not believed to have any opinions, beyond those on housekeeping problems, that were worthy of consideration.

The odds against a Chinese woman's chancing upon happiness seemed to be high, as the risks were infanticide, being sold into slavery or whoredom, educational neglect, arranged marriage to an unknown husband, a mother-in-law's tyranny, being spurned for a concubine, and permanent subservience to males who practically owned her, first her father and then her husband. Yet it cannot be said that Chinese women as a whole were noticeably any unhappier than women of their time elsewhere, or any more beset by neuroses.

Chinese poetry, to be sure, contains laments over love grown cold, lovers thwarted and lovers parted, as does ours. Chinese poetry and novels also record tender instances of love requited and enduring. What does seem clear, however, is that Chinese women, like their men, were exceptionally adaptable and enduring under adversity. They were also much more of a force in society than their submerged condition suggested. They were not so in any fashion resembling The League of Women Voters. Rather, their influence was exercised individually, personally, and privately through their menfolk.

The traditional Chinese family system was hard on individualism. The Confucian hierarchy in relationships and the Confucian ethic were restrictive, so that the Chinese tended to be inhibited, particularly the women on whom the repressions were by far the heavier. Yet the Chinese have often been described as distinctly individualistic.

The fact of the matter is that the Chinese were both inhibited and individualists. This was only one of the many paradoxes about these extraordinary people. It was related to the ability of the mundane, conventionalized Confucianist to be at the same time, or in his spare time, a mystic, placidly anarchistic Taoist. The Chinese gentleman was not in revolt against either of the opposing views. He simply yielded to and enjoyed living a contradictory life. Such an accomplishment is offensive to our Western fixation with consistency. But for the traditional Chinese, living a contradiction was sensibly taking advantage of opposites.

And so the traditional Chinese male could be punctilious in all of his ramified family roles—meek and solicitous toward his father, respectful to his uncles, a martinet with his wife, full of stern advice to younger brothers, ruinously indulgent to his small son, and moonstruck with his fifteen-year-old concubine. This still left him considerable scope for individuality in his relationship with friends. His other life, that of friendship with his peers, was one in which obligations, save those of decorum, were comparatively light. Here his personality could blossom with few inhibitions or compulsions.

Nor should it be thought that the family system denied all self-expression. The father, obviously, had extensive license to individualistic behavior, within the limits of his own family. For who but the head of the *pao chia*, or the magistrate, or the emperor was to gainsay him? And he was quite aware of the needs of his ego.

So, too, it was with the old mother in her realm, clucking over and pecking at her covey of daughters, daughters-in-law, certainly her grandchildren, even her sons and, only to be mentioned behind the hand, the patriarch himself. Down the line, the play of individualism was the privilege of the males. They were indulged over their sisters, down to the level of spoiled rotten.

The pressures of family convention were so heavy on the younger females of the family that individualism could find expression only through intrigue or open revolt. Here was not the easy ambivalence of the traditional Chinese male, quite unconcerned at living simultaneously two, or even more lives. The standard for a daughter of the family was single, straight, and narrow. If she sought to express her personality in any but a prudish, conventional fashion, she moved into rebellion, secret or overt, not into the casual inconsistency practiced, condoned, and even admired, in her brothers.

Curiously enough, the institution which for some probably commanded the deepest allegiance, next to the family, was the secret society. Although relatively few were members, every Chinese knew of the secret societies. For over the course of centuries, there had been many such organizations, composed mostly of men from the lower culture, in many cases disreputable types. Much folklore had grown up around the secret societies, about their forays against the rich and their benevolence to the poor.

But few Chinese knew much in detail about the secret societies. Some of these organizations were religious in origin. Some were formed for mutual assistance. Others were revolutionary or, contrariwise, were used by the government, as the so-called Boxers were in 1900, egged on by the dominant elements of the Manchu Court to attack foreigners. Finally, there were the broadly predatory secret societies, operating traditionally as brigands, or by the 1930s as a city gang, like the Green Gang which functioned freely in Shanghai as a crime monopoly and dispenser of charity.

Because most of the secret societies were clandestine and because the size of their membership changed with circumstances, accurate statistics of the number involved in these organizations are unknown. As a rough estimate, over-all membership might have fluctuated between ten and thirty million, well under 10 percent of the population. Thus, relatively few participated in secret societies, took blood oaths of brotherhood, and in fraternal company performed terrible and noble deeds. Such adventurous behavior, contrary to Confucian ethics, greatly appealed not only to those so embroiled but also to the feeling for vicarious romance of most other Chinese. Here then was another paradox, another contradiction of the stereotype of the placid, conformist Chinese.

Given the nature of the secret societies, it is not surprising that a number of those who rose high in the ranks of the Communist oligarchy had, before their conversion to Marxism, been active in one of the better known secret societies. Mao Tse-tung was not one of them. But in the late 1920s, he gratefully accepted volunteers from the secret societies for his ragtag and bobtail Red Army, and then in 1936 even proposed an anti-Japanese alliance with one of the organizations.

It was a marvelously intricate society through which the traditional Chinese had to sense his way. Scarcely less real than his parents was the thickly populated spirit world all about him—his ancestors, of course, and then a miscellany of ghosts and devils, insidious fox fairies who could appear in the guise of enticing maidens, mysterious omens, the eerie influence of geomancy's wind and water, portents in the skies and the kitchen gods to be propitiated. However the learned might raise their eyebrows about the supernatural, common sense dictated the wisdom of playing safe, of buying off the occult forces which were malicious, and rewarding those which were obliging. The approach to the spirit community was typically Chinese: wary, circumspect, and closely bargained to the point of retrieving sacrifices of food for consumption by the supplicants. Characteristically, the Chinese had no festival corresponding to Thanksgiving.

As with the busy supernatural throngs around him, the traditional Chinese had to manipulate his way through the swarms of living humans crowded about —his family, neighbors, friends, villagers. These were basic. Then there were his contacts with the head of his and other *pao chias*, and those whom he suspected might be secret society members and wayfarers, some of whom were good men, others fearsome. If he was of the higher culture, his associations extended in ever more ramified complexity to, if he attained court rank, the emperor.

In this mixed multitude of spirits and men, Confucian agnosticism and the Confucian code of ethics did not provide the individual with any great sense of security. The traditional Chinese quickly learned that benevolence, uprightness, righteousness, loyalty, and reciprocal altruism were not as widely practiced as invoked. Furthermore, the law courts were notoriously corrupt and ruinous to both sides in a litigation, so that no one in possession of his senses sought redress for wrongs through legal action. In any event, in this absolutist hierarchical society, there were no provisions in law for the protection of civil liberties.

Thus all Chinese below the emperor were vulnerable to mistreatment by those above them. In these human circumstances, as in those relating to the supernatural, prudence was of prime importance. Propriety should be observed and one should behave according to one's station in the hierarchy lest offense be given and animosity needlessly aroused. To fend off potential abuse, ingratiate yourself with those above you. And when victimized, try to bargain and buy your way out of trouble, enlisting if you can the moderating influences of a patron above you. If you cannot do that, try to get a middleman to intercede between you and your tormentor.

Act as a middleman yourself in disputes between others, if so invited. In so doing you earn gratitude and win public esteem. But be wary of being trapped as a defender of the losing side. Speak only in accepted homilies as one who seeks reasonable compromise in which both sides yield something, and as a practical rule of thumb, the weaker more, the stronger less.

The hazards of the traditional Chinese environment tended to foster respectful cynicism for fine phrases and noble sentiments, quick intuition for where power lay and trouble might ferment in any human situation, and a facility for lying low, evasion, passive resistance, negotiating to cut one's losses and generally surviving under adverse conditions. These qualities existed in relations within the family as in the society as a whole; in imperial China and in China under the Communists.

When a Chinese was victimized beyond endurance, his alternatives were relatively simple. He could try to kill his oppressor or he could commit suicide. Individually, the traditional Chinese seldom resorted to murder. Exceptions were female infanticide and, in the highest circles of the imperial court, assassinations. But collectively, killing—by gangs of social outcasts, by some of the secret societies, and by mobs or organized insurgents in popular uprisings—was less rare.

Suicide was a subtler means of revenge. It was the ultimate retort of an oppressed daughter-in-law. She knew that if she killed herself a resounding scandal would ensue and that her own family would be bound to seek retribution from her in-laws, even in a blood feud. This threat of suicide, incidentally, tended to curb the extent of abuse vented upon daughters-in-law and excited lively concern for their health when they took to bed with any malady not evidently attributable to natural causes.

Suicide as a form of retaliation was less common among men, but it was by no means unknown. When practiced. it was usually on the doorstep or on the premises of the oppressor. As in the case of daughters-in-law, death by his own hand rallied public opinion—rather belatedly to be sure—behind the man and against his enemy. The possibility of a suicide being visited upon one reinforced the normal Chinese disinclination to corner a man, to drive him to the wall. Especially was this so because the ghost of the deceased could be counted on to plague the offender interminably.

The traditional Chinese society not only provided limited security for the individual. It also constricted his initiative in defending himself and, what was probably more important, in finding full scope during times of peace for the expression of his individuality. In this society of allotted slots, there was no place for the gaudy ego-expansion that flowers in the American southwest. In China such exhibitionism found expression only among brigands, rebels, and emperors of ill repute.

Ambition, as we know it in the West, was suppressed. The weight of philosophic teaching was contentment with one's lot or escapism through either the Taoist or Buddhist formula. Material success, as we think of it, was ignored or scorned by the élite.

Yet *fa ts'ai*, get rich, was one of the commonest phrases and strongest aspirations of most Chinese. To pass the examinations and become an official was, of course, a much loftier goal and one even more difficult of attainment. It was a possibility only for those who could get an education, and competition to qualify for the various degrees and for official appointment was intense.

Ambition therefore, though not encouraged and though abandoned by most past twenty, was still a driving force for many. In times of tranquility, personal advancement was through conformity to an extremely conventionalized system dominated by the elderly. For age represented wisdom and power. This was so in the family, certainly. It was also the case in society as a whole, when it was not wracked by invasion or disorder. A basic and listless prescription for getting ahead was to let seniority grow on one. All that this required was patience. And the Chinese have had that quality in generous measure.

For the impatient who wanted to accelerate the process, the stratagem was to enlist the support of the influential, to find favor and bring it to bear on one's behalf. Excepting in the case of examinations where only merit counted, a man's personal performance was usually not as important as the influence he could enlist. This was grounded in the support that the ambitious young man expected and received from his family in the form of nepotism. Helping relatives to get jobs for which they had no particular qualifications was an established and respected practice.

Beyond the family, favor was sought from any source from which it could be wheedled. This might be a wealthy villager for whom some unusual favor had been done or a benign scholar whose compassion had been aroused. If the aspirant were of the privileged higher culture, then the quest for favor entered the realm of tortuous intrigue.

Whether peasant or courtier, the technique for advancement was basically the same. It began with the same quality so necessary for self-protection—the development of an acute sense of where power lay in human relations. As one sought the protection of the powerful against the aggression of others, so the powerful were necessary to support one's advancement. Having identified the sources of influence, the next step was to win them to one's side. This was by a process of ingratiation, usually through obsequiousness and such favors as could be performed by the weaker for the stronger. Often this included becoming a follower of the stronger. Thus one acquired a patron to whom one owed loyalty, at least so long as it was opportune.

The traditional Chinese was adept at this game of ingratiation, of intuitively understanding what a man wanted in order to get what he himself wanted. And he enjoyed playing this game, exploiting the more powerful so skillfully that—he hoped—the exploited was unaware of being used. That was a high form of art.

In their earlier contacts with westerners, the Chinese had little exhibited their versatility in this respect simply because there was not much that they wanted from the sea-borne barbarians, except tribute. They were not in a pleader's position, they were the bestowers of favors—including permission to trade on their own terms. It was not until the twentieth century that the Chinese fully realized that they were in the position of supplicants to the West, in need of western patrons. It was then that some of their ablest men undertook to win the favor of westerners.

Much has been made of the charm of Italians in general and the old Russian aristocracy in particular. Chinese charm, when educated to the West and focussed on the foreigner, was more persuasive for being silky, seemingly guileless, and sympathetic to the prejudices of the outlander. The Chinese usually got out of such a relationship some tangible benefit and the Westerner a conviction that he understood the Chinese and that the best of them were right-thinking and uncommonly perceptive.

In maneuvering for advancement, or for that matter in all traditional Chinese relationships, a man's "face" was of prime importance. Face was something like status, but even more cherished and much more easily bruised. You could have it, not have it, lose it, acquire it, make it, or save it.

Concern for face was related to the fact that Chinese society was gregarious and that much store was set by social harmony. In crowded living conditions, to transgress the rules of propriety by offending the self-esteem of another was to cause him to lose face—and thereby start a ruckus.

Likewise, because Chinese society was a shame culture, to embarrass or humiliate another was no joke. It was to risk shaming him. "Pu yao lien!" was one of the most serious reproaches that a Chinese child could hear. "You don't want face." "You are shameless."

The effect of a loss of face was not unlike a seizure by pangs of conscience in a righteous member of a guilt culture: secret anguish. For the guilt-ridden this involved self-reproach and usually led to a resolve to sin no more. For the shamed, there was no sense of culpability, rather a feeling of having been wronged and a need to exact amends, or failing that, to get even.

Losing face depended, of course, on where one's threshold of face began. With beggars and women it was high. That is, they had scant right to face, had little to lose and had to bear with treatment that would be intolerable to a gentleman. It followed that a man of the literati had much face. So he had a low threshold of face, suffered insult from treatment which would be borne by others without hurt, and expected a generous measure of deference.

To acquire face, in the sense of having it bestowed upon one, was what a man sought through ingratiation. Merely to be greeted by someone of higher station was to gain face. From there on any recognition of favor bestowed from above was banking face.

Making face was oneself doing something facey. In a universally laudable form, this was passing an examination. This made much face. But there were cruder ways of making face, such as keeping a bent-pole sedan chair, or flouting the established authorities with impunity. While a thief had no face, he could make face by escalating his crimes, putting on a brave show with his evil-doing and, if brought to execution, behaving defiantly before his head was cut off.

Saving face, in its most refined form, was an operation on behalf of someone who had much face and was threatened with its loss. As an example: a prominent man was so incompetent that he demoralized those with whom he was associated and threatened disaster to whatever it was they were collectively doing. The man could not be fired, for that would make him lose face and create a scandal. Even inducing him to resign would not do, for everyone would see through that. What was done, as was usual and conspicuous in official life, was to appoint Mr. Big Face to an innocuous new position ostensibly of equal or greater face. This is a solution familiar also to those in American politics and business.

Saving face single-handedly, without the considerate collaboration of others, was the less attractive alternative. It tended to involve a preemptive attack on those who would cause the loss of face. This was almost sure to arouse inconvenient rancor, lead to an unseemly spectacle, and not be very convincing. Trying alone to save one's face was therefore a last resort.

In times of turmoil, face was often overridden and the orderly technique of advancement through literary merit and ingratiation with an established hierarchy became unreliable. The unconventional man, daring and skilled in the organization of violence, rose to the top. Two great dynasties, the Han and the Ming, were founded by men out of the commonalty who joined rebel bands in the countryside and through sheer force rose to be Sons of Heaven.

Liu Pang, who became the first Han emperor, had been a village constable. In this unloved capacity, it was his misfortune that several prisoners with whom he was charged escaped. Realizing that he would be held painfully accountable, he released the remaining and less enterprising of his charges and took to the hills with those who were willing to join him as brigands. This venture bloomed into political ambition, which was not surprising because the empire was breaking up. And so, as his band and his fortunes swelled, the Mandate of Heaven descended upon the keeper-then-breaker-of-the-law, and Liu Pang made himself emperor.

The other personal initiative success story was that of Chu Yüan-chang, the founder of the Ming dynasty. A poor boy, he was orphaned at seventeen, an age at which American youths now worry about the college of their choice. Destitute, he found refuge in a Buddhist monastery where he was given menial work in the kitchen, eventually acquired some sacred book learning and prepared to become a monk. Apparently this did not satisfy him. He joined a band of rebels against the decadent Mongol dynasty and rose rapidly in the widening revolt. Obviously, Heaven was on his side for, during his campaigns, two dragons were reported to have struggled in a river, a long-tailed comet flashed across the sky, weird lights flickered in the north, and two suns were seen above. And so the beggar boy overthrew the Mongols and made himself emperor.

Naturally, the inhibited Chinese loved these stories of derring-do, of dazzling rise from son of sorrow and misfortune to Son of Heaven. Mao Tse-tung was one of those who relished these defiant and romantic episodes in Chinese history. But he went a step further, beyond reverie to action. He too rose from obscurity in a time of trouble, broke all of the rules, and by boldly organized violence made himself Son of Red Heaven.

It was characteristic of the traditional Chinese mind that, even when relations between men degenerated into violence and war, the human factor, and not weapons, remained the paramount consideration in combatting an enemy. "Do not rely on sheer military power," said Sun Tzu, the first and perhaps greatest of military theorists. Heading his list of fundamental factors in war was moral influence, "that which causes the people to be in harmony with their leaders . . ." On strategy and tactics, he observed that "All warfare is based on deception." In contrast to later doctrines of total war prosecuted through maximum concentration of force in order to wring unconditional surrender, Sun Tzu declared, "For to win one hundred victories in one hundred battles is not the acme of skill. To subdue the enemy without fighting is the acme of skill."

Common to the heroic men of action, as well as the philosophers, statesmen and men of letters, was a preoccupation with human relationships and the interaction of personalities. As for the external physical world and the realm of the spirit, they were viewed subjectively and brought into the human scene. They were meaningful only as they partook of man's experience.

This subjective approach to the physical world meant identification with nature. It was altogether to be expected that the propitious rise of Chu Yüan-chang should be heralded by two suns, otherwise inexplicable, appearing in the sky and a couple of dragons thrashing about in a river. The traditional Chinese were like the Athenians in identification with nature, but on a lower key, neither as anguished nor as frolicsome.

It follows that, while the traditional Chinese outlook toward the affairs of men was rational, the view of nature and spirits was essentially poetic and intuitive. Although the Chinese invented the compass and gunpowder, they used one to locate favorable building sites in accordance with the mumbojumbo of geomancy and the other to drive off demons. And although they produced some monumental feats of engineering—the Great Wall, the Grand Canal, and elaborate irrigation systems—physical phenomena were generally not a matter for serious investigation. The scientific attitude and method were outside of Chinese experience. This intellectual gap was to prove fatal to the traditional society.

Because the Chinese attitude toward the supernatural was a mixture of skepticism, on the part of stiff-necked Confucianists, and familiarity, for everyone else, and because China's was a shame rather than a guilt culture, the traditional society lacked the fires of spiritual compulsion that drove the West to restless, relentless expansion and proselytization. The celestial host of spirits could be troublesome. But it was not a generator of dynamism in the people of the Middle Kingdom.

Finally, the cast of traditional Chinese society did not foment economic expansion. Quite to the contrary, the prevailing contempt for business was a drag on economic progress. Opulent merchants there were, but usually their wealth was gained from government franchises for such monopolies as the sale of salt or foreign trade. Nor was there a strong tradition of reinvestment for expansion or for the introduction of innovations in business. In sum, no base was laid for either capitalism or industrialization.

And so China lurched into the nineteenth century, totally unprepared for the modern world and wanting only to be left alone with its memories of a long and glorious past.

CHAPTER *6*

The Republican Revolution

THE EXPLOSION that set off the Republican Revolution of 1911 was both accidental and premature.

On October 9 a bomb went off in the Russian concession of Hankow. Young Chinese intellectuals, plotting the overthrow of the dynasty, had inadvertently triggered the infernal machine. In so doing, they brought on their own arrest and compromised the plan for the uprising. The Manchu authorities picked up other revolutionists in Wuchang, across the Yangtze from Hankow. The Manchu viceroy caused three rebels to be executed on the following day.

Gratified by this display of viceregal grit, the prince regent in Peking sent a complimentary message to the viceroy and decorated him with the Yellow Jacket. On October 10, revolutionary elements among the viceroy's troops revolted, lest they too be apprehended. They put to flight the main body of the garrison, set fire to His Excellency's official establishment, and in so doing impelled the viceroy to flee to the refuge of a Chinese cruiser reassuringly moored close to a British gunboat. After requesting British naval assistance in preventing the rebels from crossing the river, the viceroy steamed off in the cruiser to Shanghai.

The Manchu court was alarmed by the success of the revolt. It ordered troops from the North to quell the rebellion, censured the viceroy, and stripped him of his Yellow Jacket. He subsequently died in Shanghai of, it was said, chagrin.

Meanwhile, the mutineers had frantically dug out from hiding the only senior officer who had not been smart enough to make a getaway, a Colonel Li Yuan-hung. They told him that he had been chosen as the leader of the revolution. This was an honor about which Colonel Li entertained grave misgivings and which he felt compelled to accept only after being menaced with bodily harm. Keeping their terrified leader under arrest to prevent his escape, the rebels promptly crossed the river and took Hankow and Hanyang, with its handy arsenal.

The unconventional and really quite unsatisfactory command situation was due to the absence of the professional revolutionary leadership from the scene of action during the crucial first two days of the uprising. One of the principal revolutionists was incapacitated by the explosion of the bomb. Others were out of town. And the main local figure, who had received military training, took to his heels after the bomb went off.

The national leaders of the republican movement were likewise absent. Sun Yat-sen was in the Rocky Mountains raising money and hopes for the advent of democracy to China. He knew nothing of the plans for the revolt and first learned of it from Denver newspapers. His principal collaborator, Huang Hsing, who was an experienced activist, was in South China licking his wounds after a bungled revolt in Canton.

The Republican Revolution began, then, as a headless wonder. But it was off to a dazzling start—the capture of the three Wuhan cities in two days. At last the dreams of the revolutionary intellectuals seemed to be coming true after so many disappointments.

These intellectuals who claimed the Wuchang revolt as theirs belonged to a new breed of Chinese. They detested the alien rule of the Manchus. But that was not new, nor was it confined to the young republicans. The anti-Manchu feeling was widespread among the Han people, the ethnic Chinese. It was a part of normal Chinese xenophobia. So there was extensive support for the idea of getting rid of the Manchus.

For the same reason virtually all Chinese were against the western barbarians who were persistently encroaching upon and humiliating China. What was new was the notion that there was something worthwhile to be learned from barbarians. The conclusion of the new intellectuals was that the foreign devils could be fended off only by learning and adopting the methods of the foreign devils.

These young men had been enough exposed to rudimentary information about the West to know that the foreign devils were not all of a kind. The question was from which devil to borrow to repel them all. The devil of constitutional monarchy, as in Britain? Or republicanism, as in France or the United States? The German model, perhaps, or the Japanese who had so recently and successfully adapted archaic political forms to survive and, beyond that, were themselves to embark on aggression rivaling that of the most rapacious of the civilized western powers?

How to modernize China was the question that split the new intellectuals. At the turn of the century, it divided them into nearly as many persuasions as there were intellectuals. For in addition to the variety of western political systems exciting their attention, there was an extensive range of potential theories whereby these exotic and faintly understood forms of government might be domesticated to Chinese realities.

As one of the first revolutionists, Sun Yat-sen was an early observer and student of foreign forms of government. He was introduced to western ideas as a schoolboy in Hawaii, where he was sent from Canton in 1879, and in Hong Kong, where he received a British colonial education, including a degree in medicine in 1892. His service as a healer of men was brief.

In 1894 he began his career as a political medicine man by vainly waiting upon the most prestigious of viceroys with a manifesto calling for, as summarized by the historian Chun-tu Hsueh, "the full development of men's abilities; full exploitation of the earth's resources; the full use of material things; and an unhampered flow of commerce." For this effort to change the face of a nation, Sun was neither applauded, nor was a price put on his head. His prescription was simply ignored, and probably rightly so. In any event, it lacked the zing of Liberty, Equality, Fraternity, or even Workers of the World, Unite.

Now a full-time revolutionary, Sun began his wandering overseas in search of funds, followers, and an ideology. As he collected the first two, he developed a vague doctrine. This included, of course, nationalism and democracy. Sojourning in Europe from 1896 to 1898, writes Chun-tu Hsueh, he came to realize that "to make a nation rich and strong, or to promote democracy as has been done in Europe, was not sufficient to make the people really happy." He discovered that progressive thinkers there were "still carrying on a movement of social revolution." Thus enlightened, Sun concluded, "I wish to make an all-out effort and be forever at ease by adopting the principle of people's livelihood in order to solve the problem of nationalism and democracy simultaneously."

People's livelihood was thus the sovereign remedy in Sun's developing ideology. Nationalism, democracy, and people's livelihood, these became the Three People's Principles, the summation of his contribution to political folklore. The inspiration for this ideology was out of the West, excepting for people's livelihood, which was an ancient Chinese concept. Vague and banal to occidentals, it was nevertheless a stirring, radical call to action for the young intellectuals of China.

Sun's intellectual prospecting in the West was not typical of others in the revolutionary movement. Spending most of his life outside of China, he was to a large degree an expatriate. More representative of the republican revolutionaries was Huang Hsing, one of Sun's principal lieutenants. Huang grew up in the middle of China with a classical education, topped off by such controversial innovations as geography and mathematics. In his late twenties, he was sent by a provincial government to learn about normal school education in Japan.

On his arrival in 1902, Huang was one of some five hundred Chinese students in Japan. It was a rapidly growing community of young men eager to discover what it was that had enabled these upstart barbarians to inflict a swift, contemptuous defeat on China only seven years earlier. The students were intellectually excited by the novelties of western ideas—the thrill of coming upon Montesquieu and Mill in Chinese. Political magazines, clubs, and societies were formed and, after scarcely more than butterfly life spans, superseded by more magazines, clubs, and societies.

At the inauguration of one association, a military student likened the society's office to Independence Hall. For the American Revolution was popular. So was the French Revolution. The Russian was yet to come. And for the constitutionalists who would preserve the monarchical form, Japan's Meiji Restoration was a model. But even as early as 1903, it was evident that while the immediate common goal of the revolutionary students was the overthrow of Manchu hege-mony, their broad objective was to repel all foreign aggression.

Huang Hsing was in the thick of all of this, writing, talking, plotting, and, as a symptom of his serious revolutionary resolve, engaging in target practice and querying Japanese army officers about military science. After a year in Japan, Huang returned to China.

Back in his native province of Hunan, in the middle of China, he engaged in a fairly hair-raising but foiled uprising, involving thirty insurgent members of the literati, a Chinese Episcopal rector, a bawdy house, secret societies, and Huang's disguising himself successively as a customs official and then as the traveling companion of an unsuspecting army officer. He narrowly eluded capture at every turn, ending up as a fugitive for a short time in Japan. Then back again deep into China and more revolutionary misadventures, this time gunrunning. Once more he fled to Japan.

On this visit in 1905, he met Sun Yat-sen. They immediately found them-selves in accord, whereupon they formed the T'ung Meng Hui, the predecessor of the Kuomintang. From 1907 to 1911, these men launched eight revolts, all of them fiascos. Huang directed and took part in all of them; Sun in only one.

The revolutionists were chronically short of funds, obtained mainly from overseas Chinese. Like most of their kind, before and after, they quarreled among themselves. They were poorly organized, undisciplined, indecisive in crises, and generally amateurish. They relied overly on the cooperation of secret societies, which were undependable allies. Their penetration of the army, which Huang recognized as essential, was only partially successful. But with all of their defects and failures, the rebels did stir up political feeling against the Manchu regime and win sympathy for the revolutionary cause.

Then came the Wuchang mutiny, botched by the T'ung Meng Hui leader-ship in the Wuhan cities. The revolt had initially succeeded only because the sol-dier revolutionaries had on their own acted smartly and with decision. The urgent need for the T'ung Meng Hui was to establish political direction of the revolution. This need was met temporarily when Huang arrived in Wuchang nearly three weeks after the uprising, to the vast relief of the cowering Colonel Li.

Meanwhile, the Manchu Court had been desperately seeking a dependable soldier-statesman to subdue the uprising. The logical and painful choice was a crafty general and administrator, Yüan Shih-k'ai. He had a distinguished career as viceroy, as resident in Korea, as creator of "modern" units in the army, and as confidant of the late Empress Dowager.

He had in 1898 betrayed the emperor, uncle of Pu Yi, to the vengeful old dowager as being in favor of reforms and plotting to incarcerate her. For this, Yehonala placed His Majesty under what we now call house arrest for the remainder of his miserable days. When she felt her own death to be imminent, she had him smothered to death by two eunuchs.

Yüan's disloyalty to the emperor earned him the hatred of the emperor's brother, who in 1908 became regent when his infant son, Pu Yi, succeeded to the Dragon Throne. The regent wanted Yüan's life in revenge of his brother. He was persuaded, however, to let Yüan save head and face by retiring from official life to his home in the provinces, because of a malady afflicting his foot.

This was the man whom the regent summoned in 1911, four days after the beginning of the revolt in Wuchang, to save the dynasty. Yüan's reply was a catalog of diplomatic illnesses. It is a useful reference even now for anyone wanting time to think over a proposition, or to prepare the ground before accepting an appointment, or for someone wishing to play hard to get.

After humble protestations of gratitude for past favors from the throne and remorse over his inability, because of his health, to requite the honors done him, Yüan acknowledged that he should comply with the imperial command to deal with the current crisis. "But my old trouble with my foot is not yet thoroughly set right," he revealed, "and last winter my left arm became affected." That was not all. His breathing and body showed weakness. And with the beginning of the autumnal chill, "asthma and fever, which I used to suffer from, again attacked me." As if these ailments would not suffice, Yüan went on, "In addition to this I suffer from giddiness and nervousness, and when reflecting on a matter my mind wanders."

Then came the ray of hope. He had called in a doctor to effect a cure as quickly as possible. As soon as he was "somewhat able to struggle along" he would be on his way.

The regent's reply to the man he had sought to have beheaded was as brusque as it was hard-pressed. The vermillion pencil noted Yüan's memorial to the throne and then pointed out: "Matters at Wuchang and Hankow are very critical, and the said viceroy in the past has always been a just and loyal officer and zealous in performing service." Unmoved by Yüan's eloquent decrepitude, the regent ordered him to "immediately cure himself, and in spite of his illness let him proceed, thus requiting the extraordinary confidence placed in him by the throne."

Yüan requited the extraordinary confidence by declining repeatedly his appointment as viceroy at Wuchang. Only after the regent's bid had been raised to imperial commissioner controlling the armed forces and an appointment as premier was in the offing did he find himself, some three weeks after the Wuchang mutiny, somewhat able to struggle along to take command of the campaign against the revolution. But it was more than a month after the outbreak of the revolution, when the position of the dynasty had become desperate, that Yüan cured himself enough to go to Peking to take up the burdens of office as premier.

When Yüan took over as prime minister in mid-November, most of South and Central China had overthrown the Manchu yoke and the revolution was rumbling underground in North China. The imperial forces had retaken Hankow shortly after the arrival of Huang Hsing. But that was a lonely little triumph against what the revolutionists had accomplished.

Yüan's generals regrouped and reinforced their comparatively crack troops for an attack on Hanyang. With superior force they retook the city on November 27. In so doing, Yüan demonstrated that he was a factor to be reckoned with in the rapidly changing scene. The contact that his agents maintained with the rebels during hostilities suggested that he was more than a military factor. His mind was wandering, but only from suppression of sedition to political exploitation of both sides in the conflict.

By the end of November, the fighting as well as the massacre of Manchus in rebel areas had subsided. The struggle thenceforward was in the form of political maneuver. The baffled regent resigned on December 6, and his place was taken by his sister-in-law, widow of the smothered emperor. This dowager empress was not of Yehonala's fiber. A timorous woman, she immediately yielded to Yüan's pressure for full power to negotiate with the rebels on behalf of the imperial house.

By then there were two revolutionary factions: the original one in Wuchang and a second in Shanghai. With the only troops of passable competence in the country and occupying a favorable bargaining position between the Manchus and the rebels, Yüan proceeded to negotiate. His emissaries secretly worked out on December 20 a formula with the Shanghai revolutionists, authorized by Huang Hsing, for the creation of a republican government, the appointment to the presidency of whoever first caused the downfall of the dynasty, and considerate treatment of the imperial house. Yüan continued to maintain his posture as devoted counselor to the throne. He was thus in the elastic circumstance of being loyal to both the dynasty and the revolution.

It was not until after all of this had transpired that Dr. Sun Yat-sen, the father-to-be of the republic, arrived in China, having returned circuitously from Denver via Europe. He was, on December 29, promptly elected at Nanking by the diverse rebel elements as provisional president of the republic of China, after he had privately assured Yüan that he was assuming the position only temporarily. On January 1, 1912, Dr. Sun took the oath of office at the tomb of the founder of the last native dynasty, the Ming, whose advent, heralded by flurries of natural and supernatural phenomena, had been more spectacular than that of Dr. Sun.

Now it was up to Yüan to ease the bloated Manchu establishment out of the way. This was no great problem. With the court thoroughly distraught, Yüan had only to exclude inability to cope with malign forces and sorrowfully confide to the dowager empress that the dynasty was doomed. The process of persuasion, being artful and dignified, took a little time.

So it was not until February 12 that the Abdication Edicts were issued. In them the dowager empress and the six-year old emperor handed over sovereignty "to be the possession of the whole people." They then graciously charged Yüan with organizing a provisional republican government. As for themselves, "We . . . will retire into a life of leisure, free from public duties, spending our years pleasantly and enjoying the courteous treatment accorded to us by the people, and watching with satisfaction the glorious establishment and consummation of a perfect government."

These idyllic articles of downfall did not overlook such grubby matters as a guaranteed annuity of four million republican dollars to the throne and retention by the emperor of all of his private property and retinue. He would continue to live in the Forbidden City temporarily and then move to the Summer Palace, keeping his bodyguard at the same strength as hitherto. The emperor was to be treated as a foreign sovereign. And so on went the terms of exquisite abdication in which His Majesty abandoned the cares but kept the pleasures of royalty. No provisions were made in the edict regarding concubines, but there was a stipulation that "no more eunuchs shall be appointed."

Thus far, the outcome of the Republican Revolution of 1911 can be described only as happy—compared with other revolutions. The republicans won. The monarchists saved far more face, property, and perquisites than they had earned and certainly more than had been or was to be the custom elsewhere in such upheavals. While the small Manchu minority had suffered in the process, the Han majority had been spared the anguish of a general civil war.

As for Yüan, he was now in an unassailable position. He still had decisive military power. His succession to the Manchu dynasty was legitimatized by the Manchu throne. The republicans had agreed that he should take over from the provisional president, Sun Yat-sen. And perhaps best of all, the institution of emperor had not been obliterated. It had been merely set aside in the custody of little Henry Pu Yi until, who knew, such time as a strong president might feel impelled to mount the Dragon Throne.

Yüan immediately informed Sun in Nanking and Provisional Vice-President Li in Wuchang of the abdication. "A republic," he informed the republicans, "is the best form of government." Then expansively and inaccurately he added, "The whole world admits this." Lest he had been misunderstood, Yüan proclaimed later in the message, "Never shall we allow monarchical government in our China."

Having come out uncompromisingly for the republic, bequeathed to him by the Abdication Edicts, he tactfully sought the cooperation of the revolutionaries "in the work of consolidation." Alas, he could not seek them out in Nanking, as Sun had stipulated in yielding the presidency to him, only because of "the difficulty of maintaining order in the North." This was a specious excuse and so recognized by all concerned. Yüan would not leave his base of power, and the provisional government would have to yield to him.

Accordingly, two days after Pu Yi abdicated, Sun Yat-sen abdicated as provisional president. Sun did not like the idea that the new republic derived its legitimacy from Manchu benevolence, and so informed Yüan. But his extemporaneous regime at Nanking, composed of young intellectuals, émigrés, miscellaneous army officers, and opportunists, lacked cohesion, money, and unified military authority. Ideas make for power, to be sure. But the romantic, undisciplined ideas of the revolutionists meant that they were no match for Yüan. The republicans were appealing. But they were ineffective.

Bowing before the inevitable, the Nanking assembly on February 15 elected Yüan as provisional president. Eleven days later a delegation of Nanking republicans arrived in Peking to consult with Yüan about the formation of its permanent government and the transfer of the capital to Nanking. Yüan had arranged for them to be received in a style befitting their significance. For by self-appointment they represented the people, who were now explicitly sovereign.

Consequently, the imperial portals of the great front gate of Peking were opened for them. The delegates were accompanied by a band and guard of honor through streets made festive by the flags of the new republic. After four days of this, and naturally rather full of themselves, they attended a banquet given in their honor by Yüan.

The jubilation was shattered by an outbreak of gunfire outside the banquet hall. Then the lights went out, followed by pandemonium. The guards at the function beat the guests to the living quarters of the delegation, which they happily looted. The Peking garrison then plundered the city. The disorder was allowed to spread to certain nearby cities on the following day.

Yüan had made his point, at considerable personal cost to the wise men from Nanking. The situation in the north was patently explosive and who could argue that Yüan's firm hand was not needed there to maintain order? So the delegates acceded to his inauguration as provisional president with the capital in Peking rather than Nanking.

As did others before and after him, Yüan discovered that it is sometimes more difficult to make a government function than it is to overthrow one. The provisional constitution, drawn up by the parliamentarians in Nanking, limited the presidential powers and gave more authority to the prime minister and the legislature than suited Yüan. He so humiliated the premier, T'ang Shao-yi, his most trusted collaborator, that after three months of face losing, his faithful friend simply walked out on the job.

Yüan encountered opposition from other officials and from within the parliament, particularly from those members who belonged to the T'ung Meng Hui. The transformation of this revolutionary party into the Kuomintang on August 25, 1912, involving the absorption of several minor parties, was displeasing to Yüan. It meant a strengthening of parliamentary opposition and agitation for democracy. So Yüan had Sun's subordinate, who was mainly responsible for this irksome development, assassinated. And when the parliament was an obstacle, Yüan simply bypassed it.

The provisional president's main problem was money to operate the government. The treasury was empty, revenue was insufficient, and an international loan a pressing necessity. It was over the nature and terms of the loan that much of the friction between Yüan and others in the government arose. The loan was granted in the spring of 1913.

With funds in hand, Yüan hardened his treatment of the Kuomintang. He stripped Huang Hsing of his title as General of the Army. What was more serious, he cashiered three Kuomintang military governors. With the support of Huang and Sun, one of these provincial chiefs declared war on Yüan. Several southern provinces joined the revolt in the summer of 1913. Huang even took command of this Second Revolution.

Again Yüan was too strong for the opposition. The combination of his superior military force and the newly acquired loan, on which he drew to buy off some of the rebels, disposed of the insurrection. Sun and Huang withdrew to Japan. Having proved his supremacy, Yüan used mob demonstrations to induce the parliament to elect him, on October 6, formally to the presidency. Four days later he was inaugurated.

With his status legalized and his government enjoying international recognition, Yüan felt free to tidy up around him. He began, within a month after his inauguration, by outlawing the Kuomintang. This disposed of the segment of the legislature that the president had always regarded as dangerously radical. Then in January 1914, he made it a clean sweep by dissolving parliament. Thus in less than two years after the abdication of the emperor, China had returned to despotism.

There remained the final step—that Yüan should make himself emperor. Ample precedent existed in traditional China for such a move. To overthrow a dynasty was to earn the right to put on the imperial robes. Furthermore, the restoration of imperial forms may have seemed to Yüan the only way to cope with the baffling problems of executive authority and recurrent financial crisis.

By December 1915, Yüan had rigged an allegedly representative body to call for the restoration of the imperial system. His pliant Council of State then implored him to become emperor. Ceremoniously he declined twice before accepting. His enthronement was set for early 1916.

Opposition flared up on all sides and many of Yüan's close followers deserted him. The first uprising was in Yunnan Province. Rebellion then broke out in other parts of the country and Yüan was unable to cope with widening popular defiance.

In March 1916, with enormous loss of face, he annulled the creation of his dynasty. Shamed and thwarted, he wasted away. On June 6 Yüan died.

Over a span of four years, China had been jolted from empire, to republic, to dictatorship, almost to empire again, to regional fragmentation. And yet the fabric of Chinese life had not been changed by all of this. The bulk of the population was scarcely affected by the Republican Revolution and its aftermath.

The reason was that the 1911 changeover was a political and not a social revolution. The revolution overthrew a degenerate alien dynasty, reasserted Han supremacy, and created republican institutions and procedures totally foreign to Chinese experience. But most of the values of traditional society were scarcely touched by the struggle. The integrity of the family system was left intact. Economic relationships were unchanged. Custom and tradition were barely affected. The status of the peasantry remained the same.

Peasants did not lay the groundwork for the revolution with uprisings, as they had done before in Chinese history. Nor were they mobilized to take part in it, as they would be a generation later. Sun's doctrine of People's Livelihood was a woolly dissertation that had no practical relevance to the peasants' condition. They approved of the rebellion because it was against alien domination. As for joining in the revolt, that was for those with learning and for soldiers, not for farmers. And so, while the overthrow of the dynasty was popular, it was not an impassioned mass movement.

Intellectuals, however, were involved in and affected by the revolution and its outcome. Those who belonged to the traditional literati went along with the revolution for the same reason that the rest of the population did: the restoration of Han preeminence. Initially they may have had their anxious moments over what the hot-headed, semiwesternized republicans might do to their privileged status, especially those who held official positions under the Manchus. But the rapid rise of Yüan was reassuring to the literati because he was fundamentally a mandarin of the old school. Yüan justified their confidence in him by taking care of them with jobs in the republic. The big change for these transmitters of tradition was the adoption of odd new nomenclature, a new flag, and replacement of official robes by frock coats.

In the South, where the revolutionists were the strongest, most of the literati opportunistically rallied to the republicans. In so doing they were no more than repeating what their predecessors had done in centuries past. They were adapting to an outlandish new regime, counting on their indispensability and their ability to civilize, eventually, the republicans.

To the new intellectuals, those who had been introduced, however sketchily, to western ideas and believed in modernizing China, the traditional scholar-officials were a discredited lot. They had been proven incompetent both in fending off a voracious West and in modernizing China. In this view, the new intellectuals were ahead of that part of the public which had only lost confidence in the old bureaucracy without being able to come up with an alternative to it.

The alternative was, essentially, between the new intellectuals and the generals. The intellectual revolutionists lost to the generals by default at the critical outset of the revolution, through their own irresponsibility and disorganization. The absurd Colonel Li discovered, when the shooting had stopped in the Wuhan cities and he had made himself a generalissimo, that power tasted good. So he entrenched himself in the region, connived with Yüan Shih-k'ai, became successively Sun's and then Yüan's Vice-President, but scarcely ventured out of the area he controlled and so was the prototype of the warlords who were to plague China for more than thirty years thereafter.

The revolution moved with such rapidity, not so much because of the strength of the republicans as because of the disintegration of the dynasty; whoever could decide and act the faster had the advantage. On this score, the scattered, undisciplined intellectuals were no match for Yüan and his staff. In less than two months after the start of the revolution, well before Sun had even arrived in China, Yüan had a decisive advantage over the revolutionists.

The disparity of military strength went beyond the fact that Yüan commanded the only so-called modern troops in China. The T'ung Meng Hui had no army that was under party control. It negotiated for the support of various generals. It was, therefore, dependent upon making political deals for military support. This was a treacherous business and one at which the intellectual leadership was not adept.

The revolutionary intellectuals operated under a set of complex inhibitions. They were motivated by idealistic considerations that usually placed the nationalistic, democratic objectives of the revolution above personal interest. The few times that they might have effectively challenged the generals they failed to do so for fear of jeopardizing the aims of the revolution by precipitating a new civil war and thus tempting foreign intervention. Li's and Yüan's motives, grasping power, were less complicated. The generals consequently acted with the compelling concentration of effort that a single purpose generates.

In the vital matter of foreign support, the revolutionary intellectuals won the fascinated attention and even sympathy of western countries. But they did not collect any financial backing from foreign banks or governments. All of Sun's propaganda years in Europe and North America and the fact that the T'ung Meng Hui, and later the Kuomintang, represented the only modern, democratic force in China brought the intellectual revolutionists no official backing from abroad.

Yüan won foreign support and recognition because he was a "strong man," which in the occidental official mind meant that he would create political stability. Furthermore, he had worked out an orderly transfer of authority from the dynasty to himself. Thereby he acquired the sanctified odor of legitimate succession. And finally, Yüan was there in Peking, the capital, in contact with the legations.

At every turn the generals bested the intellectuals. Even when Yüan blundered with his bid for the throne, it was not the Kuomintang which led the revolt against his vainglory. Sun was sulking in Japan and Huang Hsing was in the United States making futile statements to the press. Yüan's downfall was brought about by other generals. With that, China broke up into principalities ruled by warlords.

The dynasty had provided cohesion to the country. It had made for a certain unity in the sprawling, diverse country. But with the destruction of the imperial system, the regionalism that had always been alive in China began to flourish. The dissidence among those seeking the dethronement of the Manchus furthered the fragmentation.

The system that Yüan established in the provinces as he came to power guaranteed that the tendency toward regionalism, rather than centralization, would be reinforced. He appointed military governors in the provinces. In principle this was a sound and probably necessary expedient in a revolutionary situation. But, because his national government was initially in financial straits, he placed these generals out around the country on their own, to raise their own revenues from the localities under their jurisdiction.

This was soon disastrous to control from the center at Peking. The military governors quickly made themselves self-supporting and were able to defy any orders from Peking that they did not find convenient. Yüan could then take no disciplinary action short of going to war against them.

As the warlords became more firmly entrenched, they grew more arrogant and parochial, each in his own principality, some of which were as big as fair-sized European nations. Most of them gave lip service to the ideal of national unity. But they were in effect autonomous, already in Yüan's time in independent contact with agents of foreign powers.

In inheriting the presidency from Yüan, Li was beset by the institution of warlords. And so were his successors, until the end of this story. It was really not so surprising that this should have been so. Remembering that China is bigger than Europe, less Russia, and remembering the vicious devastation that regionalism has wrought on Europe, Chinese warlordism seems to have been a comparatively mild affliction.

Of those Chinese who were to play a decisive part in the Chinese upheaval of the 1940s, only one had a significant role in the China of 1911–1917. He was Chu Teh, who became Commander-in-Chief of the Chinese Communist armies in the war against Japan and the civil war against Chiang Kai-shek. Chu Teh's story, in terms of one man's experience, tells much about the transition from traditional to revolutionary China. It falls naturally into two parts; Chu's provincial life, recounted here, and his later activities, described in subsequent chapters, particularly Chapter 14.

In 1911, in his mid-twenties, Chu was a lieutenant owing allegiance to the Manchu dynasty. He joined the revolt against the dynasty in Yunnan, where he was stationed. The 1915–1916 uprising against Yüan Shih-k'ai was started by Chu Teh's former commanding general, and participated in by Chu, then a colonel. He carried the revolt to Szechuan and so distinguished himself that he was made a brigadier general.

Thus in 1916, while Chiang Kai-shek was money-making in Shanghai and Mao Tse-tung was attending a normal school in Hunan, Chu was fighting, in command of a regiment and then a brigade. He already had experienced five years of active military command.

Chu's parents were poor peasants. His mother came from a family of wandering actors of such lowly estate that she had no given name. She bore thirteen children of whom Chu Teh was the fourth. Thus he escaped the fate of the last five of the thirteen, who were drowned at birth because the family did not have enough to feed them. He was called Little Dog so that evil spirits, ill-disposed toward small boys, would be deceived into thinking he was not worth going after.

Little Dog feared and hated his foul-tempered father. He was therefore fortunate to be adopted by his father's childless and benign elder brother. At first this made little difference, as the family, from the grandparents on down, lived together in one house. The adoption did make a difference when the uncle insisted that the family pool its scanty resources and borrow to put Little Dog through school so that one of its members might rise out of the mire of peasant ignorance and vulnerability to protect the clan.

Therefore as a long-term family investment in future security and prosperity, Chu Teh entered a tiny school to memorize the classics. At eleven he moved to another small school where for eight years he furthered his classical studies under an old scholar with an inquiring and skeptical mind who, although he knew the modern world only through sketchy reading and hearsay, spurred Chu to prepare himself for a changing China. After Chu Teh passed the literary examinations, his family borrowed enough money to cover his expenses for a year's tutoring in the provincial capital of Chengtu, following which he would take the next higher grade of examinations qualifying him for appointment as an official.

Barefooted, to save his one pair of cloth shoes for the city, Chu Teh walked five days to Chengtu. There, going on twenty, he enrolled in the Higher Normal School to specialize in physical education. This was a grievous betrayal of his family's hopes for him. But Chu Teh calculated that the old educational system was useless and that he could not afford to buy an official position unless he married a rich girl, whose dowry could be converted into the necessary bribe. Such a young lady would certainly be old-fashioned with bound feet, and he yearned for an emancipated maiden with big feet. Therefore, it was off to Higher Normal and the newest-fangled in erudition—physical education.

Some of Chu's teachers had studied in Japan, where they had cut off their queues. Because in China this was regarded by the Manchu rulers as seditious, the teachers wore false queues. Chu was thrilled to meet these radicals. He also saw school girls with big feet. "I was a very emotional person," he later confided to Agnes Smedley, his biographer, "and I idealized girls, but from a respectable distance."

In his political questing, Chu snooped about seeking to join Sun Yat-sen's T'ung Meng Hui. Because the republican movement was cautiously underground, he was unable to make firm contact with, much less gain admittance to, its clandestine ranks. He established close relations with four fellow students from his native district and together they resolved to open a modern school in Ilung, his native district town. Chu would teach physical culture.

After a year at Higher Normal, Chu returned home. His family assumed that he had pursued his classical studies, taken his examination, and was therefore about to become an exalted being, a petty mandarin. They welcomed him with the deference bordering on awe due to one of the higher culture. Twelve years of sacrifice, saving, and debts had been justified. No longer would landlords, bailiffs, and usurers dare to prey on the Chu clan's unlettered ignorance. The returning scholar was given a room to himself and a lamp fueled with precious vegetable oil so that he might read after dark when everyone else had gone to bed.

When Chu Teh told his family what he had done and what his plans were, the reaction was at first incomprehension, then disbelief, and finally woe that all of the hopes so fondly held should now be blighted. Chu hastened to Ilung to join his fellow faculty members and set up the progressive school. Immediately the modern curriculum encountered fierce conservative opposition, most pointedly directed at Chu and his "body training." Physical exertion was for coolies. To saunter was the extent of a gentleman's exercise. The lyceum was closed down and Chu summoned before the magistrate on charges of teaching an indecent subject.

With support from the growing forces of modernization in Ilung, the new school weathered this and a series of subsequent assaults. But by 1908 Chu had decided that he must go to a military academy, become an officer, and fight for China's liberation from the Manchus and other foreigners. He would go with a friend to the new military academy in Yunnan Province. When he told his family of this patriotic decision they plainly thought that he was daft. Physical jerks were bad enough. Deliberately to immerse himself in the scum of society, the army, was the sign of an unsound mind. They suggested that he take time off to rest his brain.

In command of his senses, Chu Teh and his Chengtu friend made a rugged journey lasting some two months to Yunnan. Once admitted to the military academy, Chu sought out politically-inclined cadets and was eventually admitted to the T'ung Meng Hui. He also joined the powerful secret society known as the Ko Lao Hui. Chu was graduated from the academy in July 1911. Three months later he was in the thick of the republican uprising that overthrew the Manchu reign in Yunnan.

Although my fellow-provincial's (both Chu Teh and the author were born in Szechuan) path converged with mine at least twice—in 1908 when I was an infant in a perambulator and he in a boat stopping at Kiating on his way to Yunnan, and in 1920 when my family and I returned to the United States on furlough and passed his garrison town on the Yangtze—it was not until 1944 in Yenan that I met him, when he was Commander-in-Chief of the Communist Armies.

CHAPTER 7

The Intruders

SUMMIT DIPLOMACY between the United States and China began in 1843 with a letter from President John Tyler to the Tao Kuang emperor. Daniel Webster is generally credited with having drafted the missive for the president's signature. It is in the me-heap-big-paleface style of American diplomatic discourse.

Quite rightly, Webster had Tyler identify himself at the outset of the correspondence. He did so a little stuffily, as in an affidavit: "I, John Tyler, President of the United States of America . . ." Then, leaving nothing to chance, he named each of the twenty-six states, from Maine to Michigan. Having let the emperor know who was writing to him, and assuring him that the message of peace and friendship was "signed by my own hand," the president permitted himself, "I hope your health is good."

The amenities thus disposed of, Tyler advised the emperor that "China is a great Empire" and that "The Chinese are numerous." More explicitly, "You have millions and millions of subjects." It is not clear from the context whether Webster thought that this was an intelligence scoop worth passing on to His Majesty or that Tyler should seek to impress the Son of Heaven by his grasp of foreign facts and figures.

Next came a lesson in astronomy and geography. "The rising sun looks upon the great mountains and great rivers of China." Speeding the diurnal round, "When he sets, he looks upon the rivers and mountains equally large in the United States." Then restlessly, "Leaving the mouth of one of our great rivers, and going constantly toward the setting sun, we sail to Japan and the Yellow sea," where assuredly Mr. Webster's sun must have been also rising to look upon the mountains and rivers of China.

"Now, my words are that the governments of two such great countries should be at peace." These unsolicited words of Great White Father Tyler were bolstered by confident reference to higher authority. "It is proper, and according to the will of heaven" that the governments of the United States and China "should respect each other and act wisely." So Caleb Cushing, His Majesty was advised, was to go to Peking to deliver this letter in person.

With no more beating around the bush of platitudes, Tyler proceeded to the real purpose of the letter—trade. "The Chinese love to trade with our people," he gushed to the emperor of the Chinese. The emperor and the bureaucracy, of course, looked upon commerce as sordid and foreign trade as downright antiso-cial, particularly because of opium imports. Nevertheless, Cushing "is authorized to make a treaty to regulate trade." Tyler doubted not that His Majesty would order the treaty to be made "so that nothing may happen to disturb the peace between China and America."

Proceeding from the faintly ominous to the patronizing, Tyler advised the emperor, as he would an overwhelmed Shawnee chief, "Let the treaty be signed by your own imperial hand. It shall be signed by mine, by the authority of our great council, the Senate." Mercifully he did not add, "in powwow assembled." But he did conclude with a cheery, "And so may your health be good, and may peace reign. . . . Your good friend."

Obviously, an epistle of such consequence required a setting of consequence, even a little pomp. Beginning with the person of Cushing, there arose the question of his attire. Flying in the face of republican prejudice against ostentation, the envoy extraordinary had designed for himself an embellished version of a major general's uniform. This included white pantaloons with gold stripes, a white vest, a blue coat with gilt buttons, and a plumed headpiece.

Next, he should, of course, be attended by a suite. Webster's son, Fletcher, was appointed as secretary. Two missionaries were designated as Chinese interpreter-secretaries. Four young gentlemen, to serve without compensation, were added as padding.

Finally, there was the matter of transport. Cushing was given a naval squadron: the steam frigate *Missouri*, the frigate *Brandywine*, a brig, and a sloop of war. In this imposing company, Cushing set off in 1843 to call on Tao Kuang.

The mission had gotten no further than Gibraltar, on its way to round the Cape of Good Hope, when misfortune befell Cushing and the squadron. While the envoy, in mufti, and his suite were dining ashore, the *Missouri* caught fire. Cushing rushed aboard the burning pride of the United States Navy and saved the president's letter to the emperor. But he lost his ceremonial costume in the conflagration.

The remaining three ships, with the envoy's entourage aboard, sailed on around the Cape. Cushing, separated from finery and staff, proceeded to Suez where he took a British steamer to Bombay. There he returned to the remnants of his squadron and sailed on to China.

The Cushing mission was but one phase in the West's invasion of China's privacy. With sublime effrontery, the West had since the sixteenth century insisted that China should be "opened up." China did not want to be opened up. It wanted to be left alone.

To the seafaring people of Western Europe and North America, who lived by international exchange of goods, the Chinese attitude was perversely wrong. Obstruction of overseas commerce was a denial of the rightful way of life. And as heirs of the Inquisition, or the Reformation, or the Evangelical movement, they believed that unless missionaries from the West moved in to bring salvation, the heathen Chinese were doomed to hell's fire. Western intrusion was therefore more than justified, it was morally imperative.

China had humored the sea-borne barbarians to the extent of tolerating foreign merchants at one port only, Canton. It was the tradesman's entrance, where they were treated as disreputable peddlers not permitted to cross the threshold into the house. Chinese suspicion of the maritime West was not without some cause. The Portuguese in the sixteenth century and the Dutch in the seventeenth had preyed on the China coast. The British in the eighteenth and early nineteenth centuries had busied themselves with introducing opium from India. Other westerners, with lesser or no poppy resources, participated in the traffic on a minor scale. Among these were Americans. It should be added that the opium salesmen had no difficulty in finding Chinese officials and merchants to do business with.

Opium troubled the conscience of the West. But no more than that. The profits from the traffic spoke more persuasively. And, in any event, the big issue was getting the Chinese to loosen up so that Western Europeans and Americans could get into the country to do what they thought was good for it—and themselves.

This could not be done through reason, through a meeting of minds. Each side regarded the other as bizarre, benighted, and set in his ways. Contempt was mutual. When an effort was made at civility, the contempt was phrased as condescension, as Ch'ien Lung addressed George III and Tyler held forth to Tao Kuang.

The importunate West and the obdurate East were bound to clash. The immediate issue over which the British went to war with China in 1839 was uninspiring. The hostilities were caused by the Chinese holding British merchants in Canton hostage to the surrender of all British-owned opium in or awaiting delivery to Canton. The larger issue was what the British and all of the western governments regarded as intolerably restrictive and unjust treatment of foreign traders.

The first Anglo-Chinese War, or The Opium War, as the Chinese called it, demonstrated European military superiority. British weapons were far advanced beyond what the Chinese had. And British sailors and soldiers were better fighting men, although some Manchu and Chinese troops individually conducted themselves with great bravery. British naval tactics, blockades, bombardments, and assault landings along the China coast were far different from invasions of horsemen from across the steppe. Naval and amphibious warfare were bewildering to the Chinese. Britain won as much from widespread weaknesses within the Middle Kingdom as from English prowess.

For the British, this was a limited war. It was not one of conquest nor of extermination. They fought to chastise the Chinese and teach them to be reasonable, to be more like us. And so, in terminating the war with the Treaty of Nan-king of 1842, the Chinese government was obliged to open five ports to British trade and residence. Tariffs were to be "fair and regular." The Chinese were to recognize British officials of similar rank as their equals instead of insulting them.

And in accordance with the practices of those times, that the defeated rather than the victor should pay for all of the unpleasantness, China ceded the barren little island of Hong Kong to Britain and promised to pay twenty-one mil-lion dollars of indemnity. Of this sum, six million was reimbursement for the opium extracted from the British as ransom, three million to cover Chinese mer-chant debts to British subjects, and twelve million as the cost of the war to Britain.

Britain's right to trade in five treaty ports, and other privileges obtained in the Treaty of Nanking, aroused commercial appetites in Europe and the United States. This anxiety to get at least the same benefits that Britain had was the main reason for the Cushing Mission.

American merchants at Macao and Canton, however, did not greet the advent of Cushing with unalloyed satisfaction. They were accustomed to being on their own in dealing with the Chinese. After all, Americans had been trading at those ports since the first American ship arrived at Canton in 1784. And during the Anglo-Chinese war, the Yankee traders had turned their neutrality to cosy advantage by acting as transshippers and agents for British commerce. Cushing, they feared, might antagonize Chinese officialdom, thereby spoiling the placid relations that, through conciliation, they had developed with the Canton authorities. At least some of these merchants believed that they could quietly on their own get the same commercial advantages that the British had acquired in the Treaty of Nanking.

Upon his arrival at Macao on the *Brandywine*, Cushing sought to arrange through the authorities at Canton for his presentation of the president's letter to the emperor in Peking. He met with delaying tactics and obstruction. In turn, Cushing bluffed and inveigled. A compromise was reached. The imperial com-missioner agreed to negotiate with Cushing and took delivery of Tyler's letter.

The American envoy was in a favorable bargaining position. There was no compelling reason for the Chinese to deny to the Americans through peaceful parley what they had already yielded to the British. So Cushing got for the United States, without fighting, what the British had bought at the cost of a war. He secured most favored nation treatment for the United States and, in addition, a complacent bestowal of extraterritorial rights whereby Americans in China were to be subject to American and not Chinese civil and criminal jurisdiction. This was the first American-Chinese agreement, known as the Treaty of Wanghia, named for the village close to Macao where the document was signed in 1844.

The French were not far behind. Within a few months, they had concluded a similar commercial treaty. They obtained, in addition, permission to build

Catholic churches in the port cities opened by treaty. Outdistanced by the British and Americans in matters of trade, the French found solace in being first in the protection of the Catholic Church. The French government championed the cause of Christianity (Roman) and civilization (French) as a matter of prideful policy.

This led to concern well beyond the erection of parish houses and cathedrals. The French in 1844 pressed the imperial commissioner at Canton for toleration of Chinese converts. The commissioner memorialized the emperor regarding the French request. "On examination it appears that the religion of the Lord of Heaven is that professed by all the nations of the West; that the main object is to encourage the good and suppress the wicked; that since its introduction to China during the Ming Dynasty, it has never been interdicted; that subsequently, when Chinese, practicing this religion, often made it a covert for wickedness, even to the seducing of wives and daughters, and to the deceitful extraction of the pupils from the eyes of the sick, the government investigated and inflicted punishment . . ."

The prohibition against Christianity, the imperial commissioner concluded, was against evil-doing under the cloak of religion and not against the religion itself. Having clarified this longstanding misapprehension regarding the nature of Christianity, the imperial commissioner thought it feasible that those Chinese who practiced the religion of the Lord of Heaven might be "exempt from criminality," provided that they did not seduce wives and daughters or deceitfully take the pupils from the eyes of the sick. The emperor concurred.

Gossipy malice, however, tends to stick. Notwithstanding official clarification, the Chinese public continued to associate Christianity with eye snatching. In 1870 ten French sisters of mercy, two priests, the French Consul, and his secretary were murdered in Tientsin by a mob believing that Chinese children in a Catholic orphanage, who had died in an epidemic, had been killed for their eyes and internal organs, out of which the missionaries were alleged to have brewed an elixir. Similar tidings preceded the frenzied Boxer uprisings against foreigners of 1900.

With France assuming the function of protector of Catholicism, Britain moved to guardianship of the Church of England, placing the cross under the protection of the crown. The American government likewise took an interest in the welfare of a growing variety of denominations working in the Lord's Chinese vineyards. Along with these concerns went a solicitude for Chinese converts. This led the imperial commissioner at Canton in 1845 to an exasperated assurance, candid in the first instance, perfunctory in the second: "I do not understand the lines of distinction between the religious ceremonies of the various nations; but virtuous Chinese will by no means be punished on account of their religion." Such was the official position, "No matter whether they worship images or do not worship images . . ."

By mid-nineteenth century, the maritime West had breached Chinese isolationism. From then on, the West pushed ever more aggressively to widen the openings it had made in this closed society. The Chinese resisted, temporized, and even lashed back. But they were unable to fend off the persistent encroachment from the sea.

Trader, missionary, warrior, diplomat—these were the four intruders from across the oceans. Although the trader and the missionary looked askance at one another, each being inclined to think that China and he would be better off without the other, their differing efforts contributed to the same end: the breakup of traditional Chinese society. Commerce and religion were backed up by force, seldom applied, usually implicit, latent as an available sanction. With force available, the diplomat operated from a position of strength in his dealings with the Chinese government to protect traders and missionaries and to further what the West deemed to be their legitimate interests.

Nothing like this had ever happened to China. Unlike the barbarians from the steppes, these from the sea did not invade en masse, usurp the throne, and settle down to make China their homeland. Thus they were not assimilable. They operated from distant power bases, separated from China by vast stretches of water. So they were not accessible to the customary punitive and pacification campaigns of Chinese armies.

These barbarians appeared suddenly from over the southeastern horizon and then, when it suited them, disappeared. They left not forever, but only to return again, when it suited them. The whole performance was utterly exasperating to the land-rooted Chinese.

The diversity of the intrusion by the maritime West was also unprecedented for the Chinese. This was not a stark conquest by arms. It was subtle and multiformed encroachment: economic, religious and intellectual, military and political.

Western commercial intrusion into the Middle Kingdom developed from opium traffic and the shipment of sandalwood and ginseng, a root that the Chinese fancied as a restorative of failing faculties and functions, into more humdrum trade. The drive to expand commerce with China was stimulated by a widespread assumption that, because there were so many Chinese, they must constitute an enormous market eagerly waiting to buy.

British textile makers, for example, were excited by the thought of adding an inch to every Chinaman's gown. And some American tobacco growers were elated by the vision of displacing opium with chewing tobacco, the mouth-watering prospect of four hundred million quids a day. The illusion of a huge, rich market lying at the end of the Chinese rainbow continued to spur the western commercial invasion of China well into the twentieth century.

By the turn of the century, the original five treaty ports had grown tenfold and western business had advanced from trade to banking, inland shipping, loans for the building of railroads, manufacturing, and public utilities. Before long, village weavers found themselves displaced by textile mills in Shanghai, and boatmen on the Yangtze suffered from the competition of steamboats flying British and Japanese flags. The wrenching pains of an industrial revolution were brought to China by the maritime West, not by any elements within Chinese society. The Chinese were aware of and resentful of this.

They were also aware of the gross inadequacies of their own rulers—first the Manchu court and then the republican regimes—in coping with western economic pressures. Foreign banks extended loans for railroads and other government undertakings. Peking regularly defaulted, which brought down overseas retribution. In this manner, China lost control of its customs revenue, which came to be administered by a British subject.

Missionaries, like traders, from the maritime West had a long but erratic history of contact with the Middle Kingdom. In the thirteenth century, a series of Italian Franciscans were accepted by the religiously tolerant Mongol emperors of the Yuan Dynasty. They meekly won over no significant number of Chinese to Christianity and then faded from the scene.

Next, discreet Jesuit scholars gained acceptance by the Ming and Manchu Courts during the seventeenth century. They tactfully adjusted their theology to Confucianism and gained influence through such secular accomplishments as map making, teaching astronomy, and casting brass cannons. Their undoing came with the arrival of missionaries from other orders who accused the Jesuits of tolerating heathenish practices, particularly ancestor worship. The upshot of the dispute, brought to the attention of both the Emperor and the Pope, was the triumph of the anti-Christian Confucianists and the crippling of missionary activities by persecution and expulsion.

Unlike these early missionary activities, those undertaken after 1844 were, in Chinese eyes, imposed upon the Middle Kingdom. The right to propagate the Word of God was guaranteed by treaty between governments, reinforced by the threat of force. Thus the missionary became, like the trader, a projection of unwelcome western power. And so the message of divine love, salvation, and life eternal that he brought, a message from the Heavenly Father to all mankind, was tainted by its sponsorship—consuls and gunboats.

Apolitical in outlook and wrapped up in their calling, few missionaries were aware of their compromised position. Those who were, usually attempted to disassociate themselves from foreign governments. When their lives were endangered, however, they all were willing to accept such protection as their governments could extend. While martyrdom was a revered tradition, it would be an act of false pride to court it.

Most missionaries of the later eighteen hundreds were different from the supple Jesuits of the sixteen hundreds. Not only were they bolstered by the awesome power of the West, they tended to propagate the faith in uncompromising terms. Particularly was this true of the Protestants. And they felt freer to do this because they were in China, not on invitation nor even on indulgent acceptance, but on the basis of rights secured by treaties.

As they were theologically uncompromising, they were also convinced that western civilization, based on Christianity, surpassed any other. So the Chinese were heathen to be saved and cultural laggards to be enlightened. Therefore, along with preaching the gospel went education, the introduction of western ideas and values.

To all in the West this was a high-minded and proper undertaking. To the lettered Chinese, those of the higher culture, the nineteenth century intrusion of the missionary was a sweeping challenge. His was a far more acute affront than the encroachment of western traders. For his teachings were competitive with, when not against, Confucianism. And the claim that western civilization, based on Christianity, was superior to that of the Chinese, was an outrageous piece of effrontery to people who had always assumed that theirs was the only civilization under heaven.

For the humble folk of China, the untutored, missionaries were on first sight looked upon much as one of us would react to a humanoid debarking from an unidentified flying object. The curiosity was immense and unquenchable. At the same time, there was the calcified assumption of Chinese superiority, that there was no other right and normal existence than the Chinese, and that anyone not Chinese was a freak. However uncomplimentary this attitude, it was not so unaccommodating as the cultural haughtiness of officials, the literati, and the pretentious gentry.

The unlettered ones, therefore, once the uneasiness of meeting a foreign devil had been dissipated, were less resistant to missionaries and their proselytization. This was not surprising. In general, the concern of the foreign priest or parson for the salvation and spiritual happiness of an ordinary villager or townsman was probably the first expression of personal interest in him that the man had ever received from anyone of privileged status. Furthermore, the schools and hospitals that the missionaries provided attracted the commonalty. In many cases, material advantages also attached to being a Christian, and those who embraced Christianity for gain came to be called "rice Christians."

Measured in converts, the results of the missionary effort were unspectacular in a country of four hundred million souls. In 1850, the Catholics claimed better than three hundred thousand converts; the newly-established Protestants less than three hundred and fifty. By 1900, the Catholics had more than seven hundred and forty one thousand, while the Protestants had won about a hundred thousand. By 1920, the Catholics approached two million; the Protestants were at three hundred and sixty-six thousand. At peak strength, two decades later, Chinese Christians did not amount to 1 percent of the population.

The farthest-reaching impact of the Christian missionary movement was on the social and political outlook of those Chinese who were jarred out of Confucian bigotry by manifestations of western power and ingenuity. This resonant part of the population was stirred by the secular education, the introduction to western thought provided by missionaries as a supplement to their preaching. Most of these people were not drawn to Christian theology, but to western science, philosophy, and political theory.

Missionaries taught these subjects as a matter of enlightenment, of bringing the Chinese out of their medieval ignorance. The Chinese initially pursued these studies almost as a black magic. Thus, they imagined, they would discover the occult formula for western power. As they became acquainted with western thought, dissatisfaction with the Manchu government grew in student minds and from that the bolder turned to plotting revolt.

The missionary, therefore, with his dedication to preparing Chinese for the life hereafter, prepared them in greater numbers for revolution in this vale of tears. This continued to be as true in the twentieth as in the nineteenth century.

One of the first to be helped unwittingly by a missionary onto a career as a revolutionary was Hung Hsiu-ch'uan, born in 1813. This young man had thrice failed the civil service examinations, following which he had a vision. A spectral sage told him to save humanity. He apparently did not take this vaporous injunction seriously until he chanced upon a Christian tract. Thereupon it all became clear to him. God had summoned him to save humanity. So he baptized himself and organized friends and acquaintances into the Shang Ti Hui, the Society of God.

In search of further guidance, Hung spent two months with an American Baptist missionary, the Reverend Issachar Jacox Roberts, receiving scriptural instruction. Leaving before he was deemed ready for baptism—on which score the Reverend Mr. Roberts was quite right—Hung returned to his native place near Canton. There he and his followers made themselves socially unacceptable by smashing idols and Hung lost his position as a schoolmaster.

In a familiar pattern, the Society of God took to the hills. It engaged in preaching, hymn writing, and gathering converts to a total of nearly two thousand. Religious dissent quickly expanded into political revolt. In that, the Society was joined in 1850 by insurgent peasants who, in their misery, had risen against the Manchu authority. By then, Hung had organized a rudimentary military force.

Hung, the visionary religious fanatic, became the magnetic leader of a peasant uprising, whose origins were not spiritual longing but material destitution. The goading poverty, in turn, was caused by overpopulation and economic dislocation. Had it not been for the great groundswell of popular discontent, Hung would not have gone beyond being an obscure religious crackpot, unnoticed in history.

But in the combination of circumstances existing in 1851, he was leading a puritanical and bloody crusade to establish what he named T'ai P'ing T'ien Kuo, the Heavenly Kingdom of Great Peace. Calling for the overthrow of the dynasty and the purging of traditional institutions, the Taiping rebellion raged northward, killing, burning, and collecting recruits, as it went. By 1853, with a strength of about half a million, the rebels burned Hankow and occupied Nanking. They came within an ace of capturing Peking itself.

Meanwhile, Hung had proclaimed himself to be the T'ien Wang, or Heavenly King. He had also revised the New Testament to bolster his kingly pretensions, dropping the Holy Ghost so that he himself might assume the vacated position in the Trinity, as Divine Younger Brother of Jesus Christ.

Radical economic and social reforms were likewise promulgated by the

Taiping rebels but carried out only on a limited scale. Land and population were to be distributed so that everyone would have enough to till. A system of communal ownership of property was devised. And women were to have equal status with men.

Established in Nanking as the Taiping capital, the revolutionary leadership disintegrated in flagrant corruption. The Heavenly King secluded himself with sixty-eight wives and three hundred male attendants and was accessible only to ten or eleven subkings. The Reverend Issachar Jacox Roberts went to Nanking in 1861 to visit his former pupil, was denied an audience, and concluded from what he learned there, "I believe he is crazy . . . a wicked despot."

With the degeneration of leadership, the Taiping armies broke down into marauding bands gradually subdued by new provincial armies loyal to the throne, and by foreign soldiers of fortune near Shanghai, organized and led by an American, Frederick Townsend Ward, in what was extravagantly called The Ever Victorious Army. The outcome was defeat of the rebel forces, the suicide in 1865 of the Heavenly King, and the disappearance of the Taiping movement. Twenty million people are said to have perished during the rebellion.

Christianity was the spark that ignited a messianic fire in the volatile Hung. Christianity, distorted by the Heavenly King, was also an essential part of the Taiping mystique for the masses. It and the demands for the overthrow of the dynasty and old institutions fused to inflame millions of Chinese. The Taiping rebellion was deep and passionate. It was no reform movement, no mere political revolt, but a furious, organic revolution that flared wildly and then quickly burned down to ashes.

And yet the rickety old empire survived the fury. It did for three reasons. One was that, although the Taiping leaders could initially whip up the eager wrath of desperate peasants, they were so frenzied, disorganized, and undisciplined that they brought about their own collapse. The fatal flaw was then, as it was again to be in the future, the inadequacy of the leadership to the task that it set itself.

A second reason that the traditional system survived was that as the excesses of the Taiping rebels grew, the movement proportionately lost popular support. Many who would otherwise have been attracted to the rebellion were alienated from it.

Finally, foreign powers, which had originally been favorably disposed to the rebels because of their semi-Christian and reformist coloration, became alarmed by their extremism. Although Britain and France were at war with China while the rebellion was at its height, they came to support the Manchu dynasty against the Taiping insurgents, as they fought the imperial regime for their own purposes. When Ward, the American commander of The Ever Victorious Army, was killed, the British went to the length of permitting one of their army officers to take Ward's place—a man who became known as Chinese Gordon but better remembered for his exploits elsewhere, in the Sudan against the fuzzy-wuzzies.

The missionary intrusion did more than stimulate ideas upsetting to the ancient regime. Missionaries, especially murdered missionaries, were also exploited by governments of the West for reasons exceeding piety, justice, and compassion. A French missionary was barbarously murdered and that became for Paris a major justification for joining the British in a war against China. From it the French derived a sizable indemnity and considerable other benefits. Then in 1897, the murder of two German missionaries by bandits provided Berlin with a sought-for excuse to demand, and obtain, Kiaochow Bay and a broad hinterland as a sphere of influence.

Germany's territorial grab was only the most blatant of the aggressions perpetrated on China by the maritime powers of the West. In addition to Hong Kong, the British got a long-term lease on Kowloon, a portion of the mainland across from the island. They then obtained a lease on Weihaiwei for a naval base and the great Yangtze Valley as a sphere of influence. The French induced the Chinese to lease them a site for a naval station in South China and a sphere of influence in the areas bordering Indochina. And so it went, with even the Italians putting in a bid for territorial privileges. Western European expansionism and power rivalry had reached China and by the latter part of the nineteenth century was on a rampage.

The maritime countries of Europe were not the only nations harrying China. Two others, more determined and voracious, came to surpass the western Europeans. One was Russia; the other Japan.

Tsarist pressure was, for the Chinese, from a familiar direction. It was from the north, from across the steppe and out of the forests. Peking understood this kind of aggression, and had been, since the seventeenth century, jostled by the Russians along the Manchurian and Central Asian borderlands. Tsarist aggression was territorial in motivation. The incentive of trade was secondary. Russia exported nothing of significance to China and bought little more than tea. Nor was there an intrusion of missionaries, as there was from the West.

Russian territorial encroachments on China during the nineteenth century were larger and more significant than those of the West. They were also more adroitly, cheaply, and inconspicuously executed. Outstanding in this respect was the Tsarist acquisition of the strategic coastal expanse around and north of what is now Vladivostok. This prize the Russians received in 1860 almost as a freewill offering from the grateful Chinese, duped by a Russian envoy into believing that he had interceded and obtained the withdrawal of British and French forces temporarily occupying Peking.

In a similar fashion, Russia played the sympathetic broker following Japan's defeat of China in 1895. St. Petersburg got French and German assistance in warning Japan against holding any Manchurian territory that it had taken in the hostilities. For this favor rendered, China granted Russia a concession for the Chinese Eastern Railway straight across northern Manchuria, to connect Chita on the Trans-Siberian with Vladivostok.

With considerably less finesse, through intimidation and bribery, St. Petersburg prevailed upon Peking in 1898 to lease to Russia the strategically located southernmost tip of Manchuria, the Kwantung Peninsula. Less than three years earlier, Russia had sanctimoniously denied Japan this fruit of its victory over China. The Japanese were not at all pleased by the Russian duplicity. Regaining the Kwantung Peninsula with its naval base, Port Arthur, and its commercial port, Dalny, became a major incentive for Japan's starting the Russo-Japanese War in 1904.

Leapfrogging the length of Manchuria to the Kwantung Peninsula was atypical of the Russians. Normal Russian aggression was from Russian territory into contiguous zones claimed by China—into Central Asia, Mongolia, and northern Manchuria. The southward jump was a measure of St. Petersburg's impatience to take over all of Manchuria and to get a warm-water port on the Pacific.

The antiforeign excesses of the Boxer Rebellion in 1900 provided the Russians with an excuse to occupy much of Manchuria. This was the peak extension of Russia into China's Northeast. With the Russo-Japanese war, it was pushed back into northern Manchuria. But what was more damaging to St. Petersburg's ambitions in the Far East were the civil disturbances within Russia precipitated by the war. Confronted by a revolutionary situation, with causes much deeper and more compelling than the disgrace of military defeat, the Tsar's government anxiously turned its attention inward.

Well it might have. For the war stimulated the professional revolutionists to feverish activity. And Lenin, writing in the midst of the war as an exile in Geneva, hailed Japan's capture of Port Arthur in naively indiscriminate terms: "Progressive, advanced Asia has dealt backward and reactionary Europe an irreparable blow." Less astray from the facts, he went on, "Not the Russian people but Absolutism has suffered a shameful defeat . . . . The capitulation of Port Arthur is the prologue to the capitulation of Tsarism."

Meanwhile Stalin, that slippery conspirator, had escaped from exile in Siberia because of the internal confusion caused by the war. Back in the Caucasus and uncommitted to any one revolutionary faction, he decided to join Lenin and the Bolsheviks.

Thus a war which the Tsar's government brought upon itself by an expansionist policy in China gave impetus to revolution in Russia. More than that, it was in the first revolution that the men who made the epochal one of 1917 served their apprenticeship and began to shape an ideology and technique of revolution that some forty years later conquered China. This later conquest of China, however, was not by Russians, but by Chinese—and in the wake of a second Russo-Japanese war in which Stalin undertook to avenge the defeat suffered by Tsarist Russia.

Japan was a late starter in aggression against China. Like China, Japan had resisted the inroads of the West. But unlike China, Japan had during the latter half of the nineteenth century officially committed itself to modernization. In the phenomenal transformation of the Meiji Restoration, Japan had so made itself over by the end of the century that it was able to join the civilized nations of the West in competitive aggression against a lumbering China.

Having to make up for lost time, Japan's approach was more impetuous than that of the others. By 1895, it had defeated China in a war. A mere ten years later it disposed of the mighty Russian Empire in a war for control of Manchuria, in which China served as host country to the hostilities. During this period, Japanese pressure on Korea increased, culminating in the annexation of that country in 1910. And so, Russia having made itself a Pacific power, Japan intruded onto the Asian mainland to become a continental power.

Japan was remarkably single-minded about its aggression against China. It had no distracting interests and ambitions in Europe, the Middle East, or Africa, as did the European nations and that sprawling Eurasian empire, Russia. Japan's initial lunges onto the mainland can persuasively be represented as defensive, establishing buffer zones in Manchuria and Korea against a westward-pressing Russia. Even its later intervention in Siberia during the Russian civil war—matching similar interference by the United States—and its 1931 conquest of Manchuria may be attributed in considerable part to fear of Communist aggression, an anxiety that has impelled other countries to dispatch expeditionary forces and foster "friendly governments" in farther-away places.

When the Europeans began to fight among themselves in 1914, they neglected China. This opened for Japan vistas south of the Great Wall. Tokyo was quick to march off toward the new horizons on excursions that had little relation to the defense of the home islands. It delivered a brisk ultimatum to Berlin, advising it to hand over to Japan its Kiaochow Bay holdings, and when the Germans showed no signs of doing so, declared war and took them.

In January 1915, Tokyo confronted Peking with a shopping list of its Chinese requirements, known as the Twenty-one Demands. They ranged from demands for privileged economic arrangements and spheres of influence to the introduction of Japanese political, financial, military and, even police advisers. Had China acceded to these exactions, it would have been reduced to the level of a Japanese protectorate.

Peking temporized, and finally yielded in bits and pieces to the less exorbitant of the demands. These concessions, in turn, aroused waves of popular protest in China, particularly among students. Japan's encroachment fired nationalism and what began to be called anti-imperialism. As Japan's military defeat of Russia in 1905 added to the revolutionary potential in Russia, so its diplomatic defeats of China a decade later helped to create the preconditions for the Chinese Communist movement.

CHAPTER *8*

Manifest Destiny to Dollar Diplomacy

WHILE RUSSIA was consolidating its position as a Pacific power and Japan was striving to establish itself as a continental power, the United States conquered and held the Philippines. Thereby the United States, already a Western Hemisphere power, became also a colonial power in the Eastern Hemisphere.

If the British Empire was acquired in fits of absentmindedness, the American was picked up, secondhand, from Spain in a fit of intoxication. Just why the United States went on an imperialist binge in Asia is not entirely clear. The reasons for doing so were varied, subjectively distorted, and devious. The consequences, however, quickly became evident—entanglement in the Far Eastern power struggle.

The war against Spain began over the issue of Cuba, not the Philippines. It began in 1898, ostensibly as a crusade to liberate the Cubans from the Spanish yoke. Forthwith, to the surprise of most Americans, Commodore Dewey undertook to emancipate the Filipinos too.

A few Americans were not surprised. They were cosmopolitan in outlook, caught up in the romance and excitement of imperialism, then fashionable in Europe. Among them were Assistant Secretary of the Navy Theodore Roosevelt, Senator Henry Cabot Lodge, and Captain Alfred T. Mahan, the American geopolitician.

Impressed by the effectiveness of the British navy in imperial expansion, Mahan had developed by 1890 a theory supporting the use of naval power. He went on to point out the strategic importance to the United States of the Caribbean and Hawaiian islands and Samoa, athwart the approaches to a projected canal across Central America. Manifest destiny had moved off the land and into salt water.

Lodge and Roosevelt found Mahanism congenial to their assertive natures.

Even before the outbreak of the Spanish-American War they included the Philippines in the greater United States that they schemed for. Lodge recommended the expansionist course, what he called "the large policy," among his fellow legislators and Roosevelt took the fullest advantage of his position as assistant secretary of the navy to push what he so strenuously believed in.

Roosevelt beset easygoing President McKinley in 1897 with war plans for ousting the Spaniards from the Caribbean, thwarting the Japanese "yellow peril," and making the American naval presence felt in Manila. All of this, he forecast, could be accomplished in a mere six weeks. But to McKinley and Roosevelt's chief, Secretary of the Navy Long, so headlong a destiny was not altogether manifest.

Nothing daunted, Roosevelt continued with his plans and plots. Having decided that Commodore George Dewey was of the kind to take the Philippines, he so manipulated matters that Dewey was given command of the Asiatic Squadron. By February 1898, Long was wearied by his efforts to stave off Mr. Roosevelt's war. He decided to absent himself from the cares of office for one Friday afternoon.

That was all that the assistant secretary needed. As Long complained to his diary on the following day, "the very devil seemed to possess him yesterday afternoon." Roosevelt and Beelzebub were not alone, however, for Senator Lodge also dropped in to commune with the acting secretary of the navy.

The result of a busy afternoon were orders for the deployment of naval vessels, procurement of ammunition, acquisition of armament for a proposed auxiliary fleet, and a message to Congress asking for legislation that would provide an unspecified number of naval enlistments. Further improving his few shining hours, the acting secretary cabled to Commodore Dewey:

> SECRET AND CONFIDENTIAL. ORDER THE SQUADRON, EXCEPT MONOCACY, TO HONG KONG. KEEP FULL OF COAL. IN THE EVENT OF DECLARATION OF WAR WITH SPAIN, YOUR DUTY WILL BE TO SEE THAT THE SPANISH SQUADRON DOES NOT LEAVE THE ASIATIC COAST, AND THEN OFFENSIVE OPERATIONS IN PHILIPPINE ISLAND. KEEP OLYMPIA UNTIL FURTHER ORDERS.

Roosevelt got the war he wanted, thanks to the mysterious blowing up of the USS *Maine* in Havana harbor, and to a peculiar war wish on the part of many Americans, incited only in part by the expansionists, such as Roosevelt and Lodge, and jingoist elements in the press. No sooner had war been declared in April 1898, and Dewey victorious in Manila Bay, than Roosevelt resigned to become a lieutenant colonel in the army and second in command of Roosevelt's Rough Riders. The reduction in status from assistant secretary was more than compensated for by the thrill of being a cowboy-cavalryman in Cuba, making life miserable for his superiors, and cultivating war correspondents eager to find a hero in this misbegotten war.

Certain characteristics of Roosevelt and the Spanish-American war were to recur in American foreign affairs. One of these was an expansionist exuberance, projecting the conquest of the Far West to the conquest of the Far East. In 1898 this urge was crudely imperialistic, for acquisition of territory. In the mid-twentieth century American expansionism expressed itself less bluntly, in pressing American values and know-how on others.

This is not to suggest that Roosevelt and those who adopted "the large policy" were without moral compunctions. To the contrary, they were fairly awash with high principles. The classic example of piety in this imperialistic adventure was President McKinley's revelation of how he decided to annex the Philippines. But, first, it should be recalled that upon being told of Dewey's victory, he was not sure just where the archipelago was.

Having located the chain of islands, McKinley, as he told it, later "walked the floor of the White House night after night until midnight and I am not ashamed to tell you, gentlemen, that I went down on my knees and prayed Almighty God for light and guidance more than one night." After these vigils, the president's conclusion regarding the islands was that "there was nothing left for us to do but to take them all, and to educate the Filipinos, and uplift and civilize and Christianize them, and by God's grace do the very best we could by them, as our fellowmen for whom Christ also died. And then I went to bed, and to sleep, and slept soundly."

Fellowmen in Christ the Filipinos and Cubans may have been. But to many Americans they were an inferior form of fellowmen. The learned Senator Beveridge, opposing proposals that the Filipinos be given their independence, spoke of them as "these children" and then went on to say, "They are not capable of self-government. How could they be? They are not a self-governing race. They are Orientals, Malays, instructed by Spaniards in the latter's worst estate. . . . What alchemy will change the oriental quality of their blood and set the self-governing currents of the American pouring through their Malayan veins?"

Not from greed or lust for power did the Americans assume the white man's burden of governing lesser breeds. It was, the Senator declaimed, "the divine law of human society which makes of us our brother's keeper." God had been "preparing the English-speaking and Teutonic peoples for a thousand years" to make them "the master organizers of the world to establish system where chaos reigns. . . . He has made us adepts in government that we may administer government among savage and senile peoples."

The savage Filipinos and senile Spaniards did not agree that God had "marked the American people as His chosen nation to finally lead in the regeneration of the world." The Filipinos, who initially thought that the Americans had come to aid them in their fight for independence, soon recognized that this was not to be the case. Whereupon, the oriental quality of their blood boiled and they strove to thwart the American capture of the city of Manila.

This was the beginning of collaboration between the Americans and Spaniards against the Filipinos, those whom McKinley had resolved on his knees to uplift and civilize and Christianize. The Spaniards obligingly held off the insurgents not only in Manila but also from their outlying garrisons throughout the archipelago, until the "master organizers" could take over. Even after this, resistance persisted for years, until the Filipino nationalists were driven in turn to their knees by measures similar to those which had been resorted to by the Spaniards.

Assumptions of racial superiority recurred time after time in American foreign relations. They were often adorned with expressions of humanitarianism which made them the more galling to those toward whom they were directed. This was scarcely less true when assumptions of American superiority were less primitive, when they were that American civilization was superior—an attitude akin to that of mandarins regarding Chinese civilization. Sympathy, when expressed, and rapport, when sought, were colored by contempt.

Out of this contempt for foreigners, especially for those who were not white, or even those whites who were swarthy, stemmed a national myth that Americans could lick anyone. In the estimation of the social Darwinists at the turn of the century, Americans were the fittest in the struggle among the peoples of the world.

Inevitably, arrogance bred miscalculations. Not only Roosevelt and Lodge, but most of the McKinley administration misjudged the fighting qualities of the Spaniards as well as the Filipinos. The Americans were surprised when the Spanish fought gallantly and were totally unprepared for the tenacious resistance of "these children," the Filipinos. Military underestimation of the Filipino guerrillas at the outset of this first American war in Asia was followed by depreciation of the adversary in every subsequent conflict in Asia.

Miscalculation was compounded when put into effect by activists, like Roosevelt. An error of judgment left alone, not pushed into performance, may be cherished without untoward results. But the damage is likely to be multiplied if it is implemented with zeal.

Activism as a cult has recurred again and again after Roosevelt's ill-conceived lunge into grand strategy. The belief in "doing something" and the idealization of the man of action have insured a continuing supply of political activists.

The war against a European nation, Spain, that began in the West Indies and flared to the Southwest Pacific, came to be justified in considerable part by supposed American interests in China. Mahan, in 1900, spoke of "the world's future, centering about China" and a need for "a grip upon our special great line of communications thither." The spooky strategic concept of China as the navel of Mother Earth made the Philippines the necessary terminus of a vital line of communications leading to the Middle Kingdom.

Although China thereafter showed no signs of becoming the center of the world, Washington persisted in attributing great strategic significance to it. Somehow four hundred million people occupying a large land area must be an important power factor. This point of view was not shared by the skeptical British, but was later held by the Bolsheviks, in revolutionary terms.

In another sense China provided an alluring reason for seizing the Philippines. This was the familiar bedazzlement of what Beveridge called "China's illimitable markets." "China is our natural customer," he exclaimed. "The Philippines give us a base at the door of all the East." These expectations were feebly grounded, for American trade with China was then 2 percent of American foreign commerce.

With the Stars and Stripes flying on the threshold of all the East and the shimmering riches of old Cathay lying just beyond, American interest in China grew. So also did anxiety lest the European powers, Russia, and Japan take over China piecemeal and thus exclude the United States.

London, too, had become concerned over the threatening breakup of China and, even before the battle of Manila Bay, had sought American cooperation in opposing foreign aggression along China's coast, but without avail.

Nothing really happened on this score until a Mr. Alfred Hippisley strayed into Washington in the summer of 1899. Mr. Hippisley was an Englishman and he was on his way home to Britain for a well-earned vacation from his functions as second in command of the Chinese Maritime Customs. In Washington, he encountered an old friend from Peking, W. W. Rockhill, who had been American minister to China.

Mr. Hippisley discovered that Washington was a policy vacuum with regard to China. The secretary of state, John Hay, knew a great deal about Europe and many other things, but little about East Asia. Sensibly, he had persuaded Rockhill to act as his adviser. But Rockhill, apparently, was at a loss as to what realistic new American policy might be devised for China.

Mr. Hippisley was not at any loss in this respect, and besides, he was a voluble talker and correspondent. It was his conversations with Rockhill and Hay that persuaded them to advocate the doctrine of the Open Door—in essence, a declaration affirming the principle of equal economic opportunity for all in China. This was a British policy that London was then discarding because it had not worked. It was a Hippisley memorandum that led to presidential approval and drafting of the note that the United States sent to Britain, Germany, Russia, Japan, France, and Italy asking each nation to indicate its agreement with the Open Door declaration.

These ingenuous articles of self-denial elicited what might have been expected—a variety of evasive replies. The Russian response was barely short of a rejection. Putting an unjustifiably good face on discomfiture, as is the custom in such situations, Hay misrepresented the answers as having provided satisfactory assurances, "final and definitive." The American public was vastly impressed by the sagacity and moral force of Hay's diplomacy. He had saved China and was elevated in popular opinion to the position of a great international statesman.

While the Open Door notes were exhortations to other powers, Hay issued in 1900 a circular, approved by President McKinley, to eleven nations which committed the United States to an astonishing series of propositions. The circumstances were these. The Boxer Rebellion, a fanatical antiforeign movement, was raging in China and the legations in Peking were under siege. An international expeditionary force was being formed to relieve the beleaguered foreigners. Hay worried lest the Europeans take advantage of the disturbances and their grievances to dismember China.

Beginning his circular with a temperate statement of the American position regarding the Boxer crisis, Hay then declared that American policy was to "preserve Chinese territorial and administrative entity, protect all rights guaranteed to friendly powers by treaty and international law, and safeguard for the world the principle of equal and impartial trade with all parts of the Chinese Empire." These were spacious commitments—to "preserve," to "protect," and to "safeguard," proceeding from China, to friendly powers, to all of the world.

These undertakings ignored the organic decay within the administrative entity of China and challenged the predatory designs of most powers toward the Middle Kingdom. Furthermore, they were unsupported by the determination and the necessary means to make good on so extravagant a policy. At best, this was diplomacy by incantation.

The governments receiving Hay's circular apparently did not take seriously the American posture, for none of them bothered to respond directly to Washington. They were too busy jockeying for favorable positions in China and against one another in Europe to pay much attention to the exorcisms of imperialism and the frankincense of good intentions wafting outward from the State Department.

Although consistency is not necessarily a virtue in diplomacy, and compromise with enunciated principles is not unknown in American foreign relations, Hay's next move with regard to China does seem to have been a graceless about-face. Some four months after proclaiming American resolve to preserve Chinese territorial entity, he tried to get a naval base for the United States on Samsah Bay in Fukien Province.

But Fukien had been staked out by Japan as its sphere of influence. Tokyo's reaction was predictable. "The Imperial Government harbors no territorial designs on China . . . and they have noted with entire satisfaction the declaration made on several occasions by the secretary of state that the United States were also anxious to preserve the territorial entity of that empire." Touché, and that was the end of the naval base proposal.

At this juncture, however, it was Russia that Hay found the more trying. Using Boxer disturbances as an excuse, St. Petersburg had spread its troops all over Manchuria and there they squatted despite American and other protests. Finding Russian diplomats as slippery as their armies were sticky, Hay wearily observed to President Roosevelt in 1903, "Dealing with a government with whom mendacity is a science is an extremely difficult and delicate matter." This sentiment was to be echoed in similar circumstances forty-three years later.

So tenacious seemed the Russian hold on China's northeast that many thought the area was irretrievably lost to Peking. Hay told the president that the American minister to China "has the pessimism about Russia which is almost universal out there. 'What's the use? Russia is too big, too crafty, too cruel for us to fight. She will conquer in the end. Why not give up and be friendly?' "

Under continuing pressure, the Russians did begin to withdraw from southern Manchuria. The Japanese completed the process by force, in the Russo-Japanese war.

The Russo-Japanese War brought Theodore Roosevelt back into the East Asian scene, this time as president. He led off by asking Russia and Japan to respect China's neutrality. This was a just request because hostilities were being conducted on Chinese soil, in Manchuria. It was also a futile plea, as futile as inviting two predators to respect the prey over which they are fighting. When Roosevelt got no satisfactory reply from either belligerent, he pretended that he had.

At the outset of the war Roosevelt had been, like most Americans, pro-Japanese because the Japanese were plucky little fellows and because he wanted the Russians expelled from Manchuria. As the Russians retreated he shifted to hoping for a balance between the two combatants in Manchuria. Then as the Japanese continued to win on land and sea, he realized how he had underestimated them and sought to place restraints on their advance.

Throughout all of this he had conspired to use European states in furthering his objectives. He recommended to the Kaiser ("the only man I understand and who understands me") that together they should put Manchuria under a Chinese viceroy appointed by Germany. The German emperor's private reaction was that, among other things, "Teddy is quite a dilettante in his opinions and conclusions."

A British appraisal of Roosevelt's skipping about in power politics, that of Sir Cecil Spring-Rice, a junior diplomat in whom the president confided more freely than in his own envoys, was more indulgent. "If you took an impetuous small boy on a beach strewn with a great many exciting pebbles, you would not expect him to remain interested for long in one pebble. You must always remember that the president is about six."

Quite gratuitously Roosevelt stormed through the underbrush of European and Asian intrigue, urging peace between Japan and Russia. Eventually, having worn themselves out against one another, the belligerents accepted the insistent mediation of the American president. Whereupon the diplomatic rough-riding began.

While Roosevelt got agreement from each of the combatants on the respective advantages they were to enjoy in Manchuria, and even their recognition of Chinese sovereignty over the area, the rest of the peace settlement became the subject of acrimony. In the end, the Japanese felt cheated out of an indemnity and a claim to all of the Russian island of Sakhalin. The president won no gratitude from the Russians and became the butt of Japanese frustrations, expressed in anti-American riots. But he won the acclaim of the American people for something of no real concern to them—and a Nobel Peace award.

Notwithstanding the applause he received for this achievement, Roosevelt worried about the rise of Japanese power, particularly lest it swell to threaten the

Philippines. He had connived at the reckless commitment of American prestige and responsibility to the other side of the Pacific. Now he had to reckon with the consequences. That distant archipelago was vulnerable, inviting attack, unless the Congress would provide the costly naval protection necessary to deter a powerful aggressor. And there was no certainty that it would.

Unless the Philippines were heavily fortified and defended, Roosevelt said in 1905, they should be discarded. During the following year he confessed that he would welcome being rid of the islands. By 1907 he described them as "our heel of Achilles." More specifically, "They are all that makes the present situation with Japan dangerous."

The strained relations with Japan were worsened by insulting American restrictions on Japanese immigration. Roosevelt became so alarmed in July 1907 that he thought war was imminent. On into 1908 he considered the possibility that Japan might win such a war.

In an effort to placate the Japanese, Roosevelt had in 1905 arranged for his secretary of war, William Howard Taft, to conclude secretly a memorandum with the Japanese prime minister whereby the United States acknowledged Japanese suzerainty over Korea in return for Tokyo's assurances that it harbored no aggressive designs on the Philippines. Three years later, his secretary of state, Elihu Root, exchanged notes with the Japanese ambassador providing that the United States and Japan would respect one another's possessions in "the region of the Pacific Ocean" and accept the status quo.

The Japanese, of course, read this to mean that they would leave the Philippines alone in exchange for American recognition of the existing situation in Manchuria—Japanese hegemony. The Root-Takahira Agreement also included passages mutually pledging recognition of the Open Door and support of the independence and integrity of China. These were the provisions that Washington, of course, liked to dwell on.

Experience and responsibility sobered Roosevelt. He was no longer six. How much he had grown was shown in the advice he gave in 1910 to his successor, William Howard Taft:

> Our vital interest is to keep the Japanese out of our country and at the same time to preserve the good will of Japan. The vital interest of the Japanese, on the other hand, is in Manchuria and Korea. It is therefore peculiarly our interest not to take any steps as regards Manchuria which will give the Japanese cause to feel, with or without reason, that we are hostile to them, or a menace—in however slight a degree—to their interests. Alliance with China, in view of China's absolute military helplessness, means of course not an additional strength to us, but an additional obligation which we assume; and as I utterly disbelieve in the policy of bluff, in national and international no less than in private affairs, or in any violation of the old frontier maxim, "Never draw unless you mean to shoot!" I do not believe in our taking any position anywhere unless we can make good; and as regards Manchuria, if the Japanese choose to follow a course of conduct to which we are adverse, we cannot stop it unless we are prepared to go to war, and a successful war about Manchuria would require a fleet as good as that of England, plus an

army as good as that of Germany. The Open Door policy in China was an excellent thing, and I hope it will be a good thing in the future, so far as it can be maintained by general diplomatic agreement; but, as has been proved by the whole history of Manchuria, alike under Russia and under Japan, the "Open Door" policy, as a matter of fact, completely disappears as soon as a powerful nation determines to disregard it, and is willing to run the risk of war rather than forego its intention. . . .

However friendly the superficial relations of Russia and Japan may at any given time become, both nations are accustomed to measure their foreign policy in sections of centuries; and Japan knows perfectly well that sometime in the future, if a good occasion offers, Russia will wish to play a return game of bowls for the prize she lost in their last contest.

Taft came to the presidency with rather more than a nodding acquaintance with East Asia. As Roosevelt's secretary of war he had dealt with the strategic problems of the new American position in the western Pacific. He had conducted secret negotiations with the Japanese. He had been governor of the Philippines. Generally, he had participated in Roosevelt's appeasement of Japan and attempts to reduce American commitments in East Asia.

Yet he pursued an essentially aggressive policy in China, defying Japanese and European special interests in that country. Taft's positive course was not bellicose. In American eyes it was innocent and legitimate. It was a drive for markets and investments in China and was called dollar diplomacy.

An underlying motive for dollar diplomacy was political. If the United States could expand its economic stake in China, it could then increase its political influence in the area. Whereupon this influence would be exerted on behalf of what had become an American obsession—the preservation of China's independence and territorial integrity. Dollar diplomacy, therefore, was not only innocent and legitimate, it was also actuated, Washington believed, by the most altruistic of political motives.

The European powers, Russia, and particularly Japan, viewed dollar diplomacy in another light. Their practices in China had been that the flag followed trade. No matter how pure of heart, the Americans were not welcomed in what the Europeans, Russians, and Japanese regarded as a preserve already partitioned—and at appreciable cost to each. The Americans were hypocritical interlopers.

Dollar diplomacy was not foisted by Wall Street on a servile government in Washington. To the contrary, it was the administration which pressed and maneuvered businessmen and bankers to plunge into the Chinese market. Some financiers, notably E. H. Harriman, with ambitions for an around-the-world railroad system, were ready and willing instruments of dollar diplomacy. But most of American free enterprise, while happy to trade with the Middle Kingdom, was shy of investment ventures in a mysterious country that was the prey of fierce foreign rivalries.

As Roosevelt's slapdash impetuosity, when assistant secretary of the navy, was a foretaste of later impulsiveness in high policy, so Willard Straight was a prototype of the young man with a mission in foreign affairs. In his mid-twenties, Straight was private secretary to the America minister to Korea. There he witnessed and was shocked by Japanese imposition of a protectorate over Korea in 1905. He concluded that if the United States had large investments in China it would have greater political leverage in East Asia and thus be able to counter aggression.

Shortly thereafter he was appointed as the first American consul general at Mukden, where he strove to bring American capital into Manchuria. Being a persuasive young man, he won over Harriman and impressed Roosevelt, and then Taft.

He was soon transferred to Washington as acting chief of the Far Eastern Division of the State Department, into contact with the center of power. He was in his element in the Washington of dollar diplomacy, fomenting grand financial schemes for the benevolent penetration of China by American capital. This was expansionism, a large policy, pacifically executed and combining the attraction of supposed profit and the kindly helping hand.

Straight and Harriman collaborated to chivvy reluctant New York bankers into a combination which would deal with the Chinese government. But it was not until the Department of State officially intervened that Morgan, Kuhn, Loeb, Harriman, the First National Bank, and the National City Bank joined together as a group sanctioned by the American government to underwrite railway construction in China. Straight then became the Peking representative of this financial expeditionary force.

Although Straight and the State Department were able to force American participation in one railway consortium, the outcome was infelicitous. Popular feeling in China against this foreign loan was a contributing factor to the revolution that overthrew the empire.

Throughout these combined operations of diplomacy and finance, the bankers had the backing of the president and his secretary of state, Philander C. Knox. Both were eminent lawyers, Mr. Taft so much so that he later became chief justice of the United States. Both had that peculiar trust in the efficacy of written compacts which, while warranted in a stable society under the rule of law, is irrelevant in international society, which is essentially anarchic, without an effective system of courts and police for the administration of justice. In a staggering display of rectitude flying in the face of reality, Knox declared that whether Americans would go to war for his policy was "academic"; what was important was that the United States stick to its principles without compromise.

Knox's most celebrated legalistic exploit was an attempt to get down on paper an agreement with Britain, Russia, Japan, China, France, and Germany for the neutralization of all the railways in Manchuria. This was a lawyer's dream solution for the power struggle gnawing at the region. The British gave Knox so tactful a refusal that he chose to misrepresent it to the others as an acceptance. With the same bland self-deception that characterized John Hay's announcements about the Open Door, he continued to dissemble success when, in fact, he was being rebuffed. The irrefutable answer to Knox came in a new Russo-Japanese Treaty clarifying their respective pretensions in Manchuria—a disdainful reversal of all that the secretary of state had attempted.

Wall Street, dealing with the facts of the situation and calculating its involvement in tangible terms of profit and loss, quietly eased itself out of dollar diplomacy. When Woodrow Wilson succeeded Taft, he backed out of a proposed loan to Yüan Shih-K'ai, which that sly old military mandarin was to use in besting Sun Yat-sen's Kuomintang. Well might Wilson have shied away from this additional commitment. The bankers had made it known to the State Department that they would continue on the losing course of dollar diplomacy in China only if the government insisted that they do so.

The end result of Taft's policy of using American capital to wage power politics was a fiasco. Neither Taft nor Knox really understood the forces at work in East Asia, nor the nature of the struggle. Rather than restraining Russia and Japan, the president and his secretary of state provoked them to speed up their depredations. Rather than bolstering China's independence, dollar diplomacy undermined it, and instead of reaping rich profits, American investors encountered bafflement without rewards.

More serious than the humiliations of dollar diplomacy was a worsening of American relations with Japan. Undoing Roosevelt's belated efforts to lessen strains in these relations, Taft's policies tautened tensions between the two countries. And again, discriminatory immigration laws and attitudes aggravated Japanese resentment. Again Washington became concerned that rancor give way to war. And all of this occurred in a situation where American trade with China was declining and that with Japan steadily growing.

A decade and a half of McKinley, Roosevelt, and Taft transformed American relations with East Asia. The United States impulsively had made itself an imperial power, with a colony in the Far East nearly the size of Japan. In so doing, it thrust itself across the breadth of the Pacific on an exposed salient which successive administrations were unwilling or unable to make defensible.

The days of trading post diplomacy with China had passed and American merchants were no longer chary of official support, as the early traders in Canton had been of Caleb Cushing. The American government committed itself to the Open Door in China and to that country's administrative and territorial integrity. This commitment, by dripping reiteration over the years, became a stalactitic monument of precedents, a marvel to behold but not really a workable proposition.

And so the United States found itself deeply embroiled in East Asia. It was unprepared for such involvement. The American government, save in the latter days of Roosevelt's administration, entertained misconceptions regarding the mystic East, which may have been less picturesque than President Tyler's, but quite as misleading. Most of the men who formulated American policy had scant understanding of the gigantic forces of dissolution set in train by the intrusion of the West into China and Japan. They had less comprehension of the new impulses aborning in bitterness, frustration, and hope.

In the ensuing confusion, American spokesmen had muddled motives for American policy toward China and the Philippines. Having declared that a main reason for taking the Philippines was to get an offshore base from which to exploit the China market, after Taft involved the country in dollar diplomacy, they maintained that a positive line was imperative in China to bolster the American position in the Philippines. In this manner the myth of the strategic importance of China reinforced itself.

The big American interest in China was a state of mind. It was, first of all, spiritual. Nearly three generations of American missionaries had brought China in a peculiarly personalized manner into American homes. The American people developed a religious investment in China. They wanted it protected.

Then there was the moralistic, legalistic approach of many Americans to international relations. China had been wronged by the Europeans, the Russians, and the Japanese. Past wrongs should be righted. But if they could not be, at least future wrongs should be prohibited. And there was a moral obligation to speak up and take a stand on such issues.

Spiritual and moral interests in China created an emotional attachment to the Middle Kingdom unlike that felt for any other country. Other peoples regarded Americans as quite unbalanced on the subject of China and American statesmen were privately viewed by their foreign colleagues as rather eccentric about the Chinese.

Righteous infatuation produced policy by expostulation. This became habitual in American relations with East Asia. Washington preached to everyone, including the Chinese.

The fatal defect of this policy was the familiar one of overcommitment. However strongly the American people felt about the fate or strategic importance of China, they did not believe that their vital national interests were threatened by what was happening across the Pacific—at least, not enough so to make them willing to go to war with Russia and then Japan to stop what was happening. In such circumstances a certain moderation in diplomatic utterance was indicated.

Washington's expostulations were immoderate. As such, they deceived the American people, leading them to inflated expectations of what might be accomplished. Abroad, they devalued the worth of official American pronouncements which came to be regarded as hypocrisy or bombast.

American preaching irritated those to whom it was directed. Particularly was this true of the Japanese whose neurotic sensitivity was inflamed by racial discrimination against them. The obtuse expostulations of Washington were provocative, another infuriating insult. When preachment was without ready recourse to awesome power, and the United States was obviously unprepared to use such force it had, Washington's posturing was exposed as bluff. Whereupon, the temptation for the Japanese was to call the bluff, to translate irritation and disdain into defiance.

In the fifteen years, from 1898 to 1913, of busybody, garrulous good intentions, the United States set a pattern of behavior in East Asia that it was to follow into World War II. For no necessary reason, it contributed to the reduction of China to a shambles, ripe for the fanaticism to come, fecklessly placed itself in a compromised strategic position in East Asia, and futilely opposed the expansionism and thereby earned the vengeful antagonism of its best customer in Asia.

CHAPTER 9

The Era of Warlords and the Emergence of Communists

WHEN I THINK OF foreign intervention in other people's civil wars, I think of my mother, and the day that she stopped the fighting between two Chinese armies. Better said, she lifted a siege.

My father was away at the time, on a tour of distant small-town churches. My mother was alone with my younger brother and me, then about ten years of age, in the mission house at Chengtu, whence we had moved from Kiating. An outlying warlord had set his heart on taking this rich city, capital of Szechuan, a province bigger than Italy. He went through the normal formalities of advancing upon Chengtu with ostentation, contrived to overawe the defenders into capitulation forthwith, or at least to improve his bargaining position so that a compromise might be arranged profitable to him.

But something went awry. Whether it was an unwanted miscarriage of negotiations over the price of a compromise or a gross impropriety causing unacceptable loss of face, I do not recall. In any event, hostilities broke out and the aggressor actually attacked the city.

The firing into Chengtu, over its massive walls and huge double gates, became disagreeable. It seemed clear that we might be in for a siege. Finding bullet holes in the windows and walls of my brother's and my bedroom persuaded my mother that we should absent ourselves from the threat of shot, shell, fire, and pestilence.

Being a frontierswoman by origin and disposition, she moved directly from decision to action. She wrote brief identical notes to the warring commanders, expressing a wish to escape the oppressive heat of the summer. Would they be so kind as to grant safe passage to us to leave for the nearby hills. Somehow the letters were delivered. So one splendid, bright morning, the war ground abruptly to a stop. Soldiers of the defending forces squeaked open the enormous, iron-studded north gates of the city just wide enough for us to squeeze through, and we were outside.

Proceeding two or three hundred yards through the outskirts, we were met by a young officer of the besieging army. He assigned three of his men to escort us to the hills, a day's journey by sedan chair. I remember our flight as a genial excursion along the worn flagstone road twisting between emerald paddy fields. For several stretches I was allowed to march along with the soldiers, one of whom was amiable enough to permit me to shoulder his rifle. At the end of the journey, my mother presented our bodyguards with a little of what was customarily referred to as "wine money," but which my parents always gently and pointedly offered as "tea money."

Wine or tea—or what it was more likely to be, a small pipe of opium—no matter, our protectors left in good humor. It had been for them a detail full of diversion with the foreign devils: how we looked, what we wore, what we ate, how we spoke the comic gibberish of English. They had gotten off from the drudgery of banging away at the city. But they had not missed the up-coming capitulation of the defenders and the chance to join the ensuing sack of the capital.

My mother's interference in the course of hostilities was a benign form of foreign intervention. She was successful because of the circumstances of the warlord era. Both sides, happily, were without principles. Nationalism was not involved in the conflict. Nor was ideology and a struggle for other people's minds and hearts. The war was, therefore, neither gorged with hatred nor implacable with self-righteousness. It was, as wars go, rational. Consequently there was considerable leeway for good sense and chivalrous gesture.

Furthermore, a siege is a relatively leisurely procedure. An interruption of hostilities accommodating to my mother's wishes inconvenienced neither side. So being gallant in this situation entailed no military sacrifices.

The truce was far more easily arranged than would be the case in a modern war. The opposing warlords were there at Chengtu, one inside the walls, the other outside. Each was the ultimate authority on his side. Neither had to refer to a theater commander or a Joint Chiefs of Staff or a president. The performance was rather medieval in its simplicity. The will of each prince on the field of battle was final.

Warlords dominated the Chinese scene for something like a decade, from the death of Yüan Shih-k'ai in 1916 until Chiang Kai-shek in 1926 drove northward from Canton into the Yangtze valley in his campaign to unify China. After 1926, they were progressively reduced in number, with Chiang consolidating himself in the center of the country. The authority of Chiang's national government, however, extended to the peripheral areas only nominally, at the sufferance of a semicircle of warlords.

But in the decade of their heyday, the central government was a miserably buffetted thing, and the warlords were sovereigns, each in his principality, big or small, each with his personal army. The great powers maintained their legations in Peking, dealing with a succession of inconsequential presidents who really meant little beyond, if even within, the walls of that noble city.

They were an unlikely lot, these warlords, the kind that is thrown up in a time of trouble. One was the son of a viceroy. But most were of less imposing origins. Chang Tso-lin, who ruled Manchuria and more—an area twice the size of France—had fought, more or less, as a private in the 1895 war against Japan and then risen to power through a career of banditry. Another, a nearly illiterate minor warlord, started as a peddler on the streets of Peking, ending up, briefly, as president of China.

These were, consequently, men of widely differing dispositions and capacities. Some were ruffians. A few tried to develop and modernize the areas under their rule. Yen Hsi-shan prepared an ideological tossed salad of Confucianism, despotism, communism, and Japanese pragmatism to make his Shansi close to what he called it, "The Model Province"—that is, close to model in comparison with the scurvy regimes afflicting the rest of the country.

Feng Yü-hsiang, a hulking rustic, was also stirred by ideas and by fitful concern for the public weal. American Protestant missionaries converted him, and thereafter he was carelessly known as the "Christian General." He insisted that his troops behave themselves, and he baptized them by the platoon with fire hoses. Before long his imagination was captivated by the Russian Bolsheviks, more as a potential source of weapons, perhaps, than as an arsenal of ideological armament.

Yen, Feng, and three or four others differed from most warlords in that their concerns reached out, albeit erratically, beyond gross self-aggrandizement. They were, however, like the rest in being cunning without always being shrewd in their shifting alliances and facile betrayals of partners, and in their reliance on intrigue and violence in their official business rather than on reason and law.

It was an unstable existence. The threat of assassination was ever present. In a simple way this was borne home to me in 1933, when I was a vice-consul in Yunnan. The consul and I (there were only two of us at the post) entertained the governor, a residual and fairly noxious warlord by the name of Lung Yun. The occasion was an annual dinner symbolizing American-Yunnanese amity.

His Excellency, wizened and sallow from addiction to opium, arrived with approximately fifty bodyguards. They immediately swarmed throughout the residence to occupy all vantage points. Thus occupied, we progressed through the awkward festivities, from tepid martinis to the cramped banquet board, groaning with stilted small talk and laborious jokes.

In the midst of this carousal, the city power failed—as it often did—and the lights went out. They came back on in a matter of seconds. In the interim, the room had filled with the palace guard so that, when we could again see, we were facing drawn Mausers. Once assured that nothing was amiss, the bodyguards tactfully resumed their posts behind the draperies and around the corners outside of the doorways.

Few of the warlords lasted into mid-century. Yen, Feng, and Lung Yun did. The first two had collaborated with the Communists during the 1940s and Lung made a deal with them on the eve of their victory. These monuments of individualism were placed temporarily in a colonnade of non-Party personages adorning the facade of the new collectivized regime in Peking.

Feng expired flashily in 1948 while aboard a Soviet ship on his way to Russia. The cause of his death was said to have been an explosion of film during a movie aboard the vessel. This explanation was so strange as to be possibly true.

The stuff of power for the warlords was, of course, their armies. As I remember them from my childhood, these armies were composed mostly of buglers. Every dawn was ushered in with a blare, with brasses heralding the advent of a new day. A company of buglers mounted the city wall blowing like an array of stuck whistles. No sprightly reveilles, no trilling notes. Steady long blast on one note until all air had been expelled from the lungs and the trumpeters were puce in the face. Then the next note, and the next, and the next. Finally backing down the scale, still in steady unison, still with some flat, some sharp. Over and over again. After the sun had been thus blown aloft, silence fell briefly. Then the activities of the day began, with echoes still oscillating in the ears.

The next most memorable trait of warlord soldiery was the goose step. The goose step with jackboots is one thing; with straw sandals another. With one it was thuds; with the other thumps. But the imposing symmetry of the outflung, upflung legs neatly wrapped in puttees, was the same—at any rate not far off.

The warlord soldiers enjoyed this phase of army life. It made them feel that they were on stage. Most Chinese have a tremendous sense of theater, notwithstanding the prissy attitude of Confucianists towards dramatic arts. Tootling and goose-stepping were for the troops the closest in their mean existence that they got to play-acting. Bugling was the privilege of only some. But all could and did goose-step. This was not prosaic, like walking. Nor was it tiresome, like marching from one place to get to another. This was going nowhere, but being on display, striding out a broad theatrical convention with the whole parade ground as a stage.

The rest of life for the warlord soldier was, alas, grubby and uncertain. From the time he was hauled away from the farm as a conscript, picked up by a press gang in the city or enlisted because life at home was insupportable, he was an outsider, someone apart from the normal interrelationship of the peasants, merchants, artisans, and even coolies. He was someone looked upon with contempt and fear. "Bandits come and go," according to the old saw, "but soldiers come and stay."

The soldier was ill fed, ill paid—unless he was part of an élite unit or of a general's bodyguard. He made up for his poor estate by scrounging off townspeople or farmers, and after a rare conquest, by looting. Unless he was able to work his way up through the ranks, his prospects were dim. Those soldiers who faded away were not only the old ones. They were also those who were sick or infirm—fading into neglected discard and beggary.

On the whole, the chances of a soldier being killed in action during the warlord era were slight. Battles were usually fought with silver bullets. Divisions were deployed in battle order, menacing maneuvers executed, guns even fired. While all of this pother was going on, each side would be calculating the odds. Usually it was evident to both which would be the victor should there be a test of arms.

As the two sides had been constantly engaged in unconditional negotiations, the only problem, once there was an agreed forecast as to who would win, was what the conditions would be: how much it would cost the weaker to buy off the stronger. Or it might be: how much would the stronger have to pay the weaker not to put up an unreasonable resistance costly to the stronger? This was an urbane and humane way to wage war. Especially was this so because both adversaries were usually reasonable in the price demanded, taking into account capacity to pay and delicate considerations of face—the propriety of all involved retaining at least the appearances of self-esteem.

Happy-go-lucky is not the way to describe the Chinese soldier of the warlord epoch. Literally speaking, he was neither. No one ever asked him how his morale was. He was not expected to have any. But he did have an enviable capacity to enjoy small gratifications available to him. He had that extraordinary Chinese gift for enduring, adapting, and making do with bits and pieces. He concocted moments of pleasure as a Chinese cook can create a gourmet's delight out of scraps. A cricket in a tiny straw cage, a shadow play manipulated by an itinerant puppeteer, gambling a pittance on games of chance, or listening to the fluted tones of flights of pigeons, each with a whistle tied to a leg—any one of these was enough to make an off-duty afternoon.

Excepting for the relatively few who belonged to élite detachments, the attitude of the warlord soldier toward martial affairs was indifferent, if not evasive. Indoctrination? No one ever heard of it. Learning a little how to shoot, close order drill and, rarely, maneuvers in the field—that was it. Why was he a soldier and what was he fighting for, when he fought? He was a soldier because he had enlisted as a last recourse or had been grabbed and made to be one, and because, if he was strong enough to carry a gun and walk, any attempt on his part to stop being a soldier, any attempt to slip away, would probably end up with his being caught and thoroughly beaten, unless he joined a band of brigands.

When he fought, everyone knew that he fought with circumspection, either to preserve or to expand the warlord's wealth and sources of continuing revenue. He also fought, when the opportunity occurred and the risks were not unfavorable, to do a little looting and extorting on his own. The booty rarely amounted to much. If it did, it was largely expropriated by those higher up. How high up depended upon how much it amounted to. War was, to adjust Clausewitz to the circumstances of Szechuan, nothing else than a continuation of money-making transactions intermingled with different means.

All of this is not to suggest that the soldiery of this era was exceptionally squeamish about blood-letting—when it was the blood of others. With all of their ethical and humanistic traditions, the Chinese reacted to killing with less shock than we do—or perhaps one should now say, than we did. Having so much of both about them, the Chinese took birth and death in their stride.

Still, death was the ultimate and most intense event in the mundane Chinese existence. Thus, public executions were always well-attended spectacles. They were so attended not in morbidity, as they would be in a sanitized society. People went as a matter of uncomplicated curiosity, to view an arranged and formalistic acting out of a melodrama that was meant to convey to them the majesty of con-stituted authority and the lesson that crime does not pay.

They got the message. It was, after all, blunt enough. But with all of that, the reaction was detached. Unless the principal actor was a local hero—which was rare—there was little sense that this might have been a tragedy that was wit-nessed. Nor was there any feeling of ramified symbolism that is conveyed and felt in a bullfight. A man had been charged with a grave offense against the law, he had been paraded through the streets, he had been made to kneel, and then his head had been lopped off. That was it—raw theatrics, and taken in a two-dimen-sional, matter-of-fact way.

It was against this kind of background that the warlord soldiers usually approached the matter of killing. Not routinely, but still, with no great repug-nance, remorse, or enduring fury. They were not seized by the mass frenzy that possessed Taiping or Boxer rebels. For they were not inflamed by a cause beyond themselves and with which they could identify.

The young educated élite of the warlord era were inflamed. Their cause was nationalism. They identified themselves with it, intellectually and with excite-ment.

Their ideas came from everywhere. They came from out of the infinite Chinese past, out of Han ethnocentricism, the serene arrogance of simply being Chinese. Even as humiliations by the West stirred rational doubts about the worth of traditional Chinese civilization, the idea of innate Chinese superiority persisted, emotionally surcharged by that very humiliation.

The ideas of the educated élite came also from those Chinese of the new wave, who had made the first breakthrough to western systems of thought, espe-cially those who had been students in Japan, Europe, and the United States. Among them was Hu Shih, American-educated, a temperate man, a scholar with charm. As one of the first Chinese with a cosmopolitan look, it was natural that he should have been, in 1917, a moving spirit in launching the Chinese liter-ary revolution.

Hu Shih's most memorable contribution to the new literature of realism and concern with contemporary problems was in communication. In 1917 he took the lead in adopting the vernacular for literary and political writing. Hitherto written expression had been elegantly constricted by the classical vocabulary, syntax, and style. It was a privileged preserve for the literati. Hu Shih liberated intellectual expression for those who had something to say and intellectual comprehension for those who would read. It was as if in modern Italy all literature were in Latin, pedantically reciting the virtues of ancient Rome, when suddenly a cluster of vibrant young men began to write about the whole range of contemporary experience and hope in the language that everyone understood. This unfettered the Chinese mind.

The flood of ideas agitating the new generation came also from outside of China, as it had in the preceding decades. Particularly stimulating were Woodrow Wilson's 1918 visions of democracy, self-determination, and a humane world order. Then two years later John Dewey and Bertrand Russell each visited China. These sympathetic scholarly interventions from out of the West greatly pleased the Chinese intellectuals.

But this did not compensate for wide disillusionment with the western democracies because of what had happened to China at Versailles in 1919. The Chinese, believing in Wilson's lofty generalities, had expected that the peace treaty following World War I would provide for the return of full Chinese sovereignty to the coastal province of Shantung. For in ousting the Germans early in the war from their limited hold on the province, at Kiaochow Bay, the Japanese had moved to dominate all of Shantung. The Chinese, quite understandably, wanted the Japanese out and the province freed.

When Wilson yielded to Japanese, British, and French pressure on April 30, and acquiesced in Japan's keeping what it had taken from Germany in Shantung, the Chinese were outraged. On May 4, thousands of students rampaged through Peking looking for "traitors," cabinet ministers whom they charged with having connived with the Japanese. They destroyed the house of one and nearly lynched another. A movement was born—the May Fourth Movement.

More demonstrations followed in Peking and elsewhere in China. Students marched and shouted slogans, lay down on streetcar tracks, and finally frightened the cabinet into resigning. This was essentially a movement of educated youth. But it was not confined to them. For the students roused the indifferent or cautious townsfolk into support of nationalism. Thus the May Fourth Movement was a suggestion of mass action to come, of a nationalist revolution.

At the outset, the nationalist movement was not identified with any political party. It was spontaneous, essentially unorganized. While the intellectuals regarded the divisive warlords with shame, their dominant emotion was hatred of the outlanders for aggression against China and "unequal treaties" imposed on the Middle Kingdom.

Sun Yat-sen's Kuomintang, with its nationalist tradition, played no significant part in the opening phases of the May Fourth Movement. It had lapsed into flatulence. And the good doctor himself was preoccupied in credulous negotiations with warlords whereby he might—but never did—come to power.

As for Chiang Kai-shek, the future leader of Chinese nationalism, he had since the Republican Revolution of 1911 dedicated himself to brokerage in the financial world of Shanghai. Chiang and his official biographers have been reticent about these years of his young manhood. It does seem to be generally agreed, however, that this junior army officer of modest antecedents enjoyed the sponsorship of at least one wealthy merchant. If, indeed, he was associated with the Green Gang, the powerful secret society and crime syndicate in the metropolis, he presumably acquired much face by this affiliation. The Green Gang was well known for its philanthropic activities. In any event, the Chinese outlook on these matters was more akin to that of Syracuse, Sicily, than to that of Syracuse, New York.

With all of his involvement in money-making, Chiang had not neglected his contacts with Sun Yat-sen. On one occasion at least, in 1918, he served as an officer in one of Sun's unsuccessful military campaigns in South China. Tentatively he was resuming his army career.

Meanwhile the October Revolution had exploded in Russia. Its first shock waves swept almost imperceptibly into China. By 1918 and 1919, however, Chinese intellectuals had become aware of the revolution's significance, especially the few who had a smattering of Marxist learning. The rise of the Soviet regime became a melodramatic demonstration of how a minority group, preaching a new and "scientific" creed, offering categoric answers to everything, could overthrow an ancient regime, confound foreign intervention, and make over a country.

This was heady stuff for impatient young radicals in China, seeking a short-cut to utopia. To those of such disposition, Marxism-Leninism was more appealing than the groping gradualism and exacting freedom offered by the democratic way of the West. But their understanding of this new ideology was both sketchy and highly theoretical . As they leaned toward communism, they continued to cling to an array of previously-held beliefs.

Peking National University was the center of intellectual pulling and hauling. Into this tumult, in 1918, plunged Mao Tse-tung. He was then twenty-four, self-assured, inquisitive, an advocate of physical culture, and an ardent patriot.

The years between his youthful fling at soldiering, during the Republican Revolution, and his arrival in Peking had been spent in his native province of Hunan, pursuing education. The pursuit began in a highly erratic fashion, propelled mostly by newspaper advertisements for a series of institutions of dubious academic stature. He led off by matriculating at a police school, then darted to a soap-making academy. He quickly left in a lather of enthusiasm for studying law at a school which guaranteed its graduates appointments as mandarins at the end of a three-year course. After registering for this conveyance to power and prestige, he switched to an institution preparing its students for a career in commerce. As most of the instruction was pretentiously imparted in what was represented to be English, with which Mao had a negligible acquaintance, he quit after a month.

Mao's next educational sampling lasted longer. He attended a high school for six months. But the course seemed to him restrictive. So he decided to educate himself by selected readings at the Hunan Provincial Library. There, at the age of eighteen, he saw for the first time a map of the world. There also he discovered the histories of foreign countries and introduced himself to Adam Smith, Darwin, John Stuart Mill, Spencer, Rousseau and Montesquieu, in translations. This heavy fare, Mao admitted, he diluted with Chinese poetry and romantic literature.

While Mao deemed his self-instruction as richly satisfying, his father did not. This was but one of many differences Mao had with his father, a barely literate, self-made, well-to-do farmer. So young Mao searched the advertisements for a school appropriate to his then prevailing ambitions, which were to be a teacher. He found it: a Hunan provincial normal school. There, astonishingly enough, he stayed for five years, long enough to be graduated. He was uninterested in and therefore slighted the natural sciences. But he took enthusiastically to the social sciences.

Two of Mao's teachers strongly influenced him. One was impudently called Yang the Big Beard. With considerable contempt for Mao's initial literary efforts, he finally managed to teach the young rebel to write acceptably in the classical style. The other, Yang Ch'ang-chi, had studied in Britain. At the normal school he lectured in ethics, a Hunan Matthew Arnold. The impressionable young Mao was inspired by this scholar's idealism and morality.

During his normal school years, from 1913 to 1918, Mao permitted himself no frivolity. He had no patience with small talk. His thoughts, he told Edgar Snow twenty years later, dwelt upon "large matters—the nature of men, of human society, of China, the world, and the universe."

Otherwise he was fussing about everyone's physique, especially his own. For national salvation, for the future of China, everyone must be physically fit. And so with like-minded youths he hiked over hill and dale, stripped to the waist in rain, wind, sun, and cold. He even lay down to sleep, at least symbolically, amidst the frosts.

Mao's drive to organize others had already begun to show itself. He became secretary of the Students' Society, put together a student self-government association to keep the faculty in line, and led what was grandiosely called the students' volunteer army to protect the school, with pointed bamboo staves, against possible raids by marauding soldiers. Finally, he took part in forming a restive study group, not unlike a revolutionary party cell.

Brimming with physical culture, idealism, radicalism, and militancy, and traveling on borrowed money, Mao arrived in Peking. This was in the latter half of 1918. His ethics teacher had preceded him and was established at Peking National University as a professor. With the help of Professor Yang, the eager young provincial with his bumpkin Hunan accent got a job as librarian's assistant.

Here he was in the center of intellectual excitement, among the men who made the literary revolution and those of the political avant-garde. He had read their writings and had admired them from afar. It was a great thrill. But he was unknown, an impecunious rube from a provincial normal school. As a reading-room attendant, he was snubbed by most of the intellectual élite.

In Peking Mao shared a small room with seven others. They took their repose compactly on a single k'ang, a species of brick platform faintly heated in winter by a fire underneath it. Uncomfortable as this must have been, it was at least better than stretching out freely on a bed of frost.

The plum blossoms and palace parks in the early spring compensated somewhat for his physical discomforts. Besides, he had fallen in love with Professor Yang's daughter.

Mao had other compensations for snubs and cramps. He managed to join the university's philosophy and journalism societies and this enabled him to audit courses. Thus he met an assortment of students. Diffidence, it might be said in this connection, was not one of Mao's personality problems. Among those schoolmates were some who were to become revolutionary comrades, others his enemies. But in Peking at that time they were all groping in political confusion. Mao, for example, underwent an infatuation with anarchism. It did not take over his philosophy; he simply added anarchism to his intellectual baggage.

Nor were the leading lights on the faculty much help in clearing up the confusion. Two of them, including Mao's chief, the head librarian, were to be the prime movers in the creation of the Chinese Communist movement. And yet at this stage, 1918–1919, they were still working out a system of beliefs: neo-Confucianism, benign Marxism, and a touch of John Dewey. They had none of them yet gotten to the rip-saw techniques of Leninism in action.

By early March, Mao was out of Peking on his way south. His stay in the capital had been brief. But it had been an intense experience both intellectually and emotionally. He was confirmed in his revolutionary path, however ill-defined. And he was no longer a mere provincial youth. He had been at the most prestigious university in China and had consorted, even if on the fringes, with the best minds in the country.

On his trip south to Shanghai, Mao made pilgrimages to historic sites along the way, among them the grave of Confucius. In sopping up China's past, he spent all of his money before reaching his destination. Then his only pair of shoes was stolen. Fortunately, he encountered a fellow-provincial. As Hunanese stick together, when they are not at one another's throats, this man lent the barefooted Mao money for shoes and the remainder of his passage.

In Shanghai Mao bade farewell to friends who were leaving for France to study. Although he had worked to make these overseas studies possible, Mao stayed behind. Whether this was because he felt that he had little aptitude for foreign languages, was essentially uninterested in foreign peoples and places, or was absorbed in what he might do in China, we do not know. It was probably something of all three, with the heaviest emphasis on inward-turning to his own country.

From Shanghai, back to Hunan, back into the heartland he went. Immediately he threw himself into political action. No sooner had he done so than news came of Japan's besting of China at the Paris Peace Conference and then the May Fourth Incident in Peking. Mao redoubled his efforts, taking a leading part in the organization of a student association and anti-Japanese boycotts.

He was also a moving spirit in setting up a nationalistic, anti-Japanese organization of students, workers, and merchants. This was an important step in the direction of a mass movement. And, as might be expected, the articulate Mao managed to become editor of a newly established weekly, written in Hu Shih's plain language, ventilating Mao's angry protests.

All of this was distasteful to the warlord governor of Hunan, a blackguard who had connections with the dominant clique in Peking, which in turn was collaborating with the Japanese. The governor cracked down on the anti-Japanese organizations and closed Mao's magazine after five issues. But not before the pamphleteering Mao had made an impression, not only on literate Hunanese, but also on intellectuals elsewhere in China.

Feeling the political heat in Hunan oppressive, Mao slipped off to Peking. There he represented his Hunan affiliations, making propaganda against the warlords, particularly the governor of Hunan. Fleetingly he became head of a correspondingly transient news agency, anti-militarist in its slant.

On this second visit to the capital, in the winter of 1910–20, Mao read newly issued translations of the first part of the *Communist Manifesto*, Karl Kautsky on Marx, and Kirkup's history of socialism. On top of this, he pored over whatever he could lay his hands on about the Russian Revolution. The variety of ideas that once sloshed about in his mind were now precipitating into Marxism.

At this point something should be said parenthetically about "Marxism" and "Marxist" as applied to non-Europeans, and certainly to the Chinese. In these pages the two words are used impressionistically. For Asians filtered the peculiarly nineteenth-century European pseudo-science of Marx through their own cultural experience and predilections. They had done the same with the western ideas of democracy and republicanism, producing something identifiably different from the original. Chinese communism eventually came to be more precisely termed Maoism. But in its early phase it carried the name of the German dogmatist, a semantic absurdity here perpetuated in the interest of convenient communication.

From Peking Mao went to Shanghai to seek out Ch'en Tu-hsiu, former dean of the Faculty of Letters of Peking University, a theoretical Marxist of sorts and one of the men Mao most admired while librarian's assistant at the university. Their conversation ranged from ideology to concrete political action in Hunan. Thus, when he returned to Hunan after the overthrow of the governor by another warlord, and had found employment as a principal of an elementary school, Mao turned to political organization. He created a branch of the Socialist Youth Corps, and a Marxist revolutionary cell, opened a bookstore for radical publications, and even tried his hand at organizing workers. He was deep in plotting again, this time bedeviling the new governor, his patron.

Later, looking back on this period, Mao told Snow that by the summer of 1920 he had become in theory and to some extent in action a Marxist. At any rate, from then on he considered himself to be a Marxist.

1920 was also, in another sense, a significant year. For in 1920 he married

Miss Yang, the daugher of his old ethics teacher. In so doing, he discarded a wife, six years his senior, to whom his parents had married him at the age of fourteen. He claimed that he had never lived with her, which may very well have been true in view of his many other distractions. His second and loved wife was killed, some ten years after their marriage, on the orders of one of Chiang Kai-shek's more doggedly anti-Communist generals. This, of course, contributed in some undefinable measure to Mao's intractable feud with Chiang.

Mao's conspiratorial activities in Hunan were matched by similar undertakings by others elsewhere in China. Marxist revolutionary cells were formed, first in Shanghai by Ch'en Tu-hsiu, then in Peking, Wuhan, Canton, and Tsinan. The membership was minuscule, earnest, floundering, and amateurish.

This new stripe of Chinese had not been without foreign professional counsel. Gregory Voitinsky had slipped into the Chinese scene in the spring of 1920. He was a representative of the Comintern, the Communist Third International. With imperceptible logistic support and no public relations, he was a Russian advance agent for world revolution.

He seems to have had a part in establishing at least the Shanghai cell in May and the Peking unit in September. Guiding these ardent, naive Chinese intellectuals, Voitinsky tried to teach them that communism was more than an open-ended seminar, leading them from theoretical Marxism to the first steps in applied Leninism. As Russell and Dewey expounded on individualism and freedom, Voitinsky argued for party discipline and the dictatorship of the proletariat.

Meanwhile, early in 1921, a small group of Chinese students in France met at Paris to form the China Socialist Youth Corps. Among the members were several who later became prominent in the Communist movement in their homeland. Outstanding among these was Chou En-lai.

Inevitably, the next move was the formal establishment in China of a Communist Party. Availing themselves of the hospitable consequences of an unequal treaty, the founding fathers met in July 1921, in the French concession of Shanghai. This was customary—to repair to the relative security of an imperialist enclave in order to plot against one's fellow countrymen in power and one's imperialist hosts.

The rendezvous of the conspirators was a girls' school, closed for vacation. Thirteen delegates attended, including Mao. So did Voitinsky, and another Comintern agent, a Hollander with experience in Java, named Henricus Sneevliet, alias Maring. These two foreigners participated as ones who knew how.

Police suspicion was aroused by the insinuation of so odd an assortment into a seminary for young ladies. When the French concession authorities introduced an undercover operator into the borrowed meeting place of the Communists, the delegates quickly decamped. They reconvened some days later aboard a boat on a lake in an adjoining province, pretending to be a band of jolly vacationers on an outing. In this carefree guise the First Congress of the Chinese Communist Party continued its deliberations.

The resolutions adopted by the boating party were primitive four-square Marxist: organize the workers, crush the capitalist classes, and set up the dictatorship of the proletariat. This was to be done virtually single-handed by the proletariat, led by the Communists, who then numbered well under a hundred in all. Furthermore, even the delegates were far from being of one mind, and they were not notably disciplined. Several of them later broke with the party.

The two foreigners representing the Comintern operated in low key. Correspondingly, the advice of Voitinsky and Sneevliet was listened to, but it was not taken as law. The two Moscow agents were not even present at the closing session of the Congress.

CHAPTER *10*

Soviet, Japanese, and American Intervention in East Asia

WHAT PROPELLED Voitinsky and Sneevliet into the Middle Kingdom was an idea. Prior to the October Revolution, Russians had not bothered to intervene culturally in China. The Russian Orthodox Church had not sought to proselytize the celestial heathen. There was an Orthodox church in Peking, to be sure, but it was primarily for resident Russians and other believers. Nor did the Russians press their education or political ideas on the Chinese, as did the maritime West. With the longest common frontier in the world, China and Russia had remarkably little cultural interchange or influence on one another during modern times.

More than six centuries after the first Franciscan missionaries arrived in Peking, propagators of a new creed came to China bent on making converts. Holy Mother Russia, no longer holy but now the mother of Communism, began to intervene in the troubled mind and spirit of China.

Ideological aggression by the Bolsheviks was not limited to China. Their compulsion to transform society was universal in scope. Their revolution in Russia was only the prelude to a series of uprisings which they expected to occur in other countries—the world revolution—and it was their duty to promote this process.

Communist agitation and conspiracy were one phase of Bolshevik dynamism. There was a second phase to the Soviet outward thrust. This was the centuries-old inclination and habit of a virile, expanding people to push their frontiers forward, or at least to dilate their influence over bordering countries. Under the Tsars this had been a Slavic expression of Manifest Destiny. It was partly defensive. But mostly, especially in East Asia, it had been sheer expansionist enthusiasm—until deflated by the Japanese in 1905.

Expansionism in the classic nationalist sense faded in the early years of the Soviet regime. The new government felt itself weak. And the Bolsheviks, obsessed by what they proclaimed to be the evils of imperialism, were inhibited in their aggressive appetite.

Dualism in Bolshevik motivations had its counterpart in the dualism of Soviet institutions. The Bolshevik oligarchy, which may also be called the Kremlin, ruled through the Party and through the government. The Party was literally the senior institution. And it was the more powerful because it controlled the other instrument of power, the government.

Party-government dualism gave the Bolshevik oligarchy greater operational flexibility than that available to other sovereign authorities. But the Party-government combination also contained elements of contradiction. The Party was universalist in its outlook. The government was nationalist. The institutional conflict between the two, however, was generally kept under control by the Kremlin and by the accepted superiority of the Party over the government.

By far the more important conflict between the interests of world revolution and the interests of the state took place within the ruling oligarchy itself. Personal points of view differed over issues between dogmatism and pragmatism, between expansion and consolidation, between offensive and defensive strategies. These issues arose early, were kept in bounds by Lenin, but became fiercely contested in the late 1920s after his death.

Antedating Voitinsky's and Sneevliet's missionary endeavors by several years, the first significant Soviet move towards China was a governmental, not a party policy statement. On July 4, 1918, Georgi Chicherin, the commissar of foreign affairs, dwelt upon the Soviet attitude towards China. With revolutionary abandon he renounced "the conquests of the Tsarist government in Manchuria," all indemnities, and special interests. In the expansive mood of a revolution newly burst and a regime shakily looking for support from any quarter, Chicherin went on to offer the return of the Chinese Eastern Railway, if part of the money invested by the Russians in building the shortcut across Manchuria were paid back.

A month later, replying to a letter from Sun Yat-sen applauding the October Revolution, Chicherin envisioned the Russian and Chinese revolutions going the same way. "Our success is your success," Chicherin exclaimed in immoderate fraternalism. "Our ruin is your ruin."

This pledge of brotherhood to Sun was less than undying. About a year later, on July 25, 1919, the Council of People's Commissars drafted a statement of policy regarding China directed not only to Sun's insurgent regime in South China but also to the flyblown government in Peking, which pretended to represent all of China. The Soviet statement, known as the Karakhan Manifesto, after Chicherin's deputy, Leo Karakhan, offered to establish friendly relations, discuss cancellation of unequal treaties, and return to the Chinese people "without any kind of compensation" the Chinese Eastern Railway and all concessions.

Shortly after this outpouring of generosity, the Kremlin had second thoughts, tightfisted nationalist thoughts. For when the manifesto was published, the offer of the railway was omitted. But Peking received months later by roundabout means the original version. It reacted coolly to the fluctuating Soviet overtures. The Chinese public, that portion of it that was literate, greeted the more liberal interpretation of Soviet intentions as Moscow had hoped that it would. To these influential Chinese the new and radical regime in Russia seemed to be the only foreign government that was willing to make amends for past injustices and do the right thing for China.

The People's Commissariat for Foreign Affairs, or Narkomindel, functioned more or less as other foreign offices did—excepting that it was rather more involved in subversion than was normal in the others. The Kremlin felt the need, however, of an agency less conventional than the Narkomindel for the prosecution of revolution abroad. With considerable ingenuity, the Bolshevik oligarchy put together an elusive organization outside of the Soviet government and Party and for whose actions both could disclaim responsibility.

This was the Comintern, or Third International, which pretended to be a communist successor to earlier socialist internationals. As such, it was nominally an independent body, although the Communist Party of the Soviet Union was represented in it and the Bolshevik oligarchy controlled it. It was the Kremlin's instrument for ideological aggression.

Hurriedly the Kremlin assembled the Comintern in March 1919, less than a year and a half after the Russian Revolution began and while the Civil War was still raging. As there were in those days few Communists outside of Russia, the Kremlin turned to what was readily at hand. It drafted delegates to the First Congress of the Comintern from among the alien riffraff available in Soviet-held territory.

These were prisoners-of-war and foreigners resident in Russia for a variety of peculiar reasons. The Chinese plenipotentiary was an obscure Mr. Lao. At the inaugural sessions he nevertheless held forth in the name of hundreds of millions of oppressed Chinese toilers. A Mr. Rutgers was given the distracting assignment of representing the Netherlands, Japan, and a small sect of American radicals. The two Italian delegates, let out of prisoner-of-war camps on leash, were subsidized after the convocation to go home and make trouble for the Italian socialists. Instead, no sooner had they arrived in Milan than they dissipated their Moscow gold in riotous living.

From this harum-scarum beginning the Comintern settled down to become a polyglot bureaucracy administering Communist agitation and subversion outside of the Soviet Union. It was under Comintern auspices that Voitinsky and Sneevliet went to China to lend a guiding hand in the establishment of the Chinese Communist Party. Later, some Chinese came to Moscow to join the Comintern staff. But direction of policy and operations was firmly retained by the Kremlin.

Lenin—and the other Marxists, too, for that matter—had always had trouble in fitting China and the underdeveloped countries into the Marxist scheme of things. They were impressed by the multitudes of Asia, assuming that an enormous potential for power existed there. They were also titillated by evidences of unrest in Asia, by peasant revolts and nationalist uprisings. But how could the backward countries have a Marxist revolution if they had not developed a capitalist economy with an industrial proletariat? For this proletariat was, by doctrine, the only force that could execute a Communist revolution.

Rightly, Lenin judged that the scrawny Chinese proletariat was not up to such an assignment. Furthermore, he was, along with his fellow Bolsheviks, transfixed by the prospect of big revolutions in the West, particularly Germany. In 1920, Lenin was still waiting for the European upheaval. If the European workers cast off their chains, then there need be scant concern about the colonial and semi-colonial countries, of which China was one. For as imperialism was destroyed in the West, the oppressed peoples of the East would be liberated and they would become the beneficiaries of the dictatorship of the proletariat in Europe.

Lenin was more than a visionary and theoretician. He was also a practical man and a calculating strategist. The colonial and semi-colonial peoples, he believed, should not idly await their Marxist salvation through revolution in Europe. They should earn their passage. While the proletariat could do little, much might be accomplished by their so-called bourgeoisie and the peasantry.

Overriding the shocked opposition of some of his comrades, Lenin advocated at the Second Comintern Congress, in the summer of 1920, temporary alliances with bourgeois democracy in the backward countries. This was on the assumption that the semi-colonial bourgeoisie was nationalist and hence would be disposed to do the imperialists in the eye. Once the imperialists were ousted in a struggle of national liberation, the Communists' tactics were to shift to assault on their erstwhile allies, the national bourgeoisie. It was a strategy of conflict by stages: combining with one enemy to defeat another, and then turning on the remaining one.

At the same time Lenin proposed an active role in backward countries for the peasantry, so despised by Marx. After all, Lenin had found in the Russian revolution that the peasants were an essential element in his success. Asia swarmed with peasants. Without them the Communists could not win. He admonished the Second Congress of the Comintern to work for peasant revolutions, even for setting up peasant soviets.

Lenin's prophetic message did not get through to the Chinese Marxists. They were then in their debating society stage of development. Several months later Mao was organizing, not peasant soviets, but city workers. By the summer of 1921, when the Chinese radicals held their boating party to form a Communist Party and adopt a stiffly Marxist line, Lenin was yet another step ahead of them.

He addressed the Third Congress of the Comintern in July of that year, justifying a frantic compromise with Marxist orthodoxy. Scarcely mentioning international communism, Lenin rationalized a tactical retreat that he had just made from communism inside of the Soviet Union. He had backtracked from disastrous attempts at a Party-controlled economy toward a freer market called the New Economic Policy.

Thus preoccupied with domestic tribulations, it is not surprising that in the

Comintern meeting of 1921 Lenin had little constructive to offer to his general staff of world revolution. He perfunctorily claimed that the colonial and semi-colonial countries had been aroused and their masses converted into active factors in world politics. And at the very time that the Chinese Communist Party was aborning, he pinned his hopes on India which was, he said, "at the head of these countries, and there the revolution is maturing."

Mongolia, like Manchuria and Turkestan, was part of the long contested borderlands between China and Russia. In their drive to the Pacific, the Russians had made colonials of the Buriat Mongols in the Baikal region, as they did with other Asian minorities. The Chinese expanded north of the Great Wall to take over and colonize Inner Mongolia. Sandwiched between the two was Outer Mongolia. Here China had claimed suzerainty for centuries.

Without having been asked to do so by the Mongols, the Soviet government announced in 1919 that Outer Mongolia was an independent country and invited the dilapidated descendants of those who had subdued both the Russians and the Chinese to enter into diplomatic relations with the Soviet people and to meet with representatives of the Red Army. Nothing immediately came of this bayonet-wreathed overture. The Red Army was then busily fighting counterrevolutionaries in Siberia. And Outer Mongolia was soon occupied by a Chinese army whose vicious commander demanded and got the surrender to Chinese dictates of such autonomy as Outer Mongolia had.

Japan, too, coveted Outer Mongolia. Tokyo was aroused by the opportunities that turmoil in Russia seemed to offer. Outer Mongolia was a salient deep into Asia, slicing between China and Russia, outflanking both the Soviet Far East and North China. If Japan could dominate this zone, it would be in a position to encircle Peking and the North China Plain or to strike north to Baikal, cutting the Trans-Siberian Railway and thus isolating from the rest of Russia the expanse spreading from Baikal to the Pacific.

While Chinese and Russian ambitions in Outer Mongolia were evident, those of Japan were veiled. They were, nevertheless, scarcely less intense. Particularly was this so with the Japanese army, naturally inclined toward a continental and westward, rather than oceanic and southward, policy. Consequently, Tokyo sniffed about for such elements on the mainland as might further its designs.

One was those Chinese who might, for a consideration, be willing to advance Japanese interests. The then-ruling group in Peking played this game with Tokyo. The Chinese occupation of Outer Mongolia was at the initiative of this cabal, and the unanswered question is how much its Mongolian move was at Japanese instance.

Anti-Bolshevik Russians were a second element which Tokyo sought to turn to Japanese advantage in the Chinese-Russian borderlands. One of these was the Cossack chieftain, Grigori Semenov, an impudent young man commanding a very small horde of Cossacks, Mongols, and Serbian prisoners of war.

While Semenov could be bought but not be owned by anyone—and certainly not the Japanese—he served Tokyo's purposes well enough in the early phase of the Russian Civil War. He was a zestful troublemaker and a plague to the Bolsheviks. This suited the Japanese, who wanted turbulence from Manchuria westward. So they furnished him with a liaison officer from the Imperial Army and just enough aid to keep him pesky.

Semenov's reputation as a counterrevolutionary scourge exceeded his attainments in this respect. The British and French, briefly captivated by what they imagined to be his potential as a bulwark against the red tide, skimpily supplied him. Even President Wilson, on the basis of sluggish and faulty American information, became worked up in his reticent fashion about the Semenov promise.

While Semenov created ructions to the east and north of Mongolia, it remained for one of his henchmen to capture the capital of Outer Mongolia. In February 1921, Baron von Ungern-Sternberg took Urga, now known as Ulan Bator. Not without cause was he called the Mad Baron. Boasting descent from Genghis Khan, he also affected belief in Buddhism and accepted Japanese support in his ambitions to establish a pan-Mongol empire spreading across Central Asia. His campaign to drive the Chinese from Outer Mongolia was assisted by the Mongols, then willing to collaborate with anyone who would rid them of the Chinese leeches.

Both the Mad Baron and the Japanese were disappointed in their dreams of a greater Mongolia extending westward between China and Russia. Ungern-Sternberg promptly overreached himself with a sally northward to the region of the Soviet frontier. The Red Army had by that time sufficiently consolidated Bolshevik authority in Siberia to have forces available for operations in Mongolia. It had fostered on the Soviet side of the border the creation on March 1, 1921, of a Mongolian People's Revolutionary Party. Less than a fortnight later this incubator party asked the Red Army to intervene in Outer Mongolia.

With invitation in hand and those Mongols who issued the invitation in tow, Bolshevik troops swept into and the Mad Baron out of Urga. The date was July 7. Three days later the Mongolian People's Revolutionary Government blossomed forth. In November, as a final flourish, the Soviet Union concluded a treaty with the Mongolian People's Republic, as with an independent country. Chinese claims of suzerainty over Outer Mongolia were ignored. Thus the Kremlin created the first Soviet satellite, at the expense of China's colonial ambitions.

The Kremlin's intervention in Outer Mongolia was an act of richly inventive foreign policy, an adept merging of revolutionary and nationalist interests. It was later to be emulated elsewhere, and not only by the Bolsheviks. Foreign military intervention at the invitation of a minority professing to represent a people or a nation became a familiar stratagem in international relations.

Fabrication of puppet regimes—and their perpetuation by alien armies—differed from the traditional taking of a protectorate or colony. Historically, the imperial power imposed its authority over the subject state openly and at its own pleasure. Thus China, with no pretense of concern for Mongol opinion, had forcibly changed the regime at Urga.

But the Bolshevik theory was that political acts should properly be represented as expressions of popular will. The Bolshevik oligarchy pretended that it was itself a manifestation of the pleasure of The People. Extending this fiction, the Kremlin professed to treat its continental colonial populations within the Soviet borders—Armenians, Georgians, Uzbeks, Tadzhiks, Buriats, and others—as "autonomous." This was the principle of national self-determination within a union of many nationalities, a principle elaborated by Stalin before the Revolution and, immediately thereafter, administered by him as Commissar of Nationalities.

Projecting this ingenious rationalization of imperialism, it was logical that Soviet take-overs in foreign countries should masquerade as self-determination. It was for this reason that, before the Red Army entered Outer Mongolia, an indigenous Mongolian organization had to be put together which would claim to speak for The People of Outer Mongolia and would be amenable to asking for Soviet intervention. With the hospitable collaboration of a Mongolian people's party and government, Soviet intrusion into Outer Mongolia was legitimatized —even ennobled because it was in support of ostensible self-determination. The Mongolian revolutionary authorities, for their part, had reason to be grateful for the backing of Soviet power. Without it they would not have been able to liberate and then rule their compatriots.

In the dualism of motives pushing the Kremlin into Outer Mongolia, the ideological was probably less compelling than the nationalist considerations. Proselytizing the poxed, priest-ridden Mongols was a satisfying crusade, but hardly of vital concern to the Bolshevik oligarchy.

The Kremlin had real cause for concern about the security of the Soviet fatherland. With China weak and unpredictable and Japan boring westward into the continent, Moscow was anxious about the long, exposed land frontier with China and wanted reliable buffers to the south—Outer Mongolia, Manchuria, and Chinese Turkestan (Sinkiang). The Kremlin's fundamental concern over Outer Mongolia was therefore defensive. Moscow got what it wanted in Mongolia, but not elsewhere along its Asian flank.

Lenin's strategic thinking reached out beyond buffer building along the frontier with China. It went to the source of the threat to Soviet security in Asia. That was Japan and, less pressingly, the United States.

Characteristically, Lenin's approach was devious. Avoid direct confrontation with the two great Pacific powers. Rather, exploit the rivalry between the imperialists.

"Japan," he prematurely said, "has seized China." The United States would try to deprive Japan of its plunder. "The practical task of Communist policy," he went on, "is to take advantage of this hostility and to incite one against the other." More baldly stated, "If we are obliged to tolerate such scoundrels as the capitalist thieves, each of whom is preparing to plunge a knife into us, it is our duty to make them turn their knives against each other."

Japan and the United States did not turn their knives on one another during Lenin's time. Nor was Lenin able to do much in inciting them one against the other. In any event, there was no need to do so. The two great naval powers were already jostling one another down the one-way street to Pearl Harbor.

That street led through China, as Lenin implied. Obviously, China was not then in itself a power factor in the struggle among states. Because it was a victim, of imperialist rivalries, its significance lay in its very flaccidity bordering on the Soviet Union. Hence Lenin's wish to divert those rivalries eastward, out to sea, away from Soviet frontiers. And failing that, at least to have the Outer Mongolian buffer deflecting aggression southward, into China.

Although he was sometimes undercut by his fellow Bolsheviks, opposed by foreign functionaries in the Comintern, and slighted by the Chinese Communists, Lenin laid down the fundamentals of a Communist strategy for China that was ultimately to prove successful. He insisted that revolution in China must be based on the peasantry. And he advocated what was heresy to many of his collaborators—opportunistic alliance by the Communists with the nationalist bourgeoisie in such semi-colonial countries as China, the united front tactic.

With all of his miscalculations, Lenin was an extraordinary revolutionary strategist, not only with regard to Russia but also China. He was a pioneer in a new form of revolution mostly of his creation. As such he was a true innovator on a vast scale.

Starting with a theory claiming universal validity, he proceeded to its application. If it worked, the theory was confirmed. If not, he proceeded empirically and modified theory to jibe with reality. Lenin was therefore an improviser who operated with expedient flexibility. But as he compromised, zigzagged, and retreated two steps, he did not abandon his ultimate objective—the consolidation of Bolshevik power and the transformation of society.

Lenin complained that he had difficulty in finding out what was going on in China. Well he might have. His own knowledge of China was limited and his specialists in Chinese affairs did not agree on either the facts or interpretation of what was going on in the Middle Kingdom. Furthermore, Lenin's major concern was with Russia, and secondarily with Europe. China was well down the list of his interests. It is doubtful that he knew of Mao Tse-tung, save possibly as a strange name in a list of those who organized the Chinese Communist Party.

If Lenin, the man who had the greatest formative influence on Chinese Communism of any foreigner, had scant time for Chinese matters, Stalin, who was to intervene more in the affairs of the Chinese Communists than any other foreigner, had even less in the early days of the Soviet regime. As a Georgian, Stalin was a Eurasian, from the Caucasus mountains where Europe and Asia fuse. But his Asia was not that of the Far East. It was the Asia of the Far West, of Turkey and Persia, of Kurds and Azerbaijani. This early conditioning was of some help to him later in understanding the sleekly deceptive Chinese. He was better able to understand them than had he been a Norwegian or a New Englander. But not much better. For China was another and unique civilization.

In any event, during the first five years of Bolshevik rule Stalin was much too occupied with making his own career to concern himself with China. In those days he was an unprepossessing fellow. Other comrades around Lenin outshone him: Trotsky, Bukharin, Kamenev, and Zinoviev. They were cosmpolitan intellectuals for whom Soso, as Stalin had been familiarly known in Georgian, was, in Trotsky's words, a "dull mediocrity."

Dull he may have been. But mediocre, no. Methodically he made himself useful to Lenin and the bright, articulate members of the oligarchy by tending to the drudgery of organizational and personnel matters, which the others regarded as fit labor for a mediocrity.

Stalin rose to real power within the hierarchy through accumulating administrative authority and authority over administrative personnel. Inconspicuously and with the indifferent consent of his glamorous colleagues he collected a place on the Party's governing board, the Politburo. Then he took the far-reaching position of coordinator between the Politburo and the administrative directorate of the Party, the Orgburo. In the government, he attained a post of penetrating authority—Commissar of the Workers' and Peasants' Inspectorate. His appointment in April 1922 as secretary general of the Party consolidated the hold he had developed over the Party apparatus. He had laid well the groundwork for a bid to be the successor of Lenin when the gnomish giant was no more.

In addition to this grid of power conduits, Stalin had one post quite different from his other offices. That was commissar of nationalities. It was logical that he should have had this position. One of his rare theoretical exercises was the rationalization of national self-determination to the needs of dictatorship. Furthermore, as a Georgian, he belonged to one of the national minorities. His appointment, therefore, was both logical and politically shrewd. He discharged these responsibilities in favor of centralized control, which amounted to insisting on Russian paramountcy within the union. For so doing he was accused by champions of minority self-determination of being a Great Russian chauvinist.

Reinforcing Stalin's natural inclination to face eastward was the fact that many of the minority peoples with whom he had to deal were Asian. His work as commissar of nationalities served, then, to set him further apart from Lenin and most other members of the oligarchy, who from years of exile and continuing connections with the West were more internationally minded. With all of his oriental background and adult experience with a wide variety of Soviet Asians, Stalin remained essentially a parochial Georgian. In revolutionary creativity with regard to East Asia he never approached the flair of Lenin.

While Lenin was laying the groundwork for the Comintern, Woodrow Wilson was striving to create another kind of international institution, the League of Nations. Both organizations were to be universal in scope and both were directed at utopian ends. But Lenin's Comintern was to seek these ends through overthrow of the status quo by any feasible means, including violence. Whereas Wilson aspired, through the League, to a stable world order under law, in his words, "based on the consent of the governed and sustained by the organized opinion of mankind."

Wilson's dreams for the League and all of his universalized moralisms about making the world safe for democracy, replacing balance of power with something he called community of power, renouncing secret diplomacy for open diplomacy, and upholding the rights of all people to self-determination—these Wilsonian abstractions did not work out as envisioned. Even as he was exhorting others, Wilson was engaged in secret diplomacy at the Paris Peace Conference, acceding to Japanese domination over Shantung, thereby denying self-determination to the Chinese of that province. Nor did he offer self-determination to the Filipinos.

Although the League was a failure and Wilson's canons of political faith obviously illusioned, American statesmen and politicians continued on into the 1970s to indulge in bouts of Wilsonian moralizing. They did not fully profit from the experiences of World War I and its aftermath. Not having really understood the mistakes of the past, they were bound to repeat them.

Perhaps Wilson's oddest contribution to a world order under law, based on the consent of the governed, was his dispatch of an American expeditionary force to Siberia. This was the first major intervention by the United States in a land war on the continent of Asia. Wilson's intrusion into the Russian Civil War was also the first American intervention in a Communist revolution grown to the dimensions of a civil war. It was the precursor of Washington's excursions of 1945–49 into the Chinese Civil War and, more recently, the civil wars of Indochina.

Setting the tone for future interventions, the Siberian adventure was preceded by what amounted to disavowals of any intentions to intrude. On January 8, 1918, Wilson poured forth to Congress his Fourteen Points. Number six provided for "the evacuation of all Russian territory" (by whom he did not say) and an assurance that Russia would have "an unhampered and unembarrassed opportunity for the independent determination of her own political development and national policy." Less than six months later he had decided to intervene in Russia.

Why? As explained by Wilson, American troops were to be sent to assist two bodies of Czechoslovak troops, former prisoners of war released when Russia left the war, to join up in eastern Siberia for an undisclosed purpose. The essential reasons advanced by Wilson for such aid were that the Czechoslovaks were menaced by German and Austrian ex-prisoners (an exaggeration) and "sentimental" attachment to the Czechoslovaks.

In addition, the president wanted the Czechoslovaks to "get into successful cooperation with their Slavic kinsmen and to steady any efforts at self-government or self-defense in which the Russians themselves may be willing to accept assistance." Which Russians, Wilson did not indicate; whether the Bolsheviks or the various factions of White Russians, including Semenov and the Mad Baron.

As if to compound the bedlam already existing there, the president proposed to dispatch to Siberia a catchall commission made up of merchants, agronomists, labor advisers, Red Cross representatives, and Y.M.C.A. "agents." They were to do good to the natives. This Noah's Ark of well-wishers was typical of the compulsion to do something about an impossible situation rather than stay out of trouble. It was a compulsion that was to recur in similar form in American diplomacy.

American intervention, in Wilson's mind, was not to be unilateral. It was to be in collaboration with Japan. Each was to contribute a force of about seven thousand men. The chief of staff, General March, opposed the expedition on strategic grounds and because he thought that the Japanese would not hold themselves to seven thousand men and would use intervention as a spring-board for encroachments on Russian territory. Wilson brusquely overrode the General's misgivings.

Less than a month after Wilson's decision, Major General William S. Graves, a crusty, literal-minded soldier, was summoned to a fleeting rendezvous with the secretary of war, Newton D. Baker, in a Kansas City hotel room. There he was told that he would lead an expeditionary force to Siberia and that his mission was defined in a document hastily pressed upon him. This was a copy of the American *aide memoire* of June 17, 1918, which had been circulated to the allied governments and which recounted the American motives of intervention, from helping the Czechoslovaks to infiltrating the Y.M.C.A. into the wastes of Siberia. Much was made in the document of Washington's position that intervention was not intervention; that the American government could not take part in nor sanction in principle military intervention in Russia.

Armed with a baffling directive, the good and faithful General Graves sailed off to Vladivostok. On the day before he arrived the two Czechoslovak forces completed their drive to join up and promptly dedicated themselves to an alliance with Russian forces fighting the Bolsheviks. Furthermore, the Japanese distended their expeditionary army from the seven thousand originally proposed by Wilson to seventy-two thousand. And so Graves found the main purpose of his mission disposed of, those he was supposed to help embroiled in a civil strife that he was charged with eschewing, and his allies grown tenfold in strength and effrontery.

Because Graves staunchly refused to become involved in Russian internal affairs, he was plagued by the Japanese, the British, the French, and his own State Department, all of whom, for a variety of reasons, supported the anti-Bolshevik factions. As a result of his obstinate adherence to his directive, efforts were made to have Graves removed. But Baker championed him, the president stood firm, and this stubborn commander persisted in his ways until his expeditionary force was finally withdrawn in the spring of 1920.

Graves's experience was a fair sample of what happens when a woolly political decision is made, committing the country to fuzzy military action. The directive to the military commander reflects the unreality of the decision. If he is conscientious and determined, as is usually the case with a professional officer, he will doggedly try to discharge his orders to the letter. In the course of this, he makes more than his share of enemies and ends up by being attacked for doing his frustrating duty.

Wilson's intervention in Russia accomplished nothing that it set out to do. If, as has been represented, it began with the ulterior purpose of thwarting Japanese aggression, it was only partially successful on this score. What is clear is that growing American interference, with Japanese designs on the Maritime Province and Siberia, aggravated existing suspicion and animosity between Japan and the United States. Nor were matters improved by American political resistance to Japanese political and military machinations in Manchuria. Well might Lenin have concluded from what was going on in his own country and Manchuria that the two powerful maritime nations were "on the verge of war" and that "there is no possibility of restraining this war."

But there was. At least, there was a possibility of postponing it. And that President Harding's secretary of state, Charles Evans Hughes, set out to do.

The initiative in trying to stabilize the international situation was British, as it had been in the formulation of the Monroe Doctrine and, obliquely, the policy of the Open Door.

Exhausted by World War I, Britain was concerned over the naval armament race against, primarily, the United States and Japan. After calculating out its complicated relations with Japan, a partner of twenty years in the Anglo-Japanese Alliance, with the Dominions, and with the United States, the British Government on July 5, 1921, proposed that the president invite the powers concerned to a conference on Far Eastern and Pacific matters for peaceful settlement of differences, "the elimination of naval warfare, consequent elimination of arms, etc."

Itself in the process of putting out feelers for a meeting to discuss limitation of armaments, the State Department snapped up the British proposal and drew on it to broaden an American invitation to a conference in Washington. Nine states were to participate: the Big Five—the United States, Britain, Japan, France, and Italy—and in addition China, Belgium, the Netherlands, and Portugal. The Soviet Union was snubbed, which drew a tart reminder from Chicherin that Russia, too, was a Pacific power.

Limitation of armaments was the main concern of the Big Five at the Washington Conference, November 1921 to February 1922. No one was comfortable with the naval arms race. While the United States was economically best able to support it, Congress was unwilling to put up the appropriations to win it. So a deal was made whereby capital ships were frozen at a 5:5:3 ratio for the United States, Britain, and Japan (France and Italy were each an insignificant 1.7), and the three agreed not to fortify their outlying possessions in the Pacific. Thus, in exchange for Washington's not making the Philippines and Guam defensible, Tokyo agreed not to create naval bases in the former German islands placed under Japanese mandate, which lay athwart American naval communications to the Philippines.

In this manner a new balance of power of sorts was brought about in the Western Pacific and East Asia.

Then there was the perennial problem of China. Notwithstanding all of the fine words, from Hay onward, about China's administrative and territorial integrity, the United States had no intention of defending the Chinese with anything rougher than rhetoric. In the Nine Power Treaty, all concerned were converted anew to China's integrity, the Open Door, and no spheres of influence. All took the pledge, framed in detailed and explicit terms by Hughes, another eminent lawyer serving as secretary of state. But no provisions were made for punishment of a transgressor. This was left to consultation, a sense of personal shame, and the pangs of conscience.

The rising force of Chinese nationalism and a moderate government in Tokyo led to a loosening of Japan's hold over Shantung. But in Manchuria the Japanese clung to their privileges. Their Siberian expedition proved to be so costly and profitless that they withdrew in October 1922. However, Japanese forces remained in control of northern Sakhalin until 1925.

CHAPTER *II*

The Nationalist Revolution

ON MAY 30, 1925, I was walking up a side street in the center of Shanghai when I noticed ahead of me a huge crowd packing one of the main thoroughfares. I was seventeen, a student at the Shanghai American School, and curiosity drew me into the strangely silent multitude. Everyone was craning, looking toward a big intersection several blocks away. No one paid attention to me, the only white face in the packed throng.

Quietly I sidled forward through the crush. After two or three blocks of this I came to the front edge of the crowd. Before me was an empty street stretching one hundred yards to the intersection. There, facing me and the thousands beside and behind me were armored cars of Shanghai's International Settlement and British sailors manning machine guns. By then I had come to realize that, in color, I was on the wrong side of what had all of the appearances of a rather nasty confrontation.

This consideration, spurred by the temerity of ignorance, impelled me to step out from the mass and to pretend a saunter down to the bristling line in front of me. My whiteness was my safe-conduct. I was accepted without comment by the strained faces behind the guns. What was going on, I asked a British officer of the settlement police. Oh, agitators had been stirring up mobs. The police had shot several; the last one had toppled from a roof over there.

What was going on was something that came to be called the May 30 Incident. Several days earlier a Chinese workman in a Japanese-owned textile mill had been killed by a Japanese foreman. Young Chinese Communists had taken a leading role in organizing a protest demonstration. This rally provoked the British-controlled police to arrest student speakers who appeared on the scene, which in turn aroused the manifestation of May 30, demanding the release of the jailed students. The police reply was to fire on the demonstrators, killing about a dozen of them.

I had unwittingly joined the crowd sometime after this action. As I walked through the throngs, no one spoke a hostile word to me nor laid a hand on me. The reason for my immunity was much more than that I was an innocuous-looking specimen of imperialism. After all, twenty-five years earlier, during the Boxer Rebellion, foreign women and infants had been slaughtered simply because they were alien. Nor did the explanation lie in the armed force facing the crowd—I could have been done away with deep in the multitude without the police or the bluejackets knowing what had happened.

I was unmolested because the crowd was by then made up of spectators. The activists had been killed or dispersed. The mob had not been aroused to the extent that it was in motion, seeking vent or victim. It was an inert mass.

Powerful political action, however, was in the making. The small band of Communists in Shanghai—perhaps two hundred in all—and other activists went to work blowing gusts of agitation on smoldering xenophobia. May 30 became a slogan and those killed became martyrs. A general strike paralyzed Shanghai. British business was boycotted throughout the country. Demonstrations and strikes swept through the major cities of China and for months immobilized the British stronghold of Hong Kong.

So it was nationalism in its most virulent form—anti-imperialism—that animated the May 30 movement. And it was primarily students and workers who carried the movement forward. This was a novel combination for China, if for no other reason than that an industrial proletariat was new for China. Also, although factory workers were counted as perhaps a shade higher in the social scale than the traditional coolie, there was still an enormous gap between scholars, however callow, and laborers.

Moscow and its Chinese acolytes were delighted with the May 30 movement. Dogma had been fulfilled beyond expectation. The newborn proletariat had risen, even though briefly, shakily, and with much help from those young intellectuals who thought that the proletariat would help them to make history.

Like most of the peasantry, the proletariat had ample cause for discontent. During the mid-1920s China was in the early stages of an industrial revolution certainly no less brutal than the industrial revolution had been in England. Wages were near starvation level, working conditions harsh, and the hours of labor long. While poor peasants suffered solely at the hands of other Chinese— landlords, moneylenders, tax collectors and bailiffs—many of the city workers earned their pittances in foreign-owned factories. To these people the source of their woe was not so much their own countrymen as aliens. Urban laborers were therefore more susceptible than farmers to anti-imperialist agitation.

However embittered, the proletariat was the least significant of the principal elements of Chinese society in the first half of the twentieth century. How many there were of this quasi-class in the mid-1920s was never clear. This was so because it was never quite clear where the genuine proletariat left off and lumpen proletariat began, what the dividing line was between noble workers and ignoble coolies.

There may have been some two million of this ill-defined category in 1925.

This is a fairly imposing figure standing by itself or even viewed against total city dwellers. But measured in relation to the whole population of the country, it amounted to about one half of one per cent of all Chinese. Even had the proletariat been totally mobilized to political action, it still could hardly have been counted in China as a mass movement.

Without peasant participation, no political action could really be called a mass movement. Peasants were only marginally involved in the May 30 movement. A young Communist, son of a landlord, had begun to organize peasants in South China as early as 1922. But this was a local phenomenon and contributed nothing significant to the demonstrations three years later.

The bulk of the rural population was still leaderless in 1925. Although not galvanized, it was restive and much of it was ready to rise against an oppressive lot. With few exceptions, the students and older intellectuals who were to become the peasant leadership were in the cities working on one another, the bourgeoisie, and the fashionably revolutionary proletariat.

Without reference to Marx, Chinese students, too, looked with disdain on "the idiocy of rural life." To nearly all of them the countryside seemed to be politically meaningless, a sodden mound of embarrassment to the feverish young modernizers of China.

Students were, naturally, the most ready recruits for political action; not only university students, but also those in secondary schools. Patriotic and idealistic, they had the will to act. They were easily organized for this reason and because they were conveniently assembled by institutions. With their ardor and their superior standing in Chinese society, students were the inciters and directors of popular action against imperialism.

The bourgeoisie was familiar ground for the intellectuals. Nearly all of them were themselves of that class. So considerable agitation was directed at merchants and white collar workers—in Chinese terms, the wearers of long gowns. For the distinction between white and blue collar was then in China between those who wore gowns over their trousers and those who went about their business in nothing more below the waist than a pair of pants.

None of these four principal categories—the so-called proletariat, the peasantry, students, and the bourgeoisie—held power in the mid-1920s. Power was still held by warlords, backed by their armies. A few warlords enjoyed that measure of popular support accorded to benevolent despots. To all, however, manifestations such as that of May 30 were an unsettling nuisance. While most warlords paid suitable homage to patriotism, their greatest loyalty was to self.

Feebly challenging warlord rule were two rival political parties. Each was committed to the unification of China, ultimately on its own terms. But for the time being they were bound to collaboration in an alliance of convenience. One was the Kuomintang. The other was the Communist Party.

Matchmaker—and a relentless one—for this uncomfortable union was the Kremlin. Not only had Moscow played a decisive role in bringing the two parties together, it also counseled and sought to manage the connection. At the same time it busied itself in intrigues with warlords. No other foreign nation had in modern times intervened so deeply and widely in Chinese politics.

Sun Yat-sen had turned to Moscow essentially for two reasons. One was that he was frustrated in his footling attempts to play power politics against the warlords. They repeatedly betrayed or defeated him. The other reason was that, by 1922, he had begun to despair of gaining support from the western powers.

He therefore became receptive to Soviet overtures. The Comintern's itinerant Dutchman, Sneevliet, broadened his ministrations beyond the Communists to include Sun, advising him to direct his efforts toward organization of the masses. This led to a meeting in January 1923 between Sun and a senior Soviet diplomat, Adolf Joffe. The suave Bolshevik envoy assured Sun of Russian support, amiably agreed that China was unready for communism, and ventured to observe that national unification and full independence were China's most pressing needs. This went down very well with the good doctor.

Meanwhile, under Comintern tutelage, the puny Chinese Communist Party resolved at its Second Congress in 1922 to combine with the Kuomintang against the relics of feudalism. A year later at their Third Congress, the Communists decided to yield control (insofar as they exercised it) of the labor movement to the Kuomintang. They also proclaimed that their nationalist rivals should take over the leadership of the revolution.

Working through its dual channels—the foreign office and Joffe to Sun; the Comintern and Sneevliet to the Communists—the Kremlin had deftly laid the groundwork for a Chinese united front to operate out of Canton. While doing this, Moscow had not neglected its earlier connections with the principal warlords in the North, with whom it treated in conventional terms of raw military power. Thus the Kremlin was characteristically playing all of the angles.

In contrast, the United States dealt formally with the dummy government in Peking as the only possible authority in China. American consuls maintained contacts with some of the warlords, but only as local satraps. The Communists, to Washington, were an evil, unknown emanation. And Sun was treated with aloof deference and lively suspicion.

As a first step in his partnership with the Russians, Sun sent in September 1923 his "chief-of-staff," Chiang Kai-shek, on a get-acquainted mission to Moscow. Lenin was at that time incapacitated by the third of a series of strokes and was only four months from his death. Stalin, with whom Lenin had broken personal relations and whom he privately repudiated as unfit to be secretary general of the Party, was deeply involved in maneuvers to succeed Lenin. Chiang conferred with Trotsky, who was soon to be his, as well as Stalin's bitter enemy, and with lesser Soviet officials. By December, Chiang was back in Canton.

As adviser to Sun, the Kremlin sent Michael Borodin. He was a former Menshevik whose connections with Lenin and Stalin went back at least to 1905. Shortly thereafter until 1917 he lived in Chicago under his true name, Grusenberg. Following the Russian Revolution he acted as a Comintern agent in

Mexico, Spain, Scotland, and the United States and advised Mustafa Kemal during his rise to power in Turkey.

Borodin was, consequently, one of those cosmopolitan Bolsheviks. He took his new assignment with considerable aplomb, for he placed his two Chicago-born sons, Fred and Norman, in the Shanghai American School. Fred Grusenberg, who was a classmate of mine, explained that his father was a lumber merchant in Canton.

While the boys were singing "The Star Spangled Banner" with missionary youngsters in Shanghai, their father was in Canton persuading Sun and his followers to reorganize the Kuomintang along the lines of the Communist Party of the Soviet Union. He even obliged by drafting, in English, a party constitution for his Chinese friends. And he reassured them that they had nothing to fear from the Chinese Communists.

Accordingly, the Kuomintang adopted the Bolshevik principles of party dictatorship, which came to be described as "tutelage," and of democratic centralism, which meant that free discussion and debate were permissible within the oligarchy up to the time of majority decision. In its first congress, January 1924, the Kuomintang undertook to align itself in foreign affairs with the Soviet Union, to cooperate with the Chinese Communists, and to establish for itself a worker-peasant base. And members of the CCP were to be eligible for membership in the Kuomintang.

Borodin and the Comintern agents had made surprising progress in putting Kremlin theory into practice. Borodin had shaped up the Kuomintang as an instrument to carry on a bourgeois nationalist revolution against warlords and imperialists. Sneevliet and Voitinsky had curbed Communist inclinations to pursue an independent revolutionary course. Notwithstanding recurrent misgivings in both parties, some Communists became members of the Kuomintang, forming "a bloc from within."

Ultimately, some day, the Kuomintang and CCP would win the bourgeois nationalist revolution. After that, according to the Kremlin's scheme, would come the Communists' turn. They would be unleashed against the Kuomintang's bourgeois establishment in a new revolution ushering in socialism. This was the Kremlin's contrived projection of history.

Mao Tse-tung was in the midst of all this activity. He had been elected to the Central Committee of the CCP in the summer of 1923 and then became chief of the Orgburo. Having collaborated closely with the Kuomintang, he was chosen in January 1924 as an alternate member of that party's Central Executive Committee. These were considerable accomplishments for a young man just turning thirty.

His diligent work with the national bourgeoisie—Mao had even declared in 1923 that merchants should be in the forefront of the revolution—raised eyebrows among some of his Communist comrades. It would be an oversimplification, however, to attribute Mao's close association with the Kuomintang to slavish adherence to orders from Moscow. As a passionate nationalist and, at that time, a political realist, Mao may even have believed that temporary alliance with the bourgeoisie was essential to any movement seeking to overthrow warlords and oust imperialists. That he went along with the Kremlin's line did not necessarily mean that this headstrong young radical was Moscow's lackey.

While Mao was concerning himself with political matters in both parties, Chiang Kai-shek was in the spring of 1924 setting up the Whampoa Military Academy. In this endeavor, Chiang had the benefit of Soviet military advisers and equipment. Heading the Russian contingent was the able General V. K. Blyukher (Blücher or Bluecher), who in China used the alias of Galen or Galin.

Chiang was commandant of the academy. His deputy political director was Chou En-lai, a contrasting personality to Mao. Chou's origins were in the gentry, Mao's in the peasantry. Chou was an operator, a fixer; Mao was reflective and more likely to follow his own course. Chou, then in his mid-twenties, was already cosmopolitan in experience; Mao was a provincial.

After attending one of the best secondary schools in China, Chou went to Japan in 1917, ostensibly for a university education. Instead, he dabbled in the Japanese language, in history, and Marxist theory for two years, then returned to China. He registered at Nankai University, but spent most of his time in radical activities and some of it in jail for anti-Japanese agitation.

A year later Chou was off to France, nominally as a student. With no pretense at formal studies, he busied himself in the tempestuous community of Chinese students, arguing, expounding, conspiring. He worked for a fortnight in the Renault plant, organized demonstrations of his young countrymen, was detained by and escaped from the perplexed French police, became a Marxist, helped organize units of the China Socialist Youth Corps in Paris and Berlin and, finally, the European headquarters of the CCP in Paris. On Comintern orders, he pressed CCP-Kuomintang collaboration in 1923–1924, and so ingratiated himself with the conservatives that he was made a member of the Executive Committee of the Kuomintang European headquarters, also in Paris.

With these jaunty credentials, Chou arrived in Canton during the autumn of 1924. The local Communist Party made him secretary of its military committee. Continuing his double life, it was natural for him to move into support of Chiang Kai-shek as his deputy political commissar. Chou's immediate chief, a Kuomintang stalwart preoccupied with intraparty intrigue, gave the disarming young Communist a fairly free hand. As a result Chou infiltrated the political department of the academy with Communists.

At Whampoa Chou had another, and unique, relationship. That was with General Blyukher, whose secretary he was for a short time.

Canton in 1923–1924 was a boiling retort of revolutionary enthusiasm and seeming common purpose. Sun, Borodin, Chiang Kai-shek, Blyukher, and the two secondary level Communists, Mao and Chou, these and others all spoke the language of revolution. But each had his inner thoughts of what the common phraseology meant and of where China's interests and his own private ambitions lay. They were a solid front deeply fissured beneath the surface.

While with its left hand the Kremlin was stirring revolt in South China, with its right hand it continued to deal formally with the Peking government. Karakhan, the former deputy commissar of foreign affairs, negotiated the treaty of May 31, 1924, establishing diplomatic relations between the two countries, recognizing nominal Chinese sovereignty over Outer Mongolia, and providing for joint administration of the Chinese Eastern Railway. Peking appeared to have gotten concessions out of the Russians, but the real gains were Moscow's.

The Soviet Union won appreciation from the Chinese public for negotiating with China as an equal and it legalized by treaty its minimum interests in two sensitive buffer zones—Outer Mongolia and Manchuria. Six months later, Soviet representatives reinsured Moscow's position in Manchuria by concluding a similar agreement with the government of Chang Tso-lin, who ruled the Northeast. This Soviet concern with legalities, when the pact legitimatized Russian claims, was characteristic of the cautiously nationalistic facet of the Kremlin.

Mao was deep in the Hunan countryside when the May 30 Incident occurred. He had been there for nearly half a year, discovering the revolutionary potential of the peasantry. With the widespread indignation over the incident, he saw the country folk responsive to agitation and readily militant. Mao had found the basis for his eventual rise to power.

He was deep in the Hunan countryside because something had gone wrong with his 1924 stay in Shanghai. In the metropolis he continued his work as a Communist Party official and, in addition, acted as secretary of the Kuomintang's organization department. In this situation, he was the butt of sectarian criticism from both sides. Furthermore, he was still a rustic in background and manners and his worldly Kuomintang superiors were not likely to have been above putting him in his inferior social place. Whatever it was, sickness as he claimed, or weariness, or mortification, or a combination of these, he fled Shanghai for the reassuring bucolicism of rural Hunan.

Out of defeat Mao found his way: arousing and organizing peasants. This attracted the unsympathetic attention of the warlord governor of Hunan. Mao therefore decamped to Canton in the autumn of 1925. There he found the Kuomintang more interested than most of his fellow-Communists in mobilizing the peasantry. Most of the Chinese Communists, unlike the Russians, who sensed the importance of the peasantry, were still bookishly committed to the proletariat, reinforced in their belief by the successes of May 30.

Mao became a staff member and then principal of the Kuomintang's Peasant Movement Training Institute. Next he was appointed secretary and then deputy chief of the same party's propaganda department. In actuality, he ran that important office because the chief, Wang Ching-wei, in early 1926 was busy as acting head of the government.

Sun Yat-sen's death in March 1925 had opened the question of succession to his leadership of the Kuomintang. In the ensuing struggle for power, the left wing, led by Wang, had come out on top. This did not please Chiang Kai-shek, by then commander of the Nationalists' army. His ambitions were not limited to soldiering. And although he held forth in public like a Comintern agitator, his sympathies were not with those "outsiders" who would upset the structure of Chinese society.

Accordingly, when he discovered what he claimed was a plot to kidnap and ship him to Vladivostok, Chiang moved swiftly against those whom he assumed to be his adversaries. Using his troops, on March 20, 1926 he arrested a number of Communists and left-wing members of the Kuomintang. His show of force was brusque enough to intimidate Wang, who was of something less than heroic cast. Wang became diplomatically indisposed and sailed off to Europe. Chiang literally overnight had made himself successor to Sun Yat-sen.

In the course of his coup, Chiang briefly imposed on the Soviet advisers a genteel form of house arrest. This was taken as a hint of his dissatisfaction with Moscow's opposition to launching forthwith a campaign against the warlords. For the Kuomintang and at least Mao, among the Chinese Communists, wanted to move, to carry the nationalist revolution northward, eliminate the warlords and unite the country.

Stalin and Trotsky were against such an expedition. They imagined that the Japanese, British, and their warlord allies were straining at the leash. The Kremlin therefore opposed stirring up the imperialists by a revolutionary advance northward. But neither its will nor its wile were equal in this to Chiang's. His determination to launch the Northern Expedition was for the sake of China, and also for the sake of Chiang Kai-shek.

Borodin had been temporarily away from Canton at the time of the March 20 coup. And this may well have been one of the reasons that Chiang acted when he did. But having gotten what he wanted for the time being, and having poured forth ritualistic contrition, Chiang asked the portly, mustachioed Russian to come back to Canton. He still needed Soviet aid.

Back in the flat, steamy capital of Chinese revolution, a thoroughly irritated Borodin threatened to withdraw Soviet assistance unless the situation was restored to what it had been. Knowing how heavily the Kremlin banked on him, Chiang rejected the Russian's demand and so called his adviser's bluff. Whereupon a compromise was worked out. Borodin agreed to support the Northern Expedition and to restrain Communist activity in the Kuomintang. And Chiang promised to hold back the right wing.

He also demanded and got the removal of several Soviet military advisers. Chiang objected to their attempts to centralize the administration of the new "revolutionary" army, which would have strengthened the influence of the Russians. Furthermore, Chiang believed that one of the advisers had made fun of him.

Thus at the very outset of his politico-military career, Chiang proved that he knew how to outbluff foreigners who threatened to withdraw aid unless he acceded to alien wishes. He also revealed himself to be resentful of any "reform" of his method of control over his forces. And finally he showed an acute sensitivity in anything affecting his face, a readiness to take offense at any slight, real or imagined.

Notwithstanding all of this, Stalin and his man Borodin continued to back Chiang as the main hope for the success of the Chinese revolution. So did the cowed Chinese Communists, after murmuring about a countercoup and withdrawing from the alliance. The Russians could not do without Chiang because his Soviet-equipped and trained army represented power. The Communists could not face him down for the same reason. They had no army, only themselves, perhaps ten thousand of them in all of China, and uncertain control over labor and peasant organizations. Nor would Borodin release arms to them from the stock he had on hand for the Nationalists.

In Chiang's March 20 crackdown Mao was eased out of his position in the propaganda department. But he was allowed to retain his post at the Peasant Training Institute, which suggested that he was not wholly unacceptable to Chiang. Chiang dismissed Chou En-lai from his position as head of the First Army's political department, to which he had been promoted from the military academy. But because the adroit Chou had helpfully restrained hotheaded comrades and because Chiang was not ready to break with the CCP, he permitted Chou to share in the selection of the chief political officer for the Northern Expedition. Chou supported a Kuomintang left-winger, who got the appointment—and gratefully invited Chou to introduce capable young commissars for his staff.

Early in July 1926, Chiang started his Northern Expedition. He had a force of about a hundred thousand against an aggregate of half a million warlord troops. The campaign rolled swiftly forward, due as much to defections of warlord units and widespread cooperation from peasants as to the martial qualities of the revolutionary army. The popularity of the revolutionary cause and the effectiveness of the political workers, including swarms of students from the Communist Youth Corps, more than compensated for military inferiority in numbers. By October the revolutionary forces had reached the Yangtze at Wuhan.

As the Northern Expedition surged across South China toward the Yangtze, Mao was indoctrinating future peasant agitators at the Training Institute, concentrating on military subjects. But then the lure of action drew him closer to the center of struggle. After the Nationalists had planted themselves on the strategic mudbanks of the Yangtze, Mao was on his way back to "liberated" Hunan.

In July the Communists had tardily formed their own peasant department with Mao as its chief. But this office did not amount to much because Stalin insisted on its subordination to the Kuomintang. In any event, Mao's Central China activities continued through the established peasant organization of the Kuomintang. Ostensibly, this was collaboration with the bourgeois party. Actually, it was permeation and exploitation of the lower levels of the Kuomintang.

Millions of peasants had been aroused by the Northern Expedition. This was indeed the first stirrings of a mass movement, the beginning of a revolution in the lives of multitudes. Excited by what he encountered in the countryside, Mao preached not only against what both parties agreed were the evils of traditional China, such as the subjugation of women, ancient superstitions, and ancestor worship. He also lashed out against "the feudal landlord class," calling for its overthrow. For most of the Kuomintang, this was going too far.

It also went too far for Stalin. As the Nationalist officers were from or related to landlord families, dispossessing them of their patrimony might be expected to chill their devotion to the revolution. Having anticipated this awkward possibility, Stalin had in October 1926 warned the Chinese Communists against stirring up the peasantry and then sought to reassure them with visions of the peasantry's coming into its own through the success of the "revolutionary army" and government.

While Mao was mobilizing the peasants early in 1927, the split widened between the left and right wings of the Kuomintang. The left wing dominated the Nationalist Government after the administrative offices moved from Canton to Wuhan, en route to Peking, the traditional capital. Borodin and the principal Communists were also at Wuhan. It was an impressive concentration of civilians.

Chiang was east of Wuhan, at Nanchang, with an impressive concentration of troops. He felt strong enough to disregard the left wing and go his own way. This he proceeded to do.

Instead of driving further north to Peking, he followed a homing instinct and turned east toward Shanghai. This metropolis of wealth and infinite intrigue was his natural habitat. It was also an essential base from which he could draw enough revenue to make him independent of others, especially the Russians.

As his forces approached Shanghai in mid-February, the Communist organized workers of the city rose against the ruling war lord. And who had played a leading part in organizing the insurrection? Who but the general's former political aide, the agile Mr. Chou, mobilizing the proletariat to present Shanghai to the revolution and its leader, Chiang Kai-shek. Of an accommodating nature in this respect, Chiang halted his advance to allow Chou and his vanguard to do the fighting. Bravely bungling the insurrection, the workers were suppressed.

A month later, the Nationalists moved to the outskirts of Shanghai. Again the Communists summoned the workers to arise. This time they were successful, so that when the Nationalist troops entered the city, proletarian insurgents held all but the foreign concessions. Chiang's problem was now to oust militant workers rather than warlord mercenaries, with whose weapons these real revolutionaries had armed themselves.

Rather than attacking the worker militants head on with his troops, not all of whom could be trusted to shoot down comrades who had just welcomed them to Shanghai, Chiang turned to his old associates in the underworld. Armed gangsters, masquerading as fighting workers, briefly deceived some of the insurgents and were quickly followed up by reliable troops who joined in liquidating the confused labor union stalwarts and anyone else whose looks they did not like. In a matter of hours Chiang had slaughtered most of his Communist competition in Shanghai.

The slippery Chou En-lai was caught in the midst of the carnage. But he talked his way out of arrest and lived to make Chiang regret the gap in his Shanghai dragnet.

Having drawn the sword against the Communists, Chiang made plain his attitude toward the government in Wuhan. On April 18 he set up his own Nationalist Government at Nanking, surrounding himself with right-wing Kuomintang personalities. Chiang was now contemptuously independent. But he was not a mere warlord. He claimed succession to Sun Yat-sen as leader of the nation, as Stalin was then claiming to be heir to Lenin.

Ridding himself of the Kuomintang left wing, the Communists, and financial dependence on the Russians did not mean that Chiang wanted to break relations with the Soviet Union. Moscow could still be useful to him as a source of arms and other aid. So he announced that his differences were not with Moscow and that he had done no more than try to straighten out its busybody flunkeys. Chiang was still at it in July, sending one of his diplomatic retainers to assure a departing Soviet consul that he was not anti-Soviet and that he wanted to resume the traditional friendship between China and the Soviet Union.

Such blandishment was slight solace to Stalin. He had lost a great deal of face in the Kremlin because of Chiang's mutiny. His arch rival in the Soviet hierarchy, Trotsky, quickly seized upon Chiang's betrayal to represent Stalin as a dupe and bungler.

CHAPTER *12*

How Stalin Lost China

SOVIET POLICY TOWARD China had become a domestic issue in Russia in the struggle for power between Stalin and the opposition, mainly Trotsky. The dispute was carried on in doctrinal terms as tortuous as the small intestine. The argument had to be in an ideological context however primitive the private intent, because Marxism-Leninism permeated conscious thought in the Bolshevik oligarchy.

Simplifying the 1926–1927 feud in the Kremlin over China policy, the basic issue was whether the Chinese Communists should collaborate with the Kuomintang or pursue an independent revolutionary course. The difference, for the most part, grew out of vagueness in the grand strategy for colonial countries—in which China was included—drawn up in 1920 at the Second Congress of the Comintern. Lenin had advocated "temporary alliance with bourgeois democracy in colonial and backward countries," but the Communists were not to merge with it and were to "preserve the independence of the proletarian movement."

A feverish young Indian Communist, M. N. Roy, objected to Lenin's proposal. Because there was a good deal of give and take in those pre-Stalinist days of the Comintern, Roy pressed his theory that Asia, not Europe, was the decisive theater of world revolution and that the Asian Communists should not be hobbled by alliances with the bourgeoisie. The voluble Roy so wore down the delegates that the policy which emerged from the Congress bore the marks of Roy's hammering.

The ambiguities of the Lenin-Roy compromise were exploited by Stalin and Trotsky alike. Each cited what suited him in that contradictory document, the better to belabor the other—Stalin in defense of collaboration with the Kuomintang, Trotsky for Chinese Communist independent action. As the scholastic wrangle over China policy grew, each contestant, desperately seeking justification for his pretensions to be the true successor to Lenin, quoted from that infallible source: an abandoned slogan of Lenin's from the 1905 revolution in Russia, a fuzzy distinction between backward and relatively advanced countries, an irrecognizable description of the British Labour Party, an abortive policy toward Kemalist Turkey, and so it irrelevantly went.

Stalin's schooling at the Tiflis Theological Seminary stood him in good stead throughout this devious debate with Trotsky. The polemics became so intense that they took on a life of their own, obscuring the reality in China, victimizing the Chinese Communists, and making at least Stalin a near captive of his own sophistry. For Trotsky was quite right in accusing Stalin of being hoodwinked by Chiang and binding the miserable Chinese Communists to the Kuomintang chariot. The bolder Trotsky's thrusts became, the more rigid was Stalin in his stance.

One week before Chiang's Shanghai purge, Stalin had given assurances that Chiang was "submitting to discipline" and that so long as he battled the warlords he would be "squeezed out like a lemon, and then flung away." When the wily general squeezed the Communists and flung away the Wuhan Kuomintang regime, the infallible Stalin announced on April 21 that what had happened proved the correctness of his policy. The Communists should thenceforth cooperate closely with the Kuomintang left wing and the Wuhan regime.

Trotsky derided this prescription for renewed disasters. The Communists should cut loose and operate on their own. Set up soviets of workers, peasants, and soldiers, he insisted, to ride herd on and push the Wuhan regime to the left. Stalin stifled these flamboyant recommendations by simply denying them publication.

Still in a state of shock from being knocked about by Chiang, the Chinese Communists began their Fifth Congress on April 27, at Wuhan. With many qualms they agreed to cling to the Kuomintang rump. But what were they to do about the peasantry and land? In Hunan they had been strikingly successful in loosing the whirlwind of land-to-peasants. How were they to temper the blast to prevent expropriation of property owned by army officers and their relatives?

The answer was that they could not satisfy both the aroused peasantry and the propertied military. They nevertheless tried to do so by ordering the exemption of revolutionary officers and small owners from expropriation. Mao had favored a more drastic policy, but yielded to the compromise. He was also replaced by a Moscow-trained comrade as chief of the CCP's Peasant Department. As sometimes in the past when matters had not gone his way, Mao withdrew from the scene, absenting himself from the sessions of the Congress.

Another major issue faced the Fifth Congress—military strategy. For an organization with no armed forces of its own, the planning of military strategy involved figuring out how to use someone else's troops. With Chiang no longer available as a revolutionary tool, the Communists were reduced to consideration of General T'ang Shen-chih and the allegedly Christian general, Feng Yü-hsiang. T'ang was an enterprising warlord who had early joined the Northern Expedition and made himself acceptable by quickly becomg adept at revolutionary phraseology. Feng had returned the previous fall from Moscow, where he had played so well the part of a bluff, uncouth toiler of the East that the Kremlin generously furbished his army with Soviet materiel.

The Chinese Communists were suspicious of the two generals, but had no military alternative to them. Borodin suspected that T'ang might turn out to be another Chiang Kai-shek. He seemed to repose more confidence in the hulking Feng. He proposed that the Communists move to Northwest China, where Feng was based, and establish themselves there under the shelter of the Christian general's Soviet guns.

Strong forces of the Manchurian warlord, Chang Tso-lin, occupied the area between Wuhan and Feng's base in the Northwest. To join up with Feng meant having to eliminate first this blocking army. T'ang was already embarked on a campaign to do this, with the enthusiastic support of the Wuhan Kuomintang leaders. They envisioned themselves carried by T'ang to Peking and even combining with Feng to dispose of Chiang Kai-shek.

M. N. Roy, the Comintern's excitable guru, objected to Borodin's Northwestern Theory as defeatist, as indeed it was. Fresh from Moscow, he enjoyed considerable prestige and therefore added much to the confusion of the deliberations. His contribution on the score of where the Communists should go next was: south. One hundred and eighty degrees off the course recommended by Borodin, Roy wanted them to go back to Kwangtung and "deepen" the revolution among the masses.

General T'ang, in a sense, made the Communists' decision for them. His northern expedition was a fact. It turned out to be a fairly disagreeable fact because it bogged down in a stalemate between his and the Manchurian forces. At that point, the great red hope, Feng Yü-hsiang, swept down out of the Northwest, not to the rescue, but to assert his claim to Honan Province, over which area T'ang and the Manchurians had inconclusively fought.

Feng received on June 12 a weighty delegation from the Wuhan regime, accompanied by General Blyukher. He accepted a tactful appointment as governor of Honan and then sent the emissaries home. A week later he traveled east to meet with Chiang Kai-shek, immediately came to an agreement, and announced his wish to cooperate with Chiang in eliminating "militarism and Communism." Borodin, he ungratefully said, should go immediately back to Russia. Those Wuhan Kuomintang leaders who wanted to go abroad for a rest should be allowed to do so. Those who were inclined to join the Nanking government might do so. All of which was plain enough.

While General T'ang was locked in Honan battles, his subordinates were becoming increasingly short-tempered with the Communists. Peasants and workers had been flouting Wuhan Communist orders for restraint. They continued to behave like revolutionaries. So a local commander at Changsha on May 21 conducted a bloody purge of Communists and troublemakers. This so enraged the local Communists and peasant activists that, ten days later, perhaps as many as a hundred thousand men from the surrounding countryside attacked the city. The Changsha garrison routed the ill-equipped, untrained horde.

As the top Communists at Wuhan were nervously attempting to smooth things over with the military high command—a ministration in which both Mao and Chou En-lai were particularly active—a telegram arrived on June 1 from Stalin. The mastermind had spoken. From afar, from the other side of the Kunlun Range, the deserts of Turkestan, the Russian steppe, the Ural Mountains, and the Volga River came the word. And what was the word?

"Without an agrarian revolution, victory is impossible." Many new peasant and proletarian leaders must penetrate the Central Committee of the Kuomintang "to make the old leaders more resolute, or throw them into discard." Immediately "liquidate the dependence upon unreliable generals." Mobilize twenty thousand Communists and fifty thousand workers and peasants and "organize your own reliable army before it is too late."

Ch'en Tu-hsiu, head of the CCP since its foundation and sedulous disciple of Stalin's, reacted pungently to the ukase. The former dean of the Faculty of Letters at Peita is said to have remarked that "It was like trying to take a bath in a urinal." The old Chicago Menshevik, Borodin, was less irreverent in his comment, dismissing Stalin's telegram as ludicrous.

M. N. Roy also received the edict. He trotted off with the plot for undermining the Wuhan regime and laid it before the head of that government, Wang Ching-wei, ostensibly to enlist Wang's support. It is no wonder that Mao later told Edgar Snow that while Borodin was a blunderer, Roy was a fool.

Harassed by T'ang's forces, betrayed by Feng, and resisted by the Kuomintang left, the Wuhan Communists were in no position to act as Stalin willed. Nor were they of one mind. While the unhappy Mao was sent off to Hunan with instructions to curb the peasantry he had done so much to arouse, others had begun to plan for even more extensive and violent insurrection.

On July 14, 1927, the Comintern proclaimed that the Wuhan regime was turning counterrevolutionary. After expatiating on the correctness of past policy, the Comintern demanded that the Communists persuade the Kuomintang membership to get rid of its leaders, at the same time, arm the peasants and workers, and clean out of the CCP leadership the opportunists and those who had violated the international discipline of the Comintern.

One day after the hollow thunder of the Comintern resolution, the Kuomintang directed that all Communists who were members of the Kuomintang give up their membership in the CCP. This was the beginning of the formal break between the Wuhan regime and the Communists. Ch'en Tu-hsiu resigned from the Central Committee of the CCP and retired to Shanghai. Chou eased himself out of Wuhan intent on creating a military uprising to take the city of Nanchang. Mao slipped off to the Hunan countryside a month later, this time to the more congenial duties of organizing peasant insurrections. The Central Committee members who remained in Wuhan made themselves inconspicuous.

Borodin and Roy were recalled to the Soviet Union. High Kuomintang officials gave face to the man who had been their adviser for more than three years by going to the railway station to bid Borodin farewell on July 27. All concerned affably pretended that he was leaving only temporarily for a visit to Feng Yü-hsiang. And when Borodin passed through Feng's territory, the Christian general extended hospitality to him, as did minor warlords along the dismal road back to Russia.

After all, no more than Chiang did these gentlemen wish to be boorish to one who might again, for all they knew, be resident quartermaster for the requisition of Soviet arms—even though they all understood that he would sooner or later seek their overthrow. Revealing a belated appreciation of the warlord mentality, Borodin complained to a fellow-traveling American writer, Anna Louise Strong, "When the next Chinese general comes to Moscow and shouts: 'Hail to the World Revolution!' better send at once for the G.P.U. . . . All that any of them wants is rifles."

To replace the disillusioned Borodin, Stalin sent to China a young fellow Georgian, Besso Lominadze. Comrade Besso had two things that gave him great confidence: an extensive ignorance of China and orders from Stalin. Ch'en Tu-hsiu was to be made the scapegoat for Stalin's blunders, policy was to be more independently aggressive, and a new party boss was to be chosen for the CCP.

Abuse was therefore heaped on Ch'en as an opportunist. Lominadze approved plans for several Communist insurrections, but under the banner of the Kuomintang. And with less than a quorum, the Central Committee on August 7, embraced Ch'ü Ch'iu-pai, who had returned from school in the Soviet Union with an impressive knowledge of the Russian language and literature, as the new taskmaster of the CCP.

A week before the investiture of the cocky Mr. Ch'ü, the Communists had mounted their first military assault on a city. The Shanghai uprising, in which Chou En-lai had played a leading role, had been undertaken with workers. This time, at Nanchang, Chou organized a putsch with army units.

One participating general was the Communist Yeh Ting. A second general, Ho Lung, was then sympathetic to the Communists and destined to become one of the Communists' great commanders. Chu Teh, whom Chou had known in Berlin, was another conspiring officer. A decade later he was commander-in-chief of all Communist forces. One of Chou's former students at the Whampoa Military Academy, Lin Piao, was also involved in the Nanchang uprising as a twenty-year old colonel. Lin was to become a legendary fighting general against the Japanese, the Nationalists, and the Americans (in Korea), then minister of defense and heir apparent to Mao in the mid-1960s.

The military operation itself, involving some ten thousand rebels, was less than glorious. The mutineers took the city on August 1. Chou and his enthusiastic political comrades established on the next day a civil administration in the name of the Kuomintang, hoping thereby to placate Wuhan. When this did not work and Wuhan's forces continued to advance on Nanchang, the rebels scattered southward on August 4.

Badly organized and attacked from every side, the Communist retreat turned into a rout. It was far from the disciplined withdrawal to the peasant insurgent area in Kwantung and deepening of the revolution hoped for by M. N. Roy and many of the Central Committee. The main body finally reached Kwangtung where it found temporary respite. Chou again had a narrow escape, this time by junk to Hong Kong, weak from fever, penniless and bedraggled.

Notwithstanding its outcome, the Nanchang uprising was of prophetic significance. This first fumbling use by the party of organized, Communist-led military units was an intimation of what was to come, of the conquest of China by Communist armies. While the peasantry became the base from which the Communists rose to power, it was the armies, stemming from and linked with the peasantry, that forced the ultimate victory.

The Nanchang uprising and retreat, however, did not anticipate the intimate collaboration between the peasantry and the military which the Communists developed a decade later. The rebels failed to create a revolutionary rapport with the rural population. This was a major reason for the confused nature of their retreat.

As Chou, Chu Teh, and Lin Piao were making a getaway from their experiment in capturing a city through military uprising, Mao was engaged in a scheme for capturing cities through peasant insurrections. This had been done before in China. But for Marxist-Leninists, a strategy in which the countryside surrounded and took over the cities was something new.

Mao had taken part in the preliminary planning with other members of the Central Committee and Lominadze at Wuhan in July and early August. The insurrection was to be staged in Hunan and Hupei provinces, with Mao in charge in Hunan. Peasant revolutionary armies were to be put together from existing peasant self-defense militia. This loutish assemblage would be the main force of the insurrection. Bandits, secret societies, and Kuomintang army defectors might be used, but only as auxiliaries. The objective was to destroy the existing order of society, including "evil gentry," by violence and terror.

With all of the plans neatly drawn up by the theoreticians at Wuhan, Mao sallied forth to the way things really were in Hunan. The Party's membership there had been nearly decimated in the May 21 purge and the peasant associations severely shaken. The plan to spread terror throughout the province was plainly beyond the anaemic means available. Mao therefore decided to concentrate on one focal point, Changsha. Furthermore, the yokel self-defense units, poorly armed and disciplined, hardly seemed to be an irresistible main force. So Mao turned to what the planners had designated as auxiliary forces.

There were four so-called regiments: one of unemployed coal miners, a Communist-officered army unit which had missed joining the Nanchang uprising, a mixed detachment of peasants, workers, and secret society toughs, and a reorganized body of army mutineers. With this incoherent assortment, whose *esprit de corps* was that of a coalition of freebooters, Mao proposed to bring Changsha to its knees, and so informed the dogmatists in Wuhan. They were horrified and, never at a loss for words, told him that he was a military adventurist and should place his faith in the peasant masses.

With little change in his plans, Mao proceeded along the uneven tenor of his ways. A news report, dated September 8, revealed that the Changsha garrison commander had recently captured secret Communist orders to all cells in the city in which September 10 was set as the date for the insurrection. Confirming the accuracy of the garrison commander's intelligence, the coal miners moved to attack an outlying town on September 10. The other units, which were supposed to spring into synchronized action, dillydallied.

From then on the Autumn Harvest Insurrection was characterized by a few small successes, inept tactics, treachery, fighting among the insurgents, refusal to attack, and panic. Mao cannot be held responsible for the course of battle because he was not there. He had been tardy in leaving Changsha and was taken into custody by village police, who held him throughout the period of active hostilities, which ended on September 17.

Some of the stragglers took to nearby hills. There they were joined by a sobered Mao. He had concluded that the strategy of taking the cities from the countryside, at least with such forces as he had in Hunan, was hopeless. On September 19, he extracted from a majority of those Party officials present a decision to give up the insurrection and withdraw southward. With the remnants of the debacle Mao found a sanctuary in the mountain fastness of Chingkangshan, like a bandit chieftain in a romantic novel.

Back at Wuhan, the Party Central had received a report written in the heat of battle, and in Russian, from a "Comrade Ma," presumably the Chinese alias of a Soviet adviser. Tovarich "Ma" was outraged by the incompetence and worse that he saw on every side and by the contemptuous evasion with which he was treated by Chinese comrades. On the day that Mao and his strays decided to quit and go south, the party command sent stinging orders to the Hunan committee to renew the offensive. It is doubtful that this blast ever caught up with Mao. But the censure of the Central Committee in November did, months later. Mao was condemned for, among other things, military opportunism and slighting the assassination of evil gentry and was dismissed from the Politburo and other lesser posts.

Looking back on the Autumn Harvest Insurrection, nearly a decade later, Mao told Edgar Snow that his "little army" had been afflicted by poor discipline, a low level of political training, "many wavering elements," and "many desertions." He might have added sloppy security and intelligence. But the reasons for the cropper in Hunan—and that in Hupei was even more embarrassing—went deeper.

Crumbly as it was, the society in China which the Kremlin, its Comintern, and the CCP proposed to revolutionize was not as decrepit as they thought. Marxist-Leninist theory led them to underestimate their adversaries and overestimate existing forces of spontaneous revolt. Secondly, Chinese communism in 1927 was still green. It was a long way from having an organization strong enough to challenge the status quo head on.

Consequently, both the Nanchang and Autumn Harvest uprisings were doomed to failure. The Nanchang *putsch* and the Autumn Harvest concept of a constant bubbling up of mass revolt and terrorism by the peasantry defied the possible. Had Mao followed the dictates of the Party Central, and relied on the masses, instead of on his "little army," he might not have had even the semblance of an insurrection.

Deep in his mountain fastness, a fugitive not worth chasing, Mao had plenty of time to think over what had gone wrong and what should be done. He began by doing two things of fundamental significance. He took what was at hand, the thousand who had fought and run away with him and two local bands of semi-retired bandits, indoctrinated them, and combined them into another little army of three regiments. He also formed in November 1927 at the village of Ch'alin a soviet government. He was now on the right track to power: with an army, even though at that stage a ridiculous one, and a Communist-administered base area, however scant.

Stalin was still engrossed in his struggle with Trotsky. And China policy was still a vital issue in that contest. Trotsky accused Stalin of betraying the revolution in China. And as Stalin protested the correctness of his course, he veered in practice toward Trotsky's line of violent, immediate revolution.

After the failure of Nanchang, Autumn Harvest, and several less spectacular uprisings, came the most foolhardy of them all, the Canton Commune. Some, particularly Trotsky, later blamed Stalin for this blunder. In reality, the uprising seems to have been ordered at the initiative of the Provincial Committee. Ineptly planned, uncovered by the authorities, and clumsily executed, the December 11–13 insurrection was crushed by Kuomintang and militarist forces.

The Canton Commune was the last conspicuous Communist dissipation in the 1926–27 revolution. Collaboration with the Kuomintang had failed, and now so had insurrection. The strength of the movement had been wasted, from some fifty-eight thousand members in the spring of 1927 to less than twenty thousand by winter. A handful of Central Committee members, including Chou En-lai, were underground in the foreign concessions of Shanghai. They fretted about Mao's ideological waywardness in consorting with outlaws off in the mountains. So they ordered one of the Nanchang mutineers, Chu Teh, who was compromising himself in another fashion by serving with his detachment under a so-called Kuomintang army, to join Mao and straighten him out. It was on this querulous note that 1927 closed for the future rulers of China.

For Stalin, the Canton Commune was a last hurrah of world revolution. Revolution had not spread from Russia across Europe. Nor was it sweeping Asia. And now in China, the last chance, it had collapsed, not through any admitted fault of his but because the CCP was "immature" and prone to error. Stalin had lost China.

But he was about to gain Russia. Insofar as he did so on an issue, it was on that of socialism in one country. This did not mean repudiation of the doctrine of world revolution, but saying that building socialism (industrialization) in the Soviet Union really did come first. Stalin's sober proposition appealed more to the Bolshevik oligarchy than did Trotsky's strident demands for permanent revolution, especially in China where the Communist cause was so obviously faltering. Trotsky may have been right in the debate over China. But that "dull mediocrity" outmaneuvered him ideologically and organizationally, expelled him from the Soviet Union, and then patiently, quietly, years later, arranged for his murder.

Some aspects of the Soviet intervention in the Chinese Nationalist Revolution of 1926–1927 were prophetic of what was to come in American intervention in China during the 1940s.

Basically, there was the same assumption that China would be before long a powerful influence in the world and that its millions would be an important ally against hostile powers, particularly Japan.

Chiang Kai-shek and his Kuomintang regime were the chosen instrument for unifying China and starting it on a reliable course. Chiang's military force was strengthened with weapons and advisers, both in training and in the field.

Stalin (or Roosevelt) was essentially ignorant and opinionated about China. He had a concept of China's place in the scheme of things which overrode Chinese realities.

As artful dissemblers and adepts at the game in which the weak make captives of the strong, Chiang and several of his political entourage exploited their benefactors with alternating charm and insolence. One of Chiang's more supple dissimulations was his 1926 statement that neither Russia nor the Chinese Communists wanted to apply communism to China and that the Chinese revolution was part of the world revolution.

General Blyukher's reports to Moscow on Chiang became ever more disparaging the better they became acquainted. And Tovarich "Ma" (echoed by junior American officers twenty years later in China and forty years later in Vietnam) exploded with "These Chinese-style, totally sharpsterish double-dealings!"

But at the top, disillusionment with Chiang initially produced deeper commitment to him. Criticism of Chiang from representatives in China was either ignored or branded as evidence of disloyalty. And the Stalinists condemned the opposition for wanting to break with the Kuomintang.

China policy grew to be a vicious, major issue between the two domestic political factions, contributing to the defeat of one of them.

CHAPTER *13*

Yenching

AFTER TWO YEARS at the University of Wisconsin, I worked my way across the Pacific as an ordinary seaman. I jumped ship in Japan and then journeyed as a passenger to Peking. There I entered Yenching University in the early fall of 1929 for my junior year of college.

Yenching was, in a way, the peak American cultural effort in China. Supported by several Protestant churches and having a special connection with Harvard and a less formal one with Princeton, Yenching was meant to produce China's modern leadership, an élite blend of two cultures—the traditional Chinese and the best of the West. The tone of the university was set by its president, Leighton Stuart. He was himself a cultural blend; Southern gentility born in China, sensitive to human relationships, soft-spoken, decorous, devout, dark pensive eyes peering out from under overhanging bushes of black eyebrows. Twenty years later, as American ambassador, he was to be driven out of China by the Communists.

The Yenching campus was some five miles outside of the walls of Peking, in the countryside, about halfway between the city and the Summer Palace on the flanks of the Western Hills. Instruction for the five hundred men and a hundred and seventy-five women students was in English, mostly for science courses, and in Chinese. The faculty was mixed: Chinese, Americans, and Europeans.

Describing to my relatives in the United States the novel situation in which I found myself, I wrote in 1929, "The Chinese student feels that since an educational institution is being run for his benefit, he surely should have some voice in its operation. And so he takes into his own hands as much authority as he can wheedle or force from the administration. The Yenching student government, weak in comparison with that of most other Chinese universities, runs its own dormitories and refectories. It hires and fires the dormitory servants, leases the operating rights of the refectories to two caterers. . . .

"In academic matters . . . the Yenching students exert virtually no influence. In the majority of Chinese universities this is not true. It is not at all uncommon for students in the average Chinese college to so intimidate their professors that the grades given out bear no relation to the work done. And if a teacher is so headstrong as to try to establish high scholastic standards, the undergraduates are quite capable of forcing such a man out of the university. It has been done often enough."

My friends among the Chinese students were some of those who spoke English well or were on athletic teams. Having made the basketball and track teams, I found sport the easy, least common denominator of amiable association. One varsity and one interclass basketball game ended in a tie that year. I expected that the draw would be played off in the usual overtime period. Nothing happened. The game was over, both teams leaving the court delighted that the danger of losing face by defeat was so prettily avoided.

My one contact with Peking University, the Peita where ten years before Mao Tse-tung served as a library attendant and Chen Tu-hsiu as dean of the Faculty of Letters, was a three-day intercollegiate track meet, held at a field adjacent to that university. I ran the 200-meter low hurdles and spent the rest of the time mingling with spectators and contestants. Alongside the showy Yenching students, those from Peita seemed drab and reticent.

"Translations of Upton Sinclair's *Oil* and Remarque's *All Quiet on the Western Front* are the most conspicuous volumes in the bookstalls of Tung An Shih Ch'ang, the city's principal bazaar and market," I wrote. "Realistic and naturalistic novels are popular among the students, novels written by the rising school of Chinese realists as well as the translations from foreign authors. The Chinese college man reads extensively, both fiction and nonfiction. And the economic and political opinions which he forms from his reading would be branded in the United States as radical. I am speaking here particularly of the students in the government schools. Although there are several Communists at Yenching, the greater part of the student body coming, as it does, from bourgeois and wealthy families or from inland mission schools, is as innocent of what the Japanese term 'dangerous thoughts' as, shall we say, a Princeton sophomore."

Life among my fellow-students was not without moments of passion. "The other day there was a fight between two of the most westernized students. It was over the possession of an old hat. The vanquished one, who is terribly short-sighted without the help of his glasses, emerged from the fracas with a bloody nose and a closed eye. The victor was unscathed.

"The affair created something of a sensation, because fisticuffs between men of the student class is regarded as the height of bad form. Consequently, the chap who emerged conqueror was considered a boor and enjoyed a period of social ostracism on the part of the women students. The chancellor of the university issued a proclamation to the effect that further misconduct of that nature would be dealt with severely. For the loser of the battle there was only sympathy.

"To the Western eye the whole incident was not without its tincture of farce. But what interested me was the way in which the two boys finally settled their quarrel. Here they were, two young bloods priding themselves on their emancipation from 'Pooh, the old Chinese scholar,' as one student characterized the type to me, 'so stiff and impractical and bound by custom.' These boys had all of the surface indications of release from the old tradition. . . . Even the way in which they squared off to fight was typically American, as interpreted by the movies. But this altercation did not seem to explain itself away as glibly as the ones on the screen. The only way out seemed to be to follow custom and put themselves in the hands of intermediaries who would so manipulate declarations and retractions that face would be regained and the whole matter smoothed out. This they did. And the resumption of normal relations was celebrated by a feast at Ch'ang San's restaurant.

"Verbal violence delivered with appalling ferocity and the striking of threatening poses are the limits to which the average Chinese student will go in his disaffections. Very seldom are blows exchanged. Likewise in the majority of his other attitudes and habits, the ordinary student here is Chinese. He may be keen about sports . . . love the cinema . . . affect Western clothing, or he may have acquired something of the so-called scientific attitude. Yet, despite those very real indications of a new order, the Chinese student has more in common with his classical predecessors than with the students of Europe and America."

An extracurricular concern of male students almost anywhere is women. At Yenching, this interest was tamed by certain circumstances. "One of the fellows told me that probably a third of the men (students) were married and had children. This situation exists because of the custom of early marriage, many boys marrying before they are out of their teens. Furthermore, a considerable number of the Yenching women students are engaged. . . . The extremely rigid Chinese code of sex ethics acts as a further damper on the young ardents. There are rumors current, however, of 'immorality' in the universities in Peking whose discipline is not as inflexible as that of Yenching.

"The typical woman student here is, to use the port city boys' term, 'old-fashioned.' That is, she is a shy, speaks-not-unless-spoken-to person. . . . Skating seems to be the big chance for the lovelorn to get together. Those amatorily inclined look forward with the greatest expectation to the skating season. For only on ice can one appear arm in arm with a girl and not have the implication exceed the intent. . . .

"In the late fall I had my first contact with the Chinese university woman. It was at the inevitable Friday night movie. I had come in late and was groping my way down the aisle. I saw an empty row and sidled in. I sat down, then decided to move over one seat. I did so and found myself reposing on someone's lap. Very much startled, I leapt back to my proper place, apologized, observed dimly that I had settled on the lap of a woman student, and apologized some more.

"Then the lights came on for the change of reels, for there is only one machine. My situation was extraordinarily conspicuous. Here we were in a row all by ourselves, exposed to the gaze of students and village folk. . . . I thought I should apologize again . . . suggesting for the third time that perhaps I should move down several rows. To which she gave a third noncommittal answer.

"I began to puzzle over what I should do. The girl might be subjected to gossip if I stayed. Again, it might be a serious affront if I moved. . . . Being in the clutches of indecision, I stayed, sat through eight brightly lit intervals, engaged in nervous conversation. . . .

"Several days later I met her at some sort of class tea. She said to me, 'Why were you worried the other evening about sitting beside me in the movie; why did you keep saying that you should leave and sit somewhere else? Was it because I am Chinese, because you are in China?' "

Late in October 1929, I left the sheltered composure of Yenching for a weekend visit to Kalgan. North of the Great Wall, it was the historic garrison town controlling the main pass from Mongolia into the North China plain.

"Kalgan is a strange, romantic town," I observed. "Full of skins, furs, camels, ponies . . . wild and frontier-looking. The people wear big sheepskins and fur caps. And there seems to be no vegetation anywhere. I saw a motor cara-van setting out for the trip across the Gobi [desert]. Three cars: one containing five or six Russians, the next—an old Dodge touring car—smothered under an enormous pile of pukais ('bedding') and baggage. On top of this mess clung some twelve or fifteen Mongols and Chinese. The next automobile was as bad. How those old cars manage to stagger over the desert under such a load is incom-prehensible to me. The engine hood is padded with cloth to protect it from sand."

Meanwhile in October 1929, in other parts of China, other enterprises were under way. Feng Yü-hsiang, who two years earlier had snubbed Wuhan and joined forces with Chiang, was now fighting Chiang. And as Chiang's regime at Nanking, by this time internationally recognized as the Government of China, battled the "Christian General," his Foreign Office on October 25 tried to enlist the support of all signatories to the Kellogg-Briand Pact of Paris outlawing war. This was not because of Feng's offensive but because Nanking feared a Soviet attack. Nanking feared a Soviet attack because Chiang had instigated Chang Hsueh-liang, the young Manchurian warlord, in the cause of nationalism, to bait the bear by seizing the Chinese Eastern Railway, other Soviet properties, and Soviet citizens in Manchuria.

Also late in October, weak with malaria, Mao Tse-tung was politically organizing a Communist base area in southern Kiangsi and feuding by courier with the Central Committee over the proper proletariat-peasant mix in a revolu-tionary formula. And Chu Teh, having raided as far south as Kwangtung, was reeling back to the base area from a defeat dealt his guerrilla force by three divi-sions of regulars.

On October 26, suddenly reversing its cautious, niggling orders, the Comin-tern assured the CCP that a new revolutionary upsurge was starting and that as soon as it had swelled to the proper proportions the Chinese comrades should overthrow the landlord-bourgeois establishment and set up a peasant-worker dictatorship of the soviet type.

Moscow may have seen from afar a revolutionary upsurge in China. But it was not visible in Kalgan, or Peking, or Tientsin, which I visited in January.

"Another humiliation day. One of the dormitory coolies has just gone through all the men's residence halls ringing a bell," I wrote. "It is the signal for a convocation. Perhaps a third to a half, or maybe even two-thirds of the students will gather in the auditorium to listen to speeches dealing with some particular imperialistic affront or massacre of Chinese which happened a certain number of years ago today. I do not know what anniversary is being celebrated this morning. Unable to understand the speeches of the first two or three of these meetings which I visited, I don't think that I shall go today.

"Even were the oratory in my own language, I fear that I should quickly tire. . . . One ceremony early in the year lasted something like two and a half hours with speeches ranging from one made in English by a Harvard professor to one in Chinese by a warlord's henchman. The students seemed to actually enjoy the flow of rhetoric. The Americans I saw afterwards looked positively wan. I have yet to see an European or American who could outsit a Chinese at a function. Perhaps it is that we are a fidgety people.

"I am very much interested in the idea back of these humiliation and memorial days. Based on sound enough psychology, these ventures into self-flagellation have done much to arouse patriotism in the students. I have the impression, however, that the display is being overdone and that it is not as effective as it once was, when there were only two or three anniversaries of chagrin and high resolve a year. Furthermore, many of those young Chinese who feel the most deeply for their country are so discouraged over the internal state of affairs that, baffled, they have lapsed into political inaction and cynicism."

Chiang's foolish Manchurian provocation of Moscow was answered on November 17 by military force. His former adviser, General Blyukher, was the Soviet commander in eastern Siberia. Knowing the Chinese military well, he threw no more than one division across the border, promptly routing the defending army. The Chinese soon yielded to the Soviet demands for restitution. Again they had been humiliated, this time not by the rapacious West but by those who claimed to be their revolutionary friends.

As a matter of principle, the United States had intervened in this fracas between China and the Soviet Union. The secretary of state who did this was Henry L. Stimson, a most upright man. He was a lawyer who had faith in the benign efficacy of law. And he took seriously the Pact of Paris commitments to renounce war as an instrument of national policy, commitments which had been created by his superficial predecessor, Frank B. Kellogg.

After fruitlessly drawing Chinese and Soviet attention during the summer of 1929 to their obligations under the pact, Stimson invoked the treaty after Blyukher had pounced on the Manchurians. Stimson even succeeded in persuading the British, French, and Italians to join him in identical notes to both sides. Nanking replied that it had not broken the pact. The Soviet government, which Washington did not then recognize, declared that, under similar provocation, those reproaching Moscow would themselves have considered the pact not binding. Nor could it "admit interference" in the direct negotiations then underway with the Chinese. Finally, "The Soviet government cannot forbear expressing amazement that the government of the United States, which by its own will has no official relations with the Soviet, deems it possible to apply to it with advice and counsel."

No advice or counsel was offered by Tokyo to either side. This was not from lack of interest. To the contrary, the Japanese government, particularly the army, was watching intently how Chinese presumption had provided Moscow with a cause for invasion of Manchuria and dictation of terms, and how ineffectual American, British, French, and Italian protests had been in the face of the Red Army's abruptly accomplished facts.

Events in China continued to be in 1930, as they always had been, compartmentalized. The crisis in the Northeast subsided. But south of the Wall, Feng Yü-hsiang connived with the "Model Governor," Yen Hsi-shan, and some southern generals again to challenge Chiang. In their dark little compartment, the Chinese Communists were riven once more by internal dissension, with the Comintern trying to infiltrate Moscow-trained young Chinese into command positions in the Central Committee at Shanghai.

In the North China compartment, school let out at Yenching in June, whereupon I took off for Inner Mongolia to visit an irrigation project in an area recently ravaged by famine and then infested by typhus. Lice, and not wars or revolutions, were my main concern at that time. I filled a talcum powder can with sulphur. On the two days' train trip to Saratsi near the end of the line in Inner Mongolia, I ate sandwiches which I sprinkled with sulphur in the belief that fumes repellant to lice would thereupon exude from my pores. Whatever the original flavor of the sandwich—strawberry jam, cheese, or bologna—the savor that lingered was that of rotten eggs. I arrived at the construction camp belching sulphur and for two days was so sick I thought I would expire, a pillar of brimstone on the lonely steppe.

When I recovered sufficiently to move about I discovered that in this borderland the concern was not the government in far-off Nanking, nor the revolution that Mao was dreaming of, nor Soviet aggression, nor Mr. Kellogg's and Mr. Briand's Pact of Paris outlawing wars, but the irrigation ditches that were being built there and the bandits which the "Model Governor" could not or did not bother to suppress. Here American relief money, privately contributed—for this was the day before the American government engaged in such disbursements—and American engineering skills were applied to forestall famine.

It was the driving ingenuity of O. J. Todd, the American engineer in charge, that propelled the irrigation project toward completion. Todd was a true type of early American, the kind that opened the West. By the twentieth century, with most of the United States strapped down by railroads and plugged by dams, this breed of earth-moving frontiersman pushed southward into Latin America and westward, across the Pacific, into Asia. So here, on China's northwestern frontier was O. J. Todd, squat, leather-faced, intensely practical, and relentless in his job.

While his main function was building the ditches into which water from the Yellow River would be diverted, he could not get on with the construction unless he could fend off raids by bandit bands on his workers, engineers, and supplies. Without protection from the "Model Governor," whose domain nominally extended over this area on the northern loop of the Yellow River, Todd raised his own posse to maintain law and order. His engineers had been shot at by outlaws, so they kept firearms close at hand day and night. Thus Todd coped with the wild west of China in the tradition of the wild west of the United States.

Upon my return to Peking I wrote a story for *The Leader,* a Peking English-language newspaper, about Todd's irrigation project and an adjacent experimental farm. The first installment appeared in the issue of June 19, 1930. The big story of the day, however, was an account of Feng Yü-hsiang's and Yen Hsi-shan's brief victories over the forces of Chiang Kai-shek. And a front-page box carried the headline: "Gunboats, Planes Drive Reds from Cities in Hupeh" with a curt report that Communist troops had been forced out of three small towns. On the back page, a dispatch from New York told of a severe slump in the New York Stock Exchange, while on page 6, Moutrie & Co., Ltd., at 8 rue Marco Polo, advertised "Just Arrived, Popular Victor Records," including "Broadway Melody," "Sonny Boy," "Singing in the Rain," "My Blue Heaven," and "A Gay Caballero."

The second installment of my article was published on June 29, along with an account of further retreats by Chiang's forces. Then, "according to telegraphic advices," representatives of the anti-Chiang generals were planning the formation of a new government in Peking. And in Washington, President Hoover "signed the resolution passed by congress for the universal draft, designed to equalize service in wartime."

Thus the course of human happenings jolted along in disparate episodes. The squabbling within the Chinese Communist Party over insurrectionary tactics had meantime become so heated that Chou En-lai, the eternal middleman, went to Moscow in the early summer of 1930 to brief the Comintern and have confided to him the latest word on the Kremlin vacillating line. Ever striking a hortatory note, the Comintern declared that the "new upsurge" of the Chinese revolutionary movement had become "an indisputable fact."

As if making good the Comintern's pronouncements, Communist units upsurged, moving out of their base area in July 1930 to attack Changsha, which they briefly occupied, Nanchang, and even Wuhan. These offensives were quickly beaten back and the Communists retreated to their hills and valleys. So much for upsurge.

Scarcely aware of these ructions, excepting as they appeared in headlines announcing the routing of reds, I prepared to return to the United States and my final year of college at Columbia University. I bought a ticket for "hard class," the cheapest there was on the Trans-Siberian Railway, third class across middle and western Europe, and tourist across the Atlantic.

Beginning with the border inspection, the journey across Siberia was grim.

The train crew and Soviet passengers were glum, even with one another. What little food there was on the diner was nasty and cost more than I could afford. For seven days, from the Manchurian border to Moscow, I ate gritty black bread bought from trainside vendors, worn, anxious women with shawls over their heads. One day I was able to buy a small basket of raspberries, another day a yellowish lump of cake.

Of course food was scarce. Collectivization of agriculture, culminating in the liquidation of the Kulaks in 1929, had crippled food production. What a contrast this socialist paradise was to "feudal" China where a train trip was a social event, an occasion for gossip and eating—a bowl of noodles or steaming bread on the station platform, or persimmons, roasted chestnuts, or a stick of sugar cane bought through an open window of the car from caterwauling peddlers.

On and on Siberia stretched, over the steppe, past Lake Baikal, cobalt blue and rimmed with mountains, through forests of shimmering white birch, then finally the Urals, of comfortable proportions and inclinations, befitting the beginning of Europe. From there on, it was farmlands and woods to Moscow. It had been more than four thousand miles from the Manchurian border to Moscow.

A journalist friend had made arrangements for me to stay my three days in Moscow at the unoccupied apartment of the pro-Communist American writer, Anna Louise Strong, then absent from the city. I had heard of her adventures with Borodin and the Wuhan regime three years earlier. But my more lasting recollections were stories about her from my Aunt Flossie, whose schoolmate she had been at Oberlin College. Aunt Flossie could not bring herself to speak of Anna Louise without a shudder—brilliant yes, but she never washed her neck.

I wandered about Moscow on foot, not knowing Russian, simply looking. The first Five-Year Plan was under way and Stalin had boasted only two months before that the Soviet Union was about to be transformed from an agricultural to an industrial society. Moscow was therefore full of activity. But the city was dishevelled. The old was shabby; the new was raw and shoddy. And it was difficult to find a place to eat. I was not sorry to leave.

CHAPTER *14*

Chu-Mao and the Long March

AT ABOUT THE TIME that I was going from Asia to Europe, Chou En-lai was returning eastward from Moscow. We may even have passed one another on the Trans-Siberian. He knew that the Comintern was determined to depose Li Li-san, then the leader of the Chinese Communist Party. Li had incited from Shanghai the adventuristic assaults on the cities in July and had promised in support of them proletarian strikes and insurrection, which did not materialize. When this scheme fizzled, Li was held responsible.

More objectionable to the Comintern was Li's insistence that China was the fulcrum of world revolution and his disrespect for the revolutionary high command in Moscow. He was so indiscreet as to suggest that he knew more about China than did the strange assortment of Balkan, Ukrainian, and other bureaucratized firebrands who administered the Comintern. And his first loyalty was, unacceptably, to the Chinese revolution.

Chou's efforts to compromise and save Li's face no more than delayed the inevitable outcome. In the late fall of 1930, Li went to Moscow to do penance and there he was kept until introduced into Manchuria in 1945 with the invading Soviet Army. Li was supplanted by Wang Ming (whose real name was Ch'en Shao-yü) and Po Ku (Ch'in Pang-hsien).

Wang Ming and Po Ku were the callow leaders of a clique of young revolutionaries, "returned students" from the Soviet Union known as the Twenty-Eight Bolsheviks. Under the tutelage of the latest Comintern mentor, Pavel Mif, Wang Ming and Po Ku presumed to direct the CCP from Shanghai. Chou En-lai unobtrusively continued in his post as head of the Military Department of the Party.

While nominal authority resided with the theorists of the Central Committee in Shanghai, the substance and real power of the Communist movement in China was in the scorned hills and valleys of southern Kiangsi where the only proletariat was *lumpen*, the leadership rustic, and the Red Army an array of guerrilla bands. Although Mao is now portrayed as the dominant personality in the "real power faction," Chu Teh was then the better known. In the early 1930s they were popularly referred to in combination as Chu-Mao, with Chu's name always preceding Mao's.

The subsequent dimming of Chu's renown coincided with Mao's consolidation of supreme authority and his writing—and rewriting—of history. Mao was not a notably generous chronicler of the accomplishments of others. Furthermore, the general, plain as a mud wall and twice as durable, was a modest man who made no effort to compete for fame against Mao, an articulate man with a mission.

Mao's later reputation as a military strategist owes more than a little to Chu. Certainly, before joining forces with Chu in 1928, he had shown no talent, although considerable appetite for generalship. His performance during the Autumn Harvest Insurrection demonstrated this. In Kiangsi, Mao's military education was in competent hands: Chu, P'eng Te-huai, Lin Piao and others. But mostly it was Chu, the senior commander in age, who was the one most clearly associated with Mao.

Not only was Chu the oldest of the group, he was the most mature in terms of varied experience. His rise from being Little Dog, son of poor peasants in remotest Szechuan, to brigadier general at the age of twenty-nine was unusual enough. Then from 1916 until 1928, when he first met Mao, Chu went through personality changes and adventures sufficient for another lifetime.

After the 1916 defeat of Yüan Shih-k'ai's forces in Szechuan, Chu Teh remained in that province with his troops. He brought his wife from Yunnan, where he had met her. She was his ideal: a modern intellectual with big feet. She bore him a son and then died. Soon he married another of the same cast, who had been an underground revolutionist. He paid off his family's debts and brought his relatives to live with him.

Inevitably he had become involved in the intrigues and battles of rival warlords. The betrayal of republican ideals, the humiliation of China by foreign powers, and a succession of deaths—his first wife, his military mentor, his two younger brothers, his father—these all depressed him, and he sought solace in opium. By the time Chu was fairly well addicted, his and other units of the Yunnan army in Szechuan suffered severe defeats at the hands of a Szechuanese warlord. Leaving his wife and child with her parents, he withdrew in 1920 with the Yunnan forces and with them descended upon Kunming, the capital of Yunnan, to overthrow the ruling warlord.

Chu was made commissioner of public safety, remained attached to his opium, and developed something of a reputation as a wencher. Then, in swirling warlord fashion, the ousted general swept back in and Chu escaped in the nick of time, fleeing by horse through the wild mountains and tribeslands of northern Yunnan and western Szechuan. He knew what he wanted to do. He would break himself of addiction to opium and go abroad to study how to save China.

In due course he made his way in the summer of 1922 to Shanghai, cured himself of opium, and met Sun Yat-sen and Ch'en Tu-hsiu, then the dominant figure in the CCP. Sun characteristically offered to make a deal with him if Chu would bring Yunnan forces into Sun's camp. Chu declined; he wanted to study socialism in Europe. With Ch'en, Chu went straight to the point: he would like to join the Communist Party. Coming from a militarist, Chu's application did not appeal to Ch'en, who advised the general to study and dedicate himself to the cause of the proletariat.

Disheartened by this class-conscious rebuff, Chu proceeded on his way to Germany. Like Chou En-lai and many of the Chinese "students" abroad, he spent much time in feverish political discussion about China with his compatriots. It was a talkative kind of education in agitation, mass organization, and insurrection more than one conforming to a conventional curriculum. Academically, the education of these "students" in European culture was superficial, bordering on the vaporous. What Chu learned about the West came mostly from his systematic tramping about Berlin and other German cities, his laborious tours through museums, and his arrests and final expulsion from Germany in June 1926 by the Berlin police for Chinese political demonstrations.

While in Germany Chu had applied through Chou En-lai for admission to the CCP and had been accepted. His membership was secret and he passed as a veteran adherent to the Kuomintang, which he had joined in Yunnan. Consequently when he arrived in Shanghai during mid-summer 1926, he served the Party by reestablishing contact with his old warlord friends. The Northern Expedition was forging up from Canton and Chu's task was to win over to the Nationalist side, or at least to neutralize, a Szechuanese general who had once offered Chu a place on his staff and who in 1926 held a position on the flank of the Northern Expedition's assault on Wuhan.

This second-grade warlord welcomed Chu, was slow to understand that no bribe was offered for his allegiance to the Nationalist cause, but did stand aloof as the Northern Expedition moved on and captured Wuhan. He did not appreciate Chu's attempts to educate politically his army. Secretly warned that the warlord was preparing to kill him and his political workers, Chu decided that his usefulness in this assignment was drawing to a close. Without pausing for the customary civilities of leave-taking, therefore, Chu and his men slipped away to Wuhan.

On Chu went to Nanchang in January 1927. He had been assigned by the Wuhan government to command an officer training regiment in that city. This was part of a Yunnanese army stationed in Nanchang. So again he was consorting with old friends from his warlord past. Chu was also chief of public security in the city. His two positions made him a crucial figure in the Communist plotting of the Nanchang uprising in August.

With the prompt collapse of the insurrection, Chu began his retreat southward to Kwangtung, fighting most of the way. He then milled about in the Hunan-Kwangtung border area between the stamping grounds of rival warlords. He and his bedraggled forces, the size of which fluctuated from several hundred to several thousand, engaged in guerrilla actions and in setting up transient little soviets. One of his unit commanders was Lin Piao. His political commissar was Ch'en Yi, who had been a student in France with Chou En-lai, was to emerge in the 1940s as a leading Communist general, and in the 1960s serve as foreign minister of the People's Republic.

Chu also acquired during his sojourn in Hunan his third wife, age twenty-five and a political organizer of peasants. "It was not," he later explained to Agnes Smedley, "a conventional marriage." For his second wife in Szechuan was still alive. The third wife was captured by the enemy in January 1929, tortured and beheaded, whereupon her head was sent to her native Changsha and exhibited on a pole.

By the end of 1929, he had married a husky teenager. She had been an illiterate field worker on a big farm and rose in revolt with poor farmers when Chu's troops came by. Some fifteen years later at Yenan, I had the pleasure of foxtrotting with her. By then Mme. Chu had acquired book learning and been graduated from the Red Army Military Academy.

Chu's second wife lived on until she, with his son by wife number one, were executed in 1935 by warlord soldiers. His casual bigamy may have been unconventional but it was not singular. When families were separated for long periods in times of trouble, it was not unusual for the husband to take a new wife in the locality where he found himself. Likewise, when a man considered that he had outgrown his wife, as both Mao and Chiang Kai-shek did, he married afresh, someone he estimated as being more appropriate to his improved status. The deserted wife was, of course, expected to remain virtuous and faithful.

During the ups and downs of 1927–1928 in the Hunan-Kwangtung border area Chu had the support of a figure out of his warlord past, a Yunnanese army commander. Such temporary alliances of convenience were typical of these turbulent times, especially in the border zones between entrenched military realms. As Mao aligned himself with two bands of brigands on Chingkangshan, Chu sought desperately needed strength through association with an amiable military entrepreneur. This arrangement did not last long. In May 1928, Chu withdrew under hostile pressure, and at the behest of the Central Committee in Shanghai, to Chingkangshan. The Chu-Mao collaboration then began.

As all power is relative, that of Chu-Mao's Real Power Faction originally amounted to something only because the competing Communist power of the so-called leadership in Shanghai was merely verbal and the hostile power of the government was, until late in 1930, not concentrated against the Communists in southern Kiangsi. In terms of troop strength the Chu-Mao force was, at lowest ebb, no more than two thousand men, plus some eight hundred under P'eng Te-huai. This was early in 1929 after the Communists had been starved out of the mountain stronghold of Chingkangshan by a creeping blockade. They escaped into the hills and valleys to the east.

In a matter of months the force began to grow, picking up recruits from poor peasants and government army deserters as it moved about the countryside establishing a sovietized base area. By the summer of 1930, when the Communists surged forth to attack Changsha, Wuhan, and Nanchang, the combined forces of Chu-Mao and P'eng totaled about twenty thousand. Grandiosely they were designated as the First and Third Army Corps.

Military designations in China were imprecisely applied and gave only a general idea of how many men there might be in a unit. A detachment of only one or two thousand men might be called a division because indeed it had once been rightly so designated but had lost heavily through combat and desertions, or because it was starting small and its commander was thinking big. At the rare other extreme was the designation that understated troop strength. The illiterate Ho Lung at one time commanded what he took mischievous pride in calling a regiment. When asked how a force of thirty thousand men could be described as a regiment, Ho would reply with the chortling relish of a successful practical joker, "I can't count."

The upsurges against the cities in July 1930 drew Chiang Kai-shek's attention to the Communists in Kiangsi. He had weathered the attacks of his far more considerable adversaries, the Christian General, the Model Governor, and the "Young Marshal," Chang Hsueh-liang of Manchuria. He had been able to do so because they double-crossed one another. Late in 1930 he turned to the annoyance created by the Communist forces in Kiangsi. In December he launched the first of a series of Bandit Suppression Campaigns. One of his favorite generals, Ho Ying-ch'in, was placed in command of twelve divisions deployed to mop up the so-called brigands.

Ho, who looked like a noncommittal seraph in a Sam Browne belt, was well known to the Communists from the cozy 1926 period in Canton. Chou En-lai had been his political commissar. In the 1940s, Ho was to become the Nationalists' minister of war and one of Chiang's disastrous strategists in the Civil War. This bout with Chu-Mao was but one phase of Ho's long history of interplay with the Communists.

Nanking expected that Ho would clean out the Communists in short order. To the contrary, in about one month the foxy Chu-Mao combination forced the government troops to withdraw with the loss of more than two brigades and quantities of weapons of critical value to the lightly armed Communists. This was a reversal of the situation only five months earlier when the Red Army was routed in its attack on the cities.

The contending forces were essentially the same in July and December— poor quality government troops in larger numbers and with superior arms against determined Communist troops with inferior arms. So why was the outcome different? In July the Red Army had assumed the offensive in something close to positional warfare, trying to take and hold specific, constricted locations. It had neither the weight nor firepower to do so. In December, on its own broken terrain, it fought a guerrilla war of constant maneuver, uncommitted to holding any given position, determined only to confound, disrupt, and dislodge the enemy. At this the Communist forces were skilled and successful.

With forty thousand Communist troops against a hundred thousand government soldiers, the decisive factor in December was the human element. Communist generalship in strategy and tactics was decisively superior. The Communist command had also imbued its troops with *élan* and discipline so that they outfought Ho's slipshod levies. Finally, Mao had sufficiently mobilized at least the poor peasants and so indoctrinated the Red Army in fraternal relations with the common folk that the Communist troops received intelligence, transport, and supply support which the population denied Ho's invading divisions.

As Chu-Mao were disposing of external enemies, they were confronted with a revolt by a Communist unit which, weirdly enough, professed to follow the line of the recently deposed Li Li-san and accused Mao of fighting for Russia. Mao was thorough-going in his suppression of this dissent. More than two thousand of the objectors were killed. Mao's secret police played an important role in this purge. They were to continue as a vital instrument of authority when persuasion or command proved ineffective.

In Shanghai the Communist secret police apparatus had been organized by Chou En-lai late in 1930, upon his return from the Soviet Union. He had received Soviet assistance in this enterprise. The Chinese *cheka* in the cities was vital to the physical survival of the top Communists, stalked by Kuomintang agents.

It also served as a disciplinary agency. In January 1931, when the Twenty-Eight Bolsheviks consolidated their control, a small faction of the Party attempted to secede. Its forty-nine members were immediately betrayed to the Kuomintang, which, by executing the dissenters, conveniently relieved the Communist secret police of the burden of liquidating unruly comrades.

Irked by defeat in the first Bandit Suppression Campaign, Chiang followed up in February 1931 with a second, doubling his force to two hundred thousand against a Red Army reduced to thirty thousand. Again Communist generalship outsmarted the Nationalists, luring government columns into vulnerable positions, attacking, breaking off before enemy reinforcements could lumber into action, then suddenly attacking on another sector, again disappearing to repeat a baffling guerrilla pattern. After four months of this and loss of some twenty thousand rifles, the government armies gave up and left.

Chiang himself took command of the third campaign in July, committing three hundred thousand men to the operation, of which a hundred thousand were his own troops under his best generals. Once more the lurking Red Army traded fixed positions and time for the exposed flank, the unguarded rear, and the opportune moment to strike. The third campaign, however, was rougher going because of the size and better quality of the invading force.

The Communists nevertheless crippled two government divisions, but suffered heavy losses themselves. The offensive died out in September 1931 when the regime in South China made moves to march against the national government and, more significantly, Japan began its invasion of Manchuria. This was the first of many Japanese actions damaging to Chiang and indirectly helpful to the Communists.

During the third campaign top figures in the Central Committee at Shanghai began a gradual migration to Kiangsi. Chou En-lai was one of the first to gravitate to where the makings of Communist power were. Such was the prestige of the Party leadership that these gentlemen from the big city began to take over the direction of affairs in Communist Kiangsi. Chou led off with criticism of Mao's military strategy—"guerrillaism," he and Po Ku called it. The Red Army had outgrown such a hit-and-run strategy, they insisted. It should mount frontal attacks and besiege cities.

In November 1931 the Communists convoked an All-China Soviet Congress. It created the Chinese Soviet Republic. Mao was elected chairman of the Council of People's Commissars, a governmental position subordinate to the Party. Chu Teh became People's Commissar for War and commander of the Red Army.

Mao's influence continued to be eroded on into 1932. The Comintern in September discerned yet another crisis in capitalism and prophesied yet another revolutionary upsurge. The duty of the CCP was to mobilize the masses against the Japanese (whose occupation of Manchuria was disconcerting to Moscow), unite the Kiangsi Soviet area with Communist-held patches elsewhere in China, and overthrow Chiang's Kuomintang government. This suited the newcomers from Shanghai and their "forward and offensive line."

They had a chance to test their strategy when late in 1932 Chiang hurled a fourth offensive of two hundred and fifty thousand men into Kiangsi. Strengthened with new recruits, Nationalist defectors from previous campaigns, and a goodly supply of captured arms and ammunition, the Red Army joined battle on the outer limits of the Communist area instead of luring the enemy deep into soviet territory. This strategy worked. The Nationalists lost what amounted to about three divisions. In the spring of 1933 they withdrew. And Chou En-lai was designated Political Commissar of the Red Army.

Notwithstanding steady Japanese encroachment from Manchuria into North China, Chiang prepared to go after the Communists yet again. For him, the internal enemy had priority over the foreign aggressor. His own generals having been proved incapable of subduing the scrawny but tough Communists, Chiang turned for strategic guidance to the German military advisers he had hired to better his army. General Hans von Seeckt developed a new strategy for subduing the Communists. This was put into effect in the fifth campaign, beginning October 1933.

Against the Red Army, grown to a hundred and fifty thousand, the Nationalists deployed seven hundred thousand, bolstered by ample artillery and air support. The government armies undertook to strangle the Communists with a slowly tightening blockade, fortifying the closing ring as they pressed inward on the Red Army. Food and other supplies in the soviet area shrank painfully. The steadily constricting blockade, with no exposed flanks, gradually reduced the Red Army's field for maneuver and opportunities for surprise attacks. Valiantly and foolishly the Communists essayed the "forward and offensive" strategy of the young theoreticians from Shanghai, but with disastrous results. The superiority of Nationalist numbers and firepower was crushing.

It was evident in the summer of 1934 that the Communists could not hold out. They debated how to break out of the encirclement and where to go. In October, one year after the beginning of the campaign, some hundred thousand Communists—soldiers, political cadres, and skilled workers—breached a weak point in the government blockade and began the epic Long March, which was to end six thousand miles and a year later in Shensi, in the loess country of Northwest China.

Both Edgar Snow and Agnes Smedley have recounted in detail the story of the Long March as told to them by its veterans. I have nothing to add to their sagas. I would say, however, that the descriptions of hardships undergone by the Communists on this expedition seem believable.

The westernmost circuit of the vast loop made by the Long March passed through Yunnan and Szechuan. Snow and Smedley recount the drama of the Red Army's passage through this craggy wilderness, the highlight of which was its battle in crossing the Tatu River. My father journeyed thrice into the same area. Going and coming, he crossed the Tatu five times, uncontested, and once the River of Golden Sand, before it becomes the Yangtze, likewise without a shot being fired at him.

But then, his mission was meeker than that of the Red Army. His was to minister to the considerable spiritual needs of backsliding Baptist converts in Ningyuan, later called Sichang, midway between the Tatu and the River of Golden Sand. His first two journeys, before 1920, were round trips from Chengtu by sedan chair and walking, about two weeks each way. The third, in the mid-1920s, began in Kunming, the capital of Yunnan, and in travel time to Kiating aggregated nearly a month.

More concerned with trials of the spirit than with those of the flesh, my father accepted the physical hardships of these expeditions with equanimity. "Wasn't it hard-going over all of those mountains?" I have since asked him. "Oh yes, there were two high ranges to cross, but most of the way was through valleys." "How about the fierce Lolo tribesmen who Snow said caused the Communists such anxiety?" "They stopped me to inspect my luggage," he said, "then let me go on my way without demanding anything. Once I saw them in the distance gathered together and armed with spears, bows, and arrows. What I don't understand," he went on, "is how an army could go through that area and find enough to eat. Long stretches of the route were uninhabited."

Two events of political importance occurred on the Long March. One was the Tsunyi Conference of January 1935 in which the Politburo removed Po Ku from leadership and chose Mao to guide the Party. Po Ku, who knew more about dodging through city streets than mass flight through unknown mountains, encumbered the Communist retreat with such treasures as a uniform factory and printing presses. For Mao, who had been humiliated and stripped of nearly all power by the "returned students," this was vindication. But it did not mean that he dominated the Chinese Communist movement.

This became evident in the mountains west of Chengtu in July 1935, when he and his footsore horde, thinned by desertions, sickness and battle casualties to about forty-five thousand, joined with the Fourth Front Red Army of some five thousand. The Fourth was controlled by Chang Kuo-t'ao, a founding member of the Party and a rival of Mao's. While Mao was in Kiangsi, Chang had occupied a small enclave north of the Yangtze. When his position had become untenable, he moved to the westernmost parts of Szechuan. There he had replaced his manpower losses with Szechuanese recruits. For even in this scarcely peopled borderland there were young men eager to join the revolution—or simply to get away from the peasant's bleak existence.

The second event of political significance on the Long March was a break between Mao and Chang—and, strangely enough, Chu Teh. Mao was determined that the combined forces should go on northeastward to a small base area already established by a Communist detachment in Shensi. There the Party would be in a position to play a part on the national scene, arousing popular support on the issue of resisting Japanese aggression. Chang insisted on moving still further westward, if necessary into Tibet.

Mao went his way. Chang sidled westward. Chu and another Szechuanese general remained with Chang. Later, Chu claimed that he had been, in effect, kidnapped by Chang. The Chang and Chu byplay gave Mao no reason for trust in the loyalty of his comrades.

Was this military extravaganza, the Long March, necessary? Yes, because by the latter half of Chiang's fifth campaign the alternative was extermination. The government's resources were so much greater than the Communists' and the imported von Seeckt strategy so effective that the odds against the Red Army became overwhelming.

For their part, the Communists contributed generously to their own defeat. The conventional strategy imposed by Po Ku, Chou En-lai, and the Comintern's gratuitous military adviser, Otto Braun, was suicidal. Braun, who cloaked his schoolmaster and Bolshevik operative past with the alias of Li T'e, was no match for his fellow countryman, von Seeckt. Yet Chu-Mao went along with the hobbling attempt at positional warfare against vastly superior firepower.

Politically, too, the Communists bungled. At the outset of the fifth campaign they had made an alliance of sorts with a revolutionary regime in the adjacent province of Fukien. The pact was directed against Chiang and the Japanese. But when the Fukien rebels, with a competent army, revolted against the government, the Communists did not join forces with their allies. They held back because they decided that they should not make common cause with a "third way" between the Kuomintang and themselves. This dogmatism enabled Chiang to deal with the two regimes separately, first defeating that in Fukien and then turning full force on the Red Army.

Mao later acknowledged that both of these strategies, military and political, were mistaken. But he assumed no blame for the errors, probably rightly so. For during the fifth campaign his influence was at its lowest ebb.

CHAPTER *15*

From South of the Clouds to Peking and Beyond

ON NOVEMBER 19, 1931, the secretary of state, Henry L. Stimson, warned the Japanese ambassador that he considered the Japanese army's invasion of Manchuria to be a violation of the Kellogg Pact and the Nine-Power Treaty. On the same day, in somewhat lower key, the assistant secretary of state, Wilbur J. Carr, wrote to me saying that I had passed the Foreign Service entrance examinations and was eligible for appointment as a Foreign Service officer. This coincidence was, in a way, prophetic for me. For much of the next fourteen years of my life was involved in American objections to what the Japanese armed forces were up to.

My first post abroad was at Windsor, Ontario. This was across the river from Detroit, where I had been staying with my Aunt Flossie. My voyage to foreign parts, by ferryboat in January 1932, cost the United States Government ten cents. Or was it a nickel? Give or take five cents, my probationary year as a vice-consul was full of discovering immigration laws, notarial procedures, and the heady self-esteem of official position. I found that one of the perquisites of vice-consulhood was classification as eligible bachelor by the minor matrons of Grosse Pointe.

Then to Washington in the last days of the Republican dynasty and the first of Franklin Roosevelt. The banks were closed, but at least I had a job. At the Department of State about twenty of us, all novices, were lectured to for three months by a variety of practiced bureaucrats. Thus enlightened, we set out in all directions to protect and further American interests abroad. I was assigned to what was then called Yunnanfu and later known as Kunming, capital of Yunnan Province.

The route to Yunnanfu was through the port of Haiphong and by French railway from Hanoi to Yunnanfu. This was my introduction to the French empire in the Far East. Hanoi I found verdant, somnolent, even touched in spots with subdued elegance. It did not have Peking's grandeur, Shanghai's cosmopolitan surge, or Hong Kong's vertical panorama. Hanoi pleased rather than excited.

Up through jungled mountains the train climbed onto the plateau on which Yunnanfu sat, south of the clouds and beside a blue lake. The skies were high and clear, the air bracing, as befitting an altitude of six thousand feet, and the roads lined with eucalypti. In so splendid a setting, Yunnanfu was a peculiarly charmless city. And because the population was slugabed from opium smoking, the government had felt compelled to issue a decree ordering all shops and other places of business to open by nine in the morning.

Yunnan Province was regarded by the French as their sphere of influence. Their interest was strategic, for the province bordered on Indochina. It was also economic. But Yunnan was a poor mountain-locked area and the French exploitation of it was indolent. They found political advantage in maintaining a hospital, headed by a taciturn colonel of the French army medical corps, who treated high Yunnanese officials for disorders brought on by incontinence.

My chief was another bachelor vice-consul, one grade senior to me. There were only two of us and he derived satisfaction from being the senior official in charge of the consulate and me. As the province was under the firm control of its warlord governor, there was little political activity to be reported to Washington on which one might hope to establish a reputation as a keen diplomatic observer. Nor did commerce flourish between the United States and Yunnan. My only memorable effort at furthering American exports was a response to an inquiry from Brooklyn—was there a market for conch shells that whorl to the left? Indeed there was, in an almost inaccessible corner of the province. If I remember correctly, they were blown on religiously.

Bored by bureaucratic routine, I found myself looking forward to afternoons at Le Cercle Sportif Français. In white flannel trousers, Aertex shirt, with racquet tucked under arm, I punctiliously shook hands with everyone in sight— the manager of the Banque de l'Indochine, the wife of the postal commissioner, a lovely summer visitor escaping the heat and her husband in Saigon, a mysterious and natty Frenchman who always wore spats, even on picnics into the country. And so it went, maybe twenty times, "Bonjour, monsieur" or "Bonjour, madame."

Only after these salutations was it permissible to go to the courts for a smashing game of tennis. For mixed doubles I particularly enjoyed playing with Mme. Siguret, who also played the harp. Her plucked rendition of Debussy was the sole cultural event in Yunnanfu.

Beyond tennis there was riding. I bought a squat, irascible horse of the hardy variety bred in the mountains of West China. Thus mounted, I explored the fields, hills, and groves beyond the city. On one such excursion I was accompanied by an impatient French lady. We dallied in a copse, only to be overrun in the charge of a popeyed platoon of Chinese cavalry, which had hurtled over the crest of a nearby hill on maneuvers.

After three inconsequential months in Yunnanfu, I was transferred to the legation at Peking as attaché for language study. As I left in September, Chiang Kai-shek and his German advisers were readying the fifth and final campaign against the Communists in Kiangsi. Under the impact of the government's offensive the Communists would a year later begin their Long March and pass close to Yunnanfu as they swung northward to cross the River of Golden Sand. I have often wondered whether the approach of the Red horde toward Yunnanfu ever ruffled the soirées with Mme. Siguret and Debussy.

The Peking to which I arrived in September 1933 was in the last years of its ancient glory. It was, to be sure, no longer the capital. An awkward Nanking was. But Peking still had its imperial mien, an immense dignity, and self-assured grace.

Peking was in the last years of its ancient glory because the Japanese army, after conquering the three provinces of the Northeast, had advanced westward to occupy Jehol Province. An obviously predatory power was now directly to the north, looking impatiently over the Great Wall at the irresolute defenses of the dowager capital. In less than four years alien occupation would clank down on Peking.

No air of impending doom hung over the city in the crisp, bright autumn of 1933. Yet the Japanese were close and pressing. It was conceivable that they would increase their penetration of North China and take it over. But life was so mellow and satisfying that it was difficult to focus on disagreeable eventualities in the future.

The massive walls within walls of the city, the moats with pink and white lotus, the red pillars, yellow tiles, and marble steps of serried palaces, the profusion of temples, chrysanthemumed parks, and hyacinthed ponds, all arranged in spacious symmetry, enchanted the eye's mind. Life was at an unhurried pace so that one might relish these noble vistas—and eat well and lingeringly in a variety of restaurants—and converse, or gossip, at leisure until there was nothing more to be said until the next encounter.

Backed up against the huge wall separating Peking's Tartar City from its Chinese City was the Legation Quarter, in which were spread the diplomatic missions. This enclave, with memories of the Boxer siege of 1900, had its own walls. And the American legation, like the British, French, Japanese, and Italian missions, maintained military guards. In the American case, it was a detachment of five hundred marines.

I was assigned living quarters in what was called the Students' Mess. There three of us studying Chinese occupied bachelor apartments and shared a common dining room. The Mess was part of a temple remodeled on the interior to satisfy American requirements for comfort. The external architecture remained as it originally was, low buildings around courtyards and, what I remember with particular pleasure, latticed windows covered with translucent paper.

There we lived and studied. Our instruction was given by tutors. They were gentlemen of the old school, literati edifying young barbarians. They had seen enough of westerners to realize that they would never make mandarins of us. But they seemed still to cling to a hope that they might at least moderate our native uncouthness.

With unflagging composure, the three tutors moved from one to another of us, instructing us individually in spoken Chinese, reading, and writing. The writing of Chinese ideographs is an exercise in memory and aesthetics. The brush was inked from a slab on which the tip of a stick of lampblack had been dissolved by rubbing in four or five drops of water. A little rubbing produced a thin mixture of watery gray ink. With more rubbing, a thicker, blacker mixture would be achieved. Having been dipped in this goo, the brush was then grasped vertically between thumb and first two fingers and the composition of the ideograph began. The word was painted as a miniature abstract work of art.

It was not enough that the character be correctly written, stroke for stroke, which was the test of memory. It must also be composed in harmony to please the eye, which was the test of aesthetics. Within the exacting limits of the structure of the ideograph there was scope for creative individuality. Calligraphy was the art form for the educated gentleman. It was the highest form of art, surpassing painting. For even an illiterate vulgarian could paint a landscape or a portrait. Only a scholar could portray thought in the elegant abstraction of calligraphy.

Like most foreigners who studied written Chinese, I did not even approach the level of a scholar. I never got beyond the stage of childish block printing. Nevertheless, I found exasperated pleasure in trying to emulate my tutor.

Presiding over the legation was the ruddy, roly-poly minister, with a fuzz of faded orange hair on the top of his head. Nelson T. Johnson came from Oklahoma and had been one of the early language students. He had no outstanding qualifications for his position beyond an easy conviviality with visiting members of Congress. For these and other distinguished American travelers he had a stock of anecdotes meant to reveal the true nature of otherwise inscrutable orientals.

Notwithstanding his hearty informality, there was one conceit on which Johnson insisted. Upon his return from any journey of more than a day, he expected and got a ceremonial welcome at the railroad station from all of his diplomatic staff, the commandant, and senior officers of the marine detachment, with the marine band serenading him in brasses, drums and woodwinds. Travelers and hangers-on at the station were diverted by the spectacle of foreign devils bowing and scraping before an enviably fat one of their kind and then trooping off in his wake to reoccupy an abandoned legation.

During my first year as a language attaché, the counselor of the legation was Clarence E. Gauss. Earlier in his career, he had written the standard consular handbook on notarials. He was an intense man, shoulders humped forward from years of leaning over a desk, thin mouth turned down at the corners in near sneer, eyes a prismed blur as they peered out through thick lenses. When one first met him, the smile that grimaced his pallid face (I do not recall ever having seen him in the sun) was as disconcerting as his customary chill gaze.

Gauss was, of course, a man who longed for affection. He was not one of the diplomatic club either through birth and Ivy League or, inferiorly, through entrance by foreign service examinations in the American mandarin fashion. Nor had he been a language officer. He had been a consular clerk who by sheer efficiency had worked himself up through the ranks. He had none of the easy social graces and was incapable of the gassy banter on which Johnson had been wafted to high estate. All that he had to offer was bureaucratic excellence—and an analytical, skeptical mind.

This latter quality was enough to win him the respect of his subordinates. When genuine appreciation was accorded him, he relaxed his elaborate defenses sufficiently to reveal an inner warmth and gentleness of spirit. But for those who did not get to know him, Gauss remained a glacial figure, incorruptible and inexorable. Although I knew him only slightly, he had my admiration, which lasted even through my troubled relations with him when he was ambassador a decade later.

Several months before the end of my assignment to Peking, in the fall of 1935, a new military attaché arrived. He was a skinny little colonel by the name of Stilwell, Joseph W. I enjoyed his cheerfully sardonic attitude. And obviously he and his lively, closely-knit family relished being in Peking.

Stilwell had become a specialist in Chinese affairs. In the 1920s he had been an army language student. Then he had a tour of duty as a major with the Fifteenth Infantry, a regiment stationed at Tientsin to ensure that the legation would not again be cut off from the outside world, as it had been during the Boxer Uprising. Clearly, Stilwell was already an Old China Hand.

In addition to Stilwell, there were in the fall of 1935 two other army officers with whom I was later to be closely associated. Like me, they were on assignment for language study. One was Captain Frank Dorn. The other was Captain Frank Roberts.

At the age of thirty-four Dorn was still known by his cadet nickname of Pinky. He still looked like a big, blushing choirboy, a military handicap which he manfully overcame by being pithy and smarter than most of his contemporaries. Certainly he was more versatile than anyone I knew in Peking—author of a novel published in Britain, compiler during his duty in the Philippines of a pygmy Negrito-English dictionary, maker of illustrated maps, an expert chef, and already during his first year in Peking a discriminating collector of Chinese antiquities.

Unlike Pinky, Frank Roberts was not a bon vivant. Modest, thoughtful, and conscientious, he showed the qualities of the superior staff officer that he was to become. Both he and Pinky were made generals during World War II.

Of the score or so of army officers who studied Chinese from the late 1920s until the mid-1930s at Peking, at least a half dozen of them became generals. Two of them, Willard Wyman and Paul Freeman, rose to four-star rank and to command, not in the Far East, but of American troops in postwar Germany. Similarly, out of perhaps something like one hundred marine guard and marine language officers in the same period about twenty-five became general officers. Two of these, A. A. Vandegrift and David Shoup, rose to be commandants of the Marine Corps.

In the army as a whole, less than one percent of officers were promoted to the rank of brigadier general and above. The Peking record therefore stands out as remarkable, especially when the name of the military attaché is added to the list. For Stilwell won not only his four stars, but was also a theater commander during World War II, and later commander of all army ground forces.

The summit of military eminence was achieved by one who was not a member of the Peking group, but nevertheless close to it. He was a colonel, executive officer of the Fifteenth Infantry at Tientsin in the mid-1920s. His name was George C. Marshall.

Interestingly enough, no outstanding naval officers emerged from among those assigned to language duty at Peking, although the two naval attachés in the 1930s became admirals. Once a naval officer was identified with attaché or language functions, the tendency was to consider him as not in line for high command. He was usually limited to naval intelligence.

What accounted for the phenomenon of army and marine talent welling out of Peking? In the case of the army it was in part because an attaché or language detail did not commit an officer to military intelligence for the rest of his career. His channels to promotion were more open than for a naval officer. Much the same was true for marine language students. For marine guard officers, duty at Peking was at a garrison post, similar to other assignments with troops.

In these circumstances Peking was one of the most desirable assignments in both services, particularly to those of an imaginative, adventurous nature. To be in Peking or Tientsin was to be on the mainland of Asia, on the edge of the Chinese-Japanese-Soviet arena. On the assumption that the United States might well become involved in a Far Eastern war, this was the best available place to learn about potential friends and foes.

Creature comfort was a part of the Peking lure. In those terms it exerted more pull than Fort Sam Houston or Parris Island. Living was cheap, including whiskey. Even a lieutenant could, on his pay, afford the luxury of servants. In the case of married officers, madame could consign the children to an amah while she played bridge or sipped tea with the ladies of the diplomatic corps as she watched chukkar after chukkar of polo on the French glacis outside the east wall of the Legation Quarter.

This was a pretty fancy life, relatively speaking. Naturally, it acquired an added sheen once one was back at Quantico. There the captain's lady, surrounded by bits of soapstone masquerading as jade, cushions covered with post-imperial tribute silk and other mementos of a sojourn in the ancient capital, stimulated other service wives to goad their husbands into inveigling assignments to Peking.

Colonel Marshall's attitude toward China as a result of his tour of duty with the Fifteenth Infantry was not untypical of that of other officers. It would be going too far to say that he was captivated by China. But he had obviously enjoyed his stay in North China and was taken by the country and the people. His interest persisted for two decades, culminating in disillusion.

How much Major Stilwell, who served as his subordinate during the latter part of his assignment to the Fifteenth Infantry, then affected Marshall's attitude toward China is a matter of speculation. What is clear, however, is that Stilwell was an earnest observer of what was going on in China and that Marshall then developed a high regard for Stilwell. This was the beginning of a warm friendship between the two men and Marshall's considerable reliance on Stilwell's interpretation of Chinese affairs.

Peking, of course, was not China any more than Washington is the United States; Paris, France; or London, Britain. The language officers were therefore expected to take two or three trips into the provinces during their two years' assignment. I went on three such excursions in search of the "real" China.

One was southwestward into Honan and Shensi Provinces. These were some of my impressions, recorded upon my return to Peking. "This trip was through China's loess highlands. The topography was a series of geometric blocks and planes, resulting from the vertical cleavage characteristic of loess soil. Streams and roads cut deep; it was not unusual to see a road worn thirty feet below its curbs. The people of this area make good use of the loess in digging out caves for homes. The farmer's fields are often overhead, he living in the face of a small cliff, his cotton or wheat growing on the plateau up above. Evidently the rooms which can be hollowed out in this loess soil are extensive, for I saw at least one barracks and a score of warehouses along the railroad built in the faces of cliffs. The dusty tan complexion of the loess soil give the countryside a dry and rather parched look.

"This journey had a dual aspect; it was into the country of earliest recorded Chinese civilization and at the same time modern China's wild west. The latter is now the more evident. Few historic remains are in evidence. One is more conscious that here begins the Chinese frontier, which runs on out into Turkestan. The railway from the sea coast will be into Sian by the end of the year, new roads are being built out to the northwest, farmers' cooperatives are being formed, American-trained experts are improving the cotton (chief legitimate crop). Sian during the T'ang dynasty (618–907 A.D.) was the greatest and most highly cultured city in the world. . . . Here were China's greatest poets, her painting was during the T'ang at one of its most highly developed stages, the empire extended into Central Asia, the court was bright and lavish, it was China's golden age. Sian is now a large rambling city, much of the area within the massive walls being vacant land. It has most of the contrasts of the present-day Chinese city: trucks and mule carts, old craft shops open to the street and modern bookstores, the old-fashioned women with bound feet and school girls in uniforms.

"A trip of this nature, into conservative, pretty much unchanged China is not comfortable traveling after western standards. I planned to live off the country. However, I did give in to the extent of taking my own sleeping bag (inn bedding being vermin-infested), a dozen bars of chocolate, and some swiss cheese, all rolled up with my change of underwear and socks and shirt and disinfectant soap. The places at which I spent the night ranged from a village inn patronized by coolies and redolent with opium to the smartest hotel in Sian, a bare sort of hostelry with small gloomy rooms and also smelling of opium. The food, excepting in the two large cities of Loyang and Sian, was not only plain but bad in quality. Even the boiled water which I used for brushing my teeth in one place formed a scum of cabbage-mutton soup grease when I permitted it to stand and cool. . . .

"On the way west I struck up an acquaintanceship with a young Chinese from Shanghai for whom this journey was his first contact with the interior of his country. The straitened lives being lived before us were a shock to him; the first town we came to without electric lights provoked his apologies to me for the condition of his country. All of this I found rather interesting; here was I, a foreigner, more familiar with his own country than himself. He, like most young Chinese of the educated class, was ashamed of what I considered the quaint vestiges of China's yesterday, things which I regarded as charming and harmonious. A simple example comes to my mind. We were breakfasting on the second floor of a grimy old eating house at the railhead. On a balcony under the eaves hung strings of sausages drying. In the early morning light and with the railing and shop sign as a background they made a pleasant composition. I therefore proceeded to take a picture of the scene. Mr. Kiang was indignant. He exclaimed, 'This is a rotten aspect of Chinese life; why don't you take pictures of scenery, mountains, and water?' The waiter pridefully suggested a newly opened notions store across the street, gaudy with Shanghai dry goods, kerosene tins, and perfumed soap. I then tried with some difficulty to explain the philosophy of Alice Foote McDougall, that we Americans like anything that is quaint and old and if we can't get genuine old curiosities we fake them.

"The highly developed social sense of the Chinese was reimpressed upon me, the sense which has developed the idea that to be alone is melancholia, to be with others is to enjoy high spirits. The result upon behavior is that contacts are on a plane of exchanged courtesies. Even the young emancipated students responded to the old polite phrases when I initiated the conversation with them. The same was true of the railway people. The vast bulk of the population, however, still observes the ancient forms of politesse, habitually and without prompting; as witness ricksha coolies asking me to share their bowls of noodles with them (knowing, of course, that I should refuse), the reference to 'your honorable country' and 'my inferior country,' the invariably smiling and animated expression of face during the course of conversation, and one old Taoist abbot who rose slightly from his chair each time during our conversation that I spoke. My experience during the fifteen days of traveling was that even the surliest looking characters responded with surprising amiability to acquaintanceships opened in the conventionally courteous fashion.

"I was surprised on this journey to observe the extent to which attempts are being made in the direction of regimenting the youth. Even in villages one saw children in school uniform. Like soldiers they have small identification tags sewed on their uniform, name, school, etc. They marched like soldiers, used the same unison counting while marching.

"In Honan on a dusty road I passed a stern looking matron dressed in padded blue silks and riding a grey mule. Following her on another mule was a bride, all in various shades of pink satin and on a red saddle blanket, with her face modestly turned down. Behind were no more than two peasant men in blue cotton. Here was a typical bound-foot, illiterate, shy little peasant girl on her way to be married.

As I reached the top of Hua Shan, I entered the temple where I intended to spend the night. Within the courtyard I was confronted with a row of what were evidently university girls leaning over the upstairs verandah railing. I was astonished to see them there, because, in the first place, even now the average Chinese woman student does little more than shuttle between her home and her school, and this was decidedly an out-of-the-way place. And in the second place, the ascent of Hua Shan is steep, difficult, and not without danger.

"A priest showed me to a room on a facing balcony. I took off an accumulation of sweaters and was down to a slight wool tennis shirt, preparatory to washing up after my day's hike, when several girls appeared at the doorway. That I was an object of curiosity to college girls amused me, so I engaged them in light conversation. The numbers swelled until there must have been seven or eight girls and three or four men standing in the doorway watching me wash the soap out of my ears and telling me that they were from Central University in Nanking and were spending a week on the mountain sketching. They all had sketch books. When I started to shave, the girls left in giggling embarrassment. Subsequently, I talked with many of the students, one young lady even informing me that she would be coming to Peiping in about a month. She seemed very pleased when I asked her to inform me of her arrival so that I might take her to a show or a dance.

"This, to Chinese eyes, 'ripe' friendship developed in the course of about two hours before the eyes of the country youth who had packed my bedding roll up the mountain. The next morning as we were descending to the plain he said to me, 'Had you known these ladies before yesterday?' Upon my reply in the negative, he asked incredulously, 'But how could they then speak to you?' I explained that it's the modern way. He changed the subject.

"In a dinky railway station while waiting for my derailed train to get back on the track, the time was passed for me by the spectacle of the town sport calling up some pal on the station phone and saying 'Guess who's calling?' The subsequent stream of punk wisecracks and obscenity, with translation, would pass as having come from Podunk. His younger satellite took over the phone and the familiarity of his wobbly adolescent wit, as raucous as it was fundamentally bashful, left me astounded.

"New slogans have replaced many of the classical proverbs and exhortations on city walls, on scrolls in rooms, everywhere. Typical of their effect was the admonishment appearing in the gent's washroom of the best hotel in Loyang: 'Guard Health!' The washroom was one half latrine and, literally, one half pig sty, inhabited by a sow and a number of very bold rats. The flair for platitudes, nay, the genius, is probably a concomitant of a highly developed social sense."

As a postscript to this tale of travels, the young lady on the mountain top who said she would be coming to Peking, came. She took my invitation seriously and dropped in for tea. Proving that one can never know whence will come a bauble of political intelligence, she confided that she recently had been seduced by Sun Fo, the stuffy forty-three year old son of Sun Yat-sen and president of the legislature, and that he was a stingy man.

Another journey was westward into hilly Shansi Province. "Taiyuanfu, the capital of Shansi, is a modest-sized city at that awkward age—undergoing the reversed adolescence characteristic of current China, the mature going gangling. The other cities, towns, and villages of the province still bore strongly the marks of old China. Particularly Wutaihsien, a county seat. It is isolated in the hills, removed from all modern forms of transportation, and the natural conservatism of the Shansi people combined to preserve the town pretty much as it was one or two hundred years ago. It sat on the top of a small flat hill in the midst of a mile square plain. A stream flowed at the foot of the hill and mountains or loess bluffs surrounded the level area. Poplar groves were beside the stream. One entered the city by ascending a great ramp of Cecil B. De Mille proportions. The gates and walls were miniature and in good condition. The flagstoned streets, casual as to the direction they took, unexpectedly bore memorial arches. It was all very placid and something like the scenes on old blue and white willow china.

"It was the first time I had ridden in a mule litter. I did it to get from the end of the bus line to the sacred mountain, Wutaishan, and back again to the bus line. Other means of transportation, excepting for hiring individual mules, were out of the question. I was with the muleteer, his sport model, and two mules for five days. He was a hillbilly and spoke a dialect which for sentences would be unintelligible. Being cleverer than I, he seemed to understand what I said, usually. The litter is nothing more than a mat-covered stretcher carried between the backs of the two mules, one fore and one aft. On the stretcher one spreads one's bedding roll; miscellaneous articles are chucked in on the blankets and one climbs in with them, to sit up or stretch out. The animals follow incredibly rocky or steep or narrow trails without falling. I walked more than I rode, to the astonishment of the muleteer. He soon adjusted himself to my idiosyncrasy to the extent of climbing up for a ride while I was walking. This puzzled exceedingly the country people who were in something of a quandary as to which was master and which servant. The muleteer engaged the lead animal in constant monologue. 'Lilly, lilly,' meant 'to the left, if you please,' and 'K'o, k'o,' in the other direction. 'Brrr' brought the animal to a dead stop. Only once did the mules run away, and I happened to be aboard. They went lurching off across a mountain stream, leaving their master standing on the rocky banks pleading and cursing. Most of his discourse with the beasts was in the nature of imprecations, of so base a character that I was unable to understand what he was saying. The only phrase I could get was when, after telling the animal to go 'lilly, lilly,' the front mule would lead off 'k'o, k'o.' He would then scream Ha, you don't believe me, eh!,' followed by a low rumble of profanity.

"I arrived at Wutaishan, the sacred mountain, on a festival day. The small village in the valley was teeming with pilgrims and mountain folk. On the way to the temple where I planned to stay, I had to pass through the brief length of the village, its bazaars, and through the crowd in front of the open air theater. A play was on. The actors were a troupe of hill people, putting on a very creditable show despite their lack of fine manners and costumes. Their harsh features were a comic contrast to the refined decadence of Peking actors. The music, an integral part of the Chinese theater, came from stringed instruments, not unlike violins but with very heavy bows, from a bamboo flute, from drums, gourds, and clappers—no cymbals. There was a strong, even rhythm. The melody was more pronounced than in the Peking theater. The audience stood and sat in the open space and street in front of the theater. I noticed on the trip that many of the country stages face directly on main roads, thus pretty much assuring something of an audience.

"Wutaishan is one of the great pilgrim centers for the Mongols. There were hundreds of these nomad people sojourning in the various temples. The men I thought far handsomer than the women. The women seem to age rapidly; by the time they are forty they are creased and seamed crones. Both the men and the women are a distinct contrast to the Chinese in character and manner. They are direct and outspoken. They stride with a rolling gait, rather than stroll sedately. Their religious attitude verges on fanaticism. I have never before seen the rituals of religion observed with such sustained ardor. From early morning until dark the prayer wheels were turned by worshipers. There were praying boards before which the supplicant stood, raised pressed hands, and upon which he extended himself, not once, but repeatedly for hours on end.

"The buses on which I traveled were appalling contraptions, spry old American chassis with Chinese bodies, seats being long boards on each side, running the length of the truck. These vehicles were driven with a sort of brave young abandon over frightful roads, the whole hurtling mass aquiver from stem to stern. The Chinese passengers, wise to the ways of travel, lapsed into fitful slumber. Only I, with full Anglo-Saxon purposefulness, remained fully conscious and, with my head up and eyes open, desperately uncomfortable. I made some curious and worthwhile friendships on the bus trips. Especially an obese lady who suffered visibly from the presence of fresh air in the bus. Her discomfort being so evidently poignant that, for the sake of my peace of mind (her husband was quite unmoved by her contorted efforts to wrap up all of her head in two handkerchiefs) I lent her a large, woolly, air-proof scarf. Her husband was very grateful, she apparently not."

Three years later Shansi was invaded by the Japanese and Wutaishan became an important forward base for the Chinese Communist forces. As for my muleteer friend, if he was not killed by the Japanese, who knows, he and his cussed mules may have ended up in a Communist munitions train.

My last excursion was a brief one in July 1935. It was through a zone immediately north of Peking which the Japanese, in their encroachment southward, had persuaded the Chinese to demilitarize, and thence into Jehol Province, which the Japanese had made a part of their puppet state of Manchukuo. We were to have been a party of five. But one of our legation secretaries and Dr. Osvald Siren, the Swedish sinologist and art historian, dropped out. That left Cecil Lyon, third secretary at the legation, and Mrs. Cabot Coville, then wife of a Tokyo embassy secretary, and me. Mrs. Coville, who was visiting Peking, joined our safari with the highest credentials, daughter of Gilbert Grosvenor, then editor of the *National Geographic*. "Shortly after dawn the three of us climbed into a gravel truck full of Japanese wrestlers and skidded out of Peking. Fortunate for us was Mrs. Coville's fluent Japanese. Even the three burliest of the wrestlers, whose visages were certainly no later than Cro-Magnon, lapsed into amiability. They offered us hard-boiled eggs, we proffered a Hershey bar or two. By noon we had wallowed through the worst of the mud and were at the town of Miyun, in the demilitarized zone bordering 'Manchukuo.' We had a little cheese, crackers, gimlets, and chocolate and pushed on.

"Our eight traveling companions had also dined and in the process had become florid with *paikar* [a searing liquor made from sorghum]. The situation seemed to me full of possibilities. I learned later that Cecil felt the same way. Our position was particularly hamstrung since we were jouncing along on the floor of the truck with the gladiators around the sides of the vehicle, thoroughly surrounding us. Happily, the inebriation seemed to express itself in nothing more ominous than animated conversation with Mrs. Coville (who carried off the situation as if she were on the lawn at the embassy entertaining guests at tea; a masterly performance), insisting that I drink a bowl of *paikar* with them (after the first courtesy sip, I managed to have the rest sloshed out inconspicuously), singing songs which fortunately Cecil and I didn't understand, falling into drunken slumber, and wrestling languidly on top of gasoline cans. The backdrop for all of this drama, as well as scenes preceding and following it, was the lurching, swerving, heaving, and bounding of the truck as it passed over the now mud, now sand, now rocky road.

"By middle afternoon we had started to climb, and at six we reached Kupeikou, a pass in the Great Wall where some two years ago there was fierce fighting between the Chinese and Japanese. There our passports were examined and we entered 'Manchukuo.' There, too, our wrestlers left us. That night they were to perform for the Japanese troops stationed at the pass.

"Until about midnight we were flung about with mail and gasoline tins, crossing three ranges. Twice we broke down—no headlights. Fortunately I had a flashlight, which the driver used in mending the fault. Thereby we lost over an hour of traveling time. Then we arrived in Jehol city (Ch'eng Teh). We spent an hour trying to get into Japanese inns, all full or else bawdy. So we drove out to the Catholic Mission where the old Belgian father was expecting us but which we hadn't dared intrude upon because of the lateness of the hour. The servants let us in and we were awakened, after four hours of mosquitoed slumber, by five o'clock mass. The father was a winning old character of sixty-five with a great beard, an active mind, gracious manners, and a sense of humor. His fare was barely edible, but he away and above compensated for that with his hospitality.

"That day we ventured outside of the city to a series of temples and lama-series, in one of which was the famous Golden Pavilion of which Sven Hedin had an exact replica made and erected at the Chicago Century of Progress Fair. It was an attractive little number, but in my mind quite inferior to the magnificent temples at Tat'ung, and even some here in Peking. We sat on the terrace of one of the temples with the Lion Valley before us, the Tibetanish Potala with its coral walls to the west of us, and a range of betempled mountains to the east.

"Jehol city is full of Japanese. The Chinese are distinctly in the background. There are numerous little Japanese shops and cafes, shoddy imitations of the Ginza establishments. It is, otherwise, an uninteresting city.

"The next morning we went to the Peking bus line where we were told that the bus would definitely not leave that day but would leave the next morning, *if* it rained no more. While we were haggling with the bus people, in walked a young American in kimono and Japanese clogs. We were surprised to meet this other foreigner in so remote a place as Jehol. It developed that he too was trying to get to Peking and that there were three other young Americans who were with him and wanted to do the same and that they were all from Harvard, having just graduated or doing graduate work in the Law School (Cushing, Richardson, Benson, and Wood). They had come in from Manchuria by commercial plane, spoke not a word of either Chinese or Japanese, and didn't have enough cash to get out of the place (no one would take travelers' checks, not even the banks). Mrs. Coville did their Japanese translating for them and I their Chinese. The gendarmerie was exceedingly suspicious of them, evidently regarding them as spies. The little officer doing the questioning finally led up to his catch question, which, when translated by Mrs. Coville, was 'Ask the young gentlemen if they know anything about the recent trouble between Japan and China. . . .'

"The Harvard contingent decided to join us. So seven of us, four Chinese passengers, a mechanic, a Japanese bus official, and a Chinese chauffeur rode out of Jehol to the first washout, about half a mile from the city. That was filled in by Japanese army engineers who arrived opportunely. All afternoon we kept getting out of the Ford truck to push rocks out of the road, fill in crevasses, extricate the wheels from sand in rivers. One river baffled us. The car was so deep that the exhaust was puttputting under water and the springs drowned. To get out of that hole, the Japanese and the driver ordered nearby villagers to spirit us out. That took an hour. Several of the mountain ascents and descents had evidently been that same morning raging torrents, leaving behind a gutted and strewn road. At times it seemed as if the truck would lurch over into the ravine below.

"About ten o'clock at night we stuck in the sand of a river. It began to drizzle. We stretched a sleeping bag out for Mrs. Coville on the muddy bank and worked an hour on the truck. We nearly had it out and then it again went in above the hubs. At that we retired to the bank and the chauffeur and the Japanese went off in search of villagers. We ate crackers, cheese, and jam under our one umbrella, the original three of us in raincoats, the Harvard men under the umbrella. The villagers began to arrive, stood in a circle about us, watching us eat by a flashlight, the only illumination. With some twenty villagers working on the car with large poles, the car was finally freed and on shore. It was a curiously dramatic sight, these country folk in great straw hats, standing in water up to their thighs, illuminated by one dim light, shouting as they heaved at the truck. That night we slept on the ground, the Harvard lads in the truck, since they had no bedding with them. . . . We arrived at Peking [the next] afternoon. . . ."

Like Paris and Florence of the same period, Peking in the 1930s attracted foreign artists, writers, and scholars. Among them was Lucile Swan, a sculptress from Chicago, by way of the South Pacific. She had left her husband on one of the French islands and was living in a typical Peking fashion in a small house around a small courtyard behind a big red gate. Lucile was fine-featured, amply bosomed and hipped, perhaps in her mid-thirties and beloved by all who knew her. For she glowed with warmth and honest sentiment.

On the several occasions that I went to tea at Lucile's house, there was present a Jesuit priest. I had known of him during my Yenching days. He was the eminent paleontologist who at that time had participated in identifying the fossil skull of *sinanthropus pekinensis,* the so-called Peking Man. His name was Teilhard de Chardin.

Père Teilhard was a lean, patrician priest. Not the patrician of Roman marble or glazed porcelain. Rather, the jagged visaged aristocrat, rough cast in bronze. Which is what Lucile was doing.

We sat in her living room and talked, not of theology and not much of fossils or sculpture. We talked mostly of what are regarded as unimportant things and were quite content with that. With these two, it is not precisely what they said so long ago that is fixed in the memory. What I sharply remember, really as a spectator, was the unspoken communication. Shining from her face was Lucile's wordless affirmation that, withal (for there were lines of sadness by eyes and mouth), life was sweet and its delights were to be shared with friends to be cherished.

Père Teilhard's face, a noble construction of rugged angles and furrows and a sensitive mouth, illumined what he said. And when he was silent it still uttered his moods, slowly sometimes, more often in flashes. He did not withdraw from those about him. He radiated outward to them gravely, merrily, inquiringly. And always with delicate consideration for the other and no concern for self.

CHAPTER *16*

Japan Moves into China

AFTER COMPLETING my language course in the fall of 1935, I was transferred as vice-consul to Mukden. I had asked for this assignment and was fairly sure that I would get it because Mukden was a post little sought after. It was a wretched place, with the Chinese population cowering under Japanese occupation and the Japanese corrupted by conquest. Nevertheless, it was the most important city in Manchuria and our consulate general there dealt with the puppet government of Manchukuo at its capital, Hsinking.

It had been four years since the Japanese army perpetrated the "Mukden Incident." The Kwantung Army, that part of the imperial forces stationed by treaty in Manchuria, suddenly had attacked Mukden on the night of September 18, 1931. Against virtually no Chinese resistance, the Japanese troops occupied the city. The Japanese excuse for this action was that the Chinese had caused an explosion on the tracks of the South Manchuria Railway, which was Japanese-owned.

Forthwith, the Kwantung Army began to fan out over Manchuria. Methodically it extended its control northward to the Soviet border and southward to the Great Wall, encountering only a few outbursts of Chinese opposition. By the end of 1932 it had completed its occupation of the "Three Eastern Provinces."

The Young Marshal, Chang Hsueh-liang, who had inherited Manchuria from his rascally warlord father, Chang Tso-lin, was caught off balance. He was in Peking and a hundred thousand of his four hundred thousand troops were in North China making weight in his power intrigues south of the Wall. Chiang Kai-shek, the presumptive leader of the country, being unable to subdue his domestic enemies, reckoned himself unequal to resisting so powerful a foreign aggressor as Japan. He counseled the Young Marshal not to put up a fight and turned to the League of Nations for salvation.

Japan's conquest of Manchuria was the first flagrant violation of collective security between world wars, preceding both the Italian invasion of Ethiopia and the Nazi take-over of Austria. Britain and France, distant and sated imperial powers, beset by economic crises, were fundamentally uninterested in what

Japan was doing in Manchuria and certainly were not of a mind to challenge it. This alone was enough to render the League impotent. The limit to which the League went was the dispatch to Manchuria of an investigatory mission headed by Lord Lytton, which announced more than a year after the "Mukden Incident" that indeed Japan was to be blamed for what had happened. And that was the end of that, excepting for a debate at Geneva which affronted Japan to the extent that it withdrew from the League.

Soviet reaction to the Japanese take-over of Manchuria was subdued. Yet Moscow had much more reason to be exercised over the incursion than London, Paris, or Washington. After all, Manchuria was a salient pressing upward into the Soviet Union, and Russia had vengeful memories of its 1905 defeat by Japan in Manchuria. But Stalin was absorbed with domestic problems and an imagined menace from the West. He was still suspicious of France. Unlike Trotsky, who from exile prophetically warned of the rise of Hitler, Stalin was then unalarmed by the upsurge of Nazism. In any event, the Soviet Union did nothing to deter the Japanese from advancing to its frontier.

Washington's reaction to the "Mukden Incident" was conditioned by its accretion of commitments regarding China. The Kwantung Army had flouted oft-repeated American precepts to respect the Open Door and the territorial and administrative integrity of China and had violated injunctions imposed by the Nine-Power Treaty and the Kellogg-Briand Pact. Still fresh in Mr. Stimson's mind, however, were memories of his futile invocation of international law against the 1929 Soviet military intervention in Manchuria. Furthermore, he hoped that what the Kwantung Army had done might turn out to be a sort of mutiny which would be repudiated by right-thinking civilian authorities in Tokyo and that the situation in Manchuria would thereupon be rectified by the Japanese government.

So as not to embarrass the civilian officials in Japan, Stimson's initial approach to Tokyo was in low key, more in sorrow than in anger. But as the conquest of Manchuria continued and the Japanese moderates lost rather than gained power, the attitude of the secretary of state hardened. In wary collaboration with the League, he sought to mobilize world opinion, but to no avail. An economic embargo on Japan could not be imposed because that might lead to war, to which everyone in the West, including President Hoover, was sternly opposed.

Thus frustrated, Stimson did what his predecessors and successors did in such circumstances. He enunciated a righteous position. The secretary announced in January 1932 that the United States could not admit the legality of any situation, treaty, or agreement between Japan and China impairing American treaty rights—including those relating to China's sovereignty, independence, or territorial and administrative integrity. Without pausing for breath and in the same sentence, the secretary wound up his declaration with a warning that his government would not recognize any situation, treaty, or agreement brought about by means contrary to the Pact of Paris.

This was Stimson's doctrine of nonrecognition. It gave the Japanese no visible pause. Even before they had completed their mopping-up operations they set up a government of Manchukuo, which Tokyo recognized on September 15, 1932. Five months later the Kwantung Army moved into Jehol and added it to Manchukuo. On March 1, 1934, Manchukuo proclaimed itself an empire under the rule of Henry Pu Yi, who had been smuggled out of China by the Japanese and who lent himself to the role of puppet.

Stimson's doctrine of nonrecognition meant that we in the American consulate general at Mukden made believe that Manchuria was still a part of China, under the administration of the National government at Nanking. When we had to write the word Manchukuo, the rule was to enclose it in quotation marks—"Manchukuo." At the same time, we were expected to maintain informal contact with the Manchukuo foreign office. This entailed occasional trips to the capital, Hsinking, on which we pretended to be not American officials but private citizens. To leave no doubt on this score, we presented personal rather than official calling cards at the offices we visited.

The Manchukuo foreign office went along with this petty dissembling. The vice-minister with whom we dealt was himself a bit of an official fraud. He was not a Manchurian but a Japanese, Ohashi by name. He had served as Japanese consul general in San Francisco and, as a result of enduring the traditional inhospitality of Californians to Japanese, was rabidly anti-American. We put up with his calculated rudeness in the interest of stating to him, unofficially of course, the official American position on American treaty rights in Manchuria. It would have been futile to try to deal with the minister of foreign affairs, a Manchurian, as he was a cowed puppet of Ohashi's.

We had no contact with the Kwantung Army high command, which ruled the country. The top generals kept to themselves and scorned association with even the leading Japanese civilians of the South Manchuria Railway who, before the military took over Manchuria, had run the area much in the fashion that the East India Company had dominated India. To the military, Ohashi was a flunkey. And we were foes.

The mentality of the Japanese military was something outside of American experience. It could be understood only against the background of Japanese tradition.

Unlike the Chinese, the Japanese had always glorified the warrior. Yet, curiously enough, it was adoption and modification of the Confucian hierarchical arrangement that confirmed the high rank of the Japanese warrior. Although Chinese culture had been eagerly taken over by the Japanese beginning in the sixth century, it was not until the seventeenth that Japanese society was cast in a revised Confucianist mold. The Tokugawa shoguns, a line of military feudal lords who ruled without displacing the emperor, decreed this hierarchy. The warrior-administrators of the Tokugawa occupied a position of prestige similar to that of the literati-officials in China, in contrast to the low status of military men in the original Confucian order of rank.

These Japanese warrior-administrators were the samurai. They took themselves exceedingly seriously. They were not only fiercely loyal liegemen, they were also guardians of tradition—including the tea ceremony, flower arrangement, and the martial spirit. In this respect, the samurai were, in corsaged American terms, what the Daughters of the American Revolution aspire to be.

His two swords, long and short, were the samurai's symbol of status. If offended, he felt free to use them on a defenseless commoner. At the same time, he was severe in his demands upon himself. The samurai's will commanded his physical self. He must not fear death, nor yield to pain or hunger or cold, or any fleshly affliction. Appropriately, the samurai was a Zen Buddhist.

All Japanese bore enormous and complicated burdens of obligations—among them, to emperor, to liege lord, to parents, to teachers, and each to his own good name, his honor. These burdens lay heavier on the samurai than on his inferiors. His obligations to lord and emperor were more immediate and his personal honor more consuming.

Obligations, particularly for the samurai, were often in conflict: limitless devotion to the sovereign with duty to parents, obedience to parents with attachment to wife, demands of personal honor with loyalty to liege lord. Sorting out and resolving conflicts in his many obligations could be of excruciating and deadly concern. If a contradiction could not be correctly worked out and the samurai's honor was sullied, his ultimate recourse was *seppuku*, suicide through disembowelment. This was an esteemed solution, clearing the name of the deceased.

Japanese society, therefore, was even more formalistic than the Chinese. Hierarchical structure was more rigid and conformity to one's allotted station in life more strictly observed. The Japanese was also a shame society. Public disapproval was a frightening sanction, ostracism a terrifying fate, and ridicule insupportable. While the Chinese scholar-official had a calm regard for his "face," the samurai tended to flaunt his honor. Affront so pierced him that he responded with violence turned either outward against the offender or inward upon himself.

To the Chinese their emperor was fallible. If he ruled badly, the people had the right to depose and even kill him. The Japanese did not adopt the theory of the Mandate of Heaven. Their emperor was infallible and sacred. So Japan had never had a change of dynasty. Even the shoguns did not tamper with the Imperial House. They simply bypassed it.

With the end of the shogunate in 1867 and the restoration of imperial authority, reverence for the emperor was heightened. During the Meiji Restoration the emperor became the divine symbol of Japan's modern nationalism. Shinto, which had begun as nature worship, took on the character of a state religion centered on the emperor and chauvinism.

Samurai, about one hundred of them, brilliantly managed the Meiji Restoration, the transformation of Japan into a modern state. In so doing, they abolished their own class and created an army and navy modeled more or less after those of Britain and Germany. Some of the samurai became officers, but the bulk of the armed forces were drawn from the peasantry, which for three centuries under the Tokugawas had not been allowed to carry swords.

As the samurai officers died off, their places were taken by sons of well-to-do peasants and landholders. And so it continued on into the twentieth century, with country boys beginning their officer training at adolescence, saturated in a pseudosamurai mystique, dedicating themselves to fulfilling the divine will of the emperor. By the time that they reached maturity, they believed that they knew what His Majesty's will was—certainly what it should be.

In their minds this was no usurpation. For they looked upon themselves, and were widely so accepted, as pure-hearted executors of the emperor's will and guardians of Japanese nationalism. They, with their polished boots and long swords, not the white-robed dignitaries of Shinto shrines, were the real high priests of emperor worship. And so, of all the Yamato race, they were the ones who best knew what should be the destiny of the empire.

In all of the Japanese armed forces no element was more possessed with sense of divine mission than the Kwantung Army. It was the spearhead of Japanese chauvinism and expansion. The Mukden Incident and overrunning of Manchuria were of its making, a fait accompli flung in the face of the civilian government in Tokyo.

For Japanese business, especially for the big trusts, the zaibatsu, the armed forces had contempt. Merchants were moneygrubbers not to be trusted. They were not in the upright, impecunious tradition of the samurai—and the peasantry. They were, to be sure, part of the military-industrial complex on which Japanese power was built. But they must be made the subordinate partner, serving the military. So the Kwantung Army harried the South Manchuria Railway and its diversified subsidiaries, bringing them step by step under ever tighter military control.

Clever enough not to do this directly, the Kwantung Army gradually shackled the SMR through its creature, the government of Manchukuo. In effect, it pressed towards socialization of business in Manchuria. Also through its puppet government, the Kwantung Army tried to synthesize orderly mass support of the new regime. Mysteriously there appeared the Concordia Society with a concocted doctrine, a mutilation of Mencius' *Wang Tao*, the Kingly Way. Henry Pu Yi's subjects were enjoined to observe the proper relationships with one another, practice filial piety, and be diligent. This was hardly a rip-snorting program.

What the Kwantung Army had done was to draw on Communist and Nazi examples, but in reverse. Instead of beginning with a political philosophy, then proceeding to a party, which finally creates a government, the Japanese military backed into totalitarianism. The secretary general of Concordia (who might be considered the opposite number of the secretary general of the Soviet Communist Party, Stalin) was, of course, a Japanese. He was a Captain Amakasu who, in fulfilling what he deemed to be the will of the emperor, had some years earlier strangled a Japanese labor leader, his wife, and seven-year old son. Notwithstanding these qualifications, he did not make a go of the party. Symptomatic of this, the "spontaneous" demonstrations in Mukden, with smirking party members in chocolate brown uniforms, were listless productions.

During most of my tour at Mukden I lived in a Chinese-style house that had been built by one of the Young Marshal's generals. It was set back in a city block, half of which, fronting on the house, had been razed and was used as a trash dump. Next to the house a small heroin factory exuded, when the wind was right, the faintly sweet etherish smell of cooking narcotics. I never saw anyone enter or leave the factory.

But several times on my way to the office in the morning I passed corpses on the mounds of rubbish. I assumed that they were of drug addicts, for the only other place I had seen this was in the slums of Mukden, on the banks of a narrow waterway on which backed a skid row of well-known narcotic dens. There dead addicts, robbed of their final possessions, the rags they had worn, were dumped naked into the slime. The Kwantung Army and the Concordia Society, with its Kingly Way, were aware of all of this yet did nothing to curb the evil. It was difficult not to conclude that the Kwantung Army was satisfied that the Chinese of Manchuria should be debauched. Dope addicts do not overthrow governments.

Notwithstanding its macabre setting I liked my house. High walls surrounded it. And it had a big red double gate in the Peking style. But more protective than gates or walls were my two German shepherds.

Inside were two courtyards in which pomegranates and wood peonies grew. Small bells tinkled from the corners of the upswept eaves of the living quarters surrounding the courtyards. As there were more rooms than I could use, I occupied those of the inner courtyard. Although the big living room had two brick *k'angs*, complete with tunnels for heating with coal fires fed from outside the back wall of the room, I used a more efficient pot-bellied iron stove. Another stove warmed my bedroom on the side of the courtyard.

Lao Wang, a paunchy, cynical old Chinese, acted as my cook-butler-valet-cleaning man. He was of an independent turn of mind, barely able to keep a civil tongue in his head. He had no objections to my listening to Bach, Sibelius, Beethoven, and Franck on my gramophone, which I frequently did. He reproved me, however, for any of the Japanese company I kept, which was quite understandable.

Mr. Mori was one of these. He belonged to the Japanese Army's *kempeitai*, inadequately rendered into English as gendarmerie or military police. Actually, *kempeitai* functions were more akin to those of the KGB in the Soviet Union and included state security, espionage, counterintelligence, and surveillance of foreigners. Mori was an overt operative. We in the consulate general were among his charges and he was our working-level point of contact with the *kempeitai*. If an American got in trouble or could not be located, we phoned Mori-san.

So from time to time I had Mori and two or three of his *kempeitai* colleagues, all in civilian clothes, over for dinner. Then we usually made the rounds of the dance halls. This, too, was a useful exercise. Mukden was enlivened day and night by Japanese and Korean ruffians. For them my appearance in convivial company with known *kempeitai* operatives served as a deterrent more persuasive than diplomatic immunity.

While it is a matter of pride for most other people to be able to hold their liquor, the Japanese seemed to invite tipsiness. It may have been that they were more affected by alcohol than others. More likely it was that a glass, or cup of sake, in hand signaled, "I am drunk or about to be so. Therefore be it understood that the elaborate bonds of circumspection on my behavior are loosened and I am behaving innocently, as in my childhood, before the heavy burden of obligations was placed upon me."

So the Japanese drank to forget the present, but seldom in quest of oblivion. More precisely, he drank to remember, to recreate his unfettered small boy past. Because of this, he tended to be euphoric, even maudlin in his cups. The Japanese was a true social drinker.

In spite of—or perhaps because of—all of Lao Wang's and my ministrations, Mori and his pals were, atypically, guarded drinkers. They were also guarded conversationalists. What I remember now were flushed declarations that they would happily die for the emperor on the Soviet border. They really meant it. The greatest fulfillment of life was glory in death.

Mori's lackluster performance was due to the fact that he was really rather low-powered. He was not taking any chances with spilling anything to the enemy. He was a far cry from the daring masters of his craft, Kim Philby and Richard Sorge, who freely guzzled and talked without giving themselves away.

Father Burns was a young American priest belonging to the Maryknoll order. In February 1936 he was kidnaped in the Ever White Mountains, near the Korean border, by what the Japanese described as "bandits." For nine months Kwantung Army units conducted a search and destroy operation against the "bandits" in the steep forests of eastern Manchuria until, in one of the engagements, an emaciated Father Burns was abandoned by the outlaws in their retreat.

I went out to Tunghwa in the Ever White Mountains to receive, as it were, the priest from his Japanese rescuers. Manchuria had been under Kwantung Army occupation for more than four years. Yet wherever one looked on this journey there was evidence that the countryside was far from "pacified." The train on which I traveled had armed guards in every car and the last one was filled with soldiers. After dark, searchlights were beamed along both sides of the train and embankments.

Villages were fortified and, as we knew from Mukden, were organized after the old *pao chia* system, imposing collective responsibility on the inhabitants for disturbance of the peace. If any village was found to have connections with "bandits," a Japanese detachment would descend upon it and, depending upon the degree of complicity and the whim of the pacifiers, arbitrarily shoot from one to all of the men in the village. Notwithstanding these measures, "banditry" was rife away from the north-south line of communications.

I traveled the last leg of the journey to Tunghwa in a heavily-armed bus and truck convoy. We had not only a radio communications unit with us but also a crate of carrier pigeons. At the *kempeitai* headquarters in Tunghwa Father Burns, gaunt and uncommunicative, was symbolically turned over to me. The prim lieutenant in charge and a savage-looking sergeant officiated, correctly, but with evident hatred of me. Father Comber, resident in Tunghwa and who thirty years later was to be Superior of the Maryknoll order, whisked Father Burns off to his house.

Tunghwa was a town of about fifty thousand and apparently the military headquarters for a considerable zone in eastern Manchuria. The higher officers there were occupied with larger than municipal affairs. That left the savage sergeant as tyrant over the terrorized townspeople. Few people were on the streets and they moved slowly with blank faces. My one night in the town was hideous with the screams of those being tortured in the *kempeitai* building nearby. I was relieved to return to my snuggery by the heroin factory.

Everyone in Tunghwa was likewise relieved that I was gone. The Japanese were because my presence there was an official American intrusion into a zone of their military operations. They were absurdly suspicious that I would spy on them. The Maryknoll fathers and such Chinese as were aware of my visit must also have been relieved because it would mean that the *kempeitai,* under whose sadism they sought to survive, would be a little less edgy and vengeful.

The several hundred "bandits" who held Father Burns proved to have been a good deal more than mere brigands. Most were Chinese soldiers who had escaped to the mountains when the Kwantung Army swept into eastern Manchuria. They were well organized and operated from established bases under the forest cover. We later learned that they had kidnapped the priest with the hope that this would provoke American armed intervention in Manchuria, even a war between the United States and Japan in which they and we would find ourselves allies. When this did not ensue, they demanded quantities of arms and munitions as ransom for the missioner. In this, too, of course, they were disappointed.

For their part, the Japanese military were quite as fanciful as Father Burns's captors. They quickly concluded after the kidnapping that the American priest had conspired with the insurgents and had of his own will taken to the hills to join the resistance to the Kwantung Army. Not until after the army had "saved" and thoroughly interrogated Father Burns were the Japanese persuaded that he had indeed been seized against his will and was not a freedom fighter.

No census existed of the outlaws in the eastern marches. There were probably several thousand of them. Possibly ten thousand. Not all of them were freedom fighters. Some were straightforward brigands. But more were, in one fashion or another and in varying degrees, politically motivated. Those who captured Father Burns were representative of the Nationalist insurgents. There were also Communist guerrillas, both Chinese and Korean.

The situation, therefore, in the Ever White Mountains resembled that in Chingkangshan when Mao Tse-tung operated in and out of that high fastness in Central China. The circumstances differed in that the eastern marches of Manchuria were a more extensive and desolate area and that the Kwantung Army was a more formidable force than Chiang Kai-shek's legions.

Of the insurgents, it was the Communists who most concerned the Kwantung Army. The imperial forces were in Manchuria, after all, to stop the spread of communism. It was infuriating, therefore, that red guerrillas should brazenly operate behind their front.

The front was the Soviet border, a long loop of tense confrontation. The principal mission of the Kwantung Army was to defend that frontier or, should it be the emperor's will, to attack across that border in conquest of Siberia and the Soviet Far East. The Kwantung Army was Russia-oriented. It also looked westward at Inner Mongolia, but really as a flank to Siberia. China south of the Great Wall was soon to be for other and inferior Japanese armies. The élite force was in Manchuria, poised in readiness against the source of communism.

Border clashes flared almost weekly between Japanese and Soviet troops. In October 1936, by diplomatic pouch I wrote to my family: "There are indications of growing tension on the Soviet and Outer Mongolian borders, prompted perhaps by Japanese fear of a Russian attack or by Japanese indications of a Siberian adventure. It is impossible to forecast what will happen to the north because whether there will be a Russo-Japanese conflict depends upon not only the somewhat known factors of the state of Japanese and Russian military and economic preparedness but also upon (1) a complex interplay of European factors, and (2) the manias of a handful of Japanese, Russian, and German military leaders. It is generally supposed, for example, to be axiomatic that Moscow wants no trouble out here if it can possibly be avoided. But what about Bluecher [Blyukher], the Far Eastern commander; to what degree is he independent of the Kremlin, and in him is there a hankering after Bonapartism? So, you see, we shan't know much before the day of reckoning, if it comes."

I was wrong in some of this. While it was true that Japanese military leaders were capable of starting a Russo-Japanese conflict and were in the process of seizing ever greater authority in Japan, the Soviet and German high commands were docile servants to their party masters. It was Stalin and Hitler who entertained manias.

At about the time that I wrote this letter, Stalin was in the midst of preliminary moves to purge his officer corps. Several division commanders had been arrested and his secret agents were busily collaborating with their grateful German counterparts to frame the outstanding Soviet soldier, Marshal Tukhachevsky, as a traitor conspiring with the German General Staff. Reinhardt Heydrich, head of the German Sicherheitsdienst (SD), welcomed cooperation with the NKVD in this plot because, in the ineffable manner of secret organizations, he was feuding with his own General Staff and calculated that he could use the Tukhachevsky fraud to compromise the German high command.

Blyukher had by then been made a marshal and was still in command of the Far Eastern Army, facing the Kwantung Army. Eight months later, in June 1937, he was in Moscow, having been summoned there to sit on a court trying Tukhachevsky and seven other military commanders on charges of treason and, among other things, "wrecking" and endeavoring "to prepare the defeat of the Red Army." By this time Stalin had so much false testimony against Tukachevsky tortured from other senior officers that he did not need to use the elaborate NKVD-SD evidence, including artful forgeries of correspondence between the marshal and the Germans. It is not clear whether the court actually sat on the case or merely signed the verdict of guilty presented to it by the NKVD. What is clear, as was announced in *Pravda* on June 13, is that Tukhachevsky and his codefendants were executed.

One report had it that Blyukher was forced to take charge of the execution. If so, that was an embellishment by Stalin in his demoralization of Blyukher and the seven other commanders on the court. To be compelled to judge innocent fellow officers as guilty of the worst military crimes and then to sign their death warrants was sufficient to make them Stalin's accomplices in a hideous betrayal of comrades in arms and to poison army *esprit de corps.*

While Blyukher was in Moscow being induced to testify against the marshal, Stalin began his purge of the Far Eastern Army. Blyukher's turn was obviously coming up. But at this juncture the Kwantung Army, alert to Stalin's wrecking of his officer corps, made probing attacks on June 30 and in early July to test Red Army reaction. The results were inconclusive. But the skirmishes did postpone Blyukher's doom.

Stalin left him in command to cope with the Japanese threat from Manchuria but in May 1938 resumed the purge of the Far Eastern Army. The first to be eliminated were top NKVD officers and political commissars. The new staff officers and subordinate commanders who had replaced those cleaned out the year before were the next victims. In one month 80 percent of the headquarters staff, 70 percent of divisional and corps staffs and 40 percent of unit commanders below regimental level—the brains and muscles of the officer corps—were purged. Blyukher was isolated.

Again he was saved by the Kwantung Army. Early in July it attacked in divisional strength to take the strategic heights of Changkufeng. The off-and-on battle ended with a Japanese withdrawal—understandably so as Japan was then deeply embroiled in its war with China. Hostilities ended August 11. Seven days later Blyukher returned under orders to Moscow.

He was taken over by the NKVD on October 22, one of the imaginative charges against him being that he was a Japanese spy. He refused to sign a confession which, he was told, would lighten his sentence. The security operatives then worked him over on "the conveyor," that is unceasing interrogation by relays of inquisitors, until he expired on November 9. One story is that Yezhov, the monstrous pigmy who ran the NKVD, finally shot Blyukher. But that is not certain and we shall probably never know how this talented soldier, who served both the Russian and the Chinese revolutions, died, excepting that it was on Stalin's orders. As in the case of Tukhachevsky and other officers, the family of Blyukher was also punished by imprisonment or execution.

About a month before Stalin pounced on Tukhachevsky I returned to the United States on home leave, again by the Trans-Siberian, this time in the luxury of a Wagons-Lit compartment to myself. We passed on sidings at least two trains of freight cars headed east and jammed with men and women who shouted and gesticulated at us. While Stalin's military purges were just beginning, those of civilians were in full swing.

At Moscow I called at the embassy and was invited to lunch by George Kennan, one of the mission's secretaries. This was my first meeting with him and his refreshing, perceptive wife, Annelise. Kennan had been attending the second of a series of show trials that Stalin had rigged against the Opposition—The Trial of the Seventeen, including Radek and Piatakov. At lunch he described the eerie proceedings—the extravagant accusations of treason against the Old Bolsheviks and their incredible confessions. This was the first lesson in Russian psychology and Communist politics that I was to receive from an extraordinarily gifted colleague, teacher, and friend. The rest were to follow nearly a decade later.

While I was on my way back to Mukden from home leave a minor clash occurred between Japanese and Chinese soldiers near Peking on the night of July 7, 1937. As the Mukden Incident was the excuse for the conquest of Manchuria, so this Lukouchiao Incident flared into Japan's attempt to conquer China south of the Great Wall. When I passed through Japan late in July, the country was on a war footing, complete with night air raid drills. I arrived back in Mukden on July 31 and eight days later we learned that the Japanese had occupied Peking. The second war between China and Japan was joined and headed toward catastrophe for both.

Neither Japan nor China declared war on the other. Cheekily enough, the Chinese Communists, while beleaguered in Kiangsi, formally had declared war on Japan in 1932. The Japanese did not bother to respond in kind.

Mao maintained thereafter his aggressively anti-Japanese stance for both patriotic and tactical reasons. Because of his fiercely nationalistic bent, he was against Japan at least as much as against his domestic enemy, Chiang Kai-shek. He was anti-Japanese also because he was appealing to the many Chinese who felt the same way and were disappointed that Chiang did not fight back. This theme of nationalistic resistance to the alien invader became one of the most telling Communist stratagems against the Kuomintang regime.

No more than Mao did Chiang like the Japanese inroads. But, in his obstinate fashion, he was until 1937 determined to rid himself of the internal Communist enemy before turning to resist the invaders. In one sense, he was right. Domestic dissent should have been, ideally, first quelled, and then the government could face the external enemy without fear of foes from within.

But the situation, as is usually the case, did not lend itself to ideal solutions. Chiang's preference for civil conflict against the vociferously patriotic Communists over resistance to Japanese aggression was not popular. Nevertheless, he prepared for another round of "bandit suppression" when the Communists settled in Shensi late in 1935, following their Long March.

Meanwhile, Chiang's old admirer, Stalin, had decided to follow a united front policy. He began this policy of alignment with bourgeois and social democrat elements in 1934 when he became disturbed by Nazi, Japanese, and other forms of aggression, which he thought might threaten the Soviet Union. In such parlous circumstances he was pleased to pick up allies whenever he could find them. By August 1935, at the Seventh Congress of the Comintern, the united front policy was publicly formalized.

So far as the Chinese Communists were concerned, the united front tactic was one which they were already pursuing. They were trying to rally all Chinese, short of the right wing Kuomintang, to them on the issue of resistance to Japan. They so declared themselves anew in December 1935.

As Chiang lined up his bandit suppression forces to crush the Reds, the Communists approached those ordered to eliminate them proclaiming that "Chinese must not fight Chinese." Those to whom the slogan was directed were receptive. Particularly was this true of the Manchurian troops of the Young Marshal, Chang Hsueh-liang, then in the Northwest, far from their homeland. They did not want civil war; they wanted to drive the Japanese out of the Northeast. As for the Young Marshal, he even received Communist representatives in his headquarters.

Irritated by the recalcitrance of his punitive force, Chiang went to its headquarters at Sian in December 1936. His intention was to spur action against the Communists. Settling down for a series of conferences with his commanders, the Generalissimo moved into quarters outside of Sian, into a lodging suffused with tender memories. It was the hot springs love nest where, during the T'ang dynasty, the exquisite concubine Yang Kuei Fei entertained her emperor. The establishment had since been converted into a fancy tourist hotel.

Two years before the Generalissimo's arrival I had tarried there during my tour of Shensi. Where once had bathed the most celebrated beauty of Chinese history, I too took a bath—with no marked benefit to my appearance. It was in this steamy, idyllic setting that the first scene of the so-called Sian Incident opened.

Before dawn on December 12 the Generalissimo was awakened by a band of the Young Marshal's bodyguard shooting it out with his own surprised bodyguard. Barefooted and in his nightshirt, Chiang made a hasty getaway through a window. He fled up the side of a hill and there he hid. Before long he was captured, chilled to the marrow, his feet cut and bleeding. His captors took him to Sian.

The Young Marshal and his co-conspirator, General Yang Hu-ch'eng, told the Generalissimo that they had impounded him only to persuade him to stop repressing domestic opposition and to unify the country by taking charge of resistance to Japan. They announced publicly that they sought to "stimulate his awakening." But not everyone in Sian was so concerned with the Generalissimo's awakening. Many of the young Manchurian officers, together with other military elements in the city, wanted to execute their commander-in-chief as one who had betrayed China to the Japanese.

In this volatile situation, the Young Marshal found an ally in the Communists. Shortly after Chiang's capture, Mao sent Chou En-lai, Po Ku, and General Yeh Chien-ying to Sian. The Communists had mastered their first impulse to celebrate and demand the liquidation of their arch enemy. On second thought, they concluded that this was no time to be carried away by emotion, especially as some of Chiang's subordinates in Nanking had begun military moves against Sian threatening civil war. So the Communist emissaries urged moderation.

A week after the Generalissimo's capture, the Communist Party formally stated its position: the Young Marshal and Yang had acted with "patriotic sincerity"; immediately effect a truce between Nanking and Sian; convoke in Nanking a peace conference of all parties, in preparation for which all factions would present their proposals for resistance to Japan, national unity, and "the disposition of Mr. Chiang Kai-shek."

Moscow did not go along with using the person of Chiang as a bargaining counter. It had, with uncommon speed, reacted through its controlled press two days after his capture, demanding that he immediately be set free. His captors were called traitors and rascals. It appeared that Stalin was agitated over what might happen to his former protégé.

On the other side, in terms of the survival of the Generalissimo, were those elements in Nanking which had put armies in motion toward Sian, bombed a town near the city, and were straining to begin an all-out offensive against the "mutineers," including the bombing of Sian itself. Foremost among these militants was Chiang's trusted minister of military affairs, Ho Ying-ch'in, the seraphic little general who had led the first Bandit Suppression Campaign in Kiangsi to defeat. Opposing these sly heroics were Chiang's relatives and others concerned with getting the Generalissimo back alive.

Mme. Chiang, naturally, was in the forefront. This was not the simple woman whom Chiang had married in his youth and then discarded. It was the Americanized, Wellesley graduate, Soong Mei-ling, whom he wed in 1927 as suitable to his newly acquired status as a modern, world figure. Endowed with a temperament which in an earlier epoch would have propelled her to the Dragon Throne, Mme. Chiang flew to Sian to deal with her husband's captors.

By then, however, a compromise solution was being worked out among Chiang, the Young Marshal, General Yang, and Chou En-lai. The Generalissimo refused to submit formally to the demands made upon him while held under duress. From conflicting subsequent accounts of the deal that was made, it seems that his captors agreed to release Chiang in return for statements by the Generalissimo that he was against civil war and was working for unified national resistance to Japan.

Whatever the bargain may have been, on Christmas day the Generalissimo,

Mme. Chiang, and the Young Marshal flew to Nanking. There Chang Hsueh-liang submitted himself to trial by the Military Affairs Commission (headed by Ho Ying-ch'in), was sentenced to ten years imprisonment, was immediately pardoned by the Generalissimo, following which Chiang Kai-shek placed him incommunicado under house arrest, in which situation the no longer young marshal has lingered to this writing.

Custom required that the Generalissimo go through the ritual of regaining the face he so heavily lost at the hot springs. The punishment of the Young Marshal was not enough. He therefore offered his resignation several times. His government repeatedly begged him to remain on the job. His indispensability was thereby reaffirmed and his face restored.

The Bandit Suppression Headquarters at Sian was calmly closed. But National government troops trusted by the Generalissimo moved into Sian and up against the southern flank of the Communist area. Although this caused the Communists in their new capital at Yenan some anxiety, it turned out to be a static blockade which lasted until the end of the war with Japan.

Mao took the initiative in presenting terms for collaboration between the Communists and the National government. Yenan asked, on February 10, 1937, for an end to civil war, resistance to Japan, respect for civil liberties, and related concessions. In return, the Communists offered to quit insurrection against the National government, to change the name of their soviet government to government of a "special region," to drop the name "Red Army" and adopt National government military designations, to accept Nanking's military "guidance," to institute democracy and universal suffrage, and to halt confiscation of land from landlords.

Responding on February 21 to the Communist offers, the Kuomintang's Central Executive Committee echoed what Yenan said, but in a blustering tone. Its answer was a Resolution for Complete Eradication of the Red Menace, demanding the abolition of the Red Army and the Soviet government, the stopping of Communist propaganda, and the termination of class struggle. This exchange between the Communists and the Kuomintang was progress toward a united front. It was followed by the movement of emissaries between Nanking and Yenan and bargaining behind the scenes.

If any one event in China precipitated Japanese intervention in force, it was the Sian Incident. Chiang captured by the intensely anti-Japanese Northeasterners, their conniving with the Communists on the conditions for his release, Moscow's demands that the Generalissimo be freed, and all of the coming and going between Yenan and Nanking—this jugglery aroused the darkest suspicions of Tokyo. The Japanese government, in the grip of the military, saw the conciliatory Chiang snared by the Communists in the united front and set against everything that Tokyo had demanded: recognition of Japan's unique protecting role in East Asia, economic privileges in China, a halt to anti-Japanese agitation in China, and Sino-Japanese cooperation in combatting the spread of Communism. From early 1937 a military showdown with China was almost inevitable.

Japan's invasion in July brought to fruition in China what had begun at Yang Kuei Fei's thermal baths. In August the National Military Council appointed Chu Teh as commander of the national Eighth Route Army, which was the new name for the Red Army. It was a sleight-of-hand performance. The substance was as it had been. Only the appearances had changed.

Meanwhile the Generalissimo and Chou En-lai had been negotiating the terms of the second united front. They settled, essentially, on Yenan's proposal of February 10, plus a Communist undertaking to work for the realization of Sun Yat-sen's amorphous Three People's Principles. It was a mistrustful coalition on both sides and could be effective, both knew, only so long as a foreign invader pressed them to a more or less common cause.

CHAPTER *17*

Hankow Before Its Fall

FROM MUKDEN I was transferred to Hankow in May 1938. With war fronts across the normal routes of travel to Hankow, through Peking or Shanghai, I swung down by way of Canton. It had been heavily bombed and was blacked out when my train slunk through at night.

Up the Canton-Hankow Railway we chuffed through green and tranquil valleys. The line had been bombed but labor gangs along the way had kept it open. As we neared Wuchang, the train suddenly stopped, an alarm sounded, and we all took to the fields in search of ditches. Soon a ragged flight of Japanese bombers passed overhead, disregarding our crouching forms and the train in plain view.

The flight formation had been ragged because, I later learned, the aircraft had been intercepted and routed by Chinese and Soviet fighters. Thus the bombers had fled over us in retreat, with no time or inclination to pay us heed.

So it was that even as I approached Hankow I was introduced to the three principal elements of the international struggle then raging in East Asia. The Japanese were attacking. The Chinese were resisting. And the Russians were backing the Chinese, with cautious, limited help. But in the arena larger than this strip of field and sky, and in a time span longer than the few moments of a day in May, Japan had not been intercepted and routed. It was winning.

Japan was lunging southwestward into China. As it did so, it was acutely aware of dangers on its flanks. To the west was its old and nearest enemy—Russia. As a guarantee against any possible Soviet attacks, the truculent Kwantung Army crowded the frontiers of Manchukuo. To remind the Kremlin that it, too, had another front to worry about, Tokyo had concluded with Berlin in 1936 an Anti-Comintern Pact in which Japan and Germany agreed to work together against the Comintern menace. On Japan's eastern flank, across the Pacific and in Guam and the Philippines, was its naval rival and the sentimental friend of China—the United States. As a guarantee against the emotional unpredictability of Washington, the self-confident Imperial Navy concentrated in the northwestern Pacific.

China—the China of Chiang Kai-shek—also thought itself pressed on three fronts. The Japanese invasion was one. Although Moscow was aiding China in various ways against the Japanese, it was also nibbling across China's northwestern borders at Chiang's pretensions of control over Sinkiang. This the Generalissimo considered to be his second front. His third front was internal. Notwithstanding the truce between him and the Communists, he still regarded them as active enemies. Because Chiang also viewed the Communists as lackeys of Moscow, the Soviet and internal fronts were, in his eyes, essentially one.

Communist China—a scattering of small enclaves—looked upon Chiang's blockading armies as its main front. Japanese pressure against Communist base areas behind the forward Japanese lines constituted a second front. A third and immaterial front was against the Soviet Union, against Kremlin pressure on Mao and his confederates.

Moscow's two principal fronts were Germany and Japan. Germany, yet uncommitted in 1938 to attacking either west or east, was Moscow's greater concern. Japan was beginning to overextend itself into China and so was a lesser cause of anxiety to Moscow so long as China, in a strategic retreat that the Russians understood so well, drew the Japanese southward away from the Soviet Union. The Kremlin's interest in East Asia was therefore to make sure that Chiang continued as an undertow to the Japanese. Stalin also wanted to project Soviet influence into the Chinese Government and get control over the Chinese Communists.

Still trusting its moats of oceans on either side, the United States did not think in the stark terms of fronts. Franklin Roosevelt in October 1937 spoke of "the epidemic of world lawlessness" and called for a "quarantine" against its spread. His secretary of state, Cordell Hull, less infectiously deplored "the rising tide of lawlessness" in 1938, and reaffirmed "our deep concern for, and our advocacy of, the establishment everywhere of international order under law. . . ." The most effective contribution that the United States could make would be "to have this country respected throughout the world for integrity, justice, good will, strength, and unswerving loyalty to principle."

"The foregoing is the essence of our foreign policy," Hull droned on. "The record is an open book." Unhappily, it was not a best seller. The aggressors did not buy it. The epidemic spread and the tide rose.

By May 1938, the Japanese had captured Peking, Tientsin, Shanghai, and Nanking. The Chinese government had fallen back to Hankow. The enemy then had more than twenty divisions, at least half a million men, deployed in China. As for the defenders, no one knew how many Chinese soldiers there really were throughout the country. We may comfortably assume that there were between two and three million.

This vagueness was not due to anyone's inability to count, as the Communist general, Ho Lung, claimed for himself—although it should be added that inexactitude was a prime cultural characteristic of the Chinese. The vagueness was due to two things. One was a matter of definition: what was a soldier? Was a village militiaman, for example, a soldier? And what about a guerrilla?

Another reason for imprecision was that most divisional commanders, unlike Ho Lung, maintained their units at below authorized troop strength as good business practice. They collected from the government pay for a full complement and pocketed the difference. This was not true, it should be added, of the Chinese Red Army.

Whatever their exact number, soldiers were scattered all over China's broad expanse, many more of them than Japan was bringing to bear in its invasion. The discrepancy in number of divisions was also pronounced. A Chinese division was nominally just under ten thousand men; a Japanese more than twenty thousand. Because most Chinese divisions were understrength, it took three or four Chinese divisions to equal the manpower of one Japanese division.

The quality of Chinese divisions varied from fair, in the case of the thirty belonging to the Generalissimo and trained by German advisers, to rabble, in the case of some provincial units. Shanghai was defended by a number of the better divisions, which fought bravely for three months until outflanked by the enemy. And north of Nanking at a small town called Taierchuang, the Chinese even won a major battle in April 1938.

But after nearly a year of war, many of the capable units had been chewed up in combat. In the process they lost weapons and equipment along with men. The losses of materiel were more serious because the Chinese were critically short of even basic arms like artillery and because men were more easily replaced in China than modern weapons.

While the Japanese had thoroughly mauled the defending forces, the Chinese victory at Taierchuang was a nasty shock to them. At the same time they began to suspect that they had miscalculated the magnitude of what, with typical understatement of the disagreeable, they called the China Incident. This disrespect for the size of their task was infinitely more serious than Taierchuang, for it was to be one of the principal causes of their undoing in China. The Japanese were beginning to discover that, while they could take the lines of communication and the cities, they simply did not have the manpower to garrison and control the huge areas between and behind the narrow corridors that they held, and that within these areas resistance was springing up.

Therefore, the Japanese lashed about in the countryside of North China and then moved on. In their pacification sweeps they behaved with such vengeful barbarity that they transformed the normally compliant peasantry into outraged enemies. As these search-and-destroy operations proceeded, the invaders regrouped and received reinforcements for the campaign against Wuhan. The drive on the three cities in the center of China began in early September 1938. Fourteen divisions were committed to the effort, with air and naval support. One force pushed westward from Nanking up the Yangtze. A second advanced southward, down the Peking-Hankow Railway.

The American consulate general at Hankow, to which I was assigned, was in the Asiatic Petroleum building on the Bund, or river front boulevard. The consular offices and staff occupied the upper floor of the building. My small apartment looked down across the street on the pleasant gardens and houses of the British consulate general.

Jammed in with us that summer of 1938 was what was left of the embassy, after its retreat before the Japanese, first from Peking and then from Nanking. There was the ambassador, Nelson Johnson, who had lost little weight and amiability in flight. In addition to three secretaries, he was supported by his service attachés. Colonel Stilwell, tense and tight-mouthed, pored over maps and papers in a back room. Frank ("Pinky") Dorn, as his assistant military attaché, alternated with him on trips to the fighting fronts. And Major James M. McHugh, a Marine Corps specialist on China, acted as assistant naval attaché.

Although the ground war was that summer still distant from Hankow, the air war came sometimes to us. At midday the sirens sounded, whereupon some of us climbed to the flat roof to watch for the oncoming attack. Through the streets people ran for home or dashed into houses and doorways for there were no public shelters. Then came quiet. No one moved and if people talked it was in whispers. They were listening for the first sounds of the coming storm.

Antiaircraft batteries to the east opened up first, daubing the sky with white puffs. Soon the silvery specks of bombers drifted toward us. Nearby batteries shattered the stillness in the streets. More puffs in the sky, yet on the bombers—twenty or more—floated toward and over us. Above Hanyang's iron works and arsenal or Wuchang's administrative centers and airfield the bombs were let away. Flashes and thunder were soon over. Towers of smoke rose and swelled and sometimes blackly spouted for hours.

The antiaircraft artillery was ineffective. I do not recall having seen any Japanese planes shot down. The batteries were quite useless on night raids as they relied on sighting the enemy aircraft. While the searchlights put on a dramatic show, they helped but little the errant marksmanship of the artillerymen.

Interception and air combat were erratic. The Chinese Air Force had been decimated in some ten months of fighting. Even at the beginning of the war it was a hodgepodge outfit. A few American and Soviet-trained pilots were competent. The majority, taught by Italian instructors loaned to Chiang by Mussolini, were wildly incompetent. And the aircraft reflected Chinese shopping sprees among American, Italian, German, and Soviet manufacturers.

By the time the air war reached Hankow the Italians had long since departed and the Chinese were receiving in-combat guidance from an extraordinarily talented fighter pilot who had been retired from the American Army Air Corps, Captain Claire Chennault. With a face of cold lava, the Captain was a daunting figure who greatly impressed the Chinese, including the Generalissimo and Mme. Chiang. But Chennault did not have at Hankow the personnel, equipment, nor the time to remake the Chinese Air Force.

In contrast to most of the Chinese fliers, the Soviet "volunteers" were skilled, disciplined, and well equipped. Occasionally some of them came into the city, dressed in clumpy civilian clothes, wandering about downtown Hankow shopping for watches. Timepieces, incidentally, seemed to arouse an acquisitive passion in the Soviet military, as later the liberated peoples of Europe were to discover.

Although designated as volunteers and garbed as civilians, the Russians belonged to Soviet Air Force units. They were part of the four fighter and two bomber squadrons that Moscow sent to China in the autumn of 1937. These squadrons were rotated every six months. The Kremlin sent them not only to help Chiang resist the Japanese invasion. They went also, as Soviet air crews and planes had been sent to Spain two years earlier, to be trained and tested under combat conditions—in Spain against Germans and Italians, in China against Japanese.

Soviet aid to China went well beyond the rotating air squadrons. About a month after the Japanese invasion began in 1937, the Soviet Union concluded a nonaggression treaty with China. In 1938 Moscow made two loans to China of fifty million dollars each, a third of a hundred and fifty million dollars in 1939, and delivered to China, across the land route through Central Asia, war supplies, including four hundred combat aircraft.

Stalin made available to Chiang as advisers some of the most promising of his officers who had survived his purges. Among them were Generals V. I. Chuikov and G. K. Zhukov. Chuikov later became the defender of Stalingrad and Zhukov drove across Germany to take Berlin. At a maximum, the Soviet advisory group numbered about five hundred. But as the Generalissimo made little use of this talent, the Russian officers were gradually recalled to the Soviet Union where they had much work to do trying to repair the shambles left by Stalin's executioners.

Zhukov, it is worth noting, was sent in the summer of 1939 to take command of Soviet and Mongolian forces in a laboratory war on the Mongolian border with Manchukuo. This was the so-called Nomanhan Incident which began in May with a Kwantung Army attack that gave the defending units a bad time. In August, reinforced to thirty-five infantry battalions, twenty cavalry squadrons, with nearly five hundred tanks and about five hundred and fifty aircraft, Zhukov smartly smashed a somewhat weaker Japanese concentration, inflicting eighteen thousand casualties on it. In winning this first big test of Soviet arms pitted against a comparable adversary, Zhukov used Tukhachevsky's dashing tank tactics, discredited since the purge of their author.

All Soviet aid to China went to the National government. None went to the Chinese Communists. Stalin acted as he had a decade earlier. Reckoning that Chiang was the strongest figure in China, he supported only the Generalissimo, this time as the one best able to organize containment of the Japanese in China. Material assistance from the Soviet Union continued until shortly before the Nazi attack in 1941. From then on until the end of the war in Europe, Stalin was preoccupied with Soviet survival and victory in the West.

Before the dispatch of Soviet military advisers to China, Chiang had made use of a German military mission from 1928 to 1938. This was a much closer relationship than that with the Russians. A series of able German officers served

Chiang well. They not only played a large part in planning his only successful punitive campaign against the Communists, but had also guided the training of some thirty divisions owing allegiance to the Generalissimo. The competence and discretion of the Germans won them Chiang's confidence.

When von Seeckt returned to Germany in 1935, he was replaced by General Alexander von Falkenhausen. Then came Japan's all-out assault on China in 1937. Notwithstanding the kinship between Tokyo and Berlin created by the Anti-Comintern Pact, the German advisers, about seventy in all, stayed on with Chiang and, what is more, counseled him and his generals on the operational conduct of the war.

Advising the Generalissimo and his commanders was an exasperating business, as Blyukher had earlier discovered and Stilwell was before long to experience. For example, von Falkenhausen had advocated a war of maneuver. Instead, the Chinese clung to untenable positions in which they were decimated by superior Japanese firepower and in which they lost much of their scanty materiel. The Germans concealed their irritation. But then, they were not under the strain that Blyukher was, caught up in the Stalin-Trotsky conflict, nor that Stilwell later felt himself under as Chiang's nominal chief of staff responsible for producing results for an impatient Washington. The Germans were employees of the Generalissimo with responsibilities essentially no greater than those of hired technicians.

Such ties as von Falkenhausen and his staff had with Berlin were largely personal and legacies of those enjoyed by the more prestigious von Seeckt. The Reich minister of defense, Field-Marshal von Blomberg, the commander-in-chief of the Army, General Werner von Fritsch, and the chief of staff, General Ludwig Beck were all favorably disposed toward the von Falkenhausen group. But then in February 1939, as Stalin was in the latter stages of purging his generals, Hitler bore down on his, but less savagely. He ousted von Blomberg and personally took over the war office; he had von Fritsch framed by the Gestapo on implausible charges of homosexuality, following which he replaced the commander-in-chief with someone more pliable. Beck, who was strongly anti-Nazi, was on his way out and finally resigned in protest to the plan for the invasion of Czechoslovakia. And so the advisers in China were deprived of powerful patrons at home.

Hitler swung in early 1938 from neutrality in the conflict between Japan and China to support of his anti-Comintern ally, Japan, and when Chiang declined his offer to mediate between the two, Hitler ordered the von Falkenhausen group to return to Germany. Some refused to obey the order and remained with the Chinese. Von Falkenhausen eventually complied. But he was still in Hankow when I arrived, a lean, erect old gentleman with thick *pince-nez* and a stern mien.

Hankow's buildings were plastered with brightly colored posters of shouting young men, guns held aloft by brawny arms, summoning the populace to resist the enemy. Slogans abounded. Wuhan (Hankow, Hanyang and Wuchang) must be another Madrid. Arm the workers and the students to fight in the streets. Scorch the earth in front of the advancing foe.

This was the work of the Communists. With the new united front in effect, they were operating above ground and with frantic energy. They found response in the educated youth desperately looking for aggressive leadership. These activities, however, did not find favor with the Generalissimo because of their sponsorship and because he had more confidence in soldiers than partisans.

No one really thought that Hankow would be another Madrid. Still, in June and July many had not yet abandoned hope and there was an unreasoning exhilaration in crisis, a collective wish that there just might be another Taierchuang. The foreign correspondents were alert to the drama of the situation and one of them was an impassioned actress on the scene.

She was Agnes Smedley, an American who wrote for the *Manchester Guardian* (and who later wrote a biography of Chu Teh). Agnes had arrived in Wuhan several months earlier from Yenan and then Shansi, where she had visited Chu Teh as he fought the Japanese. This was before she had been employed by the *Guardian*. She arrived without a job and was nearly destitute. In compassion, the American Episcopal bishop gave shelter and sustenance in his home to this fairly notorious woman, whom the more anxious intelligence functionaries regarded as a Communist agent. Agnes and the Right Reverend Logan Roots were thereafter known as the Moscow-Heaven Axis, and she addressed him with great good humor as Comrade Bishop.

Agnes loved to wear an Eighth Route Army uniform because she wished she were an Eighth Route soldier—also because she was a militant women's rightser and because she enjoyed shocking the stodgy. The getup was a slumped fatigue cap pulled down to her ears over her lank bobbed hair, a wrinkled cotton tunic and trousers, neatly wound cotton puttees, and cloth shoes. This ensemble would be unflattering to any woman, but for Miss Smedley, not endowed with beauty of feature or figure, it was aggressively unbecoming.

In addition to acting as *Guardian* correspondent, Agnes worked for the government-sponsored Chinese Red Cross, trying to get and dispatch medical aid to the wounded, whose plight wrung her heart. Getting little from the International Red Cross, she canvassed the foreign community pleading for medicines, bandages, money, anything that might succor the casualties of war. She was not at all humble in her begging. To her fellow Americans it was "The United States is selling oil and scrap iron to Japan, so you are contributing to the killing of Chinese. Give something for those wounded by our greed."

One of Agnes's greatest admirers was the British ambassador, Sir Archibald Clark Kerr (later Lord Inverchapel). Sir Archie had the usual British upper class predilection for the eccentric and so immediately recognized her as a collector's item. But being also intelligent and imaginative, Clark Kerr appreciated the valiant spirit of this abrupt woman and saw that she possessed insights into the Chinese Communist movement and burgeoning guerrilla activities that he could not get from his conventional sources. She was included, therefore, in invitations to luncheons at the embassy where Sir Archie listened and everyone else talked. He was also one of her most effective volunteers in getting money and medical supplies for her relief work.

As O. J. Todd, digging his irrigation ditches, was the typical American earth-mover transported to China, so Agnes was an authentic American in the tradition of Tom Paine, the suffragettes, and the wobblies. For a radical, she was curiously unconcerned with doctrine. She said that she was not a Communist. I supposed that she probably was not, for she was too softhearted and unruly to be a party member. She told me that she admired the Communist soldiers—Chu Teh was her hero—but that she did not like the political leaders in Yenan. With a slight grimace, "They're too slick."

Later, as the Japanese were closing in on Wuhan, I asked Agnes about her plans. She said that she would go into the countryside to be with the guerrillas. "That's where I belong."

I lectured her, saying that she was giving herself to a revolution that was then on the upsurge. At that stage it was idealistic, full of high resolve and a warm feeling of comradeship because of danger from powerful adversaries. But if the revolution succeeded and the revolutionaries came to power, corruption would set in and she would be disillusioned and betrayed. Why didn't she quit this kind of life and operate as the other correspondents did? There were tears in her eyes. "I can't. There is no other way for me."

As people moved out of Hankow in anticipation of its fall, I inherited a cavernous apartment in the Hong Kong and Shanghai Bank Building. Friends foregathered there: Stilwell, Pinky Dorn, Till Durdin of the *New York Times*, Arch Steele of the *Chicago Daily News*, Yates and Natalie McDaniel of the Associated Press, Edgar Snow (whose *Red Star Over China* had only recently appeared), Paul Josselyn (my melancholic boss the consul general, who suffered from dyspepsia and looked like the man in "An American Gothic"), the military spokesman for the National government (whose name I have forgotten), Chang Han-fu who eventually became vice-minister for foreign affairs of the Communist government in Peking, Jack Belden of the United Press, Agnes, a confused political gypsy by the name of Freda Utley, and Evans Carlson (a Lincolnesque Marine Corps captain who was a dear friend of Agnes's, had spent months campaigning with the Eighth Route Army, later founded the Marine Corps unit called Carlson's Raiders and introduced the Communist slogan "gung ho" into the English language).

It was in Hankow this summer of 1938 that I first met Chou En-lai. He was the principal Communist representative there, maintaining liaison with the National government. Mao stayed in Yenan. Under the united front arrangement Chou was even designated as vice-minister for political training of the National Military Council. With a shrewd appreciation of public relations, Chou made himself accessible to foreigners, particularly correspondents. Even with his hair cropped—as he wore it that summer—and dressed in a sagging nondescript uniform, he was an impressive man. This was because of thick black eyebrows above lively black eyes, a quick wit, a deft grace of manner, and emanations of vibrancy.

Po Ku was also in Hankow at the same time. He was one of the "returned students" clique and it was he whom Mao, early on the Long March, replaced as head of the Party. Po Ku looked like a caricature of a modern Chinese intellectual—peaked, myopic, and with a shock of hair that stood upright as if he were undergoing electrocution. Yet he was full of bounce. And he was one of the originators of the Let's-Make-Wuhan-Another-Madrid rallying cry.

Wang Ming, too, was in Wuhan during 1938, but I do not recall having met him. The previous year, with the establishment of the united front, he had returned to China from Moscow where he had been resident oracle on Chinese affairs and a member of the Executive Committee of the Comintern. He was regarded as Stalin's candidate for leadership of the Chinese Party. He advocated a greater measure of CCP subordination to Chiang than Mao was willing to grant. He was no match for Mao and over the course of the next five years found himself being pushed steadily into limbo.

CHAPTER *18*

Under Japanese Occupation

By LATE SEPTEMBER the exodus from Wuhan was in full swing. The embassy had long since gone up the Yangtze on one of our little gunboats to Chungking, the provisional capital. Every train going south and every plane to Hong Kong was filled with those fleeing the invaders. The flow of refugees from downriver rose as the Japanese bore in on Wuhan—refugees who could not afford or get transportation and so shuffled through the city on foot with a few belongings and their babies on their backs.

Hundreds of wounded and sick soldiers from the front were dumped on the river bank. They were more unlucky than the many more who were left on the battlefield whose misery was already over from having been bayoneted or shot by the enemy. Those who had been brought to an illusory safety now lay neglected in their own filth too weak to move. Crowds passed by glancing down with the remote curiosity of the fatalistic.

Each passer-by had his own worries; if nothing else, his plans for flight ahead of the advancing enemy. He could not stop to lend a hand, for to touch someone in trouble was to become involved. And once involved, there would be no end to it. One would be held to account if something went wrong. In any event, there was so much of this personal disaster that there was no stopping place. One would be overwhelmed.

Collectively, the passers-by could have helped. But there was no bond amongst them. They were fragmented with apprehension, like cattle beginning to stampede.

So what could be done? Telephone the military hospital, pleading with a voice at the other end of the line to pick up the casualties. And in doing that one knew that the only change in the condition of those dying on the riverbank was that they would either expire from inattention under a roof and out of sight of the crowds or, if they survived, they would be shot by the invaders when they took the hospital.

Now the young soldiers with the fixed imploring eyes knew all of this. They had not reasoned it out. They simply and profoundly understood that there was little mercy in life and none in war—at least for a Chinese soldier. In defeat, you were on your own. Wounded or sick you were abandoned, helpless as an infant left in a lonely place to die of exposure or to be devoured by dogs.

As the invaders came close to the city, no more gravely sick and wounded were cast ashore. Then appeared the deserters, the stragglers, the men separated from their units. They had thrown away their arms and were empty-handed. Some were lightly wounded, many of them sickly, all of them dazed, not knowing where to turn in their dumb, groping search for a hiding place, a postponement of the shot in the head.

This was the Chinese army in rout. Each man was alone. None drew courage or strength or even comfort from his companions. To the contrary, each slunk away from the other, clad in the incrimination of uniform. Civilians shunned them as doomed men, sure to excite vengeance from the oncoming conquerers.

In the third week of October 1938 the Japanese pincers had closed on Wuhan. Those of us who were left behind made the last fussy preparations for the entry of the invading army. We were a few missionaries, foreign business-men, and consuls, several American, British, and French gunboats—cocky little flat-bottoms to show the flag—and hundreds of thousands of terrified Chinese who were too poor, too young, too old, or too full of despair to flee.

The Communists swore that they would blow up Hankow. They planted their dynamite. Hankow would be made a scorched earth. But then property owners and building caretakers removed most of the explosives. So Hankow was only a little singed, and that in the former Japanese concession where the Communists had their headquarters.

Early on the morning of October 26, 1938 I walked over to the consulate general. There was no traffic and only an occasional pedestrian. From the office I watched dive bombers lazily working over something downstream on the river bank. A column of black smoke surged upward. The bombers went away. It was quiet again. Then Japanese patrol craft roared up the river.

Before long a Japanese destroyer slid into sight, followed by four or five more, heading toward us. As they glided past no life was visible on their decks. Their guns were trained on the city, but ships and shore were silent. Then in about an hour the transports began to arrive, loaded with troops. All afternoon they came and anchored in midstream.

This would be the test. For when the Japanese occupied Nanking they had gone on a rampage of unchecked looting, raping, and killing which lasted three or four days. Would Hankow, too, be subjected to unrestrained savagery?

When the troops started to come ashore I went up the Bund to where they were landing. I did not approach them and they paid no attention to me. At the corner of a side street opening onto the broad boulevard of the Bund I noticed two unarmed Chinese soldiers cringing up against the closed doors of a shuttered shop. I strolled over to an adjacent shop where a couple of civilians, with unquenchable Chinese curiosity, were watching the troop-landing from behind a quarter-opened door. Hurriedly I said, "Get those men inside and into civilian clothes." There was not a flicker of response. The door closed.

Not wishing to draw attention to the street corner or to appear furtive, I walked casually toward the swelling concentration of troops. So many had come ashore that what had been a clear passage along the Bund was now filled with soldiers assembling by units. It was not until I had passed through part of the confusion that an officer, red in the face and glaring like any officer in any army in such irregular circumstances, yelled at me. In my best Mukden Japanese I identified myself and said that I was on my way back to the consulate general. Whereat he, joined by other nearby officers, bayed me on my way with bad language. My preliminary conclusion was, therefore, that this was starting out as a disciplined occupation.

Later, from our gunboat officers I learned what happened to several Chinese stragglers, probably including the two I saw. The Japanese shoved them to the river bank at the stern of our gunboat, there shot them in the head, and then roared with laughter as the wan bodies slumped into the swift current and were carried away. This was sport—and also, assumably, meant to edify the American navy.

Shortly after dark one of the Chinese on our staff came to me saying that his niece was in a part of town where the occupying troops were being billeted. Would I take him to pick her up? We got into my consul general's car and drove across the French concession—the only settlement in Hankow still administered by a foreign power.

At the far end of the concession we came upon the local Maginot Line, a barbed wire fence and a sandbag fort housing one machine gun. At the gate was a thin-skinned old armored car. The total defending force numbered perhaps forty men, mostly Tonkinese colonial mercenaries, with a sprinkling of French businessmen and sailors from the gunboat.

This beau geste outfit was confronted across the street by three Japanese tanks, quite as many machine guns behind sandbags and a horde of infantry. The French, of course, still had in 1938 the advantage of a martial reputation, the best army in Europe, and therefore the world. I asked permission to pass through these ramparts of mystique. The French shrugged, opened the gate, and I drove off on our excursion.

No Japanese challenged us or even showed interest in our passage. Soldiers milled about on the sidewalks along our route, moving into private houses. I assumed that they were getting ready to make themselves comfortable for the night. But there were no sights or sounds of violence. At our destination no Japanese were in front of the house. The young woman scuttled into the car and we got her back, past the bored French defenders, to her parents' quiet house.

Hankow was not another Nanking. The troops had orders to behave themselves. And quite as important, the occupying forces brought their whores with them. We were told, but unable to verify, that among the first transports to arrive at least one carried the army's prostitutes. Other armies may have travelled on their stomachs; the Japanese army traveled on its libido.

Life under Japanese occupation was more restricted in Hankow than it had been in Mukden because Wuhan was in a zone of active warfare. By the same token it was more stimulating. One of my functions was reporting on military and political developments, which I enjoyed. But my principal task was contact with the Japanese consular and military authorities. It meant advising them where American citizens and American properties were in areas of hostilities and protesting Japanese mistreatment or damaging of them.

My assignment to protection of American interests led to two trips out of Hankow. The first was to arrange for and assist the evacuation of Americans from a mountain resort called Kuling, which was held by Chinese guerrillas and which the Japanese were preparing to assault. I went in style aboard a gunboat, the U.S.S. *Oahu.* As this was an Anglo-American rescue mission, a British vice-consul also made the trip, but in his own gunboat—H.M.S. *Cricket, Cockchafer, Aphis,* or *Mantis.* I do not remember which—at any rate, one of the insect class men-of-war.

My British colleague and I, together with the two skippers, negotiated arrangements with the Japanese for the rescue. The two vice-consuls would go up to Kuling, arrange with the Chinese guerrillas for the departure of those foreigners who wished to leave, and accompany those departing through the opposing Chinese and Japanese lines to the river port where the Japanese would provide steamer transport to Shanghai. When the day came for the ascent to Kuling, the two old salts pulled rank and, not speaking a word of either Japanese or Chinese, climbed the mountain, leaving the two vice-consuls to mind their fighting ships.

Four or five days after the ascent of the skippers, the British vice-consul and I went by prearrangement up the mountain at the head of some three hundred coolies who were to carry down the baggage of the evacuees. I bore one of the *Oahu*'s American flags to signify to the Chinese irregulars our innocent intent. Halfway up I was challenged by a nervous young guerrilla and his two companions. As I was explaining my humanitarian mission, and he denying any knowledge of it, rifle fire broke out from Chinese lookout posts on the ridges, and the mob of coolies rounded a bend into view. The guerrillas obviously thought they were about to be attacked through some strange ruse and excitedly ordered me to go back downhill.

Foreseeing a bloody mess, I shouted to my colleague to turn the coolies around and retreat. Then with as much dignity as I could muster, and flag held high, I marched jerkily down the mountain like a patriotic duck moving across a shooting gallery. Back at the Japanese lines we waited for the master mariners. After two or three hours they came bouncing down the slopes in high spirits, rather full of their exploit. The diplomats then dragged back up the mountain, like a couple of straw bosses, leading the bedraggled coolies to the baggage. So ended one of the last exercises in China of gunboat diplomacy.

Back in Hankow, in an official despatch I summarized my fortnight's observations in and around Kuling's port city, Kiukiang, and attempted to interpret the mentality of the occupying forces. This, in part, is what I said:

"Kiukiang was practically an intact city when abandoned by the Chinese in July 1938. It had suffered only slightly from Japanese aerial bombing and Chinese demolition. The first Japanese men-of-war to appear off Kiukiang subjected the town to a senseless and wasteful shelling. That accounted for a certain amount of destruction. With the arrival of Japanese troops and naval landing parties there began the thoroughgoing vandalism and looting which has continued to the present.

"Houses were broken into, articles of value pillaged, and other objects smashed. An American resident of Kiukiang stated that the streets of the town, well known for its ceramics, were littered after Japanese occupation with broken chinaware. The loot was shipped down river in vessels which had discharged their cargoes of troops and military supplies. With the advent of autumn, the Japanese began demolishing houses to obtain wood for fires. This destruction was carried on indiscriminately so that in February large sections of the city were badly wrecked.

"The native population, with the exception of a few thousand refugees who sought shelter in foreign missions, fled before the approach of the Japanese. Shortly after their arrival, the Japanese sought to evict the refugees and move them to a refugee zone established in the outskirts of the city. The night before the transfer was to be made, it was necessary for the American doctor at the Water of Life Hospital to post five men at the hospital well to prevent women refugees from committing suicide.

"The main part of the city was, when visited in January and again in February, reserved for the Japanese. The only Chinese to be seen on the streets were a few hawkers with special passes and girls impressed as waitresses in six or eight drab little bars and cafes. Very few Japanese civilians were visible. The fronts of most shops and homes not demolished were broken in and the buildings used as storehouses, garages or stables. Soldiers were seen warming themselves over fires built on the dirt floors of vacant houses and fed by furniture, torn-up floorboards, and other structural parts of buildings. There was a heavy traffic of military trucks and staff cars. Sentries were posted at the entrance to billets and at important street corners. On the water front gangs of Chinese coolies under Japanese supervision unloaded military supplies from barges. Oil and other supplies were stacked high along the foreshore.

"An upper middle class Chinese who had assumed an important position in the Japanese-inspired Kiukiang local regime confessed to an American there that he bitterly regretted his association with the puppet government. He said that he had believed that he was aligning himself with a permanent and stabilizing force.

Association with the Japanese military and Army Special Service Section, he declared, had disabused him of those beliefs. 'How can a dissolute organization like the Japanese army,' he asked, 'be expected to hold and govern four hundred million people?'

"As an example of the experiences of thousands of Chinese in the country-side surrounding Kiukiang, there was described by an American the recent history of a village woman who had sought refuge in an American mission. In the autumn this woman lost two nephews, young peasants, who were machine-gunned and killed by Japanese aircraft while crossing a small river by ferry boat. Then her son was taken away as a supply-bearer by a passing detachment of Japanese troops. Sometime later her home was burned by a Japanese punitive expedition. Finally, Japanese soldiers discovered one day the hiding place of her three nieces. Two of the young women succeeded in reaching a nearby pond before being caught and there committed suicide through drowning. The third was caught but, because she resisted assault, was killed, disemboweled, and her entrails strewn on the road.

"It is such manifestations of violent lechery and sadism on the part of Japanese soldiery, too often reported from reliable sources throughout the occupied areas of this district to be doubted more than in minor detail, that so dismays and horrifies the average Chinese. The not infrequent cases of several Japanese raping one woman are particularly bestial in Chinese eyes. Their own irregulars and bandits are hated mostly for financial exactions and looting, the Japanese troops mostly for their treatment of Chinese women.

"The Japanese gendarmerie have in Kiukiang, as they have in Hankow, exerted themselves to curb the excesses of Japanese troops. The behavior of Japanese soldiers in the city has been therefore somewhat less disorderly than in the country. . . .

"Punitive expeditions to a village suspected of having given aid to guerrillas follow the same saturnalian procedure on the Yangtze as on the Sungari [in Manchuria]: a certain part of the male population (depending upon the 'guilt' of the village) is shot outright, the women are raped and some killed, the houses are burned. . . ."

I viewed these atrocities with moral indignation—and a sense of national superiority. For surely American soldiers could not descend to such behavior. Still, why did Japanese soldiers behave with such savagery? My 1939 analysis was this. "The Japanese military in China obviously have a conviction of divine mission. Primarily, this mission is, of course, the fulfillment of duty to the emperor and the bringing of glory to the empire through martial conquest. Secondarily, but of major importance in contributing to a psychological conflict in the military, is the idealistic belief that the mission is also a crusade to liberate the Chinese people from the oppression of their own rulers. Opposition to the crusade is, by Japanese logic, to be expected from the Chinese government and its armies and grateful gladness from the Chinese people.

"To the Japanese soldier the resistance from armed peasants, the flight of most of the population from him, and the unmistakable resentment and fear of those whom he does succeed in 'liberating' are a shocking rejection of his idealism. The psychological conflict is thereby precipitated and is certainly not lessened by the continued insistence of official pronouncements on the theme of idealism. What critical faculties he may have been endowed with at birth having atrophied through nonuse, the average Japanese soldier is unable to resolve this psychological conflict through revolt or decent cynicism. He benightedly vents the conflict in vengeful action against the people whom he believes have denied his chivalry.

"The excessive forms which this vengeance takes need further interpretation. They are perhaps largely explained by the transition of the average Japanese soldier and officer in China from a social system in which the police and family dictated most phases of his behavior to a war situation in which there are no constant social checks. Never having been encouraged to appraise independently moral values, he is in China without apparent moral judgment. This moral infantilism, with all of its ramifications of primitive glorification of the sword fetish and bloodletting, and low regard for human sensibilities, especially in respect of women, accounts in a large measure for the odious reputation of the Japanese army and navy forces in this district."

My second journey in Japanese-occupied territory away from Hankow was about six months later, in August 1939. Writing to relatives, this was my story. "Hankow has been devoid of thrills, the work has been drudgery, relieved only by a sixteen-day jaunt through Kiangsi to investigate the position of American citizens and property under East Asia's new order. I was conducted on the trip by Mr. Asahina, who is dark-complexioned, well-bred, and a Japanese vice-consul, and Mr. Fujimaru, who has flashing gold teeth, a gentle manner, and is of the military police.

"It had taken more than a month to persuade the Japanese that they should let me go. And after they were persuaded, it took them two weeks to decide just when they would let me go. Then it took them several days to decide that I would carry no bacilli and viri to my ports of call. In August the Japanese were haunted by a fear of cholera. They demanded and I presented them with a clean and sweeping bill of health from the doctor of the U.S.S. *Guam*. And a cholera inoculation certificate. Next, with some embarrassment, they asked for a stool specimen. . . .

"Two hours before we were due to leave, Mr. Asahina called and with an air of quiet distraction announced that a Japanese army doctor wanted to look at me to see if I were healthy. Knowing at the beginning that I was licked anyway, I nevertheless pretended to argue over why the *Guam* certificate was not recognized.

"I finally went with him to some epidemic office of the Army's where I was sprayed with carbolic-phenol solution from a fire extinguisher as I entered. We stood in a small dark basement room waiting. There were sentries in the corridors. The floor of the room was wet with disinfectant. After five or ten minutes an unshaven individual in underwear was brought out from behind some shelves. Mr. Asahina bowed ceremoniously and the individual sat down in front of us. He scrutinized me as I tried to bloom with health. He asked me through Mr. Asahina if I were sick. I replied truthfully that I was not. The individual got up and went away. Sighing softly, Mr. Asahina said that we might now depart.

"As I left his car to enter my office, Mr. Asahina said hesitantly, 'About your stool—.' My heart stopped. 'We must have a specimen,' he murmured. 'But I just sent you one this morning.' 'Yes, that was forwarded to an institution. The Army now demands one for the ship.' 'There is only forty-five minutes before we must go aboard,' I protested, 'you can't be so impromptu about this matter.' 'You can,' he almost whispered, 'order one of your Chinese staff to produce a specimen.' I must confess to having been taken aback at this suggestion of chicanery and my face must have shown it, of course. Laughing, I said, 'I prefer to trust myself in a crisis like this.'

"When we arrived the next afternoon at our first port of call, Kiukiang, we had a quarantine inspection. A nice little man clomped down the deck in a pair of bedroom slippers and a soiled white coat, badge of his office. Our small party was lined up next to a bevy of battered Korean harlots and their promoters, apparently being assigned to a new detail at Kiukiang. The doctor went through his inspection in a perfunctory manner. He was anxious to get to the dining salon where there was a high pile of midget sunkist oranges and custard cakes awaiting him.

"On shore we proceeded to the Japanese consulate where I met again Mr. Komori, the acting consul, an old friend from February when on the *Oahu* I had visited Kiukiang in connection with the evacuation of Americans from Kuling. Here at the Consulate was repeated the old business of Japanese determination that I should follow a course contrary to the orders I had received and/or common sense (American variety). The details of this parting of minds are too tedious to recount. The result of a two-hour conference in which I resorted to Aristotelian logic, wheedling, humor, moral indignation, and just plain sitting and waiting was, of course, a compromise.

"Soft limpid eyes like those of a fawn are the outstanding features of Lieutenant Nakamura's face. I knew him first in Hankow where he told every occidental he met that he had been a professor of international law at some college in Japan, the name of which was unfamiliar to me. He was also, perhaps pardonably, conceited over being a graduate of St. John's, Brooklyn. He had a clipping proving it, which he showed all callers. On Kuling, where he was in charge of relations with 'third power nationals' (I suppose that Chinese are second power nationals) he is quoted as claiming to have been a professor at Tokyo Imperial University and a graduate, no longer of St. John's, but of Northwestern and Columbia.

"He puzzled his 'third power' protégés.

"Late this spring some of the foreigners called on him one night saying that a Chinese civilian had been badly wounded by Japanese soldiers at the Botanical

Gardens. Lieutenant Nakamura led several soldiers the six or eight miles to and from the gardens, late at night, bringing the wounded man back to the community hospital. The next morning he called to see how the man was. When told that the patient had died, his eyes filled with tears and he wept.

"On one of his visits to the American School campus, which now houses the hospital and an orphanage, he observed the nineteen-year-old daughter of a Chinese Episcopal clergyman. He apparently found her winsome, for one evening he sent a servant to bring her back to him. This overt approach failing, he called several days later on the cultured and dignified missionary in charge of the school saying that he had a 'secret matter' to discuss with Miss —— and that he would appreciate her being sent to his residence. The missionary replied that he was sure that if Lieutenant Nakamura had anything to say to the young lady, he could take the matter up there on the campus with her mother present at the interview. Lieutenant Nakamura dropped the subject.

"I have mentioned an orphanage on Kuling. It takes care of Chinese children abandoned by desperate parents and children whose parents have been killed. There was a small girl about four years old playing on the lawn with other children the day I visited the campus. She limped badly. Her home had been in the hills below Kuling. The Japanese this spring entered the peasant hut in which she lived, killed her parents, and bayonetted her five times—four times in the thighs and once in the vagina. The hospital patched her up. She still cries with fright when she sees a Japanese soldier.

"From Kuling I returned to Kiukiang where I stayed ten days at the Standard-Vacuum oil installation, three or four miles below the city. I was waiting to see whether the Japanese were going to take me to Nanchang, by air, as we wanted for sufficient reasons, or by fishing smack as they desired. I had nothing to do with these negotiations; my boss had referred the question to the Department of State which turned the matter over to our Tokyo embassy. So I sat and waited.

"Next to the Standard-Vacuum installation was a Shell installation. Then there was a British merchant vessel which, because the Japanese had closed the Yangtze to any commercial shipping but their own, had been at its berth off the Shell installation for more than a year. There was also a British gunboat, H.M.S. *Aphis,* which had been at the installations for some four months.

"The life of my hosts, the two Standard Oil men, was representative of the rest of this marooned community, save that of the gunboat, which had its own routine. They got up at 8:30, had breakfast, and then went down to the installation office just as if there were work to be done. Of course, there was none. So after puttering around for about forty-five minutes, they would go back to the house. They would read magazines or newspapers months old. Then play with a kitten. Then talk with a minah bird who could say, 'where are you going?' and 'what's that to you?.' It was too hot to exercise. As there was no electricity in the daytime and hence no fans, it was too hot even to sit still for long in one place. At last lunch came and it was a major event.

"After lunch they lay down for naps, but could not sleep because they had slept so much during the past months. About four they would come downstairs, read a ten-day old Shanghai paper which came on alternate days, and have tea. The kitten and the bird served to occupy some more time. At about six it was cool enough to go for the same walk through the countryside which they had taken day in day out for months. Back from the walk they might have a drink with some other of the castaways. In the evening they played bridge, kept on drinking, or reread old magazines.

"Viewing the boredom as more pernicious than schistosomiasis, I went in swimming in a backwash of the Yangtze one morning. I hired a small boat, expertly sculled by a young Chinese, to take me into clear water. 'How old are you?,' I asked. 'Eighteen,' he replied. 'How many mouths in your family?' 'Grandmother, mother, and little sister; I must provide a living for them and myself. Last year when we were at Hukow (down-river from Kiukiang) before the place was captured by the Japanese my father was alive. We had enough rice then to eat, we had a new boat, and fishing was good.'

"I asked him if he had been attacked by airplanes. He said that often he had. He and the other fisher folk would hug the cliffs of the river bank. Many of them were one time caught on shore without shelter. The elders and old women were in front, they all fell on their knees, knocked their heads on the ground until lumps appeared, held their hands clasped upward in supplication, and pleaded in loud voices with the aviators, begging them to go away. ' "We are only common folk," we shouted to the planes circling above us so low we could see the heads of the aviators peering down at us; "there are no soldiers amongst us," we cried.' The planes went away without harming them, he said, although on other occasions they had been machine-gunned.

"A bomber one day flew heavily over his and other fishing boats. It dropped bombs and his boat was sunk, along with many others. The family was then without means of support. The elder brother was conscripted to be a soldier. 'We haven't heard from him since,' the fisherboy said, 'There isn't a family from our village that hasn't been scattered or had a member of it killed.' The final calamity was the death of his father from illness. That left him, as he explained at the beginning to me, the sole support of the three women in the family.

"With the help of friends he patched up an old abandoned boat and resumed fishing. Fishing was poor and constantly interrupted by the hostilities. The family nearly starved; they ate roots from the hillsides, being too poor to buy rice. Life was very bitter.

"He was very interested to know the answer to one question—'When will all of this trouble and grief cease?' I told him that I did not know. 'Why doesn't your honorable country,' he asked, 'mediate between China and Japan and bring about peace.' I asked what good he thought that would do. 'After the fighting stops the Japanese will all go home,' he explained. I told him that I was afraid that would not be the case.

"Why had he not joined the guerrillas? Because, he declared, he was a fisherman and knew nothing about fighting. Furthermore, he must support the women of his family. He said that he knew nothing about the guerrillas on the north bank of the Yangtze; he regarded them as little if any improvement over plain old-fashioned bandits. He was afraid to enter their territory. His whole attitude was one of defeatism, he had no apparent will to strike back, the Japanese had him cowed—the Japanese and the problem of keeping his family and himself alive.

"Although he had Japanese identification papers and licenses, he and all of the other fishermen, he said, kept their Chinese fishing licenses because they more than half felt that ultimately the Chinese Government would return to power in his area.

"At seven fifteen on the morning of August 23, the captain's gig of H.M.S. *Aphis* drew alongside the *Tsukasu Maru*, I tossed my baggage to Asahina and Fujimaru and shinnied up the sides of the ship and over the gunwales. The *Tsukasu Maru* was gray from the color of its paint and an accumulation of grime. It was powered with a crude oil engine which shook the vessel like an aspen leaf. About ninety feet in length, it was packed with Japanese soldiers and military supplies. They viewed me with more indifference than hostility. Mr. Fujimaru made me comfortable on a beer crate behind a steel plate which protected the small wheel-house. There I read *Life* and *The New Yorker* and admired the view at the mouth of Poyang Lake. The Japanese soldiers exclaimed, 'How pretty!' and must have been reminded of Japan—blue water and mountains.

"The soldiers were quiet and bored. They talked very little among themselves and joked even less. A few read romantic novels or movie magazines; many slept. I lent one or two near me copies of *Life*. An illustrated appraisal of Mr. Petty's art and diagrams of how the *Squalus* was raised most interested them. The uniforms of most of the soldiers were old and patched.

"We arrived at 2 p.m. at Wucheng, half way down Poyang Lake. A handsome green tiled pavilion on a hill had several fractured (by shell fire) pillars supporting its roof, with the result that it looked like a man with his hat knocked off onto one side of his head. The town was a shambles. Whether from bombing or shelling I did not learn. We proceeded to gendarmerie headquarters, established in one of the few intact buildings in town. Most of the Japanese there were dressed in Chinese clothes. They were an evil-looking crew. We were taken to an officer's rest house for lodging. The back side of the building had been blown away. The view from the front verandah was of demolished houses and piles of debris.

"Cheerful small Chinese boys, like those at gendarmerie headquarters, prepared us a Japanese style bath which did much towards curing the fatigue from which we were suffering. After the bath we sat around in kimonos with two or three officers back from the front. They got drunk, were affable but uninteresting.

"The next morning we boarded a fishing smack, whose motive power was also a crude oil engine. I sat on my suitcase, wedged between a cavalry groom, who fell asleep and blew foam bubbles as he breathed, and a student from Meiji University, the only other civilian. The awning which was supposed to shield us from the sun was so low that it hung about our ears at times. The Meiji youth was very diffident in the presence of the soldiers, he was always doffing his cap. He carried a knapsack of the variety used by Japanese students going on a hike, wore shorts and woolen stockings which were gone at the heels.

"It was a very hot and wearisome trip. Asahina, Fujimaru, and I huddled together at about 1 p.m. for lunch consisting of a can of spaghetti which I had brought along and left in the sun to get heated, a can of Japanese ham, and a can of pineapples. I gave the Meiji lad a can of spaghetti with some trepidation lest he refuse it. Even though he was obviously without food I was afraid that his pride was stronger than his hunger. He accepted it with reserve, but as soon as my back was turned he joined a group of soldiers with alacrity and pooled the spaghetti with their Japanese rations. I never found out why the Meiji youth was traveling to Nanchang. . . .

"We arrived at Nanchang at 2 p.m. I landed with the grooms, privates, corporals, and navvies and was met in incongruous style by a major on the Nanchang headquarters staff and the chief of military police who whisked me off to gendarmerie headquarters in a staff car. Major Ishihara, like Colonel Maeda at Kiukiang, was that unique modern psychological phenomenon—a Japanese army officer, zealous and consecrated as a Jesuit under the Inquisition, but more arrogant. I enjoyed meeting Major Ishihara as I had enjoyed meeting Colonel Maeda and others of their kind; they were real men, not pleasant men, to be sure, but men with force and positive personality. . . .

"Major Ishihara, like Colonel Maeda, was charming to me. It suited his purposes to be so. And I was as genial as I could be. But I knew that my guts were hated. I think we understood one another. We spoke rather bluntly two or three times. When I left, the major and the Chief of the Gendarmerie smiled and bowed repeatedly even as the plane started to jounce off down the runway and I smiled and bowed in return.

"The plane was a recent model Beechcraft flown by a competent young man in a small boy's canvas sun hat. The Japanese are good aviators and having been, as babies, strapped on their mothers' backs has not affected their equilibrium."

CHAPTER *19*

The Great Collisions

IN OCTOBER 1940 I reported for duty at the Department of State. I was assigned to the China Desk of the Far Eastern Division. The chief of the division was Maxwell Hamilton. Twenty years earlier he had been a language officer in Peking, he had served at Canton and Shanghai and came to the department in 1927, where he slowly worked his way up to head the Far Eastern Division. He possessed the virtues of a model head clerk: prim, meticulous, and most respectful toward higher authority.

Well he might have been diffident before Stanley Hornbeck, his immediate superior. Dr. Hornbeck took his carefully garnered academic degrees only a shade less solemnly than he did his position as adviser to the secretary of state on Far Eastern political relations. In his official capacity Dr. Hornbeck was overbearing and sometimes vindictive. I suspect this came from a suppressed realization that his recognition as a great scholar-statesman was thwarted by his own inadequacies. The man was, unhappily, not much more than a vigorous pedant.

It was these two, Hornbeck and Hamilton, neither with experience in Japan and both China-oriented, who were the top professionals in the department on our relations with Japan, China, and the other countries of East Asia. It was they who finally evaluated and interpreted the flow of information from the Far East and offered policy guidance to the secretary of state and the president. In so doing, it was Hornbeck who played the dominant role, Hamilton a dutifully supporting one.

My functions were menial and varied. I read and sometimes commented on despatches and telegrams from China, acted as expediter for outgoing messages, drafted answers to routine congressional and public inquiries on matters affecting China, and coordinated with other divisions proposed actions likely to have effect beyond the Far East. In 1941 I had won Hamilton's confidence to the extent that he allowed me to draft the weekly summary of events in the Far East. As this was done for the perusal of the secretary, my composition was edited by my senior on the China desk, George Atcheson, an unusually competent and quick-witted Foreign Service officer.

In a small room off Dr. Hornbeck's outer office sat his assistant, a composed and tweedy young man looking like a college instructor reading through a pile of term papers. His name was Alger Hiss, and while he was pleasant to those of us who were juniors in the division, he did not invite familiarity. This was not surprising as he was not a professional in foreign affairs, but had been a law clerk to Mr. Justice Holmes and therefore came from a realm apart. We were all on first name terms, and I remember going to a brimming cocktail party at his house and the gentle charm of the hostess, his wife Priscilla. I was therefore as disbelieving as many others some years later when Whittaker Chambers accused Hiss of espionage.

As often happens in specialized organizations, the dozen or so members of the Far Eastern Division tended to be ingrown. This natural tendency in the department to move in cliques was also characteristic of other geographical divisions. The Near Eastern Division with its Arabists was one. And the rest of us felt that those who dealt with Western European affairs regarded themselves as a cut above us.

Because of my working contacts with other divisions, I knew quite a few people in the department outside of my own group. But they remained casual acquaintances and my leisure time was spent with friends unconnected with the State Department or with other China or Japan specialists. My aunt Flossie, who was woman's editor of the *Detroit News*, introduced me to the Washington correspondent of that paper, Jay Hayden. Through him I met other Washington newsmen and so became acquainted with the flurries of political gossip that gusted through Washington. Through Hayden and others I continued to broaden the association with newsmen which I had begun in Mukden—John Gunther, William Henry Chamberlin, and J. P. McEvoy—and furthered in Hankow with those I met there. On the whole, I found newsmen more engaging and stimulating than most of my colleagues.

During the period 1940–41 I also met various New Dealers, one of whom was Lauchlin Currie. He was an administrative assistant to the president. An economist from Harvard, Currie was a prototype of the professor come to a position of influence in the White House. Like McGeorge Bundy, Walt Rostow, and Henry Kissinger, who followed and outdid him two and three decades later, he was a voracious consumer of information, confident in his intellectual prowess, schematic in his approach to foreign affairs, and bent upon translating ideas into action.

At the request of Chiang Kai-shek, Currie went to China in January 1941 to look into the Chinese military and economic situation. I assumed that the invitation had been inspired by T. V. Soong, Mme. Chiang's brother, who was in Washington lobbying for aid to China. He needed a pipeline into the White House to supplement Harry Hopkins. In any event, Currie flew off to Chungking in a boyish spirit of high adventure, armed with travel agency advice from me about climate, clothing, and disorders of the digestive tract.

He returned some six weeks later. The Chinese had feted and flattered him, confided to him their many real needs, and assured him that they were manfully preparing to receive and put to use what they were asking for. Currie seemed to have accepted what he was told at face value. The Chinese were not different from us, he told me. In the tone of one to whom some occult truth had been revealed, he said that the Chinese with whom he talked thought just as we did. Like most visiting American dignitaries who were granted audiences by the Generalissimo and his consort, Currie was captivated by Madame Chiang, who understood American men better than she did her fellow countrymen. And he was awed by what she said her husband said—for Chiang spoke no English and she was the interpreter.

After Currie's return to Washington, he telephoned me from time to time or asked me to drop by his office requesting information or expedition of some action he was seeking. Understandably, my superiors did not appreciate these direct approaches from the White House to one of their subordinates. I was uncomfortable in this situation but felt that I could not rebuff requests from someone in Currie's position. What went on here was typical of the helter-skelter Rooseveltian style of doing business.

Far more important than Currie's out-of-channels dealing with me was the president's treatment of his secretary of state. Instead of replacing Cordell Hull with someone in whom he had broader confidence, he undercut the secretary by dealing directly with the under secretary, Sumner Welles. And Roosevelt's principal White House assistant, Harry Hopkins, freewheeled in blithe disregard of the bureaucratic hierarchy. Because of the president's failure to vitalize the State Department, as he had the War Department with the Stimson-Marshall combination, and his fancy for manipulating as well as formulating foreign policy, the conduct of American foreign relations had already in 1940 and 1941 begun to pass from the Department of State to the White House operators, the War, Navy, and Treasury Departments, and special agencies.

The fall of Hankow marked the conclusion of the first stage of Japan's attempt to subdue China. Thereafter, by political maneuvers, creation of puppet regimes, and military blockade, Tokyo tried to bring Chiang to terms. This strategy lasted nearly two years, without success.

During this period the macabre dance of deceit, aggression, and war swayed to and fro across Eurasia in two-front symmetry. As Japan tried to subdue China, it probed by frontier attacks Soviet power and will. As the Red Army lashed back at the Kwantung Army, the Kremlin negotiated with the British and French for an alignment against Hitlerite Germany. When Stalin concluded that London and Paris were trifling with him and wanted Hitler deflected eastward against Russia, he suddenly made a deal with Hitler which partitioned the lands lying between them, freed Germany to expand westward, enabling the *Führer* to say "For the first time in history we have to fight only on one front," and briefly permitted Stalin the status of spectator as the imperialists went for one another's throats.

In September 1940 Japan made its first southward move outside of China. With France under the German heel, Japan wrung permission from Vichy to deploy forces in the northern part of French Indochina. This blocked the railroad to Yunnan, leaving China only one ground connection with the British Empire and the United States—the scraggly road from Rangoon to Kunming. More significantly, the Japanese armed forces were obviously in a ready position to advance further southward.

Immediately after occupying northern Indochina, Japan signed on September 27 a treaty of alliance with Germany and Italy. The Germans sought to reassure the Russians about the intention of the Tripartite Pact, saying that it "would probably serve as a damper on the warmongers, especially in America . . . and perhaps . . . serve the restoration of world peace." While it was clear that the alliance was a warning to the United States, it also reminded the Soviet Union of its two fronts, on which its two adversaries were now in military collusion. For the Japanese the pact might be counted on to restrain the Russians from taking military advantage of Japan when Tokyo turned its attention more fully to southward expansion.

Having failed in the Battle of Britain to win on only one front, and unsuccessful in persuading Stalin to yield Soviet interests in the Balkans to Germany in exchange for Berlin's airy recognition of Soviet *lebensraum* in India, Hitler decided that he must fight on a second front, that he must dispose of the Russians before returning to overwhelm the British. Hitler thought that the Red Army could be defeated in less than six months. His *Wehrmacht* invaded the Soviet Union in June 1941.

Incredibly, Stalin did not expect the assault. The Red Army at first reacted sluggishly and ineptly, but then rallied. Aided by Russian space and climate and Hitler's mistake in dispersing his strength, the Red Army stalled the *Wehrmacht*.

This was the situation between Germany and the Soviet Union when Japan attacked the United States at Pearl Harbor.

Japan had taken the precaution well before December 7, 1941 of concluding a nonaggression pact with the Soviet Union. With this agreement of April 13, 1941, Tokyo felt less apprehensive over its western flank and freer to advance southward and against the United States. Moscow's benefit from the pact was the release of considerable forces in the east for transfer to European Russia in the event of a Nazi attack.

On July 2, ten days after Hitler catapulted the *Wehrmacht* into the Soviet Union, the emperor of Japan presided over an Imperial Conference attended by the inner circle of his foremost military and civilian officials. The decisions reached were, in sum:

Bring pressure on the Chiang regime from the Southern approaches in order to bring about its surrender.

Advance into the Southern Regions, initially Indochina and Thailand, by negotiations, but if these break down, do not be deterred by the possibility of war with the United States and Britain;

Delay entry into the German-Soviet war, unless the conflict "should develop to our advantage . . ."

Plans with regard to the Soviet Union must not obstruct "our basic military preparations for war with England and America."

Eight days after these decisions, and as ignorant of them as Japan had been of Hitler's plans for invading Russia, the German foreign minister, von Ribbentrop, instructed the German ambassador at Tokyo to urge that Japan and Germany "join hands on the Trans-Siberian railway before the winter starts."

Washington, during the late autumn of 1940, was exhilarated by the drubbing that the RAF had given the Luftwaffe in the Battle of Britain. But in the State Department most of our thoughts were anxious and even gloomy. The Germans had demonstrated such tremendous power and the British were so beleaguered that unless the United States quickly bolstered Britain's strength, we thought, Hitler would triumph and organize Europe against the United States. The exchange in September of fifty American destroyers for bases on British territory in the Western Hemisphere had been only the first step in what needed to be done.

China, too, required American help, as we in the Far Eastern Division were acutely aware. But its plight was not so dramatic or critical as that of the United Kingdom. And Japan, by moving into northern Indochina and joining the Axis, seemed to be readying itself to let the China Incident simmer while it undertook some new adventure.

In spite of all of the sympathy for Britain aroused by Nazi abominations, RAF valor, and Churchill's eloquence, isolationist sentiment in the United States was still strong. Most Americans had been disillusioned by our last intervention in Europe—World War I—and had been given no reason by European statesmanship to think better of the Old World. Furthermore, they had been led to believe that exportation of arms would surely draw the country into foreign wars. Many thought that to go to Britain's aid would not only entangle us in a dirty foreign mess but also be futile, as Hitler was going to win and his New Order was the wave of the future. The United States, they argued, should remain strictly aloof, neutral.

Strangely, the isolationist passivity toward German expansionism in Europe was not matched by like aversion to embroilment in the Far East. No outcry was raised lest we become caught up, because of the Philippines, in a faraway war against Japan. Manila, more than seven thousand miles from San Francisco, was twice as far from us as Liverpool. In measurements more significant than mileage, in cultural, economic, and strategic terms, we were infinitely closer to the United Kingdom than to the Philippines. But our flag flew over the remote archipelago in the western Pacific and that, somehow, seemed to make the Philippines more vital to us than the British Isles.

Because of isolationist feelings, Roosevelt regularly assured the American people that he was trying to keep them out of the war in Europe, that there was "no demand for sending an American expeditionary force" but that "we must be the great arsenal of democracy." Following these tactics he managed to get congressional approval in March 1941 of lend-lease legislation enabling the administration to send material aid to Britain, China, and later, the Soviet Union.

To counter Nazi naval operations against shipping, he began inching his way across the Atlantic and into belligerency. In April the American Navy began to patrol the western Atlantic. In May Roosevelt declared that the United States would deliver goods to Britain and that a state of unlimited national emergency existed.

The news of Hitler's assault upon Russia broke like a Wagnerian blast of brasses and kettle drums. This would be war on a vast and savage scale. Would the Russians hold and what would it all mean for us and the British and the Japanese and the Chinese?

As the Russians began to pull themselves together and the Red Army stiffened its defenses, we watched for the next move by the Japanese and worked on scraping together military assistance to China. Aid to China was low on the list of American priorities. First, we had to equip our own neglected forces, especially those in the Philippines. Then came the British and, after the German attack, the Russians. Being in last place did not sit well with Chiang Kai-shek, but it did not deter him from asking for more than we could supply—or than he could put to use.

In the fall of 1940 the Generalissimo had sent one of his air generals, accompanied by Captain Chennault, to ask for 500 basic trainers, 10 transports, ammunition, ordnance, and supplies necessary to build 14 airfields and 122 landing strips. By March 1941 T. V. Soong, the Generalissimo's brother-in-law, increased the request to 1,000 aircraft. He also asked for arms sufficient for 30 divisions and a great variety of transportation material, from that necessary to build a railroad between Burma and China to cargo planes.

These and other applications received sympathetic attention in government offices for a number of reasons. One was strategic—strengthening China to keep Japan occupied and out of mischief elsewhere. A more pervasive reason was the sentimental feeling that most Americans had always cherished for China, heightened by pity for the Chinese as victims of aggression.

Somehow a legend gained currency that the Chinese had fought with persistent valor and that, if only weapons were placed in their hands, they would push the Japanese back into the sea. On top of this was an American sense of shame that, rather than helping the gallant victims of aggression, we had provided the Japanese the wherewithal to mangle the Chinese. Finally, Madame Chiang, T. V. Soong, and other Chungking representatives shrewdly exploited this jumble of sentiments in American officials.

The Chinese did not get all that they asked for. This was not simply because they were at the bottom of the priority list. It was also because some of the things they asked for they could not effectively use—for example, tanks that were too heavy for all but a few bridges in China and B-17 heavy bombers for which they had no adequate air fields.

By far the most valuable aid that China received in 1941 was the American Volunteer Group. The AVG was formed in the spring by private recruitment of crews from the military services to fly and maintain one hundred P-40 fighter aircraft which had been made available for the AVG. This was essentially a mercenary force under commercial contract and not under either American or Chinese military discipline. Chennault was designated as the commander of the group, with the diffident title of "supervisor."

Naturally, something as irregular as the AVG could not have been created without the gentlemanly collusion of all American officials concerned, from the president, Hopkins, and Currie to personnel officers at airbases and the crews of naval ships that escorted past the Japanese mandated islands a Dutch merchantman carrying the volunteers. After all the Chinese lobbying for air support and the considerable American effort to put together the AVG, Chungking neglected to prepare for the reception of the group anywhere in China. When the first AVG contingent debarked at Rangoon in July it, therefore, accepted the hospitality of the RAF and established itself at a Burmese airfield. There the AVG assembled and received training from Chennault in his tactics. The volunteers still were there when Japan attacked Pearl Harbor.

Meanwhile those officials dealing with aid to China were troubled by the impracticality of the military requirements presented by Soong and his subordinates. The need was felt for American officers and technicians in China to advise the Chinese government and keep the American government informed regarding China's true requirements for equipment. Brigadier General John Magruder, a thoughtful, urbane China specialist, was therefore sent to Chungking in October as head of the American Military Mission to China (AMMISCA). Being well acquainted with the country and the people, Magruder took the Chinese way of doing things in his stride. But some of his staff, especially those who were new to the scene, were shocked by their encounters with incompetence, indifference, and corruption in both the army and the management of the vital line of communications with Burma.

At least one of these officers, Lieutenant Colonel George W. Sliney, a blunt, prosaic artilleryman, drew some broader conclusions on the basis of extensive investigation of the Chinese army in October and November 1941:

> Several Chinese officers have stated to me that they believed China might be able to win this war without further fighting. They expected international diplomatic pressure to force Japan out of China. . . .
>
> The general idea in the United States that China has fought Japan to a standstill, and has had many glorious victories, is a delusion. . . . The will to fight an aggressive action does not yet exist in the Chinese Army. . . .
>
> Many small things all pointing in the same direction have caused me to have a feeling, stronger than a suspicion, that the desire of the Chinese for more modern material was not . . . for the purpose of pressing the war against Japan, but was to make the central government safe against insurrection after diplomatic pressure by other nations had forced Japan out of China.

While Chiang Kai-shek was in 1941 concerned about the insubordination of some residual warlords, his long-range anxiety was centered on the Communists. In October of the preceding year he had confided to Ambassador Johnson that the Communists were taking advantage of the situation created by the Japanese invasion—as indeed they were—and that he feared them more than the Japanese. At the turn of the year, government troops suddenly attacked and destroyed the headquarters element of the New Fourth Army, a Communist force created to operate on the fringes of and behind the Japanese lines in the lower Yangtze Valley. This action, clearly unrelated to the war against Japan but directed, rather, at eliminating competition for postwar control of Chiang's home territory, cracked the facade of the united front.

On the eve of Pearl Harbor, then, while Soong was goading guilt-ridden American officials and clamoring for equipment from meager production, ungainly Chinese armies squatted in passive resistance before their overextended enemy. Prophetically, the most significant military action in China during 1941 was the New Fourth Army affair, a premonition of civil war.

After Tokyo had decided on July 2, 1941 to expand southward, keep open its choice of action against the Soviet Union, and prepare for war with the United States, it extracted from the impotent French government at Vichy agreement to Japan's deployment of military forces in southern Indochina. When Japanese warships and transports were seen approaching Indochina, Washington reacted on July 26 by freezing Japanese assets. This order, in effect, embargoed the shipment of oil and other strategic materials to Japan. In so doing Washington forced Tokyo into a countdown toward ignition of hostilities with the United States.

Japan's stock of oil, the Navy's chief of general staff told the emperor at a Privy Council meeting on July 28, was sufficient for only two years. The choice for Japan, then, was submission to a steady drain culminating in collapse, an agreement with Washington, or war. The first was out of the question. The second was the chosen goal. But agreement must be quickly attained because time was steadily running out on its alternative, war, which must be resorted to if negotiations failed.

From the end of July onward, the Japanese ambassador tried with mounting anxiety to strike some sort of a bargain with Roosevelt and Hull. But he had no success. The Japanese and American positions were irreconcilable. And the reasons went deep.

Japan had been in the nineteenth century forced out of self-contained isolation by the West. We were accustomed to congratulating ourselves on how Commodore Perry, less than one hundred years earlier, had "opened" Japan with a naval show of force. The benighted Japanese had been urged to learn from and emulate the civilized West. They did.

By the early twentieth century, Japan had developed a strong sense of manifest destiny. But by then, because most of the less advanced peoples and their lands had been taken over by the civilized nations, and because Japan had become modernized later than the Christian West it was cheated out of the easy pickings. For those with a conviction of manifest destiny, however, the road to empire was not altogether closed and the United States had at the turn of the century shown the way. In taking the Philippines it had demonstrated how to acquire colonies by despoiling a weaker civilized nation of its overseas possessions.

After World War I the United States, Britain, and France tried to give imperialist expansion a bad name. This was, in part, because they were sated with colonies and, naturally, wanted everyone else to stay put. The western democracies were content with their lot, so why should not everyone else be with his? What was more, the western democracies had impenitently come to see that imperial conquest was improper, and they had even contrived to make it illegal.

To the colonial have-nots fired with manifest destiny, particularly to Japan, the attitude of the western democracies, particularly that of the United States, was monumental hypocrisy. Japan was convinced that it needed to expand as much as England had needed to expand beyond its islands, and certainly far more than the United States had needed to reach across the Pacific for Guam and the Philippines. As the United States claimed a Monroe Doctrine over the Western Hemisphere, so Japan believed that other powers should stay out of East Asia. If the Americans disapproved of new empires, then Japan would call the area over which it sought hegemony something else—the Greater East Asia Co-Prosperity Sphere.

The Greater East Asia Co-Prosperity Sphere was not merely a semantic dodge for the word "empire." As the Japanese believed that they had embarked upon the China Incident not simply in search of fortune and glory, but also to save the Chinese people from misrule and Communist conspiracy, so they thought of the Greater East Asia Co-Prosperity Sphere in terms of the hierarchical Japanese family, with Japan in the role of the much wiser elder brother sternly administering the affairs of the younger East Asian brothers for the benefit of all in the fraternal group. This conceit was not greatly different from France's civilizing mission, the white man's burden borne by Britain, and McKinley's subjugating the Filipinos so that, "by God's grace" we could "do the very best we could by them, as our fellowmen for whom Christ also died."

Japan's compulsion to expand was therefore reinforced by a belief that the extension of its sway was a good, even a virtuous ambition. It followed that American objections to Japanese claims of hegemony over East Asia were to Tokyo more than wrong, they were insufferable. After Washington froze Japanese assets, followed by similar British and Netherlands East Indies measures, Japan felt clutched. The Dutch action was even more provoking than the American because Tokyo had regarded the oil of the Indies as the alternative to the American supply—and the Indies were in the projected Co-Prosperity Sphere.

Everyone in Washington dealing with Far Eastern matters understood that the Japanese felt themselves to be in a crisis, for our embassy at Tokyo made us well aware of this. But only a handful had sure indications of how desperate and resolved the Japanese government was. The president, Hull, Stimson, Marshall, Secretary of the Navy Frank Knox, Chief of Naval Operations Admiral Harold R. Stark, and a few others regularly read intercepts of the most secret Japanese diplomatic cables, the code of which our cryptographers had broken.

Realizing the gravity of the situation and our military unpreparedness in the Philippines, Marshall and Stark urged that the president and Hull prolong negotiations in a play for time so that our neglected trans-Pacific defenses might be strengthened. But time was the last thing that Tokyo could concede—unless we would relax our oil embargo. That we would not do, short of Japan's backing out of Indochina and China. This was out of the question for Tokyo, even more out of the question than getting Washington twenty-five years later to back out of Vietnam.

As Hull preached to Ambassador Nomura about Japan's besetting sins, urged the necessity of repentance, and exhorted Tokyo to seek national salvation through embracing a set of vaporous political beatitudes, the Japanese Army and Navy proceeded with their countdown. On November 3 the chief of Naval General Staff approved the Pearl Harbor attack plan. On November 5, before a reluctant and troubled emperor, an Imperial Conference decided that if the Americans did not respond acceptably by November 25 to the final Japanese proposals, a decision on whether to go to war should be presented to the emperor. In any event, the armed forces were to be ready for war at the start of December. On November 26 a Japanese carrier task force set forth in the direction of the Hawaiian Islands. On December 1 a silent emperor lent his presence to an Imperial Conference, presided over by the premier, General Hideki Tojo, at which the decision was made to go to war.

The intercepts read in Washington contained no military timetable. But they did indicate that the crisis would reach its head after November 25. Upon learning from Hull that negotiations had practically broken down, the War and Navy Departments on November 27 alerted the American commanders in the Pacific to the possibility of hostilities beginning at any time. But our military and diplomatic officials in Washington—and in the Pacific—were looking intently in the direction of Southeast Asia, not at the Hawaiian Islands, for the first flash of war.

The Sunday morning air strike of the Japanese at Pearl Harbor on December 7 found our forces there unprepared for the visit. And Washington was thunderstruck. So less than six months after Stalin and his armed forces had been stunned by a surprise German attack, Roosevelt and his commanders in Hawaii were caught off guard by the Japanese.

Japan's Hawaiian assault temporarily crippled the Pacific Fleet and army air units, and stirred unseemly displays of consternation on the West Coast. But it was meant as a one-shot operation only, to clear the flank of Tokoyo's offensive into Thailand, Malaya, Borneo, the Indies—and the Philippines. Here too, in the Philippines, our commanders were caught flatfooted by the Japanese. General Douglas MacArthur, commander in the Far East, and his air commander, Major General Lewis H. Brereton, were warned after the blow at Pearl Harbor nine hours before the enemy attacked Clark Field, yet half of their aircraft were destroyed on the ground. This was particularly inglorious because the War Department had begun to believe that the few B-17 Flying Fortresses earlier rushed to the islands had greatly strengthened its defenses. And MacArthur had declared that the risk involved in attacking the Philippines had become too much for Japan.

Such, then, was the sorry beginning of American participation in World War II. This very humiliation of Pearl Harbor and Clark Field, however, angered and unified the American people. The declaration of war, in accordance with the Tripartite Pact, by a jubilant Mussolini and a loath Hitler widened the war for the American public to two fronts and made it possible for Roosevelt to argue persuasively, as he otherwise could not, that the defeat of the German enemy should have precedence over the defeat of Japan. Thus, if the United States was bound, as it probably was, to become involved in the fighting that was raging in Asia, Europe, and Africa, it is difficult to imagine any more favorable psychological initiation into global war than that provided by Japan, Germany, and Italy.

Still, the haunting question remains. If only Washington had been more flexible, if only someone other than Hull, a sterile Wilsonian dogmatist counselled by the starchy Dr. Hornbeck, had conducted the negotiations, could not the war with Japan have been avoided? The answer is no. The conflicting forces at work in both countries were so strong and deep that they could not have been reconciled no matter who the negotiators might have been.

Japan was on the march to ever greater empire. The United States objected to Japanese expansion into China and Southeast Asia because it feared the growth of Japanese power—and for sentimental reasons—a long-standing infatuation with China and the Stars and Stripes flying over the Philippine folly. Washington could not accede to what Tokyo wanted—withdrawal of support of Chiang and acceptance of the Greater East Asia Co-Prosperity Sphere, even when the Japanese promised to respect American sovereignty over the Philippines. Nor was Washington in a position to coerce Japan because it did not have in the Far East the necessary bargaining counter—a tremendous military force in being, backed by an evident will to use it.

In this untenable situation the American government complained, moralized, and bluffed. That could not and did not stop the Japanese. Nor did the United States get out of Japan's way. So they collided.

CHAPTER *20*

Rout in Burma

SEVERAL DAYS AFTER Christmas 1941 I had dinner with Stilwell and Pinky Dorn. Stilwell, then a major general, had been summoned to Washington from his command of the Third Corps on the west coast. Pinky came as his aide-de-camp. I did not know that Marshall and Stimson had chosen Stilwell to command an American invasion of North Africa. I did gather, however, that he was not bound for the Far East. After dinner, while walking to my car with Pinky, I asked him whether the general might be willing to take me along as some sort of diplomatic attaché to the commanding general, as Stilwell had once been military attaché to an ambassador. Pinky thought that this could be done.

While Stilwell was working on variants to a North African landing, Marshall consulted him on January 1, 1942 on the selection of a general to head a yet undefined mission in China. Lieutenant General Hugh A. Drum was under consideration and Stilwell noted in his diary Drum's qualifications: "Pompous, stubborn, new to them [the Chinese], high rank." Looking at himself as an alternative to Drum, he perceptively added: "Me? No thank you. They remember me as a small-fry colonel that they kicked around. They saw me on foot in the mud, consorting with coolies, riding soldier trains. Drum will be ponderous and take time through interpreters; he will decide slowly and insist on his dignity. Drum by all means."

How right Stilwell was, and how apprehensive Chiang Kai-shek was of Americans who knew China, emerged five days later in a letter from T. V. Soong to the assistant secretary of war, John J. McCloy. The American officer to be sent to China, Soong pointed out, "need not be an expert on the Far East; on the contrary, he [Chiang] thinks that military men who had knowledge of Chinese armies when China was under war lords operate at a disadvantage when they think of the present Chinese national armies in terms of the armies of the war lords." Thus at the outset of the Chinese-American relationship as allies, Stilwell and the Generalissimo were in fundamental agreement regarding the type of man who should head American military representation in China.

Unfortunately, Drum was pretentious with Stimson and Marshall and so lost their confidence. They turned to Stilwell. The concept of the China assignment had grown to include, vaguely, acting as the Generalissimo's chief of allied staff, command of some Chinese troops, and even of British, Chinese, and American forces in the defense of Burma. After a quiet evening alone with Stimson on January 14, Stilwell wrote in his journal that the secretary of war thought that the Chinese would accept an American commander but that he, Stilwell, doubted it.

This visit brought Stimson to share Marshall's high regard for Stilwell. Two days later the chief of staff called in Stilwell. Marshall wanted to know whether he would take the Chinese assignment, which by this time had expanded into saving Burma, about to be invaded by the Japanese. Stilwell's response to Marshall was that he would go where he was sent. He thought that the chances for getting results in China and Burma were good, provided that he was given command. At Marshall's request, Stilwell drafted a War Department message to the Chinese designed to test the Generalissimo on the command issue. Chiang agreed on January 21, the day after the Japanese burst out of Thailand into Burma, that Stilwell should exercise executive authority over British, Chinese, and American units, especially in Burma, and that he would serve as chief of the Generalissimo's nonexistent allied staff.

The chief of staff asked Stilwell on January 23, "Will you go?" The reply was, consistently, "I'll go where I'm sent." Thereupon agreements and orders were drawn up assigning to Stilwell functions and authority which would never be realized as fully as written. Soong confirmed that his mission was primarily "to supervise and control all United States defense-aid affairs for China; under the Generalissimo to command all United States forces in China and such Chinese forces as may be assigned to him; to represent the United States on any international war council in China and act as the chief of staff for the Generalissimo."

Stilwell's laconic orders of February 2 from the War Department, in part, designated him as "Chief of Staff of the Supreme Commander of the Chinese Theater" (Chiang Kai-shek), and appointed him "Commanding General of the United States Forces in the Chinese Theater of Operations, Burma, and India." Marshall amplified this with injunctions to "increase the effectiveness of United States assistance to the Chinese government for the prosecution of the war and to assist in improving the combat efficiency of the Chinese army."

The need to help the British defend Burma imposed yet another web of responsibilities upon Stilwell. By a decision of the Combined Chiefs of Staff (Anglo-American), if Stilwell should enter Burma at the head of Chinese troops, he was to function under the American-British-Dutch-Australian Command. This was the hastily thrown-together headquarters charged with saving Southeast Asia. It was headed by General Sir Archibald Wavell, to whom Stilwell would be subordinate and for whom the American general was to act as a go-between with the Generalissimo.

Having been touchingly "God-blessed" by the secretary of war, treated to "just a lot of wind" by the president, whom he found "very unimpressive," and congratulated by Harry Hopkins ("a strange, gnomelike creature") on embarking upon a "great adventure," Stilwell took off for Asia on February 11. He was flying into a shambles. Hong Kong, Guam, Wake, and Manila had fallen; Singapore would capitulate in four days; two weeks later Wavell would abandon Java and dissolve the ABDA Command—and the Japanese were snaking through the Burmese jungles toward Rangoon.

While the western democracies were being shoved out of their East Asian colonies, fantasy suffused Chungking and stagnation settled over the rest of the country. Within hours after the attack at Pearl Harbor, the Generalissimo called in Generals Magruder and Chuikov, Ambassador Clark Kerr, General Dennys, the British military attaché, and others to launch a program for the combined prosecution of the war against Japan. Chuikov soon dropped out of the subsequent conferences and Stalin informed Chiang that he was not yet ready to fight the Japanese. The Generalissimo's proposal envisaged combined planning and command, with Chungking, at least initially, as the center of the collective effort.

Being without an agreed, comprehensive war plan, Washington and London were as unprepared for this Chinese political blitz as they had been for military surprises sprung on them by the Japanese. To gain time for composing Anglo-American thoughts, Roosevelt and Churchill sent Major General George Brett and General Wavell to plumb the Generalissimo's strategic concept. Chiang raised with them on December 23 sweeping issues on which the two generals were not empowered to take positions. Madame Chiang dwelt upon China's needs for assistance. But what cast a blight on the conference was an infelicitous refusal by Wavell of most of the forces offered by Chiang for the defense of Burma. This outraged touchy Chinese sensibilities. The anti-British resentment thereby aroused in the Generalissimo and Madame Chiang was to linger and corrode Anglo-Chinese relations.

At this unfortunate conference Chiang unveiled his master plan. In essence, he advocated concentration by all, including the Soviet Union, on the defeat of Japan in 1942. Naval and air action should halt the enemy in the South Pacific and then move to blockade Japan. The air war was to be conducted from Alaska, the Soviet Far East, and Chinese coastal provinces. After these actions had cut off the Japanese forces in China from their homeland, then the Chinese would destroy them. The plan was uncluttered by considerations of supply, command, or what should be done about the inconvenient war with Germany.

Reluctant to turn the conduct of the war over to the Generalissimo and having little in military hardware which could be spared to slake Chiang's thirst for sophisticated weaponry, Roosevelt heaped honors on Chiang. He, Churchill, and the newly created Combined Chiefs of Staff, in an act of redundant superlatives, appointed the Generalissimo Supreme Commander of the China Theater of War, which added Thailand as a bonus to the geographical expanse in which

Chiang had already conducted war as supreme commander for four and a half years. This bestowal of an honorific was symptomatic of Roosevelt's outlook with regard to China and Chiang.

What the current realities of the situation in China were was not of prime concern to the president. For Roosevelt's approach to China was rooted not so much in what existed as what should be. Like so many Americans before him, he thought less in terms of the actuality than of the potential of five hundred million Chinese. China was to be treated as a great power so that it would become a great power, a grateful friend eventually helping the United States to keep order and peace in the Far East. And Chiang Kai-shek was to join him, Churchill, and Stalin to make a Big Four.

Churchill did not think much of this point of view. He and his military leaders were exposed to it at the Washington conference going by the decorative code name of Arcadia (December 22, 1941–January 14, 1942). Some eight years after the event, in *The Hinge of Fate*, he summed up his reactions:

At Washington I had found the extraordinary significance of China in American minds, even at the top, strangely out of proportion. I was conscious of a standard of values which accorded China almost equal fighting power with the British Empire, and rated the Chinese armies as a factor to be mentioned in the same breath as the armies of Russia. I told the president how much I felt American opinion overestimated the contribution which China could make to the general war. He differed strongly. There were five hundred million people in China. What would happen if this enormous population developed in the same way Japan had done in the last century and got hold of modern weapons? I replied that I was speaking of the present war, which was quite enough to go on with for the time being. I said that I would of course always be helpful and polite to the Chinese, whom I admired and liked as a race and pitied for their endless misgovernment, but that he must not expect me to adopt what I felt was a wholly unreal standard of values.

The early 1942 realities in China were outlined by General Magruder in February messages to the War Department. The Chinese, he reported, had no intention of assuming the offensive against the Japanese in China because this would expend the economic and political worth of their forces. It was difficult to work with them because they ignored logistic considerations, which they did not understand. Air power was their cure-all, even though their transport facilities could not take care of a tenth of the planes they were asking for. The War Department told Magruder that it was aware of the state of affairs that he reported and that it confirmed its estimate of the situation.

The president was anxious to keep China in the war. But he showed no sign of recognizing that after December 7 Chiang had no reason for capitulating to the Japanese—or for fighting them. Only in Burma, in defense of his vital line of communications to the outside world, was it worth his while to spend any of his military strength. He did, however, have much to profit from adopting the posture of faithful, neglected ally to the United States, asking for the talisman of air power to confound the Japanese then (and the Communists later), while yielding to the Americans the glory and cost of grinding down the common enemy.

American Baptist missionary house, Kiating, Szechuan, in which author was born.

The author with wet nurse,
Fu Ta Niang. Circa 1908.

The author ascending sacred mountain,
Omei Shan, with Yü Hai-san. Circa 1910.

Junk being pulled upstream through Yangtze rapids. Circa 1912.

Old swimming hole, Omei Shan, circa 1915. The Reverend John P. Davies (far left), fellow missionaries, and the author (center).

Yenching University basketball team, Peking, 1929. Left to right: Hsueh, author, Ma, Verevkin, Liu.

Tie finish in 400 meters race. Eugene Verevkin and author,
Yenching University, Peking, 1930.

Donkey Boy, at Peitaiho, 1930. *Photo by JD.*

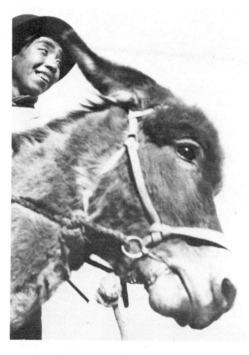

Beside the Trans-Siberian Railway,
August 1930. *Photo by JD.*

Charles Shadrach Reed II, American Vice-Consul, Yunnanfu, preparing to enter the Consulate's official sedan chair on Bastille Day, 1933.

Mr. Chang, tutor to JD when Attaché for Language Study, U. S. Legation, Peking, 1933–35. *Photo by JD.*

Japanese wrestlers, our companions on a trip to Jehol Province
from Peking, 1935.

The author scans hills west
of Peking, 1935.

Author (in boots) with Harold Caccia, then second secretary and later Lord Caccia, of the British Legation at the site of Yang Kuei Fei's thermal baths.

The author (seated second from left) making merry with two colleagues, Andrew Edson and Sabin Chase, members of the *kempeitai*, and convivial waitresses. Mori is in back row, second from right. Mukden, 1935.

Dance hall hostess, Mukden, 1936. *Photo by JD.*

Top right, left to right: German Consul, Raymond P. Ludden, and the author. Mukden, 1936.

Left to right: Unknown; Sergeant Kawai; Lieutenant Kobayashi; Father O'Donnell; Father Burns; the author; Mori; AP correspondent Mitchell; Father Comber. T'unghua, Manchuria, November 1936.

Author on his porch at Hankow, summer 1938. *Photo by Walter Bosshard of* Neue Zuercher Zeitung.

Students demonstrating for defense of Wuhan a fortnight before capture of three cities. Hankow, October 1938. *Photo by JD.*

American Embassy and Consulate General, Hankow, July 1938.
Top row: Vice-Consuls Staten, Taylor, Davies; 3rd Secretaries Jenkins, Drumright; 2nd Secretary Aldridge; Clerks Lafoon and Wiens.
Bottom row: Assistant Military Attaché Captain Dorn; Consul General Josselyn; Ambassador Johnson: Assistant Naval Attaché Captain McHugh; Assistant Military Attaché Captain Mattice; Consul Stevens.

Edgar Snow at Hankow, 1938. *Photo by JD.*

After dinner at author's apartment in Hankow. Left to right: Agnes Smedley; Captain Frank Dorn; F. McCracken Fisher (then a newsman); Chinese military spokesman (mostly obscured); Jack Belden (then free-lance newsman); A. T. Steele, *Chicago Daily News;* Captain Evans Carlson, USMC; Freda Utley; Chang Han-fu (a Communist editor); JD. Summer 1938.

At author's apartment, Hankow. Left to right: Colonel Joseph W. Stilwell; Jack Belden, free-lance newsman; M. N. Rogoff, Tass (Soviet) correspondent. Summer 1938. *Photo by Donald M. Davies.*

Agnes Smedley and Captain Frank Dorn at JD's apartment. Hankow. Summer 1938.

Fleeing before the invader. Hankow, 1938. *Photo by JD.*

Vice-Consul Asahina and author at Japanese officers' rest house, Wucheng, Kiangsi. August 1939.

At Ramgarh (India) Training Center for Chinese Army in India. Left to right: Major General Liao Yao-hsiang; Colonel Willard Wyman; JD. 1942 or 1943.

Somewhere in India. Left to right: Captain Richard Young, aide to General
Stilwell; Brigadier General Frank Merrill; General Joseph W. Stilwell.
1943 or 1944. *Photo by South East Asia Command photographer.*

Lieutenant General Joseph W. Stilwell, Commander of U. S. Forces, China-
Burma-India, with some of his staff. Author is on right. *Photo by Wide World.*

Author at airbase in Assam waiting to go over the Hump, 1943.

Patricia Grady Davies and her tum-tum (Indian dog-cart), New Delhi, 1944. Left to right: Alim, the bearer; Mme. Bovary, the mare; the syce; PGD.

Left to right: Chou En-lai, Chu Teh, JD, Mao Tse-tung, Yeh Chien-ying.
Yennan. October 1944.

Yeh Chien-ying, Chief of Staff of
Communist forces (inscribed "with esteem"
to JD by Yeh, December 15, 1944).

American Delegation at Moscow Meeting of Foreign Ministers. Front row, left to right: James B. Conant, Benjamin Cohen, James F. Byrnes, W. Averell Harriman. Standing: Unidentified colonel, JD, John Carter Vincent, Edward Page, H. Freeman Mathews, Charles E. Bohlen. December 1945.

Patricia and John Davies, Christmas 1945, Moscow.

Because of the war in the Pacific and enemy command of coastal China, Stilwell journeyed eastward, as had Caleb Cushing ninety-nine years before, to his mission in China. Like the first American envoy to the Middle Kingdom, Stilwell traveled by way of Egypt and India. His aircraft arrived in Karachi on February 24.

The Japanese had crossed the last river barrier to Rangoon and were moving on that Burmese port, the last shipping access to China. With its loss—which occurred on March 6—India would become the base from which the United States would struggle to bolster China against Japan and support positions in China from which Americans might strike at Japan.

Here, then, was Stilwell, an American general without combat troops, advancing on Japan from India, about to do battle with Japanese in Burma in defense of China, and hoping to hurl an offensive from deep within the Middle Kingdom at the then dominant naval power in the world. This was scarcely the way Teddy Roosevelt, Henry Cabot Lodge, and Admiral Mahan had envisaged manifest destiny when they committed the United States to Asia. It was a bit of black comedy not plotted in the scenario of their "large policy."

Stilwell, now a lieutenant general, was in Calcutta on February 28 to meet a downcast Wavell on his way from the collapse of the Dutch East Indies to take over as commander in chief in India. Three days later Stilwell briefly joined Chiang Kai-shek and Chennault at Lashio, a frontier town in the eastern mountains of Burma. The Generalissimo was delivering inspiration to Chinese generals sent to defend the supply lines from a doomed Rangoon. They were there because events had brought Wavell to realize that Burma needed all of the Chinese that Chiang had proffered in December.

At Kunming on March 4, Chennault accepted service under Stilwell's command and the early induction of his AVG into the Army Air Force. On the same day Stilwell arrived in Chungking. Thereupon his headquarters, United States Army Forces, China-Burma-India was activated, absorbing Magruder's AMMISCA.

Stilwell was now nominally ready for business as a combat commander. He was to control three Chinese armies composed of nine divisions. He was not only without American troops, he barely had a staff—only a few exceptionally able China and Japan specialists, the small AMMISCA group, together with a scattering of newly arrived officers. He would have the AVG, weary and depleted from three months of superb fighting against heavy odds. And that was it.

The concept of Stilwell's commanding Chinese troops was delusive. To begin with, it was an insult to the Chinese. It assumed that, in spite of the unbroken series of American disasters from Pearl Harbor and the Philippines to the Java Sea, an American ex-military attaché knew better how to fight the Japanese than any general in the Chinese army. While that prejudice might have been overcome, what could not be overcome was Chiang Kai-shek's manner of conducting war.

In matters of military science the Generalissimo was an eccentric—tea shop aphorisms drained from the classical strategist Sun Tzu. He was morbidly defensive-minded. He fretted, vacillated, and indulged in bouts of bad temper. If he had kept this all to himself and his headquarters staff, his vagaries might not have done irreparable damage. Unhappily, he broadcast them in daily bursts of orders, often contradictory, across the chain of command to his bewildered and apprehensive generals in the field, even down to division commanders.

In his meetings with the Generalissimo in early March Stilwell was uncomfortably aware of Chiang's off-again on-again mentality. Actually, the supreme commander was treating the American general no more disruptively than he treated his own officers. On March 11, with assurances from the Generalissimo that he would be in command of Chinese forces in Burma, Stilwell flew to Lashio. By far the most pugnacious character on the allied side, he was determined to prove what he had always believed—that the Chinese soldier, when properly led, fed, and equipped, was the equal of any.

Pinky Dorn was as good as his word. He arranged for the War Department to ask the Department of State for my services. On February 10, 1942 my department designated me as Second Secretary of Embassy at Chungking and detailed me to Stilwell's "mission."

Before leaving Washington on February 25, I had a farewell conversation with Currie. Present also was Owen Lattimore, back in Washington from serving as the Generalissimo's personal adviser. Currie and Lattimore stressed the importance of India, to which material for China was being diverted since the loss of Rangoon. This diversion had to be made to keep a door open to China. Lattimore said that he agreed with Chennault and Chiang that it was useless to concentrate our feeble efforts on the Japanese spearhead, that we should strike at the enemy flank. Currie then asked me to tell Chennault that he must play ball with General Arnold, commander of the Army Air Corps. If he did not cooperate he would get no equipment. Arnold had to be humored for he was tremendously influential. Chennault must be willing to sacrifice for the cause. They also wanted me to assure Chennault that he was appreciated.

With six officers and a sergeant also destined for China-Burma-India, I boarded a Pan American clipper at New York. We flew the newly established air ferry route to the Far East, via Brazil, Liberia, Nigeria, Chad, the Sudan, Egypt, Palestine, Iraq, Sharjah, and India. For me this was all new territory, fascinating, full of color and contrast. Thirteen days after leaving New York we arrived at Calcutta.

Keyed up for the rigors of campaigning in the jungle, I encountered a bottleneck in transportation to Burma and so accepted the hospitality of our consul general, George Merrell, an old friend from Peking and Harbin. "My host and Bob Buell," I wrote in a letter, "are playing backgammon and the eight servants are preparing martinis for before-dinner drinks. . . . My host has just returned . . . from Government House where around the swimming pool he chatted with Eve Curie. . . . All sorts of people whom I have known turn up. An Englishman I knew in Manchuria stopped me on the street—I didn't recognize him in uniform. He had escaped first from Hong Kong and then from Singapore under harrowing conditions. Someone else who got away from Singapore, then Batavia, then Ceylon. And others from Burma. Their composite story would be a large part of the history of the past three and a half months."

In another letter—"This noon at lunch at Firpo's . . . with orchestra playing soft music and an enormous luncheon at one's command I felt very clearly (1) how remote the war seemed, even more remote than when I was in Washington and (2) how insulated we Americans and Europeans here are from the mass of life around us, a great ocean surrounding an atoll. I felt the same thing at the Saturday Club last evening . . . their regular afternoon dance."

After ten days of this my turn to enter Burma came. At Lashio I encountered Frank Roberts, whom I had known with Pinky in Peking, and Haydon Boatner, another China specialist. Both were lieutenant colonels, Frank performing solo without any subordinates as Stilwell's intelligence staff, and the aggressive, outspoken Boatner acting as rear echelon headquarters of the American effort in Burma. As Lashio was the junction of the Burmese rail and highway system with the rugged road on into China, it was a strategically vital place. It also was the site of a Chinese General Staff mission, which contributed to the babble of orders issued to the three Chinese armies nominally assigned to the command of Stilwell. What with corruption rampant in the traffic to China and meddling by the General Staff mission, Haydon Boatner was a busy man.

While awaiting automobile transport to headquarters at Maymyo, I was given a jeep tour of Lashio by an AVG ground crewman. He was a pistol-packing young man from Tennessee happy to be away from his duties but with no explanation of why he was more than a day's journey from his base. But then, the AVG was noted for its informality. His objective that day was to collect a case of gin, and as he went about his search he drank Scotch and ate fruit salad. When his mouth was not full he dropped hints of pilfering and sale of AVG equipment.

That same day two Chinese medical corps generals arrived on a tour of investigation. No provisions had been made for hospitalization of Chinese wounded and the British were unprepared for this problem. In the evening another Chinese, General Tseng Yang-fu, with whom I shared a hotel room, discoursed on the importance of the political aspects of the war. The Burmese, he said, did not pay attention to the Government of Burma radio, but they did listen to the Japanese broadcasts. He advocated the creation of a Burmese anti-aggression league. I could see the need of counterpropaganda but believed that any such effort would come a cropper on the colonial problem—the Burmese had no desire to fight for the preservation of British rule over them.

Stilwell's headquarters at Maymyo was in the American Baptist Mission Rest House. I felt quite at home when I arrived on May 22. As Dorn was at the front with the general, I occupied his room. Maymyo was a hill station in the Burma uplands, with pine groves, hedges of blooming poinsettias, a profusion of other flowers, an abundance of strawberries, rolling grasslands, and a lake.

On the following day I went down onto the plain to Mandalay, which reminded me of parts of Kyoto—the weathered natural wood houses, not the white and gold temples, the men in pink shirts, nor the women in tight gauze bodices. On the way back to Maymyo we overtook an AVG convoy on the way to China. It was what was left of the unit at Magwe, caught on the ground the day before for lack of a warning net by a skilled and intelligent succession of enemy air strikes. The men and their Anglo-Burmese girls were a morose, bedraggled lot. With them, and the RAF knocked out at the same time, went what little air cover our ground forces had.

Back at the Baptist Rest House I encountered Stilwell, who greeted me with brisk warmth. At dinner he asked if I had met the governor of Burma. I had not. Dorn explained to me the friction between the British and Chinese over command. General Harold Alexander, subordinate to Wavell in India, was commander in Burma and assumed that he commanded not only British, Burmese, Indian, and Gurkha troops, but all allied forces in this British possession. The Generalissimo did not accept Alexander's authority over Chinese troops. Stilwell, however, was willing to recognize British overall command. And the British, according to Dorn, had demonstrated a cooperative attitude toward the Americans.

My diary entry for March 24 read: "General Stilwell in his bare room off the bare upstairs porch said, 'Sit down.' Each in a wicker chair, he said, 'There's nothing I can tell you about how to run your job. You're a free agent. All you have to do is to keep things running smoothly between the civil authorities here and us.'

"The rest of the morning and most of the afternoon was aimless. Until 4:30 when Fullerton [a young captain] and I called on Major Richmond, the governor's military aide, who was napping when we called. He roused himself to escort us to tea on a spacious verandah in the company of Miss Gibb, a gibbon fidgety as a thirteen-year-old human female while awaiting the cake and tea, which the major served her along with us. He didn't seem to have a great deal of respect for [British] headquarters intelligence; said a Jap convoy, including two carriers, was apparently heading for the Andaman Islands.

"At General Ho's headquarters the general said that the Chinese were holding only a line of communications to a very narrow front and that they were preparing to expand outward on either flank. This move was difficult, however, because of the hostility of the Burmese population. Japanese infiltration, he said, was aided and guided by the Burmese.

"I had my first job to perform. It was to find out what was being done to prevent improper use of jeeps and to regain control over those jeeps from unauthorized hands! Richmond said that the police had checked on this not only here but also in Mandalay—and had gotten into hot water as a result with the Chinese. . . .

While I had been at tea with Miss Gibb, Stilwell had been conferring with Major Generals Raymond Wheeler and Lewis Brereton and Brigadier General Earl Naiden. The able and engaging Wheeler was setting up supply and transport bases in India. Brereton and his chief of staff, Naiden, were getting Brereton's Tenth Air Force into action. After losing about half of his planes on the ground in the Philippines on the first day of the war, Brereton had fallen back to Java with the remnants and from there to India. He told Stilwell that he hoped to be in business by about May 1, a long time off the way things were going in Burma. At breakfast next morning Brereton revealed to us that Japanese aviation was skilled and intelligent. Also he favored intermittent American air strikes on Japan from Chuchow in East China.

My March 26 diary entry read: "A call on the governor's secretary, Mr. Binns, was not particularly fruitful. He is an old ICS [Indian Civil Service] man, was actually at his desk at 3 p.m., and revealed that he was of Unitarian origin. When I observed that my position was a rather unusual one, Binns said that General Stilwell's appeared likewise to be rather unusual. General S had introduced himself as commander of the Chinese Fifth and Sixth Armies. General Tu [commander of the Fifth Army] in his call on the Governor had introduced himself in much the same way. And General Alexander naturally felt that he had inherited supreme command of troops in Burma. Finally, by the constitution of Burma, only the governor is charged with the defense of Burma, he alone. I did some genial evading of the issue, talked solemnly of cooperation and remarked that this was an unorthodox war.

"I asked Binns about the Cripps visit [Sir Stafford, Lord Privy Seal, had been sent by London to India to win support for the war by a qualified offer of independence]. He was very gloomy—ah, that religious rift. It took us centuries to get over our religious wars and then only because we lost interest in religion. The East will have to do that. . . .

"Schnare's [American Consul General from Rangoon] nice old gentle Anglo-Indian clerk says that there are rumors in town that China and the US are to take over Burma and that that will be better than British rule. . . . The rumor is probably among Indians. He touched on the bitterness which the Indians feel over their betrayal in Burma by the British, mentioning the destruction by the British of a bridge which left about a thousand Gurkhas caught on the other bank of the river and the abandonment by British employers of their Indian employees. Tactfully he did not mention Americans—and his own case?

"This community at Maymyo is curious. Hundreds of really quite attractive houses and bungalows . . . inhabited by retired members of the very highly paid Burma Civil Service. And many of them are Anglo-Indians, speaking with a curiously cadenced pseudo-upper-class English accent and venerating a sort of pathetically secondhand and shabby Victorianism. . . .

"The British troops one sees are not what one would call a cocky, aggressive lot."

On the following day I was received by the governor of Burma, Sir Reginald Hugh Dorman-Smith. "Cheery military aide Grenadier Guard Capt.Cook took me in to his Excellency who, with quite a show of cordiality, greeted me in his spacious office, the windows of which opened out onto the sloping lawn and handsome old trees. Birds were singing very pleasantly and the whole atmosphere was quite agreeable, especially when H.E. ordered two large pink gins. The Governor not only turned on the charm at the beginning but kept it on—he's been described as a sort of second power Anthony Eden.

"We roamed over a variety of topics—the confused command in Burma (He showed me a rather bad bit of doggerel composed by his aides), the mistrust with which he viewed Tseng Yang-fu [the anti-aggression league advocate], why he regarded the Burmese man as 'a butterfly,' the gloomy outlook for the Cripps mission, why Burma could not be granted any great degree of autonomy, what Wavell really said to Chiang Kai-shek (Keep after the Japs in China and with the reinforcements which we have coming—but which did not come—we can hold Burma), the Chinese hostility toward the British, my contention that Stilwell is not a man to want to grab authority out of a fondness for it *per se*, the necessity of being on guard against rumors designed to create rifts among us."

Then came a visit to Fifth Army headquarters at Pyawbwe, south of Mandalay. This is what I recorded after the trip: "Major Nowakowski [American liaison officer] was alone with a collection of rather mangy Szechuanese guards. He was sitting under a slowly revolving fan gazing listlessly at some maps. The heat was really pretty terrific. We had some warm water with fresh lime squeezed into it by a Szechuanese corporal. After a while the alert went. No one paid much attention to it after the first few minutes of listening for planes. We looked at the fairly adequate shelter under a tree and at the shallow pits under the oleanders for the sentries. . . .

"While talking with a Colonel Chang and his personable young interpreter (who had been reading Andersen's Fairy Tales in the shelter and who still clutched the volume rather proudly under his arm) the second alert went. After listening closely for a while we went into the quite well constructed shelter. Before that I overheard a soldier say: 'We were told yesterday that we were to see friendly planes today but they have yet to come. If only we Chinese soldiers were supported in the air, how elated we would be.'. . .

"On the way back we picked up a young Eurasian [Anglo-Burmese], nineteen, who had left school to join the Burma Division. He had been on the Sittang front. The Burmese had apparently been of great assistance to the Japs. British patrols or small units camping at night would find themselves ringed by fire and outside the ring of flame Burmese with big knives waiting. Much of the fifth column work he laid to the native priests. . . .

"Apparently divisional commanders [Chinese] are referring orders given them [by Stilwell] back to Chungking for check."

Until General Alexander visited Chungking late in March, the Generalissimo had rejected the right of the British to exercise overall command in Burma. On March 28 Stilwell learned that Chiang had changed his mind. His wife, in a hand that rocks the cradle performance, dropped the American general "just a line to let you know . . . the High Command of Burma will rest in General Alexander's hands."

On March 30 I was back in Lashio. General Tseng told me that he had formed his anti-aggression league, which must have confirmed the governor's suspicions that Tseng was subverting an exhausted British authority. But this artificial contraption could accomplish little even if the allies were not in retreat. In the situation then existing it was futile. The next day, after two air raids, I joined Stilwell and Dorn on a flight to Kunming, where we picked up Chennault, and thence to Chungking. Stilwell had come to the capital to have a showdown with the Generalissimo over disregard of Stilwell's orders by army and division commanders.

CHAPTER *21*

Gloom in Chungking,
Disarray in India

AT CHUNGKING I was again in the Red Basin of Szechuan, where I had not been since childhood. I had forgotten how pretty were the verdant bordering hills, the rivers, the paddy fields and groves of bamboo. Stilwell and his immediate staff lived in one of T.V. Soong's Chungking houses, one with a superb view of river and hills. Dorn and I shared a dank room. The headquarters were in another building which, I noted, was "impressively spacious—more so than the Foreign Office." Continuing my April 1 notations: "I went over to the Air Force rest house and there found Chennault. I told him what Currie had to say about Arnold and the desirability of his playing ball. He said that the AVG had a contract which provided for their way home at the termination of the agreement. If they were to be inducted [into the Army Air Corps], they wanted to be inducted at home after they had gone back and seen their relatives. If they were not inducted they would of course continue to fight. He seemed to feel that the AVG had a grievance. He could do with a hundred and fifty men what would take the army a thousand. Newspapermen had gotten from some of the boys their story on induction but he had held out on it in the interests of harmony. The AVG record far excelled that of the RAF. When told that the AVG was after all only using RAF tactics, an AVG boy said, 'Well, why doesn't the RAF use those tactics?' "

Back at Stilwell's billets, the comment that I got from Dorn was that after Chennault had welcomed induction, if only to bring about some discipline in the AVG, he had come to resist it, playing petticoat and other politics. The petticoats in this instance were those of Madame Chiang Kai-shek. The Generalissimo and she wanted Chennault to be free of Stilwell's overall command. The airman had been a favorite of the Chiangs' since 1937 and they found congenial his theories for defeating Japan by air power.

That same day I went across the river to the embassy: "It looked very grubby after the pretentiousness of the military offices on the other bank. Jack [Second Secretary John S. Service] and John Carter [Vincent, Counselor of Embassy] prepared me for my entry into the Ambassadorial Presence. The first thing I did was to present Mr. Gauss with my instructions which were read with a Gausspish derisive smile. In this first conversation and during lunch I gathered that Mr. G felt that our military were given to encroaching upon diplomatic matters . . . that other special emissaries detracted from his mission and created confusion in the minds of the Chinese as to just who was representing the US, and that he rather wished that he were back home. It would seem that the fault is not so much with the new outfits (which certainly attempt to fill a very real need) but with the system that does not integrate our efforts. And that fault is primarily in Washington. There could, of course, be a considerably greater degree of integration here than now exists.

"I am told that Mr. G does not enjoy social gatherings and that therefore he has not seen H. H. Kung [Finance Minister and Chiang's brother-in-law] since November . . . and that he has very few contacts with Chinese and British officials of any description. He will not consider opening an office in the city."

Gauss, Stilwell, Chennault, these were the three principal figures of the American effort in China. They had in common driving energy, professional competence each in his own field, obstinacy, and a readiness to take offense. Three such strong-willed, prickly personalities were bound to clash or, at best, to be standoffish with one another.

Stilwell called on the Generalissimo on April 1—with the ubiquitous Madame Chiang present—to tell him that certain Chinese generals had not carried out orders in Burma. He did not say that this was because Chiang himself had countermanded Stilwell's instructions. The American general declared that in the circumstances he would have to be relieved of command. The Generalissimo professed to be puzzled by the disobedience. The upshot of a jarring confrontation was that the next day Chiang appointed yet another of his generals to act as Stilwell's executive officer. And he offered to go to Burma with Stilwell to tell his field commanders to obey the American.

Again I lunched with the ambassador and a couple of his staff. "Carping, gloomy atmosphere," I afterward noted. "His Excellency was cheerful only in the telling of his exploits in Australia." I concluded that we needed a new ambassador and thought of retired Admiral Yarnell, whom I had met at Hankow and who had greatly impressed me by his breadth of interests and quietly commanding presence.

In the evening I dined with our naval attaché, General Magruder, Ray Clapper (the columnist), and several others. "The theme was the incompetence and venality of the Chinese," I wrote. "The familiar note was again sounded that our route out will be through the Tibetan highlands and the USSR. Gen. M was all for liquidating the oriental endeavor and concentrating on opening a western front for the Russians."

Stilwell's thoughts were not of falling back in any direction. He was absorbed with getting the Chinese in Burma to attack, to push to Rangoon. The intensity of his concentration pressed silently down on the seven of us living with him. "The atmosphere . . . is pretty grim and barren. There are quiet spells of some length during meals. Pinky and Colonel Bergin [Adjutant General] occasionally lighten things up. We gather in the afternoon for tea on the roof, then down to the characterless drawing room—all of the time never animated conversation. The general is very preoccupied, constantly thinking, occasionally firing a quick, pointed question. He lightens up over Chinese food which some of the others take like good soldiers. The sergeants' mess is supposed to have refused to permit Chinese food to grace their board."

Madame Chiang received me on April 3 to accept letters that I had brought her from Currie and Lattimore and a pair of walking shoes from Mrs. Lattimore. I was met in an anteroom by Hollington Tong, vice-minister of information, official biographer of the Generalissimo, and the Chiangs' general purpose contact-man for dealing with Americans. He was a graduate of the Missouri School of Journalism and cultivated a breezy informality calculated to establish intimacy of understanding with foreign visitors. With me, it was the "usual pleasantries, excepting for a disquisition on British duplicity—he could talk frankly to me and I to him and we would know the innermost thoughts of one another. But not with the British. (This line was strangely reminiscent of what many a Japanese has said to me; it must be a widespread Oriental experience.)"

When Tong discovered that I knew Ray Clapper, who was then interviewing Madame Chiang, he suggested that we go in and join them. "They were finishing tea in a sort of American upper middle class drawing room. Missimo arose in a stately fashion and moved forward with a flashing smile and the old charm turned on. I presented the letters and the pair of shoes. Much light talk. Ray finished reading drafts of her articles for the *Atlantic* and for the *N.Y. Times* magazine. Madame Kung [Madame Chiang's sister] came in as Ray departed. She was younger and gentler than I had been led to expect. Not nearly so forceful in this meeting as was Missimo. I tried to lead Mme. out on India but she wouldn't talk. I said I thought it was fortunate that Gen. Stilwell not only knew China well but also that he was a first-class fighting general. She said that the latter was important (she probably feels that China has had too many who thought they knew China and not enough who really knew warfare). I glimpsed two cold, appraising looks which quickly disappeared. She flashed the charm again on my departure. Mme. Kung was still demure and almost shy."

As Stilwell was preparing to return to Burma, I considered how I might be most useful to him. My contact with the government of Burma had persuaded me that there was precious little that I could do for him with that placidly disintegrating civil authority. Nor did I see any great need for me in Chungking at that time. Stilwell, who very much kept his own counsel, showed no disposition to use me in his dealings with the Chinese. In India, however, I saw what I thought was a job badly in need of doing.

The general had no one on his staff who was well-informed about India. Yet we were counting on India as the vital staging and even production area from which to supply China and as a base from which to mount the reconquest of Burma, if that colony were lost. We were vaguely aware that the Indian people were disaffected from the British raj, but we did not know how serious their discontent was. If the Indians were as hostile as the Burmese, then we had real cause for concern. Especially if the Japanese attacked India.

I presented to Stilwell on April 4 a case for my spending some time in India, getting for him a firsthand estimate of the political and economic situation there. Henry F. Grady, former assistant secretary of state, was heading a special mission due soon to make an economic survey of India. I could be sent initially to establish liaison for Stilwell with the Grady mission. The general nodded his head in his vigorous, quick way and told me to write a letter to Grady for his signature.

The next morning I took off for India by way of Lashio, where a detachment of Gurkhas with bagpipes and drums were lined up as a guard of honor for the Generalissimo. He followed in the next plane, accompanied by Madame Chiang, Stilwell, and eleven Chinese generals. They were to spend the next two days in conferences at Maymyo with the Chinese field commanders and General Alexander. The Generalissimo would make plain to his generals that Stilwell's orders were also to be obeyed.

Clare Boothe Luce had arrived at Lashio ahead of our two planes. She had come in the guise of a correspondent for her husband Henry's publications, traveling appropriately in an aircraft carrying five million dollars' worth of bank notes destined to cope with China's money shortage. She, too, went to Maymyo where, I was later told, her queenly charms rivalled those of the Missimo. I went on to Calcutta.

Calcutta was in more of a flap than I had expected. Sir Stafford Cripps was making no progress in his attempts to procure the support of Indian politicians for the fight against Japan in exchange for qualified independence. More immediately alarming, a Japanese task force was roaming the Bay of Bengal unopposed, sinking allied shipping at will. The port of Calcutta had been partially cleared of ships in anticipation of a possible attack. And on the day of my arrival a second enemy task force composed of five carriers, four battleships and accompanying cruisers, destroyers and tankers had hurled an air strike at Colombo. Stripped of its defenses by the demands of the Middle East and Burma, India lay exposed and vulnerable.

From Calcutta I went to New Delhi to acquaint myself with American officialdom in the capital of India. It was all newly arrived. For prior to the Japanese having made us and the British allies, the British raj had forbidden foreign representation at New Delhi, rather as the Chinese emperors had denied barbarian envoys residence in Peking. We were now making up for lost time.

As India was not an independent nation, we could not have an embassy or legation. But we had the Office of the Personal Representative of the President of the United States. The occupant of that Office, the personal representative himself, was Colonel Louis Johnson. A former national commander of the American Legion, Johnson was a bruisingly aggressive politician who had gotten to be assistant secretary of war and was eventually, in 1949, to become an ill-chosen secretary of defense.

Although Johnson had arrogated to himself claims of authority over all American activities in India, including military, his real task—at least as he envisaged it—was to induce the British to give the Indians immediate independence. He was a crude expression of Roosevelt's concern over "the Indian problem." The president had on March 10 "with much diffidence" recommended to Churchill that Britain contrive for India an interim government similar to that of the thirteen American states under the Articles of Confederation. Roosevelt, it seemed, believed that what had been good for the American colonists would be good for three hundred and fifty million Indian colonials, smoldering with ancient, explosive antagonisms of race, religion, and caste.

To further this naive vagary, Roosevelt had sent Johnson, a man uniquely unsuited to deal with the British and the Indians. Coarse, bombastic, and essentially ignorant regarding matters into which he was muscling, Johnson could only make trouble between the president and the prime minister, to mention but two. For India was the subject on which Churchill and Roosevelt were most at odds, with the prime minister determined that the King-Emperor should maintain his sway.

When I called at the office of the personal representative, I learned from George Merrell, who had been transferred from Calcutta, that Johnson had been openly intervening in the Cripps negotiations on the side of the Indians, who themselves were far from agreement with one another. Merrell, a very proper diplomat, was horrified by Johnson's "goddamning" to the British and "goddamning" of the British to the Indians. The personal representative thought that his roughshod tactics had worked and on April 9 had said to Merrell, "Well, now that this is all fixed we can go home."

By April 11, Cripps's negotiations with the Congress Party cracked up over British unwillingness, particularly in defense matters, to grant self-government immediately. On the next day Cripps left for home. Johnson stayed on to continue muddying the waters.

After Cripps the question was, what would the Indians do? In a baffling new environment, we Americans were confused and anxious. British officials maintained their aplomb; the viceroy, the dinosaurian Marquess of Linlithgow, went on a tiger shoot. But some of his senior advisers were privately wrought up, indignant that the Congress Party negotiators and all activists had not been clapped in jail. The educated and politically alert Indians were of as many distraught and brooding minds as there were Indians of their kind.

This subcontinent was a miasma. There were no ready explanations of its nature that satisfied me. The British were not unbiased expositors because they were India's proprietors. And they had a love-hate relationship with this land of fantastic contrasts. As for the Indians themselves, their extraordinarily diverse outlooks, their subjectivity, and their persecution complexes, yielded no immediately coherent explanation of what India really was.

During the next nine months I was to spend much of my time traveling the subcontinent inquiring into the nature of India. I started with some of the most knowledgeable British officials in New Delhi and then went on to Nehru, Gandhi, Jinnah, Rajagopalachari, Mrs. Naidu, and many others—Hindus, Muslims, Sikhs, princes, untouchables, Communists and, accidentally via parachute, headhunters. This inquiry, I discovered, took me into a realm quite apart from the entangled relationships of America, China, Russia, and Japan. The story of my Indian incarnation therefore lies beyond the scope of this narrative.

A number of things that I learned did have a bearing on Stilwell's broad responsibilities. One was that both the Indians and the government of India were facing in the wrong direction for the war we were in. Like the big guns of the Singapore bastion, fixedly pointing out to sea and therefore captured from behind, the government of India had for generations braced itself for attack over the northwest frontier—from Russia. It was wholly unprepared for an assault from the east, for surely no enemy could get past Singapore.

Insofar as the Indians looked beyond themselves, it was westward: the Muslims to the Islamic countries, the Hindus and others to Europe. They were astonishingly ignorant of and indifferent to both China and Japan, notwithstanding centuries of common ties in Buddhism. This was summed up by a trivial incident. In a conversation with me, Gandhi groped for the proper form with which to identify Madame Chiang. He said: "Madame Kai-Shek—er—Madame Shek."

While five hundred million Chinese reciprocated the lack of interest in them of three hundred and fifty million Indians, there did exist a common bond between the Chiang establishment and at least some of the Congress Party leaders. It went beyond the thin sentiments that they were fellow Asians. After all, the Japanese were then stridently pan-Asian and spectacularly successful ones. The common bond was impotent hatred of the British. In the case of the Chiangs, the bill of particulars began with the Opium War and carried through to the inconsiderate incompetence of the British in protecting China's communications through Rangoon and Wavell's making the Generalissimo lose face.

In February, the Chiangs made a state visit to India, ostensibly to rouse their fellow Asians in support of the war. In meetings and correspondence between the Chinese and Indian nationalist leaders, each side stimulated the anglophobia of the other. This reciprocal goading of resentments did not find favor with all Indian nationalists. The pragmatic Rajagopalachari told me in May that Chiang "had written a letter to Nehru recently in which he complained of the British conduct of the war in Burma, pointing out their many faults. 'What good does that do?' Rajaji asked."

Of obvious interest to Stilwell was Indian reaction to the American military presence on the subcontinent. Gandhi's objections to us were growing. I summed them up in a radio message to Stilwell on June 14: "Our troops entered India without Indian invitation or asking Indian leave, their presence contributed to [the] strength [of] British domination, he [Gandhi] anticipated no political support from United States which was under [the] spell [of] British diplomacy."

Gandhi was evidently preparing for civil disobedience. In a letter to Currie on June 18 I observed: "The situation is too far deteriorated . . . for any hope. If Gandhi acts, I suspect that the British will be very tough. Their solution is apparently going to be force rather than conciliation, unless pushed awfully hard from Washington. Of course, Gandhi and Nehru (wretched spectacle) may be staging a tremendous bluff to frighten us into turning the heat on the British, but I don't think so. I'm afraid that they mean business."

They did mean business. The question, then, was whether the government could maintain order. In August Gandhi's Congress Party created widespread disturbances. Thereupon the government jailed Gandhi, Nehru, and other leaders instigating disorders. And that was the end of the trouble. The British had proved their contention that they were able to rule India, not because they were strong but because the Indians were so weak—and divided.

The ability of New Delhi to maintain domestic order under conditions of invasion or sustained air attack was not tested. The government of India was spared the revealing ordeal undergone by the government of Burma. For the Japanese task forces moved away after their sweep through the Bay of Bengal and air strikes at Ceylon.

I noted on April 13 reports that they had "disappeared off southern India. Madagascar?" There were fears that the Japanese might even move northward in the Indian Ocean to interdict the movement of Persian Gulf oil to the Middle East front. But no, we were now overestimating as we had underestimated Japanese power. The enemy task forces returned to the Pacific to ready themselves for the decisive sea battles with the Americans. The Japanese naval withdrawal from the Indian Ocean, incidentally, disappointed the Germany Navy which had hoped for a Middle East link up between the two forces.

General Brereton, with his nine heavy bombers and seven fighters, discreetly refrained from challenging the marauding task forces. He was awaiting badly-needed parts and reinforcements for his newly created Tenth Air Force. He maintained his headquarters in the Imperial Hotel. I visited his air intelligence to find it "amateurish" and to "learn little."

Also in the Imperial were various liaison officers for Stilwell and a military intelligence mission from the War Department which was vainly looking for highways to China. I encountered a Colonel Edwards who seemed to have a more pessimistic orientation. Seeking escape routes, he was trying to get a map of Afghanistan and asked, "That's the country northwest of here, isn't it?" I told him that he was on the right track.

When Grady arrived on April 17 he found that Johnson claimed authority over Grady's American Technical Mission. The personal representative said that Roosevelt had told him to "assume command" in India. He had interpreted literally the president's careless expansiveness—what Stilwell dismissed as "just a lot of wind"—during the customary farewell and laying on of hands. Grady was well acquainted with the way official Washington functioned, was backed up by the State Department, and so declined to be corralled.

Nor was he overcome by the prevailing dejection that he encountered. After Grady had talked with Johnson, I noted in my diary, "He had been presented with the theory that (a) Calcutta was about to be lost, (b) the bulk of Indian industry is concentrated in the Calcutta area, (c) therefore, why do anything, let's go on home." Undeterred by this and more of its kind, Grady and his small staff went about their investigation of the Indian economy and calmly finished their task on schedule at Bombay in the latter half of May.

It was the only performance I observed that year that was expert, orderly, constructive, and above the petty rancors that assailed it. In part this was because it was a manageable undertaking. But more importantly, Grady was wise enough not to attempt more than could be accomplished. And controlling all was the character of the man—a gentleman, considerate of the sensitivities of others, modest, and discerning.

The findings of the Technical Mission confirmed that there were severe limits to what India could contribute in production to Stilwell's war efforts further east. Furthermore, the lines of communications northeastward from Calcutta into Assam, the now vital staging area for air lift to China, were thin and rickety. What India could adquately do was to feed, clothe, and accommodate a considerable body of Chinese troops.

Meanwhile in Burma four Japanese divisions, with strong air support, were beating nine Chinese divisions, two Burmese, and five Indian infantry brigades, one British armored brigade and six British infantry battalions, with skimpy air support. The Japanese were clearly superior in morale, fighting qualities, firepower, maneuverability, intelligence operations, supplies, transport, and command. They also had the considerable help of the Burmese people. Late in April they surprised the allies with a flanking movement that captured Lashio and so cut off the only motor road into China.

This, in effect, ended the first Burma campaign. Alexander's demoralized imperial forces retreated as best they could to India. Seven Chinese divisions escaped back to China and two made their way out to India.

Stilwell, Dorn, Belden, and a handful of others stuck it out to the end. Having endured continuing disobedience on the part of the Chinese generals and erratic orders from the Generalissimo, Stilwell was in a state alternating between wrath and exasperation. After Lashio fell, the Chinese generals disregarded Stilwell altogether and took off on their own. In danger of being trapped by the enemy, he sent out on the last two planes as many of his staff, wounded men and refugees as could be gotten aboard. With nobility of spirit, but questionable command judgment, he remained behind with those who were left. He took command of surely the most irregular force ever led by a three-star general—about one hundred and fifteen in all, including eighteen American officers and five enlisted men, the resourceful Dr. Gordon Seagrave and his gallant nineteen Burmese girl nurses, stray British and Chinese officers and men, Indian cooks and mechanics, an American Baptist missionary, seven British Quakers, a couple of Anglo-Indian refugee maidens, and Jack Belden who, with his *Retreat with Stilwell*, was to become the Homer of the Stilwell odyssey. Rushing to avoid Japanese encirclement, they started out for India by trucks and jeeps. These they soon abandoned because of broken bridges and bad roads. Beginning May 6 they marched through jungles and hills, next rafted down a river and crossed the Chindwin, then struggled through tropical rain forests and over high mountains, arriving at Imphal, India on May 20.

In New Delhi on May 25 Stilwell summed up his evaluation of the Burma campaign and his strategic concept for the future. "I claim we got a hell of a licking. We got run out of Burma and it is humiliating as hell. I think we ought to find out what caused it, go back, and retake it."

This was, to be sure, a wordier exposition than MacArthur's "I shall return." But then it said a good deal more—not the least about the man himself.

With Stilwell and MacArthur reeling from Japanese assaults—one on the western flank of the enemy advance, toppled into India, the other on Japan's southern front, back onto his haunches in Australia—the crestfallen American Navy on the eastern flank prepared its first revenge for Pearl Harbor. Nine days after Stilwell's New Delhi statement, an American carrier force under Admirals Spruance and Fletcher decisively defeated a Japanese carrier force near Midway Island. The enemy ships and planes were commanded by Admiral Nagumo who had led the attack on Pearl Harbor, then the strikes against Ceylon, and now at last was confounded in mid-Pacific. Four Japanese carriers and one heavy cruiser were sunk in this encounter as against one American carrier.

Japan's first defeat significantly took place in the Central Pacific area, for it was against the enemy's eastern flank that American power was most effectively to be applied.

CHAPTER 22

Politics Rampant

EVEN BEFORE his retreat to India, Stilwell was planning his next Burma campaign, a counteroffensive. He sent on April 16, by liaison officer, a proposal to the Generalissimo to transfer about a hundred thousand selected Chinese soldiers to India. There they would be provided with lend-lease equipment and trained by Americans. He also recommended that their commanders above regimental level be Americans. This harked back to the Taiping Rebellion, to Chinese Gordon, and to Frederick Townsend Ward and the Ever Victorious Army. It was a suggestion which Stilwell should have known would be offensive to the Generalissimo and all Chinese senior officers.

Stilwell optimistically estimated that after four to six months of training in India, this force would be committed to an offensive in two phases: 1. recapturing Burma with supporting action from China, and 2. "ejecting" the enemy from Thailand. According to Brigadier General William R. Gruber, the American liaison officer, the Generalissimo approved the proposal "in general," with reservations about broad American command and the possible use of Chinese troops in support of the British against Indian civil disturbances.

On May 25, after his retreat from Burma, Stilwell asked Marshall and Stimson for American troops—one or more divisions. He would use them, with the Chinese he had asked Chiang for, to drive through to Thailand. Thereafter he would push within China to a coastal triangle defined by Canton, Hainan, and Hanoi. From this vantage he would stab the enemy's north-south sea and air artery.

Stilwell's plea and optimistic promises were those of a frustrated American fighting man, longing for his own kind of soldiers. He wanted them for the fresh, familiar strength they would bring, as an earnest of American commitment to the China-Burma-India area, as a consequent bolstering of his bargaining position with Chiang and Wavell, and as a stimulus to the dispirited Chinese and British. But he was foredoomed to disappointment, for CBI was then near the bottom of the list of both strategic priorities and logistic accessibility. In answering Stilwell's request, the War Department told him that it had neither the men nor the shipping.

In the opinion of the influential Operations Division of the War Department, land access to China had to be opened as that country could never be adequately supplied by airlift. Retaking Burma, OPD reckoned, was for the British to do because Burma and India were in their area of responsibility. The American role should be a supporting one.

Returning to Chungking, and sickened by jaundice, Stilwell nevertheless entered upon a series of conferences with the Generalissimo. At the first session on June 4, Stilwell presented Chiang a paper, "Notes for the Generalissimo," in which he diagnosed what ailed the Chinese Army and proposed remedies. As used by Stilwell in these conversations—and by the War Department in its communications—"Chinese Army" was a courtesy title. In a sense, there was no national army. There were Chiang's troops, a variety of warlord or provincial troops, and Communist troops. The Generalissimo could order his own divisions, but he had to negotiate with the others, and then could not count on them. Least of all, could he interfere with their internal organization.

Stilwell was keenly aware of all this, and so was Marshall and OPD. To preserve Chiang's face, the Americans went along with the fiction that the Generalissimo really commanded the three hundred understrength divisions scattered about China. But in the June conferences, when speaking of the Chinese Army, Stilwell was actually talking about those forces over which Chiang exerted at least some degree of authority.

The Chinese Army was weak, Stilwell told the Generalissimo, for more reasons than lack of equipment. Beginning with what was at hand, divisions should be merged to create full strength units, whereupon all available weapons should be distributed as far as they would go among the reconstituted divisions. As only a few division and army commanders were efficient and possessed moral courage, the rest should be purged, or else "the Army will continue to go down hill, no matter how much material is supplied for it."

There must be unity of command in future operations, Stilwell continued in his "Notes for the Generalissimo." One man should be chosen, whose "absolute control of the troops must not be infringed upon." Furthermore, supply, transport, communications, and medical services needed reformation. And finally, rewards and punishment should be promptly administered.

After scanning Stilwell's paper, Madame Chiang exclaimed that this was what the German advisers had told the Generalissimo. At another meeting on June 24 she said that Stilwell's recommendations could not be acted on, one had to be "realistic," and the "head cannot be lopped off otherwise nothing would be left." Some five years earlier, when Chennault had urged drastic measures against incompetence and corruption, she had answered, "He [Chiang] says that the Chinese are the only people he has to work with, and if we get rid of all those people who are at fault, who will there be left?"

So Stilwell was not the first to irk the Generalissimo with recommendations for reforming his military forces. Even before Chennault, von Falkenhausen, and von Seeckt, there had been Blyukher and his Soviet advisers. They had all learned the limits of criticism and advice that they might press upon Chiang. They remained within those bounds. But then, none of them had been charged with the staff and command responsibilities borne by Stilwell in an allied war situation.

He took these maddening responsibilities as bounden duty, particularly Marshall's injunctions to "increase the effectiveness" of American aid and to "assist in improving the combat efficiency of the Chinese Army." Because of his soldierly and uncompromising nature, Stilwell strove to push through what he had been told to do. This put him on a collision course with the Generalissimo and the military system on which Chiang's power rested. For Chiang, to improve the combat efficiency of the Chinese Army, i.e. the forces accepting his orders, meant not only some heads being lopped off. It also meant cashiering for incompetence most of those who retained their heads. Confronted with a purge, most Chinese generals would have ceased to take orders and either have turned on the Generalissimo or simply assumed the character of warlords, their troops staying with them.

The system was therefore unalterably opposed to its reformation. Knowing that he could not make over his army on the American—or German or Soviet—model without a major upheaval wrecking his power base and endangering his life, the Generalissimo refused to tamper with the system. He wanted, instead, to compensate for his blighted military forces with the most advanced implements of war—flying machines, tanks, and heavy artillery. But he had neither sufficient skilled personnel nor facilities for sophisticated military equipment. And Stilwell, who advised the War Department on lend-lease needs and managed final delivery to China, was averse to supplying Chiang with this equipment excepting as it could be effectively used. Marshall, after all, had told him to "increase," not to disregard, "the effectiveness" of American aid.

Consequently, Stilwell and Chiang were at loggerheads over both improving the combat efficiency of the Chinese Army and substituting American weaponry for organizational reform. What Stilwell wanted Chiang to do, the Generalissimo would not do. What the Generalissimo wanted to do, Stilwell resisted.

Chiang felt thwarted also by Washington. Through T. V. Soong he had in April asked for Chinese representation on the Combined Chiefs of Staff, quoting a barbed remark by Gandhi, "Why, they [the Anglo-Americans] do not even admit your country to their staff talks." Chiang's request was turned down. This meant that China failed to gain a place on the Munitions Assignments Board in Washington, which was under the CCS. Consequently, Chungking had no direct voice in the allotment of material as it became available. These rebuffs were deeply resented by Chiang as an affront to China's newly conferred status as a "Great Power."

On top of this exclusion, the Anglo-American combination began to repossess the accumulation of lend-lease supplies which had been assigned to China but could not be sent there because of the loss of Rangoon. In addition, new assignments of lend-lease were being reduced, if for no other reason than the limitations on moving equipment by air into China. To cap it all, development of the air transport system lagged far behind hungry Chinese expectations, and little progress had been made in expanding air power in China.

T. V. Soong, a clever and aggressive man, was alert to the decline in China's supply fortunes. He was well informed of what went on in Washington because, like his sister, Madame Chiang—but without her flashy regality—he had a manipulative understanding of Americans. In his position as Chinese foreign minister, resident in Washington, he had ready access to the White House, principally through Hopkins, and he was attentively served by a variety of American sinophiles and retainers with broad contacts in the American government.

Soong was therefore well acquainted with the reasons why China was on short rations: the surface access route via Burma had been lost, the airlift substitute had at best limited capacity, and other war fronts had first claim on both supplies and transport. Yet, when a committee of the Munitions Board took into account, in June, the large stockpile of supplies in India awaiting airlift to China and concluded that July assignments of new equipment for China should be reduced or eliminated, Soong professed to believe that this was done at Stilwell's instigation. He went beyond this, and announced on June 20 to Roosevelt and Churchill that if the scheduled 3,500 tons of supplies per month were cancelled, cooperation among the allies in the form of the China Theater would be terminated. Under instructions from Hopkins, the Munitions Board backtracked. Soong kept the Generalissimo provocatively advised of Anglo-American slights to China and his dark suspicions of Stilwell.

The day after Soong sent his ultimatum to the president and the prime minister, Tobruk fell. The British loss of this Cyrenaic town in their desert war against the Italians and Germans triggered an American action in India which flared into a crisis in Chungking between the Generalissimo and Stilwell.

What happened was this. With the stunning defeat at Tobruk, the allies feared that the redoubtable General Rommel might crash through to Cairo and the Suez Canal. All possible reinforcements were rushed to Egypt—including Brereton's heavy bombers and supporting transport aircraft from India. In addition, a flight of A-29 bombers destined for China was detained at Khartoum.

It was Stilwell who, on June 26, had to bear these tidings to the Generalissimo. Chiang was coldly and insultingly furious with Stilwell because of the bomber diversions, ordered by Washington. Furthermore, he and Madame Chiang said that Soong had reported that Stilwell was the reason that only a trickle of supplies was flowing to China. Madame Chiang concluded with a blend of oriental indirection and American bluntness: "The pro-Japanese element is very active [in Chungking]. The Generalissimo wants a yes or no answer to whether the Allies consider this theater necessary and will support it."

Roosevelt's reply to the yes or no query posed by the lady was bland and reassuring. Delivering it to the Generalissimo on June 29, Stilwell received in return Chiang's Three Demands, as they were later called.

1. Three American divisions should arrive in India between August and September to cooperate with the Chinese forces in restoring the line of communications through Burma.

2. Beginning in August the American air force in the China Theater of War should consist of five hundred planes continuously fighting at the front. Their strength must be maintained without interruption by necessary replacements.

3. Beginning in August, the monthly aerial transportation should be five thousand tons.

"Rain for dust," I wrote in a letter on June 22, "moist heat for arid, verdure for dun wastes, malaria for . . . heat prostration." I had come from New Delhi to Assam on my way to Chungking, whence Stilwell had summoned me. I was at the Dinjan airfield, then the only base for the airlift to China. Some thirty C-47 transports operated from this small field, skimming over the mountains on the Burmese border, the hills and valleys of northern Burma, and the jagged ranges of westernmost Yunnan, between which plunged the stygian gorges of the Salween and the Mekong. This topographical barrier between India and China came to be called the Hump. It was the terrain which T. V. Soong had, in a January 31 memorandum to the president, described as "comparatively level."

In May and June the transports were moving less than a hundred tons a month. The Generalissimo's demand of five thousand tons beginning in August was out of sight. There was a shortage of aircraft and parts, new airfield construction was slow, and during the monsoon season planes were often grounded.

Three days after my arrival at Dinjan I was still in Assam's Brahmaputra valley, with the Himalayas at my back, Burma and China beyond the ranges in front of me, the monsoon rains pouring down, huge clouds churning up against the mountains, and no plane daring to fly into that tumbling murk. "I sleep in a one-room school house with seventeen young Americans, with lights and a picture in color of George, R.I., but no water, save that gushing down the gutters and the moisture of damp bedding." To relieve boredom, I drove by jeep through the tea plantation countryside surrounding the airfield.

The planters' "bungalows are prettily set on stilts above green, green lawns bordered by very English hedges and flaming hibiscus and flowering trees. The tea bushes rise chest-high, a plateau of crisp, geometric greenness. As the plantation houses are several miles apart, each area within a radius of ten or fifteen miles has its own golf course and club." It all seemed deserted, for most of the British men were off to war and their women and children at hill stations or home in Britain. And some of the plantations were doomed to be cleared to make airfields.

Arriving in Chungking on June 25, I found Stilwell's residence full, and so stayed at the officers' mess where "the principal recreations are eating, poker, and singing." The officers occasionally "wander through Chungking's really dreary, squalid streets and venture into Sing Sing (really Hsin Hsin, i.e. Heart Heart) where one pays the equivalent of fifty cents for a dish of ice cream flavored like a cosmetic and where one may see one or two pretty Chinese girls of an evening. Sing Sing once had upholstered chairs, but the authorities decided that such comfort incited easygoing ways, so one must now sit on hard chairs. Sing Sing and the other cafes were closed down for some time after some of the AVG boys shot up one of them in a manifestation of misplaced exuberance.

"On the fourth of July I drove out of town . . . to share General Chennault's last luncheon as the commander of the AVG [prior to induction in the Army Air Corps]. It was a pretty drive through the hills which surround Chungking and past the villages where now many city people live and which show the effect of city folk. At one spot the road commanded a view of a plain hundreds of feet below. Low clouds let the sun through in spots on the bright green paddy fields, the clumps of trees shading tiny hamlets, the winding flagstoned paths threading through the paddy fields. And when one sighted a line of peasants working barelegged in the rice and a line of carriers with wide-brimmed straw hats carrying baskets on the end of poles, the scene took on an almost staged quality. . . . The sheeny rice fields were fringed with tufted, waving sorghum like bangs on the glossy head of a Chinese country girl. We crossed a small stream bordered by feathery bamboo and supplicant willows. It was a lush, well-groomed countryside . . . intimate because everywhere was evidence of generations of loving cultivation.

"Our host [Chennault] was, of course, a great personality. He is lean, rugged and, like Uncle Joe [Stilwell] possesses that quality which I have found to be very rare—dynamic leadership."

While Stilwell was engaged in his conferences with the Generalissimo, I began sniffing Chungking politics. I first checked with the embassy. The ambassador was "most genial and friendly," and I spent a talkative weekend with him and John Carter Vincent, his counselor. Gauss, I wrote in a July 13 letter, "is a very frank man. And a man of almost unbending will. . . . The past week I have been moving between the ambassador and the general as a thin binding tie."

They were not antagonistic, for they had known and respected one another for years. But Stilwell was so engrossed with his military problems that he had little time for Gauss, who remained aloof, across the Yangtze from Chungking. In one of their rare conversations Stilwell inadvertently mentioned, twelve days after the event, the Generalissimo's Three Demands, and only after repeated questioning by Gauss did he reveal what they were. This was typical of the general's mistaken secretiveness with Gauss, which restricted the ambassador's usefulness to him as an ally.

My situation was awkward, being assigned to the ambassador, yet detailed away from him to Stilwell. Gauss was not one to be jollied into rising above what he regarded as the general's slights. And I was not yet sure enough of my position with the brooding Stilwell nor of the reasonableness of the ambassador's pique to suggest to the general that he confide more in Gauss. The ambassador had also made it plain to me that he thought I was frittering away my time with the military, that I should be put back to work behind an embassy desk. So rather than being bond, I was burr. In a July 6 letter I wrote, "Uncle Joe said to me the other day with a chuckle, 'Well, I had a talk with the ambassador this morning. He said that he wanted you back. I told him that he didn't have a prayer.'"

Having checked with the embassy on the political scene, I proceeded on my own to make inquiries and seek interviews. As in India, I specialized in the outs, the opposition, and for the same reason. In both countries, our Foreign Service staffs maintained active relations with those in authority. Quite properly our diplomats were circumspect and limited in their contacts with those of whom the government of the country disapproved. Because of my peculiar status, I had more latitude. I could afford to be unorthodox without the embassy's having to take the blame, for I was with the military and all kinds of indiscretions were excused in the military on the grounds that they advanced the war effort.

Chou En-lai was in Chungking as the principal Communist representative at the capital. I sought him out on June 29 at the Central Hospital where he was convalescing from an operation. He was in a small whitewashed room, lying on a bed of rope "springs," and in a good humor, his expressive eyes bright and vital. In a memorandum to Stilwell I reported what Chou had to say:

"Since the beginning of the Pacific War ... he has not been called in for consultation with the Central Government authorities. During the past three weeks, as the expectation of a Japanese attack on Siberia increased, the Central Government's blockade of the Communist area in the northwest has tightened. General Hu Tsung-nan commands an army of 441,000 maintaining this blockade ...

"General Chou did not anticipate a Japanese attack on Kunming. He pointed out that the Japanese knew that the decisive subjugation of China would be a never-ending task and, in effect, that more important objectives still lay before them. Current Japanese operations he regarded as an interim campaign preceding a major effort against either Siberia or India. An attack on Siberia he considered to be more likely.

"He declared that others may be able to seek peace with the Japanese, but never the Generalissimo. He remarked with a significant smile that rumors of the Chinese being prepared to accept Japanese peace offers were staged for effect. ...

"Unified command is the most important factor, General Chou stated with emphasis, in any attempt to retake Burma. He said half-laughingly half-seriously that if the Generalissimo would permit him, he would take Communist troops under his command for a Burma campaign and 'I would obey General Stilwell's orders!'"

During the next few days I interviewed five other persons: Chang Han-fu, editor of the Communist newspaper, who had been at parties in my Hankow apartment; Madame Sun Yat-sen, widow of the deceased national hero and sister of Madame Chiang, Madame Kung, and T. V. Soong; Sun Fo, son of Sun Yat-sen by his first wife and president of the Legislative Yuan; T. F. Tsiang, political vice-minister of the Executive Yuan; and T. C. Lin, a professor acting as "consultant" to an American intelligence agency, the Office of the Coordinator of Information. I summarized for Stilwell on July 5 the views of this diverse group, including those of Chou En-lai:

"Both Communist and Kuomintang officials interviewed anticipated a Japanese attack on Siberia in the near future . . . based upon a belief that (1) Japan must round out its defensive position, therefore the threat of Siberia must be eliminated; (2) as the defeat of Germany would have disastrous effects upon Japan, a Japanese attack on Siberia to ensure a prompt German victory over the Soviet Union is indicated; and (3) time is operating against the Japanese, consequently they must act promptly.

"None of the Chinese interviewed suggested that the outbreak of Russo-Japanese hostilities would be seized by the Chinese as an opportunity for taking offensive action against the Japanese. . . .

"The Chinese interviewed all displayed what was to me, after talking to some of our officers, a strange confidence that the Japanese would not and could not knock out China. Chou En-lai said, and I think accurately, that even though the Generalissimo were forced to fall back into northwest China he would never capitulate to the Japanese. . . .

"Dr. Sun Fo and Mr. T. C. Lin sought to minimize the significance of the blockade [against the Communists] and suggested that the Communist forces could not be considered effective and modern fighters."

In retrospect, the concern of both Communist and Kuomintang officials over a possible Japanese attack on the Soviet Union seems unreasonable. We know now that the turning point in the war against Japan had been in early June, at Midway. But that was a naval battle and for the Chinese, landlocked in the fastness of their western mountains, it was far, far away. They were more aware that the Japanese were holding all that had been so easily taken, that the Germans in North Africa had humiliated the British and in the Soviet Union were advancing toward the oil fields in the Caucasus. The massive Russian victory at Stalingrad that cost Hitler three hundred thousand men was still six months away. In the summer of 1942, to the land-minded Chinese, the Japanese Army still seemed awesome, the Soviet Far East drained of its strength and ripe for plucking. And, indeed, had the Japanese then had the extra power, it would have been strategically wise for them to have joined the Germans in an attempt to bring down the Russian giant and secure their rear.

My next memorandum, July 11, was of a conversation with General Yang Chieh, who had been president of the Military Academy and then ambassador to the Soviet Union:

"The experiences of General Yang in connection with . . . Russian aid for China in the early phases of the Sino-Japanese hostilities were illuminating and significant in connection with our own program of lend-lease aid to China. He said that the day after his arrival in Moscow he stated China's needs to the Soviet authorities. In a matter of two or three days the main outlines of what form this aid was to take had been decided upon. Prices were not mentioned in the initial negotiations and when they were, they were lower than those asked by American and British commercial organizations. The supplies promptly began to move and, as we know, arrived during the early phase of the war at Haiphong, Hong Kong, and Lanchow by the thousands of tons.

"But then came the Russian disillusionment. They discovered that the aircraft were misused and cracked up by inexperienced personnel and that the other material seemed scarcely ever to find its way into combat against the Japanese. It disappeared and no accounting was given. The Russians reproached him [General Yang] for misrepresentation and he found himself in a most uncomfortable position.

"We Americans must be on guard against a repetition of the Russian experience, General Yang warned. We must take steps to insure that the material which we supply China is used for the purpose for which it is given. If this is not done, lend-lease supplies will be hoarded by the Chinese Government (for civil warfare, maintaining the dominance of the regime now in power, and for increasing China's military strength against the day when it can be used as a counter at the peace table?).'We Chinese have thick skins,' General Yang stated, 'and you have been too polite with us.' "

CHAPTER *23*

Special Envoys

SINCE MAY, a month before the Three Demands, the Chiangs had been asking for a visit from Harry Hopkins and, as an afterthought of Madame Chiang's, Currie. The Generalissimo told Roosevelt that he wished to "acquaint him [Hopkins] with the situation and consult you intimately through him." This was a transparent effort to short-circuit Gauss and Stilwell. But Hopkins was too frail for so arduous a journey and his services were needed in more vital matters.

Currie warmly recommended himself to Roosevelt for the pilgrimage as "special envoy"—"I am personally congenial to the Generalissimo" and "I know intimately Stilwell." After Washington's attention had been caught by the Three Demands, the president dispatched Currie to placate the Chiangs. Gauss and Stilwell were forewarned by Washington of the visit but did not know what the special envoy would be up to. The general turned me over to Currie for what assistance I could be to him, and to learn from him what would be of interest to Stilwell. In a letter dated July 25, from my temporary abode with Currie, I wrote: "Lauch [Currie] has gone off to the South Bank to commune with and lay calm hands on the fevered brow of the Gmo. So I am quietly alone in the modest splendor of one of T. V.'s [Soong] Chungking houses which we are now occupying. . . .

"It is surprising to encounter in a person as genuinely, if perhaps sometimes ostentatiously, simple as Lauch occasional flashes of pomposity. He is susceptible to deference and flourishes. Probably because of their novelty . . . John Carter Vincent and I had quite a struggle to persuade him that on his initial call on the Gmo he should wear long trousers and a tie. But I couldn't change him on his call on the minister of war, whom he saw in a pair of khaki shorts and a gray sports shirt which was giving away in the back. That elderly kewpie, General Ho, surrounded by clicking aides, didn't raise a nonexistent eyebrow."

Currie rummaged about in the issues between Chiang and Stilwell. What the Generalissimo had demanded by August was agreed upon as vaguely distant goals and Chiang was mollified. It also developed in the course of the conversations that the Generalissimo had been unaware of the extent of Stilwell's authority over lend-lease supplies assigned to China. This was because Soong had modified Roosevelt's message to Chiang on the subject. It likewise appeared that the foreign minister had not explained to the Generalissimo the Soong-Stimson agreement of January defining Stilwell's various functions. In extenuation, Soong was not alone in his reluctance to bear unwelcome tidings to Chiang. Stilwell was repeatedly told by responsible Chinese that no one dared to tell the Generalissimo the truth.

Currie asked me to accompany him early in August on a call at the Soviet embassy for a conversation with the ambassador, counselor, and military attaché. In an otherwise routine interview, the military attaché said, in response to a question from Currie, that a foreigner could not successfully command Chinese troops. He continued: "A system of advisers, however, could serve a useful purpose. But such a system calls for advisers in all of the various units, from armies and divisions on down. The ranking adviser must have at his disposal his own channel of information from and advice to the smaller units." Asked whether the Chinese were willing to accept advice, the military attaché shrugged his shoulders and said that yes they would, usually.

This was the system that both the Russians and the Germans had used. Neither had attempted to take over command. Even during the Autumn Harvest Uprising of 1927 when the Russian "Comrade Ma" was advising Mao Tse-tung's guerrillas—and going wild with frustration—the Russians had not attempted formal command.

Like the Generalissimo, Chou En-lai wished to acquaint Currie with the situation in China. An intermediary from Chou told me that the Communist representative had no forewarning of the special envoy's advent and was consequently puzzled when, after nearly a year of being ignored by Chiang, the Generalissimo suddenly asked to see him. Chiang expressed solicitude for Chou's postoperative health and urged the Communist representative to make use of the Generalissimo's residence on Mount Omei, nearly two hundred miles from Chungking. Chou was at a loss to explain this unexpected concern over his welfare until he learned that Currie had arrived later that same day.

In response to Chou's requests to see the man from the White House, I passed on through Chou's intermediary the reply that Mr. Currie considered it impolitic at that time to meet the Communist representative. I then became the channel through which Chou conveyed his point of view to Currie. I assumed, of course, that the sleek retainers hovering about the house and grounds were government agents and that they reported that I was the contact man with the Communists.

Chou had two special messages for Currie. His first was, as I reported to Currie on August 6, to the effect that "the Chinese Communists hope that the American government will take steps which will insure the use of lend-lease supplies in accordance with the purpose of such American aid. The fear was expressed that unless the American government maintained a firm and constantly watchful attitude on this score, lend-lease supplies would be hoarded for use after the war in maintaining the position of the ruling faction." This added nothing to our information or resolve. Magruder and then Stilwell, with Gauss approving, had been since the inception of the program alert to the risk of lend-lease equipment being hoarded and otherwise misused.

Chou's second message was an invitation. The Communists would welcome the visit to areas controlled by them of one or several American officials. It was suggested that the Generalissimo could reasonably be requested to grant permission for such an inspection tour on the grounds that the American government should, in view of the possibility of a Japanese attack on Siberia, have firsthand information with regard to this vital border region and the Communist armies. American Army officers were mentioned as the most logical officials to be sent. As I had for some months been hoping to make an investigatory visit to Yenan before the year was out, I was personally pleased that the invitation had been issued. Currie was mildly interested; his mind was occupied with weightier matters.

On the last day of Currie's sojourn in Chungking, August 6, I said in a letter: "I have been acting rather as Lauch's aide—arranging his appointments, writing some of his letters, and listening to a few of his confidences. He doesn't ask my advice very often but is tenacious of the memoranda I write. . . . My trouble, of course, is that I have too many bosses. None of them tells me anything much for fear that I shall repeat what I hear to one of the others—which I do. My first boss [Gauss] knows nothing, anyway, excepting what he is told by his juniors. So he has nothing to tell me. My second boss [Stilwell] knows a good deal but says little unless he is asked. But if asked, he will talk. This last one [Currie] is involved in high policy a little in the best medieval Italian tradition —sans poisoning—and so can tell me hardly anything. But I get a good deal of it through the other channels, due to man's fatal need of unloading to someone. If a wife is not present, then a friend. This afternoon I had the exquisite pleasure of writing for the Gmo's signature a paragraph of a letter to the president in which I launched out on the virtues of my latest boss.

"My general impression is that the weightiest affairs of state are sometimes decided in a shockingly haphazard way. I always suspected it. . . .

"My only prolonged contact with the Gissimo was over a watermelon. He had a very impressive and at the same time charming open air dinner for Lauch out in the hills after which the minister of education (a prime reactionary) and the vice-minister for foreign affairs and I sat around melons at a small table discussing Chinese country theatre. The Gissimo descended upon us in a flowing white gown and to our honor and slight distress sat down. . . . We sat in immobile silence for some five minutes until he spoke. It was all highly deferential and formal. Madame was very chatty and charming. But my favorite is still Madame Sun."

Before this al fresco repast, Currie was given an imposing going-away present. Chiang asked him to convey to the president and the Combined Chiefs of Staff a manifestation of grand strategy known as the Pacific Front Plan. He could scarcely have made a more flattering gesture to the special envoy. Actually, the plan was Stilwell's, an elaboration of his May 25 proposal to Marshall and Stimson and a more refined project, of July 18, for a Burma offensive.

In brief, the Pacific Front Plan of July 29 envisaged an offensive by one American, two Chinese, and three British divisions driving from India into Burma, synchronized with an attack by twelve Chinese divisions from Yunnan. These converging forces would sweep the enemy out of Burma and then overrun Thailand. Meanwhile nine Chinese divisions would push from Yunnan to Hanoi and Haiphong. The allied advance northward from Australia and American naval assaults on Japanese communication lines would be coordinated with galvanizing allied forces on the mainland.

Three days later I wrote a memorandum for Stilwell, "The China-Burma-India Theater—A Reappraisal." In this paper of July 31, I made no mention of the Pacific Front Plan, but did outline as the most ambitious of three possible courses of offensive action a scheme resembling that plan. Unduly concerned over the likelihood of Japan's joining Germany to knock Russia out of the war —which would have had disastrous effects on the British and us, at least in Europe—I concluded that "coordinated operations" on the mainland and in the Pacific would distract the Japanese away from Siberia. The other two courses of action that I summarized were alternative air offensives in and from China.

Stilwell gave me free rein in expressing my opinions in memoranda. Never during my assignment to him did he attempt to alter my politico-military comments. I told him that in my reports I tried, in so far as possible, to support his position with political exposition and argumentation. Nor did he ever complain to me about the widening distribution I gave to my reports; to the contrary, he encouraged it.

Currie did not reveal to either Gauss or Stilwell the full nature of his conversations with the Generalissimo. I sensed from Currie that he was unfavorably disposed toward Stilwell. The general was also suspicious of what recommendations would be borne to Washington. The upshot was that in mid-August I returned to the United States with Currie in the hope that I might learn something of his intentions and the results thereof.

I failed in this mission. Currie was affable, communicative on such matters as movement of lend-lease supplies, but gave me no clear indication of what he would say to the president about Stilwell, the command issue, and the reformation of the Chinese Army. He did not tell me that on August 24, three days after our arrival at Washington, he had recommended to Roosevelt the removal of Stilwell, Gauss, and T. V. Soong.

Even if on that date he had wanted to bring me into his confidence, he would not have found me. For I had taken the day off on a personal matter. On August 24, Patricia Grady—a peerless young woman—and I were married. I had known her in 1941 as a reporter and columnist for the *Washington Post* and as a daughter of Henry F. Grady. As we were both earnest about the war, we decided that we should forego a honeymoon and so went back to work the next day.

Most of my time on this visit to Washington was spent in consultation in the Far Eastern Division. I found the Department of State a backwater with little influence on the wartime rush of events. My colleagues were discouraged and restive.

I learned after August 24 that Currie had recommended Stilwell's recall. My reaction was summed up in a September 24 letter: "He [Currie] wants old Joe removed; I not. For reasons of personal attachment—not valid—and because no one better has been suggested."

I did not know that Currie had also approached Marshall with a suggestion that Stilwell be transferred to another theater—a suggestion that the chief of staff calmly rebuffed when it became apparent that Currie was speaking on his own initiative and not with the authority of the president. But Currie was apparently persistent in seeking the relief of Stilwell. Well after my return to CBI, Marshall observed on October 6, in a memorandum to the president, "I know that Mr. Currie feels that Stilwell should be relieved but I do not believe Mr. Currie realizes what this is going to mean towards the accomplishment of our military objectives in Burma."

While I was in New Delhi during the latter part of September interviewing Indian politicians, Stilwell radioed me to come to Chungking to help him with the impending visit of Wendell Willkie. Having been defeated by Roosevelt in the 1940 presidential elections, Willkie was barnstorming through Africa, the Middle East, and the Soviet Union with Roosevelt's blessing and in the nonpartisan cause of allied solidarity. He was about to descend upon Chungking. At the close of Willkie's visit, I summarized on October 6 for the preceding special envoy, Currie, my impressions of his successor's performance:

"I got back just in time. A few hours after Willkie arrived. There was a great crush at Paishihyi [airfield]. . . . The ambassador was inundated by pressmen who caught Mr. W's fancy. This was an inauspicious beginning. Then instead of going over the river to spend his first night with CEG [Gauss], WW, being human, decided to stay at Yi Yuan [Chinese Government residence]. CEG left in a huff, muttering that he didn't care if he never saw him again. They got down to the ferry at about midnight to find the pontoon black with people waiting for a ferry. All traffic on the river had been suspended in expectation of Mr. W's crossing. Third Secretary Sprouse got ahold of a police captain telling him that WW was not going to cross the river so it was all right for the ferry to operate. The crowd, which was by this time practically anti-American, swarmed on and still more to come. So His Excellency decided that he, JCV [Vincent], and others would take a sampan. They had to scramble some distance upstream along the river bank to find one, were mulct as to price, were carried by the turbulent Yangtze well below the landing near the embassy, had to pole upstream, ducking under hawsers, and were confronted at the landing by large crowds sleepily waiting for Willkie. No chairs [sedan]; so up the hundreds of steps His Excellency climbed to find detachments of police drawn up to welcome and protect WW. Sprouse said it was like the retreat from Dunkirk and quoted the ambassador as having exploded upon arriving at last, one a.m., back at the envoy's catacomb, 'By God, I would have voted for Willkie last election, but in 1944, I'm voting for that Socialist fellow, Elmer Thomas [sic]. . . .

"As John Fairbank [then collecting publications and comforting needy Chinese scholars] observed in his quietly analytical way, 'One makes a tour such as Mr. W's to make the maximum ephemeral impression on the press, newsreels, and radio, or to make a few close friends and contacts, or to gain as much information as possible. Mr. W. seems to be doing the first of these.' . . . His [Willkie's] spontaneity and his demonstrativeness have made a hit with the public. What the shrewd, sophisticated people that count think I don't know. But I imagine that they are satisfied.

"There is little doubt that Little Sister [Madame Chiang] has accomplished one of her easiest conquests. Presiding at a relief organization tea, with the cloak of an air marshal thrown over her shoulders, she admitted with disarming feminine frailty that Mr. W. was a very 'disturbing influence,' a confession which visibly gratified the president's personal representative. At the same function he kissed a little girl and presented her with a cake. Then he did it over for the movie cameras. Yesterday he kissed a girl guide. Then, according to Central News, 'he later spotted several co-eds and jokingly remarked to the interpreter: "Very good-looking. Tell them that I've travelled all over the world and have seen many girls, but I think they are the most good looking." ' It's interesting the influence which enforced celibacy has on judgment—and the course of political events.

"There have been several conversations with the Gmo. Neither the ambassador nor the general has been informed of their nature. The general had several appointments, but they were postponed. This afternoon WW finally granted the general an interview for half an hour during which he expounded on general subjects, asked no questions, and told a funny story. He has been closely chaperoned. The top floor of Yi Yuan, where he is housed . . . swarms with Foreign Office and other officials. His program is in their hands. . . . His hosts were intelligent enough, though, to let him see Chou En-lai."

One of the curses of the airplane is that it made possible global junketeering by politicians. Before the day of transoceanic flights, a voyage to Asia was a long, tranquilizing experience, enabling a man to collect his thoughts and even engage in reflection. This discouraged most politicians from travel to foreign parts. But, with the advent of ocean-hopping, the way was opened for all manner of political flitting about.

Willkie's fluttering across three continents was one of the first of such performances. It was of no visible benefit to the United States. It did not even enhance Willkie's personal reputation with the Chinese who dealt with him. "The young Chinese Foreign Office official who acted as Willkie's shadow," I wrote in an October 9 letter, "observed that he didn't see how anyone as 'unstable' as WW could have been a successful businessman, much less a serious contender for the presidency. WW offended most of the Chinese officials who entertained him or showed him their establishments by snubbing them and concentrating on the American pressmen."

In the last analysis, what Chinese officials thought of Willkie as an American statesman on display did not matter much. Willkie was getting what he wanted—headlines and pictures in the papers back home and material for his image-building bestseller, *One World*. Chinese officials could afford to bear with slights and insults because the Chiangs were getting through Willkie what they wanted—pressure on Roosevelt and the War Department to remove Gauss and Stilwell and to perform in accordance with the Generalissimo's wishes. In my October 9 letter I wrote of Willkie that Madame Chiang had "wound him around her little finger causing him to implore her in the presence of her austere husband to accompany him to the U.S., promising her all the planes she wanted." In lieu of Madame Chiang, however, Willkie got a letter for the president from Chennault about aircraft and air power.

In this communication of October 8, Chennault promised Roosevelt that he would "accomplish the downfall of Japan" if only he had 105 fighters, 30 medium bombers and 12 heavy bombers, backed by a modest 30 percent fighter and 20 percent bomber replacement. In the process of toppling Japan, he could in between six months and a year "destroy the effectiveness of the Japanese Air Force." To do all of this he would require a "very small" amount of supplies brought in on an augmented airlift over the Hump. Also, he would need "full authority as the American military commander in China."

Everything considered, it was a dazzling presentation in the first person singular: I, Chennault, against the Japanese Empire. In China "I can destroy Japanese aircraft at the rate of between ten and twenty to one. When the Japanese Air Force refuses to come within my warning net and fight, I will strike out with my medium bombers against their supply line to the Southwest Pacific. In a few months the enemy will lose so many aircraft that the aerial defense of Japan will be negligible. I can then strike at Japan . . . . My air force can burn up Japan's two main industrial areas . . . . The road is then open for the Chinese Army in China, for the American Navy in the Pacific and for MacArthur. . . .—all with comparatively slight cost."

The concept of an air offensive from Chinese bases against the Japanese in China, Japanese shipping, and Japan itself was not new. Only from airfields in eastern China was Japan then in range of American bombers. In 1942 and on into 1943 the Joint Chiefs of Staff counted on an eventual American air offensive from bases and forward landing strips in China. But the accomplishment of this depended on reopening surface communications through Burma to supply the gluttonous demands of a force strong enough to do the job. In addition, the quality of Chinese ground forces and their equipment needed to be greatly improved to enable them to protect the bases and forward landing strips against enemy ground attacks designed to neutralize American air power.

Chennault's letter to the president was therefore less than a balanced presentation of what was needed and what could then be done in the way of an air offensive. In his vainglory he slighted two drab but decisive considerations: logistics and ground defense. And in so doing, Chennault may not even have been wholly disingenuous, for he was unschooled in logistics and impatient of ground fighting. As Stilwell was more soldier than theater commander, Chennault was more fighter pilot than air force general.

His effrontery in recommending himself to Roosevelt for full authority as American military commander in China was insubordination not only to Stilwell but also to Brigadier General Clayton L. Bissell, who had succeeded Brereton as commander of the Tenth Air Force. Chennault was under Bissell. His China Air Task Force, activated in July with 56 P-40s and eight B-25 medium bombers, was a part of the Tenth Air Force.

Here was another personality conflict in the cantankerous CBI Theater. Chennault was a combat airman, Bissell a desk flier. Chennault, who was not constituted, or at least was not conditioned, to be one of the coterie that ran the old Army Air Corps, despised Air Corps brass for that very reason. And as far as he was concerned, Bissell was a particularly scheming and gouging member of that cabal, fettering the intuitive genius of honest airmen. This was unfair to Bissell who at least understood the complexities of administering a large air operation and the limitations that logistics imposed on what Chennault could do.

And so it was that a scant three months after being inducted into the Army Air Corps, Chennault boldly advised the president, in effect, to oust the theater and air commanders and turn over American military authority to him. In this move he had potent backing—the Generalissimo and Madame Chiang. To the Chiangs Stilwell was an irritant, forever probing the incurable failings of their power structures and nagging them to do the organically impossible. Whereas Chennault—here was the man who would take over the war for them and give them an effortless victory.

When Madame Chiang arrived in the United States on November 27 she was met by Hopkins, who noted, "She thinks that Stilwell does not understand the Chinese people and that he made a tragic mistake in forcing Chiang Kai-shek to put one of his best divisions in Burma where it was later lost. She said Chiang Kai-shek did this against his best judgment. . . . She does not like Stilwell and expressed the greatest admiration for Chennault." Currie, then Willkie, and now Hopkins, the pressure on Roosevelt to oust Stilwell and favor Chennault was mounting.

Stilwell's central objective in the autumn of 1942—to train, equip, and ready Chinese troops for combat against the Japanese—was far from realization.

A plan for thus fitting thirty divisions had been under consideration with the Chinese since November 1940. In October 1942 Stilwell doubled the project to sixty divisions, even though the Generalissimo's headquarters had not completed a list of the units for the first thirty.

This was due to more than incompetence in Chungking's high command. The rapid development of even thirty well-armed élite divisions would upset the intricate, sensitive power equilibrium within China, and not necessarily to Chiang's advantage. For example, among those who were represented as his own generals, which ones, if any, could Chiang trust with the extra power proposed by the Americans?

The two depleted divisions that had retreated from Burma into India were another matter. Chiang conceded them to Stilwell for training and outfitting at Ramgarh, in the tawny, rolling countryside southwest of Calcutta. The General-issimo even provided fillers, flown from China by American aircraft, to bring the units up to strength and later added reinforcements to what was known as the Chinese Army in India. The Ramgarh operation became an extraordinary accomplishment, creating from two beaten, emaciated divisions and their anaemic, scabious additions a stalwart corps far superior to any other Chinese unit.

In Stilwell's calculations, the Chinese Army in India would be the spear-head of the Chinese offensive across northern Burma to open a ground line of communications to China. The main attack, however, should be on the Japanese flank by elements of the hoped-for thirty divisions program in Yunnan. Much larger than the Ramgarh detachment, the projected Yunnan group was desig-nated as Y-Force.

Looking even further ahead, Stilwell envisioned the Y-Force's returning to China from victory in Burma and then undertaking a campaign for the recapture of Hankow. This would be followed by the seizure of the strategic Hsuchow area in East China whence there would be mounted "an intensive and continuous bombing of Japan." It is difficult now to understand how anyone with a knowl-edge of China could think that such vaulting expectations were attainable. Why did Stilwell think them to be possible?

To quest, to dream the impossible dream—no, it was not simply quixoti-cism that impelled him to joust with Chinese windmills. Nor did he close his mind to the possible futility of it all, believe that it was not his to reason why, and charge into the valley of frustration. It was a little of both, plus a Cromwellian zeal to create a New Model Army. But most of all, it was a traditional American conviction that almost anything was possible if you only had enough gumption and stick-to-itiveness.

Stilwell's big mistake, in which I sometimes went along with him, was to think that he could strike a bargain with the Generalissimo: Stilwell could arm and train sixty (later ninety) divisions and enlarge the Chinese Air Force if only Chiang would reform his military establishment and take the offensive against the Japanese.

Had Chiang been able and willing to do what Stilwell asked, China might well have emerged from the war in fact a great power. And of more primitive concern to the Generalissimo, he might have been able then to fend off the Communists. As Chiang could no more reform his power base than overcome his idiosyncrasies, the bargain was doomed—as was Chiang.

CHAPTER *24*

Unconditional Surrender and TRIDENT

UNCONDITIONAL SURRENDER was a war aim, Roosevelt declared on January 24, 1943 at a press conference at Casablanca where he had been meeting with Churchill and the Combined Chiefs of Staff.

Unconditional surrender made little sense in an infinitely conditional world. In excluding compromise, it barred a negotiated peace and so the possibility of creating some sort of international equilibrium through a balance of power. It assumed that the Soviet Union and China were also champions of tolerance, decency, freedom, and faith, and would join us after victory in creating our kind of peace. Meanwhile political considerations could await decision until after the war was won. Finally, unconditional surrender ensured a longer and bloodier conflict than would have been the case had the war been fought for the limited objective of restoring some sort of balance of power.

Significantly, unconditional surrender stirred scarcely any criticism when Roosevelt announced it. It suited the American notion of war—concentrate on crushing the enemy, the source of evil, whereupon virtue and plenty can prevail. This was essentially the same moralistic and utopian approach that Wilson took in World War I.

For most of the American high command the aim of total victory and imposing unconditional surrender was congenial. Roosevelt had informed the Joint Chiefs of Staff of his intention to advocate unconditional surrender a fortnight before his Casablanca declaration. The JCS did not even study the implications of this decision. The president's pronouncement, after all, spared the generals and admirals the distractions and inhibitions of fighting for conservatively calculated political goals.

What seemed more important at the time were the immediate strategic decisions regarding Europe and the China-Burma-India area. The fall of 1943 was provisionally chosen for a Burma campaign, designed to support the exercise of air power from Chinese bases. And the president and prime minister emphasized the urgency of sending air reinforcements and personnel to Chennault.

Field Marshal Sir John Dill, Lieutenant General H. H. Arnold (chief of the American Army Air Corps), and Lieutenant General Brehon B. Somervell (Chief of the American Army Services of Supply) were delegated to proceed to Chungking to make the Generalissimo privy to these familiar intentions. Arnold, on whom Chiang concentrated his attention, got a dose of what Stilwell had for a year been subjected to: demands for a then impossible increase in Hump tonnage, disregard of logistics, independent status for Chennault, five hundred aircraft by November, and threats of a separate peace with Japan unless his wishes were fulfilled. Arnold politely held his ground and the Generalissimo finally, at the last session, agreed to join the fall offensive.

Chiang sent T. V. Soong and Ho Ying-ch'in, minister of war, for further consultation on February 9 at Calcutta with Dill, Wavell, Arnold, Somervell, Stilwell and Bissell.

My diary entry of February 9, Calcutta, noted a meeting at the Great Eastern Hotel with Stilwell "after the little Casablanca conferences were completed": "He told me to come on up with him and talk to him as he changed. He asked me what would happen in India. I said, among other things, that Gandhi [then jailed by the Government] would not fast—which Mr. G. promptly proceeded to do some twelve hours later (this is being written after the fact).

"There were three useful things that I might do—(1) Call on Mr. Jinnah [Muslim leader] ('Yeah, yeah', the Old Man nodded), (2) go up into Assam to find out what could be done about neutralizing fifth column activities when we go back into Burma, (3) take the Shensi-Shansi [Communist region] trip.

"The Old Man was lukewarm about the last, didn't see that it would pay immediate dividends. . . .

"By this time he was in the tub, bathing himself as he does everything—vigorously, jerkily. Ferris [Brig. Gen. Benjamin G., Stilwell's Deputy Chief of Staff] was dressing his amiable, flaccid self in the other room.

"My exposition on neutralization of fifth column activities and psychological warfare . . . roused Stilwell's interest. He croaked from the depths of his tub: 'Be careful there or you're going to sell yourself a job.' Ferris had come into the room. So he suggested setting me up under Benny [Ferris] in New Delhi with . . . espionage and counterpropaganda in my charge. I would presumably be a part of Pape's [Col. Robin Pape] G-2. Benny thought Robin a very sound, solid fellow. So do I. Almost too much so. As the General was buttoning himself up, I suggested my going with Somervell to Bombay where I would see Jinnah. Worth the try, I thought. 'Okay, yep, yep.' "

Not wishing to act on Stilwell's naked inspiration that I become part of Pape's stagnant bureaucracy, I allowed the subject to lapse until March 6 at Chungking. There I proposed a vaguely supervisory function over psychological warfare and related activities. The general gave his assent.

Meanwhile other issues seemed to me to have become more important. One was the problem of Stilwell himself. It was threefold: his role, his personal limitations, and his resultant critics. His role, as he interpreted it, was unplayable. He could command and somewhat reform that small portion of the Chinese army that was in India, but not any part of it that was in China.

The Stilwell personality was complex and contradictory. To me its dominant feature was pent-up intensity. Stilwell's devotion to his family and to what he considered to be his duty was intense, as was his hatred of his enemies, foreign and domestic. He liked to regard himself as a simple man, identified with common folk. In reality he was surprisingly sophisticated. But he was so contemptuous of hypocrisy and those who gave themselves airs that he exaggerated his plainness.

More than once Stilwell praised certain of his officers to me as "good haters." Yet, one of the qualities in Dill that he most admired was Sir John's "human kindness." A common criticism made by his subordinates was that he was vindictive. But my observation was that he was also often indulgent to a fault. Suspicious, secretive, and intolerant, Stilwell was at the same time forthright—indiscreetly so with the Generalissimo and the press—and receptive to reason.

Disagreement with those he did not respect as men brought out his negative qualities. This is what the Generalissimo, Roosevelt, Chennault, Hopkins, and Currie encountered in Stilwell. It turned them against him and made the president and his assistants the more receptive to Chiang's and Chennault's conniving against Stilwell.

This situation worried me, particularly as the Chinese-Chennault lobby in the United States, then led by Madame Chiang, was finding fault with Stilwell and accusing him of shackling Chennault. In a letter to my wife of February 22, I expressed "fears that the Old Man has about outplayed the role of angry, uncompromising old John Brown, that he can't storm Harper's Ferry, and that he has made far too many enemies." I then proposed, if the atmosphere seemed propitious, to talk to Stilwell "like a Dutch nephew."

My opportunity came on March 7, a two-hour session after dinner at the general's house in Chungking. Cryptically, in my diary I recorded, ". . . by the light of a glaring acetylene lamp we started to talk. I had it written down in a loose leaf notebook, which I tore out sheet by sheet." First came enemies. I listed them. And said that in addition to the professional job [Stilwell's military functions] and the Chungking political whirlpool, there were the Washington currents and crosscurrents. They had to be faced up to. The psychological problem [of our dealing with the Chinese] was almost insoluble. We knew how to handle horses and machines, but not [other] humans.

I then described to him the obtuseness of many of his officers in their dealings with the Chinese, particularly at Ramgarh. Next I got to the nub of the matter—the criticism that I had heard from his subordinates about himself and his senior officers: his neglect of his overall command responsibilities, his preoccupation with scattered minor combat and administrative activities, his poor judgment in choice of principal subordinates, and the flabby incompetence of many of those officers. "The only punch pulled," I wrote, "was vindictiveness, which came at the end. There wasn't the heart for that. . . . The most cruel phrase [which I do not recall] was repeated upon request. Little lines were drawn, triangles sketched, not a trace of anger or resentment. In the middle—'You didn't think I could take it?' Hand shading eyes from the glare, but no flush or blanching."

Then the general began to talk. Brereton and Chennault, neither of whom he had asked for, "were rated as s.o.b.s." Of other senior officers, he recognized their weaknesses but at the same time, in some cases, their abilities. "It is a one-man show because he can't trust," I wrote in summing up Stilwell's conclusions. "Things go to pot if the master hand is removed."

Who, Stilwell asked, should be on the next promotion list? I named several. Who they were, I have now forgotten, save for one. He was the only one of whom the general approved—Colonel Frank D. Merrill, a Japanese language specialist, who had been in and walked out of Burma with Stilwell and was later to command the jungle unit known as Merrill's Marauders.

What could be done about the Chiang-Chennault agitation against Stilwell in the United States? During Madame Chiang's visit to the United States, the anti-Stilwell propaganda had spread beyond the White House and into the public print, beginning with *Time*. I suggested that the general send Haydon Boatner, Colonel Mason Wright, his public relations officer, and me temporarily to the United States to tell his side of the story to influential members of the press. He did not accept this suggestion; he was "disinclined to weigh that risk heavily."

Two days after my conversation with the general, I handed the ambassador a memorandum in defense of Stilwell's position. Gauss was returning to Washington on consultation and I hoped that this would provide him with ammunition to support the general. Before delivering the memorandum, I showed it to Stilwell, who "remarked that it expressed what he tried to say. But he always became involved in sons-of-bitches and bastards in his phraseology." "All I want to do after this war," Stilwell said, "is to go walking in the woods with my dog and not see another human being."

Rarely did the general show me any of his communications from the War Department and I never asked him for this type of information. On April 1, at New Delhi, he handed me a message from Marshall. In it the chief of staff passed on to Stilwell part of a March 8 letter from the president to Marshall. In the original full text Roosevelt had indicated that Stilwell's recommendation that we bargain sternly with Chiang was "exactly the wrong approach in dealing with Generalissimo Chiang who, after all, cannot be expected, as a Chinese, to use the same methods that we do." Having imparted to Marshall this insight into a people for whom bargaining was a way of life, the president delivered a concise lecture on Chinese history, politics, and psychology. It was these two paragraphs that Marshall passed on to Stilwell:

All of us must remember that the Generalissimo came up the hard way to become the undisputed leader of four hundred million people—an enormously difficult job to attain any kind of unity from a diverse group of all kinds of leaders—military men, educators, scientists, public health people, engineers, all of them struggling for power and mastery, local or national, and to create in a very short time throughout China what it took us a couple of centuries to attain.

Besides that the Generalissimo finds it necessary to maintain his position of supremacy. You and I would do the same thing under the circumstances. He is the chief executive as well as the commander-in-chief, and one cannot speak sternly to a man like that or exact commitments from him the way we might do from the Sultan of Morocco. [Marshall tactfully changed it to tribal chieftain in his message to Stilwell].

From this nearly irrecognizable description of China, Roosevelt proceeded to criticize Stilwell for neglecting air action in China and to emphasize his belief in the strategic value of operations by Chennault in 1943 and his desire that the airman have adequate supplies and "complete control over his operations."

With reticence I summarized in my diary the substance of Marshall's message to Stilwell, closing with "Finally, couldn't so and so be replaced, he could be guaranteed a good job in a pleasanter clime. Jesus, the gal really did turn on the heat." Now, twenty-seven years later, I translate that entry as signifying that Marshall also informed Stilwell that Roosevelt had requested Stilwell's reassignment elsewhere, and that I had assumed that in her February visit to the White House Madame Chiang had induced the president to move against Stilwell. "I said [to the general] 'You can't debate.' Let it ride and hope it will be forgotten with the passage of time. Temporize. Again the proposal of a Boatner-Davies visit. No sale. I suppose it's a question of not wanting to stoop to politics back home. The feeling on the subject [Stilwell's reaction to the Marshall message] was terribly inflamed—combined with anxiety."

Ten days later Stilwell told me that I was to go to Washington with the proficient and astute Colonel Frank Merrill, who was to consult with the War Department. "It was interesting," I noted, "that the Old Man gave me no explicit orders." I assumed that he wanted me to tell his story. Coincidentally, also on April 10, the Generalissimo asked Roosevelt to summon Chennault to Washington to present to the president a Chiang-Chennault plan for a China-based air offensive. Thereupon, Marshall asked Stilwell to come to Washington. Thus, by chance, I was on the fringe of the China consultations of April 30 and early May and the Anglo-American Trident Conference which followed.

Before they left China, Chennault (now a Major General and his Task Force grown to the Fourteenth Air Force) denied to Stilwell knowledge of a joint air plan with the Generalissimo and knowledge of Chiang's request that Roosevelt summon him. By the time that Chennault and Stilwell arrived in Washington, the Generalissimo had sent to the president his latest strategic opinion. Delivered on April 29 by Soong, now back in Washington, it was this. The entire airlift into China for May, June, and July should be devoted to building up fuel and other supplies necessary for a decisive air offensive. As air transport shortage had been "the only obstacle" to prompt unleashing of such an offensive, dedication of all Hump tonnage to the air effort would remove the only impediment to the onslaught. As for a Japanese reaction, the Generalissimo proffered his personal assurance that an enemy ground advance on Chinese air bases "can be halted by the existing Chinese forces."

It was precisely on this issue, the ability of existing Chinese forces to protect air bases, that Marshall and Stilwell had differed with Chennault, Chiang, and now Roosevelt. The chief of staff and his CBI theater commander believed that existing Chinese forces could not halt determined Japanese advances on Chinese air bases. This had been demonstrated a year earlier when the enemy, annoyed by Doolittle's provocative and ineffectual raid on Tokyo, swept with ease over the bomb-Japan bases in East China. Only after the combat efficiency of Chinese ground forces had been greatly improved, to the extent that they could defend forward bases, could a serious air offensive be sustained.

Chennault's air plan, dated April 30, proposed a phased air offensive, beginning in July with an attempt to wrest air superiority from the Japanese in China and progressing finally to bombing Japan itself late in 1943. The paper he presented ignored the line of communications problem from the Hump freight terminal at Kunming to the distant takeoff bases in East China. He was given no pause by a Japanese reaction on the ground, the possibility of which he recognized. Nor did he raise the need of strengthening in any way the ground forces protecting forward air bases.

Roosevelt received Chennault several times and was much taken by the impressive commander of the Fourteenth Air Force and the spectacular promises of what he could accomplish with air power. As Chennault later wrote, he assured the president that if he got ten thousand tons of supplies a month, he would sink and severely damage more than a million tons of Japanese shipping, whereat Roosevelt "banged his fist on the desk and chortled, 'If you can sink a million tons, we'll break their back.' "

The president was not at all taken with Stilwell, who brought no formula for quick, dramatic successes, but only problems and urgings that Roosevelt do what was distasteful to him—bargain with Chiang. After the meeting, as recorded in my diary, Stilwell told Ambassador William Phillips "that he had tried to hold the conversation but that FDR had taken it away from him. Also that when he told FDR some of the things CKS [Chiang] had said about us, the president had been shocked." The burden of Roosevelt's discourse, Stilwell said to me, was a description of "the war against Japan as, geographically, a piece of pie with Tokyo as the apex." The president had also "shown him a letter from CKS in which the latter had demanded that space across the Hump during May, June, and July be devoted exclusively to air supplies."

This was not an agreeable encounter for the general. In such a situation, it was in his character to become dour and withdrawn. Currie saw Roosevelt after the meeting and told me that the president had remarked "He is not a well man." Stilwell had worsened his position with the commander-in-chief. But he was still staunchly supported by Marshall and Stimson, as he always had been when attacked by Roosevelt and Chiang.

The upshot of the Washington consultations on the Chennault Plan was that the airman should be given a chance to show what he could do. Admiral William D. Leahy, chief of staff to the president, recalled in his memoirs that he had sided with Roosevelt in favoring Chennault, but that the rest of the Joint Chiefs of Staff, Marshall, Admiral Ernest J. King, and Arnold, had inclined toward Stilwell's views.

Just what Leahy imagined the situation in China to be is a matter for wonder. For in recording his first sight of the Generalissimo late in 1943, he wrote, "Chiang Kai-shek was a slight, studious-appearing man with no resemblance whatever to the bandit that he was reported to have been before the war commenced." But then Leahy seems to have been bandit-prone in his biographical knowledge of the Big Four. With considerably more justification in the case of Stalin, he wrote "Most of us [assumably the Joint Chiefs of Staff, at least], before we met him, thought he was a bandit leader who had pushed himself up to the top of his government." The president's strategist in residence then went on to concede rather handsomely that he had misjudged the old accomplice of Tiflis bank robbers.

Roosevelt sent Chiang a preliminary reply to the Generalissimo's demand for all Hump tonnage for May, June, and July, saying that Chennault could not have all of it. Madame Chiang, who was staying at the White House, immediately summoned John J. McCloy, assistant secretary of war, to impress on him that Chiang's wishes should be fully complied with. Soong backed up his sister with a letter in the same vein to the president and then, on May 17, before the Combined Chiefs of Staff, resorted to a familiar Chiang-Soong threat—a separate peace with Japan—unless China was backed wholeheartedly. The Generalissimo commanded the China Theater, Soong said, and should have his way.

As a political decision by the president, not a Joint or Combined Chiefs of Staff decision, Chennault was allotted, in effect, the bulk of Hump tonnage.

During and after this wrangling I was briefing newspapermen, a publisher (Henry Luce), congressmen, and bureaucrats on the CBI Theater and Stilwell. Following one of these sessions, with a group of functionaries of the Board of Economic Warfare, I was told that something of what I had said in this confidential meeting with American officials had been reported to Soong and that the foreign minister was displeased. I, therefore, called on Soong and told him that I was disturbed by exaggerated reports which I knew had been made to him. As noted in a memorandum that I made that day, June 5, he replied: "There are no secrets in Washington. Rest assured, Mr. Davies, that no conference takes place regarding which I do not have accurate and complete information."

Soong's statement was both boastful and exaggerated. Its crudity exhibited the broad un-Chinese streak in him that frequently caused him trouble with other Chinese, conspicuously his brother-in-law, the Generalissimo. For like his sister, Mei-ling, his Chinese self was in conflict with his impatient, aggressive westernized self. This made for uneven performance. The language and tone of Soong's comments to me also revealed his contempt for American officialdom and for the ease with which he could subvert Americans to his use.

I was able to persuade Stilwell to accept an invitation from Eugene Meyer, publisher of the *Washington Post*, to meet a selected group of journalists. I also found myself in the position of conciliator between Currie and Stilwell. My diary notations read: "I reported to the Old Man . . . that Lauch had said, 'How can I make my peace with the General?' Old Joe was rather sour but agreed to receive him. . . . Old Joe had little to say. But then he never does. Lauch remarked afterwards, 'The General played his cards awfully close to his chest.' Lauch's game is to play in with the general, to try to guide overall Asia policy, and to set up his own little intelligence group."

On May 10, I recorded that I had "attended one of Lauch's bi-weekly conferences on Far Eastern affairs. Not a very significant meeting beyond the implication of Lauch's assembling the State, Board of Economic Warfare, Office of War Information, Army and Navy Far Eastern experts under his wing."

While I was a Stilwell partisan in the Stilwell-Chennault feud, I admired the commander of the Fourteenth Air Force as a fighting man and was unhappy over the dissension between the two. Consequently, after I arranged for Stilwell to talk to Hornbeck at the State Department, I also made an appointment for Chennault with the political adviser on Far Eastern affairs. Hornbeck's conclusion was that "both should have what they want." This benign but not very helpful judgment was followed by an observation that Stilwell and I "were poor salesmen. We should emphasize the positive approach instead of the weaknesses of the Chinese." There was some truth in Hornbeck's comment. At the same time, it was a recommendation to lay stress on the encouraging aspects of decomposition.

Churchill, with a train of admirals, field marshals, air marshals, generals, and lords, arrived in Washington on May 11 for the Trident conference. Madame Chiang, ever alert, quickly got word to him that she would be pleased to receive him in New York, where she then was. To spare the prime minister this pilgrimage, Roosevelt invited the Missimo to lunch with his guest at the White House. "The invitation," Churchill later recalled, "was refused with some hauteur." Which "somewhat vexed" the president. But, Churchill concluded, "in the regretted absence of Madame Chiang Kai-shek, the president and I lunched alone in his room and made the best of things."

My diary entry for May 13 was: "With Mr. Churchill's arrival, the issue ceased to be air vs. ground in the China Theater and became the U.S. vs. Britain. Frank [Col. Merrill] said today that in Europe we seem to be preparing to do what the British want us to do. As for Asia, Wavell is here to get us out of Burma, not into it. His job is to explain how impossible it is to retake Burma."

"I hated jungles—which go to the winner anyway—" Churchill later wrote. He thought "in terms of air power, sea power, amphibious operations, and key points." And so the British delegation at Trident was opposed to the planned Burma campaign. Nor had the prime minister's opinion of the Chinese risen. "The president and his circle still cherished exaggerated ideas of the military power which China could exert if given sufficient arms and equipment. They also feared unduly the imminence of a Chinese collapse if support was not forthcoming."

In the case of Europe and, to a lesser degree, Burma, the Anglo-American differences were the outgrowth of contrasting philosophies of warfare. For the Americans, war was science and technology, production of weapons and fighting men, assembly and direct application of force. For Churchill, who dominated his military professionals, war was an art. It was making do with scant resources, maneuver, wile, using others, and biding his time.

The American approach derived naturally from a society of plenty, in which material and human resources were abundant and the national character was self-confident, aggressive, and impatient. Britain, however, had been terribly bled in World War I and was now into its fourth year of a second mangling struggle. In these circumstances, the British had to husband their strength. Curbing their native ardor, they preferred to spend time in circuitous routes, if these would save casualties. Beyond this elemental calculation, and with a far shrewder understanding of history than Roosevelt and his high command, Churchill and his staff were alert to the political advantages to be gained by certain peripheral operations.

The prime minister's eagerness to invade Italy was not simply to overthrow Mussolini and to thin out Hitler's defenses against OVERLORD by drawing German divisions south of the Alps. It was also to gain a flanking position on the Balkans, against the Germans who were then there—and the Russians who soon enough would be there. His fascination with Turkey, Greece and Yugoslavia came from an urge to preempt them, to deny the Soviet Union a position on the Mediterranean. And his inclination, revealed at Trident, to bypass Burma—which would go to Britain anyway—in favor of amphibious operations against Sumatra or other objectives closer to Singapore, was more than military leapfrogging and a reluctance to allow a hemorrhage of English blood in Burmese jungles. If MacArthur was obsessed with returning to the Philippines, Churchill was scarcely less determined that Singapore should be retaken by British arms. He had no desire to risk an entanglement in the tropical underbrush of Burma delaying British repossession of Singapore, the symbol of Britain's imperial power and authority in Asia.

Most of the Americans who had an inkling or more of British political preoccupations thought them to be indecent. We were fighting a war, they exclaimed, and men were dying. We should concentrate all possible forces and drive headlong across the channel and France into the Ruhr, across Burma into China, through the frontal depth of Japanese defenses onto Luzon, and into the enemy's eastern flank in the Marianas. If the politicians wanted to plan the postwar world, let them do so. But they should not meddle in serious military operations. There would be time enough for political finagling after the war was won, after unconditional surrender.

Trident ended in compromises. Whether to invade the Italian mainland was left undecided, although Churchill eventually had his way. A major effort in Burma was postponed, but Stilwell would push forward in North Burma to protect the Assam airfields and the road and oil pipe line being built toward China.

China still loomed in American minds as a position of major strategic importance. An American Strategic Plan for the Defeat of Japan was presented by the JCS to the May 14 session of the Combined Chiefs. It provided for a convergence on Canton-Hong Kong, with the Americans coming from the east and the British and Chinese from the west. The combined forces would then advance to North China, whence Japan would be heavily bombed. If this did not force a capitulation, it would be necessary to invade Japan. Reiterating the strategic judgment about China, Marshall told the combined chiefs on May 20 that "the retention of China as a base for the defeat of Japan is a vital necessity."

This concept of China as a decisive location from which to defeat Japan persisted until late 1943. Doubts began to arise, however, in the early fall of 1943 as American naval strength increased and it became apparent that the Marianas might be seized, from which industrial Japan would be within range of the new B-29 long-range bombers. On September 1, in a letter to my wife, I hinted that China might be bypassed—"and rightly so." On October 18, the War Department's planners broached the possibility of "an approach [to Japan] from the Pacific rather than from the Asiatic mainland." But the Mariana landings were, at the end of 1943, more than six months away and concern with China as a lodgment from which to bomb Japan continued well into 1944.

Dissatisfied with the loose, conflicting command situation with regard to India, Burma, and the rest of Southeast Asia, Churchill began in June to agitate for a unified command in that part of the world. What finally emerged in October was the South East Asia Command (SEAC), with the glamorous vice-admiral Lord Louis Mountbatten as Supreme Allied Commander, South East Asia (SACSEA). Stilwell was designated as acting Deputy SACSEA. The appointment of the admiral, who had been Britain's chief of combined operations, suggested that Churchill's intention was that SEAC should be an amphibious rather than a land theater, Sumatra rather than Burma.

The creation of SEAC-SACSEA did not improve matters. The China Theater remained under the Generalissimo. The CBI Theater, affecting only American forces in the area, continued to be under Stilwell's command. India was independent of Mountbatten, with Wavell promoted, successively, to field marshal and then to viceroy, and General Sir Claude Auchinleck succeeding him as Commander-in-Chief, India. So SEAC amounted to yet another overlapping command area. For logistic support SACSEA depended on India and CBI. For troops he depended mostly on India and China, and for combat aircraft, to a large measure, on CBI.

It is small wonder that, in search of a spread of his own, Lord Louis before long set up his headquarters in Ceylon. It was the most idyllic command post of World War II, reposing in a botanical garden at Kandy, hidden in the mountains at the center of that lovely tropical island. The seclusion was not spoiled by even a landing strip. It was in this lush fastness that a burgeoning Anglo-American headquarters planned the reconquest of Burma, while dreaming of Sumatra and Singapore.

His new position as acting deputy to Mountbatten did not greatly affect Stilwell. Nominally, it meant that he had yet another chief. But most of Stilwell's time was spent on his functions as Joint Chief of Staff for the Generalissimo, commander of American forces in the CBI Theater, commander of the Chinese Army in India, and dispenser of lend-lease supplies to China.

CHAPTER *25*

My Forebodings and the Cairo Conference

MOST OF THE TIME since 1935 I had lived among people ruled by occupying armies, in Manchuria and Central China, or by colonial administrators, in Burma and India. I was therefore acquainted with the circumstances of oppression, from ferocity in the Ever White Mountains to paternalism in Travancore. I had also listened to the longings for freedom of these people, from the fisher lad on the Yangtze, who simply wanted foreign soldiers to leave him in peace, to Indian intellectuals brooding over a frayed bondage and bitter about anticipated betrayals after the alien war had been won by their white masters.

The peace that would follow the war troubled me. My upbringing in the Puritan ethic predisposed me to sympathy for the common folk, wherever they were, and to want a peace that would protect them. Before Trident, on March 26 at Kunming, I wrote to my wife with inconsiderate *weltschmerz*: "An extensive but not sharp melancholy has settled on me . . . from the stupidity and misdirected passions of most humans, the slowness of the war, the evil that will be spawned from the peace, the civil strife that will probably follow in this miserable land [China], and our incapacity to cope with the problems which will confront us. It's the old, old story of human history. Only, this time it's going to be of wider scope and greater upheaval. The only course is to do as well as one can and be stoic about what one can't do."

On April 4, from New Delhi, I continued: "We are going to blunder through to a victory in this war—even though it may be only a temporary victory which will be followed by another war well within our time. I don't know which is more important at this juncture—ensuring the victory or planning for what we are going to do with the victory. I am inclined to think that the latter is the more important. And the thing that alarms me about the planning is the personnel engaged in it. . . . They are people with impeccable intentions, a mass of written material, and no direct contact with the problems which they are setting out to solve. Inflation, shortage of consumer goods, and political reaction in China are things they have on graphs and charts, not things that they rub shoulders with. And until they do, the graphs and charts are likely to confirm them in the error of their theoretical ways."

My first exploration of the uncertain future was a survey of the rivalry between Chiang's Kuomintang government and the Communists, the likelihood of a civil war, and the risks of Soviet-American involvement in that struggle. The paper was dated June 24, 1943 and was written during my stay in Washington after Trident. In part, I said: "The Kuomintang and Chiang Kai-shek recognize that the Communists, with the popular support which they enjoy and their reputation for administrative reform and honesty, represent a challenge to the Central Government and its spoils system. The Generalissimo cannot admit the seemingly innocent demands of the Communists that their party be legalized and democratic processes be put into practice. To do so would probably mean the abdication of the Kuomintang and the provincial satraps.

"The Communists, on the other hand, dare not accept the Central Government's invitation that they disband their armies and be absorbed in the national body politic. To do so would be to invite extinction.

"This impasse will probably be resolved, American and other foreign observers in Chungking agree, by an attempt by the Central Government to liquidate the Communists. This action may be expected to precipitate a civil war from which one of the two contending factions will emerge dominant.

"If Chiang and the Communists were to fight a civil war without external aid to either side there is little question that, unless it had by then been rendered impotent by the exhaustion of the prolonged war against Japan and by the centrifugal tendencies referred to above, the Central Government by sheer weight of arms would be able to crush the Communists. Such an eventuality is, however, unlikely for the reasons mentioned below.

"It would only be natural that, should Chiang attack the Communists, the latter would turn for aid to their immediate neighbor, the Soviet Union. And as such an attack would probably not be launched until after the defeat of Japan, the Communists might expect with good reason to receive Russian aid.

"This would be so because, following the defeat of Japan, Russia would no longer be threatened on its eastern borders, because the Kremlin's present need of Chiang Kai-shek's cooperation would have passed, because Stalin would then presumably prefer to have a friendly if not satellite Chinese Government on his flank, and because the Soviet Union would then have surplus arms in abundance for export.

"A Central Government attack would therefore in all probability force the Communists into the willing arms of the Russians. The position of the political doctrinaires who have been subservient to Moscow would be strengthened by such an attack. The present trend of the Chinese Communists toward more or less democratic nationalism—confirmed in six years of fighting for the Chinese motherland—would thereby be reversed and they could be expected to retrogress to the position of a Russian satellite.

"In these circumstances they would not be a weak satellite. With Russian arms, with Russian technical assistance, and with the popular appeal which they have, the Chinese Communists might be expected to defeat the Central Government and eventually to take over the control of most if not all of China. It may be assumed that a Russo-Chinese bloc, with China as a subservient member of the partnership, would not be welcomed by us. The effect of such a bloc upon the rest of Asia and upon world stability would be undesirable.

"Chiang Kai-shek and his Kuomintang lieutenants fully realize the risks of an attack on the Communists. This may explain the reported statements of high officials in Chungking that they must prepare not only for the coming civil war but also for the coming war with Russia. Chiang and his Central Government recognize that they cannot defeat the Communists and the Soviet Union without foreign aid. Such aid would naturally be sought from the United States and possibly Great Britain.

"We are of course already supplying lend-lease war materials to China. All of this equipment is being channelized to the Central Government. None of it goes to the Communists. Ironically enough Russian military supplies to China, also delivered only to the Central Government, have reportedly been given to the four hundred thousand Government troops now understood to be blockading the Communist territory—and thus immobilized in the war against Japan. American lend-lease supplies may be expected ultimately to be used for a similar purpose.

"American lend-lease equipment already delivered and to be delivered during the future course of the war will probably, however, not be sufficient to guarantee a Central Government victory in a civil war in which the Russians would be aligned against Chiang. In these circumstances we may anticipate that Chiang Kai-shek will exert every effort and resort to every stratagem to involve us in active support of the Central Government. We will probably be told that if fresh American aid is not forthcoming all of China and eventually all of Asia will be swept by communism. It will be difficult for us to resist such appeals, especially in view of our moral commitments to continued assistance to China during the postwar period.

"It is therefore not inconceivable that, should Chiang attempt to liquidate the Communists, we would find ourselves entangled not only in a civil war in China but also drawn into conflict with the Soviet Union."

I concluded this paper with a recommendation that we establish points of direct contact with and observation of the Communists in their area.

On my way back to CBI in July, I stopped off for several days in London. There I listened to some of our military planners who had been conferring with their British opposite numbers on future operations against Japan. Drawing on this information, a conversation with Ambassador John G. Winant, and subsequent ruminations in India and China, I analyzed in a memorandum of September 17 policy conflicts among the British, the Russians, the Chinese, and ourselves. After reading my fifteen pages, Stilwell said that he hoped that the president would look at the memorandum, even though he did not read anything over a page in length. I sent a copy to Currie, who passed it on to Roosevelt on October 20. Beyond that I do not know what happened to the paper.

British policy, I wrote, was directed at conservation of British manpower, repossession, and possible expansion of empire, "preventing China from developing into a major power," and "reducing Russia's strength . . . by delaying the opening of a second front." Chinese policy was preoccupied with postwar consolidation of Kuomintang power, and dreams of industrialization and territorial expansion into Outer Mongolia and northern Burma.

"Absorbed in their struggle with the Germans and realizing that they cannot depend upon Britain and the United States to defeat the Wehrmacht for them, the Russian policy appears to have been less political than that of the British and the Chinese. In its singleness of purpose—confined to the defeat of the enemy—it has resembled ours.

"But while we follow such a policy from choice, the Russians have done so from necessity. A mortal struggle for survival leaves little slack for political picking and choosing. British policy in 1940 and 1941 and Chinese policy before Pearl Harbor had the same attributes of simplicity.

"Once the Russians feel, however, that they have won their fight for survival and that they have some leeway for maneuver, it will not be surprising if they begin to make their military strategy subservient to an overall political policy. That point may already have been reached.

"It is perhaps not too early to suggest that Soviet policy will probably be directed initially at establishing frontiers which will insure Russian security and at rehabilitation of the USSR. There is no reason to cherish optimism regarding a voluntary Soviet contribution to our fight against Japan, whether in the shape of air bases or the early opening of a second front in Northeast Asia. The Russians may be expected to move against the Japanese when it suits their pleasure, which may not be until the final phases of the war—and then only in order to be able to participate in dictating terms to the Japanese and to establish new strategic frontiers.

"At this point it may be worthwhile to insert comments on our bargaining positions. As the Soviet Union's peril diminishes, its need for our aid diminishes. In direct proportion as the Kremlin feels its need of American assistance lessening, our bargaining position becomes weaker and we are less able to persuade the Russians to act as we desire. We appear to have made little use of our bargaining strength with the Soviet Union because, perhaps, we were not prepared to force through what we wanted and because we would not have been prepared to exploit our advantage even had we done so. Now we find our bargaining strength with the Russians slipping away, as it has been slipping away with the British since Pearl Harbor. Our strong bargaining position vis-a-vis the Chinese remains. But we have never employed it on any major issue; rather, the Chinese have us on the defensive because of a guilt complex we have with regard to China. . . .

"The Soviet Union's suspicions of the intentions of the United States and

Great Britain are certainly reciprocated by the Western Democracies. These Russian suspicions, together with the resurgence of Russian nationalism, would seem to make it more likely that the Soviet Union will continue to play a lone hand in international affairs.

"This possibility arouses in politically informed minds in the United States, Britain, and China concern lest the Soviet Union, in seeking to establish its new strategic frontiers, will expand into territories which the other three powers, also for strategic reasons, wish to remain independent or which one of them (China) claims. How far does the Soviet Union intend to penetrate into Middle Europe in pursuit of the Germans? What are Soviet intentions in southwestern Asia? What are Russian plans for the use of their Korean divisions? And if the Chinese Communists are driven to seek Russian aid because of Chungking attacks, does the Kremlin intend to utilize as satellites the Chinese Communists and any territory which they may with Russian arms hold or capture? North China and Manchuria, for example. . . .

"One thing is sure. We are not heading for a brave new world. For the conduct of the war is shaping the conditions of the peace. If there were to be a brave new world through moderate and rational transition, it was incumbent upon the United States and Great Britain to take the lead. We started with the Atlantic Charter, the "Four Freedoms" and Mr. Wallace's noble conception of the era of the common man. As we began to enjoy military successes, however, the voice of liberal humanism faded. Mr. Churchill assumed and has maintained the lead in expressing the determination that imperialism of the British brand shall not perish. By our silence we have, in so far as the rest of the world is concerned, acquiesced in this point of view.

"Mr. Churchill's change of complexion is understandable. Britain cannot make the concessions necessary to allay Soviet and Chinese suspicions, fear, and antagonisms nor satisfy the desires of its Asiatic colonials without reducing itself to the position of a third-class power. This Mr. Churchill has never been prepared to do. Rather, his intentions would seem to be quite the opposite. And he has our support in all of this.

"Whether or not a brave new world could have been brought into being is now a question for academic debate. The opportunity for a moderate, humane, and equitable transition to a better world system has passed. The lines of future conflict are being formed by the course of the present one. We can now be assured of further war and revolution in our time. Like it or not, we are up to our necks in power politics."

On October 20, at New Delhi, I had a free-ranging conversation with the head of the British Political Warfare for the Far East, John Galvin, and others. Galvin plainly indicated that the British Government was determined to regain all of its empire. I said that Stilwell's designation as Mountbatten's deputy and our participation in retaking British colonies would cause the American people to ask "why our boys had to die to repossess British colonies for Great Britain."

Turning to the future of Japan, I asked, "Is it desirable that Japan be completely crushed?" as many Americans were then advocating, "Cannot Japan be used in the future as a counter against the Soviet Union and China?" While Galvin agreed with this, he nevertheless anticipated that Japan would be on the Asian side in an eventual war between the Anglo-American bloc and a Soviet-Chinese-Indian-Japanese coalition.

Our commitment to "recreate Britain as a first-class power," I commented in a memorandum of the conversation, was laying the groundwork for a future war between revolution and counterrevolution. "Britain can be a first-class power only as it has the empire to exploit. Imperial rule and interests mean association with other peoples on a basis of subjugation, exploitation, privilege, and force. It means a constant struggle between the urge to revolt and the compulsion to suppress. It means a turning by the colonial peoples to any nation or group of nations which can promise them a change, nations to whom the colonial peoples would not turn were it not for their servitude."

Some weeks later I received a letter, dated November 30, from Currie, in which he said: "Just a note to tell you that I passed your latest consignment of dynamite along to the Boss [Roosevelt]. He returned it with a cryptic little note saying he wanted to talk it over with me, but, for reasons which you can imagine, the opportunity has not yet arisen so I am not sure what the reaction was. However, I expect the soil was reasonably fertile and that the memo should bear some fruit. By the way, we don't talk about our cousins in quite such strong terms in Washington."

Roosevelt and Churchill met with Chiang at Cairo, and then with Stalin at Tehran in November 1943. Upon his return to the United States from these conferences, the president delivered a speech by radio, a Fireside Chat, on Christmas Eve, 1943. In it he disclosed his efforts at personal diplomacy, by which he laid much store for the conduct of the war and the future of mankind. He spoke of his and Churchill's spending four days with Chiang going over the complex situation in the Far East and "long-range principles which we believe can assure peace in the Far East for many generations to come."

Those principles are as simple as they are fundamental . . . restoration of stolen property to its rightful owners, and the recognition of the rights of millions of people in the Far East to build up their own forms of self-government without molestation. . . . Never again must our soldiers and sailors and marines . . . be compelled to fight from island to island. . . .

I "got along fine" with Marshal Stalin. . . . I believe that he is truly representative of the heart and soul of Russia; and I believe that we are going to get along very well with him and the Russian people—very well indeed.

Britain, Russia, China, and the United States and their allies represent more than three-quarters of the total population of the earth. As long as these four Nations with great military power stick together in determination to keep the peace there will be no possibility of an aggressor Nation arising to start another world war.

Stilwell took Frank Merrill, John Liu (his Chinese liaison officer), and me to the Sextant Conference at Cairo, about which Roosevelt spoke in his Fireside Chat. On the first leg of the journey out of Karachi I was astonished to discover that the general had no prepared statement or plan ready for the conference. Therefore, on November 19, at our overnight stop in Iraq, on a piece of Shatt-al-Arab Hotel stationery, I sketched out a plan for a 1944 offensive. As I now vaguely recall it, the proposed campaign was directed at the capture of Canton, in coordination with the Navy's westward advance in the Pacific, and called for the contribution of one token American division. I showed my essay in war planning to Merrill and Stilwell. Neither thought much of it.

The next morning on the plane, Merrill took my Shatt-al-Arab piece of paper and in about an hour brought me two-and-a-half pages of rewrite in proper War Department style. This he turned over to Stilwell for final drafting in the general's punchy style. At Cairo on November 21, Merrill and I borrowed a typewriter and paper from the Air Force, condensed the plan to one page and gave it to Stilwell, who put it in his hip pocket and left. I also drafted a paper on the political considerations involved in China and Southeast Asia, in which I recommended that the United States avoid involvement in the reconquest of British, Dutch, and French colonies. The next morning Merrill and I typed the final version of the plan, with copies made from smudgy carbon paper salvaged from a torpedoed ship.

We then sped to Mena House, the hotel at the Pyramids which served as conference headquarters, and the name of which impelled me to call the conference the Mena Pause. There we passed out copies to officers we knew among the Army, Navy, and Air Corps planners. Next we called on General Patrick J. Hurley, the former secretary of war who was then acting as a roving representative of the president in the Middle East, and whom I had met in New Delhi when he was on his way to Chungking to make arrangements for the Generalissimo to go to Cairo. As Hurley was about to visit Roosevelt, we pressed copies of both papers on him. While Merrill went off to buy an accordion, I proceeded to the American legation where I left copies for Ambassador Winant, who had come to the conference from London.

Sextant opened on the morning of November 23, with the Big Three, Madame Chiang, and the top military, including Stilwell, Mountbatten, and Chennault. I was of much too lowly rank to attend. But I was filled in after this and later sessions by Stilwell, Merrill, or my friends from the Operations Division of the War Department, principally Brigadier General Frank Roberts, whom I had known since 1935 in Peking.

At the first session, Lord Louis presented a SEAC plan for a modest Burma campaign. The Generalissimo raised several objections. Decision on the SEAC proposal was postponed.

In the afternoon Marshall presented to the Combined Chiefs Stilwell's dark horse entry out of Shatt-al-Arab, graciously representing it as the Generalissimo's plan. I was told that the American JCS were pleased with it. But Mountbatten and the British Chiefs, who were taken by surprise, criticized the plan as logistically unfeasible. General Sir Alan Brooke, Chief of Imperial General Staff, dismissed it as "fantastic." The plan was shelved for study.

This was no great loss. The drive through the Central Pacific had gained lodgment on the Gilbert Islands three days earlier. The preference of the planners for the amphibious advance westward across the Pacific was being justified. And on December 2 at Cairo, the Anglo-American Combined Planners submitted an Overall Plan for the Defeat of Japan. They assumed that "invasion of the principal Japanese island may not be necessary and the defeat of Japan may be accomplished by sea and air blockade and intensive air bombardment." Furthermore, "The main effort against Japan should be made in the Pacific." SEAC's supporting operations for 1944 were to capture northern Burma. The principal action from China would be long-range B-29 raids.

Roosevelt, Churchill, Marshall, Hopkins, and others who had not had the adventure of dealing directly with the Generalissimo became acquainted, at Cairo, with his capriciousness. Chiang reversed himself several times on the SEAC plans for 1944. Mountbatten, who now had the excitement and suspense of trying to elicit a firm decision from the Generalissimo—to Stilwell's vast relief —remarked in his diary on November 27, that Churchill, Roosevelt, and the Combined Chiefs "have been driven absolutely mad, and I shall certainly get far more sympathy from the former in the future." Chiang left that day. Lord Louis pursued him to Ramgarh, where the Generalissimo was inspecting the Chinese Army in India. There the Supreme Commander, South East Asia, had the pleasure, however transient, of witnessing the Supreme Commander, China Theater, change his mind once again, this time in favor of the SEAC operation.

Roosevelt and Hopkins, together and separately, had at least four private meetings with the Generalissmo and Madame Chiang. No minutes were kept by the Americans of these conferences, which was harder on those other Americans having to deal with Chiang and his government than it now is on historians. The State Department had belatedly rushed a senior, Chinese-speaking diplomat, Willys Peck, to Cairo to assist the president in the meetings with Chiang, but he was sent packing back to Washington.

A Chinese summary of one of the conferences recorded that Chiang thought that after the war the Japanese should choose their own form of government and that Korea and Indochina should be independent. Roosevelt and Chiang agreed that Formosa should be "restored" to China, according to the summary. Elliott Roosevelt, the president's son, who was present at another meeting, listed Chinese unity—the Communist problem—as a topic discussed. The younger Roosevelt also mentioned the future of Malaya, Burma, and India as subjects of an earlier conversation. On December 6, Hopkins told Stilwell and me, as an aside in our conversation, that the Chiangs had revealed to him strong anti-British feelings and great nervousness about the Russians. He thought them childish in many respects. They wanted Outer Mongolia, whereat he laughed.

After five days of consultation with the Generalissimo, Roosevelt and

Churchill left on November 27, accompanied by the Combined Chiefs of Staff, to meet with Stalin at Tehran. Those of us having to do with China and SEAC stayed behind. Merrill now had a chance to practice on his accordion, I wrote to my wife, "playing 'O, Come All Ye Faithful,' 'The Halls of Montezuma,' and 'Old Folks at Home.' Hideous." In another letter: "Old Joe came in and tried the instrument—very earnest, very loud, but a little in need of practice. . . . John Liu, who is one of our sight-seeing party, bought a violin yesterday. . . . I am looking wistfully at a cornet. We may return as Joe and His Three Hot Jivesters."

Our sight-seeing extended, in Uncle Joe's Chariot, to Jerusalem and Bethlehem. Then it was Memphis and Saqqara and the tombs, where "the Old Man was all over the place, peering, shooting questions and showing sharp appreciation of some lovely bas-relief. . . . 'Archaeology is something that could really get to you, especially if you had a few successes.' " So we needs must journey to Luxor where we were swept along by the intense Stilwellian inspection of Theban splendors. The general was having a glorious time. The Anglo-American delegations returned from Tehran on December 2, greatly impressed by Stalin and the gigantic scale of the war on the Russian front. Stalin's figures were 330 Soviet against some 260 Axis divisions. For the Burma campaign we were talking in terms of a score or so of allied divisions against 5 or 6 Japanese.

Stalin's assurance on November 28 that the Soviet Union would join the war against Japan after the defeat of Germany was welcomed by the American army high command. Marshall had looked forward with distress to the cost in casualties of subduing the last fanatical resistance not only in Japan, but perhaps also in North China, Manchuria, and Korea, should the Russians remain aloof. While I was relieved by what Soviet action would mean in American lives saved, I was still troubled by the prospect of Soviet expansion in northeastern Asia and all of its implications.

Churchill used Stalin's pressure at Tehran for the earliest opening of a second front in France to induce Roosevelt to join him in cancelling a SEAC amphibious landing on the Andaman Islands in the Bay of Bengal. Landing craft for this operation, Churchill argued, would be needed in Europe. The prime minister was also well aware that abandonment of the Andaman action, which the Generalissimo asserted was indispensible to a Burma offensive, would give Chiang an excuse for withdrawing from the planned land offensive in Burma, which neither of them liked.

Stilwell took me with him on the morning of December 6 in Cairo to seek guidance from Hopkins. We were received by the frail Hopkins, lounging in his bed under a pale green counterpane. On the attitude of the British toward China, he said that they no more wanted the Chinese strong than they wanted the Japanese strong. However, they wanted Japan built up after the war. But, said Hopkins, Japan would be our enemy again. Because of this we must have bases in Formosa, the Philippines and "anywhere we damned please."

Our aim is that China be a great power, Hopkins continued. It will need

American aid in rehabilitation. Our government should be studying now what we can do. The Far East will be the most important area in American foreign relations. Hopkins recognized that the Chinese and the British are both dependent on us. We can therefore have our way. As for the Russians, they have no territorial ambitions in Asia. Stalin has no fear of Chiang and only contempt for the Chinese fighting forces.

I pointed out the need of clear direction from Washington to those of us abroad. Hopkins admitted that our ambassadors are handicapped for lack of guidance and because of duplicating agencies. He said that what was needed was a small, closely-knit group to run American foreign affairs. Secret directives on policy should be sent to key officials abroad. Hopkins said that Stilwell and I should immediately get the word about policy directly from the president.

At 12:45 on the same day the general and I were received by the president. "Hello, Joe," he said. He shook hands with a display of warmth. The Andaman operation was all off, he began. He had fought for it, but the prime minister would not yield. At Tehran Churchill had given in to Stalin and him on an early cross-channel invasion of France. As the conference at Cairo could not now be allowed to end in an impasse, the Andaman operation was out. This, I thought, was a political swap, revealing Roosevelt's unwillingness to dictate to Churchill.

Things weren't so bad, the president went on. The airlift would grow. We would work on arming and training ninety Chinese divisions (Stilwell had suggested this project to Chiang in early November and Roosevelt had vaguely endorsed it in a Cairo meeting with the Generalissimo). We would also build up the Fourteenth Air Force and a new project for B-29 bases in West China. Chiang asked for a billion dollar loan. He told the Generalissimo that it probably couldn't get by Congress and that he might manage fifty million for currency stabilization.

What should our policy toward China be, Stilwell asked. Roosevelt rambled in reply, but in sum it was: we want a strong China. In contrast, when he said to Churchill that four hundred and twenty-five million Chinese could not be ignored, the prime minister snorted, "Four hundred and twenty-five million pigtails." Churchill insists that he will not lower the Union Jack over any part of the Empire. Therefore, in the case of Hong Kong, Roosevelt would agree to the British flag being raised, but then as a generous gesture, the British should the next day declare it to be an open port.

I asked the president how the seeming "nobility" of the Russians in Asia could be explained. They were like us, he immediately replied. They had all of the land they needed. As I was not thinking of land hunger, but of security, I inquired whether they might not seek for Manchuria a status similar to that of Outer Mongolia. No, definitely. He had advised Stalin that he was confident that Chiang would declare Dairen to be a free port and that Siberian trade could then transit this warm water port in bond. Although he did not think that the Soviet Union would seize Chinese territory, he assumed that Stalin would not allow the Chinese Communist army to be put upon.

Roosevelt said that he had bluntly asked Chiang if he wanted Indochina. The Generalissimo replied that he did not, under any circumstances. Should Indochina be repossessed by France, he had asked Stalin, and the answer was no. The president seemed to be thinking in terms of trusteeship. This would also apply to Korea, which he said was not ready for self-government.

Hopkins, who had wandered in during the conversation, inquired how we should react if Japan suddenly capitulated. I asked how we should react if the Chiang regime disintegrated. Roosevelt immediately responded. We should bolster the next in line. Who would that be? Stilwell and I agreed that there was no obvious one man, that it might be a group. Stilwell added that we need not search for successors, they would come to us.

On Japan, what Hopkins seemed to be really interested in was the position we should take with regard to the emperor. I remarked that the emperor might again be made a tool of fanatics. Roosevelt appeared to concur and then told us about one of his ancestors who had passed through Japan when the Mikado was without power. It had taken only some seventy years to build up the emperor, he remarked. Then the president regaled us with anecdotes about his ancestors in the old China trade. This lore of Cathay appeared to be the most vivid part of his knowledge of China.

Roosevelt next meandered into stories about loan negotiations with Dr. Kung, Chiang's finance minister and brother-in-law. Inexplicably, from that he moved to an exposition on postwar aviation between Britain and Australia via the United States. Hopkins asked scattered economic questions about China. At no point did either give the general a coherent statement of what they wanted him to do, particularly in light of the cancellation of the Andaman operation.

Hopkins asked me if I knew the Chinese language. I said that I did. Near the end of the conversation he told Roosevelt that they needed a small, closely-knit group that would not talk and would do what needed to be done. On our departure, I was startled to hear the president say, "Remember, you're both ambassadors, both ambassadors."

As we rode back to our quarters, Stilwell held his head in his hands.

CHAPTER *26*

Postwar Plans, ICHIGO, and GALAHAD

FORTY-SIX YEARS after the Battle of Manila Bay, the second American conquest of the Philippines began. The second Roosevelt, unlike his cousin, was not inspired by callow imperialism. It was in his larger policy to take the Philippines in order to give them back to the Filipinos. In so doing, he hoped to set an inspiring example: how an imperial power should conclude its stewardship over dependent peoples.

This posture was not unpopular with the American citizenry. Americans had long since found that the rewards of empire were not as satisfying as had been represented at the turn of the century. The Philippines had not yielded great riches to the United States. For some American farmers, at least, Filipino agricultural products were resented competition. By 1934 the United States had been sufficiently disillusioned with the colony to promise independence in 1946.

Having made a virtue out of a disembarrassment, there remained an older American vestige of the white man's privilege in the Far East. That was extraterritorial rights in China, the rights of Americans in China to be tried by an American and not a Chinese court. The United States relinquished these rights in January 1943.

Thus the American government cleansed itself of colonial ambitions in the Philippines and semicolonial privileges in China. It had moved a long way from the policies of Tyler, Cushing, Theodore Roosevelt, Lodge, and Taft. It no longer imagined China to be a fabulous market, nor demanded "unequal treaties" to protect American traders and proselytizers. Gunboat and dollar diplomacy were unmentionable, unworthy of the new plane of trust and collaboration to which American-Chinese relations were to be elevated. The Open Door policy would be honored as a matter of course, for China would be one of the four great powers, dealing with an even hand among all seeking commerce with her.

The four great-power concept, begot by Roosevelt, embraced by Chiang, endured by Churchill, and tolerated by Stalin, took form in a manner traditionally favored and trusted by American statesmen—a public declaration. This declaration of November 1, 1943 was issued at the conclusion of a meeting at Moscow of the American, British, and Soviet foreign ministers and co-signed by the Chinese ambassador to the Soviet Union. In it the four governments pledged, among other things, "united action" after the war for "the organization and maintenance of peace and security."

The ailing Hull was gladdened by this rhetorical accomplishment. He had prevailed upon Molotov to let the Chinese sign the declaration and so be identified as peers of the mighty. He had told the conference that isolation was suicidal and that they should all prepare for postwar international collaboration and a world power under law. He had assured Molotov that nothing could prevent the United States and the Soviet Union from becoming fast friends, with which the Commissar professed entire agreement. Americans and Russians, the secretary expatiated, shared in large measure the same tastes, the same jokes, and in general were very congenial.

A conversation on October 30, with Stalin performing as the mellow statesman, produced something akin to euphoria in Hull. First, Stalin said that the Soviet Union would join the war against Japan after the defeat of Germany. Then, responding to the secretary's lament that isolation had almost ruined the United States and the Soviet Union, Stalin referred "in the most sympathetic and favorable manner" to the great necessity for American-Soviet collaboration. Hull's memorandum of the conversation continued, "I said that this was wonderful . . . that our two people were very much alike . . . that there need be no serious difficulty at all in promoting close understanding and trust and friendship . . . to all of which he agreed."

Returning to Washington, Hull told a joint meeting of the Senate and House of November 18 that "as the provisions of the four-nation declaration are carried into effect, there will no longer be need for spheres of influence, for alliances, for balance of power. . . ." Spheres of influence and balance of power were regarded as immoral in the Department of State—and the White House. In his memoirs, Hull exclaimed, "I was not, and am not a believer in the idea of balance of power or spheres of influence as a means of keeping the peace. . . . and I was grounded to the taproots in their iniquitous consequences."

Three months after Hull told the Congress that there would be no more need for alliances and balance of power, I wrote a memorandum, dated February 19, 1944, advocating a touch of *realpolitik* in our Asian policy, saying in part: "Nowhere does Clausewitz's dictum that war is only the continuation of politics by other methods apply with more force than in the Asiatic theater. If we are to plan intelligently the conduct of our war against Japan we must clearly define and understand our long-range political objectives in Asia.

"Presumably we seek in Asia (1) the greatest possible stability after the war, and (2) an alignment of power favorable to us when we again become involved in an Asiatic or Pacific war."

Peace and security, both Roosevelt and Hull assumed, could be had only through generous collaboration among the Big Four. Roosevelt personalized this ideal. While Churchill was difficult, with his cynicism about the Chinese and his dedication to recreating Britain's imperial grandeur, he could be counted on to stick with Roosevelt on postwar collaboration. Chiang's dependence on Roosevelt's favor meant that he would go along with Big Four peace keeping. Stalin was the suspicious, uncertain element in the foursome. But Roosevelt thought that Stalin was, as Robert Sherwood quoted the president, "get-atable;" if reasonable Soviet claims such as access to warm water ports were accepted, Stalin could be won over to cooperation in keeping the postwar peace.

What disposition should be made of colonies in Asia? Roosevelt believed that Japan should be stripped of its possessions. Formosa and Manchuria should go to China, to which Chiang readily agreed. So should the Ryukyu Islands, even though Chiang had at Cairo suggested a joint Chinese-American administration under trusteeship.

The Soviet Union should get southern Sakhalin (Karafuto) and the Kurile Islands, as desired by Stalin. Korea, which was not ready for self-government, should be placed under trusteeship administered by China, the Soviet Union, and the United States. The mandated islands would also come under trusteeship, with the United States maintaining military bases where needed. Thus Japan would be stripped back to its original size.

After his return from Tehran and Cairo, Roosevelt said on January 12, 1944 that Stalin, Chiang, and he saw eye to eye on all major problems of the Pacific and that he anticipated no postwar difficulties over control of the Pacific.

Disposition of certain territories belonging to allied nations was a more delicate proposition than parceling out the enemy's possessions. While Chiang was to get Dairen as a part of Manchuria, Stalin also wanted it—plus the nearby Port Arthur naval base and operating control of the South Manchurian and Chinese Eastern railways. He aimed at a restoration of pre–Russo-Japanese War rights. Roosevelt hoped to arrange for a gentlemanly three-way compromise whereby making Dairen a free port would be matched by a similar arrangement for Hong Kong. Outer Mongolia was even more touchy. Chiang wanted it, but Stalin insisted on recognition of the status quo.

At Tehran, Roosevelt confided to Stalin that he thought the best solution of the Indian problem would be reform from the bottom, somewhat along Soviet lines. Stalin observed that reform from the bottom would mean revolution. This exchange suggests that the president had given up his Articles of Confederation formula as the answer to the Indian question.

Roosevelt, Stalin, and Chiang agreed that Indochina should not be returned to the French. But Churchill was determined that the French and Dutch should get back their colonies. The president described the Indochinese to Stalin on February 8, 1945 as like the Javanese and Burmese—of small stature and not warlike. These quaint and placid little people, Roosevelt decided, should be placed under the protection of trusteeship for twenty or thirty years. The details could be worked out after the war.

Meanwhile, in whose theater of war was Indochina to be? Originally, it was regarded as part of the China Theater. Then with the creation of SEAC, Mountbatten wanted it within his scope of operations. The Generalissimo sharply contested this at Cairo, but conceded that, when the time came, SEAC might attack Indochina from the south as the Chinese invaded from the north, with the boundaries between the two theaters to be decided at the time. This was acceptable to Roosevelt, who had on November 9 told the State Department that the matter of Chinese forces entering Indochina "should be left to the discretion of the Joint Chiefs of Staff and the commanding officers in the area. This is essentially a military problem."

It was not. Military dispositions conditioned postwar political events. The assignment of southern Indochina to Mountbatten resulted in occupation of Saigon in September 1945 by the British. They promptly restored French colonial rule and, in collaboration with the defeated Japanese, ousted the indigenous popular front regime established the month before. In northern Indochina, however, Chiang's occupation forces tolerated the Vietnamese regime, headed by Ho Chi Minh, until the French had been established in the south and claimed the rest of their colony. Whereupon the Chinese withdrew, loaded with booty.

The decision on what Roosevelt regarded as "essentially a military problem" led to the Indochina wars. Roosevelt did not live to participate in later decisions which might have deflected the French from their folly and, ultimately, the Americans from their colossal blunders. A neophyte President Truman, attended by a European-oriented assistant secretary of state, James C. Dunn, told Madame Chiang on August 29, 1945—as the British advance elements were moving into Saigon—that no decisions had been made with regard to Indochina. We had started our ride on the Indo-Chinese toboggan.

In the CBI theater units of the Office of Strategic Services (OSS), Office of War Information (OWI), and Board of Economic Warfare (BEW) were being expanded by a stream of newcomers, each eager to make his contribution to the war effort. The embassy at Chungking and the mission at New Delhi supervised OWI propaganda in those two capitals. The embassy assisted BEW in its purchases of strategic materials for the United States, such as wolfram and tin. But BEW collection and analysis of economic intelligence regarding the enemy was primarily on behalf of the American military. As a paramilitary organization, OSS was entirely answerable to Stilwell.

The senior officers of the two CBI headquarters, forward echelon at Chungking and rear echelon at New Delhi, looked askance at their new auxiliaries, particularly OWI propaganda teams in support of combat headquarters in Assam. These army old-timers shared Stilwell's view that the only way to beat the enemy was to kill him and that psychological and economic warriors had to prove their worth in body counts. On this basis, OSS secret operations got a passing grade. OSS secret intelligence, research, and morale operations were indulged, even though secret intelligence and research overlapped with the army's G-2 activities, and morale operations, meant to befuddle and dishearten the enemy, seemed farfetched.

From my contact with the first arrivals of the OWI, BEW, and OSS contingents, I concluded that their activities needed political guidance and a sympathetic channel to Stilwell. Late in the spring of 1943 I suggested to the general that he ask for four more Foreign Service officers so that the five of us, under his command, might supervise political, economic, and psychological intelligence and warfare operations. He gave his assent. While in Washington at the time of the Trident Conference, I discussed the matter at the State Department and on May 29 presented the department a memorandum on the subject.

Of the four Foreign Service officers asked for, three were detailed to Stilwell on the same basis as myself. The fourth was withheld because of poor health. The three who joined me were John K. Emmerson, a Japan specialist, Raymond P. Ludden, and John S. Service, both China specialists. As we were all of approximately the same age and rank, I did not wish to assume authority over them. We therefore functioned ecumenically, although I was regarded as the senior among equals because of my longer association with the military.

My formalistic concept of our role in the theater was not put into effect. By the time Emmerson, Ludden, and Service received their orders in the late summer of 1943, the two headquarters had worked out supervisory arrangements, primarily through G-2, with OWI, OSS, and FEA, the Foreign Economic Administration which replaced BEW. We therefore operated in an informal advisory capacity on political issues to these agencies and the headquarters officers dealing with them.

Emmerson spent some time with an OWI propaganda team in the northern Burma combat zone. He also investigated intelligence collection from and propaganda use of Japanese prisoners of war in Burma, India, and China. Ludden likewise visited the combat area in Burma and later acted as political adviser to the Twentieth Bomber Command at Chengtu, the long-range strike force meant to attack Japan itself. Service began by traveling about the theater, mostly in south China, and then settled in Chungking where he was available to the headquarters and functioned in much the same fashion that I did when I had been in Chungking.

Emmerson I had not known well before this association in CBI. But Service and I had grown up together in Chengtu and Shanghai. And Ludden and I had served together at Mukden. As Service and Ludden had been language students at Peking at the time that Stilwell was military attaché, they already knew him and the China specialists among the army officers in CBI.

With OSS I developed a special relationship. William Phillips, who took the place of the untoward Louis Johnson as the president's personal representative in India, had as military aide a Lieutenant Colonel Richard P. Heppner. A presentable young gentleman, Heppner had been a junior member of William J. Donovan's law firm. It was through Heppner, I think, that I met the exuberant Donovan who, with the rank then of brigadier general, headed OSS. Donovan was in early 1943 attempting to expand his operations into the CBI Theater, was encountering the headquarters indifference which I mentioned, and was puzzled as to whom he could put in charge of OSS activities in CBI. I offered to help where I could and suggested Heppner as his representative in the theater.

Heppner seemed to be a logical choice. He was very much a Donovan man, was liked by Phillips and both the diplomatic and military staff in New Delhi, and was politically informed. Donovan accepted the suggestion and Stilwell gave his assent. Consequently part of my time in Washington during May and June 1943 was spent in being introduced to the OSS apparatus. It was a pungent collection of thugs, postdebutantes, millionaires, professors, corporation lawyers, professional military, and misfits, all operating under high tension and in whispers. I found OSS, then and later, a diverting contrast to Hull's stupefying department, and Donovan's way of doing business—dinners at his house and luncheons at the F Street Club—preferable to negotiations over a desk.

Returning to CBI after the Trident Conference, I traveled with Heppner and Captain Duncan Lee of the OSS Washington headquarters. En route, they introduced me to some of the OSS people in London. I remember the son of J. P. Morgan and the son-in-law of Andrew Mellon, sent by Donovan to cope and connive with the British upper class which thickly populated Britain's secret intelligence and operations. Then I met their men in Algiers and Cairo, where we stopped over in veiled elegance at OSS villas.

Back in CBI, Lee and I, in company with Eric Sevareid, William Stanton (an economic warrior), and a score of GIs, started across the Hump. The aircraft malfunctioned and we were forced to jump. Although a cloak-and-dagger man, Lee was no more of a parachutist than I. But his native resourcefulness was to pay off. As he floated downward, he hung his musette bag on his toes. Just before hitting the ground, he gently shuffled off the bag. Freeing himself from the harness he dashed to the bag to find his ingenuity rewarded. The bottle of gin therein was intact. This OSS operation must be rated in paramilitary annals as uncommonly adroit.

The OSS operatives who appeared on the CBI and SEAC scene were a richly diversified group. One, for example, was a reflective newspaperman, Edmond Taylor, who had written *The Strategy of Terror*. Another was S. Dillon Ripley, a blithely urbane ornithologist, and later the secretary of the Smithsonian Institution. Then there was Tolstoy's grandnephew, Ilya, who tried but failed to establish a pack animal supply-lift to China through Tibet. Julia Child, yet another, was engaged in dark activities in Kunming and was to become years later the French Chef on American television. These were among the more civilized elements of OSS. There were others not so nice.

Competitive with OSS in China was Navy Group, China, headed by Captain Milton E. Miles. Navy Group weather- and ship-watched. It also combined with elements of the Generalissimo's secret police to form an organization named SACO, Sino-American Special Technical Cooperation Organization, and pronounced socko.

Miles was a strange personality who flaunted a pennant designed by himself, displaying three question marks, three exclamation marks, and three asterisks in line. He also revelled in barking out "SACO" and claimed lurid successes for SACO's guerrilla and sabotage activities. Miles boasted to me in 1942, I believe it was, how his agents had poisoned several Japanese naval officers in

Hankow—sing-song girls who dosed the victims with aspirin, he said. He asked Stilwell for ten thousand daggers with which to arm SACO agents assigned to stab Japanese in Indochina.

Miles had placed himself in the hands of Tai Li, the unsavory head of Chiang's secret police, whose main function was to hunt down individuals suspected of being anti-Chiang. Tai's organization reached into Japanese-occupied China, particularly the big cities where its principal enemy was the Communist underground.

For Tai, Miles was a willing source of the most advanced small arms and communications equipment. In return for this bonanza, Tai was pleased to furnish the captain with reports of exploits against the Japanese. Listening to Miles, I was always reminded of a self-proclaimed Chinese intelligence agent who regularly visited me in Hankow with cheering and unbelievably precise reports of Chinese accomplishments against the Japanese, which tidings I was in no position to verify. But all that spy ever got was a cigarette, a cup of tea (free of aspirin), and a thank you.

Miles, who was fundamentally ignorant about China, refused to have on his American staff anyone who spoke Chinese or had experience in China. Thus Tai —and the Generalissimo—enjoyed in the entire U.S. Navy Group what Chiang had, through Soong to McCloy in January 1942, asked for in the position to which Stilwell was finally appointed—someone unencumbered by an understanding of China. Furthermore, Miles resisted authority by the theater commander over his activities. He was able to do so because his operation was under the patronage of Admiral King, chief of naval operations, and his backup man in Washington, Captain J. C. Metzel, another hush-hush personality, dealt directly with King.

After I had become acquainted with Miles, Stilwell asked me to try to bring the captain under supervision of the CBI command. Miles would have none of it. Donovan, who had snarled ties with Miles, attempted to incorporate SACO within OSS, and was rebuffed.

Ambassador Gauss suffered many indignities in the new diplomacy. He had put up with Washington's placing under his supervision an animal husbandman sent to provide American know-how on artificial insemination of Chinese camels. But SACO was too much. Miles had been "accredited as attached to this embassy," Gauss reiterated on February 9, 1944 in one of several complaints to the Department of State, but "he makes no reports to the ambassador and information regarding the activities of his office is limited to rumor and report from other sources." Nor did Gauss like the embassy's being implicated through Miles with Tai Li's "dreaded secret police . . . and general 'Gestapo' agency." He recommended that Miles be detached from the embassy, which was eventually done.

Miles outlasted both Stilwell and Gauss in China. He continued to be a source of no joy to the senior American officials. Stilwell's successor, Lieutenant General Albert W. Wedemeyer, wrote to the War Department on July 5, 1945

"If the American public ever learned that we poured supplies into a questionable organization such as Tai Li operates, without any accounting, it would be most unfortunate indeed. . . . Miles has been Santa Claus out here for a long time."

The fighting phases of the war in China and Burma sputtered on. Eager to prove his boasts to Willkie, Hopkins, and Roosevelt, Chennault hurled the Fourteenth Air Force at the Japanese air arm in Central China in July 1943 before he had built up adequate supplies and reserves. He did not knock the enemy out of the skies. To the contrary, the Japanese gave him a bad time and in about three weeks he had to break off the offensive. In the exchange, however, the Fourteenth took a respectable toll of Japanese aircraft and shipping, although only a fraction of the exaggerated claims made by its pilots.

After regaining its strength, the Fourteenth resumed the attack and in November even raided Formosa. Chennault was stinging the enemy. But in planning for his 1944 operations he again derided the contention that the Japanese, in reaction, would knock out his forward bases by a ground offensive. Imperial General Headquarters in Tokyo reckoned differently. In January 1944 it decided to go after the bases and those segments of the railways from Peking to Canton which had been left to the Chinese. The operation, called ICHIGO, began in mid-April and during its nine months' course employed in all fifteen divisions and five independent brigades.

Chennault had also asserted that the Japanese could not mount a ground offensive without drawing reinforcements from their armies fighting the Americans in the Pacific. To the contrary, the flow of reinforcements was in the opposite direction and the compensating strength needed to back up ICHIGO came from temporary transfers out of Manchuria and recruits from Japan. When Chennault became aware of the enemy deployment for ICHIGO, he was smitten with gloom. This, he exclaimed, was the most threatening enemy buildup since Pearl Harbor; the Chinese armies were weak and he doubted that he could deal with the air assault and also provide adequate air support to the Chinese ground forces.

The first phase of ICHIGO, north of the Yangtze, was an easy Japanese success over superior numbers of Chinese troops with no stomach for a fight. South of the Yangtze at Hengyang, during July, Chinese resistance stiffened. General Hsueh Yueh, the Chinese area commander, had some forty divisions available against eight Japanese divisions driving down the Hankow-Canton Railway. Contrary to Chennault's predictions, Japanese air action was weak and so the Fourteenth was able to concentrate on support of the Chinese ground forces. This it did with conspicuous success. Nevertheless, on August 8 the enemy captured Hengyang.

Halfway through the siege, the unit of the Fourteenth assigned to support the Chinese was hampered by a shortage of fuel and supplies, even though Stilwell had early in June reallocated Hump tonnage to give Chennault the ten thousand tons per month that he and the Generalissimo had asked for. Hsueh Yueh, too, complained of insufficient weapons and ammunition. But Hsueh, whose name had been linked with T. V. Soong in 1943 in a plot against the Generalissimo, was in Chiang's bad books. Hsueh was also suspected of conspiring with other disaffected generals in southeastern China against the Generalissimo. Therefore Chiang opposed the dispatch of supplies to Hsueh, even when his favorite, Chennault, pled on behalf of the area commander. Stilwell, and later Wedemeyer, abided by the Generalissimo's preference to lose territory to the Japanese rather than supply one of his own generals whom he mistrusted.

After Hengyang, the Japanese continued to disprove Chennault's and Chiang's various assurances to Roosevelt. Notwithstanding command of the air, which Chennault had in the latter half of 1944, and Chinese superior numbers on the ground, the enemy swept up the bases at Kweilin and Liuchow, ventured westward into Kweichow Province (to Chiang's alarm), joined up with the Japanese forces in Indochina, took over the railways in southeastern China and occupied all but one of Chennault's advanced bases. For an army that was on its last legs and only six months from unconditional surrender, it was quite an achievement.

To say that ICHIGO was a clear-cut success is not to belittle the accomplishments of the touchy Chennault. While he had grossly overstated what he could do, his Fourteenth Air Force had, indeed, been a major factor in the China war. Although it did not halt, it tactically crippled the movement of the Japanese armies in Central and South China. What was of more far-reaching significance —though not recognized by either Chennault or Washington at the time—the Fourteenth strategically hurt Japan without dropping a bomb on it. In its work-a-day raids on Yangtze shipping, it sank enough ore carriers from mid-1943 to mid-1944 to cut Japan's iron ore imports in half.

Roosevelt's enthusiasm for Chennault waned as it became apparent that the Fourteenth Air Force would not provide a shortcut to victory. By 1944 his fancy had been captured by a project for using B-29 long-range bombers taking off from West China, to attack the Japanese home islands. It was a cumbersome enterprise. The big bombers were based in India for security. For their raids on Japan they were serviced at four airfields near Chengtu, hand-built by some three hundred thousand peasants. The first assault was on June 15, 1944 against steel works on Kyushu. The Air Corps had looked to cutting Japanese steel production in half by such attacks. The postwar assessment was that, operating from China, the B-29s of the Twentieth Bomber Command had reduced Japanese steel supply by less than two percent.

So it might be said that the Fourteenth Air Force did more strategic damage to Japan than did the strategic bombers, solemnly commanded from Washington by the Joint Chiefs of Staff as a superforce, which the War Department likened to the Pacific Fleet. It was not until the B-29s began operating in November from the Marianas that they demonstrated their awesome destructive power.

Fighting on the ground in CBI was coalition warfare at its worst—contradictory, tangled, and strategically insignificant. American-Chinese-British plans and operations inordinately occupied Roosevelt, Churchill, and their military staffs. And if the president was disappointed in Chennault, he became irritated with the Generalissimo.

Churchill had been disturbed in 1942 that Roosevelt considered the Chinese Army as comparable to the Soviet Army. By 1944 the president had been disabused of this figment. But he and his military and diplomatic advisers continued to worry about "keeping China in the war." The Chiang-Soong threats to quit the war were meant to play on American anxiety and did elicit American supplies. The Chinese, having been already well bought by Roosevelt's promises of Manchuria and Formosa and his intention to make China a great power, had nothing to gain by getting out of the war and certainly had no intention of doing so.

At the same time, Chiang had even less desire in 1944 than in 1941 to fight the Japanese. The defeat of Japan by the Americans was in sight as was, consequently, his showdown with the Communists. So he was in early 1944 holding back on commitment of his forces in Yunnan to a Burma campaign. He had, however, given Stilwell command of the Ramgarh-trained Chinese Army in India.

This was enough for Stilwell to start driving across northern Burma. Returning from the Cairo conference, he found the CAI stalled, just over the Indian border, in Burma. It had been clearing the enemy from in front of the road that American engineers were building from Ledo in India toward the northern Burmese town of Myitkyina and eventually China. The route of the prospective road was some three hundred miles from Ledo to Myitkyina, over mountains and through jungles. A veteran Japanese division, the Eighteenth, which dominated the capture of Singapore, opposed the untested Ramgarh graduates. In these circumstances no one expected Stilwell to get very far.

By prodding, inspiring, and shaming them, Stilwell moved the CAI to the offensive. They were small-scale actions, battalion and company-size engagements at first. On several occasions Stilwell went up to battle areas, to the horror of the Chinese officers. He persuaded his charges to maneuver in enveloping tactics. When they discovered that they could surprise and outfight the Japanese, they overcame their diffidence and became aggressive. But the two division commanders periodically received messages from the Generalissimo, as had been the case in the first Burma campaign, and were fitfully palsied thereby.

In this second Burma campaign Stilwell had the tremendous advantage of command of the air. The Tenth Air Force ruled the skies over northern Burma. This made possible close-in air support of ground forces and a then novel technique in jungle warfare, air supply of mobile columns and air evacuation of wounded.

A second factor of assistance to Stilwell in his 1944 offensive was effective British support. It was in two forms. Involuntarily, the main British force on the India-Burma border south of Stilwell contained and exhausted a major Japanese assault by four divisions. This so occupied and then weakened the enemy that he could not reinforce the Eighteenth Division. Voluntarily, British long range penetration groups—the dashing Major General Orde Wingate's Chindits—and other irregular units operated behind the Japanese lines to the distraction of the enemy. These British exploits in 1944, and the final British triumph in Burma, are a story beyond the scope of this account, but are here acknowledged as having been essential ingredients in Stilwell's North Burma accomplishments.

Stilwell had yet another advantage. This was about three thousand American combat soldiers, officially designated as the 5307th Composite Unit (Provisional), assigned the resplendent code name of GALAHAD and, because Frank Merrill was the commander, given by the press the inevitable comic strip title of Merrill's Marauders. The élite outfit was made up of volunteers from jungle-experienced forces in the Caribbean area and the South and Southwest Pacific and had received the benefit of some two months' training under Wingate. In size, the unit was a good deal short of the three American divisions that Stilwell had so longed for. Nevertheless, as a mobile strike force operating against the enemy's flanks and rear, it was expected to be an exemplar and spur to the CAI. In February, Merrill began his wide-ranging operations through the jungle.

During April and the first half of May the main Chinese forces poked reluctantly forward against stubborn Japanese opposition. Again the Generalissimo was warning his division commanders, behind Stilwell's back, to take no chances. In these galling circumstances the impatient Stilwell decided to hazard a surprise attack on Myitkyina by Merrill's unit. This involved crossing a high, choppy mountain range and pouncing on Myitkyina from the north while the CAI strove to push the enemy's main force from the route of the road, down the Mogaung Valley, well to the west of the strategically important town.

But the American outfit was near exhaustion. In two months of operations it had trudged and fought five hundred miles, had lost half of its men, and Merrill had suffered a heart attack. The unit was brought back to strength by addition of two Chinese regiments drawn from divisions sent from China to reinforce the CAI and three hundred Kachin tribesmen, trained by OSS and at home in the Burmese mountains. Merrill, whose will was stronger than his heart, resumed command.

Starting out in three columns in the last days of April, the mixed task force struggled up through the high jungle and down again, destroying several Japanese outposts. Guided by a Kachin scout, one column advanced close to Myitkyina without being detected. The enemy was caught off guard, the airfield was taken, and the operation was, thus far, a brilliant success. The cost had been high. Most of the Americans were sick—ulcerous jungle sores, dysentery, malaria, and deadly scrub typhus. They were in poor condition to fight. Then Merrill was stricken by another heart attack two days after the initial victory and had to be evacuated.

The follow-up of success at the airfield failed. Fresh reinforcements and supplies were scheduled and urgently needed to rush the Japanese garrison in the town before it got organized and also received reinforcements. Instead, the first arrivals by air on May 17th were a company of aviation engineers and its equipment and an antiaircraft battery, neither of which was needed. Only then was a battalion of Chinese infantry flown in. The next morning, the American air commander, Major General George E. Stratemeyer, further bungled the flow of reinforcements by gratuitously sending in two British antiaircraft detachments.

And so it went as the advantage of surprise was dissipated and the tough, canny Japanese dug in deep to hold the town. There were probably less than a thousand of them on the 17th. A fortnight later reinforcements had raised the enemy garrison to about twenty-five hundred and later to as high as perhaps thirty-five hundred. American intelligence consistently underestimated the opposing force as being approximately five hundred men.

As soon as the airfield was secured on the afternoon of the 17th, and before his second heart attack, Merrill tried to press home his advantage by an assault on the town, drawing on the only troops then at hand—his bedraggled task force, some of whom had not eaten for several days. The Chinese battalions advanced on the town, became lost, were confused by Japanese fire, and ended up fighting one another. The next day the whole regiment from which these two battalions had been selected attacked Myitkyina and did the same thing, only on a bigger scale.

These two affrays set the scene for the siege of Myitkyina, which lasted two and half months. Underestimating Japanese strength, the Americans kept expecting the enemy to collapse. So they and the Chinese made repeated attacks on the strongly entrenched Japanese, only to be thrown back. The task force did not have sufficient heavy artillery for effective massed fire. As the only means of supply was by two-engine air transports, no tanks were available to harden the infantry assaults. Tenth Air Force fighter-bombers worked over the Japanese position to little avail.

Consequently it was up to the foot soldiers. The original two Chinese regiments were reinforced by five more. They were indifferent quality, as the best troops were pushing down the Mogaung Valley against the Japanese main force. Because the 5307th Composite Unit was the only American combat outfit in CBI, no qualified American reinforcements were at hand. Late in May Stilwell desperately sent in two makeshift battalions of engineering troops pulled off their road building jobs and a weak battalion drawn from twenty-six hundred newly arrived GALAHAD replacements from the United States.

These green soldiers were flown into Myitkyina during the monsoon rains and stepped off the transports into a nightmare. They entered a battlefield of mud from which the veterans of the airfield victory were being flown out by the scores, wounded and diseased. For an American to qualify for evacuation on account of sickness, he had to maintain a temperature of 102 degrees for three consecutive days. So desperate was the need for anyone who could pull a trigger. GALAHAD survivors were vomiting most of their K rations and some fell asleep during battle.

The sight and stories of the Americans they had come to sustain disheartened the newcomers who, even had they been in high spirits, were unconditioned for the grinding fight that lay in wait for them. In several of their early encounters with the enemy they broke and fled. In short order some fifty replacements cracked up psychopathically. The rest settled down and acquitted themselves well. But losses were heavy. One of the engineer battalions suffered 41 percent casualties.

In the two and a half months of the siege, Stilwell made three changes of command. Merrill's successor, Colonel John E. McCammon, was relieved after he came down with pleurisy. Haydon Boatner, who was in command of the American-Chinese sector of northern Burma, was also given command at Myitkyina, but he was laid low by malaria. Boatner was replaced by Brigadier General Theodore F. Wessels, who had the good fortune to take over just as the CAI drove the main body of the Japanese out of the Mogaung Valley and thus emerged in a position where it could readily send support to Myitkyina and, by the same token, block enemy supplies and reinforcements to the beleaguered Japanese garrison. Slowly that garrison was ground down until its commander, with never a thought of surrender, ceremoniously committed suicide on August 1. Two days later the Chinese and Americans overcame the last spasms of resistance, taking 187 prisoners, most of whom were incapacitated by wounds or disease.

After the capture of Myitkyina, the 5307th Composite Unit (Provisional) was disbanded. It had been expended. Only two hundred or so of the original unit, under its first commander, the doughty Colonel Charles N. Hunter, lasted out the siege. The other survivors had been hospitalized in rear areas and, when convalescent, were defiant of discipline. They had believed unauthorized assurances that after arriving at Myitkyina they would be relieved. When that did not happen they became recalcitrant.

The siege had been an inglorious climax for GALAHAD. These troops were neither equipped nor trained for the siege. And they were physically spent, and then decimated by disease. GALAHAD was, after May 17, a victim of the devouring exigencies of war—in this case caused by erroneous intelligence and, derivatively, faulty generalship. But in the three months that the unit performed in the role for which it was designed, it operated with distinction and rightly earned the Distinguished Unit Citation which it was awarded.

GALAHAD the exemplar—that was another matter. The Chinese were not greatly impressed. The Americans were more skilled, but they were no more brave. And they were less durable. The statistics on evacuation for sickness during the siege showed 980 Americans (of which 570 were GALAHAD) and 188 Chinese. Remembering the stringent interpretation of illness imposed on the Americans—in reality, virtually all of GALAHAD needed hospitalization—and the far larger number of Chinese troops engaged, the actual ratio between the two was much more to the disadvantage of the Americans than the statistics suggest.

Only once before the GALAHAD episode had American combat troops engaged in a campaign on the Asian land mass. That was the expedition in 1900 that fought its way to Peking to rescue Americans during the Boxer Rebellion. The American military intervention in Siberia during the Russian Civil War was not comparable, as General Graves was ordered to avoid involvement in the conflict and did so. The Korean War was the third occasion in which American ground forces campaigned in Asia. And the fourth was the Indochina War. In only one of these were Americans and Chinese allies, and that was during the brief GALAHAD campaign.

CHAPTER 27

Salween Campaign and My Third Trip to Washington

MERRILL'S CAPTURE of the Myitkyina airfield was the first spectacular allied success in CBI. It was the more satisfying because it was a surprise. Together with the slow, solid advance of the CAI into Burma, it showed that the American-Chinese combination could outmaneuver and outfight first class Japanese troops.

With the Myitkyina airfield denied to the enemy, the airlift to China could take a lower passage over the Hump and carry more tonnage. Now there could be little doubt that northern Burma could be cleared of the enemy and a road and pipeline built to China without waiting for the expulsion of the Japanese from southern Burma. How quickly this could be done depended on the Generalissimo.

But Chiang balked at moving the twelve divisions of his Yunnan expeditionary force against one understrength Japanese division strung out across his path into Burma. Instead, he had since Cairo been nagging at Roosevelt for the billion dollar loan and for more aircraft and more Hump tonnage. The president's messages to the Generalissimo began to be a little tart, even to verge on what he had so condemned in Stilwell—stern bargaining with Chiang. "If the Yunnan forces cannot be employed," he radioed the Generalissimo on January 14, 1944, "it would appear that we should avoid for the present the movement of critical materials to them . . . and curtail the continuing buildup of stockpiles in India."

The next day, before receiving Roosevelt's terms, Chiang called in Gauss and presented the ambassador with a message to the president which outdid Roosevelt's attempt at stern bargaining. He gave the president a choice of coming across with the billion dollar loan, or paying all expenses incurred by the American Army in China (which included airfield and other construction) at the official exchange rate of Yuan 20 to $1.00. The open market rate was then fluctuating around Y200 to $1.00 and rising. If neither of his alternatives were accepted, Chiang continued, reciprocal aid to the American Army in China would be terminated and the Americans would have to shift for themselves.

In leading up to his final threat, the Generalissimo called the attention of the president to the semifact that, after Cairo, "I have even gone to the length of delaying reopening the Burma route so that essential amphibious equipment should be diverted to European theater of war, thereby disappointing all sections of my fellow countrymen who still bear in memory the scar of the fiasco of the last Burma campaign thru which China lost great quantities of equipment and men thru no fault of her own."

After handing the ambassador the message to Roosevelt, Chiang said that the cutoff date, if his conditions were not met, would be March 1. Thereafter China would carry on as best it could until its inevitable economic and military collapse. Gauss was not a man to be stampeded. His concluding comment to Hull on the message to Roosevelt and Chiang's oral statements was that "we should maintain a firm position, declining to be coerced by threats and petulant gestures."

Chiang's ultimatum riled the War Department to the point that it was willing to have a showdown with the Chinese, and, if necessary, pull out of China. Both Major General Lucius Clay, Somervell's Director of Materiel, and the Treasury Department thought that the Generalissimo was bluffing. Those who spoke for the Department of State thought not and advocated conciliating Chiang. Hornbeck emphasized the importance of preserving Big Four solidarity.

In Chungking the issues raised by the Generalissimo's ultimatum were negotiated principally by Gauss and H. H. Kung, the Finance Minister. Kung, who had in all respects waxed fat in office, was a lineal descendant of Confucius of the seventy-fifth generation, a graduate of Oberlin College, married to Madame Chiang's and T. V. Soong's oldest sister and, at least in his own estimation, adept at dealing with Americans. On February 3 it was his turn to make the American flesh creep. This was not an easy assignment, with the ambassador's gimlet eyes drilling into him. So almost in a tone of banter he raised the possibility of China's economic collapse and the old specter of a separate peace with Japan, adding lamely that the Japanese had been making "some very good offers." Gauss reported without comment what Kung said.

Roosevelt wisely remained aloof from the haggling over the Generalissimo's ultimatum. By deflecting the negotiations in Washington to the strangling lower levels of government, he quietly called Chiang's bluff. But he had not given up on getting the Yunnan force into the battle for northern Burma. Stilwell, whose offensive the president was following with new respect, and Mountbatten, whose four divisions in the sector southwest of Stilwell were reeling under the attack of three powerful Japanese divisions, joined in asking Roosevelt and Churchill to press Chiang for an offensive out of Yunnan. Roosevelt responded with an eloquent message on March 17 to the Generalissimo, urging him to seize the opportunity to go after the lone division on the Yunnan front.

But Chiang's thoughts were far away. He had on March 17 communicated to Roosevelt his manifold anxieties arising out of an alleged attack by aircraft bearing Soviet insignia on Sinkiang provincial troops near the border of Outer Mongolia. "This cannot be construed as a local incident," he warned, "but is a very significant indication of the Soviet Far Eastern policy both now and in the future." Furthermore, the Chinese Communists were "evidently preparing" to revolt and take Sian. They would not dare to do so, he went on, "without some understanding having been reached between the Soviet and the Japanese." Lastly, the Japanese were preparing for an offensive on the Peking-Hankow Railway—as indeed they were, with the initial deployment of ICHIGO.

Roosevelt's message brought Chiang's attention back to the uncongenial business of taking the offensive. But the Generalissimo would have none of that. Again he radioed the president his qualms over Sinkiang, the Russians, the Outer Mongols, the Communists' intent on bolshevizing China, and the Japanese ready to take over Szechuan and Yunnan if he did something beyond his power to do. No, China must, among other things "prepare herself for the day—may it not be distant—when Allied land and naval forces can be dispatched to the China coast." For these reasons, and "bearing in mind our obligations to the Allies and our duty to ourselves," Chiang concluded in some confusion, "it is impossible for our main forces to undertake an offensive from Yunnan." He would, however, send reinforcements to India for Stilwell's drive into Burma.

Reacting to this March 27 message from Chiang, the president radioed on April 3, "It is inconceivable to me that your YOKE [Yunnan] Forces, with their American equipment, would be unable to advance against the Japanese Fifty-sixth division in its present depleted strength." If these forces were not used in the common cause, Roosevelt went on, "our most strenuous and extensive efforts to fly in equipment and to furnish instructual [sic] personnel have not been justified."

In Stilwell's absence at the Burma front, his chief of staff, Major General Thomas G. Hearn, delivered the president's communication to Madame Chiang for presentation to her husband. Several days later, at a reception, she told Hearn that she was afraid that the president's message might diminish the likelihood of YOKE's being ordered into action. Assuming, probably rightly, that she may have withheld Roosevelt's radio message from the Generalissimo, Hearn so informed Marshall on April 10. When the chief of staff passed this on to the president, Roosevelt demanded that from then on his communications to Chiang be presented by the ranking American army officer in Chungking directly to the Generalissimo. He never did receive a reply from Chiang to his April 3 message.

Even before hearing from Hearn, Marshall had on April 7 advised Stilwell that if YOKE did not act, its lend-lease supplies should be cut off. This was repeated to Hearn and indirectly made known to the Chinese high command, which apparently had no inkling of Roosevelt's lecture to Chiang. Pinky Dorn, now a brigadier general and in command of the Americans advising and assisting the twelve YOKE divisions, was in Chungking at that time conferring with the top Chinese staff officers. He invited them to be his guests on the evening of April

12 and at the conclusion of the conviviality—for among his many accomplishments Dorn was a connoisseur of Chinese food and wine—Ho Ying-ch'in, chief of staff and minister of war, indicated that he was disposed to put the matter of an offensive to the Generalissimo. Two days later Ho officially authorized the Chinese Expeditionary Force to move against the enemy.

It should not be thought that Dorn's bestowal of libations was more persuasive than Marshall's withholding of hardware. But Pinky's merrymaking with the high command did facilitate face-saving in an awkward situation. As Ho insisted to Marshall on April 14, "Decision to move part of YOKE Force across the Salween was made on initiative of Chinese without influence of outside pressure." The supply of lend-lease equipment was quietly resumed.

A month later the Chinese Expeditionary Force, along a hundred mile front, went down into the gorge of the Salween and crossed uncontested the deep swirling river. Not until they had climbed the western slopes of the gorge did the Chinese encounter Japanese resistance. Then for a month they disregarded the tactical advice of Dorn and his advisers to take advantage of their greatly superior numbers and air-supplied mobility, to bypass the widely separated enemy strong points, and to send columns forward to meet the [CAI] driving toward them. Instead they sought out and frontally assaulted Japanese positions. In mid-June they were stalled along a front a scant twenty miles west of the Salween. The Japanese, as usual, fought with skill and incredible fortitude.

The twelve Chinese divisions were part of the first thirty that, for nearly two years, Stilwell had been pleading with Chiang to reorganize so that they could be properly trained and armed by the Americans. They were not reorganized. Nor did the Americans in Yunnan have adequate control over training or sufficient equipment. So the Expeditionary Force was inferior to the CAI. Generalship was atrocious, manpower was squandered, ammunition wasted, and weapons misused and neglected.

Impressed by what the president had said to Stilwell and me—that should the Chiang regime disintegrate we should support its most likely successor—I examined in a memorandum dated December 31, 1943 our relations with that regime. I began by saying, "The Generalissimo is probably the only Chinese who shares the popular American misconception that Chiang Kai-shek is China." After analyzing the unsoundness of his position, I concluded that, "in this uncertain situation we should avoid committing ourselves unalterably to Chiang. We should be ready during or after the war to adjust ourselves to possible realignments in China."

I acted on Hopkins's request to be kept informed by sending him a copy of the memorandum. In a letter to Currie on January 2, 1944, enclosing another copy, I wrote that "politically and militarily we are nowhere in so false and vicious a position as in China and India. I think our involvement in South East Asia is far more inexcusable and likely to be repudiated by the American people than the Graves adventure in Siberia ever was."

Several days later, in New Delhi, I dined with Major General Albert C.

Wedemeyer, then Mountbatten's deputy chief of staff, and the senior American officer on SACSEA's staff. Prior to this appointment, he had been a senior planner in the War Department. He delivered his opinions with flat self-assurance. After the conversation I noted: "Al stated that he thought the British and we should permit the Germans and the Russians to beat each other into pulp. He expressed briefly Mr. Churchill's feeling that Britain and the United States were the guardians and legatees of the only civilization worth preserving."

I asked whether we should refrain from crushing Japan "so that in the post-war world we could use Japan as a counter to the Soviet Union. He said definitely yes."

As for the current phase of the war in CBI and SEAC, Wedemeyer maintained that we should be unable to join up with MacArthur's and King's drives on Japan if we became tangled in a Burma jungle campaign, and that the only way in which we could hope to synchronize ourselves with MacArthur and King would be to go around through Singapore.

My greatest concern remained with what I believed was the oncoming civil war in China, Soviet exploitation of it, and our lack of firsthand information regarding and contact with the Chinese Communists. Following up on my recommendations of the previous June, I again laid out on January 15 the reasons for sending American observers to the Communist areas and attached a suggested message from the president to the Generalissimo asking permission to do so. I sent copies to Hopkins and Currie. Whether I discussed this memorandum with Stilwell when I saw him several days later, I do not recall. If so, it was perfunctorily, for he had approved of such a mission in earlier conversations and was now absorbed in the beginnings of his drive across northern Burma.

In company with the CBI deputy chief of staff, Brigadier General Benjamin G. Ferris, I flew on January 19 to Combat Headquarters in Burma to receive orders from Stilwell for a trip to Washington as part of a small group headed by Ferris. Naturally, Stilwell was not at headquarters, but somewhere down in the bush. "The Old Man came in the next day by liaison plane, wearing a Chinese army cap, a lumpy field jacket, dirty khaki pants, leggings, and boots. He looked gray and tired but bounced about with all the symptoms of vitality."

The group being sent to Washington was to solicit continuing support for Stilwell's current offensive and to ask for pressure on the Generalissimo and the British to attack in force from Yunnan and India. It was being sent in advance of and in competition with a SEAC mission, headed by Wedemeyer, to London and Washington. The SEAC mission was to argue for essentially the strategy that Wedemeyer summarized to me.

I had misgivings about the composition of our group and privately told Stilwell that I thought it needed Haydon Boatner, "who knew from firsthand the history of the Ramgarh experiment, had been through two monsoons on the Assam-Burma border, had directed the operation in the Hukawng valley, and had the dramatic qualities that would appeal to the president if he had the opportunity to see him." Stilwell agreed. "As he left the basha [jungle house of boughs] he told Benny [Ferris] that he had definitely decided to send Haydon. He hopped into the command car and whizzed off to the landing strip to catch the liaison plane for the front." Again he had said nothing to me about what I should do.

Back in New Delhi and two days before my departure for Washington, I was awakened in the middle of the night by the servants announcing that my wife had arrived. She had been some three months on the way and for the last several weeks I had lost track of her. Because she was traveling on her own, her route had been opportunistic and roundabout: Panama, Peru, Argentina, Brazil, across the South Atlantic by a tiny Swedish freighter, and then up the length of Africa from Capetown to Khartoum, next Aden, Karachi, and so to New Delhi. I barely had time to introduce her to my most hospitable host, George Merrell, who turned over my quarters to her, before I flew off to where she had been.

Again in Washington, I functioned on a variety of fronts. Foremost was presentation of Stilwell's plea for a concerted offensive across northern Burma. On February 7, Haydon and I went in to see Frank Roberts, now chief of Army planners, sitting in a big room behind a glossy desk, with a battery of phones and buzzers, two flags, a big globe, thick carpets, indirect lighting, and a low-voiced secretary. Haydon stated our case. Frank agreed with it. To me he said that we could not, of course, expect American troops beyond GALAHAD.

Having received confirmation that our point of view was not out of line, I pulled Boatner out of the Pentagon, where he was "roaring around being scornful of all of the plush," and began introducing him to newsmen and legislators at small informal luncheons and over drinks. "Haydon is refreshing and crunchy like a good tart pickle," I had written my wife, "or celery with lemon." Although not as outspoken as Stilwell, he was a convincing witness.

Ferris took me on February 17 to present our case to the secretary of war, whom I had admired, from the time that he was secretary of state, as an American patrician. "As we entered the room, Mr. Stimson tottered in our direction, vaguely shook hands with us and asked us to be seated. He wanted to know what Benny had to say. What followed was a confused conversation, Benny talking about our problems of getting the British to act, and Mr. Stimson apparently lagging behind. The secretary did recognize, however, that there had always been a reluctance on the part of the British to initiate Allied action against Burma. After much talking around the subject and after we had made two trips across the room to look at wall maps, it developed that Mr. Stimson had not been informed of South East Asia Command's latest proposal. . . . I must confess to having been taken aback by this. The secretary appeared to be a little embarrassed when he realized that he had been left in the dark on this score. I left the meeting feeling that it had been altogether inconclusive and marvelling that the president should wish to retain a fumbling, tired old man in the position of secretary of war."

I did not fully appreciate at the time that Stimson also had his hours of intellectual vigor. In any event, he had not been chosen to administer the War Department—the superb Marshall and assistant secretaries did that. Stimson, a

Republican, was secretary of war as a venerable symbol of national unity, a model of personal integrity, and much of the time a source of sage counsel. Still, it was remarkable that both the secretary of state and the secretary of war should be of failing faculties and the president's most influential confidant, Hopkins, an invalid.

On February 18, Boatner saw the president. "Haydon was very pleased with the results," I wrote my wife. "Apparently he grabbed the ball and ran with it."

Boatner and I were received by the under secretary of state. Stettinius, with all of his engaging qualities, was a let-down from Summer Welles, his predecessor. In the presence of Welles one felt that here was a brilliant, incisive, disciplined, and objective mind. In fifteen minutes he covered more ground than the ordinary interviewer would in an hour, simply because he knew which questions to ask, in what order to ask them, and kept the conversation to a central theme.

After listening to us with slight comprehension but much show of dynamic concern, Stettinius sent us the next day to see Joseph C. Grew, former ambassador to Japan and then special assistant to Hull. Grew was very much interested in what we had to say and appeared to be anxious to go to bat on the question. Stettinius had asked him to prepare a memorandum which would be taken over to the White House. I spent most of the day drafting a memorandum for Grew stressing the necessity of turning the heat on both the prime minister and Chiang in order to bring about the activation of the Imphal and YOKE forces. What finally happened to my draft I do not know.

Partly as a result of my public relations activities on Stilwell's behalf, the press carried several stories critical of British inaction on the Burma front. I say partly because other officials were finding the British at fault in this respect, and news correspondents and commentators were themselves already aware that the British were holding back while Stilwell was advancing. At any rate, the press criticism produced an indignant British reaction, and my friends in the Pentagon and at the State Department told me to ease up on my background briefing of the press.

Currie, who had become disenchanted with the Generalissimo and thought that we should pull out of China excepting for the air effort, told me that Roosevelt was annoyed by Churchill's negative attitude regarding a northern Burma offensive. British inaction, the president told him, was not the fault of Mountbatten but was at the instance of the prime minister.

General Magruder, who had headed the American Military Mission to China, and Colonel McHugh, formerly naval attaché in Chungking, were now serving at OSS headquarters, where I met with them on February 23. Unlike Captain Miles and his SACO, these two veteran intelligence officers wanted to conduct espionage without the Chinese being aware of what they were up to, because they rightly believed that Chinese security was poor. "It is a problem which we have explored for two years without solving," I noted. "Their best bet seems to be the use of the Fourteenth Air Force as cover." It developed during our meeting, however, that two OSS officials in China had, without consulting one another, assigned the same secret intelligence project to two different Fourteenth officers.

Not all of my time on this visit to Washington was spent on strategy, lobbying, and intelligence. On February 24 I lunched "with Professor Blakeslee and his cheery band of postwar planners. They struck me as being a mediocre, academic, partially-informed array." This was a pity. But it was indicative of the attitude of the top levels of the government. Having adopted an inspirational approach to ordering the postwar world, they were disinterested in—or even had a distaste for—a rigorous examination of plausible and workable objectives. Planning for the future, therefore, was relegated to a mousey committee in the out-buildings of the State Department.

By March, Wedemeyer had arrived from London, charged by Churchill, but not the skeptical British Chiefs of Staff, with pressing for a SEAC offensive towards Singapore. The American Joint Chiefs turned down the proposal for much the same reason advanced by their British counterparts—it was out of phase, too far behind the projected advance of the Pacific Fleet and MacArthur. Wedemeyer told the JCS on March 21, 1944 that the northern Burma campaign could hardly succeed—even as Stilwell and Merrill were disproving his predictions.

Mountbatten wanted an integrated Anglo-American staff, one like Eisenhower's with American and British officers intermingled. I believed that, given SEAC's obvious mission, the reconquest of colonies, Americans should not be implicated in the eyes of Asians with the reimposition of imperial rule. Particularly was this true in the case of propaganda and other forms of psychological warfare. I was relieved at a March 7 meeting on psychological warfare, presided over by Wedemeyer, to hear him state that he was against an integrated Anglo-American operation in this sensitive function. As illustrative of the level at which many of these conferences proceeded, Benny remarked, with regard to some British officer, that "the trouble with him was that he was 'pro-British'."

Frank Roberts told me on my arrival in Washington that he was working on the matter of the Observers' Mission. Laughing, he said that with all of the trouble with the Generalissimo (wrangling over Chiang's billion dollar ultimatum), it was a fine time to broach the question of visiting the Communist area. From the Asiatic section I learned that my memorandum on the Observers' Mission had been bucked by Hopkins to the president, who had attached to the memo a note to Leahy instructing him to discuss the matter with Marshall and take action.

Roosevelt's message to Chiang was dispatched on February 9, a slightly abridged and revised version of my suggested text. In Chungking, the phlegmatic Hearn put the message in the form of a memorandum from himself to Madame Kung, asking her to pass the president's communication to her sister, Madame Chiang for the Generalissimo. This traffic of Roosevelt's missive through the

304   *Dragon by the Tail*

boudoirs of the Soong sisters occurred before the president had ordered direct delivery of his messages to Chiang.

Meanwhile the Department of State had lost track of what was going on. It had, of course, a copy of my memorandum. And I had reported to the Far Eastern Division that the president had charged Leahy and Marshall with action. Beyond that I was not then informed, having turned my attention to other affairs.

Puttering along at its own pace, the department decided to give my proposal qualified support. Six days after Chiang had answered Roosevelt, Stettinius wrote to Stimson in the style used to communicate with a foreign, but friendly, government. On balance, he favored sending observers to the Communist areas. Would the War Department please inform State "of any decision reached and of any action taken by General Marshall concerning this proposal." Stimson replied on March 7, recapitulating what had been done, adding that on March 1, "the White House informed the Generalissimo that we shall plan to dispatch the Observers' Mission shortly."

Thus almost a month after the president had first acted, the torpid Department of State learned, thanks to the Pentagon, what the White House had been doing in a matter of major importance to American relations with China and the Soviet Union.

CHAPTER *28*

Wallace and Mountbatten

"THE TWO great lands of China and Russia are glorious in the present," Vice-President Henry A. Wallace proclaimed on May 20, 1944 as he started on a visit to China and Siberia. Envisioning China not only as a Great Power, but also as a Good Power, Wallace announced that "The future of China belongs to the world and the world in justice and peace shall belong to China." And of his Siberian expectations, soon to be realized by inspection of a forced labor camp, he intoned, "I shall feel the grandeur that comes when men wisely work with nature."

This discharge of political flatulence signaled the beginning of an effort by the Roosevelt administration again to buck up the Generalissimo and to manufacture goodwill between China and the Soviet Union. The president was not enthusiastic about Wallace's going to the Soviet Union and told his emissary to stay away from Moscow. Roosevelt's main concern was China. Chiang's whining for a billion dollars, his forebodings of conflict with the Russians and the Chinese Communists, and the incompetence of his armies in dealing with ICHIGO aroused the president's anxiety. He asked Wallace to explain to Chiang that it was primarily at Hull's insistence at the Moscow Conference that China had been recognized as one of the four Great Powers and that the Generalissimo could not let the United States down after America had pinned such faith and hope on China as a world power.

The vice-president was met at Tashkent in mid-June by the American ambassador to the Soviet Union, W. Averell Harriman. The ambassador passed on to Wallace Stalin's views on China, as expressed in an interview on June 10 with Harriman. Stalin had agreed with Roosevelt's opinion that Chiang was the only man to hold China together. Harriman had said to Stalin that Roosevelt felt Chiang should be encouraged to settle with the Chinese Communists and to liberalize his internal policies. Stalin, who could hardly have forgotten his 1926–1927 attempts to manage Chiang as the leader of the Chinese Nationalist Revolution, had observed that "This is easier said than done."

Under existing circumstances, Stalin had reiterated, Chiang was the best man available in China. But his faults must be kept in mind. His army was very weak and many of his entourage were crooks and even traitors. Furthermore, he refused to use the Chinese Communists against the enemy. The Chinese Communists were "margarine" Communists, but they were patriots who wanted to fight the Japanese.

Did Stalin have any suggestions as to a joint American-Soviet policy toward China, Harriman had asked. Yes, Chiang should be brought more strongly under American influence. The United States should and could assume leadership in regard to China. As for Moscow's relations with Chungking, they were based on a treaty of friendship and nonaggression. The Sinkiang-Mongolian border incidents (about which Chiang had complained to Roosevelt) were not the fault of Chiang but of the provincial governor. Soviet forces would, however, back the Outer Mongols if Sinkiang troops again crossed the border.

Wallace arrived in Chungking on June 20 and on the following afternoon met with the Generalissimo and Soong, who acted as interpreter. To none of the Wallace-Chiang meetings was the ambassador invited, which was as unwise as it was rude. The vice-president quickly got down to business, saying that Roosevelt assumed, because the members of the Kuomintang and the Communists were both Chinese, that they were basically friends. To back up this fallacy, Wallace quoted references by the president to the Bryan Treaty, Al Smith, and Charles Francis Adams, which allusions could only have been to Chiang as unconvincing as they were mystifying. If these Chinese friends could not get together, Wallace went on, they might "call in a friend" and that friend, Roosevelt had indicated, might be none other than himself. This was Washington's first dabbling mediation in the whirlpool of enmity between Chiang and the Communists.

Continuing his recitation, Wallace relayed Roosevelt's comments that the British did not consider China as a Great Power, that the Russians were cool regarding China, but that the president wanted China to be a Great Power in fact as well as theory. The vice-president then observed that no question which might result in conflict between China and the Soviet Union should be left pending. This prompted Chiang to suggest that Roosevelt act as arbiter or middleman between China and the Soviet Union. The Generalissimo said that he wished for a friendly understanding with the Soviet Union. Wallace mentioned Harriman's conversation with Stalin whereat Chiang, according to Soong's translation, asked to see a copy of the memorandum of the talk. Saying that he did not have a copy, Wallace told the Generalissimo simply that Stalin had emphasized the need for a unified China in the war effort and suggested that Soong talk over the matter with John Carter Vincent.

Vincent, then chief of the Division of Chinese Affairs of the State Department, was one of several officials whom the vice-president brought with him on his mission. Following the Chiang-Wallace-Soong meeting, Vincent gave Soong an inoffensive account of the Harriman-Stalin conversation, in which he mentioned the old tyrant's enticement of the Americans to assume leadership in the

Far East. With characteristic presumption, Soong asked Vincent for any notes he may have made of Harriman's report on the conversation. Also during that evening, Vincent cautioned Wallace against making any commitment that Roosevelt would act as an arbiter between China and the Soviet Union. Therefore, the next morning before breakfast—for Wallace had an ostentatiously rustic approach to diplomacy—the vice-president hastened to disabuse the Generalissimo of any idea that the United States would go beyond offering good offices in China's relations with the Soviet Union.

Vincent had earned his passage by his advice to the vice-president. Before his departure from Washington, Vincent had been charged by Hull with restraining the vice-president from making promises that the American government could not live up to. Attempting to arbitrate between Stalin and Chiang would have been just that—and would have aroused far more rancor on all sides than did the first Roosevelt's 1905 mediation at the close of the Russo-Japanese War.

Wallace brought up at the June 22 meeting the painful subject of the poor showing being made by Chinese troops in Central China. Chiang replied in familiar terms—after seven years of wartime hardship the Chinese had looked to aid from abroad, but Roosevelt had let him down by withdrawing from the projected amphibious campaign against Burma. He then turned to the matter of the American army. Its officers lacked confidence in China, but he "continued to have confidence in his army." For his part, Chiang said, he lacked confidence in Stilwell's judgment.

The Chinese Communists, the Generalissimo asserted, were subject to Comintern orders. The low morale of the Chinese people and army was due to Communist propaganda. The Communists wanted a breakdown of Chinese resistance to Japan so as to strengthen their position. The Soviet Union would not feel secure if the Communists were not in power in China. In contrast to Stalin's statement about margarine Communists, Chiang laughingly characterized the Chinese Reds as more communist than the Russian Communists.

With regard to the intermittent negotiations between the Kuomintang and the Communists, the Generalissimo said that the Kuomintang's proposal was: support the president (Chiang), support the government, and support the war effort. The government required obedience, incorporation of Communist forces within the Chinese army, and integration of the Communist areas with the rest of China under National government administration. If the Communists would accede to these requirements—and here Chiang switched to the request for an Observers' Mission—the group of American officers would be permitted to go to North China. But they would be under the auspices of the National government, would train "converted" Communist troops (although Washington had not asked for this), and would have no direct contact with the Communists—by which the Generalissimo presumably meant independent relations with the top Communists.

The best contribution that the Americans could make to a settlement, Chiang said, would be to display "aloofness" to the Reds. Later in the conversation, he again advised American "coolness" toward the Communists. And he said, "Please do not press" in the matter of the observers.

The next morning Wallace and Vincent did press in the matter of the observers, stressing the American need for military intelligence from out of North China, particularly in connection with B-29 operations. Whether this line of argument was persuasive, or some other consideration moved him, the Generalissimo suddenly consented to the dispatch of observers without regard to progress in relations between the Kuomintang and the Communists. But they would go under the auspices of his National Military Council.

In leaving Chungking, Wallace was accompanied by the Generalissimo and Madame Chiang on the hour-long drive to the airport. Amidst a good deal of ceremonial amiability, Chiang said that although the Communist problem was an internal Chinese matter, he would welcome the assistance proffered by Roosevelt. While he would not regard the president's participation as meddling, he warned that the Communists would not live up to their assurances, which would greatly damage Roosevelt's prestige. Beneath the show of courteous compliance, Chiang opposed Roosevelt's acting as a friend between friends.

Through Currie and Willkie, the Generalissimo had tried to bring about the removal of Gauss and Stilwell. With Wallace he attempted to have the ambassador and theater commander at least short-circuited. In his contact with the president, Chiang complained to Wallace, there were too many channels through the State Department. And while Chennault was most cooperative, Stilwell had no understanding of political matters. Could not Roosevelt send a personal representative to handle both political and military matters? With this thought in mind, Wallace took off for Kunming.

While the vice-president was making his way through Siberia and Central Asia to China, I had been in New Delhi, with side trips to Kandy, dealing with CBI's political and propaganda relations with South East Asia Command. Stilwell was down in the Mogaung Valley, slugging away at the Japanese and worrying about the dragging siege of Myitkyina. Just as Wallace arrived in China, Stilwell ordered me and one of his public relations officers, Captain Paul Jones, to hurry to Chungking to attend the vice-president. The general declined to leave his war to wait upon Wallace, whom he regarded as another junketing, big-noise Mr. Fixit from Washington.

By the time that Jones and I arrived in Chungking, the vice-president was well into his series of meetings with the Generalissimo and the answer to my invitation for him to visit Stilwell in the jungle was deferred. Later, in a summing-up of the Wallace tour in China, I wrote to Stilwell, in part, " . . . Jones and I were given the best job of runaround I have ever been up against. It was done by two of Claire's [Chennault] boys. I blew up with Chennault about it, uttering a few homely truths about the damage done by the Chennault-Stilwell feud. To his juniors I read the same line and added that I had as little use for Chennault's disciples who needled Chennault on Stilwell in the belief that they thereby won

Claire's gratitude as I had for Stilwell enthusiasts who did the same thing to the theater commander. It seemed to jar them somewhat so that on the night of June 26 when Wallace, Chennault, Glenn [Chennault's Chief of Staff], and the two stooges discussed with me the possibility of the VP visiting you in the Valley, Chennault and Co. were very reasonable and decent . . . Decision by VP was against because of weather uncertainty and tight future schedule."

Easily could the vice-president, as well as Chennault, afford to be reasonable and decent about the difficulties of Wallace's visiting Stilwell in Burma. For Wallace had earlier that day sent a radio to Roosevelt recommending the elimination of Stilwell from authority in China. The vice-president, at first, had wished to supplant Stilwell and, in effect Gauss, with Chennault, "in whom political and military authority will be at least temporarily united" and with the right to "deal directly with the White House on political questions." When he realized that the appointment of Chennault would be opposed by the War Department, Wallace suggested in his message to the president the name of Wedemeyer. The vice-president, Chennault, and his staff were tactful enough not to mention any of this to me.

While Wallace deemed it inconvenient to become acquainted with the man whose removal he was recommending, he did find time after his talks with Chiang to visit Chengtu and to spend three days as Chennault's Kunming house guest. We also inspected one of Chennault's doomed forward bases, at Kweilin, farther from Kunming than Stilwell's headquarters in the jungle. Nor was the vice-president acquainted with Wedemeyer. So his ill-advised counsel to the president regarding American representation in China was a piece of airy irresponsibility.

It was not so received at the State Department by Joseph W. Ballantine, deputy director of the Office of Far Eastern Affairs. In a memorandum dated June 29, concurred in by his chief, Joseph C. Grew, Ballantine recommended to Hull that the president accede to Chiang's request for a personal representative. The "military officer of high rank" so designated, Ballantine said, "might be able to establish a very close and cordial relationship with the Generalissimo and be able tactfully to guide and advise him." In political matters, however, the representative "should work in close harmony with the ambassador," who would be retained. As an ambassador is by definition a personal representative of his sovereign or chief executive, Chiang would then be blessed with two presidential emissaries—a silly arrangement inviting mischief.

In the Pentagon, the Chiang-Wallace scheme for ousting Stilwell contributed to a determination to increase the theater commander's power in China. The Joint Chiefs of Staff on July 4 presented the president with a memorandum scathingly critical of Chiang and Chennault in their resistance to ICHIGO. Stilwell, the JCS stated, was the only man "who has been able to get Chinese forces to fight against the Japanese in an effective way." The Joint Chiefs recommended to the president that he send a message, which they had thoughtfully prepared, urging the Generalissimo "to place General Stilwell in command of all Chinese armed forces." They also asked Roosevelt to promote Stilwell to be a full general for two reasons. He had "conducted a brilliant campaign with a force, which he himself made, in spite of continued opposition from within and without and tremendous obstacles of terrain and weather." And the higher rank would give him needed prestige for the larger responsibilities proposed for him.

Roosevelt took the advice of the JCS rather than that of Wallace and on July 6 radioed Chiang asking him to place Stilwell in command, directly under the Generalissimo, of all American and Chinese forces in China, including the Communists. Replying on July 7, Chiang agreed in principle, but said that there must be a preparatory period before Stilwell took over. He asked for the personal representative to "adjust the relations between me and General Stilwell."

In this context the president saw merit in the Generalissimo's request for the unguent services of a personal representative. On July 13 he replied that he would look for a suitable man and urged Chiang to prepare for Stilwell's assumption of command at the earliest possible moment. Roosevelt then sailed off to Honolulu for conferences with General MacArthur and Admiral Chester W. Nimitz, the Pacific Fleet commander, who were fighting the only decisive actions against the Pacific enemy. Marshall and Stimson began the search for a peacemaker between Stilwell and the Generalissmo.

After my futile dance of attendance upon the vice-president I returned to New Delhi. For sound functional reasons, the principal CBI headquarters had been shifted there from Chungking. In charge was Major General Daniel I. Sultan, a calm, sensible army engineer, recently assigned to CBI as deputy theater commander. From New Delhi I sent to Stilwell a Dutch nephew letter. The marginal comments are Stilwell's.

I do not now recall whom I quoted in disdain of Stilwell's four Gs, or section chiefs of personnel, intelligence, operations, and supply. In any event, I was of the same mind as Stilwell regarding G-3. Merrill, who had been G-3 before commanding the Marauders, was succeeded by Colonel Dean Rusk, whom I admired and believed to be an outstanding staff officer. He later served Kennedy and then Johnson as secretary of state.

"Dickie Mountbatten, impulsive kid," Roosevelt said to Stilwell and me on December 6, 1943, in referring to the Supreme Allied Commander, South East Asia. Fresh and driving enthusiasm, however, was one of Lord Louis's qualities that had most recommended him to the prime minister and the president for appointment as SACSEA. And it was the quality that Stilwell found most congenial in the admiral.

While Stilwell made private fun of Mountbatten's lordly station in life and his splendid tailoring, this was no more than traditional republican parochialism. What did incense Stilwell was something for which Lord Louis was not, fundamentally, responsible. That was Churchill's strategy of bypassing Burma, to which SACSEA was bound. Consequently Mountbatten was committed to withholding from Stilwell the full extent of support of which he was capable during late 1943 and early 1944.

Stilwell's resentment was reciprocated by SACSEA when the American general stole a march on him by sending Boatner, Ferris, and me to Washington ahead of the SEAC mission headed by Wedemeyer. Mountbatten regarded this as insubordination because Stilwell was his deputy, although never formally so designated. Criticism of SEAC in the American press also irked Lord Louis— and Churchill—both of whom wrongly attributed its origin to Stilwell. Relations between the supreme commander and his deputy became so strained that Marshall instructed Stilwell on March 2 to go to Mountbatten and reestablish cordial relations, which he did.

In a March 7 minute to Field Marshal Sir John Dill, Mountbatten said of Stilwell, "He really is a grand old warrior but only the Trinity could carry out his duties, which require him to be in Delhi, Chungking, and the Ledo Front simultaneously." It may even have been that the grand old warrior outdid the Trinity. In commanding the Chinese and American units in North Burma, Stilwell was answerable to himself as (a) the Generalissimo's Joint Chief of Staff and (b) Commanding General of CBI. But because Burma was within SEAC's sphere, he also served as a corps commander under two layers of British authority— Lieutenant General Sir William Slim (whom Stilwell liked and respected), commander of SEAC's Fourteenth Army, and General Sir George Giffard, SEAC's commander-in-chief of ground forces. Yet, Slim and Giffard were, at the same time, subordinate to Stilwell in his capacity as deputy supreme commander.

That such a lunatic chain of command functioned at all in SEAC was due mostly to the fact that, as Lord Louis put it to Dill, Stilwell "had never really done anything about those duties" as Deputy SACSEA. To rationalize the hierarchy, Mountbatten suggested to Dill that "Stilwell's command should be confined to China" and that Wedemeyer or Sultan, Stilwell's deputy in CBI, should take over as the senior American in SEAC. Then in June, General Brooke, Chief of Imperial General Staff, told Marshall that SACSEA wanted a replacement for his deputy.

Thus while Chiang and Wallace were seeking to get Stilwell out of China (Wallace suggesting he be confined to India-Burma) and asking for Wedemeyer as his replacement, the British wanted Stilwell sent back to China, with Wedemeyer replacing him in SEAC. The combination of pressures roused the Joint Chiefs of Staff to rally around the only commander on the Asian continent fighting a winning campaign against the enemy. The JCS did concede, however, in its July 4 recommendations to Roosevelt that, if Stilwell went to China (to command all Chinese armed forces), Sultan should command the Chinese in Burma under Stilwell's direction, and the capable General Wheeler, who had moved from serving as CBI supply and engineering chief to acting as principal administrative officer of SEAC, should take Stilwell's place as Mountbatten's deputy. Wedemeyer was not mentioned.

On August 1, while the Generalissimo was stalling on giving him command

APO 885, July 17, 1944

Dear General-

What I have been hearing during the past two or three months makes me think that perhaps it is again time to act as an objective reporter on what is being said about you and your problems. I do this because I know from experience that, unlike many men in very big jobs, you do not want to be insulated from critical comment. So here goes.

Theater or Sector Commander: It is probably no news to you that there has been and is criticism of your preoccupation with the North Burma sector. This criticism is encountered in the air, ground and supply forces, from Kweilin and Chengtu to Delhi, and it is increasing. I hear it asked when you intend to come out of the woods and take over as theater commander. The explanation that there is no one else who can make the Chinese perform is not accepted at full value. The question is asked - "If Boatner cannot do it, why not give Cheeves or Bergin two stars and tell one of them he's got to do it."

Simply because the G-mo won't have it. I hope now he will accept Sultan.

CBI's Role in the War Against Japan: It is felt that back in Washington there is a growing tendency to discount CBI's potential contribution to the attack on Japan (I've written you my own ideas on the subject). It is said that "Stilwell's playing the Burma sourdough" contributes to the Washington impression that there is not the leadership in CBI to rate a place in the major league. The rebuff which we got to our inquiry about the forthcoming Pearl Harbor talks, even if routine, may be an indication of Washington's estimate of our potential value. I hear it said that CBI is slipping from the position of a second class to a third class theater; that only you can effectively champion its case; but that you can do that only if you get out of the tactical realm and step vigorously into the strategic one. Which brings us back to the preceding paragraph.

UNFAIR TO ORGANIZED LABOR.

"GUILTY."

Have we really a strong argument?

Your Staff: General Sultan is generally considered the best thing that has happened to the theater for a long time. But by and large, your senior staff officers are regarded as a garland of millstones around your neck. Hearn's return was viewed with surprise and dismay. Same true of Ferris. Your four Gs are looked upon as varying from pleasant mediocrity to senile incompetence. Creasy of Planners not included. An officer today talked to me along these lines: *(GOOD OFFICERS ARE SCARCE.)*

YES.

COULD BE WORSE.

Right. And we are trying to do something about it.

Granted that CBI has become the dumping ground for men whom Eisenhower and MacArthur did not ask for, still, that's no reason for the present appalling staff and command situation. There is in this theater enough talent to remedy the situation: the few obviously superior officers like Merrill and Timberman plus hidden or misused talent needing only an intelligent G-1 to bring it out. There are too many square pegs in round holes. But first of course the Old Man must rid himself of dead wood. Politically FDR

YES.

NOT NEARLY UP TO M.

Where?

Don't forget about the little matter of RANK.

McCammon — OUT.
Boatner — OUT.
Wessels — will soon be.
who else shall I fire?

may be able -- if at considerable cost -- to get away with
Ma Perkinses in his cabinet; militarily JWS can't afford to
keep on the incompetents he has in responsible positions.
There is more at stake than the feelings and reputations
of generals and colonels. He will have to learn to be as
ruthless as Eisenhower or MacArthur.

TRUE.
Name a
GOOD
theater
G-2
!!!

Intelligence: One of the better informed newspapermen
recently back from the States said that he heard a good
deal of unfavorable comment in Washington about CBI, but
that where this theater was most criticized was in the field
of intelligence. He was told that more intelligence is
coming out of the Central Pacific than out of CBI, which
should not be so.

I would here interpolate on my own. The inadequacy
of our intelligence has been and is being painfully revealed in the Central China campaign. We weren't sure that
the blow was coming, when it came we didn't know how far
it was going and now we don't know whether it is over.
That's a hell of a state of affairs.

Pinkney, JICA's air man and apparently a very able intelligence officer, diagnoses the trouble as a lack of centralized control resulting in duplication of effort, withholding of information, failure to cross-check and general
confusion. He points to the well-coordinated British system with all intelligence funnelling into a central agency
as an example from which we can learn.

Sincerely,

John

John Davies

Drysdale is going home.   *G - 1*
Hunt is now on for G-2   *G - 2*
I think the G-3 stuff has   *G - 3*
   been pretty good. (I
   insist on doing my own
   in the field.)
We are looking for him.   *G - 4*
Are you thinking of
Cheves? If so, who
will run Calcutta?

P.S. These memos are
   always welcome.
           J.W.S.

in China, and when it was clear that the siege of Myitkyina was about to end in victory, the grand old warrior emerged from the jungle as a four-star general and descended upon the luxuriant SEAC headquarters at Kandy to do something about his duties as Deputy SACSEA. For Mountbatten, who was leaving for London on consultation, had in a pro forma fashion invited his number two to take over in his absence. To the astonishment of Supremo, his deputy accepted. And so Stilwell came to preside over the military garden of Eden, with its smartly-tailored officers, its crisp and lovely English WRENS and WAAFS, and a botanical display surpassing Gauguin and Rousseau.

What Deputy SACSEA did about his duties soon became evident. Because he did not take the inflated headquarters at Kandy seriously, he turned the operation of SEAC over to its chief of staff, Lieutenant General Sir Henry Pownall and in effect went on a hard-earned vacation. Pownall, after all, had the credentials to run the show. He had been British commander in chief in the Far East at the outset of the war and then Wavell's chief of staff during the debacle at Singapore and in the Dutch East Indies.

The enormous black Cadillac assigned to him Stilwell relegated to his mess sergeant, Gus Renard, a former chef at New York's Stork Club, who went victual shopping in it at the local market, while Deputy Supremo buzzed around town, sight-seeing in a jeep. He read *Life in a Putty Knife Factory* and *A Tree Grows in Brooklyn*, and even lent his abstemious presence to several cocktail parties. The general was not as stimulated as he had been by Egyptian antiquities, but he was more lighthearted, for he had won some battles in Burma—and in Washington.

As the SEAC staff did not quite know what to make of Deputy Supremo, he was treated with a wary deference. But then, SEAC officers were accustomed to treading warily. Mountbatten, with all of his charm and grace, was temperamental and capable of nobly upbraiding an offender.

My impression from a visit to Stilwell, as well as others that I made to Kandy, was that circumspection was more pervasively necessary between the British and American staff officers lest national sensibilities be bruised. A similar need for tact existed between the British who had come out from home, and had never been in Asia, and the British colonials, particularly Indian Army officers. The newcomers were impatient with the colonials whom they regarded as Colonel Blimps, as indeed many of them were. And the old India wallas harrumphed that, dash it, these chappies from Mayfair would come to no good end trying to hurry the East.

While Mountbatten's dissatisfaction with his deputy—a fifth wheel—flared sporadically, his discontent with his commanders-in-chief—the operating heads of SEAC's navy, army, and air force components—was more constant. He had asked London to replace Admiral Sir James Somerville and General Giffard, but had refrained from doing the same with regard to Air Chief Marshal Sir Richard Peirse only because he thought it not politic to fire all of his principal subordinates at once. Somerville, a ruddy old tar, did not wholly accept Lord Louis's authority over his fleet. He was inclined to treat Admiral Mountbatten, who had never commanded any naval vessel more imposing than a destroyer—and that sunk from under him—as chairman of a commanders-in-chief committee. As for Giffard, SACSEA rightly thought him not nearly aggressive enough.

My impression was that Wedemeyer, as deputy chief of staff, stayed aloof from the personality conflicts in SEAC. He regarded himself as a global strategist, qualified for far more significant responsibilities than those offered by his out-of-the-way post. He had hoped for command of an armored or airborne division in Europe as a necessary combat step in his advancement. When this was not offered him and he was assigned to SEAC, he felt that he was being eased into a backwater because of what he was pleased to regard as his too open nature.

SEAC was neither a tight nor a happy ship. It was not Mountbatten's fault. In a sense, it was Mountbatten's misfortune that he was relatively young and inexperienced and that he was bolstered on all sides by veteran and strong-minded professionals. But the trouble with SEAC went deeper than personalities.

It was a command suffering from an inner conflict. It was designed for an amphibious offensive aimed at Singapore, but instead was dragged northward into land warfare in the mountains and jungles of the India-Burma border. Even if it had not been so deflected, it could not have in 1944 discharged its amphibious mission. As Somerville's naval force lacked the requisite sea and air power, and sufficient reinforcements would not be available until after the defeat of Germany, SEAC was not only in conflict with itself, it was also frustrated.

When SEAC was set up it was not evident that Nimitz and MacArthur would pick up the momentum that they did in the advance across the Pacific. Had the Pacific pace been slower and had the war against Japan dragged on for a year or more beyond the defeat of Germany, there would have been a real amphibious role for SEAC. Consequently the creation of SEAC as a contingency command made sense.

My several contacts with SEAC were as a member of Stilwell's staff—Stilwell in his manifestation as commanding general of CBI, not as Deputy Supremo. This metaphysical distinction was important as it meant that I was not involved in SEAC, but that I treated with it. I dealt principally with Maberly Esler Deming, Lord Louis's decorous political adviser, who later became British ambassador to Japan, and with Air Vice-Marshal Philip Joubert de la Ferté, who was in charge of psychological warfare. They treated me with suave courtesy and understanding in my efforts to keep the United States from being identified in Asian eyes with the British reconquest of empire.

Mountbatten was aware that I resisted in this respect his basic concept of SEAC as a totally integrated command. Yet he was always gracious in his relations with me. And so I found the atmosphere at Kandy decent and considerate even in our differences.

CHAPTER 29

Mao: We Must Cooperate

BEFORE STILWELL had completed his four weeks at Kandy, he sent me on another trip to Washington, this time as impresario for Frank Merrill. We arrived in Washington to find the Pentagon and the White House determined to push through Stilwell's command over Chinese troops in China itself. For Washington this was the crucial military issue in CBI and SEAC. Stilwell's relationships with other commands, including Mountbatten's, were of lesser importance.

Roosevelt told Chiang, as of August 23, that he did not think that the Chinese forces "to come under General Stilwell's command should be limited except by their availability to defend China and fight the Japanese." To further this sweeping behest, Stimson and Marshall had selected Major General Patrick J. Hurley to be the president's personal representative to the Generalissimo. Roosevelt told Hurley to promote harmonious relations between Chiang and Stilwell and to facilitate Stilwell's command over Chinese armies assigned to him.

But Hurley was not to be alone in his eminence. Personality conflicts in the War Production Board necessitated, for domestic political reasons, the removal of its chairman, Donald M. Nelson. Roosevelt wanted him out from under foot and so was inspired to appoint him to be personal representative to Chiang for economic matters.

When I arrived in Washington the twin emissaries were poised to fly to China, by way of Moscow. In explaining the Russian detour, Hurley revealed to the startled State Department that he wanted to tell Molotov and, if possible, Stalin why he was going to China and to solicit Soviet advice on "the line which he should adopt in his dealings with Chiang Kai-shek." On August 25 I wrote to my wife: "Called Hurley night before last. . . . He asked me to leave with him today, by way of Siberia. Broke my heart to say no. He wants me to hurry up to China. . . . The Nelson appointment is viewed with wry amusement. . . . China is apparently to the American political scene what Siberia is to the Russians. Only Roosevelt's technique is quicker and more humane."

Hurley had given the impression to the Eastern European Division that the president had approved of his visit to Moscow for consultation with Molotov. Roosevelt denied that Hurley and Nelson were going to Moscow on his instructions. Nelson nevertheless opened the conversation with the foreign commissar by saying that Roosevelt had asked him and Hurley to go to Molotov and acquaint him with the reasons for their missions to China.

When I saw Hopkins in early September, he was ribald and derisive in his comments about Nelson. His cynicism about Nelson, whose official environment he well understood, and his romanticism about Chennault, whose operating circumstances were remote from his own experience, were symptomatic of the contradictions in this sensitive, ferrety personality.

On the major issue of Stilwell's role Hopkins observed, as I recorded after our meeting: "The Generalissimo's latest messages seemed to indicate that he is willing for General Stilwell to assume command of all Allied troops in China, including the Chinese. He [Hopkins] suggested that it was felt that only a foreign commander such as General Stilwell could command both Central Government and Communist troops. I remarked that in view of his experiences in the first Burma campaign I found it hard to believe that General Stilwell would not be skeptical of the degree of control which he could exert over Chinese army commanders. I said that I foresaw his authority being undercut at every turn.

"This comment apparently came as a surprise to Mr. Hopkins. He declared that General Stilwell had not indicated any doubt of his ability effectively to command Chinese troops. He asked whether or not the American command of Chinese forces in north Burma had not been a success. I replied that it had been but that in India and Burma we had far more control over Chinese units than we have had or will have in China. I went on to say that General Stilwell might successfully exert command but that all of the way it would be a hard battle against Chinese recalcitrance, lethargy, and indifference, and that I was sure General Stilwell would be the first to admit this. Nevertheless, full of pitfalls as such an arrangement might be, it seemed to me that the alternative—which was to leave the Chinese to liquidate the Japanese armies in China—was a pretty hopeless solution, and I thought that General Stilwell felt the same way.

"Mr. Hopkins stated that General Stilwell would have a great deal of power because the White House would in this arrangement work directly through General Marshall to General Stilwell."

At the end of September, Merrill and I returned to New Delhi by way of Iceland, London, over liberated France, then through the Levant to India. By this time, the military enterprises initiated in June—the Normandy landings, the Russian summer offensive, and the capture of Saipan—had proceeded successfully. The western Allies had pressed the Germans back nearly to their borders. The Soviet juggernaut, twice the weight of the Anglo-American war machine on the western front, had rolled into East Prussia, Poland, and Rumania. And in the Pacific, the American amphibious advance had reached Palau, on the threshold of the Philippines.

Only in China, on the allied side, were matters in unnerved disarray. By mid-September the Generalissimo's forces were crumbling before ICHIGO. Belying the confidence in his armies which he had asserted to Wallace, Chiang was so disconcerted that he wanted to bring his expeditionary force back over the Salween, lest the Japanese move on Kunming from the east.

Embarrassing and unsettling as the ranging offensive of the Japanese was to Chiang, it was not his only worry. His corrosive rivals, the Communists, and his clamorous allies, the Americans, deeply disturbed him. The Communists were a subversive force from below because of their popular appeal and their organizing genius among the masses. The Americans threatened his ramshackle power structure from above.

They did so in two respects. Roosevelt's insistence that Stilwell be given control over all Chinese armed forces menaced the queasy political balancing by which Chiang maintained a qualified paramountcy over the various military forces in China. This system, and his own high command, which the Generalissimo had in 1942 indulgently described to Stilwell as semieducated, lazy, and prone to error, could not be expected to withstand the stringency of Stilwell's authority—if the American general were granted effective command.

The second American threat was the Observer Group. It had on July 2 arrived at Yenan, the Communist "capital." Although not intended as such, it was available as a channel of direct communication for Mao Tse-tung to the top American representatives in China and to Washington. Because the Generalissimo had objected to the designation of the unit as a "mission," it was named the Observer Group and, alternatively, Observer Section. Also, because for some months my colleagues and I had sportingly called the Communist area Dixie—a rebel territory—the observers were also referred to, among Americans, as the Dixie Mission.

The Observer Group was headed by Colonel David D. Barrett, a China specialist and former assistant military attaché. He was admirably suited to this responsibility for he not only spoke and read the language but also had an unusual facility for establishing rapport with Chinese. He was accompanied on the initial flight to Yenan by six officers, a sergeant, and my colleague, John S. Service.

When I made the proposal in January to send the observers, I had planned that Service should be the first of the four foreign service officers detailed to Stilwell to go to Yenan. Fortunately, Ambassador Gauss was of the same opinion. Service was fluent in Chinese, the ablest political reporter among the China specialists, and a prodigious worker. My thought was that he would stay at Yenan to report from the center of Communist authority.

With the second contingent of nine to Yenan, on August 7, went Raymond P. Ludden. From our time together in Mukden I knew that he had a solid understanding of guerrilla operations in harsh country. Furthermore, as he was of an adventurous spirit, he was the logical one to go into the field with the Communists and with them to penetrate behind the Japanese lines. I had confidence in his ability to make a realistic appraisal of Communist organizations, operations, and potential in the decisive countryside of North China. On October 6, with three American officers and a sergeant, Ludden left Yenan for a four-month tour of some twelve hundred miles by mule and on foot through Communist-held territory.

Less than a week after his arrival at Yenan, the indefatigable Service submitted the first of what was to grow into a torrent of political reports, which George F. Kennan was later to describe as "an absolutely outstanding job of reporting." Service recorded that the observers felt "that we have come into a different country and are meeting a different people." He quoted an officer born and brought up in China as saying, "I find myself continually trying to find out just how Chinese these people are." Service continued: "To the skeptical, the general atmosphere in Yenan can be compared to that of a rather small, sectarian college—or a religious summer conference. There is a bit of the smugness, self-righteousness, and conscious fellowship. . . . One cannot help coming to feel that this movement is strong and successful and that it has such drive behind it and has tied itself so closely to the people that it will not easily be killed."

Naturally, the Communist oligarchy was gratified by the arrival of the Dixie Mission. The presence of the Observer Group was an official American acknowledgement that the Communists were taken seriously, at least militarily. But that was not enough for Mao. At a dinner on July 26, welcoming the Americans, he asked Service whether there was a possibility of establishing an American consulate at Yenan. As matters stood, this would have amounted to *de facto* recognition of the Communist regime. Mao said that he wanted the consulate as a form of American representation that would continue after the conclusion of the war against Japan and the withdrawal of the Observer Group—when there would exist the greatest danger of a Kuomintang attack and civil war.

Service asked Chou En-lai on the following day whether an allied commander over all forces in China was advisable or practical. Service reported:

He replied with a strong affirmative but qualified it by saying that the time for the suggestion had not yet come. We should wait until American supplies and men are coming into China in significant magnitude and the counter offensive is actually in sight. The commander should be American and would be welcomed by the Communists, if agreed to by the Central government.

Regarding the possible enlargement of the scope of activities of the present Observer Section, Chou said that such expansion toward active collaboration would of course be welcomed by the Communists but would, unless there were a radical change, be opposed by the Central government. However, the door was now opened a crack and it might be possible, by following a slow and careful course, to move toward modified collaboration. For this reason the granting of permission for the Observer Group was a milestone. (I was interested that here, as well as in other parts of the conversation, Chou was careful to recognize the authority of the Central government and the, at least, potential leadership of the Generalissimo. He obviously had no expectation that we were going to immediately start on a program of direct support of the Communist forces.)

Mao gave Service a month to become acquainted with the Yenan environment and then invited the junior American diplomat for a conversation on August 23. In retrospect, over the span of a quarter of a century, this discourse was of greater significance than all of Roosevelt's and Wallace's conversations with Chiang. Mao, the man who before long was to rule China as Chiang could only dream of doing, pled with a second secretary of embassy for a deal between Washington and Yenan. This extraordinary overture emerged in the latter part of the eight hours of the interview.

In pedantic and verbose fashion, characteristic of Communist argumentation, but at the same time with a bluntness not unlike Stalin's, Mao proceeded from an exposition of the situation in China to his questions about American policy—will the United States return to isolationism, is Washington really interested in democracy in the world, and what is its attitude toward the Chinese Communists? It is from this final broad question that the following quotations are excerpted. Said Mao, as reported in summary by Service:

We could not raise this question of [U.S.] recognition [of Yenan] before. In a formal sense it is still premature. We only ask now that American policy try to induce the Kuomintang to reform itself. This would be a first stage. It may be the only one necessary; if it is successful there will be no threat of civil war.

But suppose that the KMT does not reform. Then there must be a second stage of American policy. Then this question of American policy toward the Communists must be raised. We can risk no conflict with the United States. . . .

Every American soldier in China should be a walking and talking advertisement for democracy. He ought to talk it to every Chinese he meets. American officers ought to talk it to Chinese officers. After all, we Chinese consider you Americans the ideal of democracy. . . .

Finally, any contact you Americans have with us Communists is good. Of course we are glad to have the Observer Section here because it will help to beat Japan. But there is no use in not pretending that—up to now at least—the chief importance of your coming is its political effect on the Kuomintang.

(I noted his emphasis on Americans landing in China and suggested that the war might be won in other ways and a landing not necessary.)

We think the Americans must land in China. It depends, of course, on Japanese strength and the development of the war. But the main Japanese strength is in the Yangtze valley and North China—not to speak of Manchuria.

If the Americans do not land in China, it will be most unfortunate for China. The Kuomintang will continue as the government—without being able to be the government.

If there is a landing, there will have to be American cooperation with both Chinese forces—KMT and Communist. Our forces *now* surround Hankow, Shanghai, Nanking, and other large cities. We are the inner ring; the KMT is further back.

If there is to be this cooperation with both Communist and KMT forces, it is important that we be allowed to work in separate sectors. The KMT is too afraid of us to work with us. Their only concern will be to checkmate us. When we are in separate sectors, the U.S. Army can see the difference: that we have popular support and can fight. . . .

Soviet participation either in the Far Eastern War or in China's postwar reconstruction depends entirely on the circumstances of the Soviet Union. The Russians have suffered greatly in the war and will have their hands full with their own job of rebuilding. We do not expect Russian help.

Furthermore, the KMT, because of its anti-Communist phobia, is anti-Russian. Therefore KMT-Soviet cooperation is impossible. And for us to seek it would only make the situation in China worse. China is disunified enough already! In any case Soviet help is not likely even if the KMT wanted it.

But Russia will not oppose American interests in China if they are constructive and democratic. There will be no possible point of conflict. Russia only wants a friendly and democratic China. Cooperation between Americans and the Chinese Communist Party will be beneficial and satisfactory to all concerned. . . .

[I jokingly remarked that the name "Communist" might not be reassuring to some American businessmen. Mao laughed and said that they had thought of changing their name but if people knew them they would not be frightened.]

Even the most conservative American businessman can find nothing in our program to take exception to.

China must industrialize. This can be done—in China—only by free enterprise and with the aid of foreign capital. Chinese and American interests are co-related and similar. They fit together, economically and politically. We can and must work together.

The United States would find us more cooperative than the Kuomintang. We will not be afraid of democratic American influence; we will welcome it. We have no silly ideas of taking only Western mechanical techniques. Also we will not be interested in monopolistic, bureaucratic capitalism that stifles the economic development of the country and only enriches the officials. We will be interested in the most rapid possible development of the country on constructive and productive lines. First will be the raising of the living standard of the people (see what we have done here with our limited resources). After that can come the "national defense industry" that Chiang talks of in his *China's Destiny*. We will be interested in the welfare of the Chinese people.

America does not need to fear that we will not be cooperative. We must cooperate and we must have American help. This is why it is so important to us Communists to know what you Americans are thinking and planning. We cannot risk crossing you—cannot risk any conflict with you.

CHAPTER 30

Roosevelt's Ultimatum to Chiang

MAO TSE-TUNG's extraordinary bid for a working arrangement with the United States was ignored by the American government. Aside from the State Department's China specialists, Washington took little, if any notice of Mao's overture. And so a historic point in American-Chinese relations was passed unperceived.

The American government was absorbed in the final phases of a global war. In this context China had become a disappointment and a nuisance. Reluctantly Washington had given up hoping that China would be of any strategic importance in the defeat of Japan—unless Stilwell were given effective command of Chiang's armies.

Even so, the enemy was to be overcome by blockade, bombardment, and finally, invasion from island lodgments in the Pacific. Air operations from China would, if possible, be in marginal support of the mighty oceanic effort. The Japanese armies on the mainland would be mopped up, if necessary, after the Russians had overrun at least Manchuria and the Americans had subdued resistance on the home islands of Japan.

As Chiang's authority in China deteriorated—lost to the Japanese and the Communists—and as China's strategic importance dwindled, the American attachment to the Generalissimo began to take on the nature of a fixation. Exasperated as Roosevelt had become with Chiang, he found himself bound to the Generalissimo as the imagined personification of all China and phantom member of the Big Four. For perpetuation of the Chiang myth had become essential to the Roosevelt-Hull prospectus for a world of international-interracial peace and harmony. The United States, near its peak of wartime might, was close to being in its relations with Kuomintang China a captive nation.

At the same time, the American government recognized the realities of decomposition in China. These were inflation, shortage of consumer's goods, rampant corruption, peasant revolt in Honan, alienation of the educated class, warlord and regional plottings against Chiang, latent treachery among those around him, immediate fear that the Japanese might in extremity lash out to take Kunming or Chungking, and the looming horror of a civil war in which the Russians would intervene in support of the Chinese Communists. It was this last prospect that most acutely concerned Washington.

Somehow the American government had to reconcile unreality with reality. There was the vision of a benign Chiang presiding over a unified, democratic, and powerful China and acting in felicitous concert with Stalin, Roosevelt, and Churchill to dispense justice and tranquility to a troubled world. The conflict between this Elysian concept and the squalid facts of China had to be resolved. The decision of the American government was to make reality conform to unreality.

To accomplish this, Chiang Kai-shek and his regime had to be reformed. The American government set out to do just that. The missionary undertaking was not systematically defined and implemented as was subsequent proselytization elsewhere. It tended to be sporadic and uncoordinated. Nevertheless, two major ministrations were evident, one political, the other military.

Following Vice-President Wallace's admonitions to the Generalissimo to seek political salvation through making up to the Communists and getting along with the Russians, Ambassador Gauss cautiously broached with Soong, the foreign minister, and then Chiang, on August 30, a proposal that the Generalissimo "bring competent representatives of other groups or parties to participation in the government." Chiang replied perfunctorily that the suggestion might be worth studying. It was clear that he was preoccupied with bringing the Communists to heel, not in conciliation.

Washington, he told Gauss, did not understand the Communist problem in China and it was the embassy's duty to see to it that it did. Furthermore, the American government's urging that differences with the Communists be resolved only made the Communists more recalcitrant. And since the arrival of the observers at Yenan, Chiang complained, the Communists were becoming arrogant. The American government, through the Observer Group, should tell them to submit to the National Government.

Commenting on his fruitless conversation with the Generalissimo, Gauss observed, in part, that Chiang did not appear to realize that "Time is on the side of the Chinese Communists; that as time goes on the Kuomintang Government's influence and control in free China is deteriorating if not yet disintegrating; and that if the Soviet Union should come to make war upon the Japanese . . . defeat of the Japanese continental armies would probably leave the Communist forces and their regime in a strong political and military position in those areas [North China and Manchuria] . . . placing them in the category of a *de facto* regime for a very large section of this country, having Soviet approval and probably Soviet support."

Hull radioed Gauss on September 9 that the president and he thought that the ambassador should make a "positive, frank, and friendly approach to Chiang" regarding the situation in China. Roosevelt and Hull felt that the Generalissimo's August 30 conversation with Gauss indicated "a discouraging lack of progress in Chiang's thinking." They suggested that the ambassador tell the Generalissimo that, if he would arrange a meeting, Gauss would urge upon the Communist representative in Chungking the necessity for Chinese unity in a spirit of "tolerance and good will—of give and take." The observers in Yenan were on a military mission and unsuitable for making representations to the Communists.

Continuing, the secretary assured the ambassador that the president and he approved of the proposal made by Gauss to Chiang that representatives of minority parties be brought into the government. The end to be sought, not only on behalf of China, but also the United States and the United Nations, was a "strong but representative and tolerant government" under which the "physical and spiritual resources" of the Chinese would be utilized "in carrying on the war and in establishing a durable democratic peace."

The scrupulous Gauss met with Chiang on September 15 and said that he would be willing to talk with the Communist representative in Chungking. The Generalissimo wanted the ambassador to tell the representative that the Communists should submit unconditionally to Chiang. Gauss wisely pointed out that he could not mediate; all he could do was to voice the American views on the need for unity in China. And he would talk with the Communists only if the Generalissimo so wished.

Nor did the ambassador make any progress in his suggestion that the Generalissimo create some sort of coalition war council. He reported to Hull and the president that he did not feel that Chiang had "acquired any realization that it would be practicable or desirable to work for unity in China by other than the means he has pursued through the years of disposing of opposition."

Hull sent the president the ambassador's report of the Chiang conversation, and a covering memorandum. While admitting that the Generalissimo's attitude was "not encouraging," Hull saw some hopeful indications. Among them were the permission given to several American journalists to visit Yenan and more open discussion in some political circles. These developments occurred largely because of "American press criticism and friendly official approaches." Therefore American pressure for reform was having an effect, it should be kept up, and there was reason for guarded optimism. This unflagging search for rays of sunshine amidst the murk was characteristic of American policy toward China then and for five years thereafter.

In contrast to its diffident approach to Chiang on the subject of political reform, the American government's treatment of the Generalissimo in the matter of military reform had become exacting. This was due, in part, to the nature of Stilwell, but also to the belief of the president and the JCS that military considerations were almost always overriding. Washington's brusque tone was also caused by irritation with Chinese military incompetence.

The Generalissimo had no need to fear a coup d'etat by his units at Ramgarh or in Burma, separated from him by mountains and Japanese. Across the

Hump he could afford to yield, provisionally, authority to Stilwell, even though he continued to issue tactical orders to his officers behind the American general's back.

Notwithstanding the distinction between Chinese units in Burma-India and those in China, of which Marshall and Stilwell were aware, both men hoped that Chiang would be willing to give Stilwell command of all Chinese forces to stem the rampaging ICHIGO offensive. Stilwell would have to make some emergency reforms if the enemy was to be checked. He could not, in the time available, reorganize, train, and equip the ninety divisions that he had proposed to the Generalissimo. But even minimal reform turned on Stilwell's being given command.

I doubted that Stilwell would get effective command. What I had said to Hopkins on September 4 was a cautious expression of my skepticism. I had long been dubious over the possibility of American command of Chinese troops, even in Burma and India.

In my diary on February 17, 1943 I had noted: "One of our major mistakes is attempting the impossible—command over the Chinese. We have the weapons, which makes the Chinese willing to string along with us much further than they ordinarily would. We have our ideas of how they should be used and our ideas of command and organization. We want to impose them on the Chinese because we consider the Chinese inefficient and incompetent. We are approaching them with the mentality of Gordon and Ward during the latter half of the 19th Century. And it doesn't go down. Chou [homonym for Joe—Stilwell] talks about bearing down, discipline, enforced discipline. And then—he is left hanging in air."

Now, many years later, I am puzzled why Stilwell did not advise against Washington's fateful attempt in mid-1944 to have him put in command of all Chinese forces. I have no record of and do not recall any discussion with him on the subject. Such matters the general kept to himself and I did not, with all of my plain-speaking on his other affairs, inquire into what may have passed between him and the White House or the War Department.

The initiative on the command issue, as later revealed, came from Marshall. The chief of staff was beset by Wallace's and Mountbatten's maneuvers against Stilwell, together with Chiang's and Chennault's failure to halt the Japanese onslaught in Central China. In these circumstances, on July 1, Marshall radioed to Stilwell in Burma asking whether he thought that he could do some good by moving across the Hump to deal with the situation in Central China and concentrate on "the rehabilitation and in effect the direction of the leadership of the Chinese forces in China proper." In a wintry reply on July 3 Stilwell said that "The harvest of neglect and mismanagement [of the Chinese Army] is now being reaped. . . . There is still a faint chance to salvage something in China," but only if the president forced the Generalissimo to give Stilwell command. "Without complete authority over the Army, I would not attempt the job." He closed with, "The chances are not good, but I can see no other solution."

I can understand Marshall's and Stilwell's anxiety over the Japanese offensive. I can also understand Stilwell, the faithful soldier, sensing that his commanding officer hoped he would volunteer for an impossible assignment and dutifully doing so. But I am surprised that he apparently believed that the Generalissimo could be induced to give him "complete authority" over the Chinese army.

Chiang could not give anyone control over the Chinese forces simply because he did not himself have complete authority over most of them. And those that he did effectively command he would not relinquish to anyone. For the jealous manipulation of them, by which he nimbly stayed atop the heaving political heap, would then no longer be his, and he would be toppled.

Roosevelt's demand of Chiang on July 6 that he give Stilwell authority over his troops was an affront to the Generalissimo. And the president's phrase, "including the Communist forces," could only have been intolerable to Chiang. For the pesky American general to establish an operational relationship with Chiang's enemies would at least give them face and probably result in the Americans arming them.

This was not something new in Chiang's relationship with Stilwell. In September 1943, anticipating a Japanese ground reaction to Chennault's air attacks, Stilwell recommended that the Generalissimo order the Communists' Eighteenth Group Army and Nationalist troops in the Northwest—including elements assigned by Chiang to blockade the Communists—to launch a diversionary attack along a broad front designed to distract the enemy from retaliating against Chennault's airfields. Madame Chiang later informed Stilwell that he was in trouble with the Generalissimo because of this recommendation and that he should have known that the Communists would not take orders. "Told her," Stilwell wrote in his diary, "it would show them up to the world if they didn't."

Now in 1944 he was again thinking of using the Communist and Nationalist forces in the Northwest, as he radioed Marshall on July 3, to harry the enemy's flank and give pause to ICHIGO. The immobilization of large bodies of Chinese troops in sterile confrontation with one another disgusted Stilwell. He wanted them put to use. He observed to Marshall with regard to the Communists that "Two years ago they offered to fight with me."

While Chou En-lai had on June 29, 1942 told me, as I reported to Stilwell, that he would be willing to take Communist troops into Burma and "obey General Stilwell's orders," the employment that Stilwell was now considering was quite another matter. It would involve, assuming Chiang's concurrence, sending meagerly equipped Communist forces into a major offensive for which they did not have sufficient reserves of materiel and which the Americans would be unable, for logistic reasons, adequately to supplement.

Whatever the real attitude of the Communists in 1942, in 1944 it was that American command over at least their own forces should await the arrival in volume of American supplies and troops and the imminence of a counteroffensive. This was Chou's position in his July 27 conversation with Service. What Yenan wanted was a direct pipeline, not one through Chiang, to the American military supply gusher and direct dealing with American authority, whereupon it might be willing to accept, at least nominally, an American commander in chief over Communist as well as Nationalist forces.

Mao's insistence, in his August 23 discussion with Service, on the importance of American landings on the China coast was an integral part of the Communists' hopes for direct supply from and bilateral relations with the United States. Yenan showed little interest in being supplied from over the Hump, the prospects for which would be, at best, a thin trickle over Chiang's objections. Its interest was in a port, through which equipment could flow directly to them in volume. Similarly, Mao's emphasis on the Communists and the Nationalists functioning separately, each in its own sector of the country, meant that the Reds alone would deal with the Americans in that section of China controlled by them.

I do not know whether Stilwell saw Service's reports out of Yenan and what he thought in August his chances were of command over the Communists' troops. Whatever his expectations, it now seems evident that Yenan had no intention during the summer of 1944 of giving Stilwell immediate and unconditional authority over its forces.

The pair of personal representatives of the president, Hurley and Nelson, breezed into Chungking on September 6, 1944. During the Hurley-Nelson stopover at Moscow, Molotov had revealed to them on August 31 that some impoverished Chinese called themselves Communists, but they had no relation whatever to communism. Nor should the Soviet Government be blamed for or associated with these elements. The Soviet people, Molotov continued, would be very glad if the United States would help the Chinese economically and militarily, and toward unification. In addition, the Soviet Government would welcome the United States' taking a lead in Chinese affairs, politically, militarily, and economically.

Brimming with optimism and self-confidence, and favorably inclined toward Stilwell, with whom he had established a salty rapport, Hurley sat down on September 7 at his first conference with the Generalissimo. He radioed to the president what had transpired: Chiang said that he was prepared to give Stilwell actual command of all forces and his complete confidence. But, Hurley reported, "we have not yet ironed out any of the details, some of which will undoubtedly be difficult to solve." Chiang "seemed deeply concerned about the so-called Communist troops in China." Hurley thereupon sought to assuage the Generalissimo's fears.

I was able to report to him that Molotov had said that Russia is not giving support to the so-called Communistic organization in China. In fact, Molotov states that the so-called Communists of China are not Communists at all. We were able to report also that Molotov stated that Russia desires more cordial relations with China; notwithstanding all this the Generalissimo still seems skeptical regarding the Communists and stated definitely that any so-called Communist troops serving under General Stilwell would have to submit definitely to the control of the Generalissimo and the National Military Council.

Concluding his message to the president, Hurley declared: "There is a good prospect for unification of command in China and the Generalissimo shows a definite tendency to comply with your wishes."

Later, in a letter to Hull, Gauss touched on what Hurley had vouchsafed to him of the personal representative's initial efforts at mediation between Chiang and Stilwell. The ambassador's understated reaction was, "I do not share General Hurley's optimism." And he quoted a Chinese friend, "it is not so difficult to arrive at understandings but exceedingly difficult to implement them."

Being of an expansive nature, Hurley was not content to deal only with those matters defined by the president as his mission—to harmonize Chiang-Stilwell relations and facilitate Stilwell's exercise of command. Alone, these two items of business were of formidable complexity and delicacy. But emboldened by ignorance of China, Hurley presented on September 12 to the Generalissimo a ten-point agenda, only the last four topics of which bore directly upon Stilwell's powers, including the control of lend-lease. The first six items were:

1. The paramount objective of Chinese-American collaboration is to bring about the unification of all military forces in China for the immediate defeat of Japan and the liberation of China.

2. Cooperating with China in bringing about closer relations and harmony with Russia and Britain for the support of the Chinese objectives.

3. The unification of all military forces under the command of the Generalissimo.

4. The marshaling of all resources in China for war purposes.

5. The support of efforts of Generalissimo for political unification of China on a democratic basis.

6. Submission of present and postwar economic plans for China.

This was a prospectus not for reform but for transformation of China. Soong, who was present at the conference, promptly objected to the phrase in item 5, "on a democratic basis," which was duly eliminated. Chiang disposed of the first six items by accepting them as "objectives." Stilwell's powers were another matter; they should be defined by international agreement.

Stilwell was not waiting for the terms of an international agreement. He was already sketching out for himself what he would initially do as a commander of China's field forces, and for Hurley, a draft of what the commander's powers should be. His jottings to himself indicated that, among other things, he hoped to order counterattacks in Central and North China, to establish new troop training programs, to take over provincial troops, and, after conferring with the Communists, to supply them by air from Chengtu. These were bold expectations. Stilwell's outline of his powers, drafted for Hurley's information, was correspondingly sweeping.

More in pursuit of his instructions to facilitate Stilwell's command than of those enjoining him to promote harmony, Hurley laid before the Generalissimo in mid-September two documents. One was a suggested order to be issued by Chiang appointing Stilwell as Field Commander of Ground and Air Forces. The proposed order authorized Stilwell to "reward and punish, to appoint and relieve." It also empowered him "to issue orders for the operations of the ground and air forces."

The second document was a draft directive from Chiang to Stilwell. The American field commander was instructed to "proceed at once with the reorganization and relocation of ground and air forces." In so doing he was authorized to activate and equip new units, to disband old units, and to transfer individuals and units from one command to another without regard to existing jurisdictions. Finally, Stilwell was directed to improve the living conditions of the troops and to requisition supplies, for which receipts would be given, for redemption by the government.

Hurley's two documents, reflecting Stilwell's wishes, bespoke reform with a vengeance. To put them into effect would bring down Chiang's rickety power structure. Even the proposal to better the lot of the troops, in a military system that habitually and deliberately underfed, exploited, abused, and profited from its soldiery, would be rejected by most officers above company grade and, if their objections were overridden, would swamp the inflation-logged economy. Nor could the Chinese treasury afford to pay for supplies requisitioned by army units in the localities where they were garrisoned or deployed.

Hurley would have been aghast had he understood the implications of what he was asking of the Generalissimo. But he had only the sketchiest knowledge of China and what he was proposing, in American terms, seemed to be little more than a wholesome job of housecleaning in the interests of military efficiency and getting on with the war. Stilwell, however, could not have been unaware of the significance of the proposals to Chiang. His attitude was that he had been asked to take on the responsibilities of command and if he was to fulfill those duties, by God, he had to have the authority to do so.

The abolitionist streak in him was ascendant. Come hell or high water, he would abolish the corruption and incompetence that enslaved the soldiery. Not all of it, of course, for there was too much foulness for any one man to cleanse in so short a time. But enough of it to perhaps set the enemy back on his heels. Even for that he needed full power, though he probably would not need to draw upon all of it.

In this mood Stilwell flew to Kweilin for a quick look at the shambles on the South China front and to order the demolition of air bases in the path of the Japanese offensive. His visit was strictly military. He did not concern himself with the separatist movement in South China, which Gauss then thought might "set up some sort of autonomous organization" behind the Japanese lines. Returning to Chungking, Stilwell was on September 15 urgently summoned by the Generalissimo. Chiang was in a panic over the Salween front. He wanted to withdraw his expeditionary force across the gorge and, in effect, abandon the attempt to open the supply line from India.

Furious, Stilwell immediately reported to Marshall this quailing development and the tale of Chiang's bungling interventions in the South China fiasco. He concluded his radiogram with:

I am now convinced that he [Chiang] regards the South China catastrophe as of little moment, believing that the Japs will not bother him further in that area, and that he imagines he can get behind the Salween and there wait in safety for the U.S. to finish the war. Our conferences on command are dragging, and tomorrow we are going to try some plain talk with T. V. Soong, in the hope of getting to the Gmo some faint glimmer of the consequences of further delay and inaction.

In his diary entry for September 16, before summing up his plain talk with Soong, Stilwell recorded an exchange between Hurley and Soong on lend-lease negotiations.

The G-mo insists on control of Lend-Lease. . . . T. V. says we must remember the "dignity" of a great nation, which would be "affronted" if I controlled the distribution. Pat [Hurley] told him "Horsefeathers." "Remember, Dr. Soong, that is our property. We made it and we own it, and we can give it to whom we please." . . . Pat said there were one hundred and thirty million Americans whose dignity also entered the case. . . . (If the G-mo controls distribution, I am sunk. The Reds will get nothing. Only the G-mo's henchmen will be supplied, and my troops [trained by Stilwell] will suck the hind tit).

Accompanied by Hurley and Sultan, Stilwell met with Soong on September 16. He took with him a memorandum of what he would and did say to the foreign minister. On the subject of the overall or field commander he warned:

I hope that the Generalissimo will realize that I do not seek the job; I have been delayed, ignored, doublecrossed, and kicked around for two and a half years in my attempt to show the Chinese how they can hold up their heads and regain their self-respect. I have looked forward for forty-four years to getting a chance to command American troops, and I could have had it if I had not been a real friend of China and the Chinese people. I am still ready to do anything I can, but only under conditions that make a solution possible.

The central issue in the conference was "nothing less than full power" for Stilwell, as was laid down in the two Hurley proposals, and "The Generalissimo must refrain from any interference in operation." Soong was shaken by the American requirements. He disclosed what he said the Generalissimo had in mind. This would amount to making the commander, as Stilwell later put it, "an overall stooge." Stilwell said that if he could not have authority, he could not accept responsibility. "And the Gmo would have to keep his fingers out of the pie. We gave TV quite a shock."

With the reluctance of Chiang's subordinates to bear bad tidings to their testy chief, it is not certain that Soong transmitted the full voltage of his shock. Whether he did or not, the Generalissimo could hardly have been complacent over the American pressures on him. He had asked Roosevelt for a personal representative to "adjust the relations between me and General Stilwell." In just over a week of negotiating, the Generalissimo found himself horns locked with Stilwell, and Hurley, the conciliator, backing his adversary.

Stilwell's report of current conditions in China, forwarded to Marshall at Quebec, arrived as the Octagon Conference decided that the prospects for a vigorous offensive in Burma were promising. News of the Generalissimo's latest antics therefore created a particularly deplorable impression. Marshall and the president reacted immediately and on September 16 dispatched a caustic message from Roosevelt to Chiang.

"My Chiefs of Staff and I," the president stated, "are convinced that you are faced in the near future with the disaster I have feared." Roosevelt then took Chiang to task for failing to reinforce and support his Salween front and threatening to withdraw across the river. If he did not correct these deficiencies, "we will lose all chance of opening land communications with China and immediately jeopardize the air route over the Hump. For this you must yourself be prepared to accept the consequences and assume the personal responsibility."

"I have urged time and again in recent months that you take drastic action," the president continued. "Now, when you have not yet placed General Stilwell in command of all forces in China, we are faced with the loss of a critical area in east China." In the final paragraph Roosevelt said, "I am certain that the only thing you can do now . . . is to reinforce your Salween armies immediately and press their offensive, while at once placing General Stilwell in unrestricted command of all your forces."

Although Hurley was in Chungking as the president's personal representative, the War Department did not relay the message to him for delivery to the Generalissimo. The radio went, as had previous presidential communications to Chiang, with no indication of deviation from the procedure ordered by Roosevelt after he discovered in May that Hearn had been dropping off his messages to one or another of the Soong sisters for presentations to the Generalissimo—that is, the senior officer present was to hand the communication to Chiang. In these circumstances it was correct that Stilwell should act as the messenger, which he did.

It would have been more politic had Hurley delivered the message, which Stilwell characterized as "hot as a firecracker." The personal representative might have, although this cannot be said with assurance because of Hurley's unpredictable temperament, muffled the explosion a little by a discreet and sympathetic presentation. But this would not have altered the acrid coercion of Roosevelt's intervention.

As bearer of the presidential missive no one, unless it had been Mao Tsetung, could have been more repellent to the Generalissimo than was Stilwell. And the setting of the Chiang-Stilwell encounter could hardly have been more calculated to humiliate the Generalissimo. For Stilwell arrived in the midst of a conference between Hurley and Chiang, attended also by Soong and senior officers of the Chinese high command. Before Chiang's scheming subordinates, Stilwell "handed it to him." The Generalissimo read the attached Chinese translation, and (continuing Stilwell's record made that evening): "The harpoon hit him right in the solar plexus, but, although he turned green, he never batted an eye. He just turned to me and said: 'I understand.' . . . I got out promptly and came home."

Stilwell was elated. The president was aggressively supporting him. And what was more, he, Stilwell, had paid back in kind what he had long endured from the Generalissimo—loss of face. He did not seem to care, or perhaps even recognize, that, having inflicted so flamboyant a loss of face on Chiang, the Generalissimo's enmity toward him was now wholly vindictive. Nor did he seem to realize that while the strong might be able to prevent the weak from acting, inducing the weak to act was quite another matter.

Stilwell and others of us had miscalculated the power of the United States to impel the wasted regime of Chiang Kai-shek to perform as ordered by Washington. Here the president had berated and threatened the Generalissimo, attempting to goad him to action. And if Chiang did not wish to act, as he did not, all he had to do was stall and go limp, which he did. The only positive action to which the Generalissimo was now committed with passion was to rid himself of the outrageous Stilwell.

CHAPTER *31*

The Final Squandering of Stilwell

SERVICE recommended to Stilwell, in a report from Yenan dated August 29, "the extension of American military aid to the Chinese Communist armies." Among the arguments that he advanced in support of supplying and training the sparsely armed Communists was that they would thereby be enabled to expand their guerrilla actions against the Japanese in North and Central China. As they wanted light weapons, military aid to them would be comparatively economical. Anticipating obstinate Kuomintang objections to arming the Communists, Service said, "We must decide whether the gains we can reasonably expect from aiding the Communists will justify the overcoming—or disregarding—of this Kuomintang opposition."

I do not know whether Stilwell saw this report, or if he did, when he did. A copy went to Gauss, who nearly a month later, observed to the Department of State, "It appears that we are to be faced inevitably with the problem of determining whether the Chinese Communists are to be supplied with American arms and equipment in the struggle against Japan." The ambassador weighed the problem in the context of Government-Communist relations, in the course of which he commented:

An attempt to supply the Chinese Communists with American arms and equipment without first obtaining the sanction of the Kuomintang government in Chungking—which we have in the past and continue to recognize as the Government of China—would produce serious repercussions, if indeed it did not bring about the collapse of the Chiang Kai-shek regime. On the other hand, our compliance with Kuomintang wishes not to supply the Chinese Communists . . . might be expected to hamper the conduct of military operations against the Japanese and perhaps prolong the war.

This was a gnawing dilemma. The happy solution longed for by Americans dealing with China was a Kuomintang-Communist reconciliation. Gauss presented it as a possibility. But he was much too hardheaded to repose his faith in it. He saw as "the only alternative . . . a continued and progressive distintegration . . . followed perhaps by chaos and a consequent grave impediment of the prosecution of the war against Japan." Gauss did not, however, answer the question—should the United States arm the Communists if there were no reconciliation?

Unbeknown to Service at the time he recommended arming the Communists, the War Department was seriously considering much the same thing. By September 4 it had informed Stilwell that it anticipated the problem of administering lend-lease to the Chinese forces, including the Communists. While Stilwell wanted to supply the underequipped Communists, he indicated to Hurley on September 13 that the assignment of materiel should be to "the first two groups of thirty divisions each"—sixty of the ninety Nationalist divisions that he had so long sought to equip and train. This would indefinitely delay supplies for the Communists. Nevertheless, on the same day Stilwell received the Chungking representatives of the Communists and said to them that he would visit Yenan.

Ten days later, after Stilwell had handed Chiang the "hot as a firecracker" message from Roosevelt, General Ho suggested to Stilwell that perhaps the Generalissimo was disgruntled because he did not have control of lend-lease. Hoping to break the deadlock with Chiang, Stilwell thereupon worked up an agenda for renewed talks with the Generalissimo, the salient points of which were:

1. That I [Stilwell] be sent to Yenan to make the following propositions to the Reds:
   a. The Reds to acknowledge the supreme authority of the GMO, and to accept command through me.
   b. The Red Forces to be employed north of the Yellow River, out of contact with the Central Government Troops.
   c. Equipment and ammunition to be furnished five divisions with supporting artillery.
   d. Keep those Red Divisions at full strength.
   e. Both the KMT and the Reds to drop discussion of political matters until the Japanese are beaten.

2. That lend-lease materials (military) be turned over to the GMO on delivery in China for distribution, with the understanding that:
   a. The "X" and "Y" Forces [India-Burma and Yunnan armies] have first priority.
   b. That the remainder of the first thirty divisions, the Reds, and the Kweiyang Force (to be formed) have equal priority.
   c. That no other units be equipped until after these units are fully outfitted. This includes maintenance.

3. That the command question be settled by the publication of orders as suggested by General Hurley.

The War Department had considered supplying the Communists in the context of all Chinese forces being under Stilwell's command and, implicitly, with the Generalissimo's approval. Stilwell's proposed agenda clarified and went beyond this position. He would ask the Communists to acknowledge Chiang's authority, he would turn over lend-lease distribution to the Generalissimo, but then he would expect Chiang to arm his enemies. To be sure, only five Communist divisions would be supplied as against sixty Nationalist divisions. Still, it was a proposition that would be wholly unacceptable to the Generalissimo.

By this time Hurley's self-confidence was dented, even though he had sought to reasure the president by repeating his quotations from Commissar Molotov and asserting that "while the situation is difficult a harmonious solution is possible." Consequently, Hurley welcomed Stilwell's proposed agenda as the solution of the impasse with Chiang. Using one of his favorite expressions to describe an event of conclusive effect, he exclaimed, "This will knock the persimmons off the tree."

The Generalissimo, however, remained unshaken when Hurley called on him on September 24. Chiang had devised a formula of his own—one demanding Stilwell's recall. This did knock the persimmons off the tree.

Stilwell had insulted him, the Generalissimo told Hurley. By handing him the president's message, Stilwell had made him a subordinate to Stilwell. Therefore their relationship was impossible. And were Stilwell made field commander, Chiang feared that his army would mutiny.

Backing up his oral rejection of Stilwell, the Generalissimo gave Hurley an *aide-mémoire*. The personal representative read it, considered that its language would be offensive to the president, and asked that it be rewritten. The revised version, accepted by Hurley, accused Stilwell of having no intention of cooperating with Chiang, believing that he was being appointed to command the Generalissimo, and being unfit for the duties envisaged. Were Chiang to appoint him, "I would knowingly court inevitable disaster." The Generalissimo asserted that he would, however, accept any qualified American officer as field commander.

Downcast by his failure to conjure harmony, Hurley transmitted the revised document to the president on September 25. Stating what was evident, he advised Roosevelt that Chiang and Stilwell were incompatible. Stilwell was incensed by Chiang's charges and told Marshall so. By now he was also mistrustful of Hurley.

Although the Generalissimo had him on the ropes, Stilwell, unlike Hurley, was still struggling to gain the initiative. From his contacts in the high command, Stilwell learned that maybe the root of the Generalissimo's displeasure was Stilwell's wish to arm the Communists. It was only a guess, as Chiang was not telling his senior officers what he was up to and was working only with Soong. The worried Stilwell grasped at this plausible surmise and in writing, on September 28, informed Ho Ying-ch'in, the war minister and chief of staff, that: (1) The suggestion for using the Communist troops was raised because it seemed advisable to make use of any and all military assets in this crisis and that Stilwell was not insisting on the use of the Communists as a condition for agreement, and (2) The matter of using the Communists can be dropped, and we can proceed advantageously with our other plans.

Whereupon Stilwell, who with all of his feuding was of an affirmative nature, outlined a training and equipment program for Nationalist troops. "This plan can be started at once . . . give us the security we want . . . [and] the nucleus of a force sufficient to take the offensive within six months." Stilwell had yielded on American control of lend-lease; now he backed away from using the Communists—and by that token, arming them. But the accommodation he sought with the Generalissimo was not forthcoming. Chiang and Soong were nervously waiting to learn whether Roosevelt would recall Stilwell.

A telegram to the Generalissimo from Kung, who was acting as Chiang's personal representative at Washington, broke the stalemate. Soong passed on to Hurley on October 1 Kung's report of an encounter with Hopkins at a dinner party. In the course of conversation, the casual Hopkins, according to the Soong-Kung account, observed that, as "the sovereign right of China" was involved in the matter, "the president intended to comply with the Generalissimo's request for the recall of General Stilwell."

This was enough for Chiang. The next morning he met with his politburo, the Standing Committee of the Central Executive Committee of the Kuomintang. He was in an agitated frame of mind, pounded the table and ranted that Stilwell "must go," that all lend-lease must come to him, and that if there were to be an American commander of all forces in China, he must have contact with only those put at his disposal by the Generalissimo. The Americans were trying to infringe on China's sovereignty, Chiang declaimed. "This is a new form of imperialism."

As the Generalissimo warmed to his subject he accused Stilwell of boasting that, if he went to Yenan, he would be able immediately to get the cooperation of the Red Army. "That is nonsense . . . there can be no compromise with the Communists." And as a parting word of assurance, "Do not be afraid if the Americans will not do as I want them to do; we can get along without them." In so saying, Chiang reciprocated the sentiments of the War Department about the Chinese—but not those of Roosevelt, who could not in his plans for peace get along without Chiang.

The president finally, on October 5, radioed the Generalissimo. He agreed to relieve Stilwell as chief of staff and as distributor of lend-lease supplies. But he wanted the general kept as commander on the fighting fronts of Yunnan and Burma.

Chiang quickly retorted on October 10 that he stood on his original request that Stilwell be relieved. The general was not qualified and not deserving of his confidence. Once Stilwell was replaced, "the policies which you advocate will then be executed without delay."

Accompanying the Generalissimo's message was an *aide-mémoire* addressed to Hurley but directed at the president. It was a tedious, distorted, and bad-tempered survey of Stilwell's alleged shortcomings as a strategist. Coming from Chiang, with his wartime military record of crashing incompetence, the critique was ludicrous.

Hurley had spent the weekend cloistered with Chiang and Soong at the Generalissimo's residence as they composed the direct and indirect messages to the president. Emerging from this immersion, the personal representative offered his counsel to the president. He reminded Roosevelt that "you had decided to sustain the leadership of Chiang Kai-shek." Then, with all due deliberation— "cutting my throat with a dull knife," as Stilwell described the message—Hurley continued:

In studying the situation here I am convinced that there is no Chinese leader available who offers as good a basis of cooperation with you as Chiang Kai-shek. There is no other Chinese known to me who possesses as many of the elements of leadership as Chiang Kai-shek. Chiang Kai-shek and Stilwell are fundamentally incompatible. Today you are confronted by a choice between Chiang Kai-shek and Stilwell. There is no other issue between you and Chiang Kai-shek. Chiang Kai-shek has agreed to every request, every suggestion made by you except the Stilwell appointment.

Chiang and Soong had been correspondingly impressed by Hurley's attributes. So Soong sent through Hopkins a request from the Generalissimo to the President asking that Hurley's assignment be on a more permanent basis. "I am relying upon him for assistance in negotiation with the Chinese Communists," Chiang confided. "It is my purpose to increase the Communist troops in the regular forces of the National Army," he volunteered. "General Hurley has my complete confidence. Because of his rare knowledge of human nature, and his approach to the problem, he seems to get on well with the Communist leaders."

On October 17 I arrived at Chungking. Stilwell filled me in on the crisis. Two days later I wrote in a letter to my wife: "My plans for the immediate and distant future remain altogether nebulous. . . . I haven't yet asked my boss about my fate because there are bigger issues afloat. This evening I am seeing Hurley. I shall attempt to persuade him to take himself and me to Yenan.

"Hurley is unhappy, I think. If he isn't he should be. You know that his job entailed the maintenance of harmony. He has not been successful. A crisis of considerable proportions has arisen. It is now commonly known among informed Chinese . . . that he [Chiang] has said that JWS must be replaced, anybody else will do, just so long as it is somebody else. The rest of what I know is not common knowledge so must be withheld . . .

"This locking of horns has created quite a mess. JWS is holding up very well . . . I have reason to believe that I am on a Chinese list of those tarred with the JWS brush and that if they can arrange it I go with him—if he goes. Which is all right by me. New horizons."

My next letter began: "Ten minutes after pouching a letter to you . . . saying that I didn't think the issue would be joined until after the elections, I got the news that the Old Man had been told that he was out. So that's that."

When I saw him, Stilwell was grim and matter of fact. "What the hell," he said, "you live only once and you have to live as you believe."

The immediate problem was to get his side of the story to the American public, for obviously the firing of an American theater commander by one of the Big Four was bound to create something of a sensation. So Theodore H. White, then *Time* correspondent, and Brooks Atkinson, the drama critic covering another kind of theater for the *New York Times,* were invited to Stilwell's residence where the general briefed them. They were plainly moved by the denouement that was unfolded before them, for they, like virtually all of the press corps, had come to regard the general with affection.

In his October 18 communication to Chiang, Roosevelt was cool and businesslike. Stilwell was being recalled immediately. CBI was to be split into two theaters, India-Burma under Sultan, China under Wedemeyer. No American would assume responsibility in a command position for the operation of Chinese forces in China. Wedemeyer's responsibilities would be limited to acting as the Generalissimo's chief of staff and to command of American forces in China, including Chennault and his Fourteenth Air Force.

Chiang had won. Stilwell had lost. And he had lost because Roosevelt had let him down. It was in these intensely personal and contentious terms that those of us at Stilwell's headquarters thought and spoke.

Even in Washington, remote from the venomous confrontation and in the midst of a multitude of other problems, some of this feeling existed. As Roosevelt moved in early October to recall Stilwell, the judicious Stimson considered that a grave injustice was in the making, recorded his belief in "Stilwell's courage and sagacity," and noted that "Marshall today said that if we had to remove Stilwell he would not allow another American general to be placed in the position of chief of staff and commander of the Chinese armies, for it was so evident that no American would be loyally supported."

The simple fact was that Roosevelt had no choice in the matter. Even if he had wanted to do so, Roosevelt could not have forced Stilwell upon Chiang. For Chiang had demanded Stilwell's recall on the only grounds allowing of no debate —that of his personal privilege as chief of state. The president could not, in those circumstances, loyally support Stilwell against the Generalissimo. The least damaging move that he could make was to withdraw the general.

We were wrong to have blamed Roosevelt for the outcome of the Chiang-Stilwell imbroglio. In seeking the broader cause rather than an individual culprit, the command crisis over Stilwell may be said to have been the inevitable result of two illusions. One was an American romantic image of China. The second was an assumption that the United States could pretty much work its will on China.

Bathed in sentimentality about China, and in self-reproach for not having gone to China's rescue when it was first invaded (as Stimson had urged in 1931), the American public and government after Pearl Harbor looked upon the Chinese as needing only American assistance to launch a spirited counteroffensive. Americans attributed to the Chinese the impatient pugnacity then animating themselves. In reality, the war against "the common enemy" was a side issue for Chiang and his regime. His main concern was to conserve such strength as he had, add to it from American bounty, and prepare for civil war against the Communists.

General Magruder in his 1942 reports from Chungking tried to dispel the illusion of Chiang rampant and tugging at the leash. And Churchill, who in 1942 "had found the extraordinary significance of China in American minds, even at the top, strangely out of proportion," attempted to persuade Roosevelt to a more realistic view. But it was all to no avail.

The second illusion, that the United States could, to a significant degree, shape as it wished the course of events in China, was related to the first. Mistakenly assuming an identity of intent and dynamism, Americans likewise assumed in early 1942 that the Chinese would, in a spirit of cooperation and eagerness to learn, welcome tutelage, even though by a nation which had until then undergone nothing but humiliation in fighting the Japanese. Within the government it was realized that intrusion of American authority into Chinese internal affairs could be an exceedingly touchy business with a people who, for good reason, were hypersensitive about foreign intervention. But this was slighted because, after all, we were allies and the American Government could therefore take liberties with a wartime partner which in other circumstances would be impermissible. Although Stalin quickly disposed of this assumption with regard to the Soviet Union, Washington persisted in it toward China.

In some respects American-Chinese relations in 1941 were reminiscent of the nineteenth century. It was the same old story of the importunate West and the obdurate East. The era of forcing China open to trade, of dollar and gunboat diplomacy, had passed. But the missionary compulsion to persuade the Chinese of the error of their ways and to walk the straight and narrow path persisted. In World War II the missionary dedication had spread to political and military proselytization. The approach was still highminded, full of abstract love and concern for the Chinese, and unconsciously self-righteous.

Chiang reacted to this suffocating attention much as had the Manchu Court —seeming compliance accompanied by stubborn evasion. He was, with all of his revolutionary pretentions and conversion to Methodism, a traditional Chinese who detested barbarians and wanted to be left alone.

Because Americans in 1942 imagined China as a fiercely fighting ally and Chiang as a bellicose comrade-in-arms eager for the touch of the guiding American hand, the American government believed that only a dynamic, fighting general would do as the principal military representative in Chungking. This was a grievous misapprehension. What was needed was an inert, ceremonious old general, laden with honors, whose mission would have been to maintain a languid liaison between the Chinese high command and the War Department.

Having said this, it is only fair to sketch a scenario of what might have developed had Washington adopted an approach to China radically different from that actually chosen. The American government would have recognized that China had fought alone against Japan, off and on, for a decade and that Chiang had thereby won the right to turn his attention to internal matters of more pressing concern to him. The liaison officer's directive would have forbidden him to broach the subject of the war against Japan to the Chinese, unless instructed to do so by the War Department. Contact with the Generalissimo would have been through the ambassador. In sum, official American relations with China would have resembled those with the Soviet Union, in which Harriman was in practice the personal representative of the president, and the chief of military mission functioned in a subordinate liaison capacity.

Such an arrangement would have avoided the inflamatory issues of an American chief of staff to the Generalissimo and American command over Chinese troops, both of which concepts were unworkable. Thus the senior American military man in China would have been spared operational responsibilities, frustrating when his authority was undercut and circumscribed, and stultifying when it was withheld.

As China would not have been fancied a significant factor in the war against Japan, there would have been no need for a directive to any American general to increase the effectiveness of American aid and to assist in improving the combat efficiency of Chinese forces. Token lend-lease equipment could have been supplied the Generalissimo by air—there would have been no need for opening land communications across North Burma. Chennault could have been permitted to continue with his American Volunteer Group, as he wanted to do, and supported by the War Department to the degree that he could provide air defense to West China and undertake limited offensive action, short of stinging the Japanese to retaliate on the scale of ICHIGO.

With regard to India and Burma, the 1942 campaign in Burma would have been better left to the British and Chinese to work out between themselves, even if it might have meant a swifter Japanese conquest of the colony. As it became available, American air power would have been, as it was, assigned to the defense of India. The overextended Japanese salient in Burma could have been, as Churchill wished, left to wither. The decisive advances of Nimitz and Mac-Arthur, far to the east, would have eventually forced the Japanese either to pull out or be cut off.

With all of the benefits of reasoning after the event, this was the way it might better have been. But it was not; not simply because of Roosevelt, Stimson, Marshall, and Stilwell. The American people and government, with their fiery vision of Chiang and China, expected aggressive, can-do American military leadership in China. They got it in Stilwell, probably the fightingest general, the most conscience-ridden, duty-driven officer in the United States Army. Off he was sent on a self-defeating mission.

The pity of it all was the waste. Deplorable enough was the grinding misuse of a man of vibrant force and dedicated spirit. Transcending the waste of Stilwell was the squandering of men, money, and things in the American wartime effort for China. This futile, and ultimately self-destructive, paying-out of American resources was not unique in American relations with East Asia. Before China was the Philippines. After China was Indochina.

CHAPTER *32*

Dixie

THE DAY AFTER Stilwell's recall I wrote to Charles E. Bohlen, the principal Soviet specialist at the department, telling him that I would like to be transferred to the embassy at Moscow.

My plan was, while awaiting a decision, to go to Yenan to get a firsthand impression of the Chinese Communists. Then if Wedemeyer, who would not arrive in Chungking until the end of October, wished to take me over from Stilwell, well and good. If not, Sultan wanted me at New Delhi, headquarters of his new India-Burma Theater. In either case, I preferred only a brief assignment, as I hoped to get to Moscow before mid-1945, in time to observe the entry of the Soviet Union into the war against Japan and the workings of international communism in the subsequent civil war in China.

Gauss had never reconciled himself to my detail to Stilwell, nor to my having arranged for the assignment of three other Foreign Service officers to the general. Because of my strained relations with the ambassador I had no desire for an assignment to the embassy at Chungking. Yet, ambivalently, I respected and was fond of Gauss.

He had been treated more shabbily by Washington than had Stilwell. The general, after all, had received the stalwart support of Marshall and Stimson. Gauss had the creaky backing of the irrelevant Hull. While Roosevelt finally came to champion Stilwell, he behaved as if Gauss scarcely existed.

What was worse, the president had dispatched a preposterous series of plenipotentiaries to China—Currie, Willkie, Wallace, Nelson, and Hurley—undermining the ambassador's position as the only personal representative of the president. These vagrant Pooh Bahs, after conniving with the Chinese, returned to Washington to disparage Gauss and urge his removal. Hurley was an exception in that he did not go back to Washington while Gauss was ambassador, although he had already pulled strings to succeed him.

In contrast, Gauss was imbued with a selfless sense of duty. Following Wallace's barnstorming through Chungking, the ambassador advised Hull that "in connection with Chiang's desire for appointment of a personal representative of the president . . . if it is desired I am of course prepared without question to step aside as ambassador to China in the interest of setting up here an effective coordination and direction of our vital diplomatic and military activities in this country." Rather than replacing Gauss, the president sent others to duplicate an existing function, thereby deranging matters.

As Gauss had endured all that in self-respect he could take, he resigned and left Chungking on November 14. Six months later he retired from the Foreign Service.

Like Stilwell, Gauss was a Yankee puritan, a man of integrity, resolution, and fidelity. He knew too much about China for the liking of the Chiang-Soong dynasty and could not bring himself to the adulation that the Generalissimo and Madame Chiang expected of Americans. His reporting on China, supported by an outstandingly able staff, was dispassionate, balanced, and, viewed in retrospect, perceptive.

When Hurley was first being considered as the mediator between Stilwell and Chiang, the under secretary of state reported to Hull on August 3 that Hurley had "appealed to me" (Stettinius) to present to Hull the possibility of Hurley's being made ambassador to China.

Hurley's inclinations were less ambassadorial than viceregal. Having laid out in his ten-point agenda on September 12 a program for making over China, he brashly moved to dispose of the seething conflict between the Kuomintang and the Communists, even as he negotiated to harmonize relations between Chiang and Stilwell. At the height of the command crisis, while conjuring up "the verdict of history" as one of many reasons for achieving harmony through firing Stilwell, Hurley reassured the president that "I have the so-called Communist question under discussion at the present time and am satisfied that we will arrive at a solution of that problem."

Having helped Chiang to ease Stilwell out of Chungking, Hurley informed Roosevelt on October 23 that, "With the advice and consent of the Gissimo we are having conferences with the leaders of the Communist Party and the Communist troops." This senatorial statement requires clarification. The use of "we," to which Hurley had become partial, did not refer in this case to Chiang and himself. It was a stylistic affectation that he used interchangeably with the first person singular. Nor were his conferences with Mao Tse-tung and Chu Teh; they were with the Party's representatives in Chungking.

Freed of the burden of reconciling Chiang and Stilwell, Hurley was able to devote all of his talents to reconciling Chiang and Mao. In this self-imposed undertaking he had the benefit of Chiang's and Soong's solicitous advice. Not since he had been in Washington had Soong had so impressionable an American to work on. It is no wonder that Soong had passed to his old friend Hopkins the Generalissimo's request to the president for Hurley's "more permanent" assignment so that he could help out in negotiations with the Communists. But it was hardly Soong's wish that Hurley should establish independent contacts with Mao.

Enroute to Dixie [Communist area]
October 22, 1944

Dear General Hurley—

I am very sorry to have gotten away without seeing you and at least saying goodbye. I called your house this morning and was told that you were away over the week-end. . . .

In view of the important, if not decisive, role which these people up north are going to play in China's future, I hope that you wll see your way clear to come up for face-to-face talks with their leaders. I think the president should have a fully rounded picture of the major personalities in China. If the Communist leaders are phonies and small time operators, the president should know it; if they've got what it takes, he should know it. And you're the one to make the estimate for him.

I'll have the welcome mat out.

John Davies

We were a mixed group traveling to Yenan on the headquarters' C-47, piloted by Captain Jack Champion. There were my colleague, John K. Emmerson; Theodore H. White of *Time*; Koji Ariyoshi, a nisei sergeant assigned to OWI; and I, going for a stay of a fortnight or more. With us were a half dozen or so officers, headed by Brigadier General Malcom F. Lindsey, on a sight-seeing tour of the next best thing to Lhasa, and due to return the next day with the aircraft. The quotations that follow are from a journal I kept of this visit to Yenan.

"October 22, 1944   It was necessary to slosh through mud and slime walking from #6 officers quarters at Chungking to the main gate of the headquarters. It was a gray drizzly morning. The road to the airfield was muddy. So was the airfield. We sloshed around loading while a group of Chinese officials in Chungshan [Kuomintang] uniforms stood nearby on the edge of the field observing everything that went on.

"Champ took off, hurtling away from the precipice which drops into the river, skimming and skidding over roofs and around hill edges. We passed over Sian, dun, geometrical and not as big as I had remembered it. Then as we proceeded north of the Wei River we began to eye the horizon surreptitiously for Zeros.

"The topography was loess canyons and plateaus. Champ let us down until we were one hundred or so feet above the plateaus, whereupon we began wheeling around the crests of several plateau islands preparatory to diving into the canyon into whose walls are dug the caves which constitute the town of Yenan. Down we swooshed into the canyon and began to follow its winding course. On both sides stood people at the mouths of their caves waving and staring. We went still lower, flew over the bombed-out ruins of the original town, and then buzzed the crowd surrounding the airfield and the field itself. Champ then turned the transport around in the confines of the canyon as if the ship were a fighter—to the alarm of most of us—and buzzed the field once. Then he went away. Back down the canyon. By the time we had turned around and come back, again flicking off bystanders' hats with our wing tips, the field was cleared and we came in for a humdrum three point landing.

"One of the first things I saw out of the window as we taxied to a stop was Jack [Service] sprinting around a cabbage patch in excellent 440 style to be first at the door of the plane. When all of the colonels and Atlantic City weekenders began piling out, he remarked to me, 'Why didn't you bring some sulfa drugs instead of all this horseflesh?' I took him aside by the tail of the plane and told him what had happened to the Old Man. He said bitterly, 'It was worse then than I thought.' I told him that he was going home. He accepted the news without great enthusiasm.

"Yeh Chien-ying, [chief of staff], Po Ku [Politburo member in charge of propaganda], and a large company of lesser luminaries were on hand to extend a welcome. Yeh, in his brindle, shapeless homespun, did not make initially a strong impression, excepting for his slightly occidentalized features. Ramshackle trucks driven by Eighth Route Army [preunited front designation of Eighteenth Group Army] soldiers backed up expertly to the plane and were loaded. There were pictures being snapped by miniature photographers dressed in the sloppy, cotton wadded garments which seem to be the commonest form of dress. Present also were three or four female comrades in the same garb and wearing visored caps set at rakish angles. Jack said, 'I defy you to find a woman wearing a skirt; all in pants.'

"We clambered onto the trucks and went lurching down the dusty road, the sun bright overhead, not a cloud in the sky and the tawny loess hills glistening in the sunlight. The people alongside the road were robust, so were the horses, so were the mules, so were the dogs. Our officers exclaimed over the contrast to Chungking.

"The truck forded the river; we passed down a dusty road past a row of twenty or thirty shops and turned in through a gate in a mud wall, guarded by a husky young soldier wearing a long sheepskin coat, and arrived at our Dude Ranch. The quarters provided us were eight rooms in a brick, stone, and adobe house with a narrow front porch and chrysanthemums, tomatoes, and tobacco growing in the front yard. The roof of the house was flat with weeds and bushes growing on it as camouflage. There was a separate little building which served as a dining room. The latrines were, of course, out of doors, foreboding a chill and drafty winter.

"Jack took me in with him and JKE [Emmerson] shared a room with Maj. [Ray] Cromley, an OSS wallah. Our room, like all of the others, had a tunnel-like ceiling. Hence the house is described as a cave-house (most of the population lives in real caves). Our room has a dirt floor, papered windows and door, whitewashed ceilings and walls and is thirty by twelve feet. The beds consist of one or more boards set on sawhorses with a straw tick and cotton-wadded comforters as bedding. The furniture is of wood, sturdily made and finely varnished.

Our illumination at night is a small kerosene lamp and candles. A charcoal brazier provides heat and carbon monoxide. A large earthenware receptacle outside the door is filled with hot water in the morning and from it we get our wash water for the enamel basin in which we perform our ablutions. A captured Japanese sake bottle sits on the window sill holding drinking water.

"Our attendants are Eighth Route Army orderlies whom one does not address as 'boy' but as 'chao tai yuan,' literally 'entertain-the-guests officer.' They unobtrusively and efficiently keep the quarters neat.

"Most of the our first afternoon was spent in conference with Jack and laying lines for our extrication from the debris caused by the Stilwell downfall. Dinner we had as guests of General Chu Teh [commander in chief] and Chou En-lai at the Reception House. It was a big affair with prominent party and army personages, the two Central Government delegates (commonly referred to as spies), foreign correspondents (including two shabby *Tass* [Soviet news agency] representatives), our whole Observer Section (including the sergeants), and various Eighth Route military; Chou was host at our table; Chu Teh at Barrett's [Colonel David D. Barrett, commanding the observers] and Lindsey's table; Po Ku at still another table; and finally there was a fourth table at which sat the Central Government general and colonel plus a nondescript collection of people. The dinner waxed merry with toasts and finger [drinking] games. After standing up to pears and grapes in the reception room, the party broke up—part to go to the movies brought up on the plane; Lindsey and Dave to visit with Chu Teh; Jack, JKE, and I to confer with Chou and Mao Tse-tung.

"Ch'en Chia-k'ang, our tiny long-eyelashed contact man, aide, guide and interpreter, took Jack, JKE, and me from where the truck stopped by the auditorium, back up the side of the canyon a way. Oh yes, Chou was with us. Our way was lighted by kerosene lantern. We passed a guard, went through a gate, and found ourselves on a cleared courtyard effect in front of several cave entries. There seemed to be five or six rooms facing onto the courtyard. This was Chou's house.

"He took us into his study, somewhat smaller than the room Jack and I share. Books were profusely stacked and scattered. A pot of white chrysanthemums stood on the clean brick floor. There was a photograph of Madame Sun and one or two persons I did not recognize. Oh yes, one of Mao. Mrs. Chou entered. She is a homely, friendly, self-assured woman, an intellectual and revolutionary in her own right, a veteran of the Long March. She was dressed in wadded gray trousers and jacket with a white knitted cap on her head. With hospitable warmth she poured out tea into the little cups, passed pleasantries with Jack and me, and then left the men to their talk.

"Mao soon appeared. He is big and plump with a round, bland, almost feminine face. With the direct, friendly manner of the Chinese Communists he strode up to each of us and shook hands. He sat on a little stool on my right; then came Chia-k'ang; then Chou, JKE, Jack, and I completed the circle. I stretched back in a steamer chair. We talked frankly for two or three hours. Chu Teh came in when we were about half way through.

"Those three men sitting around the table, their faces in the half light of a feeble kerosene lamp, showed up in dramatic contrast. Mao with the slow gestures, the big soft frame and face, the master of dialectical argument, the incandescence of personality which develops not in the twinkling of an eye but of easy perception. There is an immense, smooth calm and sureness to him.

"Chou has a leaner facial architecture. And he has three well-defined features: heavy eyebrows, brilliant black eyes, and a full well-formed mouth. His is the personality full of mobility, his anger, his earnestness, and his amusement fully set forth in his face. He is the one of quick, deft gestures. He will make a photogenic foreign minister.

"Old Chu is the shambling, slow, shrewd peasant. His face is flat, broad, and homely as a north China mud wall. Yet it has tremendous character. His frame is square and his gait is a rolling waddle, the product of his heavy width and decades of wearing wads and wads of cotton padded pants. In repose his face is tough. But it breaks into a wide pervasive laugh when he is pleased or entertained. While he looks and acts the primordial peasant, he is quick and sensible of perception and decision. That came out in our talk.

"It was an inconclusive talk in that no definite decisions resulted. But both sides benefitted from the exchange of ideas. I got the impression that here we were dealing with pragmatists—men who knew their limitations as well as their strength. And they were confident—confident and patient. They have waited a long time to get where they are now. They are willing to wait much longer.

"We rode back after midnight standing up in a truck, the cold night air sharp on our faces."

I did not, as I should have done, make a memorandum of the conversation with Mao, Chu, and Chou. My memory of this meeting is that, in the context of sizing up the ruling group at Yenan, I tested Mao on his August statement that American forces should land on the North China coast. What support would the Communists give to such a landing? He replied that they would collaborate fully —provided that the American effort was a major one and included supplying them. But the concept needed further study. Chu and Yeh, the chief of staff, would explore the possibilities with me.

The next morning I dashed off a letter to my wife, to be carried out by the aircraft on its return trip that afternoon. She was tending my New Delhi office as a conscripted volunteer. Briefly I mentioned the conversation of the previous evening, and then added: "The net result of the talk was nothing affirmative. As Jack will tell you, it looks like no dice unless we act on a grand scale. If we don't, they are still calmly confident in their growing strength.

"I see little for me to do here unless we act in such a way as to use this area. The reporting job has been pretty completely done by Jack—and superbly. All that is left are surveys, as Jack says, of such subjects as taxation. The negotiating side is moribund. Therefore, I foresee a short stay at Yenan this trip."

"October 23   Shivery ablutions in the crisp morning air, clumping around in

flying boots. Breakfast with chopsticks—scrambled eggs, fried sliced mantous (steamed unleavened bread), coarse toast, honey, congee, and Nescafe. Pears were the fruit.

"We sat around in the front yard, sunning ourselves as we sweated out letters to catch the plane.

"At ten-thirty we went across the river to headquarters for lunch. Present: most of the visitors, Dave, Jack, JKE, Mao, Chu, Chou, and Yeh Chien-ying. Cowan [one of the visiting officers], chortling over the days when the Communists had a price on his head as a Standard Oil capitalist sucking the blood of the Chinese masses, persuaded the four big Reds to have their picture taken with him in their midst. Which led to an orgy of photography. The dignitaries lent themselves to the festivities with considerable zest.

"After lunch we climbed into a bus with sleazy blue curtains and an orange-tinted rear window and lurched off to the airfield. There was one bodyguard riding with the driver and four in the rear. After all, it was a top classification load.

"The goodbyes were spontaneously warm, everybody seemed to like everybody. The co-mingling of great, near great, and no account was as evident here as everywhere in Yenan. Mao and Chu were in there rubbing shoulders with young students and truck drivers. The plane was loaded down with outgoing luggage plus parcels to friends in Chungking, including bundles of coarse local wool yarn. Everybody stuck around for the takeoff which was magnificent in a cloud of enveloping dust. We watched the ship turn around away down the valley and then fly back over our heads. As it disappeared over the distant loess hills I had a sense of desertion and isolation. We piled into the jeep and rode home.

"It was very quiet in the brilliant early afternoon sunlight of our front yard. JKE, Ariyoshi, and I, who were the newcomers, began to adjust ourselves to our new companions and environment. Colonel Barrett, former asst. military attaché at Chungking and Peiping and recently G-2 of the Z Force, is commanding officer. India-born St. Louis surgeon Major Casberg is the doctor. Major Cromley is the Jap OB [order of battle] man and has a Japanese wife and two children still in Japan. Nomura and Nakamura are two niseis. Remeneh is the radio operator and Cady is the weather man. All four are sergeants, I believe."

On the following day I started my fishing expedition for an estimate from the Communists of their military capabilities. What cooperation could they offer a hypothetical American landing somewhere on the coast between Shanghai and Chefoo on the Shantung Promontory? I had gathered from my Washington visit of the month before that the War Department had slight interest in a landing on the China coast. But I had begun to think of the political by-products of such a landing—an American-Chinese Communist military collaboration that might forestall a Soviet take-over of North China when Russia entered the war against Japan.

"October 24   At the request of General Yeh I went across the river with

[Ch'en] Chia-k'ang and had a long talk with him and Yang (Yang Shang-r'un, Chu Teh's secretary). We talked about the war in Europe and Asia. With an intent look on his face he took detailed notes. He is the most obviously alert, forthright, and outgiving of the big four. A good man for an American to do business with. None of the smirking smoothness of his Chungking counterpart. Straightforward, bluff, and eager to discuss and learn. I suggested specific statements of capabilities. He accepted the idea. When I got back I broached it to Dave and he agreed to take the matter up if we were approached.

Our food is uniformly good. No feast stuff, plain cooking of good quality foodstuffs, in abundance and variety. In eating Chinese food like this day in and day out what one misses are desserts. I speak from previous experience, not this brief encounter. Yet, I have heard no complaint from our group.

"October 25   Dave and I went over to Gen. Yeh's quarters where we talked with Chu and Yeh. Old Chu sat back and listened most of the time. Obviously Yeh is the man who will do most of the work.

"Yeh's office and home are apparently of one piece. A conscientious, though silent, participant in our conferences is Niu Niu, the chief of staff's three-year-old daughter. A bright-eyed, red-cheeked little beauty encased in layers of garments and wearing a white knitted peaked cap with a red star à la russe on the front, Niu Niu hangs over the arm of a chair with the tips of her fingers pressed together gravely listening to discussions of strategy. She can be distracted, however, by a dried melon seed or the zipping of my flight jacket. She is obviously adored by her father and is also able to take considerable liberties with grandpa Chu.

"The children one sees around headquarters are so healthy looking. Healthy and clean. Furthermore, they are well-mannered. No shouts of foreign devil. They say, 'Ah, there goes an American.' Or 'That is a foreign friend.' Almost too good to be true. I suppose it's the party line.

"This evening after dinner we piled into a truck and rode off to the theater. Dave, Chia-k'ang, JKE, Ariyoshi, and myself. We had seats on the front row. The only other person there whom I recognized was Mrs. Chou En-lai, who sat behind us knitting. The theater was cold. I had on a wool shirt, leather jacket, and fur-lined flight jacket and still felt chilly. My thick rubber-soled shoes protected me from the cold brick floor. The seats were wooden benches. There were probably five hundred people in the auditorium.

"The thin blue coolie cloth curtain rose on a wild mountainous scene with a lone guerrilla lookout gazing from a peak. The scenery was realistic and, considering the shortages which confront this area, extraordinarily well done. There were a lot of real weeds and overripe daisy bushes which I eyed with allergic misgivings.

"The plot was based on actual occurrences in Shansi. The Japs invaded a village. As a result the villagers took refuge in the hills where they hid out for weeks, exhausting their supplies. The partisan leaders argued against their going back into the village, arranged in cooperation with a small group of Eighth Route regulars to raid the village for supplies. Then the whole town remained away and developed a new life out in the hills. The Japs became desperate because they were then in effect living in a desert. The troops and the guerrillas finally drove the Japs away. This is a skeleton outline of the plot. The meat of small incidents and characterization is left off. It was a cast of twenty or thirty—all sorts of peasant and village types, partisans, regulars, Japs. The acting was fresh and zestful. And of a very high quality. The partisan leader was a matinee idol type. But more virile. Perhaps more like a cowboy hero. There was no love interest. It was a play with a purpose, more designed to instruct the peasant in the meaning of the war, the technique of resistance, and the importance of Chinese solidarity.

"By the second act the weeds and daisies got me. There was so much violence, stampeding, flight and leaping exultation going on in the play that the scenery was almost constantly agitated. The pollen flooded into my face in great waves. I sneezed with wracking and appalling regularity throughout acts two, three, and four, a matter of a mere two and one half hours. My discomfort was accentuated by my fright. In their striving toward realism, the producers had a fire on the stage as much and as often as possible. There was a torchlight convocation in the first act on which the non-asbestos curtain fell. Then to give the impression of cold—which was entirely unnecessary—fires were built on the stage before which the genuinely shivering actors huddled. Finally, a paper snow storm deluged the stage—and the fire.

"Last night, I forgot to record, I knew was Patricia's broadcast night [weekly commentary for OWI] from All India Radio. So I kept the radio operator up until 10:15, the equivalent of 9:45 Delhi time, and his little generator going so that I could listen. It wasn't very clear, too much interference. Remeneh thought that maybe we had one of the subsidiary wave lengths and would do better next time if we could find the proper place on the dial.

"*October 26*   Dave and I again went over to headquarters for more talkee-talkee. Present were Yeh, P'eng Teh-huai (vice commander of the 18th Group Army and commander of the Southeast Shansi base area), Nieh Jung-chen (commander in Chin-Cha-Chi), Lin Piao (commander of the 115 Division), Yang Shang-k'un, and Chia-k'ang. We soon saw that they did not know quite how to go about the job [of stating their military capabilities in a form acceptable to us]. So we suggested that we would give them three hypothetical cases on which to base their statement. P'eng Teh-huai gave us an eloquent background lecture and then we left. Dave and I drew up one case and as he typed up that case in more or less final form I outlined a second. The third, we decided, could be based on the first. Chia k'ang took the papers over in the afternoon and we sat back to await results.

"Brother Cromley [working on Japanese order of battle] is regularly visited by Japanese prisoners. They come wandering in one or two at a time dressed in Eighth Route uniform and without a guard. One fairly new prisoner who was considered to be yet incompletely converted was accompanied by a prisoner who had seen the light, armed with a slender walking stick. They sit around a table with Cromley, smoking his cigarettes, and with all the pretty little Japanese courtesies, tell him all. It's a pleasant, chummy atmosphere."

While awaiting an answer to our question on military capabilities, my mind turned in search of other areas of possible common interest between the United States and the Chinese Communists. In addition to military cooperation, how might we draw them away from future reliance on the Soviet Union and into dependence upon the United States? Mao had insisted to Service that he wanted American help in industrializing a future Communist China. In terms of their own interests, I tried indirectly to induce Chou to spell out their concept of economic collaboration with the United States.

"October 27   This morning I rose quickly from my desk, having been moved by what I am pleased to call an inspiration and strode briskly to Chia-k'ang's quarters. As we walked up and down the big front yard I suggested that he present for Comrade Chou's consideration the advisability of drawing up and publicizing a Communist postwar economic program. I said that T.V. and Papa Kung had been talking awfully big in the U.S. about how they were going to reconstruct China after the war and how anxious they were for American capital to come in and do the job. I observed that their promises were based upon a politically uncertain situation which might well betray any American investments made through them. The Communists are now on the verge of coming of age. They are able to talk with increasing assurance about the political destiny of at least North China. With the growing assurance of political power and stability there devolves upon them a responsibility for economic planning. It must be large-scale long-range economic planning. Their immediate preoccupation must necessarily continue to be the livelihood of the masses in their bases: agricultural production, cottage industries, relations between the landlord and the peasant, cooperatives, and makeshift industry. But at the same time they must begin to prepare for the big economic problems of the future. And if they give these plans publicity they are bound to attract the attention and interest of the American ruling classes. Their terms to outside capital can be no tougher than the Russian ones were. Which were not so tough that many of our big businessmen were unable to do business with the Russians. Actually, the Chinese Communists will probably offer much more attractive propositions. Now is the time for them to state in outline form, in terms of general principles, their economic postwar plans.

"Mondays, Wednesdays, and Fridays are bath days. We go over to an officers' bath house tended by a handsome young soldier with a lame leg—battle wound—and two hsiao kwei (little devils: orderlies). We sit in the anteroom warming ourselves before the charcoal brazier, sipping tea while the bath is drawn. Two of us bathe at a time because there are two big cement tubs to a room. There is a dressing room with a brazier and towels spread on a brick platform on which one can lounge after the bath, smoke, drink tea, and converse—

for a bath in China is to only a lesser degree than in Japan, a social event. The room in which the tubs are is in the rear and has only one small window away up. The atmosphere is therefore rather dark and gloomy. Nothing is quite as clean as it should be. One feels that the bottom of the tub has not been scrubbed to the degree of immaculateness which one might wish. The washcloths seem to have been only dried out since used by a previous bather. And the towels are well on the grimy side. Therefore I sluice off afterwards with a basin from the home-made tap, don't use a wash cloth, and dry off with my own towel."

Believing that the balance of power in East Asia would shift against us when the Soviet Union moved eastward against Japan—unless we quickly countered by preemptive collaboration with Yenan—I radioed Hurley on October 27: "Of such immediate and long-range strategic importance that it warrants your personal visit is info that can be obtained here and which you cannot get in Chungking. I do not know, in wake of the recent wreckage [recall of Stilwell], what offer on salvage plans officials at Chungking may be making but I do know that you can take significant information and proposals back to the president vitally affecting the war and future balance of power in Asia and the Pacific, if you will visit Yenan. This I know after comprehensive talks with our observers back from the field and with Chinese leaders here."

CHAPTER *33*

The Communists Offer Joint Operations

Resuming my journal:

"*October 28*   Dave and I again visited Gen. Yeh in his quarters. We talked a little more in detail about what his staff and commanders were doing. He had nothing ready for us, however. Performance in China takes time. Niu Niu was present throughout the meeting but had little to offer beyond a shy smile or two. She expressed the opinion that she had no interest in riding in either an airplane or a jeep.

"Her daddy in his vigorous straightforward manner, even in matters regarding food, took us in to lunch. There we joined Chu Teh and Teddy White. Teddy had apparently been interviewing the commander in chief. It was a jolly lunch. Excellent plain food and much joking and laughter. Old Chu was rather quiet throughout the chow but joined in all of the laughter. It was a good atmosphere —everybody himself and at ease. Not a strained moment or a false sentiment. Which is very rare in any luncheon with people who are not all old friends. These Communists have a great sincerity, a faculty for creating a straightforward genuine atmosphere.

"Yesterday JKE went over to the Workers and Peasants School. Koji Ariyoshi went with him. I kid them about their proletarian school days. They were provided two shaggy ponies for the trip. They came dragging in about an hour after dinner. They had been thrown coming and going, had lost their horses, and finally themselves. It was quite a story. But they were enthusiastic about what they had discovered at the school. It is for Japanese prisoners. The story is one of even more profound regeneration of the prisoners than was the case in Burma. They all want to go back to Japan to build a new Japan. And they are peasant boys—allegedly the most difficult to convert. Their reports about conditions in Japan indicate that things are really in a very bad way, not enough to wear, not enough to eat, and considerable unrest. What keeps them going is the conviction that there is no way out, that the Americans intend to erase Japan, kill all of the males between the ages of fifteen and fifty. I suspect that the secret of the Eighth Route success with their prisoners is that the indoctrination is done by other Japanese. They will believe one of their own countrymen where they would not believe a Chinese or American. Our persuasive element is the niseis.

"The nisei boys here are greatly impressed by Okano Susumu [pseudonym of Nosaka Sanzō], the Japanese Communist leader here, formerly a delegate to the Comintern. Okano is apparently a highly intelligent and attractive person. I met him several days ago but have not yet had an opportunity to talk to him in any detail. He is supposed to have lived in England for some time. John says that he has a good command of English. He has a Chinese wife who learned Japanese here.

"After dinner we crossed the rickety little bridge by the light of a bright nearly full moon to the Army auditorium where a dance was scheduled. The jam session was in full swing when we arrived. The band, composed of a mouth organ, several Chinese fiddles, and some unidentified percussion instruments, sat solemnly on the stage playing 'Marching Through Georgia.' With equal solemnity wadded couples were gravely circling around on the mud dance floor. People who had caps wore caps, everyone was in wadded pants and jackets, including the girls. Sex was undeterminable save by the cut of the hair. There were two idiosyncrasies in garb. One was a young lady in a whitish knitted coverall bunny suit, the other was a maiden with a small blue ribbon in her hair.

"General Lin Piao, looking like a nondescript and shabby little soldier, was one of the most persistent and expert among the dancers. He also had an eye for beauty, such as was discernible and available. The chief of staff didn't miss a dance. He performed with a slightly tango-like step. Grandpa Chu sat on the sidelines watching the proceedings with vast benevolence, comfortable in his faded blue cotton uniform, his blue cotton army cap shoved back on his head. He said that he wasn't dancing because he was suffering from a slight stomach complaint. The ubiquitous Niu Niu was there having a high old time with others of the youngest Communists between dances. A prisoner Japanese police dog ran interestedly about sniffing the guests, apparently completely reconciled to having betrayed his emperor and joined the Reds.

"Several young ladies were introduced to me and I was urged to dance. I made it as plain as was consistent with courtesy that I had no desire to fox-trot to Yankee Doodle, but hospitable comrades insisted that I enjoy myself. So I had a dance with the 'best dancer in Yenan.' She was a young woman of twenty-six who some three years previous had slipped through the blockade to this loess canyon paradise. And she was in truth a very good dancer. As she had undergone part of her schooling in Shanghai, I guess that she learned the light fantastic there. Then a thoroughly plain female comrade came up and asked me to dance. She was, as might be suspected, an English teacher at the local foreign languages school. Next a youngster of twenty-three (I can say that now that Patricia is twenty-four) was pressed upon me. She too had taken the pilgrimage through the blockade. Finally, Mrs. Chu Teh strode up and asked for the pleasure. For a Hunan peasant girl who was a veteran of the Long March she danced well. She is much younger than the C in C, plumpish, plainly nice and has a good direct manner. Oh yes, there was another lady comrade who sought my company on the dance floor. She wore a white sweater. But a Yenan sweater girl is quite different from a Hollywood one. The sweater is but the final one of many shapeless layers.

"My head was by way of being fairly well turned by all of this attention until I realized that I was considered by the majority of the young ladies as an acceptable subject on which to practice their English. Most of the lady comrades were students at the Foreign Languages School.

"The whole thing was rather like a church sociable with everybody seeming to know everybody else, fellowship at a high pitch, and Grandpa Chu (the Red Scourge of the 1920s and 30s with a price of tens of thousands on his head), smiling benignly at the antics, sipping tea, and letting children climb over him. He said to me, 'We are very informal here; some of our more old-fashioned countrymen would not approve of these goings-on.'

"Our little nisei sergeants were having a good time. They asked some of the Chinese girls for dances and stayed on long after Dave, JKE and I got bored and left. So did Ray Cromley, who is seizing this unparalleled opportunity to learn to dance.

"I neglected to say that we were taken to the dance by two of the unique people at this North China New Jerusalem. They are Dr. and Mrs. Michael Lindsay [Lord Lindsay of Birker]. Michael is the son of the Master of Balliol College and an economist by trade. Mrs. Lindsay is a Chinese with a sweet face and two pigtails and a baby daughter by Dr. L. Michael taught at Yenching University where the present Mrs. L. was a student. During that period before Pearl Harbor he branched off into physics and chemistry and taught the guerrillas how to blow up railways. Come Pearl Harbor, he and his wife joined the people he had been teaching how to blow up railways and proceeded to Chin-Cha-Chi where he expanded into radio communications. He is now the principal radio technical adviser here.

"Michael and his wife had drinks in JKE's and my room before rice this evening. It was rum and hot water and scotch and hot water because it is Saturday night and because it is cold.

"*October 29*   Chia-k'ang walked me up the valley to Yang Chia Ling where Party headquarters is and Chou En-lai's cave is to be found. This walk was in response to an invitation from Chou to come and talk economic programs with him.

"Chou just sat and listened to me expound. Mrs. Chou, like a competent and sensible American housewife and clubwoman, bustled in and out, seeing that tea and fruit were on the table, and even spilling before us a handful of precious candy from Chungking. I told Chou that we would like to know what program they had for the postwar reconstruction of China. Assuming that they would come into power, what specific economic principles would they put into effect. For example, what was their policy going to be with regard to communications, industry, foreign investments, and foreign trade. These were questions which, I knew, they had not formulated answers to. I told him that their problems were rapidly becoming more complicated in the economic field. That while they would probably have to continue to concentrate a large share of their attention on the immediate problems of the landlord-peasant relationship, cooperatives, and cottage industries, and how to circumvent the Kuomintang blockade, at the same time they had to begin to prepare for the economic responsibilities which will hit them all of a heap if they attain political power and stability in urban North China. Chou listened with great interest as I rambled on. Obviously, he had nothing ready and was just getting a clear idea of what I wanted.

"He said that they are not worried about getting technicians and administrative personnel if and when they get the cities. He said that even now there are many Chinese engineers and others with scientific training who would come to Communist territory if the blockade were lifted. On sending people to the U.S. for technical education, he believed that mature men who had already had practical experience were the ones to be sent for training rather than students. Students, he felt, wasted too much of their time on subjects aside from their specialty. He said that initially, of course, there would be need to import foreign experts and advisers. His only positive trade comment was that there would be a great need for coastal shipping and our old rolling stock.

"Chou was full of questions about the American government and American politics. Like all of the Communists he was a strong Roosevelt man. And like all of them he was intensely interested in the forthcoming elections. We got into the mysteries of the electoral college system. That beat me. This conversation carried on into lunch, which, for some strange reason, was held down the hill a bit in an auditorium rather than in their own quarters. We were—Chou, Mme. C., Chia-k'ang, and I—the only people eating in a big room which had a Ping-Pong table at one end of it. After the meal, Chou took Chia-k'ang on in a fast game of Ping-Pong. Mme. Chou and I conversed on the side. She wanted to know where my wife was. And when I told her, she insisted that Patricia come up for a visit.

"*October 30*   The captive Japanese police dog pranced into our front yard, creating consternation and pandemonium among our three adolescent mongrels, imaginatively named: Whitey, Brownie, and Pinkie. The prisoner was a precursor of General Chu who came to call. He [Chu] stopped for five or ten minutes at our interpreter-aide's house and then with massive, waddling dignity ambled over with his secretary, Chia-k'ang, and Hwang Hua [English-speaking liaison official; in 1971 Chinese delegate to the United Nations]. He sat for about two hours, sipping tea, smoking cigarettes, eating candy, eating pears, eating apples, and talking. We all did the same. The conversation was essentially social and inconsequential. His call was largely a courtesy one. At the end he went into a long discourse about the value of guerrilla warfare.

"Chu's visit demonstrated one of the characteristics of the Communists—an old-fashioned tempo. It's a Chinese peasant movement. And it has the Chinese peasant habit of moving deliberately. I have never seen Chu or any of the other leaders look or act hurried. The chief of staff is the only one of the bunch who has a brisk manner. And that only occasionally. That Chu could amble over with two bodyguards and spend two and a half hours shooting the breeze with us indicates either that he delegates everything excepting the very important questions or that there is really very little happening over at headquarters. I suspect that the latter is true. It is a loose, decentralized administration.

"After lunch Teddy picked up Doc Ma [Ma Hai-teh, pseudonym of George Hatem, an American physician who cast his lot with the Communists], Dave, Chia-k'ang, Hwang Hua, and me and took us into town to the Shen-Kan-Ning [Shensi-Kansu-Ninghsia Border Region—Communist base area] Parliament Bldg. where Mao was to address a cultural, educational, and medical gathering of delegates from throughout the SKN district. We arrived to find the open ground in front of the largish brick auditorium filled with candidates and party members clad in faded and dusty blue wadded garments. A monotonous uniformity. Excepting in the faces. All kinds. Intellectuals myopically peering from beneath peaks of workers caps. Peasant leaders, stalwart and bronzed, their heads shaved in the country manner halfway back from the forehead. Party workers and soldiers.

"We were checked in past the soldier at the door and the man who registered our names. We sat in the front row. The meeting took some time to get under way. One group of delegates was in the wrong seats. New benches had to be set down in front of us. Small boys passed out tea to the favored few in front. Chou En-lai and the competent good-looking Gen. Nieh came in and sat down on the other side of the aisle. After we had waited for fully half an hour Comrade Mao arrived looking smart in his trim uniform of dark brown homespun. He went along in front of us, shook hands, and sat down.

"The two tables of earnest and unattractive comrades at either end of the stage got their papers and pencils ready. They were apparently the press. Then from left center there emerged a gnomish figure in an oversize great coat, double-breasted with but one button secured and the sleeves hanging well beyond his finger tips. On his head he had a grey cap of the same material as the coat. It sat squarely and low on his wizened skull and was kept from slipping down over his neck by two flamboyant ears of the color and texture of dried mushrooms. From his chin and the sides of his face drifted wisps of dirty grey beard. He had a long nose and as much of a pouch under each eye as a Mongol can muster. This figure from the ghetto stepped forward and said in a clear voice, 'The meeting is opened. Comrade Mao will speak.' The chairman was identified to me as the vice-minister of education for the Shen-Kan-Ning District.

"Amidst warm applause, Mao got up, disappeared back stage, and then emerged on the platform. He did not speak easily at first. He was thinking as he went along, cleared his throat a lot, and stalled some. After five or ten minutes he warmed up. His manner was familiar and direct. His language was homely. He made fun and everybody laughed. He used simple similes and illustrations. He walked around the stage and gestured inelegantly but expressively whenever he felt like it. He mimicked. He stopped to pour himself a drink of water two or three times—very deliberate. He fumbled around in his pocket to pull out his notes, paused for a minute or two as he read them before going on. It was all informal and very effective. Some public health man had apparently done an exceptionally good job in his county. Mao went into some detail to extol the man but wasn't quite sure what his name was. He looked through his notes. Several people in the audience volunteered the man's name (who was probably sitting in the audience), but there didn't seem to be agreement. For some time there was a little doubt as to just who the hero was who was being singled out for particular honor.

"The speech was mostly about witch doctors, old-fashioned superstitions, and feudal abuses. Early in the talk, however, he drew especial attention to us. He was talking about how the delegates came. 'How did you come?' he asked. 'On your two feet,' he answered himself as he trudged a few steps across the stage. 'How far did you come from?' 'Four or five hundred li [a li is one-third mile].' 'How long did it take you?' 'Five or six days.' 'Now we have here some foreign friends. They came in here by airplane. And how long does it take them to come from America? Six days, maybe,' and he looked a little inquiringly in our direction. Chia-k'ang corrected him incorrectly, I should say (unless one came by Murmansk or Alaska), 'four and a half days.' The audience gasped with pleasure at this remarkable contrast.

"After the meeting we went up to the guest house where we sat on the terrace in front of Teddy's quarters and drank his whisky which Doc Ma enjoyed very much. It is a fine view from that terrace—the market street below, the cliffs and caves across the valley with the bright afternoon sun on their glistening buff surface, the Yenan pagoda in the distance, teamsters cracking their long whips over four horses pulling a heavily laden two-wheeled cart, and nearby coolies working at a fast pace digging out the side of the hill to make another terrace.

"Dave, Chia-k'ang, Hwang Hua, Doc Ma, and I walked the dusty road home. Doc Ma said that these people are worried about the British and what they may do in South China. They greatly fear that, using Chiang, they may divide China. Return to the old spheres of influence. Therefore the Communists wish to move slowly, make every attempt to compromise to avert the splitting of China in two. I see that I have embroidered what Doc Ma had to say.

"But I haven't explained who Doc Ma is. He is a Syrian or Armenian American who has heretofore been very mysterious. I believe he comes from one of the Carolinas. He got his medical training in Switzerland. Ed Snow brought him in here in the middle 1930s sometime. And here he has been ever since. I remember when at the Hankow Consulate General in 1938 or 1939 we got an inquiry about a certain Hatem or something or other. That was Ma Hai-teh. We identified him as that mysterious individual at Yenan. Well, here he is, a nice, sensitive, apparently normal American levantine with large black eyes, a long nose, and prematurely—for his thirty-four years—grey hair. He has married a Chinese girl and has a child by her. He is detailed to live with us, be at our service, and returns home only for the weekends. The impact of this group on him— American language, American breeziness, American cigarettes, field jacket, GI boots—has made him homesick, I suspect, and regret a little his alienation.

"*October 31*   Chou and Yeh dropped around in the evening to drink tea, eat pears, and talkee-talkee in general rather than specific terms. I suppose these calls are largely to show that, although they have not yet got the plans ready, they are interested and friendly. They went in to listen to the program in Chinese from San Francisco and after awhile left laughing. The program was about Mussolini, which subject they seemed to feel was a waste of time.

"*November 1*   This afternoon Chia-k'ang took me to the tower room of Party headquarters at Yang Chia Ling. There I met Liu Shao-ch'i, whom Teddy describes as the Stalin of the Chinese Communist Party. He is a member of the Politburo and apparently is in charge of party organization. Chia-k'ang says that he was one of the original founders of the Chinese Communist Party, veteran of the Long March, organized some of the Central China base areas.

"Liu is about the same height as I, slightly stooped, looks to be in his late forties, has undistinguished bland features, kept his hands in his sleeves folded across his front, wore his cap rather low on his forehead so that he peered from beneath the visor. He was a little suspicious of me at first, but later opened up to a considerable degree. We talked about the underground. At the end when he got enthusiastic he stood up and, to emphasize what he was saying, would bring his padded arms up from his sides or off from his stomach in stiff little gestures. It is impossible in padded cotton garments to make the graceful agile gesture.

"On the way back, scuffing through the dust of the river bank road, past the lumbering two-wheeled carts, past the blacksmith shoeing horses, past the gully where goats were being slaughtered, past the stinking hides drying in the sun, Chia-k'ang and I talked about the new-found cockiness of the Communists. When did the Communists stop being afraid of civil war, I asked him. After the New Fourth Army incident in 1941 (when the Central Government attacked the New Fourth in the Yangtze valley), Chia-k'ang said, the Communists realized that they had to make themselves strong enough to stave off any attack. After two years of preparation, they felt at the end of 1943 that they were powerful enough to take care of themselves. Which accounts for the cockiness which I reported last winter.

"*November 2*   After lunch I had my first talk with Yelacic (or Yellacich). Mr. Y is a Yugoslav with a Russian mother. When I first saw him I thought he was an

Eurasian. He has the mongoloid eye and indeterminate complexion of an Eurasian. He wears a North China teamster's grey felt cap with a long flap for the back of the neck, a peaked visor flap, and two ear flaps, all turned up and tied on top. His jacket is very old and worn with leather patches on the elbow. But the material is an Esquire check and plaid. Must once have been very sportif. His trousers are wadded cotton.

"Mr. Y says he has lived twenty-odd years in China, that he worked in or ran some garage in Tientsin, and that he escaped from Jap territory into the helping hands of the Communist guerrillas some months ago. They brought him here, a trip of many months' duration. He has the background of a not-quite-accepted member of treaty port society. Something like a Russian manager of a British-American tobacco company factory. I was interested in what he would have to say about the Communists because I felt that he would view them with a critical eye.

"He did. Of the Eighth Route Army he said that it was far from being a modern fighting force. Obvious. The simple matter of time. Impossible to have precision in operations because most of the officers do not have watches. The measure of time within the twenty-four hour span is: morning, afternoon, or night. And the tempo is slow. What's the rush, was the comment which met his agitated efforts to hurry up. Although officers wear no insignia, there is distinction between officers and men. The former eat better and live better. Do they beat the men, I asked. No, there they are good; not like other Chinese armies. The Army also takes the people too much into account. In any conflict of policy between the people and the Army, the people are always adjudged right. Too much toadying to the masses by the party and army. And everything must be decided by K'ai huei (opening a meeting). Too much time wasted in government-army relationships by talkee-talkee.

"The Japanese have a very effective measure (as in Manchuria) for deterring sabotage against the railroads. Group responsibility of the villages along the line. Any sabotage and fierce punitive measures are taken against the villages in the vicinity of the railway. This means that not as much sabotage is done as should be.

"Mr. Y has been up to the oil wells north of here. Too much politics there as in the army. The technical expert was under the party man, who was an ignoramus. Yes, he thought that the party people realized that the technician must have the say in industry. They would make that adjustment when they got big factories. They were muddling along now because the industrial problems were practically nonexistent.

"He was high in his praise of the fighting quality of the Shantung units of the Eighth Route Army and Shantung guerrillas. The Shantung people love fighting and are not afraid of shooting guns, the way the southerners are. He thought that all of the northern Communist armies and militia could, if given enough ammunition, tie up Jap communications.

"San Francisco radio carried the presidential announcement of the JWS recall.

"*November 2*   Dr. Fry is an Austrian Jew emigré who fled Tientsin to work with the Communists. He has been with them two years. Like Yelacic (I forgot to say) he does not believe that the Central Government can crush the Communists. Preposterous [he said]; I underestimate the strength of armed and determined masses.

"Dr. Fry believes in acupuncture. Says that he has cured malaria with it. They have no medicine. All they can do is stick them with needles. Acupuncture has been successful both as a preventative and a cure. Doc Casberg snorts with disbelief.

"This afternoon we went over for the big staff meeting at which we were to be given one of the statements of capability. Chu, Yeh and Chou. Chia-k'ang, Hwang Hua and, curiously enough, Doc Ma for the translation. Yeh presented the case simply and effectively. Then Chou had a few things to say. He said them impressively—honest, direct, and sensible. Dave and I felt that it was a very good job. Two others were there, I forgot to say, Yang and Liu Hsiao [Party official introduced to me as an authority of the Shanghai underground]. We had dinner with them (and of course Niu Niu, who strangely enough had been left out of the staff meeting). Then we went home.

"Liu Hsiao went home with us. For two hours we sat around Dave's charcoal brazier, eating peanuts, candy, pears, and drinking tea. Liu had a lot of very important things to say.

"When brushing my teeth in the yard after the conference broke up I was hit by the combination of the carbon monoxide and all I'd eaten and passed gracefully and briefly out. Doc Casberg told me to puke, which I did, and then I was all right. He said that the charcoal fumes have a cumulative effect. They certainly did."

There on November 2, puking on the Reds' good earth, I ended my Yenan journal. Why I wrote no more in it during the six remaining days of this visit I do not remember. Probably it was because, when not caught up in the constant palaver so characteristic of life in Yenan, I was drafting four papers. One outlined the statement of Communist capabilities presented at the staff conference on November 2. Three summed up my salient impressions of the Communists.

Yeh's presentation of Communist capabilities, which I reported on November 3, proceeded from my hypothesis of an American landing in the vicinity of Lienyunkang, the coastal terminus of the east-west Lunghai Railway south of the Shantung Promontory. He assumed two and a half Japanese divisions within a radius of about one hundred miles of the port, doubling in strength by D-plus-3, three days after an American landing. To insure unquestioned Communist-American superiority, Yeh postulated the commitment of five American divisions to the operation. In close support of the landing, the Communists would throw in fifty thousand of their regulars. In addition, with regulars and militia, they would assume the offensive generally in North China, disrupt communications, and undertake to tie down the enemy away from the invasion zone. The port, Yeh emphasized, must become a supply base for the Communists, whose limited materiel would be quickly drained in the inevitable Japanese counter-offensive, and whose principal need would be captured Japanese ammunition and light arms.

Following Yeh, Chou En-lai observed that if the American authorities preferred another port in the Communist area, similar all-out cooperation would be forthcoming. An American decision to land in the Communist area must be followed by staff talks and a cover plan. The Communists would fight with total strength, Chou continued, and they would mobilize the population within a two hundred mile radius of the landing to provide labor and foodstuffs for the American forces. In sum, the Communists offered all of the cooperation within their power to give. Barrett and I were assured that this was presented with the concurrence of Chu Teh and Mao.

The three other papers that occupied me were my political appraisals of the Communists. "How Red Are the Chinese Communists?" I asked in the title of one memorandum. Not very, was my conclusion. I thought that "they have now deviated so far to the right that they will return to the revolution only if driven to it by overwhelming pressure from domestic and foreign forces of reaction." There may have been some truth in this. For who can say how the orientation of the Yenan oligarchy would have developed had the United States, instead of reacting in late 1945 as Marxist-Leninist doctrinaires expected that it must, accepted Mao's invitation to cooperate? Be that as it may, it is obvious in this memorandum that I underestimated the influence of ideology on Communist behavior.

In the second memorandum, "The Chinese Communists and the Great Powers," I stated that "the Communists no longer feel that their survival or extinction depends upon foreign aid or attack." I did not rate the Soviet Union or Britain as decisive as the United States in Yenan's calculations. Substantial American aid would hasten the extension of Communist control over China. At the same time, "We are the greatest fear of the Communists because the more aid we give Chiang exclusively the greater the likelihood of his precipitating a civil war and the more protracted and costly will be the Communist unification of China."

"Will the Communists Take Over China?" was the title of a third memorandum. To me this was the sovereign question about China. The relevance and significance of all that the American government was doing and planning in and about China turned on the outcome of the struggle between Chiang and Mao. Power was the decisive factor in my consideration. The Communists had expanded, I wrote, "by a process, which has been operating for seven years, whereby Chiang Kai-shek loses his cities and principal lines of communication to the Japanese and the countryside to the Communists. . . .

"From control of some hundred thousand square kilometers with a population of one million and a half they have expanded to about eight hundred and fifty thousand square kilometers with a population of approximately ninety million. . . .

"The reason for this phenomenal vitality and strength is simple and fundamental. It is mass support, mass participation. The Communist governments and armies are the first ... in modern Chinese history to have positive and widespread popular support. They have this support because the governments and armies are genuinely of the people.

"Only if he is able to enlist foreign intervention on a scale equal to the Japanese invasion of China will Chiang probably be able to crush the Communists. But foreign intervention on such a scale would seem to be unlikely. Relying upon his dispirited shambling legions, his decadent corrupt bureaucracy, his sterile political moralisms, and such nervous foreign support as he can muster, the Generalissimo may nevertheless plunge China into civil war. He cannot succeed, however, where the Japanese in more than seven years of determined striving have failed. The Communists are already too strong for him. . . .

"Since 1937 the Communists have been trying to persuade Chiang to form a democratic coalition government in which they would participate. Should the Generalissimo accept ... [they] may be expected to continue effective control over the areas which they now hold. They will also probably extend their political influence throughout the rest of the country—for they are the only group in China possessing a program with positive appeal to the people.

"If the Generalissimo neither precipitates a civil war nor reaches an understanding with the Communists, he is still confronted with defeat. Chiang's feudal China cannot long coexist alongside a modern dynamic popular government in North China."

I came away from my sixteen days at Yenan impressed by the force, cohesion, and pragmatism of the ruling Communist group. All the indications were that Mao was firmly in command. His former rivals of the Russian-trained faction—"The Twenty-eight Bolsheviks"—were no longer a threat to him. Po Ku had capitulated to Mao, and Wang Ming, Stalin's man, was isolated and assumably undergoing reeducation.

Mao's Rectification Campaign, begun in February 1942, was in full swing. Through intensive indoctrination, Mao was trying to do two things. One was to tighten party discipline in a sprawling, expanding movement. The other was to give a Chinese character to Marxism. Without denying Marxist internationalism or turning against Russian Communism, the Chinese Communists were veering toward ideological autonomy.

While I was aware of the Rectification Campaign, I did not inquire into it. My attention was fixed on the issue of power, and what the United States might do to attract Yenan away from the Soviet Union.

Obviously the Chinese Communists wanted military collaboration with the United States, assumably for the weapons that we could supply them. These would not only better their chances against Chiang, but would, I calculated, also foster their independence of Moscow.

In somewhat longer perspective was the question of American economic aid. My efforts to whet Chou En-lai's appetite for collaboration with Wall Street produced only a reserved and generalized response. Although Mao had said that he would welcome foreign investments, the idea of issuing an economic prospectus took a little getting used to for those who had so long demanded the confiscation of foreign interests. I do not know what if any effect my dangling of capitalist benefits before their eyes had on the Communists. But I did believe it important to encourage them to think that Mao was right in seeking an American alternative to reliance on Moscow.

CHAPTER *34*

Sustaining Chiang

WITHOUT ADVANCE NOTICE, Hurley flew to Yenan on November 7, 1944. More than a fortnight had passed since an aircraft had come from Chungking. And so, like the inhabitants of a Pacific atoll flocking to the beach to greet the arrival of a trading vessel, the Observer Group and many Yenan worthies gathered at the airstrip to greet our only contact with the outside world. The plane landed, the door opened, and there stood Hurley, tall in the saddle, as it were. In a sharply pressed uniform of a major general, he was drawn up to his six-feet-three, his bushy white moustache glistening in the sun.

At some point in the ensuing confusion Mao arrived on the scene to welcome the personal representative of the American president to the rebels' lair. No one more than Hurley was aware that this was an historic occasion. Harking back to his Oklahoma frontier origins—of which he was insistently proud—he suddenly stiffened and gave forth a Choctaw war whoop. He offered no explanation of what had moved him to screech—whether it was the parched landscape reminiscent of a dust bowl or the company in which he found himself. Everyone was dumbfounded. As the echoes in the canyon died down, Hurley put all at ease by strutting genially among the assorted Marxists. I performed some of the initial introductions and turned him over to the commander of the Observer Group, Colonel Barrett.

The personal representative had not come in response to my pleas that he visit Yenan to inquire and evaluate. He had come on a mission of reconciliation, as mediator between Chiang's regime and the Communists. Some ten days before his arrival he had composed a Basis for Agreement between the antagonists. It provided, in brief, for military unification, Chiang's supremacy, and legalization of the Communist Party. Point three would commit the adversaries to "support the principles of Sun-Yat-sen for the establishment in China of a government of the people, for the people, and by the people." Both sides already professed adherence to Sun's vague Three People's Principles: nationalism, people's rights, and people's livelihood. Hurley's Gettysburgian revision of Sun introduced a new and unsettling element, for while Sun Yat-sen's principles envisaged government for the people, they did not prescribe government of or by the people.

Before coming to Yenan, Hurley had submitted his proposal for the Generalissimo's approval. Two of Chiang's factotums revised it somewhat. The personal representative thereupon took the proposal with him to Yenan for presentation to the Communists.

On the afternoon of his arrival I had a brief talk with Hurley and told him that he should not expect the Communists to yield to terms acceptable to the Generalissimo. They would be tough to bargain with, I warned him. Hurley did not take kindly to my cautionary advice and in a fatherly manner suggested that it would be better if I returned to Chungking on the aircraft the next day, which I did.

A similar endeavor by another to be helpful aroused Hurley's murky suspicions—he who brought unwelcome tidings must be personally hostile. Hurley made this friendly attempt at assistance a matter of record:

8 November, 1944

Theodore White, correspondent for *Time* and *Life*, told me that he had just talked to Chairman Mao and Mao had told him that there was not any possible chance of an agreement between him and Chiang Kai-shek. White told me many reasons why Mao should not agree with the National Government. White's whole conversation was definitely against the mission with which I am charged.

Hurley conferred with Mao, Chu Teh, and Chou En-lai on November 8, 9, and 10. Colonel Barrett sat in on the parleys and has provided an animated account of them in his monograph on the Observer Group. A Sergeant Smith, Hurley's stenographer-batman, was also present. This glum young man was probably the recorder of the minutes of the first two meetings, the authorship of which later mystified the historians compiling the diplomatic papers of 1944.

After Hurley had presented his proposal, the first question Mao asked, according to the minutes, was "whose idea" the proposition was. The personal representative answered that "it was his idea, the basis was his idea, but it had been worked on by all of us." Assumably "us" meant Hurley, Chiang, Soong, and company.

The essence of Hurley's exhortations to the Reds was that, because both they and Chiang were patriotic and democratic, the Kuomintang regime and the Communists should join together to create a unified China. Apparently feeling that the personal representative did not understand the situation in China, Mao delivered a lecture on the conflict within China, laying the blame on the Kuomintang regime. Hurley was taken aback and said that he had not realized that "the feeling was so deeply engrafted. . . ." He then indicated that Mao's statements were "what the enemies of China have been saying." Disregarding the fact that his was a self-imposed mission, he complained that "it was asking too much to ask an outsider like him to do all of the work in fixing an agreement."

Mao was not moved to pity for Hurley. Irked by the crack that his comments were those of the enemies of China, he reminded the American that

Roosevelt, among others, had been critical in the same terms of conditions in China. Hurley backtracked, saying that "if Chairman Mao will work with him [Hurley] and they can get Chiang Kai-shek to work with them, they can bring about union in China. . . ."

Out of this jawboning there emerged, at the invitation of Hurley, a Communist revision of the original proposals approved by the Nationalists. The refinements introduced by the Reds included reorganization of Chiang's National Government into a coalition government and the National Military Council into a united high command, in both of which the Communists would be represented. Furthermore, foreign supplies were to be equitably distributed, meaning that the Reds would receive lend-lease equipment.

Barrett recalls that on November 9 Hurley told Mao that the Communists' amendments—which would have at least undermined Chiang's regime—were entirely fair. Indeed, he thought that they did not go far enough. He would like to suggest on the following day some additions.

Hurley was in the tradition of the many American political celebrities who lay great store by sonorous pronouncements. He also had excessive pride of authorship. With dubious justification he claimed to have written the 1943 Declaration on Iran, in which the United States, Britain, and the Soviet Union affirmed the sovereignty of Iran. Now in Yenan was an opportunity to make a place for himself in history as the wordsmith of Magna Charta for a new China.

Having borrowed from Lincoln for point three of his original proposal, Hurley expanded that section by drawing on the Bill of Rights and Roosevelt's Four Freedoms.

The Coalition National Government will pursue policies designed to promote progress and democracy and to establish justice, freedom of conscience, freedom of the press, freedom of speech, freedom of assembly and association, the right to petition the government for the redress of grievances, the right of writ of Habeas Corpus, and the right of residence. The Coalition National Government will also pursue policies intended to make effective those two rights defined as freedom from fear and freedom from want.

The Communists were much taken with Hurley's lavish additions. If accepted by Chiang, they would knock the persimmons off the tree—for the Communists. Chiang's faltering authoritarianism could not adapt to democracy. Now the Reds, who had long been using the slogans of democracy to shake the Chiang regime, had the prestigious support of the personal representative of the president of the United States. And if a real attempt were made to put into effect a coalition government of the kind embroidered by Hurley, the Communists would probably, through superior organization, discipline, and popular appeal, take over power through political maneuver within the government rather than having to fight for it.

Agreement having been attained on what was now a new proposal, Mao wrote a letter to Roosevelt saying that, "It is with great pleasure that I express my high appreciation for the excellent talent of your personal representative and his deep sympathy towards the Chinese people." Mao reassured the president of Communist devotion to democracy, Chinese unity, and the "deep-rooted friendship" between the Chinese and American people. Not to be outdone, Hurley left with Mao a letter lauding his host for "splendid cooperation and leadership" and his "qualities of mind and heart."

In a buoyant atmosphere, Hurley and Mao signed in duplicate their Five-Point Proposal. One copy of this documentary oddity was retained by Mao, the other Hurley took back to Chungking with him on November 10 to present to the Generalissimo for his signature.

On the 11th, the personal representative sent Soong a copy of the Hurley-Mao protocol. The foreign minister reacted immediately and in a state of agitation visited Hurley, who was confined to his quarters with a cold, protesting that the personal representative had been "sold a bill of goods by the Communists" and that "The National Government will never grant what the Communists have requested."

On November 13 a still rheumy Hurley received me and brought me up to date on developments. I reported the conversation to Vincent at the Department of State, writing that the negotiations between the Generalissimo and Chou were being "conducted through General Hurley, who is acting as mediator." Continuing with what the personal representative had told me, "General Hurley stated that the Chinese Government desires that the conversations be kept secret as they are placed in an embarrassing position by the Communists. . . . He said that the proposals . . . are eminently fair and that if there is a breakdown in the parleys it will be the fault of the government and not the Communists.

"The General stated that he believed the Generalissimo was willing to reach an understanding but that the Generalissimo's wishes were being sabotaged by the men around him. He said that he [Hurley] was being told one thing by Chiang and another thing by his subordinates.

"One of the conditions which he and the Generalissimo agreed to in connection with the removal of General Stilwell, General Hurley stated, was that the Generalissimo would undertake to reach an agreement with the Communists."

Before commenting on the bargain he thought he had struck with Chiang over Stilwell, Hurley had lashed out against Soong. Hurley was loath to believe that Chiang could oppose the formula he had worked out with Mao. He attributed the resistance he was encountering in Chungking to machinations by Soong. It was the foreign minister, whom he described as "a crook," who was turning the sympathetic Chiang against acceptance of the Yenan proposals.

As he had recorded a black mark against Theodore White for telling him the truth about Mao's attitude, so Hurley denounced to me the innocuous British ambassador, Sir Horace Seymour, for allegedly suggesting that he could not bring the government and the Communists together and "pointing out that for centuries China had been divided and gotten along well enough." This he took as sufficient proof that Sir Horace and the British empire were seeking to divert him from his mission. But "Sir Horace was a clumsy diplomat," he snorted, for he, Hurley, had seen through the stratagem.

Official American evaluations of the internal situation in China during the final months of 1944 were diverse. So were the opinions of what policy should be followed.

One point of view was held by those who had studied the international Communist movement, the ablest of them being some of the Soviet specialists of the Foreign Service, officers who were or had been posted at the American Embassy in Moscow. They had a shrewd understanding of Stalinism and were thoroughly familiar with the history of Comintern activities and the current operations of European Communist parties. They correctly described the European parties as being under the disciplinary control of the Kremlin.

These highly competent students of Communism tended to regard the Chinese Communists as Asian counterparts of European Communists, as "creatures of Moscow." In so doing they slighted the particularist features of Chinese Communism. For seventeen years the CCP had maintained its own armies and, however fleetingly at times, governed territory under its authority. The Kremlin had not for nearly a decade been able to insinuate its men into the central command of the CCP. To the contrary, Mao had neutralized all Soviet attempts to penetrate the Yenan apparatus, which he kept firmly under his control. And Mao, with all of his faith in Marxism-Leninism, was passionately nationalist.

Laying stress on the ideological affinity between Moscow and Yenan, and little acquainted with the organizational separation between the two, the American experts on communism regarded the Chinese Communists as wholly subservient to the Kremlin. Therefore they viewed any growth of Chinese Communist strength as an expansion of Soviet power into Asia. It followed that to aid Yenan in any fashion, particularly with military supplies, would be to contribute to the extension of Moscow's rule—and therefore would be against the national interests of the United States.

There were, naturally, many shades of opinion in this interpretation of Yenan-Moscow relations. Curiously enough, military intelligence did not adopt a definitive stand on the issue until July 1945, when it produced a lengthy exposé, more political than military in character, in which it took the orthodox Kremlinologist position regarding the Chinese Communists. It so neglected the military factors in the equation that, on the eve of the civil war, it did not in this revelation estimate the relative capabilities of the Nationalists and the Communists.

On the scene, in China, the orthodox view was held by Wedemeyer, if his retrospective assertions are to be credited. At the time, however, in November and December of 1944, he was preoccupied with his new responsibilities in China. He gave the impression of being without definite opinions regarding the Chinese Communists, of welcoming whatever evidence was available. He went so far as to present to the Generalissimo modest plans for arming the Communists, which Chiang rejected.

Chennault (or a ghost writer) was more articulate. In one of his personal letters to the president, that of September 21, 1944, he warned Roosevelt of the dangers of a civil war, in which Yenan "has an excellent chance of emerging victorious." Looking beyond such an eventuality, he prophesied that "a government in China, closely tied to Moscow, would upset the balance of power in the Pacific." He saw only one way to prevent this from happening. "That is for us to sponsor thorough political reconstruction at Chungking, followed by true unification between Chungking and Yenan." Chennault admitted that this would be "immensely difficult" and he gave no hint of how the opposing regimes were to be unified.

In the Office of Far Eastern Affairs of the State Department judgments regarding the degree of Yenan's subservience to Moscow differed, but were not in the forefront of official concern. The Asian specialists concentrated on how civil war in China might be averted. They clutched the straw of reconciliation between incompatibles. If only Chiang would reform his regime he might be able both to strengthen his position and reach some sort of accommodation with the Communists. But if that did not work, the State Department would improvise policy.

Hurley's approach to the baffling problems of China was uniquely his own. He declared with mounting emphasis that his mission was "to sustain" Chiang as the paramount leader of China and prevent the collapse of the National Government. With what authority he asserted this is not clear. There is no record of its having originated with the president—then absorbed in bringing the war against Hitler to an end and preparing for the complications of victory in Europe—or from the Department of State—which feared that Chiang might be undone at any moment and was consequently wary of irrevocable ties to him and his regime.

Unlike other American officials, Hurley believed that Moscow was uninterested in the Chinese Communists. He continued to accept what Molotov had told him, that the Soviet Union disdained the Chinese Communists. And he was confident he had changed the Generalissimo's mind, from a conviction that the CCP was an instrument of the Kremlin to acceptance of what Hurley had been drumming into him—that Moscow was indifferent to Yenan and benign in its intentions towards Chungking.

Hurley did not think that Yenan was so strong that it was destined to take over China. Underestimating Communist strength, believing that Moscow would not back Yenan, and convinced that there were no fundamental ideological conflicts between the Reds and Chiang's regime—for both were, in his opinion, devoted to government by, for, and of the people—Hurley expected that Yenan would yield to unification under Chiang. To the dismay of the embasssy staff, whose apprehensions I shared, Hurley involved himself and the American Government ever deeper in the fatal struggle between Chiang and the Communists.

My own estimate of the situation in China in November 1944 was starker than it had been in the spring of 1943. Chiang's Kuomintang regime was doomed to defeat by the Communists, I now concluded, either through the violence of civil war or through political conquest in a coalition.

In appraising the character of the Yenan regime I mistakenly described it simply as "democratic." The Chinese Communist dispensation was not democratic in the sense that the word is understood in the United States and Western Europe. It was then, however, a popular regime, attracting rather than exacting the allegiance of the peasantry with which it came in contact. For it identified itself with the people in depth.

Yenan provided the great mass of the population, which had been without hope, an affirmative, personal way out of the swamps of despair. The way out was through rustic nationalism, based on organized guerrilla resistance to the Japanese invaders, and a novel feeling of having some say in the shaping of one's individual destiny. The Communists brought the peasants into consideration of and seeming decision on all matters affecting them. Never in Chinese history had the people been so personally and systematically taken into account in the processes of government. While this was not democracy in the American sense, the people were truly the nourishing water in which the Communist fish swam.

Notwithstanding the ideological kinship between Moscow and Yenan, I thought that the Kremlin did not then control the Chinese Communist movement. But I assumed that Moscow wanted to dominate the Chinese Communists and that once the Soviet Union joined the war against Japan it would act to do so. Troubled by this prospect, I wrote a memorandum on November 15 surveying possible American courses of action in the next six months. "We should not now abandon Chiang Kai-shek. . . . But we must be realistic. . . . We must not indefinitely underwrite a politically bankrupt regime. . . . We must make a determined effort to capture politically the Chinese Communists rather than allow them to go by default wholly to the Russians. Furthermore, we must fully understand that by reason of our recognition of the Chiang Kai-shek government as now constituted we are committed to a steadily decaying regime and severely restricted in working out military and political cooperation with the Chinese Communists."

Making a bow to Hurley's efforts, I said that a mutually agreed-upon coalition would be "from our point of view the most desirable possible solution." Certainly, it was preferable to a devastating civil war from which the Communists would also emerge victorious. "Meanwhile we have no time to lose. . . . While being careful to preserve the Generalissimo's 'face,' we should without delay begin to expand our limited representation and activities at Yenan. Then, if a coalition government is established, we shall have the groundwork laid to launch immediate large-scale military cooperation with the forces in North China [Communist]. If the present Chiang-Communist negotiations break down, we shall have existing well-established relations with the regime which will probably inherit North China and Manchuria. . . . If the Russians enter North China and Manchuria, we obviously cannot hope to win the Communists entirely over to us, but we can through control of supplies and postwar aid expect to exert considerable influence in the direction of Chinese nationalism and independence from Soviet control."

All of this was a long way from Hurley's sustaining Chiang and preventing a collapse of the National Government. It was also a denial of the orthodox Kremlinologist dogma about the nature of Chinese communism—at least until the Russians moved into China. I overstated what we might be able to do in recommending that we strive to "capture" the Chinese Communists. But then, I was also still persuaded of what I had written on November 7, "If we continue to reject them [the Chinese Communists] and support an unreconstructed Chiang, they see us becoming their enemy."

Back in June, when Stilwell got wind of Mountbatten's unsuccessful intrigue to have him replaced by Wedemeyer, the old warrior jotted in his diary, "Good God—to be ousted in favor of Wedemeyer—that would be a disgrace."

Now that had happened, at the instance of Chiang, and Wedemeyer arrived at Chungking on October 31, 1944 to assume command of American forces in the China Theater. His mission was more restricted than Stilwell's. The JCS defined it to him in a directive dated October 24:

a.   Your primary mission with respect to Chinese forces is to advise and assist the Generalissimo in the conduct of military operations against the Japanese.

b.   Your primary mission as to U.S. combat forces under your command is to carry out air operations from China. In addition you will continue to assist the Chinese air and ground forces in operations, training, and logistical support.

The third injunction by the JCS was an unusual and prophetic restraint:

c.   You will not employ United States resources for suppression of civil strife except in so far as necessary to protect United States lives and property.

Finally, Wedemeyer was "authorized," not instructed, "to accept the position of chief of staff to the Generalissimo."

Nothing was said in Wedemeyer's directive about increasing the effectiveness of American aid, improving the combat efficiency of the Chinese Army, or commanding Chinese troops. In essence, Wedemeyer's function was to be complimentary and advisory to the Generalissimo, helpful to the Chinese armed forces, and supervisory over Chennault and Major General Curtis E. LeMay, commanding the Twentieth Bomber Command operating out of Chengtu. The new theater commander and chief of staff to Chiang (which position he accepted) was in some respects well suited to these formal responsibilities. He had the broad approach of a global strategist, was an orderly administrator, and comported himself with ponderous solemnity, even when affecting a bucolic simplicity supposedly characteristic of his native Nebraskan farmers.

As soon as I returned from Yenan I called on Wedemeyer on November 8. "He was cordial and indicated that he wanted me," I wrote to my wife. "But Uncle Dan [General Sultan, commanding Burma-India Theater] had asked for me. As Uncle D outranks him, it's up to me to talk my way out of Uncle D's kindly toils." This I soon did.

Meanwhile, sharing Gauss's annoyance over my rambunctiousness, Vincent had initiated a State Department request on November 8 to the War Department that I be released by the Army for transfer to Colombo, Ceylon as consul.

To complete the jumble, I learned on November 14 through the military and diplomatic grapevine that Harriman, assumably at the instance of Bohlen, had asked for my assignment at Moscow. Stimson settled matters with a November 22 letter to Stettinius stating that Wedemeyer "indicates that it is his conviction that unless these three officers [Service, Emmerson, and Davies—Ludden was on an extended tour behind enemy lines] are retained, military activities will be hampered." So I stayed on with the Army, under Wedemeyer, as I then preferred to do, but hoped to move on to Moscow after a few more months in China.

Like Stilwell, Wedemeyer made no attempt to prescribe my functions. I therefore operated much as I had with his predecessor. As I did so, I watched with approval his efforts to establish cordial relations with the Generalissimo and the Chinese high command. The Chinese, anxious to demonstrate that Stilwell had been the only impediment to smooth and productive relations, tried to reciprocate.

Wedemeyer had been in Chungking only ten days when he radioed Marshall that "the disorganization and muddled planning of the Chinese is beyond comprehension." Then, at the end of November, he asked the Generalissimo whether he might supply arms to General Hsueh Yueh, Chennault's favorite who was fighting the Japanese in East China. Chiang told Wedemeyer to disregard Hsueh's plea for equipment. Wedemeyer's next request was to arm and activate the Communists, which was turned down by the Generalissimo.

After a month in China, Wedemeyer's comments to Marshall about the Chinese high command, although more forgiving of Chiang, had begun to read like Stilwell's.

The Generalissimo and his adherents . . . are impotent and confounded. They are not organized, equipped and trained for modern war. Psychologically they are not prepared to cope with the situation because of political intrigue, false pride, and mistrust of leaders' honesty and motives. . . . Officials surrounding the Generalissimo are actually afraid to report accurately conditions for two reasons: their stupidity and inefficiency are revealed, and, further, the Generalissimo might order them to take positive action and they are incompetent to issue directives, make plans, and fail completely in obtaining execution by field commanders.

Writing to the chief of staff on December 16, in the midst of prevailing alarm that the Japanese would advance on Kunming and Chungking, Wedemeyer unburdened himself:

The Generalissimo is striving to conduct the war from Chungking. The management of affairs of state in itself would require a Disraeli, Churchill, and Machiavelli all combined in one. The Gissimo will not decentralize power to subordinates.

In early conferences with the Generalissimo, I pointed out that we should . . . insure the defence of the Kunming area. I presented a plan for this purpose and he approved that plan. . . . Now I find that he is vacillating—in fact, he has ordered movements of divisions from the Kunming area without my knowledge. . . .

If he [Chiang] goes to the Kunming area, the governor of Yunnan may kidnap him or at least place him under protective custody. . . .

It is the influence and chicanery of his advisers, who have selfish, mercurial

motives and who persuade him when I am not present to take action which conflicts with agreed plans. . . .

It is amusing and also tragic to note that many high-ranking Chinese officials
are asking me to facilitate their evacuation to America by air. . . . Self-sacrifice and
patriotism are unknown quantities among the educated and privileged classes. . . .

The Chinese soldiers are starving by the hundreds. . . .

If only the Chinese will cooperate! . . . The Generalissimo often asks me to
move by air fifty thousand men from A to B. . . . We make appropriate arrangements. Suddenly he will order a change. . . . Neither he nor his advisers really
understand supply and movement problem. But they ask for the most astounding
troop movements to implement their strategy, which is really piecemeal, uncoordinated employment of forces.

Wedemeyer, therefore, seemed to be aware of at least some of the shortcomings of the Generalissimo and his stalwarts. Yet, taking his chief of staff designation very seriously, he strove mightily to make something of military significance out of China's incoherent levies. He was not required to do this. To the
contrary, the wording and the tone of his directive from the Joint Chiefs of Staff,
in contrast to the mission given Stilwell, was restricted, almost passive. Why,
then, did Wedemeyer assume so positive a role?

As a soldier, it was in his training that he should discharge his duty with all
vigor, he should overfulfill, accomplish more than was expected of him. His conditioning in this respect was reinforced by the presence of Hurley, a frenetic
activist, who regarded himself as Wedemeyer's patron and acted as his preceptor.
Perhaps more importantly, Wedemeyer was acutely, impatiently ambitious. His
ambition was goaded by the fact that he, a colorless, junior desk general, was
taking the place of a grizzled campaigner, to many a martyr-hero. He was determined to succeed where Stilwell had failed.

So driven, Wedemeyer plunged into the Chinese maelstrom, identifying
himself—and his country—with the survival of Chiang and his regime. With
Hurley he would "sustain" Chiang. Like Hurley, he thought this was an attainable goal because he grossly underestimated the potential of the Chinese Communists. He was shocked by the plain-spoken pessimism of Gauss about the situation in China, when he called on the ambassador shortly before Gauss's departure. He was unimpressed by my recommendations that the United States beware
of continuing commitment to a bankrupt regime and that Washington pragmati-
cally hedge its investment of power in China by more affirmative relations with
the rising force, the Communists.

T. V. Soong had won, late in 1944, the Generalissimo's suspicious acceptance of him as agent for dealing with the inscrutable Americans. Although
Chiang's brother-in-law had the title of foreign minister, the Generalissimo
restricted Soong's authority. With ample reason, Chiang did not trust his brilliant, semi-American relative.

He knew that Soong coveted his power and had plotted to shunt him aside
into an honorific position and take over governing authority. Late in 1942 Soong
had urged Stilwell to cultivate two generals favored by the foreign minister—

Ch'en Ch'eng and Hsueh Yueh. Boldly he sought to enlist Stilwell's support for a deal which would have, among other things, given the foreign minister extensive powers over the Chinese military establishment. Stilwell reacted with noncommital reserve, and nothing came of the proposal.

In one of the tactical reversals so characteristic of conspiracies within the Chiang-Soong dynasty, Soong turned against Stilwell. He began sniping at the general and then on September 15, 1943 during a sojourn in Washington, presented Roosevelt with a reorganization scheme for the China Theater. This would assign two unspecified Chinese officers as supreme commander and as chief of staff. Chiang would thus be replaced as supreme commander, but left with his title as chief of state, and Stilwell would be eliminated. The president referred this flight of fancy to Marshall, who dismissed it.

As Soong, in Washington, was concocting a new order for the China Theater, two of his sisters in Chungking, Madame Chiang and Madame Kung, puzzled Stilwell by suddenly, on September 13, offering themselves as his guardian angels. Anti-Stilwell rumors were spurting in Chungking and Stilwell had been deficient in ceremonious treatment of the Generalissimo. Little and Big Sister undertook to treat on his behalf with Little Sister's husband. Stilwell accepted their advances and surmised that they had come to his rescue at the behest of brother, T. V.

The intrigue in which the Soong siblings and Stilwell were involved was symphonic in complexity. Slighting the contrapuntal contributions of factions in the Chinese army officer corps, cliques in the Kuomintang, Soong's tiny coterie of civilians, and Chennault, this appreciation concentrates on the dominant theme.

The second movement began with Soong's passage through India in mid-October 1943 on his way to Chungking. There he encountered Mountbatten, also bound for Chungking as the newly appointed SACSEA, and General Somervell, dispatched by Roosevelt to introduce Lord Louis to the Generalissimo. Having told a surprised Somervell that the president had consented to withdraw Stilwell, and Mountbatten that the appointment of Stilwell as Lord Louis's deputy would create "disastrous irrevocable repercussions," the foreign minister scurried on to China.

The second movement rose to a crescendo on October 17. The Generalissimo, as interpreted by Soong, advised Somervell that Stilwell should be recalled. Quickly, on the following day, the two sisters intervened with Chiang in defense of Stilwell. General Ho, the war minister and chief of staff, whom Stilwell had repeatedly tried to oust, likewise came to his support. None of these three Chinese had any reason to back the foreigner for his own sake. But each of the three had reason to preserve the distribution of power in Chungking as it was— Madame Chiang to keep her husband in his position of paramount authority, Madame Kung to protect her husband, the finance minister, whom her brother wished to push aside, and Ho because he feared Stilwell less than an ascendant Soong—and Soong's candidate for chief of staff, General Ch'en Ch'eng.

In this impassioned passage, a lyric motif was briefly introduced. The sisters induced a reluctant Stilwell to reassure the Generalissimo that he fully recognized Chiang's commanding position. This was done, *obbligato,* and the Generalissimo's face was thereby celebrated. Whereupon Chiang, in a thunderous climax to the second movement, cast out Soong. The hysteria of this October 18 encounter, with the Generalissimo screaming and smashing his teacup and Soong upbraiding his brother-in-law, was disproportionate to the issue of Stilwell. So was the concurrent relief of General Ch'en Ch'eng from his field command for alleged reasons of health.

Madame Kung, as imperturbable as she was shrewd, confided to Stilwell two days later that she had been compelled to choose between "her own flesh and blood" (meaning her brother) and the good of China (meaning the good of herself, of Dr. Kung, and of Chiang Kai-shek, in that order). Soong's power lust had challenged the hierarchical order of the dynasty, and those threatened reacted together against the would-be usurper. The rash foreign minister was lucky not to have been executed, and he knew it.

The third movement was a pastorale, with Soong permitted for appearances' sake to retain his title of foreign minister, but ostracized by the Generalissimo. Thoroughly cowed, Soong remained out of sight. But not for long. During the visit of Vice-President Wallace in June 1944 the Generalissimo brought him out on short leash to serve as interpreter.

In the process Soong recovered his confidence sufficiently to advise Wallace that Chiang was bewildered and his authority disintegrating, that it was "five minutes to midnight," and that the government needed reformation. Much impressed, the vice-president took Soong with him on his pilgrimage to Chennault. On the flight to Kunming, Wallace was casting about for the name of someone whom he might recommend to replace Stilwell in China. John Carter Vincent, who accompanied the vice-president on his tour, later stated that Soong may have been the one who volunteered the name of Wedemeyer. In any event, the Chinese foreign minister appears to have participated happily in the vice-president's scheming for a reshuffle of the American military command in China. Soong was back in his stride.

Wallace had found the foreign minister to be a kindred Chinese spirit— "pro-American," "efficient," and above all "western-minded," in contrast to Chiang, whom he described as "eastern-minded." Soong fostered the image of himself as a "modernist" who should be the chosen American instrument to guide China out of the war and into the postwar world. This was a vain pretension, for Soong did not have the sinews of power.

If he had any following, it was a timid handful of westernized bankers and technicians. They were a tiny fraction of the thousands of American and European-educated Chinese who could be termed modernists, but the majority of whom were politically inactive. Soong's American claque, conspicuously Wallace, inflated the foreign minister's insignificant coterie to include Ch'en Ch'eng and Hsueh Yueh, both relatively outstanding generals, and several others. But these men, who did dispose of appreciable power, were not Soong's followers.

Like virtually all of their colleagues, they were opportunists, receptive to political propositioning, provided that the proposition seemed profitable.

To gather to him these significant forces, Soong had to show them more strength than he had. This he could do if he were able to deliver the Americans. Soong had the support of Chennault, who characterized him as a modernist and urged Roosevelt "to sponsor thorough political reconstruction at Chungking. . . ." But the foreign minister had not been able to muster Chennault's balky superior.

Therefore, Stilwell had to be gotten rid of. On this score, the Generalissimo and Soong were in agreement in 1944. But for different reasons—while Chiang wanted no more of Stilwell's humiliating spurs in his sides, Soong wanted any American who would collaborate with him in "reforming" Chiang's regime as he saw fit. For essentially conflicting reasons Chiang and Soong combined in the autumn of 1944 to accomplish Stilwell's downfall.

Hurley and Wedemeyer did not turn out to be all that Soong had hoped for. Soong and Hurley got along well at the outset of their relationship. In a message to the secretary of state, dated August 18, 1945, Hurley recalled:

> Dr. Soong was not in good standing with his government when I arrived in China. I found very few Chinese who were western-minded. Dr. Soong's Harvard education, his eleven years' banking experience in the United States, and long official service there has given him an insight into the American situation that is unsurpassed by any Chinese I have ever known. . . . I turned instinctively to a Chinese who could understand what I was saying and make the Generalissimo understand. Conversely he could make me understand the Generalissimo.

The communion between Soong and Hurley was soon marred by the foreign minister's criticism of the Hurley-Mao Five-Point Proposal to the Government. The personal representative's chronically swollen and tender vanity was thereby bruised. Thereafter he regarded Soong with hostile suspicion—and yet remained dependent upon the foreign minister in his relations with the Generalissimo.

Soong's relations with Wedemeyer were less close, if for no other reason than that the general tried to function through military channels. His view of Soong was naturally colored by Hurley's. And his own contacts with the foreign minister did not arouse enthusiasm in him for Soong.

The determination of Hurley and Wedemeyer to "sustain" Chiang hardly contributed to a realization of Soong's ambitions. Yet Soong had preferred them to Gauss and Stilwell. Now he was discovering that they were even less likely than the two stubborn old China hands to support his aspirations, for Gauss and Stilwell had not, at least, committed themselves to keeping Chiang in power. In the new situation, so much of his own making, Soong was compelled to choke down his ambitions and serve the Generalissimo as a technician for coping with foreign devils.

The position of the so-called modernists, of whom Soong was the most prominent, was not unlike that of the Twenty-eight Bolsheviks in the Communist camp. Both were foreignized, the modernists by American education, the Twenty-eight Bolsheviks by indoctrination in the Soviet Union. Neither could challenge with any hope of success its more indigenously-rooted ruling group. The big difference, aside from ideology, between the Twenty-eight Bolsheviks and the Modernists was that the Communist faction was organized and programmatic while Soong's category was not. For the modernists were really a cultural category rather than a cohesive political faction.

Soong was neither a plausible successor to the Generalissimo nor a feasible middle choice between Chiang and the Communists. He was acute rather than wise, tricky rather than deft, arrogant rather than poised, alien rather than persuasively different. He could not make it. By the end of 1944 China was so polarized between Chiang and Mao that there was no third way. It was one or the other.

CHAPTER 35

Hurley and I Disagree

ROOSEVELT radioed Hurley on November 17 that he would like to appoint him ambassador. "Your intimate knowledge of the situation there, both from the military and diplomatic standpoints . . . eminently qualifies you." Hurley immediately accepted.

Two days later Hurley hinted to me that he would be made ambassador and wanted me on his staff. On November 21 I wrote my wife, "General Hurley indicated to me this morning that he would like to have you come to Chungking." Then, as I informed her on November 26, even before his appointment had been confirmed, Hurley ordered a Cadillac flown in to him. In a two-hour session with me on December 1, he described how he was going to repaint and refurnish the ambassador's residence—he wouldn't have his dog sleep in Gauss's bed—and evict the five staff members to whom Gauss had given shelter in an overcrowded Chungking. "Now that he thought of it," I reported to Patricia, "he'd like to have us live with him."

Because of alarm aroused by a Japanese column advancing westward, Hurley said to me on December 8 that my wife should postpone her move to Chungking. It is just as well that this was the case as Soong was increasing his pressure on Hurley to get me out of China. Within a fortnight after Stilwell's departure the foreign minister had told the personal representative, I was reliably informed, that he had received an intelligence report from Yenan that I had sent Service to the United States to recommend, in conjunction with Stilwell, the withdrawal of recognition of Chiang's government and the recognition of Yenan. Hurley apparently believed this mendacious and obvious concoction until my informant explained to him that the Chinese had the habit of playing off individuals as well as nations against one another.

The personal representative remembered this lesson. When he fulminated to me about Soong on November 13, he said that the foreign minister was overly fond of intrigue and attempted to play personalities, trying to get Hurley off the track "chasing rabbits" with allegations against other Americans, the minister of war, and Tai Li. Now in early December Hurley revealed to me that Soong was still pressing for my departure, declaring that Chiang thought that I had already left, and asking when I was going. On one of these occasions, Hurley said, he replied, "All right, let's ask the Generalissimo." Whereat Soong backed away from doing so. The new ambassador then told the foreign minister that he planned to have my wife and me stay with him, and "enjoyed watching T.V. squirm."

After reporting this byplay to my wife, I wrote: "I intend to get away (but not as a refugee, God damn it.) George [Atcheson, embassy Counselor] said that he was tired of frustration. He wanted to go to a country where we weren't having to back up all of the time. An affirmative atmosphere, I said. Still, I wouldn't change this experience—for a while. I am just fully comprehending in my conscious, rather than my subconscious, the medieval quality of this situation."

While Hurley filled me in on a part of what he was up to, he did not bring me fully into his confidence or make use of me. He was determined to bring about a reconciliation between Chiang and the Communists single-handed. I hoped that he might succeed, but he knew I greatly doubted that he would.

Because of the American clamor for reform in Chungking and the Hurley-Mao *démarche* calling for a Bill of Rights and more, Chiang felt that he had to make a gesture in response. On November 21 cabinet changes were announced, the most important of which was the appointment of a chastened General Ch'en Ch'eng as minister of war. Of far greater significance was the delivery to Hurley that day of the government's counterdraft to the Hurley-Mao proposals. It had gone through three writings, ending up as a document that repeated some of Hurley's declamatory prose, but introduced a provision requiring the Communists to "give over control of all their troops to the National Government." Obviously, this would be unacceptable to Yenan.

As Chou En-lai was preparing to leave Chungking in disgust, Hurley brought in Wedemeyer and Wedemeyer's chief of staff, Major General Robert B. McClure, to meet with Chou and quite gratuitously involve the United States more deeply in this internal Chinese affair. Hurley and Wedemeyer tried to persuade Chou that the Communists should accept the government's terms, and trust that Yenan's interests would be safeguarded by the one Communist officer whom the government would allow on the National Military Council. Chou was unmoved.

Colonel Barrett, who had participated in the meeting, accompanied Chou to Yenan. At Hurley's request, he conferred with Mao and Chou on December 8 in a futile effort to convince them that they should yield to Chiang's conditions. Mao observed that to accept these terms would be "tantamount to complete surrender" and that it would mean that "we give up our only means of self-defense, which is our army." Other comments by Mao, as recorded by Barrett, were:

General Hurley also says that acceptance of representation in the National Military Council will give us "a foot in the door." . . . All we can say is that "a foot in the door" means nothing if the hands are tied behind the back. . . .

We find the attitude of the United States somewhat puzzling. General Hurley came to Yenan and asked on what terms we would cooperate with the Kuomintang. We offered a five-point proposal of which the basis was the establishment of a coalition government. General Hurley agreed that the terms were eminently fair, and in fact, a large part of the proposals were suggested by him. The Generalissimo has refused these terms. Now the United States comes and earnestly asks us to accept counterproposals which require us to sacrifice our liberty. . . .

General Wedemeyer says that if we come to an agreement with the Generalissimo, he can give us arms. . . . We would welcome such assistance with all our hearts, but we cannot be expected to pay the price which the Generalissimo demands. . . .

The United States believes that Chiang Kai-shek must be retained in power at all costs. . . . If on his record, the United States wishes to prop up the rotten shell that is Chiang Kai-shek, that is her privilege. We believe, however, that in spite of all the United States can do, Chiang is doomed to failure. . . .

We are not like Chiang Kai-shek. No nation needs to prop us up. We can stand erect and walk on our own feet like free men.

Whereat Mao strode back and forth. When speaking of a foot in the door and hands tied behind the back he flung his hands to the rear upon his buttocks. This was typical Maoist acting out a train of thought. Mao continued:

If the United States abandons us, we shall be very, very sorry, but it will make no difference in our good feeling toward you. . . . We would serve with all our hearts under an American General, with no strings or conditions attached. . . . If you land on the shores of China, we will be there to meet you and to place ourselves under your command.

If the United States will not help us, there is still England and the Soviet Union.

When mentioning the Generalissimo, Mao permitted himself outbursts of wrath and name-calling, even descending to the indecent vulgarity of calling Chiang a turtle's egg. This performance, too, was typically Mao, and convincing because it came naturally to him.

At the close of the symposium, Mao reminded the long-suffering Barrett that it was Hurley who had suggested that Mao and he sign the Five-Point Proposal on November 10 as evidence that they both considered it fair. "Much as we would dislike to do this," Mao cautioned, "there may come a time when we feel we should show this document, with the signatures, to the Chinese and foreign press." Upon his return to Chungking on the following day, Barrett dutifully reported to the ambassador, and conveyed Mao's somewhat less than subtle threat. As recounted in Barrett's chronicle, *Dixie Mission*, "I was afraid for a moment he [Hurley] might burst a blood vessel. 'The mother————,' he yelled, using an expression now in rather common use but seldom heard at the time, 'he tricked meh!' "

In a stodgier vein, that same day and quite coincidentally, I directed a memorandum to Wedemeyer with a copy to Hurley in which I said in part: "The Generalissimo realizes that if he accedes to the Communist terms for a coalition government, they will sooner or later dispossess him and his Kuomintang of power. He will therefore not, unless driven to an extremity, form a genuine coalition government. . . .

"The Communists, on their part, have no interest in reaching an agreement with the Generalissimo short of a genuine coalition government. They recognize that Chiang's position is crumbling, that they may before long receive substantial Russian support, and that if they have patience they will succeed to authority in at least North China."

Three days later, after I had learned the substance of what had transpired at the Mao-Chou-Barrett meeting, I began another memorandum to Wedemeyer and Hurley with, "The negotiations looking to an agreement between the Generalissimo and the Chinese Communists have failed." In a cut-the-Gordian-knot approach, I recommended that we tell Chiang that we would work with and supply whatever Chinese forces we thought would most contribute to the war against Japan, provided that they did not show an inclination to precipitate civil conflict. We would keep the Generalissimo informed of the supply distribution. But we would "refuse to become further involved in and party to Chinese domestic political disputes."

Hurley called me in on the following day, December 13, and asked me to go over a message he was sending to Washington reporting the Communist rejection of the Government's counterproposals. As Hurley kept his exchanges with the president and the secretary of state to himself, I was surprised at being consulted. The message as finally dispatched was brief and factual with only one optimistic note—"I do not believe that the door is definitely closed to further negotiations."

It was out of bafflement, I suspect, that Hurley turned to me. For at about this time he had confided to me one of his pieces of folk wisdom. "Why do the leaves turn red in the fall? Because they were so green in the spring." My bleak view of the situation, however, could not give him the answers that he wanted. He was still determined to bring Chiang and the Communists together, to unify China, and to do it himself. He was critical of Gauss for having refused to be involved in the poisonous melee between Chungking and Yenan. As later, on February 18, 1945 he radioed the secretary of state, he believed in "implementing" the suggestions he made to the Chinese. The only question in his mind was how far he might go in "inducing or compelling the unification of Chinese armed forces"—under Chiang.

In my opinion Hurley was making a conceited and foolhardy commitment of the United States to a futile and dangerous course. Although I was not so blunt as this with the ambassador, he recognized my lack of sympathy for his policy. I was not astonished, therefore, when he indicated in mid-December that I should soon leave China. Describing the incident to my wife, I wrote: "I saw Hurley and asked him what about Chip's message [Bohlen had radioed that Harriman was expecting me at Moscow]. He said that he thought it would be useful for me to go and before February [as I had planned]. But that it must be secret as it would make Rhumba [Soong] exquisitely unhappy [to learn that I was going to Moscow rather than being banished to an obscure post]. I haven't yet taken the matter up with General W as he is away. . . . Hurley will tell Rhumba that, as desired by Rhumba, I am being returned for transfer—Basra or Aden perhaps!"

Satisfied that he would gain credit with Soong for my departure, the mercurial ambassador regaled me on December 15, for the second time, with an account of how Soong had urged him to arrange the transfer of Lieutenant Joseph W. Alsop (a journalist acting as Chennault's aide) for assignment to Hurley. The ambassador guffawed, "T. V. figures that you know too much; he wants to set up his own pipeline to me."

In the company of Barrett and Lieutenant Colonel Willis H. Bird, an OSS secret operations officer, I flew to Yenan again on December 15. At the time I had only a vague notion of what the other two were up to. I did know that Barrett was bearing a message from Hurley to the Communists regarding the moribund negotiations with the government. As Barrett did not volunteer more than that I did not pursue the matter. In OSS tradition, Bird was appropriately uncommunicative, but I had heard at headquarters that he had some sort of plan for using Communist guerrillas.

My reasons for going to Yenan were slighter. As I now recall, one was to inquire whether the Communists had information about a possible tacit agreement between Chiang and the Japanese to cease offensive action against one another. My other reason was to get a final personal impression of the dominant Chinese Communists before going to Moscow. I particularly wanted to sense the temperature of attitude toward Americans and the United States.

Not surprisingly, Chou thought that there might be a tacit nonaggression understanding between Chungking and the Japanese. Parenthetically, when Wedemeyer confronted Chiang on January 10, 1945 on this score, the Generalissimo neither denied nor admitted it: "His spontaneous reaction was a dry cackle." I was impressed anew by the intelligence, force, and confidence of the top Communists. And those with whom I came in contact were demonstratively cordial.

Well they might have been. For it has since been revealed that, aside from bringing a plea from Hurley to Chou to keep the Five-Points secret and to reopen negotiations with the government, Barrett also brought word from Wedemeyer's chief of staff of a plan to introduce four to five thousand American airborne troops into Communist territory for demolition operations and to organize and lead Communist guerrillas. McClure wanted Yenan's reaction to the plan before trying to clear it with the Chungking government.

But this was not all. Bird had his OSS plan. It now appears to have involved sending in OSS units, also for demolition and diversionary attacks, equipping up to twenty-five thousand guerrillas, establishing a school for clandestine warfare, developing a radio net in cooperation with the Communists' Eighteenth Group Army, and supplying the People's Militia with one hundred thousand simple pistols.

What the Communist responses to these propositions were, I do not know.

The McClure proposal, with no offer of materiel and its emphasis on American command, was hardly what the Communists hoped for. But, if accepted, it might lead to more forthcoming American cooperation. The OSS plan, however, was an attractive enough bid in itself, even though the Communists would have much preferred rifles to cloak-and-dagger pistols.

Both projects were discarded in mid-January. It is sufficient to say here that Hurley became entangled and befuddled in scheming by both Chungking and Yenan, claimed that he had not been advised of the planning consultations with the Communists, and in a paroxysm of suspicion fired off a radio to the president virtually accusing McClure, Barrett, and Bird of conspiring behind his back, wrecking the negotiations, and encouraging the Communists to bypass him. When Wedemeyer, who was absent during this unedifying performance, returned he was indignant over the slanderous charges against his officers and reproached Hurley for trespassing in military matters. But Wedemeyer did issue an order prohibiting all officers from assisting or negotiating with Chinese political parties or persons without his permission.

It might be added that Hurley later upbraided Wedemeyer for trespassing in political matters when the general, in a message to Marshall, spoke of Hurley's negotiations as having been unsuccessful. The ambassador, then living with Wedemeyer, punished the general for the wounding transgression by refusing for days to speak to him. In the unwonted hush Wedemeyer found solace in the thought that he was no less capable than Hurley of "understanding the political situation, particularly the implications of Communism, in China."

It was I, however, who was the first object of Hurley's wrath, a wrath kindled by frustration over the negotiations with which he had so overweeningly identified himself. His vanity would not permit him to admit that he had blundered, that the negotiations could not succeed. Consequently, when the parleys faltered, some fell influence must be at work, someone was undermining his efforts. Soong was eager to tell him who that was.

The letter from Chou En-lai to Hurley that Barrett brought on our return from Yenan on December 17 was friendly to the ambassador, agreeing not to publish the Five-Point Proposal, but keeping pressure on a jumpy nerve by saying that it might be necessary later to do so. Chou laid all blame for the deadlock in negotiations on the Kuomintang and its "lack of sincerity." The Communists, he said, "never closed the door of negotiation." Revealing an understanding of Hurley, Chou stated, "The Central Committee of our party and Chairman Mao wish to register here their gratitude for your enthusiasm in unifying the Chinese people." And he sent "our very best wishes" to the ambassador, Wedemeyer, and McClure.

However gratifying the Chinese blarney, the fact remained that Yenan was holding to the Five-Point Proposal, to the pain of its principal author. The first hint of Hurley's mortification came to me on December 19 when he said, as I wrote to my wife, "that in view of a talk he had this morning he thought it would be a good thing all around" for me to proceed to Moscow. I assumed that the talk had been with Soong.

Wedemeyer was now back at Chungking so I asked him to release me for prompt transfer to Harriman because of my difficulties with Soong and now Hurley. The general was astonished, felt that I should not leave because of Soong, and asked me to stay on. I explained that I could not function in my political field in the face of the foreign minister's relentless hostility and his influence over Hurley. Wedemeyer then consented and I gave him a letter asking formally for detachment from detail to him.

On December 21 I informed my wife: "There is in the mill a message that Al [Wedemeyer] has released me for the Moscow detail. His reply to my letter came in today. And a very nice one it was too. Thanking me for my efficient and loyal service."

Two days later I again wrote: "Yesterday I had quite a blowup with the ambassador [Hurley]. He accused me of sneaking off to Yenan on this last trip to wreck his negotiations. T. V. had told him so. And apparently he accepted T. V.'s explanation. Who [Soong] had said that I had advised the Communists not to pay any attention to Hurley because he was an old fool. Very nice. We had an half-hour argument on the subject, I talking quite frankly. I left with the impression that I had persuaded him of the preposterousness of T. V.'s charges. But I am not sure. His mind is not as clear as it once was. And I think that he is a little confused by the maelstrom of intrigue in which he finds himself. I'll tell you all of the fantastic details when I see you. I must confess that, hardened as I am to the incredible deviousness and scheming of the Chungking scene, I had not anticipated anything quite like this."

"I have not seen His Excellency for several days so do not know what his latest reactions may be," I told my wife on Christmas Day. "I am not worried, only philosophically amused and historically depressed." I found out, vaporously, what Hurley's latest reactions were at a merry Christmas party at the embassy where "the genbassador with a sprig of evergreen at the back of his head led off a snake dance around the room, emitting Choctaw whoops. Shortly before that impressive spectacle . . . he summoned me over, lifted his glass and said sententiously 'Here's to you, John.' It was the peace pipe. As he left he said, 'I'm going to stop—I've forgotten the word, raising hell with or riding or something like that—you. And you stop doing the same with me.' "

Hurley sent the secretary of state on December 24 a summary of his position and the situation in China. He repeated his concept of his mission, mainly "to prevent the collapse of the National government," "sustain" Chiang, and "unify all the military forces of China." He implied that he had nearly persuaded Chiang that the CCP was not an instrument of the Soviet Government and that Moscow did not recognize the CCP as Communist. "When I first arrived it was thought that civil war . . . was inevitable. Chiang Kai-shek is now convinced that by agreement with the Communist Party of China he can (1) unite the military forces of China against Japan and (2) avoid civil strife in China."

After summarizing the course of negotiations, the ambassador restated his conviction that "there is very little difference, if any, between the avowed principles" of the National government and the Communists. "The greatest opposition to the unification of China," he continued, "comes from foreigners." These were "the imperialist nations" and their representatives in Chungking. Also, "there are some American military and diplomatic officers who believe that the present Chinese government will eventually collapse and that there can be no military or political unification of China under Chiang Kai-shek."

In cataloguing the alleged opinions of these Americans, Hurley asserted that they believed that the Communists "should" not unite with the National government, nor "permit" Communist troops to be united with the Chinese Army, and that the United States should deal with the CCP but "not with the National government."

Returning on December 29 from a quick visit to Yenan, Colonel Barrett brought me a letter from Chou En-lai. It was written in English, probably a translation from Chinese as Chou's knowledge of English was sketchy. It was in response to a note I had sent him informing him of my impending departure.

I left Chungking for good on January 9, 1945. On the way to the airport I stopped off to say goodbye to Wedemeyer and Hurley. I wished the ambassador luck in his negotiations and then, as I now remember it, incautiously expressed the hope that he would not be caught in the tangles of Chinese intrigue should the negotiations fail. It would be a pitiable end to so distinguished a career.

Apparently I had struck a responsive chord in Hurley. He became quite florid and puffy, shouting that he would break my back and other pleasantries. "You want to pull the plug on Chiang Kai-shek," he repeatedly bellowed. The ambassador's blast furnace approach raised my temperature and the exchange between his fulminations and my remonstrances was heated. As to all conversations, an end came to this one and Hurley and I parted with a civil handshake.

I wondered at the time whether the frenzy of the ambassador's reaction to my concern for his place in history may not have been caused in some part by a memorandum that I wrote on January 4. It was an exercise in viewing the China scene as if from the Kremlin. Here are some passages from it.

The current situation in China must afford the Kremlin a certain sardonic satisfaction.

The Russians see the anti-Soviet government of Chiang Kai-shek decaying— militarily, politically, and economically. . . .

The Russians have witnessed the instructive frustration of American efforts to bring about by exhortation a Chiang-Communist agreement. If by our refusal now of military cooperation to the Communists the potentially pro-American and nationalist group at Yenan has lost prestige and those doctrinaires favoring reliance upon the Soviet Union have been further strengthened, the Kremlin doubtless knows it.

The Russians need not regret their present hands-off policy. From Chinese Turkestan to the China coast events seem gratuitously to have served the Kremlin well. . . .

December 28, 1944.

Dear Mr. Davies:

Thank you for your nice letter and gift which you sent us. We hope that you have thoroughly enjoyed your Christmas holidays and will have a very happy New Year.

I deeply regret to hear that you may be leaving China on a new assignment, at the same time I hope your hopes may be fulfilled and that you will soon come back. We hope, however, to be able to keep in touch with you through Mr. Jack Service who, we have heard, is coming back.

I wish that you will not forget us when you get back to Washington. Let me hear from you from time to time and send us some of the current magazines and literature, books and other material that you can spare or have finished reading.

Colonel David Barrett will be able to give you more details about here when he gets back so that I will not go into details.

My wife joins me in wishing you a very Happy New Year and continued success. I look forward to seeing you very soon among us.

Yours,

Chow En-lai

The [Chinese] Communists have amply demonstrated a capacity for independent, dynamic growth. However Marshal Stalin may describe the Chinese Communists to his American visitors, he can scarcely be unaware of the fact that the [Chinese] Communists are a considerably more stalwart and self-sufficient force than any European underground or partisan movement....

It is presumably evident to the Kremlin that ... we seem to be committed to (1) reliance upon only Central Government forces for the conduct of the war against Japan on the continent and (2) unconditional support of Chiang Kaishek. Yet Chungking can contribute little. ... And as for Chiang's being able to unite China, the Russians are scarcely likely to cherish illusions on that score.

No one is perhaps more aware than Marshal Stalin of the fallibility of foreign loyalties to the Soviet Union. Or of the potency of nationalism. And perhaps no one more than Marshal Stalin appreciates the malleability of a revolutionary movement.

It is therefore difficult to believe that the Kremlin does not recognize certain conditions in Communist China which the United States might, if it would and could, exploit to its own great advantage. They are:

(1) The eagerness and the capability of the Communists to cooperate with the United States....

(2) The strategic position of Communist China extending deep into Japan's inner zone.

(3) The present nationalistic feeling among the Communists which, with practical American encouragement, would probably become the dominant motivation of the Communists, but which, with continuing American indifference to Yenan, will be superseded by a sense of persecution, isolation, and dependence upon the Soviet Union.

(4) The present moderate social and economic program of the Communists, the mass support which they command and their outstanding vitality....

(5) The Communists' need of foreign capital ... and the inability of the Soviet Union to fill that need for some time....

Moscow may well doubt that we will and can exploit these conditions so favorable to us. ... The necessary sensitivity in a democratic system of the administration to public opinion makes it unlikely that American policy can be anything other than a vacillating compromise between realism and wishful thinking.

It is difficult to escape the conclusion that we are in Russian (and British) eyes the victims of the insularity and international political immaturity of our people and of the unwieldy processes of democracy. By our unwillingness and inability to engage in *realpolitik*, the Kremlin may well believe, we stand to lose that which we seek—the quickest possible defeat of Japan and a united, strong, and independent China. And the Soviet Union may stand to gain ... a satellite North China. The Kremlin is not likely to be unaware of what is at stake in this situation —the future balance of power in Asia and the Western Pacific.

CHAPTER *36*

Moscow

IT WAS DUSK when we landed at Moscow. Snow covered the ground and haze blurred the hulking, shabby buildings lining the way to the center of the city. Only a few cars moved on the streets and pedestrians, swaddled in black greatcoats or gray quilted jackets, hurried on their way with downturned heads.

My wife and I had left the radiant winter of New Delhi on February 9, 1945 and then, under Tehran's Persian blue skies, waited until March 23 for Soviet visas. We had basked in our due of light and warmth when we boarded a Soviet C-47 at Tehran. In a Russian roulette takeoff, with a comrade lounging on the auxiliary gas tank in the cabin, a glowing cigarette hanging from his lower lip, we headed for Baku. After overnighting there, and fortified by a breakfast of caviar and garlic sausage, we flew to the desolation of Stalingrad and thence to Moscow, arriving on March 25.

Ambassador Harriman generously took us in and gave us a room in the uncertain splendor of Spaso House, his residence. We were lodged directly above a salon in which movies were shown after dinner. They were meant to relax the American colony and hold high our culture to fellow diplomats and the handful of Russians permitted or ordered to associate with foreigners. Wartime difficulties of transportation between Moscow and the United States limited the cinematic repertoire. *Casablanca*, with Humphrey Bogart, was an oft-repeated favorite. There was no escaping the casbah. Patricia and I would seek the quiet of our room, only to be pursued through the booming floorboards by a snarling Bogie.

The ambassador seldom used his office in the chancery. He also had an office in Spaso House. My dominant memories of Harriman are of a handsome figure in a dressing gown, late at night in front of the fireplace of his bedroom, humped over in an easy chair methodically penciling corrections on the pages of an outgoing message strewn on his lap. It was mostly in this cozy setting that he wrestled through communications issuing from his embassy.

Along with others of the staff I worked at the chancery. This was housed on the lower floors of a ramshackle, seven-story edifice of typically shoddy Soviet construction. The building faced a corner of the Kremlin and Red Square. The upper floors were used as quarters for staff members. Patricia and I came to occupy a duplex apartment on the top floors with a theatric view of Kremlin towers and onion domes, Red Square, and St. Basil's.

As minister-counselor, George Kennan directed the operations of the embassy. Working for him was an exhilarating experience, for his was an intuitive and creative mind, richly stored with knowledge, eloquent in expression, and disciplined by a scholarly respect for precision. It was a delight to watch him probe some sphinxlike announcement in *Pravda* for what might lie within or behind it, recalling some obscure incident in Bolshevik history or a personality conflict within the Party, quoting a passage from Dostoevsky on Russian character, or citing a parallel in Tsarist foreign policy. His subtle intellect swept the range of possibilities like a radar attuned to the unseen.

Like most of the foreign service specialists on Russia, Kennan regarded Roosevelt's policy toward the Soviet Union as, at best, credulous. Harriman, although privately having serious doubts about it, was outwardly a stern supporter of the president's course and showed slight if any interest in what Kennan thought on the big issues. Unable to influence Washington away from self-deception, the sensitive Kennan suffered agonies of frustration.

He and his colleagues had been deeply affected by two revelations in 1937 of the Roosevelt administration's attitude toward relations with the Soviet Union and White House suspicion that the Russian specialists were prejudiced against the Bolsheviks. One was an affliction visited upon them in the form of an ambassador, Joseph E. Davies. He was opportunistic, married to an heiress, and a deserving Democrat, and so was casually rewarded by Roosevelt with the Moscow embassy. The Foreign Service officers of the embassy staff were appalled by the ambassador's toadying to the Soviet oligarchy and crass representation of himself as one who knew how to get along with the Kremlin. It seemed to them that his appointment to so intricately exacting a position was an indication of at least presidential frivolity.

The second 1937 disclosure of the Roosevelt administration's attitude was an abrupt order uncomfortably issued by the under secretary of state, Sumner Welles, doing away with the Division of Eastern European Affairs. Attention to Soviet developments was relegated to one junior officer occupying half a room in a newly-created Division of European Affairs. Robert F. Kelly, the chief of the abolished division and one of the best informed men in the West about the Soviet Union, was transferred to Turkey. The division's special files were ordered destroyed and its unique library scattered into the Library of Congress. To the Foreign Service officers who were and had been reporting on the Moscow purges, what happened to their division in Washington had a faintly familiar stench.

I had a feeling of kinship with the Russian specialists. But my functions in the embassy, initially, were not directly related to American policy toward the

Soviet Union. My job was to comment on the situation in East Asia and to report on Soviet developments affecting that part of the world.

For the ambassador, the foremost East Asian problem was getting the Soviet Union into the war against Japan. In this he reflected the wish of the president and the Joint Chiefs of Staff. Harriman did not bring me into his consideration of and activities in this endeavor. He worked with his Military Mission, headed by the competent Major General John R. Deane.

My friend Major General Frank Roberts was a member of the Mission. With the war in Europe in its final phases, Roberts had been transferred late in 1944 from his senior planning duties at the Pentagon to Moscow as leader of an Army-Navy-Air team to plan in deep secret with the Soviet high command coordination of the final phases of the war against Japan. The Russians were so secretive and aloof that the Roberts group had scarcely any contact with Soviet officers. Nothing like the combined Anglo-American planning was attainable with the Russians.

My ideas on Soviet intervention in what had become our war against Japan had not changed since I first expressed them in 1943. I still thought that Soviet participation would turn the situation in China to our disadvantage and the balance of power in East Asia against us. Nor had I altered my assumption that the Russians were determined "to move against the Japanese when it suits their pleasure, which may not be until the final phases of the war. . . ." I continued to believe that anything that the United States might say would not alter Moscow's basic intentions or timing one way or another.

The official American view was that we needed Soviet help against Japan to shorten the course of hostilities and save American lives. Washington reckoned that to insure Japanese capitulation an invasion of the home islands would probably be necessary. Unless the million and a half Japanese troops in China proper, Manchuria, and Korea were disposed of by the Russians—for Chiang's forces were utterly incapable of this—they would eventually reinforce the fanatical resistance to American invasion, or hold out indefinitely on the mainland. The effect of the then projected atomic bomb on Japan's will to resist was unknowable and so not considered.

Even so, some American naval officers doubted that an invasion would be necessary, calculating that a combination of naval and conventional air action would bring Japan to its knees. Marshall's rebuttal to this was that it would mean a prolonged war of attrition, which the American people would not accept, for they wanted the quickest possible victory.

The Yalta meeting of Roosevelt, Churchill, and Stalin occurred in February during my final days in India and first days in Iran. I arrived in Moscow ignorant of what had been decided at the conference regarding East Asia, and I remained uninstructed until the end of the Pacific War. Consequently, for some six months after the Crimea Conference I did not know how far we had gone in paying Stalin, at the expense of others, to do what he was determined to do—enter the war against Japan.

Actually, the political conditions that Stalin laid down to Roosevelt on February 8, 1945—lest, as the old tyrant said, it be difficult for him and Molotov to explain to the Soviet people why Russia was entering the war against Japan—were less greedy than, in 1943, I had thought likely. When I had written of Russia's moving against Japan to establish new strategic frontiers and expand into territories claimed by China, I had assumed that the Kremlin would unilaterally act to realize Tsarist ambitions for, at a minimum, suzerainty over at least Manchuria and Korea. Otherwise, as Stalin implied, why join someone else's war?

Signed on February 1, 1945 by Stalin, Roosevelt, and Churchill, the Yalta Agreement provided for Soviet entry into the war against Japan "on condition that": the status quo in Outer Mongolia be preserved; the former rights of which Russia had been deprived "by the treacherous attack" of Japan in 1904 be restored (southern Sakhalin, Dairen, Port Arthur, and the Chinese Eastern and South Manchuria railways); and the Kurile islands be "handed over" by Japan to the Soviet Union. The Big Three acknowledged that the Mongolian and Manchurian concessions would require the concurrence of the Big Fourth, Chiang. And Roosevelt assumed the incubus of obtaining, "on advice from Marshal Stalin," the Generalissimo's acceptance of the arrangement. This was to be delayed until Stalin gave the signal, because no one trusted the Chinese to keep a secret.

In return for the benefits demanded, the Soviet Union expressed "its readiness" to conclude a pact of friendship and alliance with the National Government of China.

Churchill, it should be noted, considered the agreement to be an American-Soviet arrangement and signed it as a matter of form.

The Yalta Agreement and attendant arrangements were a transaction in which the Americans, acting as promoters, engaged the Russians to go to war against Japan. For services thus rendered, the Americans undertook to present the bill to the Chinese for payment to the Russians. The anticipated profits to the promoters were an earlier defeat of Japan and a saving of American lives. This promotional scheme, however, was flawed in several respects. It was not needed to bring the Russians into the Pacific War. It did not hasten Japan's defeat, nor save American lives. It made Washington appear to be Moscow's collector in Chungking. And it needlessly legitimized, at least in the careless concession of all the Kuriles, an extension of Soviet power in the Pacific.

In extenuation, the Yalta Agreement may have restrained the Kremlin, which, had it not been for the Crimean deal, might have been more predatory.

Unease descended upon Moscow with the death of Roosevelt on April 12. The ordinary folk sorrowed, for they regarded him as a benefactor. Notwithstanding official Soviet efforts to conceal from them the magnitude of American aid—materiel, industrial equipment, and massive quantities of food—the Russian people knew that the Americans were helping them mightily. What would happen now with Roosevelt gone? Would the new man care about them? For the

Kremlin the question took a different form. Would the new president, a disturbingly unknown factor (possibly even to Truman himself), be as "get-atable" as Roosevelt?

Into this atmosphere came one who was spasmodically "get-atable." On his way back to China from stormy consultation in Washington, Hurley stopped off in Moscow three days after the president's death for a powwow with the chiefs of world communism. The subject was to be his problems with Chiang and those whom Molotov had assured him were not Communists, and to enlist Stalin's support of his endeavors.

Hurley came well-recommended. For Roosevelt had told Stalin at Yalta that Hurley and Wedemeyer were having much more success than Gauss and Stilwell had enjoyed in bringing Yenan and Chungking together and that the fault for delays lay more with the Kuomintang and the Chungking government than with "the so-called Communists." Responding to this confidence, Stalin— who had been outfoxed by both Chiang and Mao in his 1927 united front machinations—told Roosevelt that Chiang should assume leadership in a united front and professed mystification over why the united front of "some years ago" (presumably 1937) had not been maintained.

So that he might have some points of reference in his contacts with Hurley, I prepared for Harriman on April 15 a paper on the situation in China. After a preliminary analysis, I concluded that China probably could not be unified under Chiang. If not, could Chiang's government, as a rump regime in South China, be so strengthened as to become "a dependable balance and buffer in eastern Asia"?

My answer was that it might if it were underwritten militarily, economically, and politically (I was thinking of the United States and perhaps Britain), but that an assumption of responsibility on that scale "might well be repudiated by the electorates of the underwriting governments." I could not envisage the American people being willing, immediately after the defeat of Japan, to commit themselves anew to another ghastly Asian crusade.

In discussing the Chinese Communists I ventured to assert, "Mao Tse-tung is not necessarily a Tito simply because he is a Communist." This turn of phrase, written when Tito was regarded as one of the most sedulous of the Kremlin's foreign stooges, might better have been worded, "Mao and Tito are not necessarily Stalinists simply because they are Communists." Be that as it may, I raised the question of American collaboration with Yenan, but added that this did not necessarily imply abandonment of Chiang. We could work with both.

I then asked, "Will the Chinese Communists be willing to cooperate with us on terms equal to or better than those which they will extend to the Soviet Union? In other words, will they be voluntary creatures of Russian foreign policy? We do not know. And the operations of Communist-dominated regimes in Europe [then emerging] do not give us convincing indication of how the older and more self-sufficient Chinese Communist regime would react to American overtures. . . .

"What can be said at this juncture, however, is that if any Communist regime is susceptible to political 'capture' by the United States, it is Yenan. . . .

"A policy of aid to and cooperation with the Chinese Communist regime . . . will involve competing with Russian drawing-power rather than seeking to block it off, as would be the case were we to bolster Chiang as a balance and a buffer."

Such a course, I continued, would entail a considerable outlay of economic aid and integrated political effort. But if the Soviet Army entered North China, political domination by Moscow would probably follow, as it was then following the sweep of Soviet arms through eastern Europe. "However, the Red Army is not likely to invade North China without excuse. The excuse is the presence of Japanese troops. And it is one which, presumably, we are not prepared to attempt to remove either through military or political action."

Here was the germ of an idea which I had formed in Yenan when discussing American military collaboration with the Chinese Communists. It was one of joint American-Communist operations in and occupation of North China, meant to forestall Soviet incursions into that area. I had thought of the same for Manchuria but dismissed the concept because I assumed that the Russians would overrun the Three Eastern Provinces before Yenan and we could establish the Chinese Communists there.

At the time that I wrote this memorandum for Harriman I was unaware that in March Chu Teh had indicated to Service that he expected the Soviet Army to attack only into northern Manchuria and not attempt, because of logistic problems, a flanking operation into North China. Nor did I know that, contrariwise, Stalin had told the ambassador and Deane on October 17, 1944 that Soviet strategy called for, in addition to direct assaults on Manchuria, an envelopment proceeding from Baikal, through Mongolia to Kalgan, and thence south of the Wall.

Although I do not know, I suspect that Chu Teh was not privy to Stalin's plans. That the Soviet Army did not sweep south of the Wall was due, I assume, not to logistic limitations but to the fact that the war ended so quickly and that Stalin did not wish to excite Washington by occupying the Peking-Tientsin sector.

I did not develop my concept of combined American-Chinese Communist operations in North China and Manchuria. The prevailing outlook of the American government did not encourage elaboration of such thoughts.

What was real, in contrast to my theorizing, was the garish presence of Hurley. In the company of Harriman he conferred with Stalin and Molotov on the night of April 16. The United States ambassador to China expatiated on his interpretation of Soviet policy toward China, the political scene in China, and the objectives of American policy—to support the National government of China under Chiang for the unification of Chinese armed forces and the establishment of a free, united, democratic government.

"Stalin stated frankly," Hurley reported to the secretary of state, "that the Soviet government would support the policy." Stalin spoke kindly of Chiang, saying that he was "selfless" and a "patriot" and "that the Soviet in times past had befriended him." Chiang's old befriender also wanted Hurley to know that the United States "would have his [Stalin's] complete support in immediate action for the unification of the armed forces of China." Hurley exclaimed that this was the best news he had received.

On the morning of April 17 at Spaso House, where he also was staying, Hurley was exultant. He made no mention to me of his conversation of the night before. Avoiding touchy subjects, we were elaborately genial with one another, as we had been from the time of his arrival in Moscow. Harriman and his daughter Kathleen, a gallant gentlewoman who acted as hostess at Spaso House, departed early that day for Washington. This left my wife responsible for the well-being and entertainment of the distinguished guest who, five or six months earlier, had suggested that she serve as his hostess in Chungking.

With the Harrimans on their way, Hurley turned to the task of transfiguring the notes taken by my spirited colleague, Edward Page, at the meeting with Stalin into a formal communication to the secretary of state and the president. Page, who had spent the hours after the nocturnal interview with Stalin in prolonged social intercourse, remembered having placed the notes in the Spaso office safe. But when he assayed opening it, the combination did not come to mind. Whereupon word was hastily sent to Patricia to distract and detain Hurley with all of the wiles at her command. At this juncture I decided that my presence on the scene at the moment of truth could only inflame the ambassador, and so I slipped off to the chancery.

As Page frantically juggled combinations, Patricia opened Hurley's floodgate of memories, interviewing him in depth on his life story. Occasionally he would rise to do his duty, but she would prevail upon him to linger and tell just one more anecdote. Meanwhile urgent radios were sped along the American military communications net in search of the Harrimans, begging Kathleen to recite the combination. Before the Harrimans were tracked down in North Africa and Hurley had wearied of talking about himself, Harriman's secretary dropped into the office and, when told of the crisis by the haggard Page, reached into the briefcase she was carrying and produced the Hurley-Stalin notes.

After dispatching Hurley's message to Washington and bidding its author Godspeed to Chungking, Kennan pondered the ambassador's report of the interview with Stalin. Because it disturbed him, he called me in and, with my cooperation, drafted a radio to Harriman in Washington. Perhaps the essence of this message of April 23 was, "In Ambassador Hurley's account of what he said to Stalin there was of course nothing to which Stalin could not honestly subscribe, it being understood that words mean different things to the Russians than they do to us." And with regard to what Stalin said, "It would be tragic if our natural anxiety for Russian support at this stage, coupled with Stalin's cautious affability and his use of words which mean all things to all people, were to lead us into an undue reliance on Russian aid or even Russian acquiescence in the achievement of our long term objectives in China."

Pursuing further the mystery of Stalin's real attitude toward Chiang, I commented on an April 27th article, "Whither China?," carried in an official publication. My conclusion was that the Kremlin was not then disposed "to classify the Generalissimo with London Polish leaders and other 'enemies of democracy.'

"This is in contrast to Yenan's identification of Chiang with the forces of reaction. This relative reserve and obvious caution with which Moscow continues to treat the person of Chiang is open to a number of interpretations. In particular if Yenan is considered here [Moscow] to have been exhibiting undue political health and outward independence, then Moscow's tolerant attitude toward Chiang may represent a delicate warning that the Kremlin had more than one string to its Chinese bow. It would not be out of accord with established Russian methods to hold open and exploit the possibility of collaboration with Chiang as a means of impressing Yenan with the necessity for hewing closely to the line of solidarity with Russia."

Victory in Europe was distrustfully announced by the Soviet government on May 9, two days after the German surrender in the West. The next morning the people of Moscow went out in the streets to celebrate. This they did by taking a walk. For in a country where everything was arranged, spontaneous manifestations of group emotion were scowled upon. As the Party-Government apparatus had not ordered dancing in the streets, there was no dancing in the streets.

With full hearts and empty faces the celebrants strolled sedately past the chancery. The embassy staff, in a happy mood, stood at open windows looking down at the passersby. At midmorning the atmosphere in the street dramatically changed when several dozen young Russians halted in front of the chancery to wave and exchange shouted congratulations with us. Soon there were hundreds and by noontime thousands of upturned, smiling faces and uplifted arms filling the boulevard and square to the foot of the Kremlin walls.

Several carloads of secret police in black leather coats tried grimly to disperse the crowd. Ordinarily, the people would have decamped at the first quiet command. But today they were in great numbers, in high spirits, honoring the triumph of Russian and allied arms, and so paid the police no heed.

Kennan, who was chargé d'affaires in the absence of Harriman, rose to the occasion and caused a Soviet flag to be run alongside the American flag on the chancery. This brought forth roars of approval and cheers. Then Kennan climbed out on a ledge at the base of the building where in Russian he shouted congratulations on the victory, whereat he was given a joyous ovation. The rest of us leaned out of windows and over balconies to cheer the crowd and sprinkle confetti made from torn writing pads.

A Russian soldier was hoisted to Kennan's perch where he embraced an American sergeant standing beside Kennan and gave the flabbergasted desk soldier a big, wet kiss. Kennan backed off into the chancery leaving our hero to be slavically treated as one—tossed overhead by the ecstatic crowd all of the way from the chancery to Red Square. Two or three other Americans, through goodwill or curiosity, ventured within reach of the crowd and were accorded the same high-flown honors.

By dusk the demonstration had subsided, although passersby still waved and shouted greetings. The enormous upsurge of shared happiness had been full of innocence and beauty. But it was now drawing to a close, and tomorrow morning the people of Moscow would walk by the American embassy without turning their faces to us and we would treat them with sympathetic circumspection lest our contact compromise them in the eyes of their rulers. The outpouring of affection between us could be only brief.

For the men behind the dark red walls of the Kremlin victory in Europe formalized a transition in their unending struggle against the independence of others, a transition in Eastern and Middle Europe from war to the use of means short of war. In East Asia a different Soviet transition was three months distant, a transition from quiescence to war, and then to political action. But in May the Kremlin's attention was focused on its imposition of puppet regimes on areas in Europe occupied by the Soviet Army.

Troubled by arbitrary Soviet behavior in eastern Europe, Truman dispatched Hopkins to plumb Stalin's intentions, mostly with regard to Poland. As for Asia, Hopkins was to ask for the earliest possible Soviet entry into the war against Japan.

During Hopkins's stay in Moscow, from late May until early June, I was summoned into his and Harriman's presence at the instance, I assumed, of Hopkins. I had been with him socially but this was my first and only business session with him—in the ambassador's bedroom command post. He was pale and wasted, for he had not much more time to live, but his eyes were brightly appraising. It was not a discursive meeting, none of the mixture of idealism and cynicism that characterized our previous encounters. Only one question—what did the Soviet Union want in the Far East?

I do not recall my answer in detail. It was, however, along the lines of a memorandum that I wrote several weeks later on the same subject. In brief, the Kremlin wanted either to dominate or have the voluntary allegiance of North China (including Sinkiang and Inner Mongolia), Manchuria, Korea, southern Sakhalin, and the Kurile Islands. At the mention of the Kuriles, a quizzical expression crossed Hopkins's face. Through my mind flashed the thought that Stalin might have indicated at Yalta or in current talks with Hopkins—about which I was also uninformed—a lack of interest in the islands. I exclaimed, "But don't they want the Kuriles?" Harriman, with obvious irritation, told me not to ask such questions. I was properly rebuked. Stalin's price for fighting Japan was still a closely held secret.

We now know what passed between Stalin and Hopkins on May 28, with Molotov, Harriman, and Bohlen also present. Stalin said that Soviet forces would be in position to move against the Japanese on August 8. When the Russians would strike, however, depended on when the Chinese accepted the Yalta Agreement. Acceptance of the agreement was necessary to justify Soviet entry into the Pacific War. Stalin would disclose the Crimea understanding when the Chinese foreign minister visited Moscow early in July.

As an aside, it may be said that this performance of Stalin's was characteristic of the old conspirator. What he intended to do anyway, and solely for Soviet advantage, he preferred to bedeck with trappings of legality and represent it as a favor done for others. He carried off this stratagem of reinsurance and high-mindedness with a shrewd understanding of both American and Chinese psychology.

Stalin agreed with Hopkins that Chinese unity was desirable but said that he had no specific plans for bringing it about. Only the United States, he continued, could give China the economic help that it needed. He did not intend to alter Chinese sovereignty over Manchuria or any other part of China. He did not think that the Chinese Communist leaders were as good as Chiang, nor could they unify China. Stalin concurred with Hopkins's statement that Chiang would have to make reforms if he were to unify China, but added that it would be necessary that the Generalissimo recognize the need of reform—and furthermore, that reform could not be fixed upon China from without. He reassured his callers that Chiang's civilian administrators would be accepted by the Soviet command in any areas of China that it occupied.

Harriman advocated American-Soviet agreement in the Far East and in that connection mentioned the Open Door policy—John Hay's hallowed doctrine which Tsarist diplomats had treated so rudely. Stalin said that the United States must play the largest part in helping China to its feet. Whereat Hopkins hastened to reassure the Bolsheviks that Washington did not wish to see any other nation kept out of the Far East.

As for Korea, Stalin accepted that it should be placed under trusteeship—comfortable in the knowledge that the only politically and militarily organized Koreans were Communist, ready for introduction into the peninsula in the wake of the Soviet invasion.

To his American visitors Stalin indicated a preference for imposing unconditional surrender on Japan, so that the enemy's military power would be crushed. He recognized that unconditional surrender would mean that the Japanese would fight to the last. Should the Japanese sue for peace and the allies accept a modified surrender, Stalin envisaged an allied occupation of Japan that would accomplish the same results that unconditional surrender would. The Soviet Union would expect to share in the occupation, with its own zone.

Hopkins and Harriman were "very encouraged" by what Stalin had told them.

CHAPTER 37

Russia Enters the War Against Japan

THE AMERICAN GOVERNMENT in mid-1945 was as ill prepared for the end as it had been for the beginning of the war against Japan. Its program for a world order was a reverie. It clung to bad policy, such as unconditional surrender, and was creating wistful new policy in East Asia—which would turn out to be unworkable. At the same time, some of the top men in the government were questioning, as they had not before, the wisdom of accepted courses of action.

A key doctrine in the Rooseveltian program was great power solidarity, more particularly as it referred to American-Soviet unity of purpose and performance. Most of the Russian specialists of the Foreign Service and State Department never believed that such unity could go beyond limited cooperation during the war against a common enemy. But these disbelievers had been little heeded. In addition to them, Harriman, Deane, and even Hull had voiced doubts in 1944. By mid-1945 disillusion was spreading.

Washington was reluctant to accept that, at best, great power unity was ephemeral. For on this misty, scudding foundation the American government had built a cumulus cloud of assurances to all peoples regarding a new world order. These promises, topped by the Charter of the United Nations, committed Washington to policies which counted on the Kremlin's being like-minded and cooperative. If it were not, then the policies would be nonsensical and the towering cloud of hopes dissipated by the heat of great power rivalry. This was an awful prospect. Washington officialdom shrank from contemplating it.

Doubts rose within the government over the wisdom of urging the Soviet Union to join the Pacific War. But Washington was tied to this policy by the Yalta Agreement. What was more compelling, the War Department deemed it necessary. And MacArthur, widely venerated as a geopolitical seer, had told James Forrestal, Secretary of the Navy, on February 28, 1945, that the American government should secure the commitment of no less than sixty Soviet divisions against the Japanese in Manchuria.

The Army was keenly conscious of the burden of imposing unconditional surrender on Japan. The Okinawa campaign had dragged on from spring into summer, in hard, bloody going. Ahead lay the harrowing prospect of invading Kyushu, and then Honshu. For seemingly, the only absolute victory in this war of absolutes, of unconditionals, was through invasion, subjugation, and occupation of the home islands of Japan.

Joseph C. Grew, acting secretary of state while the bustling, trivial Stettinius was in San Francisco helping to found the United Nations organization, broached the matter of unconditional surrender to Truman on May 28, and on the next day to Stimson, Forrestal, and Marshall. In effect, Grew said that the demand for unconditional surrender ensured prolonged and fanatical Japanese resistance and, consequently, an unnecessarily heavy toll in American casualties. If the Japanese were assured by an official American declaration that after defeat they would be allowed to determine their own political future, particularly to retain their monarchical system, they would see a way open to an orderly surrender and acceptance of foreign occupation. The preservation of the emperor was crucial, for only he could order capitulation of the Japanese armed forces.

The president and his military advisers agreed with Grew in principle. but considered such a declaration to be premature. Thus more than two months before the atomic bombings of Hiroshima and Nagasaki and the Soviet onslaught, all of which were counted on to save American lives, Truman and the Pentagon laid aside Grew's quiet suggestion that American lives be saved by giving Japan a face-saving formula for early surrender.

Meanwhile, as Stalin told Hopkins on May 28, some Japanese were putting out peace feelers. Stalin's understandable concern was that Tokyo persuade Washington to make peace before Moscow was fully ready to join in the kill and the grab. But the Kremlin's suspicions were unfounded. The Americans remained true blue to the Reds.

As time for the first test of the atom bomb approached, Stimson, McCloy, and Forrestal vigorously supported, with little effect, Grew's plea for an announcement of surrender conditions. McCloy, on June 18 at a meeting with Truman, Stimson, Forrestal, and the JCS, even suggested, to no avail, the offering of terms that would make possible a political solution of the war without prolonging the hostilities. After the bomb had been proven at Alamogordo, and mostly because of prodding by Stimson, the conditions of unconditional surrender were issued on July 26 at the Potsdam Conference in an American-British-Chinese proclamation. Like a religious tract, it pointed out the advantages of repentance, atonement, and redemption over hell's fire—"the alternative for Japan is prompt and utter destruction." Nothing was said about the emperor. But mention was made of a government "established in accordance with the freely expressed will of the Japanese people."

In desperation, the Japanese Foreign Office sought during July to enlist the good offices of the "neutral" Soviet government as mediator for a negotiated peace. Stalin and Molotov entertained the offers, and thereby themselves, into the first days of August. Informed at Potsdam of Tokyo's several overtures, the American leaders showed no disposition to discuss terms with the enemy. They were locked into a totally military resolution of the war, with two new elements added—Russian hordes on the ground and fission from the skies.

As the Russian specialists of the Foreign Service had been slighted in the dcisions on great power unity, collaboration with the Soviet Union, and imploring Stalin to enter the Pacific War, so the diplomats who knew Japan—Grew, Eugene Dooman, and Joseph Ballantine—were little heeded in vital issues about Japan. Had it not been for Grew's high position and ultimately the strong backing of Stimson, McCloy, and Forrestal, their warnings against unconditional surrender and their advice that the imperial system be retained might have been wholly disregarded. As it was, they were called "appeasers" by those who would have at least deposed the emperor.

American military policy toward China in the final seven months of the Pacific War was characterized by futility in the China Theater and indifference at the Pentagon. Wedemeyer planned counteroffensives for the Chinese, which they conducted inconclusively against the thinning Japanese ranks in South China. He found the Generalissimo unprepared for the problems that would arise from a Japanese surrender, relying on the Americans to subdue the enemy in the coastal ports and then airlift Chiang's armies thereto. This convenient arrangement with the Americans apparently suggested to the Generalissimo further politico-military excursions. He spoke to Wedemeyer on July 31 of Chinese troops being placed in Korea to thwart the Russians. Bold as he was about outmaneuvering Stalin in Korea, Chiang was timid about Stilwell (then on Okinawa in command of the Tenth Army), declaring that if American troops were to land in China they must not be commanded by Stilwell.

For the American high command in mid-1945, however, China was of trifling importance so far as the war against Japan was concerned. If the Russians intervened in August, as Stalin promised, they would take care of the Japanese main force on the continent. If they purposely delayed, as Marshall feared they might do, Chiang's armies could, perhaps, nibble at the Japanese stranded on the mainland of Asia.

Politically, during mid-1945 the critical China issue remained: what should American policy toward Chiang's Kuomintang regime and the Communists be? One course was to plug away at bringing about a reconciliation between the two sides, to support Chungking while trying to reform it, but at the same time to keep a hand in with Yenan. This was a flexible policy that left the way open to changes in course as the situation in China changed. It was the course advocated, with varying emphases, by most of the China specialists.

A second course was Hurley's sustaining Chiang at all costs. The Communists would have to adapt themselves to Chiang's wishes because Stalin wanted them to do so and because they were a puny force. Hurley had told Chiang that the Generalissimo would have no trouble in defeating them.

I tended toward the first choice, but felt that it had been outdistanced by events. The two sides were, I thought, irreconcilable. So deal separately with each. The Communists already held most of North China, the Russians would soon intervene and, if we wanted to have any influence at all with the Communists, we had to commit ourselves immediately to collaboration with Yenan. This was, in effect, a two-China policy.

No one, to my knowledge, recommended that the United States prepare to pull out of China as soon as the war with Japan ended.

Nine days after I had left Chungking for Moscow, Service returned to China and was promptly called in by Hurley, upbraided for past policy recommendations, and threatened with being broken if he so offended again. Soon thereafter Ludden arrived in Chungking from a four months survey of Communist-held territory in North China. What he had to report on Communist strength in the countryside of three provinces was of prime importance in estimating the Communist power potential.

Ludden had immersed himself in the mass of a mass movement. Those of us, including Ludden, who had been at Yenan, the center of the mass movement, had been impressed by the dynamism of the Communist directorate. All of the reports we had of the Communist hinterland indicated that the vitality and discipline of the center permeated to the far-flung outlying parts of the movement. But no official American political observer had surveyed these areas back of Yenan, in North China. Ludden was the first foreign service officer to explore the movement in physical depth.

He and five or six military members of the Observer Group left Yenan early in October 1944, traveling by mule and on foot. They were escorted by detachments of Communist regulars, from fifty to nine hundred men, depending on their proximity to the Japanese. Guerrilla scouts all along the route kept the column informed of enemy dispositions. Thus convoyed and screened, the Americans penetrated behind the Japanese forward positions in Shansi, crossed that province, and advanced to the headquarters of the Shansi-Chahar-Hopei Base Area close to Fu P'ing near the Peking-Hankow Railway.

On the road and in the villages and towns where he stopped, Ludden observed the Communist movement in basic operation—the indoctrination and organization of masses of peasants. These originally apolitical folk had been made desperate by Japanese barbarities and thereby receptive to the Communists. As patriots, not as revolutionaries, the Communists had come to the peasants and said that they need not despair, that they could organize, resist the invaders, and eventually be rid of them, and that the Eighth Route would help them do this. The Eighth Route Army (only officials and foreigners referred to the main force of Communist regulars by their new designation as Eighteenth Group Army) had a legendary fame in North China as friend and champion of the people.

When Ludden returned to Chungking, he submitted to headquarters in early February his written conclusions and orally reported to Hurley at an embassy staff meeting. His salient points were that the Communist armies and governments were genuinely united with the people; popular support of the Communist dispensation was an evident reality; the peasantry was intensively organized on a massive scale; the Communist leadership was "the most realistic, well-knit, and tough-minded group in China"; and the movement was steadily expanding. Hurley's displeasure with what he was hearing was manifested by heckling Ludden about authorization for the trip, for which Ludden had orders.

In company with Service, Ludden next conferred with Wedemeyer to whom they presented the case for a flexible policy of working with any and all elements in China that would advance the primary American objective of defeating Japan. The general said that he agreed and asked for a paper on the subject. He told Ludden that he wanted him to be available for further consultation in Washington, whither Wedemeyer would soon be going with Hurley for conferences. Outside of the theater commander's office Ludden encountered General McClure who, as Ludden recalls, "seemed to be champing at the bit to get up among the Commies with troops." The atmosphere at headquarters, therefore, was more receptive than it had been in the ambassador's office.

Service and Ludden completed their memorandum for Wedemeyer on Feburary 14. A few days later Hurley and Wedemeyer and, separately, Ludden and Emmerson left for Washington. One of the more competent China specialists, George Atcheson, became chargé d'affaires. He bravely decided that the embassy should correct the distorted picture of China that Hurley had been presenting to Washington.

Atcheson's message, an expansion of the Service-Ludden memorandum, was a collective effort, as Atcheson told the department, "drafted with the assistance and agreement of all the political officers." In part, the embassy contended that unqualified support of Chiang would accelerate the outbreak of civil conflict and that the American government should cooperate directly with, in addition to the Chiang government, "the Communists and other suitable groups who can assist the war against Japan." Atcheson suggested that the department discuss the matter with Hurley and Wedemeyer.

Ballantine and others did this, beginning March 5, and evoked predictable reverberations from Hurley. His staff was disloyal to him, the ambassador raged, State Department career officers were in collusion against him, and Atcheson's message undermined his efforts. Even so, he was confident that Chiang and the Communists would come to an agreement by the end of April.

Hurley stormed about Washington calling on Marshall, Stimson, and a stricken Roosevelt, about to begin his final journey to Warm Springs. By clamoring to these and other high officials, the ambassador got what he wanted—weary assent to, in effect, unqualified backing of Chiang. No one at the top level in Washington during the spring of 1945 was really very interested in China, certainly not to the extent of opposing the ornery ambassador. The Office of Far Eastern Affairs later issued policy papers emphasizing the need of flexibility in the conduct of relations with China. But at this critical period of American-

Chinese relations, the tetchy Hurley was running the show practically single-handed. He was to continue to do so until the end of the war.

In another respect the ambassador got what he wanted—the immediate recall of Service, Ludden, and Emmerson, and soon thereafter of Atcheson. A day or two before they were to leave Washington for Chungking, Ludden and Emmerson were told by Wedemeyer that because pressure had been brought to bear on him that he could not withstand, he was regretfully releasing them back to the State Department. Upon his return to the embassy in April Hurley browbeat the staff, ordering that nothing unfavorable about the Chiang regime be reported to Washington. The ambassador's abuse of his office prompted the senior China specialist at the department, the judicious Edwin F. Stanton, to present to Grew a catalogue of complaints about Hurley, including "we can no longer count on receiving factual and objective reports." Nothing came of this.

Soon after Hurley had assured the State Department that Chungking and Yenan would be reconciled in April, Service was in Yenan listening on March 13 to a confident Mao say that the Communists and Chiang were further apart and that the Generalissimo's refusal of coalition was the road to civil war. As Wedemeyer was telling Vincent that the Communists wanted him to command their troops. Mao was explaining to Service that while Yenan would accept American command, "it must be of all Chinese armies." Mao and Chou again asked for American support of coalition. They were also eager to cooperate directly with the United States during and after the war. In two conversations Mao restated his October theme that China (meaning his kind of China) would be dependent on American aid for postwar reconstruction.

From talks with Chu Teh and others, Service gathered that the Communists did not expect the Russians to move against the Japanese until the spring of 1946. When the Soviet Army invaded northwestern Manchuria, the Chinese Communists would then begin their infiltration of South Manchuria, for which they had been diligently preparing. Yenan expected that after the defeat of the Kwantung Army Moscow would leave the Chinese Communists in control of Manchuria. The Reds assumed that the Soviet Union would want the commercial use, without infringement of Chinese sovereignty, of Manchurian transport and port facilities.

Service had been in Yenan less than a month when, as a result of Hurley's pressure on the War and State Departments, he was ordered on March 30 to return to Washington. Out of deference to Hurley's sensitivities, he was assigned at the department to duties unrelated to China. This did not lessen Service's distress over the disastrous course that American policy was taking in East Asia, and he spoke frankly of this to nonofficial contacts. At Stilwell's instance, he had, as had I, briefed members of the press. Now, in April and May of 1945, he freely provided background information to journalists whom he considered reliable.

One of these was Philip J. Jaffe, the seemingly reputable editor of *Amerasia*, which was generally regarded as a respectable magazine dealing with Asian affairs. OSS counterintelligence, however, had secretly raided the *Amerasia* office in March and discovered classified documents which had been illegally

removed from various government departments and agencies. The Federal
Bureau of Investigation took over from OSS and placed Jaffe, who was identified
as a Communist, and his contacts under surveillance. Service had innocently
walked into a trap and when the FBI sprang it on June 6, he was picked up with
Jaffe and others associating with Jaffe. On August 10, by an unanimous vote of
20–0, a grand jury exonerated Service. Two days later he resumed active duty at
the State Department.

Although motivated by patriotic concern over an injurious policy, Service
readily admitted that he had been indiscreet in his dealings with Jaffe. Indiscre-
tion was fairly prevalent in Washington during World War II. Witness T. V.
Soong's boast to me on June 5, 1942, that there were "no secrets in Washington"
and "no conference takes place regarding which I do not have accurate and complete information." In any event, Service's involvement in the *Amerasia* case and
his motives were later distorted, first by Hurley and then by others. This was the
beginning of a seizure, a gnawing at its vitals, that afflicted the American government for a decade and more.

As the time for Soong's July appointment with Stalin approached, and without clearing his action with Stalin, Truman revealed to Soong on June 9 the
substance of the Yalta Agreement and the soothing assurances that Stalin gave
Hopkins in May. Hurley enlightened Chiang on June 15. Notwithstanding all of
the precautions for secrecy, both Soong and Chiang already had more than an
inkling of what was unveiled to them. Neither of them expressed objections to
the deal made behind China's back. After all, Stalin's attitude seemed much less
grasping than might have been expected—even obliging.

Harriman said to me after Soong's arrival at Moscow at the end of June that
he was complying with the foreign minister's request that I be denied all knowledge of Soong's negotiations. This request could not have come to the ambassador as any great surprise because in a June 19 message from Chungking Hurley
announced that "There are also rumors afloat here, that we do not credit, to the
effect that John Davies is responsible for news items in Moscow papers that
appear to be adverse to the Chinese government." The receipt of this piece of
intelligence caused Harriman to break into laughter at the vision of me as a regular contributor to *Pravda* and *Izvestia* and then to turn red in the face with indignation at Hurley's snide absurdity.

I was content to be left in ignorance of Soong's travail in Stalin's web. I
turned my hand to writing an estimate of Soviet policy in East Asia. This was an
elaboration of what I had orally outlined to Hopkins. The Kremlin would, I
thought, pursue

a unilateral policy designed to revise the situation in the Far East in its favor for
the following reasons:

A. Security against:

1. China, which can, if it develops along certain lines, emerge after one or
two generations as the greatest single threat to the Soviet Union on the Eurasian
continent;

2. Korea, as a natural corridor for an attack on the Soviet Far East;

3. The Kuriles, Karafuto, Hokkaido, and Honshu. . . . The example of the British Isles serving as a springboard for a transoceanic invasion of the adjacent continental land mass is presumably not lost on the Kremlin.

B. Naval and merchant marine expansion.

1. The need for new ports and bases to accommodate an expanded Soviet merchant marine and navy is another reason for a revisionist Soviet policy in East Asia.

2. Control over certain straits . . . is essential to the USSR if it is to have free access to the open Pacific. . . .

C. The political attraction of:
 1. The internal struggle for power in China . . .
 2. The political vacuum in Korea . . .
 3. Chaos in Japan. . . .

In discussing Soviet strategy and tactics for East Asia, I anticipated

A "correct" [Kremlin] attitude toward China . . . and Korea so as to avoid:
 1. Appearing imperialistic to Asiatic peoples;
 2. Openly provoking charges of Soviet interference in China's internal affairs;
 3. Revealing its intentions toward Korea;
 4. Incurring at this juncture intensified American suspicion and hostility.

The Kremlin would rely on Communist China, I thought, to serve its immediate ends in China. But—

It is debatable whether Moscow could have counted on Yenan's unquestioning obedience had the American government last autumn and winter (while the Soviet Union was still unprepared to act in Asia) accepted the fact of a divided China and realistically and vigorously sought to develop the nationalistic tendencies of Communist China. However that may be, it is clear that Communist China can now operate only in the Soviet orbit.

This situation is entirely satisfactory to the Kremlin because it can conduct fundamentally meaningless flirtations with Chungking while being fully confident that:

a. Yenan will resist spontaneously—and probably effectively—Chiang's attempts to establish Kuomintang authority over Northeast China.

b. Communist China will become a part of the USSR's security cordon, because, if for no other reason, it will scarcely be accepted by any other foreign alignment.

In concluding the memorandum I suggested that "anaesthetization of the United States" would be a Kremlin tactic.

For obvious reasons the Kremlin will be careful in performing its political surgery in Asia to cause during the next two or three years as little shock and pain as possible to the United States. Therefore the present "correct" attitude and other tactics designed to diffuse the one basic issue of aggressive Soviet expansion. Therefore also, the Kremlin may be expected to operate more gradually in Korea, Manchuria, and North China than it would otherwise need to. . . .

This anaesthetization will be effective in pretty much direct proportion to the degree of ignorance in which the American people are kept with regard to the issues involved.

On July 10, the date of my memorandum, Hurley dispatched a message to the secretary of state in which he appeared to place on Moscow responsibility for the success or failure of unity in China. After congratulating himself on obtaining Soviet assurances of support of Chungking, Hurley said that Yenan did not believe that Stalin would support Chiang. "Nothing short of the Soviet's public commitment will change the Chinese Communist opinion on this subject." Once the Communists "are convinced that the Soviet is not supporting them, they will settle with the National government if the National government is realistic enough to make generous political concessions." This last qualification reopened the question of where responsibility lay for unity in China.

Hurley closed the gap by stating that Chinese Communist strength—military, territorial, and in adherents—was exaggerated by State Department officials and others. Therefore, by implication, if the Communists did not have Soviet support, they "will eventually participate as a political party in the National government."

As if in answer to Hurley's prayers, Harriman reported to Washington, also on July 10, that a Soviet-Chinese treaty of friendship and alliance "in the form proposed by Stalin is satisfactory to Soong." The Chinese foreign minister had so informed him. Furthermore, Stalin had "categorically stated that he would support only the National government of China and that all military forces of China must come under the control of the government." Harriman added that "Soong is inclined to believe that if an agreement with the Soviet Union is reached this will open the way for an understanding between the National government and the Communist Party."

Two days later on the eve of Stalin's departure for Potsdam, the negotiations were suspended, with the degree of Soviet control over Dairen, Port Arthur, and Manchurian railways in serious dispute. Soong flew to Chungking to consult with the Generalissimo.

Hurley's July 10 plea for Moscow's open support of Chungking, so as to bring Yenan to heel, moved me, in consultation with Kennan, to submit a comment to Harriman. I was unaware, of course, of Soong's confidences to the ambassador. I suggested that the Soviet government could "quite easily repudiate Yenan publicly without basically altering Yenan's intransigent attitude. . . . If Yenan is controlled from Moscow, it is not by the State apparatus—the Government—but by the Party. The State can, when the Kremlin wishes, publicly follow an unexpectedly conciliatory and sedative policy in matters affecting the interests of other powers. At the same time, the Party can do just the opposite."

But even if both Government and Party turned a cold shoulder on Yenan, I continued, this did not mean that the Chinese Communists would capitulate to Chungking's terms. When far weaker, during 1927–37, "with no foreign support save huzzas and poor coaching from the Comintern bleachers, they resisted

Chiang with embarrassing persistence." Soviet influence can be overestimated, and Yenan's "strength, vitality and obstinacy" should not be ignored.

Soong had arrived back at Chungking faint of heart. "I am a broken man," he told Hurley. Then, "This proposed agreement with Soviets will be destructive politically to the man responsible for it." He did not want to return to Moscow.

Those Americans dealing with the consequences of the Yalta Agreement were not much happier. Harriman had suggested to the president and the secretary of state that a study be made of how far, in the American government's opinion, the Chinese might yield to Soviet demands. As the poor old department had no copy of the agreement or any records of conversations about it, Grew ordered up a not very helpful historical monograph "prepared on the basis of our recollection of its [agreement's] contents." A familiar unease afflicted those high officials, a sense of national guilt. The guilt over selling oil and scrap iron to Japan before Pearl Harbor had been expiated. Now was the shame of a deal with the Russians, seemingly at China's expense.

In the roaring last week of the war, the reluctant Soong reappeared in Moscow. The day after his arrival the Soviet Army began its invasion of Manchuria. Stimulated by this event—Stalin advised him that he had better agree quickly or "the Communists will get into Manchuria"—and with Harriman interceding at the Kremlin on his behalf, Soong reached an accord with Stalin on August 13. The treaty and subsidiary documents were signed on the following day—the day that Japan formally accepted the Potsdam surrender terms.

The bargain struck at Moscow conformed generally to the Yalta Agreement. Soong told Harriman that he was encouraged by the accomplishment. In Chungking, Chiang expressed to Hurley satisfaction with the treaty. The ambassador also understood the Generalissimo to have "admitted" that the treaty indicated a Soviet intention to assist in unifying the Chinese armed forces, to support China's efforts to create a strong, united, democratic government, and to support the National government. If Hurley understood Chiang correctly, they were probably the only two people who believed this.

After learning the substance of the Soviet-Chinese agreement and disturbed by what I thought was an unduly optimistic reaction of the American press to it, I drafted a message with Kennan's assistance, sent to the department on September 4, commenting on the accord. As Moscow did not need the pact to achieve what was being attained by the Red Army, I observed, its utility to the Kremlin lay in "lending legality to situations which might otherwise have led later to undesirable disputes and complaints against [the] Soviet Union." Soviet willingness, while in occupation of Manchuria, to admit Chinese to civil affairs control and to withdraw Soviet forces within three months were gestures that would not prevent the Chinese Communists from taking over the Northeast. Moscow's seeming moderation in Manchuria would serve to calm suspicions of Soviet intentions, we indicated, without halting covert Soviet activities in Manchuria, Korea, and Japan.

The war against Japan culminated in a horrendous burst of violence. On

August 6 the Americans baptized the atom bomb on Hiroshima. Two days later the great Bolshevik khan loosed his scourge upon Manchuria. And on August 9 Nagasaki was consumed by fission.

It was an extravagant four days' finale. None of it may have been necessary. By mid-July American naval and conventional air action had brought Japan to the verge of capitulation. Assurances that the imperial system would be tolerated might well have opened the way for surrender. But this did not happen.

In Tokyo what did happen in early August was a fierce last struggle for the emperor's power of decision, between some military fanatics bent on fighting to the death and conservative elements wanting a face-saving peace. The conservatives won. On August 10 the Japanese government broadcast its readiness to accept the Potsdam ultimatum on the condition that the emperor's prerogatives as a sovereign ruler were not prejudiced.

Washington, speaking for the allies, responded on the following day that the authority of the emperor and the Japanese government would be subject to the Supreme Commander of the Allied Powers, but that the ultimate form of government would be freely established by the Japanese. In confirming on August 14 its acceptance of the Potsdam terms, Tokyo informed the allies that the emperor had issued an Imperial Rescript telling his subjects of his capitulation, and that His Majesty was prepared to authorize the government and Imperial General Headquarters to carry out the surrender terms and to command all Japanese forces to cease hostilities. The formal surrender took place September 2 aboard the U.S.S. *Missouri*.

For most Russians their six-day war against Japan meant little. It was a war of revenge for a Tsarist defeat, a war for national profit, and most of all, a war on other people's land. The Russian people had been physically and emotionally mauled in the fight against the Nazis. V–J Day had none of the joyous relief of V–E Day. Patricia and I strolled up to Red Square to watch with thousands of Muscovites the salute to victory over Japan. It was salvos of artillery, rockets, and searchlights in color—but a spiritless crowd. In personal terms what did southern Sakhalin or the Kuriles mean but two more distant, disagreeable places to which one might be sent should the secret police feel so inclined?

At least, Japan's surrender meant no more fighting for Russians. And it brought peace for Americans, Britons, and, most durably, the Japanese. But for the Chinese it marked the beginning of a new and more bitter war. More precisely, it opened the way for resumption of the metamorphic civil war begun in 1927.

CHAPTER *38*

Civil War Begins

WITH RUSSIAN ENTRY into the Pacific War on August 8, 1945, the Soviet Union, the United States, the Chiang regime, and the Chinese Communists became fighting allies against Japan. Britain was part of this alliance, but had sense enough to remain aloof from the contortions that began two days later.

When Tokyo made its preliminary offer of surrender on August 10, Japan began to fade out as an enemy. As of the same date, Yenan ordered its forces to take the surrender of adjacent Japanese troops and, in so doing, began to assume openly the role of Chungking's enemy.

Also on the tenth, the Joint Chiefs of Staff ordered Wedemeyer to "assist . . . in the rapid transport of Chinese Central Government forces to key areas in China"—which meant territory occupied or claimed by Yenan. Having thus acted in support of Chiang and in conflict with the Communists, the JCS warned the general that he must not "prejudice the basic U.S. principle that the United States will not support the Central government of China in fratricidal war." Wedemeyer promptly told the Pentagon that its order was contradictory.

Chiang reacted on August 11 to Yenan's challenge. Like Canute, he commanded the Communists "to remain at their present posts and wait for further directions." But the scantily-armed Reds were beginning to move, to take such materiel as they could from isolated Japanese garrisons south of the Great Wall, but more significantly, toward Manchuria where they expected to inherit from the Russians a grubstake of weapons taken from the Kwantung and Manchukuo armies, then control of the Northeast.

At the same time, Stalin was negotiating with Soong an alliance, signed on August 14, that ignored the existence of the Chinese Communists and formally committed the Soviet government to back the National government of China. As a treaty of alliance, this went further on Chiang's behalf than any pledge to him by Washington. The lineup on the fifteenth was: Americans, Russians, and Chinese Nationalists as allies, the Japanese as fast-fading enemies, and the Chinese Communists regarded as obstructionists by Washington, unseen by Moscow, and enemies by Chungking.

By the next day the Japanese armed forces had received General Order No. 1. This directive had been drafted in Washington, cleared with allied governments, and transmitted to Tokyo by MacArthur as Supreme Commander for the Allied Powers. It was then dispatched from Tokyo as an order of "Imperial General Headquarters by direction of the Emperor" commanding the surrender of all Japanese forces. Obedient to the imperial will (Grew had been dead right), the emperor's far-flung legions prepared to capitulate—those in China to Chiang, excepting that the Kwantung Army was to surrender to the Soviet commander in Manchuria.

Dutifully the Japanese armies in North China and the Yangtze Valley, which had been victorious in every campaign, waited for the Nationalists to come and take their surrender. But Chiang's troops were far away. In contrast, the Communists surrounded the Japanese strong points clamoring for their surrender. When the Japanese declined, the Reds attacked some of the weaker garrisons, and the Japanese fought back. Therefore, in mid-August the Imperial Army in China proper remained as enemy to the Communists, but graduated to being an ally of Chiang's against Yenan. At last Chiang and the Japanese military were collaborating to prevent the spread of communism—the Generalissimo's failure to do so in 1937 having been an ostensible reason for Japan's invasion of China.

Late in August, starting with Nanking and Shanghai, the Americans began a massive airlift of Nationalist armies to key areas in China, faithfully held by the Japanese. By putting Chiang in position to accept Japanese surrenders, the Americans performed also as his allies in what was now a civil war. The Generalissimo was in no great hurry to accept the surrenders because he found the American-Japanese combination most helpful. He drew on troops lifted by the Americans and used them to campaign against the Communists, while the Japanese continued to hold for him the principal North China cities and lines of communications.

Finally, on October 10, nearly two months after General Order No. 1, the Japanese surrender at Peking was accepted. But not before the American government had begun to deploy some fifty-three thousand American marines in North China to ensure an orderly surrender and repatriation, and take over the job the Japanese had been performing for Chiang. Even after surrender, the Japanese continued to serve as reliable allies. The American consul at Tientsin reported on October 30 that the marines depended almost entirely on former puppet and Japanese troops "for maintenance of order" in towns along the railway. Congressman Mike Mansfield thought that the use of marines to garrison North China cities was "most unwise" and on the fifteenth told the State Department so—to no effect.

Chiang's Soviet allies ignored the Kwantung Army's efforts to surrender in compliance with General Order No. 1 and continued attacking in revenge for 1905. After disarming and deporting the Kwantung Army to Siberia, the satisfied Russians held the principal cities and railways of Manchuria, awaiting the arrival of the Generalissimo's men to receive China's lost territory recovered by the Soviet Army. Several hundred Nationalist officials were accepted with punctilio by the Soviet army in September and October as a vanguard of the Chinese administration of the Northeast. But they could not function until the occupying army withdrew and was replaced by Nationalist forces. Awkwardly enough for the Nationalists, Chinese Communist troops had also arrived in Manchuria, as the Russians looked the other way. Under the command of one of Yenan's ablest generals, Lin Piao, the force had already grown by November to well over a hundred thousand men, many of whom had been recruited from the former Manchukuo Army.

At Soong's request, Stalin had agreed during their August negotiations to withdraw the Soviet Army from Manchuria by November 15. Anxious to deploy his armies in Manchuria before the Russians completed their retirement, Chiang had prevailed upon the American Navy to carry his troops to Manchuria. During October American transports sought to land the Nationalists at various points along the Manchurian coast only to observe Chinese Communists lying in wait. Eschewing involvement in what Washington and Wedemeyer elegantly called "fratricidal warfare," the Americans finally debarked their charges at a North China port held by the United States Marines. The Navy Department passed to the State Department the exasperated request of the Commander, Seventh Amphibious Force, that sufficient shipping be turned over to the Chinese to operate so as to avoid any more "long wandering journeys . . . in attempts to disseminate . . . Chinese Nationalist troops."

As November 15 approached, with none of their troops in Manchuria, the Nationalists begged the Soviet Army to delay its departure. December 3, the first of several extensions, was set as the new deadline. The Soviet Army having pulled back from southwestern Manchuria, Chiang began his invasion of Manchuria on November 15. The Generalissimo had committed his best units to this adventure—heavily armed, American-trained divisions. Lin Piao's still lightly equipped Communist troops offered slight resistance, for they were not yet ready to fight the decisive battles.

Chiang's American allies had moved half a million of his troops by air and by sea, and his American, Soviet, and Japanese allies had held key areas for him. But this was not enough for Chiang. Thanks to his allies, he had picked up an enormous quantity of materiel from one million two hundred and fifty thousand Japanese in China. Nor was that enough. He wanted the equipment for ninety divisions that Stilwell and then Roosevelt had mentioned to him, but for which he was impotent to pay the price—reorganization and reform of his army.

With the flinty Stilwell out of the way and the Americans in a cold sweat at the thought of the Communists taking over China, the time was propitious for the Nationalists to press for an unqualified grant of equipment for ninety divisions. Hurley was an eager spokesman, conveying the Generalissimo's desire for the materiel to Washington on August 11. In an interview with the secretary of state, James F. Byrnes, on September 3, Soong typically demanded to know whether the United States was ready to fulfill its "commitment" to equip one hundred divisions. But because, with the end of the Pacific War, the lend-lease spigot was being turned off, Chiang had to content himself with the completion of the American wartime program for equipping thirty-nine divisions and eight and a half air groups. Thereafter he was to receive huge stockpiles of American surplus materiel to continue feeding his insatiable appetite for the instruments of war—which he hoped would compensate for a want of generalship and martial spirit in most of his armies.

Anticipating the termination of Wedemeyer's wartime command at the moment he most needed American military collaboration—for the war against the Communists—Chiang asked Truman on September 10 for an American military advisory group. The JCS recommended prompt granting of the request, proposing an initial complement of more than three thousand. Vincent, then Director of Far Eastern Affairs at State, had misgivings. Such a group might put the United States in the position of having "a semicolonial Chinese army under our direction." But planning for the group went ahead and it was established in early 1946, a model for later military advisory groups to other countries threatened by communism.

By the end of 1945, as the president reiterated American attachment to nonintervention in other people's affairs, the American government was widely and vigorously intervening in China's internal affairs. In four months intervention in the Chinese Civil War far exceeded in scope and intensity Wilson's in the Russian Civil War. But this was a particularly high-minded intrusion because it was meant to dispose of a threat to the unity of China under the National government headed by Chiang Kai-shek, the leader of all Chinese, and so acknowledged by the whole world, including Stalin.

China had not been unified since the Manchu dynasty. Chiang had tried to impose the authority of his Kuomintang government over all of the country, but had never succeeded in doing so. Nor was he to his fellow countrymen the commanding figure that Churchill, Roosevelt, and Stalin were to theirs.

Chiang's regime and the Communists were the two principal elements on the China scene. Lesser forces were: a number of residual warlords, semiautonomous provincial factions and generals, and in occupied China and Manchuria, puppet governments and armies set up by the Japanese. Political brokers, agents, and provocateurs constantly moved among these varied elements making deals, buying and selling expedient allegiances, and betrayals. As the time of testing between Chiang and the Communists approached, the squirming intrigue intensified, with the principal antagonists bidding particularly for the strategically located puppet troops in the Yangtze Valley and North China. In these accessions Chiang did better than the Reds.

The issue in China was not, as Washington proclaimed, the preservation of Chinese unity under Chiang. There was no unity in China even against the Japanese. The issue was whether Chiang might be enabled to survive in the southern half of the country or whether the Communists would overrun all of China.

Measured by armament, material resources, and the number of soldiers nominally under its command, the Chiang regime was in 1945 far mightier than the Communists. The Nationalists had the only armor and heavy artillery, the only air force, the only navy, and the only industrial base, including more than a dozen arsenals. Nominally under the Generalissimo's command were two million seven hundred thousand troops as against nine hundred thousand regulars claimed by the Communists. These figures were probably inflated. As Stalin laughingly remarked in December, all Chinese are boasters who exaggerate the size of both their own forces and those of their opponents. Nevertheless, it is probably safe to assume that Chiang had at his disposition roughly three times as many soldiers as the Communists.

And yet, the decisive fact that emerged in China from eight years of Japanese invasion and occupation was that the power ratio between Chiang's regime and the Communists had been reversed. In a fluid, not static, relationship Chiang's strength was wasting and Yenan's was expanding. Decadence and rapacity, antagonizing the citizenry, rotted the seeming strength of the National government and armies.

In contrast, the Communists were dynamic, cohesive, and disciplined. They possessed élan, popular appeal, and organizational genius. These intangibles gave the Reds overall superiority. In the course of the civil war they were to gain an ascendancy also in weapons, starting with those laid down by the Japanese and puppets, then with American arms taken from the Nationalists.

While the Generalissimo vaguely understood that Communist power had expanded, he could not bring himself to admit the full extent of that growth and what this meant to his own situation. In reality, he had two courses open to him. One was to yield to coalition with the Communists pretty much on their terms. This might have postponed his downfall. The other was to adjust his plans and actions to the power realities of 1945, to acknowledge that North China and Manchuria (which he had never really possessed) were now beyond his ability to reclaim, to accept the fact of two Chinas, and so try to reoccupy and hold no more than China south of the Yangtze. While his dynasty could hardly have hoped to last a century and a half, as had the first Southern Sung dynasty, he might have had a chance to survive in half of China, provided that he could vitalize his regime and obtain massive American aid.

To the Generalissimo these were unthinkable alternatives. Not at all surprisingly, therefore, he chose in August to act out his pretensions as the generalissimo, moral preceptor, and sovereign of all China. To do less would be to lose face, and what was worse, to become Mao's puppet or a regional warlord. Also, had not the Americans extolled him as one of the Big Four rulers of the earth? Did not the American ambassador constantly contend that all China must be unified under Chiang, did not the American general, Wedemeyer, stand ready to fly Nationalist armies to the cities surrendered by the Japanese, and had not both declared that he could subdue the Communists?

Hurley and Wedemeyer had also advised Washington before the onset of civil war that Chiang could subdue the Communists. Together, with the eccentric Commodore Miles of SACO fame, they assured the Joint Chiefs of Staff in March that Chiang could, with comparatively little American assistance, put down the Communists. In subsequent months, Hurley made light of Communist strength to the American press and the Department of State. After the civil war had started, Wedemeyer announced to the press on August 30 that he did not believe that the Communists were strong anywhere in China. "Regardless of their number or equipment," he declared, "I do not anticipate any difficulty with the Communists."

Thus the top Americans in China emitted a steady clatter of confidence in Chiang's superiority over the Communists. There was no dissenting note from within the embassy for the sufficient reason that Hurley had prohibited any such disagreement on pain of being branded disloyal. And so Washington came to be out of touch with reality in China.

As fighting broke out after Tokyo's offer to surrender and Wedemeyer began to airlift the Nationalists into conflict with the Communists, Hurley acted in desperation to bring Chiang and Mao into negotiation before all of his promises of reconciliation between the two were consumed in the flames of civil war. Being sensible about carnage, Chinese have usually been willing to negotiate as they fought. So it was between the Nationalists and the Communists in the fall of 1945. Neither side wanted to appear unreasonable or responsible for the hostilities which all Chinese, exhausted by nearly a decade of fighting, wanted no more of.

Yenan was keenly aware of the public antipathy toward more war and the advantages to be gained from appearing conciliatory. Furthermore, American and Soviet pressures for a deal with Chiang were heavy. Stalin had told Harriman on August 29 that "he believed an agreement would be reached between Chiang and the Communists." And finally, Yenan preferred national coalition to civil war, provided that the formula would ensure a Communist capture of power from within.

Therefore Mao acceded to Hurley's opportune pleas that he go to Chungking to treat with the Generalissimo. The ambassador, who went to escort him and guarantee Mao's safety in Chungking, interpreted the Chiang-Mao agreement to negotiate as a tribute to himself, "a source of gratification to us that we have been able to maintain the respect and confidence of the leaders of both parties." This mistaken conceit he announced to the press and repeated to the secretary of state.

Guarded by Hurley, Mao arrived in Chungking on August 28 and engaged in footling negotiations with Chiang. As was to be expected, no mutually acceptable compromise between these two was possible. On October 11 Mao returned to Yenan.

Meanwhile in the midst of real struggle and disaster, the Generalissimo and Hurley were off on another tangent. The ambassador reported to Washington on September 1 that Chiang had told him that "the imperialist governments France,

Britain, and the Netherlands" were seeking "an excuse for landing imperialist forces in China." In the Generalissimo's opinion, Hurley solemnly continued, "the imperialists are actually cooperating with the Communists . . . [and] the United States and the Soviet Union are cooperating with the National Government of China."

The bugbear of "imperialists" undermining his labor of conciliation haunted the ambassador—rather conveniently so. He had flamboyantly committed himself to unifying the Communists with Chiang's regime. Therefore he could not, without risking a walkout by the one accused, blame either side for the failure of his efforts. Nor could he, without appearing to have been bamboozled, turn on his trusted collaborator, Stalin. He found rationalization, therefore, for the failure of his mission in imagined foul play by weary Europeans.

After two weeks of the futile negotiations between Chiang and Mao, with the civil war ranging uncontrolled, Hurley suddenly asked the State Department's permission to return to the United States. He said that he wanted "to discuss the American-Asiatic policy" with Byrnes and Truman. "The fundamental issue in Asia today," he revealed, "is between democracy and imperialism; between free enterprise and monopoly." The ambassador stated that America was supporting British, French, and Dutch imperialism against democracy and that the imperial nations represented in China were supporting a policy intended to keep China divided against itself. "Perhaps the government has decided," Hurley taunted, "not to continue what President Roosevelt outlined as the long-range policy of the United States in regard to China."

On his departure for Washington on September 23, Hurley informed the State Department that "The *rapprochement* between the two leading parties of China seems to be progressing and the discussion and rumors of civil war recede as the conference continues." The Generalissimo, understandably anxious that Hurley should continue to sustain him, asked the president to return the ambassador. Truman replied on October 20 that he and Byrnes would send Hurley back to China because of "the confidence we repose in General Hurley's judgment and ability. . . ."

Two and a half months of civil war changed Wedemeyer's estimate of Communist strength. No longer did he maintain that the Reds were an inconsequential force. He recognized in a message to Marshall, on the day before Chiang invaded Manchuria, that the Communists were winning support because of the corruption of newly arrived Nationalist officials in North China, that Chiang was "completely unprepared" for occupation of Manchuria against Communist opposition, and that the Generalissimo should first attempt to consolidate his authority south of the Wall.

Wedemeyer undertook on November 20 to acquaint the new chief of staff, General of the Army Dwight D. Eisenhower, with the China scene. The Generalissimo was "sincere," Wedemeyer began. But—considering Chiang's background as "warlord and politician, and his oriental philosophy, his approach to problems presented would probably be inefficient, incomprehensible, and unethical by American standards." Wedemeyer then delivered a threnody on Kuomintang officialdom, repeating the mournfully familiar descriptions—unscrupulous, incompetent, worthless, conniving, intriguing, surreptitious, and corrupt. Surrounded by henchmen of such kidney, Chiang was "bewildered and impotent."

So was Wedemeyer. Continuing his narrative to Eisenhower, he had told the Generalissimo that the Nationalists did not have the strength to "recover" Manchuria. Chiang seemed to agree, and then took off into the Northeast. Wedemeyer estimated that the Generalissimo could stabilize South China if he accepted "foreign administrators and technicians" and thoroughly reformed his regime. Chiang could not stabilize North China and Manchuria for months or years unless he reached a settlement with the Communists, and that possibility appeared remote. Meanwhile, the retention of American forces in China was bound to lead to involvement in "fratricidal warfare." And his dual capacities as American commander and chief of staff to the Generalissimo were no longer tenable.

Wedemeyer asked that he be immediately relieved as Chiang's chief of staff and that either all American forces in China be removed or his directives be changed "to justify under U.S. policies their retention and employment." Three days later he told Eisenhower that if unification of China under the Nationalists was to be American policy, then "involvement in fratricidal warfare and possibly in war with the Soviet Union must be accepted," and would require more American forces than were present in China, plus a change in his directives.

Through a process of wishful and sloppy thinking the American government had by mid-November drifted into a quandary. As late as November 26, Forrestal and the new secretary of war, Robert P. Patterson, stated that "reliable information available indicates that the strength and activity of Communist forces are considerably exaggerated." Several days earlier the gung-ho Patterson had exclaimed that he saw no peril in increasing the American commitment— why, the Marines then there could walk from one end of China to the other without serious hindrance.

Most of the State Department was less carried away with imaginings of Communist insignificance. The chief of the China division, Everett F. Drumright, however, recommended that the American government should "afford all necessary assistance in recovering all lost [Chinese] territories—especially Manchuria." He marshalled an array of reasons, including the specter that a disunited China might "bring about conditions which will plunge the world into a third world war." He did not mention what obviously worried Wedemeyer, the risks of a third world war from trying to unite China. Drumright assumed that American aid would make possible the unification of China, but he did not give any reasons for that whopping assumption, how much the necessary assistance would cost, or whether the American people would support the undertaking.

Drumright's stance, which found considerable favor at the time, was typical of much policy thinking in the American government then and later. The power realities of a situation, even when understood, tended to be subordinated to what "ought to be done," what should be done because of precedents, commitments, moral compulsions, sentiment, and that great catchall, "national security." The factor of cost of a policy was thus often slighted.

The American government, however, was not yet prepared to underwrite Chiang's conquest of China. Washington policy makers were floundering. The secretaries of war and navy pressed the secretary of state for broad political decisions, suggested consultation with the Russians about Chiang's "continuing to lean on unilateral U.S. action," and decided that while the Marines should stay in China for the time being, the president and Byrnes would have to decide whether Wedemeyer should continue as Chiang's chief of staff.

Wedemeyer added on November 26 his thoughts to the quest for a policy. The conflicting orders that he had were impossible to carry out. Therefore, either give him the American forces and support necessary to unify China under Chiang, which, he snapped, would be contrary to the American policy of self-determination and American public opinion, or invoke through the United Nations a trusteeship for Manchuria and Korea, "pool the military resources of the United Nations" to repatriate the Japanese, and thereafter clear out of China, leaving the Chinese to decide through evolution or revolution their destiny.

At this tense juncture who should stalk into the confusion but Hurley. Notwithstanding the Generalissimo's plea for his sustaining presence and the confidence that Truman said he and Byrnes reposed in Hurley's judgment and ability, the ambassador did not want to go back to his post. He had told Byrnes that he wanted to resign. Now on November 26 he brought in a letter of resignation, but the secretary turned it aside and talked him into a promise to return to China on the twenty-eighth.

Late in the morning of the twenty-seventh the president conferred with the ambassador and they agreed that because of the seriousness of the situation in China Hurley should leave without delay. Some two hours later, while Truman was at lunch with his Cabinet, he was informed that Hurley had just issued to a gathering of newsmen a denunciation of the conduct of American foreign policy towards China. Absolving the president and the secretary of state from blame, Hurley charged in his statement to the press:

> The professional foreign service men sided with the Chinese Communist armed party and the imperialist bloc of nations whose policy it was to keep China divided against herself. Our professional diplomats continuously advised the Communists that my efforts in preventing the collapse of the National government did not represent the policy of the United States. These same professionals openly advised the Communist armed party to decline unification of the Chinese Communist Army with the National Army unless the Chinese Communists were given control.
>
> Despite these handicaps we did make progress toward unification of the armed forces of China. We did prevent civil war between the rival factions, at least until after I had left China. We did bring the leaders of the rival parties together for peaceful discussion.

Hurley's statement to the press was mostly excerpts from his turbid letter of resignation. In neither did he name the professional diplomats whom he was accusing. It was not until he appeared before the Senate Foreign Relations Committee on December 5 that he accused by name George Atcheson, Service, two others, and me.

Truman took Hurley's behavior as insulting to his administration. He immediately accepted Hurley's resignation. Having done this he acted quickly to offset the political uproar whooped up by Hurley. The president telephoned Marshall, who had only recently retired to the tranquillity of Leesburg. In his *Memoirs*, Truman recalls having said, "General, I want you to go to China for me." To which Marshall responded "Yes, Mr. President" and hung up. He had cut short the conversation lest Mrs. Marshall overhear and learn sooner than was necessary how brief their retirement would be.

So the most distinguished of American generals was sent to make the American dream of China come true, not through force but through persuasion. More as a tribute to Marshall than as an expression of confidence in the possibility of having one's way with China, Stalin said in December that if any man could settle the situation in China, it would be Marshall, one of the few military men, in Stalin's opinion, who was a statesman as well as a soldier. But even Marshall, with his Olympian prestige, would not be able to bring China together under Chiang. The power ratio between the two Chinas had been unalterably reversed. If Chiang was incapable of saving himself when he still had time and Stilwell was offering to help him do so, he certainly could not now, after three more years of degeneration, revivify his regime. And as for the Communists, with their virility they were destined to win all of China, either through the coalition that Marshall sought, or if that failed, through conquest. Marshall could not change these realities. The American dream was turning into a nightmare.

CHAPTER *39*

The Huge Practical Joke

AFTER THE PACIFIC WAR my attention increasingly turned to what was going on inside the Soviet Union, Europe, and the Middle East. The tumultuous events in East Asia seemed remote, stale, and foregone. Hurley's postured resignation did, however, briefly bring the China issue alive for me.

I wrote to my relatives in the United States on November 29 that I had been made first secretary of the embassy in Moscow. "Set against that are the ructions let loose by my old admirer and fellow traveler, Patrick J. Hurley. I haven't yet seen press reactions from the US (we get cables on press reactions every day—brief, but an indication). I expect some will come across my desk later in the day. In the meantime, my own reaction is that he has been so intemperate and inaccurate that he is damaging rather than helping his case. I know the man pretty well and what he has done does not in the least surprise me. It apparently surprised my present ambassador who last evening expatiated at some length and rather amusingly on the subject. I suppose that there will now be a good deal of muckraking, which won't surprise me. And most of it I expect will be beside the point.

"The point is not are you for or against communism, but granting its existence—how best to go about coping with it. I think that it has by now been pretty well demonstrated that Patrick's tactics are not working. I have learned a lot since last January and what I have learned caused me to revise some of my ideas, but on the other hand confirmed me in the belief that I was closer to being on the right track than the Paper Tiger [Hurley], as the Chinese called him. Diplomacy is one of the more fluid arts so it is of course arrant nonsense to look back and say that if from such and such a date policy had been something or other it would have flowed along a certain definite course."

My next letter was on December 14, after Hurley had denounced me by name before the Senate Foreign Relations Committee. "Since writing to you last I see that Patrick put me on his first team. It made me mad at first and I was all set to roar on back home and shoot the works. But George Kennan and Patricia dissuaded me. They told me to wait and see how the thing shaped up. Patricia's strategy, which is usually pretty sound, was to wait and let Patrick talk and talk and talk. The theory being that the more he rambled on the more he would discredit himself in the eyes of most (the Hearst-McCormick gang, of course, is hopeless). From what we know of press reactions at home, I now conclude that Patricia was probably right.

"The issues, of course, are far greater than appear out of the Hurley-burley. And they are ones that I would take delight in testifying on. Our foreign relations are in a fantastic state—wishful thinking, vacillation, secret skeletons, and pervasive confusion. For these reasons the Foreign Service is not an exhilarating business. To get out of it and be able to speak the truth would be a refreshing experience. On the other hand, somebody has to carry on with the job. We stay on hoping that things will be better, that our experience can be productive of some good. So I, and others like me, stay on. I am willing to quit, however, if matters in the FS become intolerable or if someone better than a senile mountebank makes it worth my while.

"I hope that you didn't take Patrick's outbursts too seriously. Perhaps because we are so far away and not subject to the concentrated impact of a howling press—even though it lasts for only a few days and then disappears like a Kansas twister—we looked at the phenomenon as a somewhat ludicrous performance. The ambassador made jokes about the affair. I hesitate to quote him for fear of making him sound intemperate on the subject."

Byrnes arrived at Moscow in mid-December for a conference with Molotov and Ernest Bevin, the British Foreign Secretary, a beefy, frolicsome trade unionist. The meeting had been impulsively proposed to Molotov by Byrnes in late November. Molotov welcomed the suggestion with what, for him, amounted to enthusiasm. Bevin objected for, among several reasons, the sufficient one that the time given was too short for proper preparation. But, as Byrnes was in a hurry to clear things up with the Russians, and Molotov was more than willing to accommodate the secretary of state, Bevin reluctantly acceded to the conference.

Byrnes would have done well to have collaborated closely with Bevin, who knew far better than he how to negotiate with Marxists. Instead he continued to snub his British colleague so as to curry favor with Molotov and Stalin, and relied on his Southern charm and wit to captivate the impervious Russians. Byrnes's facile qualities, productive on Capitol Hill, were inadequate for impromptu bargaining with Molotov on an agenda that ranged from tidying up the Balkans to control of atomic energy—and finding a solution to the problems of China.

Harriman assigned me to the job of contact with newsmen. Before the first press conference, the ambassador introduced me to the secretary and his retinue, which included Benjamin Cohen, counselor of the department, Dr. James B. Conant, acting as atomic energy adviser, and my colleagues, Bohlen and Vincent. "The ambassador introduced me with a big laugh," I wrote home, "as one of the dangerous characters favored by Patrick, whereupon there was much chaffing and joking."

In the same letter I reported that "Vincent asked me the other evening how

I would like the job as chief of the China Division. I said not much." I wanted to widen my horizons.

My most memorable encounter with Byrnes was during a break in the conference when the delegations were in a reception room taking refreshments. The secretary was engaged in laborious pleasantries with Molotov when he spied me. He waved for me to join them. As I stood face-to-face with Molotov, Byrnes turned to the commissar and drawled, "Pat Hurley says he's a Communist, so when he comes knocking at your door, you let him in, hear?"

Byrnes quivered with chuckles as Molotov's interpreter translated the secretary's encouragement of an assignation. Not a muscle twitched on the commissar's pasty face, composed for this social recess in a fixed faint smile. The light from the chandeliers glittered on his thick pince-nez, the bristly moustache remained rigid. Byrnes's joshing had fallen flat.

The Secretary had gone to Moscow in the hope that, with regard to China, he could get an exchange of assurances with the Russians. He would lay on the table the reasons why the marines were still in China. In return he wanted the Soviet government to say what it would do about transferring control of Manchuria to Chiang. He would try, as Forrestal had suggested to him, to talk the matter over realistically with the Russians.

The Soviet reaction was brisk. The Soviet government supported Chiang and had embodied this in a written agreement. It was under a special agreement with the Chinese government regarding Manchuria that Soviet troops had disarmed all Japanese troops there and removed them as prisoners of war to Soviet territory. Soviet troops had begun their withdrawal but had halted at the request of the Chinese government.

This, Molotov indicated, was more than the Americans had done. Putting the amiable Byrnes on the defensive, the Soviet delegation charged in writing that there were in China "up to five hundred thousand nondisarmed Japanese troops" apparently in "violation of the terms of surrender." The dates of the disarmament of these Japanese and the departure of the American forces in China had not been indicated. The Japanese troops were being drawn, the Soviet statement continued, into "military operations on the side of the troops of the Chinese government . . . into the struggle between different portions of the Chinese people."

With an air of documented self-righteousness, the Soviet bill of particulars declared that "The Soviet government adheres to a policy of noninterference in the internal affairs of China" and that interference on the part of others was leading to "an aggravation of the internal political struggle." MacArthur's General Order No. 1 prescribed that the Chinese should disarm the Japanese in the China Theater. This task should not be assigned to foreign troops. The Soviet response to Byrnes's attempt to talk the matter over realistically with the Russians ended with the recommendation that American and Soviet troops simultaneously withdraw from China in three weeks, by no later than the middle of January, 1946. Byrnes could not accept this, and so the Americans were maneuvered into an unflattering light.

As the great adjudicator, Stalin received Byrnes on December 23, with Molotov, Harriman, and Bohlen also present. Putting Byrnes, a former justice of the Supreme Court, in the role of a culprit, Stalin calmly asked why the United States did not wish to remove its troops from North China. Byrnes protested that the American government did indeed wish to get its troops out, but that it had certain obligations and certain circumstances made withdrawal difficult. Indulgently, Stalin commented that his government would have no objections if the United States wished to leave its troops in China but it would merely like to be informed.

After twitting Byrnes further, Stalin gave him some fatherly advice. If the Chinese people became convinced that Chiang depended on foreign troops, the Generalissimo would lose his influence. Apparently Chiang did not understand this, Stalin went on, but the American, British, and Soviet governments should then understand it for him. It would be much better for Chiang to rely on his own forces. However, if the United States wanted to help him, it should not help him in such a manner as to destroy his authority with the Chinese people.

Having imparted this good counsel [Yenan was making popular gains through propaganda that Chiang was depending on Japanese and American troops], Stalin offered his comments that both Chiang and the Communists were boasters about their numerical strength. Where was Chiang's army of a million and a half? (Wedemeyer had calculated two million seven hundred thousand.) Getting into the spirit of the thing, Byrnes replied that he, too, would like to know the answer to that. But there were fifty thousand (Wedemeyer calculated five armies or about a hundred thousand) Nationalist troops in North China. Stalin thought that fifty thousand should be enough to disarm the Japanese. After all, twenty-five Soviet aviators had taken the surrender of two Japanese army corps at Mukden. And so it went; Molotov did not add to the ridicule of the Generalissimo. He had on the nineteenth contributed his piece of heavy sarcasm —eight years of war should have been long enough for Chiang to learn how to handle Japanese, particularly after they had capitulated.

And so, by talking the matter over realistically, Byrnes found out what the Russians thought about the China problem. Or had he?

What Stalin thought of the China problem at the end of 1945 can only be a matter of speculation. With that caveat, my surmises proceed as follows.

His western front was more important to Stalin than his eastern. Western Europe and the Middle East were a greater potential menace and a greater prize than East Asia. In East Asia there was not much that he could do about Japan because of American domination of the islands. In Korea he would establish a buffer in at least the north of that country. As for Indochina, it was of remote strategic interest. And so Stalin slighted Ho Chi Minh. Because the Kremlin was scheming for a parliamentary take-over of France by the French Communist Party, Stalin permitted that party, for domestic political gain, to press the Vietnamese Communists to yield to the reimposition of French authority in Indochina.

Stalin's approach to the problem of China was wary, and with reason. There were his memories of how Chiang and Mao had both let him down and of Trotsky's stinging criticism of him for having lost the Chinese Revolution in 1927. He felt a need to proceed with particular caution in dealing with these perverse and elusive people. His inclination towards prudence was reinforced by a determination not to provoke openly the Americans. Their infatuation with China made them the most volatile factor in the Chinese situation. To inflame them by overt, adventuristic intervention in China would yield no calculable gain.

Consequently, Stalin's strategy was essentially negative and gradualistic. He was not attempting to bring China under his sway at one stroke. His objective was initially preventative—to prevent the emergence out of the chaos in China of an independent, unified, strong government over the vast expanse stretching south of his Asian frontiers, along four thousand miles of common border.

This preclusive strategy was dual in character. Stalin tried to detach the border areas of Manchuria, Inner Mongolia, and Sinkiang so as to reduce the physical size of China and to erect barriers between the Soviet Union and China. Secondly, within China proper, he followed a policy designed to forestall the possible development of an integrated central government independent of Soviet influence. He pursued both objectives with sly caution.

In Manchuria, Stalin had acquired, in the privileges accorded by the treaty he had negotiated with Soong, the traditional groundwork for developing a separatist regime in the Northeast. During the civil war, Moscow cultivated the inclinations toward autonomy of Mao's man in Manchuria, Kao Kang. Kao was responsive to the Soviet overtures, until the Chinese Politburo eliminated him in the early 1950s, his disappearance being politely attributed to suicide.

Soviet machinations in Inner Mongolia and Sinkiang during the late 1940s were directed at creating Mongol and Turki administrations independent of any Chinese authority, Nationalist or Communist. These stratagems failed because Mao outmaneuvered Stalin. While Mao, like Stalin, championed the right of ethnic minorities to "autonomy," each of these great power chauvinists sought to bestow such "autonomy" under its supervision. The Chinese Communists, like the Chinese Nationalists, even wanted Outer Mongolia lumped with Inner Mongolia as a part of China, and were seemingly so ill-informed and naive as to tell Service in 1944 and March 1945 that the Soviet Union recognized Outer Mongolia as a part of China.

If Mao had not anticipated Stalin's intention to detach China's border regions, obvious Soviet intrigue in the wake of Russian invasion of Manchuria and Inner Mongolia made those intentions evident. That the Chinese Communists were able to thwart Soviet stratagems in the border regions and, eventually, even oust the Russians from their privileged position in Manchuria, was due to the bargaining skill of Mao and Chou and to the Kremlin's wish to avoid a public scandal in its relations with so conspicuous a fraternal party.

Stalin did not fare any better in the second course of his preventive strategy. He failed to prevent the emergence of an independent, unified, strong government in China. But his attempt to do so was uncommonly devious and adroit.

Throughout the civil war, Stalin maintained correct relations with Chiang. He had no need to fear that Chiang's unfit regime could bring all of China under firm control. But by continuing formal recognition of the Nationalists, the excited Americans were given no overt cause to vent their frustrations on the Soviet Union. And the Soviet government retained its ties with Chiang as a vulnerable chief of state—a relationship advantageous to the Kremlin.

To make sure that Chiang remained vulnerable, Stalin allowed the Chinese Communists to glean from Manchuria Japanese weapons of little interest to the Soviet Army. But he did not go beyond this in contributing to Communist military power. For he did not want the Maoists to win hands down throughout the country and establish an independent, unified, strong China.

Contrary to Washington's assumptions that he did, Stalin did not control the Chinese Communist Party and its army. He did not have inside the Chinese Party-State apparatus Kremlin agents with power to punish and cashier. The apparatus belonged to Mao, not to Stalin. And both the Party and the Army, but particularly the Army, were intensely nationalistic. Therefore, to Stalin they were unreliable. They had to be worked over.

Who better to do this for him than Chiang and the Americans? His Chinese votaries should submit to a coalition with the Kuomintang regime. Through this humbling experience they would be persuaded to accept a greater degree of Kremlin influence in their affairs. If such a coalition were formed and it acquired authority over all of China, the Kremlin would be able, through a dependent CCP, to make its wishes felt within the coalition government.

This was the popular front formula that had failed him in China in 1927. Fallible as it was, it was preferable to either Chiang's or Mao's gaining unilateral control over China. And if it failed again, as it seemed to be doing at the end of 1945, at least it would not be Stalin, but Truman and Byrnes and Marshall who would be made to look foolish.

A protracted civil war in China would not be to Stalin's disadvantage. It would occupy American attention, distracting it from the prime arena in Europe. And in such a conflict, the Americans would, because of their support of Chiang, make themselves more hated by the Communists than were the Japanese. Such bitter enmity would naturally tend to bond the Communists to the Soviet Union.

Consequently, all that was required of Stalin was that he remain aloof, not give the Americans visible reason to turn on the Soviet Union, and allow the situation to develop of itself to his advantage. Although he could easily anticipate that the United States would become damagingly and humiliatingly entangled in China, he could hardly have foreseen the self-destructive frenzy that gripped American domestic politics as a result of the American "loss" of China.

Stalin's greatest error in judging the China scene in 1945 was underestimating Chinese Communist power. He did not think that Mao could make it. He was deceived by his own cynicism—and, astonishingly enough, his little faith in the power of a people's war.

The implosion of China, which began with the intrusion of the maritime West in the nineteenth century, was now in a final phase. The civil war—more truly a social revolution—was further collapsing the traditional society and its accretions of pseudowesternism. At this stage of social revolution, the internal conflict was intimately Chinese, notwithstanding fluttering American intervention.

Britain, which probably did more than any other nation to trigger the implosion, was comfortably back in Hong Kong and busily trading again. The British had been right about China during the war against Japan. They had doubted that Chiang could unify China or that they could change matters. Therefore they had remained aloof. The Chinese were to be "admired and liked as a race," Churchill said, "and pitied for their endless misgovernment."

Defeated Japan, which had contributed so much to the decline of Chiang and the rise of Mao, was out of the power equation in East Asia. But this could only be temporary. A people as vigorous, talented, and cohesive as the Japanese would sooner or later again make its influence felt.

The Soviet Union, which had inspired the movement then conquering China, was already one of the two superpowers and a major factor in East Asia. Its part in the Chinese implosion had been brief and spectacular. In a quarter of a century, by example and precept, but little by proselytization and material support, Communist Russia ignited a new force within China that further consumed what the maritime West had started, and then, indigenously, began the fusion of a new order in China. Stalin's gratification over this phenomenon was blighted by the fact that he did not control the process of fusion.

For more than a century the United States, now the other superpower, had lavished gifts, teaching, and care on the Chinese. In so doing it had contributed to the collapse of traditional Chinese society. But for all of its prolonged and earnest solicitude, the tremendous American effort in China failed to evoke a native movement mobilizing mass support—unless the bizarre Taiping rebellion be considered as such. Chiang and his Kuomintang, over which Washington came to assume such proprietary interest, had been in the mid-1920s inspired less by American ideas of democracy than by the techniques of Bolshevism. And to the dismay of the American government, Chiang and his Kuomintang had been launched in their bid for power by Stalin and his agents, Borodin and Blyukher.

Now, two decades later, after the greatest victories in American history, everything that Americans had striven for in China seemed to be mortally threatened. Washington could not bring itself to accept that the Chinese might reject the American example and American preaching. Baffled and indecisive, the American government vacillated between illusion and reason. Marshall had been sent to China out of illusion—to materialize the phantasma of a united China under Chiang. He wisely concluded that he could not bring about unity through mediation and returned to the United States in January 1947. Reason had won. But illusion persisted. And so a frittering American intervention with military advisers and intermittent supplies continued until the Communists finally triumphed in 1949.

A variety of influences limited in the mid-1940s the American choice of action toward China. Church-going Americans—and that was most Americans—had grown up believing that of all of the Lord's vineyards China was perhaps the most beloved. Sentimentality permeated the popular American attitude towards China. A long accumulation of unworldly policies, beginning with the Open Door and a habit of making decisions in evasion of displeasing facts, conditioned official thinking about China. Well-heeled Kuomintang lobbying in the United States and an American claque of pro-Chiang publicists and politicians agitated for deeper American involvement in the Chinese civil war.

In such an environment, it was nearly impossible for the American government to take a sensible position like that of Britain. Military and foreign policy reasons for breaking out into a position of sympathetic detachment outweighed the reasons for remaining Chiang's captive. But presidents and bureaucracies tend to prefer drifting in a blunder to undergoing the public embarrassment of reversing themselves. A Washington decision to step out of the China trap following the defeat of Japan would have raised a tumult of reproaches from the American public, especially from those who acted as Chiang's propagandists. It would have taken a president wiser and stronger than Roosevelt was in 1945 and more perceptive and less encumbered than Truman to make such a decision.

An alternative course would have been American armed intervention on a scale calculated to be sufficient to win the civil war for Chiang. The scale of such intervention would have been incalculable—a blind commitment of American power. I had thought in 1944 that a possibly effective intervention would have had to be of the magnitude of the Japanese invasion of China. With the more recent American intervention in Vietnam as an example, it may be sufficient to note that in 1945 China had ten times the population and nearly thirty times the area of the two Viet Nams. The American people have reason to be thankful that Marshall, Dean Acheson, and Truman finally decided to restrain the progression of policy towards deeper involvement, and to "lose" China rather than to try to conquer it for Chiang.

A third course would have proceeded from a *realpolitik* decision to act on the basis of, initially, two Chinas. This would have meant *de facto* recognition of Yenan's authority over North China and Manchuria, collaboration with the Communists against the Japanese, allowing Chu Teh to take the Japanese surrender in the North, refusing to transport Chiang's forces to the North, and generally aiding the Communists in their area so that they would have had no need to move towards dependence on the Soviet Union.

In the event of civil war, which the Communists would have quickly won, the American attitude would have been neutral. The main American concern throughout this hypothetical course would have been the *realpolitik* objective of creating conditions whereby the Chinese Communists might retain their independence and develop their own jealous interests as a natural counterweight to Soviet power in East Asia.

The *realpolitik* choice was unthinkable as American policy. It would have let down Chiang, supported atheistic communism, and, at best, been speedily identified as amoral and European. The American government, therefore, envenomed Communist China against the United States without altering the outcome of the civil war, ensuring that Mao had nowhere to turn but to a waiting Stalin. It consolidated China and the Soviet Union as a bloc against the United States, eliminating any possibility of a balance of power relationship in East Asia for more than a decade—until the Chinese could no longer endure the possessive Russian embrace and split with the Soviet Union.

Those Americans who, during the period 1942–1950, endeavored to reform and unify China were disillusioned, embittered, or injured by the experience. This was the case with Stilwell and Gauss. Wedemeyer became so emotionally involved in and confused over the China issue that he crossed Marshall, which may well have been the reason that he did not attain his ambition of becoming chief of staff. Hurley's facade as a statesman was demolished by his performance in China. Marshall, the organizer of triumphs over Germany, Japan, and Italy, dutifully went to China and failed to organize two Chinese— Chiang and Mao. Leighton Stuart, who had dedicated his life to educating and Christianizing Chinese, abandoned his ministrations as president of Yenching University to become the last American ambassador to China, only to be driven out by the Communists, heartbroken.

Roosevelt's China policy does not contribute to his reputation as a great president. It was illusioned and credulous in the first years of the war. During the Stilwell command crisis, with unsound advice from his subordinates, Roosevelt was impractically harsh towards Chiang. Finally, by permitting Hurley to usurp the formulation of policy towards China, he was disastrously irresponsible.

Truman, with more loyalty and drive than comprehension, continued with Roosevelt's China policy. But in the last months of 1945 he made the decisions that led to the self-inflicted wounds of American involvement in the Chinese civil war. His concept of American policy towards China was, as he fatuously summed it up to Byrnes on January 5, 1946, "We should rehabilitate China and create a strong central government there."

When in 1949 Mao triumphed in the civil war, the Americans thought that because they had "lost" China, Stalin had "won" it. Stalin knew better. But if he thought that Mao had "won" China, he was mistaken. To be sure, Mao had captivated China, and then restructured it. But he failed to attain what he wanted most, short of which, he believed, all other achievements would eventually be betrayed and dissipated. This exalted, overweening goal was, in China, to transform the elusive nature of man. With the breakdown of his Great Proletarian

Cultural Revolution in the late 1960s, Mao the Messiah "lost" China to the generals and the bureaucrats.

The truth of the matter is that China has been since the fall of the Empire a huge and seductive practical joke. The western businessmen, missionaries and educators who had tried to modernize and Christianize it failed. The Japanese militarists who tried to conquer it failed. The American government which tried to democratize and unify it failed. The Soviet rulers who tried to insinuate control over it failed. Chiang failed. Mao failed.

Epilogue

MAO TSE-TUNG AND CHOU EN-LAI secretly tried to arrange in January 1945 for an invitation to meet with the president of the United States in Washington. At Hurley's instance they were rebuffed. The president of the United States secretly tried to arrange in July 1971 for an invitation to meet with Mao and Chou in Peking. He was invited.

During the span of a quarter of a century, 1945–1971, the American people and government reversed their opinion of China and the Soviet Union as allies of the United States and of Japan and Germany as enemies. From hoping for a world order under law, Americans shifted to a conviction that power in the world had become polarized between two hostile superpowers, the United States and the Soviet Union, that China and Eastern Europe were fused in a Communist monolith controlled by the Kremlin, and that the rest of the world was "free" and either with the United States or pusillanimously neutral. By the 1960s Washington had begun to outgrow this simplistic view. Evidence of the Moscow-Peking split and the development of secondary power centers in Western Europe and Japan were persuasive.

However, the American people and government continued to think of the United States as an Asian power and to believe in the applicability and efficacy of American military force in Asian situations. This was glaringly so in Indochina. As with Mao, the American government ignored a request by Ho Chi Minh in 1945 for cooperation and aid. Postwar American support went to the reimposition of French colonial rule, the losing side. With the rout of the French, successive American administrations, hagridden by "the loss of China," involved the United States ever more extensively in Southeast Asia to prevent the "loss" of Indochina. The lesson learned from the Marshall-Truman-Acheson decision to pull back from intervention in China was not the wisdom of abstinence from Asian civil wars. Rather, it was that "losing" an Asian country to communism was a politically fatal liability at home.

The Nixon visit in 1972 to Peking opened possibilities that international relations might function not only in new patterns but also in another manner. The new patterns included diminishing the inflated position of Moscow and reducing Taipei to its properly meager dimensions. A different mode of operation became possible when Nixon announced that he sought "normalization" of American relations with China. The way was opened for the American government to pursue a policy of balance of power.

The basis for such a policy was the triangular relationship among Washington, Moscow and Peking. Each was the adversary of each of the other two. At the same time, each was the ally, at least potentially, of each of the other two against the third.

Peking's desire for relations with Washington was, in part, because it wanted a counter to the weight of Soviet malevolence. It wanted to break out of the rigid two-way confrontation with Moscow into a situation in which it could, if need be, readily solicit Washington's support. That is to say, it wanted to practice balance of power—in traditional Chinese terms, to play off the far against the near.

The Kremlin, naturally, did not welcome signs of an American-Chinese rapprochement. No longer could Moscow count on the advantage of dealing with Washington and Peking each in isolation from the other. Balance of power, which the Kremlin understood as well as the Chinese, and which both had practiced with consummate skill, could now be employed in restraint of Moscow. But should China menace international equilibrium, Moscow and Washington could join to curb Peking.

The United States was ill prepared to undertake a policy of balance of power. The legacy of Wilson and Hull, that such a course was iniquitous, remained strong. The purpose of balance of power politics—to maintain a tolerable international equilibrium—continued to be misrepresented as mischievous and inciting to war. Furthermore, public, congressional, and executive behavior with regard to China and Indochina from 1945 to 1971 had been less than cool-headed and intelligent. The record did not suggest an American aptitude for balance of power politics.

Ready or not, the American government in 1971 entered a situation impelling it toward the conscious practice of balance of power. And on a scale surpassing the Washington-Moscow-Peking triangle. For a burgeoning Japan was now a major factor to be reckoned with in East Asia.

The diffusion of power in East Asia and the opening of contacts was a healthy development. The calm American acceptance of the new trend suggested a certain maturity—or boredom—in the United States with Asian affairs. Even if only transient, it has been a welcome turning away from the overblown, vain, and apocalyptic policies of the past.

Notes

FOR THOSE wishing to inquire further into Chinese culture and history, including relations with the United States, there is a wealth of written material available, most of which is of impressive scholastic quality. John K. Fairbank's bibliography of it, included in his masterly *The United States and China* (3rd ed., Harvard University Press, 1971) is a convenient guide. O. Edmund Clubb's *Twentieth Century China* (Columbia University Press, 1964) also carries a bibliography helpful to the inquiring reader.

CHAPTER 2

The geographical statistics in this chapter draw on three of George B. Cressey's works, all published by McGraw-Hill: *China's Geographic Foundation*, 1934, *Asia's Lands and Peoples,* 1951, and *Land of the 500 Million,* 1955.

CHAPTER 5

Page 55 The quotations from Sun Tzu are taken from *Sun Tzu: The Art of War,* translated by the distinguished American soldier-scholar, Brigadier General Samuel B. Griffith, USMC, and published by Oxford University Press, 1963.

CHAPTER 6

Page 59 Chun-tu Hsueh, *Huang Hsing and the Chinese Revolution,* Stanford University Press, 1961, p. 26.

Page 68 The biographical sketches here and in Chapter 10 of Chu Teh borrow from Agnes Smedley's *The Great Road,* Monthly Review Press, 1956.

CHAPTER 7

Page 82 Lenin quotation from Bertram D. Wolfe, *Three Who Made a Revolution,* Dial Press, 1948, p. 278.

CHAPTER 8

Page 86 Beveridge speech, January 9, 1900, *Congressional Record,* 56 Congress, 1st Session, pp. 704–12.

Page 87 Alfred Thayer Mahan, *The Problem of Asia*, 1900, p. 180.

Page 90 Roosevelt, the Kaiser and Spring-Rice: Whitney Griswold, *The Far Eastern Policy of the United States*, Harcourt, Brace, 1938, pp. 106–11.

CHAPTER 9

Page 97 Roosevelt's changed views: Griswold p. 35, 123–32.

Page 104 The biographical material on Mao Tse-tung in this and later chapters derives largely from Edgar Snow, *Red Star over China*, Grove Press, revised edition, 1968, Jerome Ch'en, *Mao and the Chinese Revolution*, Oxford, 1965, and Stuart Schram, *Mao Tse-tung*, Simon & Schuster, 1966.

CHAPTER 10

Page 120 The Graves expedition to Siberia is described by the general himself: William S. Graves, *America's Siberian Adventures*, New York, 1931. George F. Kennan, in his *The Decision to Intervene*, Princeton, 1958, views this Wilsonian caper in perspective.

CHAPTER 12

Page 137 Ch'en Tu-hsiu quotation from Harold R. Isaacs, *The Tragedy of the Chinese Revolution*, Stanford University Press, 1961, p. 246.

Page 139 The Autumn Harvest Insurrection is described by Roy Hofheinz, Jr., in *The China Quarterly*, No. 32, Oct.-Dec. 1967.

CHAPTER 15

Page 164 Stilwell, who becomes a major character in this story, is the central figure in Barbara Tuchman's distinguished *Stilwell and the American Experience in China*, Macmillan, 1971.

CHAPTER 16

Page 182 Stalin's liquidation of Blyukher and other Soviet generals was but a part of a consuming horror stunningly chronicled by Robert Conquest in *The Great Terror*, Macmillan, 1968.

CHAPTER 20

In this and subsequent chapters my account of events in World War II relies heavily on two sources. One is the authoritative history, in three volumes, of the China-Burma-India Theater in the series, *United States Army in World War II*, issued by the Office of the Chief of Military History, United States Department of the Army. Solidly written by Charles F. Romanus and Riley Sunderland, the studies are entitled: *Stilwell's Mission to China* (1953), *Stilwell's Command Problems* (1956), and *Time Runs Out in CBI* (1959).

My other principal source is the Department of State's series, *Foreign Relations of the United States*, particularly the annual volumes having to do with China, 1942–45. Hereinafter they will be referred to by the abbreviation FR-Ch followed by the pertinent year.

CHAPTER 21

Pages 239–40 General Frank Dorn's *The Walkout*, Charles Scribner's Sons, 1971, provides a definitive account of Stilwell's 1942 exodus from Burma.

CHAPTER 22

Page 242 Mme. Chiang to Chennault quotation from Claire L. Chennault, *Way of a Fighter*, Putnam's, 1949, p. 77.

Page 247 JD conversation with Chou En-lai: FR-Ch-42 p. 102.

Pages 247–48 JD conversations with various Chinese: FR-Ch-42 pp. 99–101.

Page 248 JD conversation with Yang Chieh: FR-Ch-42 p. 115.

CHAPTER 23

Page 251 JD memo of statements by Soviet Military Attache: FR-Ch-42 p. 123.

Page 253 JD memo *CBI Reappraisal: FR-Ch-42* pp. 129–31.

CHAPTER 24

Page 263 JD memo for Gauss in re Stilwell: FR-Ch-43 pp. 25-29.

CHAPTER 25

Page 272 JD memo of June 24, 1943: FR-Ch-43 pp. 258–66.

Pages 273–74 JD memo of Sept. 17, 1943: excerpts in Maurice Matloff, *Strategic Planning for Coalition Warfare* (one of WWII series), Dept. of Army 1959, p. 287.

Pages 275–76 JD conversation of Oct. 20, 1943: summarized FR-Ch-43 pp. 878–80.

Page 279 My original memo of conversations with Hopkins and Roosevelt is somewhere in the bowels of the State Department. The account given in this chapter is based on declassified excerpts from the original, provided to me in the late 1950s by the then Chief of the Historical Division, G. Bernard Noble.

CHAPTER 26

Page 283 Excerpt from JD memo of Feb. 19, 1944: Hearings before Subcommittee of Senate Foreign Relations Committee, pursuant to S. Res. 231, 81st Congress, 2nd session, 1950, p. 2129.

Page 286 JD memo of May 29, 1943: FR-Ch-43 pp. 60–61.

CHAPTER 27

Page 299 JD memo of Dec. 31, 1943: FR-Ch-43 pp. 398–99.

Page 300 JD memo of Jan. 15, 1944: FR-Ch-44 pp. 307-8.

CHAPTER 28

Pages 308–9 JD letter to Stilwell: *Stilwell's Command Problems* pp. 375–76.

CHAPTER 29

Page 317 JD conversation with Hopkins: Ibid. p. 421.

Page 319 Service's first report from Yenan: FR-Ch-44 pp. 517–20. Other Service reports from Yenan appear in FR-Ch-44 and 45. See also John S. Service, *The Amerasia Papers: Some Problems in the History of US-China Relations*, Center for Chinese Studies, University of California Press, Berkeley, 1971.

Page 320 Service's summary of his extraordinary interview with Mao appears in FR-Ch-44 pp. 602–14.

CHAPTER *32*

Page 343 Stettinius to Hull Aug 3 : FR-Ch-44 p. 247.

CHAPTER *33*

Page 362 JD memo, "How Red . . .": FR-Ch-44 pp. 669–70.
Page 362 JD memo, *C.C. and Great Powers*: Ibid. pp. 667–69. JD memo, *CC Take Over?:* Ibid. pp. 670–71.

CHAPTER *34*

Page 366 Barrett monograph: David D. Barrett, *Dixie Mission*, Center for Chinese Studies, University of California Press, Berkeley, 1970.
Page 371 JD memo Nov. 15, 1944: FR-Ch-44 pp. 695–97.

CHAPTER *35*

Page 382 JD memo Dec. 12 to Wedemeyer: FR-Ch-44 pp. 734–35.
Page 383 JD second trip to Yenan: FR-Ch-44 pp. 752–55.
Page 386 JD memo Jan. 4, 1945: FR-Ch-45 pp. 155–57.

CHAPTER *36*

Page 393 JD Apr. 15 memo to Harriman: FR-Ch-45 pp. 334–38.
Page 395 Kennan comments on Hurley report: FR-Ch-45 pp. 342–44.
Page 396 JD analysis: FR-Ch-45 p. 346.

CHAPTER *37*

Pages 402–3 Two of Ludden's reports appear in FR-Ch-45 pp. 200–04; 212–15.
Page 405 See above, Chapter 29, Service monograph on Amerasia Papers.
Page 405 JD estimate of Soviet policy: FR-Ch-45 pp. 928–32.
Page 407 JD comment to Harriman: FR-Ch-45 pp. 439–40.
Page 408 JD radio to Dept.: FR-Ch-45 pp. 982–84.

Index